FROM AYN RAND'S PHILOSOPHY OF RATIONAL
SELF-INTEREST:

AMERICA: I can say—not as a patriotic bromide, but with full
knowledge of the necessary metaphysical, epistemological,
ethical, political and esthetic roots—that the United States of
America is the greatest, the noblest and, in its original founding
principles, the only moral country in the history of the world.
(Philosophy: Who Needs It)

CAPITALISM: When I say "capitalism," I mean a full, pure,
uncontrolled, unregulated laissez-faire capitalism—with a
separation of state and economics, in the same way and for the
same reasons as the separation of state and church.
(The Objectivist Ethics)

EMOTION: An emotion that clashes with your reason, an
emotion that you cannot explain or control, is only the carcass
of that stale thinking which you forbade your mind to revise.
(Atlas Shrugged)

MORALITY: The purpose of morality is to teach you, not to
suffer and die, but to enjoy yourself and live. *(Atlas Shrugged)*

DR. HARRY BINSWANGER, an associate of Ayn Rand, received his
doctorate in philosophy from Columbia University. He taught philosophy
for many years at Hunter College and gave courses on Ayn Rand's
philosophy, Objectivism, at The New School for Social Research in
New York City. He is now editor of *The Objectivist Forum*, a magazine
that applies Objectivism to philosophical and cultural issues.

THE
AYN RAND
LEXICON

Objectivism
from A to Z

Edited by
Harry Binswanger

with an Introduction by
Leonard Peikoff

A MERIDIAN BOOK

MERIDIAN
Published by the Penguin Group
Penguin Books USA Inc., 375 Hudson Street, New York, New York 10014, U.S.A.
Penguin Books Ltd, 27 Wrights Lane, London W8 5TZ, England
Penguin Books Australia Ltd, Ringwood, Victoria, Australia
Penguin Books Canada Ltd, 10 Alcorn Avenue, Toronto, Ontario, Canada M4V 3B2
Penguin Books (N.Z.) Ltd, 182–190 Wairau Road, Auckland 10, New Zealand
Penguin Books Ltd, Registered Offices: Harmondsworth, Middlesex, England

Published by Meridian, an imprint of Dutton Signet, a division of Penguin Books USA Inc.

First Meridian Printing, January, 1988

30

ACKNOWLEDGMENTS

Excerpts from *The Ominous Parallels*, by Leonard Peikoff. Copyright © 1982 by Leonard Peikoff. Reprinted with permission of Stein and Day Publishers.

Excerpts from *The Romantic Manifesto*, by Ayn Rand. *Copyright* © 1971, by *The Objectivist*. Reprinted by permission of Harper & Row, Publishers, Inc.

Excerpts from *Atlas Shrugged*, copyright © 1957 by Ayn Rand, *The Fountainhead*, copyright © 1943 by Ayn Rand, and *The New Intellectual*, copyright © 1961 by Ayn Rand. Reprinted by permission of the Estate of Ayn Rand.

Excerpts from *Philosophy: Who Needs It*, by Ayn Rand. Copyright © 1982 by Leonard Peikoff, Executor, Estate of Ayn Rand. Reprinted by permission of the Estate of Ayn Rand.

Excerpts from "The Philosophy of Objectivism" lecture series. Copyright © 1976 by Leonard Peikoff. Reprinted by permission.

Excerpts from Alvin Toffler's interview with Ayn Rand, which first appeared in *Playboy* magazine. Copyright © Alvin Toffler 1964. Reprinted by permission of Alvin Toffler.

REGISTERED TRADEMARK—MARCA REGISTRADA

Library of Congress Cataloging-in-Publication Data

Rand, Ayn.
  The Ayn Rand lexicon.

  Includes index.
  1. Philosophy.   I. Binswanger, Harry.   II. Title.
  III. Title: Objectivism from A to Z.
  B945.R233A96 1988   191   87-15291
  ISBN 0-452-01051-9

PRINTED IN THE UNITED STATES OF AMERICA

Information about other books by Ayn Rand and her philosophy, Objectivism, may be obtained by writing to OBJECTIVISM, Box 177, Murray Hill Station, New York, New York 10157, USA.

Contents

Contents

Introduction

AYN RAND WAS a philosopher in the classical sense: she was intent not on teasing apart some random sentences, but on defining a full system of thought, from epistemology to esthetics. Her writing, accordingly, is extensive, and the range of issues she covers enormous—so much so that it is often difficult for a reader to know where in her many books and articles to look for a specific formulation or topic. Even Miss Rand herself was sometimes hard-pressed in this regard.

The Ayn Rand Lexicon solves this problem. It is a compilation of key statements from Ayn Rand (and from a few other authorized Objectivist texts) on several hundred alphabetized topics in philosophy and related fields. The book was initially conceived by Harry Binswanger, who undertook it during Miss Rand's lifetime with her permission and approval.

Two different audiences can profit from the *Lexicon*. Those who know Miss Rand's works will find it a comprehensive guide to the literature. It will enable them to locate topics or passages easily, and—by virtue of its detailed indexes and cross-references—to check on their wider context and ramifications. Newcomers to Ayn Rand will find the book an intriguing introduction to her thought, one eminently suited to browsing. Many such browsers, I venture to say, after sampling the entries under REASON, SELFISHNESS, CAPITALISM, and a few more such topics, will become hooked by the logic and originality of Ayn Rand's ideas. If this happens to you, the next step is to turn to one of her books.

By its nature, this kind of project requires an editor with a professional knowledge of philosophy in general and of Ayn Rand's philosophy, Objectivism, in particular. Harry Binswanger qualifies on both counts. He is a Ph.D. from Columbia University and taught philosophy for many years at Hunter College. Dr. Binswanger was an associate of Miss Rand's. He taught Objectivism at the New School in New York City, and assisted in a course on the subject at the University of California (Berkeley). At present, Dr. Binswanger is editor of *The Objectivist Forum*, a magazine that applies Objectivism to philosophical and cultural issues.

In preparing the *Lexicon*, Dr. Binswanger has done a thorough and meticulous job. He has covered not only the familiar works of Ayn Rand, but also obscure and little-known sources. He has done the excerpting skillfully and accurately, always selecting essentials; as a result, the passages he offers are generally self-contained and self-intelligible. And he has arranged the material within a given topic in a logical sequence, each excerpt building on the earlier ones. If one reads straight through a topic, one will discover not a series of disconnected sentences, but a definite structure and development; this makes the reading even more illuminating and enjoyable.

The Lexicon is a welcome addition to the growing Ayn Rand Library, of which it is Volume IV. It is going to be extremely helpful to me personally, and I am happy to recommend it to anyone interested in the thought of Ayn Rand. She herself, I know, would have been pleased to see it become a reality.

—*Leonard Peikoff*
South Laguna, California
January 1986

Editor's Preface

THE PHILOSOPHIC WRITINGS of Ayn Rand and her associates have grown to include almost two thousand pages distributed among eight books—plus various lecture courses, newsletter articles, and pamphlets. Accordingly, I conceived the idea of creating a reference work, organized by topic, to function as an Objectivist dictionary or mini-encyclopedia.

I first proposed this idea to Ayn Rand in 1977. She was originally somewhat skeptical about its feasibility, being concerned as to whether her writings would lend themselves to the kind of excerpting that would be required. To sell her on the project, I wrote a detailed prospectus of the book and worked up a sample—the entries beginning with the letter "N." She was favorably impressed with the results and gave me permission to go ahead. She commented extensively on several dozen entries, helping me to define appropriate standards for excerpting and topic selection.

As the work progressed, Miss Rand became increasingly enthusiastic about the project. One value of the book had special meaning to her: it eliminates any shred of excuse (if ever there had been one) for the continual gross misrepresentation of her philosophy at the hands of hostile commentators. As she quipped to me, "People will be able to look up BREAKFAST and see that I did not advocate eating babies for breakfast."

Miss Rand had intended to read over the entire book, but after completing the letter "A" I had to shelve the project in order to found and edit *The Objectivist Forum*, and did not resume work on it until two years after her death. Consequently, she read only about 10 percent of the material.

I have endeavored to cull from the Objectivist corpus all the significant topics in philosophy and closely allied fields, such as psychology, economics, and intellectual history. The *Lexicon*, however, does not cover Ayn Rand's fiction writings, except for those philosophical passages from her novels that were reprinted in her book *For the New Intellectual*. Material by authors other than Miss Rand is included only if she had given it an explicit public endorsement—as with Leonard Peikoff's book *The Ominous Parallels* and his lecture course "The Philosophy of Objectivism"—or if it was originally published under her editorship in *The Objectivist Newsletter, The Objectivist,* or *The Ayn Rand Letter.* I have also made use of four *Objectivist Forum* articles that Miss Rand read and approved.

To keep the book to a manageable size, I have had to omit many passages which could have been included. I have sought to include under each heading only the essential passages, roughly proportioning the length of the entries to their scope and importance, within the limits of the amount of material available in the sources. The entry under Immanuel Kant, for instance, is as long as it is not merely because Miss Rand had so much to say about Kant's philosophy, but because of his immense influence on the history of philosophy, and thus on history proper. Miss Rand regarded Kant as her chief philosophical antagonist. Nevertheless, I may have missed some passages that merit inclusion, and readers are invited to send me any such passages c/o New American Library for their possible inclusion in future editions. For some headings (e.g., KNOWLEDGE), I give only the term's definition and rely on the cross-references to lead the reader to other topics for elaboration.

In accordance with Miss Rand's wishes, I have included statements about other philosophies only in selected instances: on Aristotle (whose system is the closest to that of Objectivism), on Kant (whose system is the diametrical opposite of Objectivism), on Friedrich Nietzsche (whose views, though fundamentally opposed to Ayn Rand's, are often taken to be similar), on John Stuart Mill (the philosophical father of today's "conservatives"), and on some influential contemporary schools: Pragmatism, Logical Positivism, and Linguistic Analysis. Those interested in the Objectivist analysis of other philosophies may consult *For the New Intellectual* and *The Ominous Parallels.*

In a number of instances, I have used oral material from Leonard Peikoff's tape-recorded lecture courses. Dr. Peikoff has edited these passages for this purpose. I have also included a few statements by Miss Rand from the question-and-answer periods following these lectures. Miss Rand's answers, which were wholly extemporaneous, are presented virtually unedited.

In excerpting from written material, I have sought to minimize the clutter of ellipses and square brackets. Where I have excised material from within a continuous passage, I have, of course, used ellipses to indicate that deletion. But I have not used ellipses at the beginning or end of entire passages, even when I have made initial or terminal cuts. Thus, the reader is put on notice that, at the beginning of a passage, some words from the start of the original sentence may have been dropped. Likewise, at the end of a passage, sentences in the original may continue on beyond where they end here.

Square brackets are used to indicate my own interpolated words or introductory notes (except that I have retained the square brackets used by Ayn Rand, Leonard Peikoff, etc. to insert their own comments within a direct quotation from someone else). In a few instances, I have deleted italics, but as a rule they are as they appear in the original texts; in no case did I add italics.

Some entry headings appear in quotation marks. The quotes are used to indicate either a concept that Objectivism regards as invalid or obfuscatory (as with "COLLECTIVE RIGHTS"), or a term used in a new or special sense (as with "STOLEN CONCEPT," FALLACY OF). The content of the entry should make clear which function, in a given case, these quotation marks serve.

Some explanation is necessary about the manner in which I have identified the sources of the passages quoted. The references include page numbers for both hardcover and paperback editions when possible (only paperback editions are currently available for *Introduction to Objectivist Epistemology, The New Left: The Anti-Industrial Revolution,* and *Capitalism: The Unknown Ideal*). I have cited the page number only for the passage's beginning even when it continues beyond that page in the original (e.g., a page reference normally given as "54–56" would appear here only as "54"). And, unless otherwise stated, all quotations are from Ayn Rand.

Note also that paperback page references for *The Romantic Manifesto* and *The New Left* refer to the second editions of these works. The first edition of the former did not include "Art and Cognition," and "The Age of Envy" was not included in the first edition of the latter.

All the books cited are available in paperback editions from New American Library. Much of the other material, including back issues of Miss Rand's periodicals and some separate pamphlets, is available from The Objectivist Forum, P.O. Box 5311, FDR Station, New York, NY 10150. (When an article published in a periodical has been reprinted in a book, only the book reference is given.)

I wish to thank Leonard Peikoff for his continued encouragement and editorial advice. Thanks are also due to Allison Thomas Kunze for identifying several passages that were worthy of inclusion and to Michael Palumbo for his meticulous assistance in assembling the manuscript.

I must stress that the *Lexicon* is not intended as a substitute for the primary sources from which it is derived. It is a fundamental tenet of Objectivism that philosophy is not a haphazard collection of out-of-context pronouncements, but an integrated, hierarchically structured *system,* which has to be studied and judged as such. For a brief indication of what Objectivism as a philosophic system advocates, the reader may refer to the entry, OBJECTIVISM. For a fuller statement, the best single source is Galt's speech in *Atlas Shrugged* (reprinted in *For the New Intellectual*).

—*Harry Binswanger*
New York City
February 1986

Conceptual Index

This index groups the topics under the headings: Philosophy, Psychology, Economics, and General. Philosophy is broken down into its branches: metaphysics (the study of the fundamental nature of reality and of man), epistemology (the theory of knowledge), ethics (the science of moral values), politics (including both political theory and more concrete public policy issues), and esthetics (the philosophy of art).

PHILOSOPHY: Metaphysics

PHILOSOPHY: Epistemology

PHILOSOPHY: Ethics

PHILOSOPHY: Politics

PHILOSOPHY: Esthetics

PSYCHOLOGY

Abbreviations

ARL	*The Ayn Rand Letter* (1971–1976)
CUI	*Capitalism: The Unknown Ideal* (1966)
ITOE	*Introduction to Objectivist Epistemology* (1979)
FNI	*For the New Intellectual* (1961)
GS	Galt's Speech, from *Atlas Shrugged* (1957), reprinted in *FNI*
NL	*The New Left: The Anti-Industrial Revolution* (1971)
OP	*The Ominous Parallels,* by Leonard Peikoff (1982)
PWNI	*Philosophy: Who Needs It* (1982)
RM	*The Romantic Manifesto* (1969)
TO	*The Objectivist* (1966–1971)
TOF	*The Objectivist Forum,* edited by Harry Binswanger (1980–)
TON	*The Objectivist Newsletter* (1962–1965)
VOS	*The Virtue of Selfishness* (1964)
WTL	*We the Living* (1959)

THE
AYN RAND
LEXICON
Objectivism
from A to Z

Abortion.　An embryo *has no rights*. Rights do not pertain to a *potential*, only to an *actual* being. A child cannot acquire any rights until it is born. The living take precedence over the not-yet-living (or the unborn).

Abortion is a moral right—which should be left to the sole discretion of the woman involved; morally, nothing other than her wish in the matter is to be considered. Who can conceivably have the right to dictate to her what disposition she is to make of the functions of her own body?

["Of Living Death," *TO,* Oct. 1968, 6.]

Never mind the vicious nonsense of claiming that an embryo has a "right to life." A piece of protoplasm has no rights—and no life in the human sense of the term. One may argue about the later stages of a pregnancy, but the essential issue concerns only the first three months. To equate a *potential* with an *actual*, is vicious; to advocate the sacrifice of the latter to the former, is unspeakable. . . . Observe that by ascribing rights to the unborn, i.e., the nonliving, the anti-abortionists obliterate the rights of the living: the right of young people to set the course of their own lives. The task of raising a child is a tremendous, lifelong responsibility, which no one should undertake unwittingly or unwillingly. Procreation is not a duty: human beings are not stock-farm animals. For conscientious persons, an unwanted pregnancy is a disaster; to oppose its termination is to advocate sacrifice, not for the sake of anyone's benefit, but for the sake of misery qua misery, for the sake of forbidding happiness and fulfillment to living human beings.

["A Last Survey," *ARL,* IV, 2, 3.]

If any among you are confused or taken in by the argument that the cells of an embryo are living human cells, remember that so are all the cells of your body, including the cells of your skin, your tonsils, or your ruptured appendix—and that cutting them is murder, according to the notions of that proposed law. Remember also that a potentiality is *not* the equivalent of an actuality—and that a human being's life begins at birth.

The question of abortion involves much more than the termination of a pregnancy: it is a question of the entire life of the parents. As I

1

have said before, parenthood is an enormous responsibility; it is an *impossible* responsibility for young people who are ambitious and struggling, but poor; particularly if they are intelligent and conscientious enough not to abandon their child on a doorstep nor to surrender it to adoption. For such young people, pregnancy is a death sentence: parenthood would force them to give up their future, and condemn them to a life of hopeless drudgery, of slavery to a child's physical and financial needs. The situation of an unwed mother, abandoned by her lover, is even worse.

I cannot quite imagine the state of mind of a person who would wish to condemn a fellow human being to such a horror. I cannot project the degree of hatred required to make those women run around in crusades against abortion. Hatred is what they certainly project, not love for the embryos, which is a piece of nonsense no one could experience, but hatred, a virulent hatred for an unnamed object. Judging by the degree of those women's intensity, I would say that it is an issue of self-esteem and that their fear is metaphysical. Their hatred is directed against human beings as such, against the mind, against reason, against ambition, against success, against love, against any value that brings happiness to human life. In compliance with the dishonesty that dominates today's intellectual field, they call themselves "pro-life."

By what right does anyone claim the power to dispose of the lives of others and to dictate their personal choices?

["The Age of Mediocrity," *TOF*, June 1981, 3.]

A proper, philosophically valid definition of man as "a rational animal," would not permit anyone to ascribe the status of "person" to a few human cells.

[Ibid., 2.]

See also BIRTH CONTROL; INDIVIDUAL RIGHTS; LIFE, RIGHT *to*; MAN; SEX.

Absolutes.   Reality is an absolute, existence is an absolute, a speck of dust is an absolute and so is a human life. Whether you live or die is an absolute. Whether you have a piece of bread or not, is an absolute. Whether you eat your bread or see it vanish into a looter's stomach, is an absolute.

[GS, *FNI*, 216; pb 173.]

"There are no absolutes," they chatter, blanking out the fact that they are uttering an absolute.

[Ibid., 192; pb 154.]

Just as, in epistemology, the cult of uncertainty is a revolt against reason—so, in ethics, the cult of moral grayness is a revolt against moral values. Both are a revolt against the absolutism of reality.

["The Cult of Moral Grayness," *VOS*, 99; pb 77.]

A moral code impossible to practice, a code that demands imperfection or death, has taught you to dissolve all ideas in fog, to permit no firm definitions, to regard any concept as approximate and any rule of conduct as elastic, to hedge on any principle, to compromise on any value, to take the middle of any road. By extorting your acceptance of supernatural absolutes, it has forced you to reject the absolute of nature.

[GS, *FNI*, 216; pb 172.]

See also AXIOMS; COMPROMISE; METAPHYSICAL *vs.* MAN-MADE; PRAGMATISM; PRIMACY *of* EXISTENCE *vs.* PRIMACY *of* CONSCIOUSNESS.

Abstraction (process of). The act of isolation involved [in concept-formation] is a process of *abstraction:* i.e., a selective mental focus that *takes out* or separates a certain aspect of reality from all others (e.g., isolates a certain attribute from the entities possessing it, or a certain action from the entities performing it, etc.).

[*ITOE*, 11.]

The higher animals are able to perceive entities, motions, attributes, and certain numbers of entities. But what an animal cannot perform is the process of abstraction—of mentally separating attributes, motions or numbers from entities. It has been said that an animal can perceive two oranges or two potatoes, but cannot grasp the concept "two."

[Ibid., 19.]

See also CONCEPT-FORMATION; CONCEPTS; INTEGRATION (MENTAL).

Abstractions and Concretes. Abstractions as such do not exist: they are merely man's epistemological method of perceiving that which exists—and that which exists is concrete.

["The Psycho-Epistemology of Art," *RM*, 27; pb 23.]

See also CONCEPTS; ENTITY; PERCEPTION; PLATONIC REALISM.

Acting. *See Performing Arts.*

Agnosticism. [There is] a widespread approach to ideas which Objectivism repudiates altogether: agnosticism. I mean this term in a sense which applies to the question of God, but to many other issues also, such as extra-sensory perception or the claim that the stars influence man's destiny. In regard to all such claims, the agnostic is the type who says, "I can't prove these claims are true, but you can't prove they are false, so the only proper conclusion is: I don't know; no one knows; no one can know one way or the other."

The agnostic viewpoint poses as fair, impartial, and balanced. See how many fallacies you can find in it. Here are a few obvious ones: First, the agnostic allows the arbitrary into the realm of human cognition. He treats arbitrary claims as ideas proper to consider, discuss, evaluate—and then he regretfully says, "I don't know," instead of dismissing the arbitrary out of hand. Second, the onus-of-proof issue: the agnostic demands proof of a negative in a context where there is no evidence for the positive. "It's up to you," he says, "to prove that the fourth moon of Jupiter did not cause your sex life and that it was not a result of your previous incarnation as the Pharaoh of Egypt." Third, the agnostic says, "*Maybe* these things will one day be proved." In other words, he asserts possibilities or hypotheses with no jot of evidential basis.

The agnostic miscalculates. He thinks he is avoiding any position that will antagonize anybody. In fact, he is taking a position which is much more irrational than that of a man who takes a definite but mistaken stand on a given issue, because the agnostic treats arbitrary claims as meriting cognitive consideration and epistemological respect. He treats the arbitrary as on a par with the rational and evidentially supported. So he is the ultimate epistemological egalitarian: he equates the groundless and the proved. As such, he is an epistemological destroyer. The agnostic thinks that he is not taking any stand at all and therefore that he is safe, secure, invulnerable to attack. The fact is that his view is one of the falsest—and most cowardly—stands there can be.

[Leonard Peikoff, "The Philosophy of Objectivism"
lecture series (1976), Lecture 6.]

See also ARBITRARY; ATHEISM; CERTAINTY; "OPEN MIND" and "CLOSED MIND"; SKEPTICISM.

Altruism.

Theory

What is the moral code of altruism? The basic principle of altruism is that man has no right to exist for his own sake, that service to others is the only justification of his existence, and that self-sacrifice is his highest moral duty, virtue and value.

Do not confuse altruism with kindness, good will or respect for the rights of others. These are not primaries, but consequences, which, in fact, altruism makes impossible. The irreducible primary of altruism, the basic absolute, is *self-sacrifice*—which means; self-immolation, self-abnegation, self-denial, self-destruction—which means: the *self* as a standard of evil, the *selfless* as a standard of the good.

Do not hide behind such superficialities as whether you should or should not give a dime to a beggar. That is not the issue. The issue is whether you *do* or do *not* have the right to exist *without* giving him that dime. The issue is whether you must keep buying your life, dime by dime, from any beggar who might choose to approach you. The issue is whether the need of others is the first mortgage on your life and the moral purpose of your existence. The issue is whether man is to be regarded as a sacrificial animal. Any man of self-esteem will answer: *"No."* Altruism says: *"Yes."*

["Faith and Force: The Destroyers of the Modern World," *PWNI*, 74; pb 61.]

There are two moral questions which altruism lumps together into one "package-deal": (1) What are values? (2) Who should be the beneficiary of values? Altruism substitutes the second for the first; it evades the task of defining a code of moral values, thus leaving man, in fact, without moral guidance.

Altruism declares that any action taken for the benefit of others is good, and any action taken for one's own benefit is evil. Thus the *beneficiary* of an action is the only criterion of moral value—and so long as that beneficiary is anybody other than oneself, anything goes.

["Introduction," *VOS*, x; pb viii.]

It is your *mind* that they want you to surrender—all those who preach the creed of sacrifice, whatever their tags or their motives, whether they demand it for the sake of your soul or of your body, whether they promise you another life in heaven or a full stomach on this earth. Those who start by saying: "It is selfish to pursue your own wishes, you must sacrifice them to the wishes of others"—end up by saying: "It is selfish to uphold your convictions, you must sacrifice them to the convictions of others."

[GS, *FNI*, 176; pb 142.]

Now there is one word—a single word—which can blast the morality of altruism out of existence and which it cannot withstand—the word: *"Why?"* *Why* must man live for the sake of others? *Why* must he be a sacrificial animal? *Why* is that the good? There is no earthly reason for it—and, ladies and gentlemen, in the whole history of philosophy no *earthly* reason has ever been given.

It is only *mysticism* that can permit moralists to get away with it. It was mysticism, the *un*earthly, the supernatural, the irrational that has always been called upon to justify it—or, to be exact, to escape the necessity of justification. One does not justify the irrational, one just takes it on faith. What most moralists—and few of their victims—realize is that reason and altruism are incompatible.

["Faith and Force: The Destroyers of the
Modern World," *PWNI*, 74; pb 61.]

Why is it moral to serve the happiness of others, but not your own? If enjoyment is a value, why is it moral when experienced by others, but immoral when experienced by you? If the sensation of eating a cake is a value, why is it an immoral indulgence in your stomach, but a moral goal for you to achieve in the stomach of others? Why is it immoral for you to desire, but moral for others to do so? Why is it immoral to produce a value and keep it, but moral to give it away? And if it is not moral for you to keep a value, why is it moral for others to accept it? If you are selfless and virtuous when you give it, are they not selfish and vicious when they take it? Does virtue consist of serving vice? Is the moral purpose of those who are good, self-immolation for the sake of those who are evil?

The answer you evade, the monstrous answer is: No, the takers are not evil, provided they did not *earn* the value you gave them. It is not immoral for them to accept it, provided they are unable to produce it, unable to deserve it, unable to give you any value in return. It is not immoral for them to enjoy it, provided they do not obtain it *by right*.

Such is the secret core of your creed, the other half of your double standard: it is immoral to live by your own effort, but moral to live by the effort of others—it is immoral to consume your own product, but moral to consume the products of others—it is immoral to earn, but moral to mooch—it is the parasites who are the moral justification for the existence of the producers, but the existence of the parasites is an end in itself—it is evil to profit by achievement, but good to profit by sacrifice—it is evil to create your own happiness, but good to enjoy it at the price of the blood of others.

Your code divides mankind into two castes and commands them to live by opposite rules: those who may desire anything and those who may desire nothing, the chosen and the damned, the riders and the carriers, the eaters and the eaten. What standard determines your caste? What passkey admits you to the moral elite? The passkey is *lack of value*.

Whatever the value involved, it is your lack of it that gives you a claim upon those who don't lack it. It is your *need* that gives you a claim to rewards. If you are able to satisfy your need, your ability annuls your right to satisfy it. But a need you are *unable* to satisfy gives you first right to the lives of mankind.

If you succeed, any man who fails is your master; if you fail, any man who succeeds is your serf. Whether your failure is just or not, whether your wishes are rational or not, whether your misfortune is undeserved or the result of your vices, it is *misfortune* that gives you a right to rewards. It is *pain*, regardless of its nature or cause, pain as a primary absolute, that gives you a mortgage on all of existence.

If you heal your pain by your own effort, you receive no moral credit: your code regards it scornfully as an act of self-interest. Whatever value you seek to acquire, be it wealth or food or love or rights, if you acquire it by means of your virtue, your code does not regard it as a moral acquisition: you occasion no loss to anyone, it is a trade, not alms; a payment, not a sacrifice. The *deserved* belongs in the selfish, commercial realm of mutual profit; it is only the *undeserved* that calls for that moral transaction which consists of profit to one at the price of disaster to the other. To demand rewards for your virtue is selfish and immoral; it is your *lack of virtue* that transforms your demand into a moral right.

A morality that holds *need* as a claim, holds emptiness—non-existence —as its standard of value; it rewards an *absence*, a defect: weakness, inability, incompetence, suffering, disease, disaster, the lack, the fault, the flaw—the *zero*.

[GS, *FNI*, 178; pb 144.]

Altruism holds *death* as its ultimate goal and standard of value.

["The Objectivist Ethics," *VOS*, 33; pb 34.]

Since nature does not provide man with an automatic form of survival, since he has to support his life by his own effort, the doctrine that concern with one's own interests is evil means that man's desire to live is evil—that man's life, as such, is evil. No doctrine could be more evil than that.

Yet that is the meaning of altruism.

["Introduction," *VOS*, xii; pb ix.]

Practice

Observe what this beneficiary-criterion of [the altruist] morality does to a man's life. The first thing he learns is that morality is his enemy: he has nothing to gain from it, he can only lose; self-inflicted loss, self-inflicted pain and the gray, debilitating pall of an incomprehensible duty is all that he can expect. He may hope that others might occasionally sacrifice themselves for his benefit, as he grudgingly sacrifices himself for theirs, but he knows that the relationship will bring mutual resentment, not pleasure—and that, morally, their pursuit of values will be like an exchange of unwanted, unchosen Christmas presents, which neither is morally permitted to buy for himself. Apart from such times as he manages to perform some act of self-sacrifice, he possesses no moral significance: morality takes no cognizance of him and has nothing to say to him for guidance in the crucial issues of his life; it is only his own personal, private, "selfish" life and, as such, it is regarded either as evil or, at best, *amoral.*

[Ibid., xi; pb viii.]

Even though altruism declares that "it is more blessed to give than to receive," it does not work that way in practice. The givers are never blessed; the more they give, the more is demanded of them; complaints, reproaches and insults are the only response they get for practicing altruism's virtues (or for their *actual* virtues). Altruism cannot permit a recognition of virtue; it cannot permit self-esteem or moral innocence. Guilt is altruism's stock in trade, and the inducing of guilt is its only means of self-perpetuation. If the giver is not kept under a torrent of degrading, demeaning accusations, he might take a look around and put an end to the self-sacrificing.

Altruists are concerned only with those who suffer—not with those who provide relief from suffering, not even enough to care whether they are able to survive. When no actual suffering can be found, the altruists are compelled to invent or manufacture it.

["Moral Inflation," *ARL,* III, 13, 2.]

Some unphilosophical, eclectic altruists, invoking such concepts as "inalienable rights," "personal freedom," "private choice," have claimed that service to others, though morally obligatory, should not be compulsory. The committed, philosophical altruists, however, are consistent: recognizing that such concepts represent an individualist approach to ethics and that this is incompatible with the altruist morality, they declare that there is nothing wrong with compulsion in a good cause—that the use of force to counteract selfishness is ethically justified—and more: that it is ethically *mandatory.*

Every man, they argue, is morally the property of others—of those others it is his lifelong duty to serve; as such, he has no moral right to invest the major part of his time and energy in his own private concerns. If he attempts it, if he refuses voluntarily to make the requisite sacrifices, he is by that fact harming others, i.e., depriving them of what is morally theirs—he is violating men's rights, i.e., the right of others to his service —he is a moral delinquent, and it is an assertion of morality if others

forcibly intervene to extract from him the fulfillment of his altruist obligations, on which he is attempting to default. Justice, they conclude, "social justice," *demands* the initiation of force against the non-sacrificial individual; it demands that others put a stop to his evil. Thus has moral fervor been joined to the rule of physical force, raising it from a criminal tactic to a governing principle of human relationships.
[Leonard Peikoff, "Altruism, Pragmatism, and Brutality," *ARL*, II, 6, 3.]

The social system based on and consonant with the altruist morality —with the code of self-sacrifice—is socialism, in all or any of its variants: fascism, Nazism, communism. All of them treat man as a sacrificial animal to be immolated for the benefit of the group, the tribe, the society, the state. Soviet Russia is the ultimate result, the final product, the full, consistent embodiment of the altruist morality in practice; it represents the only way that that morality can ever be practiced.
["Conservatism: An Obituary," *CUI*, 195.]

America's inner contradiction was the altruist-collectivist ethics. Altruism is incompatible with freedom, with capitalism and with individual rights. One cannot combine the pursuit of happiness with the moral status of a sacrificial animal.
["Man's Rights," *VOS*, 127; pb 95.]

From her start, America was torn by the clash of her political system with the altruist morality. Capitalism and altruism are incompatible; they are philosophical opposites; they cannot co-exist in the same man or in the same society. Today, the conflict has reached its ultimate climax; the choice is clear-cut: either a new morality of rational self-interest, with its consequences of freedom, justice, progress and man's happiness on earth—or the primordial morality of altruism, with its consequences of slavery, brute force, stagnant terror and sacrificial furnaces.
["For the New Intellectual," *FNI*, 62; pb 54.]

Psychology

It is obvious why the morality of *altruism* is a tribal phenomenon. Prehistorical men were physically unable to survive without clinging to a tribe for leadership and protection against other tribes. The cause of altruism's perpetuation into civilized eras is not physical, but psycho-epistemological: the men of self-arrested, perceptual mentality are unable to survive without tribal leadership and "protection" against reality. The doctrine of self-sacrifice does not offend them: they have no sense of self or of personal value—they do not know what it is that they are asked to sacrifice—they have no firsthand inkling of such things as intellectual integrity, love of truth, personally chosen values, or a passionate dedication to an idea. When they hear injunctions against "selfishness," they believe that what they must renounce is the brute, mindless whim-worship of a tribal lone wolf. But their leaders—the theoreticians of altruism—know better. Immanuel Kant knew it; John Dewey knew it; B. F. Skinner knows it; John Rawls knows it. Observe that it is not the mindless brute, but reason, intelligence, ability, merit, self-confidence, self-esteem that they are out to destroy.

["Selfishness Without a Self," *PWNI*, 61; pb 50.]

The advocates of mysticism are motivated not by a quest for truth, but by hatred for man's mind; . . . the advocates of altruism are motivated not by compassion for suffering, but by hatred for man's life.

["An Untitled Letter," *PWNI*, 123; pb 102.]

The psychological results of altruism may be observed in the fact that a great many people approach the subject of ethics by asking such questions as: "Should one risk one's life to help a man who is: a) drowning, b) trapped in a fire, c) stepping in front of a speeding truck, d) hanging by his fingernails over an abyss?"

Consider the implications of that approach. If a man accepts the ethics of altruism, he suffers the following consequences (in proportion to the degree of his acceptance):

1. Lack of self-esteem—since his first concern in the realm of values is not how to live his life, but how to sacrifice it.

2. Lack of respect for others—since he regards mankind as a herd of doomed beggars crying for someone's help.

3. A nightmare view of existence—since he believes that men are trapped in a "malevolent universe" where disasters are the constant and primary concern of their lives.

4. And, in fact, a lethargic indifference to ethics, a hopelessly cynical amorality—since his questions involve situations which he is not likely ever to encounter, which bear no relation to the actual problems of his own life and thus leave him to live without any moral principles whatever.

By elevating the issue of helping others into the central and primary issue of ethics, altruism has destroyed the concept of any authentic benevolence or good will among men. It has indoctrinated men with the idea that to value another human being is an act of selflessness, thus implying that a man can have no personal interest in others—that *to value* another means *to sacrifice* oneself—that any love, respect or admiration a man may feel for others is not and cannot be a source of his own enjoyment, but is a threat to his existence, a sacrificial blank check signed over to his loved ones.

The men who accept that dichotomy but choose its other side, the ultimate products of altruism's dehumanizing influence, are those psychopaths who do not challenge altruism's basic premise, but proclaim their rebellion against self-sacrifice by announcing that they are totally indifferent to anything living and would not lift a finger to help a man or a dog left mangled by a hit-and-run driver (who is usually one of their own kind).

["The Ethics of Emergencies," *VOS*, 46; pb 43.]

[Intellectual appeasement] is an attempt to apologize for his intellectual concerns and to escape from the loneliness of a thinker by professing that his thinking is dedicated to some social-altruistic goal. It is an attempt that amounts to the wordless equivalent of the plea: "I'm not an outsider! I'm your friend! Please forgive me for using my mind— I'm using it only in order to serve *you!*"

Whatever remnants of personal value he may preserve after a deal of that kind, self-esteem is not one of them.

Such decisions are seldom, if ever, made consciously. They are made gradually, by subconscious emotional motivation and semi-conscious rationalization. Altruism offers an arsenal of such rationalizations: if an unformed adolescent can tell himself that his cowardice is humanitarian love, that his subservience is unselfishness, that his moral treason is spiritual nobility, he is hooked.

["Altruism as Appeasement," *TO*, Jan. 1966, 2.]

The injunction "don't judge" is the ultimate climax of the altruist morality which, today, can be seen in its naked essence. When men plead for forgiveness, for the nameless, cosmic forgiveness of an unconfessed evil, when they react with instantaneous compassion to any guilt, to the perpetrators of any atrocity, while turning away indifferently from the bleeding bodies of the victims and the innocent—one may see the actual purpose, motive and psychological appeal of the altruist code. When these same compassionate men turn with snarling hatred upon anyone who pronounces moral judgments, when they scream that the only evil is the determination to fight against evil—one may see the kind of moral blank check that the altruist morality hands out.

["For the New Intellectual," *FNI*, 50; pb 45.]

See also CHARITY; COLLECTIVISM; "DUTY"; KANT, IMMANUEL; MORALITY; MYSTICISM; SACRIFICE; SELFISHNESS; SELFLESSNESS; SOVIET RUSSIA; SUFFERING; TRIBALISM.

Ambition. "Ambition" means the systematic pursuit of achievement and of constant improvement in respect to one's goal. Like the word "selfishness," and for the same reasons, the word "ambition" has been perverted to mean only the pursuit of dubious or evil goals, such as the pursuit of power; this left no concept to designate the pursuit of actual values. But "ambition" as such is a neutral concept: the evaluation of a given ambition as moral or immoral depends on the nature of the goal. A great scientist or a great artist is the most passionately ambitious of men. A demagogue seeking political power is ambitious. So is a social climber seeking "prestige." So is a modest laborer who works conscientiously to acquire a home of his own. The common denominator is the drive to improve the conditions of one's existence, however broadly or narrowly conceived. ("Improvement" is a moral term and depends on one's standard of values. An ambition guided by an irrational standard does not, *in fact*, lead to improvement, but to self-destruction.)

["Tax Credits for Education," *ARL*, I, 12, 1.]

Politically, the goal of today's dominant trend is statism. Philosophically, the goal is the obliteration of reason; psychologically, it is the erosion of ambition.

The political goal presupposes the two others. The human characteristic required by statism is *docility*, which is the product of hopelessness and intellectual stagnation. Thinking men cannot be ruled; ambitious men do not stagnate.

[Ibid.]

See also CAREER; PRODUCTIVENESS; PURPOSE; VALUES.

America. I can say—not as a patriotic bromide, but with full knowledge of the necessary metaphysical, epistemological, ethical, political and esthetic roots—that the United States of America is the greatest, the noblest and, in its original founding principles, the *only* moral country in the history of the world.

["Philosophy: Who Needs It," *PWNI*, 12; pb 10.]

Since the golden age of Greece, there has been only one era of reason in twenty-three centuries of Western philosophy. During the final decades of that era, the United States of America was created as an independent nation. This is the key to the country—to its nature, its development, and its uniqueness: the United States is *the nation of the Enlightenment.*

[Leonard Peikoff, *OP*, 101; pb 100.]

America's founding ideal was the principle of individual rights. Nothing more—and nothing less. The rest—everything that America achieved, everything she became, everything "noble and just," and heroic, and great, and unprecedented in human history—was the logical consequence of fidelity to that one principle. The first consequence was the principle of political freedom, i.e., an individual's freedom from physical compulsion, coercion or interference by the government. The next was the economic implementation of political freedom: the system of capitalism.

["A Preview," *ARL*, I, 24, 5.]

The most profoundly revolutionary achievement of the United States of America was *the subordination of society to moral law.*

The principle of man's individual rights represented the extension of morality into the social system—as a limitation on the power of the state, as man's protection against the brute force of the collective, as the subordination of *might* to *right.* The United States was the first *moral* society in history.

All previous systems had regarded man as a sacrificial means to the ends of others, and society as an end in itself. The United States regarded man as an end in himself, and society as a means to the peaceful, orderly, *voluntary* co-existence of individuals. All previous systems had held that man's life belongs to society, that society can dispose of him in any way it pleases, and that any freedom he enjoys is his only by favor, by the *permission* of society, which may be revoked at any time. The United States held that man's life is his by *right* (which means: by moral principle and by his nature), that a right is the property of an individual, that society as such has no rights, and that the only moral purpose of a government is the protection of individual rights.

["Man's Rights," *VOS*, 124; pb 93.]

It took centuries of intellectual, philosophical development to achieve political freedom. It was a long struggle, stretching from Aristotle to John Locke to the Founding Fathers. The system they established was not based on unlimited majority rule, but on its opposite: on individual rights, which were not to be alienated by majority vote or minority plotting. The individual was not left at the mercy of his neighbors or his leaders: the Constitutional system of checks and balances was scientifically devised to protect him from both.

This was the great American achievement—and if concern for the actual welfare of other nations were our present leaders' motive, this is what we should have been teaching the world.

["Theory and Practice," *CUI*, 138.]

To the glory of mankind, there was, for the first and only time in history, a *country of money*—and I have no higher, more reverent tribute to pay to America, for this means: a country of reason, justice, freedom, production, achievement. For the first time, man's mind and money were set free, and there were no fortunes-by-conquest, but only fortunes-by-work, and instead of swordsmen and slaves, there appeared the real maker of wealth, the greatest worker, the highest type of human being—the self-made man—the American industrialist.

If you ask me to name the proudest distinction of Americans, I would choose—because it contains all the others—the fact that they were the people who created the phrase "to *make* money." No other language or nation had ever used these words before; men had always thought of wealth as a static quantity—to be seized, begged, inherited, shared, looted or obtained as a favor. Americans were the first to understand that wealth has to be created.

["The Meaning of Money," *FNI*, 111; pb 93.]

America's abundance was not created by public sacrifices to "the common good," but by the productive genius of free men who pursued their own personal interests and the making of their own private fortunes. They did not starve the people to pay for America's industrialization. They gave the people better jobs, higher wages, and cheaper goods with every new machine they invented, with every scientific discovery or technological advance—and thus the whole country was moving forward and profiting, not suffering, every step of the way.

["What Is Capitalism?" *CUI*, 29.]

In its great era of capitalism, the United States was the freest country on earth—and the best refutation of racist theories. Men of all races came here, some from obscure, culturally undistinguished countries, and accomplished feats of productive ability which would have remained stillborn in their control-ridden native lands. Men of racial groups that had been slaughtering one another for centuries, learned to live together in harmony and peaceful cooperation. America had been called "the melting pot," with good reason. But few people realized that America did not melt men into the gray conformity of a collective: she united them by means of protecting their right to individuality.

The major victims of such race prejudice as did exist in America were the Negroes. It was a problem originated and perpetuated by the non-capitalist South, though not confined to its boundaries. The persecution of Negroes in the South was and is truly disgraceful. But in the rest of the country, so long as men were free, even that problem was slowly giving way under the pressure of enlightenment and of the white men's own economic interests.

Today, that problem is growing worse—and so is every other form of racism. America has become race-conscious in a manner reminiscent of the worst days in the most backward countries of nineteenth-century Europe. The cause is the same: the growth of collectivism and statism.

["Racism," *VOS*, 178; pb 130.]

The Americans were political revolutionaries but not *ethical* revolutionaries. Whatever their partial (and largely implicit) acceptance of the principle of ethical egoism, they remained explicitly within the standard European tradition, avowing their primary allegiance to a moral code stressing philanthropic service and social duty. Such was the American conflict: an impassioned politics presupposing one kind of ethics, within a cultural atmosphere professing the sublimity of an opposite kind of ethics.

[Leonard Peikoff, *OP*, 117; pb 115.]

America's inner contradiction was the altruist-collectivist ethics. Altruism is incompatible with freedom, with capitalism and with individual rights. One cannot combine the pursuit of happiness with the moral status of a sacrificial animal.

["Man's Rights," *VOS*, 127; pb 95.]

This country—the product of *reason*—could not survive on the morality of sacrifice. It was not built by men who sought self-immolation or by men who sought handouts. It could not stand on the mystic split that divorced man's soul from his body. It could not live by the mystic doctrine that damned this earth as evil and those who succeeded on earth as depraved. From its start, this country was a threat to the ancient rule of mystics. In the brilliant rocket-explosion of its youth, this country displayed to an incredulous world what greatness was possible to man, what happiness was possible on earth. It was one or the other: America or mystics. The mystics knew it; you didn't. You let them infect you with the worship of *need*—and this country became a giant in body with a mooching midget in place of its soul, while its living soul was driven underground to labor and feed you in silence, unnamed, unhonored, negated, its soul and hero: the industrialist.

[GS, *FNI*, 228; pb 181.]

A dictatorship cannot take hold in America today. This country, as yet, cannot be ruled—but it can explode. It can blow up into the helpless rage and blind violence of a civil war. It cannot be cowed into submission, passivity, malevolence, resignation. It cannot be "pushed around." Defiance, not obedience, is the American's answer to overbearing authority. The nation that ran an underground railroad to help human beings escape from slavery, or began drinking *on principle* in the face of Prohibition, will not say "Yes, sir," to the enforcers of ration coupons and cereal prices. Not yet.

["Don't Let It Go," *PWNI*, 260; pb 213.]

Americans have known how to erect a superlative material achievement in the midst of an untouched wilderness, against the resistance of savage tribes. What we need today is to erect a corresponding *philosophical* structure, without which the material greatness cannot survive. A skyscraper cannot stand on crackerbarrels, nor on wall mottoes, nor on full-page ads, nor on prayers, nor on meta-language. The new wilderness to reclaim is philosophy, now all but deserted, with the weeds of prehistoric doctrines rising again to swallow the ruins. To support a culture, nothing less than a new philosophical foundation will do.

["For the New Intellectual," *FNI*, 58; pb 50.]

America vs. Europe

It was a European who discovered America, but it was Americans who were the first nation to discover this earth and man's proper place in it, and man's potential for happiness, and the world which is man's to win. What they failed to discover is the words to name their achievement, the concepts to identify it, the principles to guide it, i.e., the appropriate philosophy and its consequence: an *American* culture.

America has never had an *original* culture, i.e., a body of ideas derived from her philosophical (*Aristotelian*) base and expressing her profound difference from all other countries in history.

American intellectuals were Europe's passive dependents and poor relatives almost from the beginning. They lived on Europe's drying crumbs and discarded fashions, including even such hand-me-downs as Freud and Wittgenstein. America's sole contribution to philosophy—Pragmatism—was a bad recycling of Kantian-Hegelian premises.

["Don't Let It Go," *PWNI*, 256; pb 210.]

Europeans do believe in Original Sin, i.e., in man's innate depravity; Americans do not. Americans see man as a value—as clean, free, creative, rational. But the American view of man has not been expressed or upheld *in philosophical terms* (not since the time of our first Founding Father, Aristotle; see his description of the "magnanimous man").

[Ibid., 258; pb 211.]

There have never been any "masses" in America: the poorest American is an individual and, subconsciously, an individualist. Marxism, which has conquered our universities, is a dismal failure as far as the people are concerned: Americans cannot be sold on any sort of class war; American workers do not see themselves as a "proletariat," but are among the proudest of property owners. It is professors and businessmen who advocate cooperation with Soviet Russia—American labor unions do not.

[Ibid., 258; pb 212.]

America is the land of the uncommon man. It is the land where man is free to develop his genius—and to get its just rewards. It is the land where each man tries to develop whatever quality he may possess and to rise to whatever degree he can, great or modest. It is not the land where one glories or is taught to glory in one's mediocrity.

No self-respecting man in America is or thinks of himself as "little," no matter how poor he may be. That, precisely, is the difference between an American working man and a European serf.

["Screen Guide for Americans," *Plain Talk*, Nov. 1947, 40.]

Tribalism (which is the best name to give to all the group manifestations of the anti-conceptual mentality) is a dominant element in Europe, as a reciprocally reinforcing cause and result of Europe's long history of caste systems, of national and local (provincial) chauvinism, of rule by brute force and endless, bloody wars. As an example, observe the Balkan nations, which are perennially bent upon exterminating one another over minuscule differences of tradition or language. Tribalism had no place in the United States—until recent decades. It could not take root here, its imported seedlings were withering away and turning to slag in the melting pot whose fire was fed by two inexhaustible sources of energy: individual rights and objective law; these two were the only protection man needed.

["The Missing Link," *PWNI*, 51; pb 42.]

A European is disarmed in the face of a dictatorship: he may hate it, but he feels that he is wrong and, metaphysically, the State is right. An American would rebel to the bottom of his soul. . . . Defiance, not obedience, is the American's answer to overbearing authority.

["Don't Let It Go," *PWNI*, 260; pb 213.]

See also ARISTOTLE; CAPITALISM; CONSTITUTION; ENLIGHTENMENT, AGE of; FOUNDING FATHERS; INDIVIDUALISM; INDIVIDUAL RIGHTS; REPUBLIC.

Amoralism.   The clearest symptom by which one can recognize [the amoralist] is his total inability to judge himself, his actions, or his work by any sort of standard. The normal pattern of self-appraisal requires a reference to some abstract value or virtue—e.g., "I am good because I am rational," "I am good because I am honest," even the second-hander's notion of "I am good because people like me." Regardless of whether the value-standards involved are true or false, these examples imply the recognition of an essential moral principle: that one's own value has to be *earned.*

The amoralist's implicit pattern of self-appraisal (which he seldom identifies or admits) is: "I am good because it's *me.*"

Beyond the age of about three to five (i.e., beyond the perceptual level of mental development), this is not an expression of pride or self-esteem, but of the opposite: of a vacuum—of a stagnant, arrested mentality confessing its impotence to achieve any personal value or virtue.

Do not confuse this pattern with psychological subjectivism. A psychological subjectivist is unable fully to identify his values or to prove their objective validity, but he may be profoundly consistent and loyal to them in practice (though with terrible psycho-epistemological difficulty). The amoralist does not hold subjective values; he does not hold *any* values. The implicit pattern of all his estimates is: "It's good because *I* like it"— "It's right because *I* did it"—"It's true because *I* want it to be true." What is the "I" in these statements? A physical hulk driven by chronic anxiety.

["Selfishness Without a Self," *PWNI,* 60; pb 47.]

[The amoralist] will walk over piles of corpses—in order to assert himself? no—in order to hide (or fill) the nagging inner vacuum left by his aborted self.

The grim joke on mankind is the fact that *he* is held up as a symbol of *selfishness.*

[Ibid., 58; pb 50.]

See also ANTI-CONCEPTUAL MENTALITY; MORALITY; SELFISH-NESS; SELF; SELF-ESTEEM; TRIBALISM.

Analytic-Synthetic Dichotomy.   The assault on man's conceptual faculty has been accelerating since Kant, widening the breach between man's mind and reality. The cognitive function of concepts was undercut by a series of grotesque devices—such, for instance, as the "analytic-synthetic" dichotomy which, by a route of tortuous circumlocutions and equivocations, leads to the dogma that a "necessarily" true proposition cannot be factual, and a factual proposition cannot be "necessarily" true.

[*ITOE*, 102.]

Objectivism rejects the theory of the analytic-synthetic dichotomy as false—in principle, at root, and in every one of its variants. . . .

An analytic proposition is defined as one which can be validated merely by an analysis of the meaning of its constituent concepts. The critical question is: *What is included in "the meaning of a concept"?* Does a concept mean the *existents* which it subsumes, including *all* their characteristics? Or does it mean only certain aspects of these existents, designating some of their characteristics but excluding others?

The latter viewpoint is fundamental to every version of the analytic-synthetic dichotomy. The advocates of this dichotomy divide the characteristics of the existents subsumed under a concept into two groups: those which are *included* in the meaning of the concept, and those—the great majority—which, they claim, are *excluded* from its meaning. The dichotomy among propositions follows directly. If a proposition links the "included" characteristics with the concept, it can be validated merely by an "analysis" of the concept; if it links the "excluded" characteristics with the concept, it represents an act of "synthesis."

[Leonard Peikoff, "The Analytic-Synthetic Dichotomy," *ITOE*, 127.]

The Objectivist theory of concepts undercuts the theory of the analytic-synthetic dichotomy at its root. . . . Since a concept is an integration of units, it has no content or meaning apart from its units. *The meaning of a concept consists of the units—the existents—which it integrates, including all the characteristics of these units.*

Observe that concepts mean *existents*, not arbitrarily selected portions of existents. There is no basis whatever—neither metaphysical nor epistemological, neither in the nature of reality nor of a conceptual consciousness—for a division of the characteristics of a concept's units into two groups, one of which is excluded from the concept's meaning. . . .

The fact that certain characteristics are, at a given time, *unknown* to man, does not indicate that these characteristics are excluded from the entity—*or from the concept*. A is A; existents are what they are, independent of the state of human knowledge; and a concept means the existents which it integrates. Thus, a concept subsumes and includes *all* the characteristics of its referents, known and not-yet-known.

[Ibid., 131.]

The theory of the analytic-synthetic dichotomy has its roots in two types of error: one epistemological, the other metaphysical. The epistemological error, as I have discussed, is an incorrect view of the nature of concepts. The metaphysical error is: the dichotomy between necessary and contingent facts.

[Ibid., 144.]

Only in regard to the man-made is it valid to claim: "It happens to be, but it could have been otherwise." Even here, the term "contingent" is highly misleading. Historically, that term has been used to designate a metaphysical category of much wider scope than the realm of human action; and it has always been associated with a metaphysics which, in one form or another, denies the facts of Identity and Causality. The "necessary-contingent" terminology serves only to introduce confusion, and should be abandoned. What is required in this context is the distinction between the "metaphysical" and the "man-made." . . . Truths about metaphysical and about man-made facts are learned and validated by the same process: by observation; and, *qua truths*, both are equally necessary. Some *facts* are not necessary, but all *truths* are.

[Ibid., 150.]

The failure to recognize that logic is man's method of cognition, has produced a brood of artificial splits and dichotomies which represent restatements of the analytic-synthetic dichotomy from various aspects. Three in particular are prevalent today: logical truth vs. factual truth; the logically possible vs. the empirically possible; and the a priori vs. the a posteriori.

[Ibid., 152.]

The theory of the analytic-synthetic dichotomy presents men with the following choice: If your statement is proved, it says nothing about that which exists; if it is about existents, it cannot be proved. If it is demonstrated by logical argument, it represents a subjective convention; if it asserts a fact, logic cannot establish it. If you validate it by an appeal to the meanings of your *concepts*, then it is cut off from reality; if you validate it by an appeal to your *percepts*, then you cannot be certain of it.

[Ibid., 126.]

See also CAUSALITY; CONCEPT-FORMATION; CONCEPTS; DEFINI-TIONS; MEANING (of CONCEPTS); METAPHYSICAL vs. MAN-MADE; NECESSITY.

Anarchism.   Anarchy, as a political concept, is a naive floating abstraction: . . . a society without an organized government would be at the mercy of the first criminal who came along and who would precipitate it into the chaos of gang warfare. But the possibility of human immorality is not the only objection to anarchy: even a society whose every member were fully rational and faultlessly moral, could not function in a state of anarchy; it is the need of *objective* laws and of an arbiter for honest disagreements among men that necessitates the establishment of a government.

["The Nature of Government," *VOS*, 152; pb 112.]

If a society provided no organized protection against force, it would compel every citizen to go about armed, to turn his home into a fortress, to shoot any strangers approaching his door—or to join a protective gang of citizens who would fight other gangs, formed for the same purpose, and thus bring about the degeneration of that society into the chaos of gang-rule, i.e., rule by brute force, into perpetual tribal warfare of prehistorical savages.

The use of physical force—even its retaliatory use—cannot be left at the discretion of individual citizens. Peaceful coexistence is impossible if a man has to live under the constant threat of force to be unleashed against him by any of his neighbors at any moment. Whether his neighbors' intentions are good or bad, whether their judgment is rational or irrational, whether they are motivated by a sense of justice or by ignorance or by prejudice or by malice—the use of force against one man cannot be left to the arbitrary decision of another.

[Ibid., 146; pb 108.]

A recent variant of anarchistic theory, which is befuddling some of the younger advocates of freedom, is a weird absurdity called "competing governments." Accepting the basic premise of the modern statists—who see no difference between the functions of government and the functions of industry, between force and production, and who advocate government ownership of business—the proponents of "competing governments" take the other side of the same coin and declare that since competition is so beneficial to business, it should also be applied to government. Instead of a single, monopolistic government, they declare, there should be a number of different governments in the same geographical area, competing for the allegiance of individual citizens, with every citizen free to "shop" and to patronize whatever government he chooses.

Remember that forcible restraint of men is the only service a government has to offer. Ask yourself what a competition in forcible restraint would have to mean.

One cannot call this theory a contradiction in terms, since it is obviously devoid of any understanding of the terms "competition" and "government." Nor can one call it a floating abstraction, since it is devoid of any contact with or reference to reality and cannot be concretized at all, not even roughly or approximately. One illustration will be sufficient: suppose Mr. Smith, a customer of Government A, suspects that his next-door neighbor, Mr. Jones, a customer of Government B, has robbed him; a squad of Police A proceeds to Mr. Jones' house and is met at the door by a squad of Police B, who declare that they do not accept the validity of Mr. Smith's complaint and do not recognize the authority of Government A. What happens then? You take it from there.

[Ibid., 152; pb 112.]

The common denominator of such [advocates of "competing governments"] is the desire to escape from *objectivity* (objectivity requires a very long conceptual chain and very abstract principles), to act on whim, and to deal with men rather than with ideas—i.e., with the men of their own gang bound by the same concretes.

["The Missing Link," *PWNI*, 53; pb 44.]

Picture a band of strangers marching down Main Street, submachine guns at the ready. When confronted by the police, the leader of the band announces: "Me and the boys are only here to see that justice is done, so you have no right to interfere with us." According to the "libertarian" anarchists, in such a confrontation the police are morally bound to withdraw, on pain of betraying the rights of self-defense and free trade.

[Harry Binswanger, "Q & A Department:
Anarchism," *TOF*, Aug. 1981, 12.]

Private force is force not authorized by the government, not validated by its procedural safeguards, and not subject to its supervision. The government has to regard such private force as a threat—i.e., as a potential violation of individual rights. In barring such private force, the government is retaliating against that threat.

[Ibid., 11.]

*See also COMPETITION; GOVERNMENT; ECONOMIC POWER vs. PO-
LITICAL POWER; LAW, OBJECTIVE and NON-OBJECTIVE; OBJEC-
TIVITY; RETALIATORY FORCE; WHIMS/WHIM-WORSHIP.*

Ancient Greece. The sound of the first human step in recorded history, the prelude to the entrance of the producer on the historical scene, was the birth of philosophy in ancient Greece. All earlier cultures had been ruled, not by reason, but by mysticism: the task of philosophy —the formulation of an integrated view of man, of existence, of the universe—was the monopoly of various religions that enforced their views by the authority of a claim to supernatural knowledge and dictated the rules that controlled men's lives. Philosophy was born in a period when . . . a comparative degree of political freedom undercut the power of mysticism and, for the first time, man was free to face an unobstructed universe, free to declare that his *mind* was competent to deal with all the problems of his existence and that *reason* was his only means of knowledge.

["For the New Intellectual," *FNI*, 19; pb 22.]

Ancient Greece tore away the heavy shroud of mysticism woven for centuries in murky temples, and achieved, in three centuries, what Egypt had not dreamed of in thirty: a civilization that was essentially pro-man and pro-life. The achievements of the Greeks rested on their confidence in the power of man's mind—the power of reason. For the first time, men sought to understand the causes of natural phenomena, and gradually replaced superstition with the beginnings of science. For the first time, men sought to guide their lives by the judgment of reason, instead of resorting exclusively to divine will and revelation.

The Greeks built temples for their gods, but they conceived of their gods as perfect human beings, rejecting the cats, crocodiles and cow-headed monstrosities enshrined and worshiped by the Egyptians. Greek gods personified abstractions such as Beauty, Wisdom, Justice, Victory, which are proper human values. In the Greek religion, there was no omnipotent mystical authority and no organized priesthood. The Greek had only a vague idea of, and little interest in, an afterlife.

[Mary Ann Sures, "Metaphysics in Marble," *TO*, Feb. 1969, 12.]

See also ART; HISTORY; MYSTICISM; REASON; PHILOSOPHY.

"Anti-Concepts."   An anti-concept is an unnecessary and rationally unusable term designed to replace and obliterate some legitimate concept. The use of anti-concepts gives the listeners a sense of *approximate* understanding. But in the realm of cognition, nothing is as bad as the approximate. . . .

One of today's fashionable anti-concepts is "polarization." Its meaning is not very clear, except that it is something bad—undesirable, socially destructive, evil—something that would split the country into irreconcilable camps and conflicts. It is used mainly in political issues and serves as a kind of "argument from intimidation": it replaces a discussion of the merits (the truth or falsehood) of a given idea by the menacing accusation that such an idea would "polarize" the country—which is supposed to make one's opponents retreat, protesting that they didn't mean it. Mean—what? . . .

It is doubtful—even in the midst of today's intellectual decadence— that one could get away with declaring explicitly: "Let us abolish all debate on fundamental principles!" (though some men have tried it). If, however, one declares: "Don't let us polarize," and suggests a vague image of warring camps ready to fight (with no mention of the fight's object), one has a chance to silence the mentally weary. The use of "polarization" as a pejorative term means: the *suppression* of fundamental principles. Such is the pattern of the function of anti-concepts.

["Credibility and Polarization," *ARL*, I, 1, 1.]

Observe the technique involved . . . It consists of creating an artificial, unnecessary, and (rationally) unusable term, designed to replace and obliterate some legitimate concepts—a term which sounds like a concept, but stands for a "package-deal" of disparate, incongruous, contradictory elements taken out of any logical conceptual order or context, a "package-deal" whose (approximately) defining characteristic is always a non-essential. This last is the essence of the trick.

Let me remind you that the purpose of a definition is to distinguish the things subsumed under a single concept from all other things in existence; and, therefore, their defining characteristic must always be that essential characteristic which distinguishes them from everything else.

So long as men use language, *that* is the way they will use it. There is *no* other way to communicate. And if a man accepts a term with a definition by non-essentials, his mind will substitute for it the *essential* characteristic of the objects he is trying to designate. . . . Thus the real meaning of the term will automatically replace the alleged meaning.

[" 'Extremism,' or The Art of Smearing," *CUI*, 176.]

[Some other terms that Ayn Rand identified as anti-concepts are "consumerism," "duty," "ethnicity," "extremism," "isolationism," "McCarthyism," "meritocracy," and "simplistic."]

See also *ARGUMENT from INTIMIDATION; CONCEPTS; DEFINITIONS; INVALID CONCEPTS; "PACKAGE-DEALING," FALLACY of.*

Anti-Conceptual Mentality.

The main characteristic of this mentality is a special kind of passivity: not passivity as such and not across-the-board, but passivity beyond a certain limit—i.e., passivity in regard to the process of conceptualization and, therefore, in regard to fundamental principles. It is a mentality which decided, at a certain point of development, that it knows enough and does not care to look further. What does it accept as "enough"? The immediately given, directly perceivable concretes of its background. . . .

To grasp and deal with such concretes, a human being needs a certain degree of conceptual development, a process which the brain of an animal cannot perform. But after the initial feat of learning to speak, a child can counterfeit this process, by memorization and imitation. The anti-conceptual mentality stops on this level of development—on the first levels of abstractions, which identify perceptual material consisting predominantly of physical objects—and does not choose to take the next, crucial, fully volitional step: the higher levels of abstraction from abstractions, which cannot be learned by imitation. (See my book *Introduction to Objectivist Epistemology*.) . . .

The anti-conceptual mentality takes most things as irreducible primaries and regards them as "self-evident." It treats concepts as if they were (memorized) percepts; it treats abstractions as if they were *perceptual* concretes. To such a mentality, everything is the given: the passage of time, the four seasons, the institution of marriage, the weather, the breeding of children, a flood, a fire, an earthquake, a revolution, a book are phenomena of the same order. The distinction between the metaphysical and the man-made is not merely unknown to this mentality, it is incommunicable.

[*"The Missing Link," PWNI*, 45; pb 38.]

[This type of mentality] has learned to speak, but has never grasped the process of conceptualization. Concepts, to him, are merely some sort of code signals employed by other people for some inexplicable reason, signals that have no relation to reality or to himself. He treats concepts as if they were percepts, and their meaning changes with any change of circumstances. Whatever he learns or happens to retain is treated, in his mind, as if it had always been there, as if it were an item of direct awareness, with no memory of how he acquired it—as a random store of unprocessed material that comes and goes at the mercy of chance. . . . He does not seek knowledge—he "exposes himself" to "experience," hoping, in effect, that it will push something into his mind; if nothing happens, he feels with self-righteous rancor that there is nothing he can do about it. Mental action, i.e., mental *effort*—any sort of processing, identifying, organizing, integrating, critical evaluation or control of his mental content—is an alien realm.

[*"The Age of Envy," NL*, 177.]

This mentality is not the product of ignorance (nor is it caused by lack of intelligence): it is self-made, i.e., self-arrested.

["The Missing Link," *PWNI*, 50; pb 42.]

In the brain of an anti-conceptual person, the process of integration is largely replaced by a process of association. What his subconscious stores and automatizes is not ideas, but an indiscriminate accumulation of sundry concretes, random facts, and unidentified feelings, piled into unlabeled mental file folders. This works, up to a certain point—i.e., so long as such a person deals with other persons whose folders are stuffed similarly, and thus no search through the entire filing system is ever required. Within such limits, the person can be active and willing to work hard. . . .

A person of this mentality may uphold some abstract principles or profess some intellectual convictions (without remembering where or how he picked them up). But if one asks him what he means by a given idea, he will not be able to answer. If one asks him the *reasons* of his convictions, one will discover that his convictions are a thin, fragile film floating over a vacuum, like an oil slick in empty space—and one will be shocked by the number of questions it had never occurred to him to ask.

[Ibid., 47; pb 39.]

He seems able to understand a discussion or a rational argument, sometimes even on an abstract, theoretical level. He is able to participate, to agree or disagree after what appears to be a critical examination of the issue. But the next time one meets him, the conclusions he reached are gone from his mind, as if the discussion had never occurred even though he remembers it: he remembers the event, i.e., a discussion, not its intellectual content.

It is beside the point to accuse him of hypocrisy or lying (though some part of both is necessarily involved). His problem is much worse than that: he was sincere, he meant what he said *in and for that moment.* But it ended with that moment. Nothing happens in his mind to an idea he accepts or rejects; there is no processing, no integration, no application to himself, his actions or his concerns; he is unable to use it or even to retain it. Ideas, i.e., abstractions, have no reality to him; abstractions involve the past and the future, as well as the present; nothing is fully real to him except the present. Concepts, in his mind, become percepts —percepts of people uttering sounds; and percepts end when the stimuli vanish. When he uses words, his mental operations are closer to those of a parrot than of a human being. In the strict sense of the word, *he has not learned to speak.*

But there is one constant in his mental flux. The subconscious is an integrating mechanism; when left without conscious control, it goes on integrating on its own—and, like an automatic blender, his subconscious squeezes its clutter of trash to produce a single basic emotion: fear.

["The Comprachicos," *NL*, 218.]

It is the fundamentals of philosophy (particularly, of ethics) that an anti-conceptual person dreads above all else. To understand and to apply them requires a long conceptual chain, which he has made his mind incapable of holding beyond the first, rudimentary links. If his professed beliefs—i.e., the rules and slogans of his group—are challenged, he feels his consciousness dissolving in fog. Hence, his fear of outsiders. The word "outsiders," to him, means the whole wide world beyond the confines of his village or town or gang—the world of all those people who do not live by his "rules." He does not know why he feels that outsiders are a deadly threat to him and why they fill him with helpless terror. The threat is not existential, but psycho-epistemological: to deal with them requires that he rise above his "rules" to the level of abstract principles. He would die rather than attempt it.

"Protection from outsiders" is the benefit he seeks in clinging to his group. What the group demands in return is obedience to its rules, which he is eager to obey: those rules *are* his protection—from the dreaded realm of abstract thought.

["The Missing Link," *PWNI*, 49; pb 40.]

Racism is an obvious manifestation of the anti-conceptual mentality. So is xenophobia—the fear or hatred of foreigners ("outsiders"). So is any caste system, which prescribes a man's status (i.e., assigns him to a tribe) according to his birth; a caste system is perpetuated by a special kind of snobbishness (i.e., group loyalty) not merely among the aristocrats, but, perhaps more fiercely, among the commoners or even the serfs, who like to "know their place" and to guard it jealously against the outsiders from above or from below. So is guild socialism. So is any kind of ancestor worship or of family "solidarity" (the family including uncles, aunts and third cousins). So is any criminal gang.

Tribalism . . . is the best name to give to all the group manifestations of the anti-conceptual mentality.

[Ibid., 50; pb 42.]

Observe that today's resurgence of tribalism is not a product of the lower classes—of the poor, the helpless, the ignorant—but of the intellectuals, the college-educated "elitists" (which is a purely tribalistic term). Observe the proliferation of grotesque herds or gangs—hippies, yippies, beatniks, peaceniks, Women's Libs, Gay Libs, Jesus Freaks, Earth Children—which are not tribes, but shifting aggregates of people desperately seeking tribal "protection."

The common denominator of all such gangs is the belief in motion (mass demonstrations), not action—in chanting, not arguing—in demanding, not achieving—in feeling, not thinking—in denouncing "outsiders," not in pursuing values—in focusing only on the "now," the "today" without a "tomorrow"—in seeking to return to "nature," to "the earth," to the mud, to physical labor, i.e., to all the things which a *perceptual* mentality is able to handle. You don't see advocates of reason and science clogging a street in the belief that using their bodies to stop traffic, will solve any problem.

[Ibid., 52; pb 43.]

See also CONCEPTS; PERCEPTION; PSYCHO-EPISTEMOLOGY; RACISM; REASON; TRIBALISM.

Antitrust Laws. The Antitrust laws—an unenforceable, uncompliable, unjudicable mess of contradictions—have for decades kept American businessmen under a silent, growing reign of terror. Yet these laws were created and, to this day, are upheld by the "conservatives," as a grim monument to their lack of political philosophy, of economic knowledge and of any concern with principles. Under the Antitrust laws, a man becomes a criminal from the moment he goes into business, no matter what he does. For instance, if he charges prices which some bureaucrats judge as too high, he can be prosecuted for monopoly or for a successful "intent to monopolize"; if he charges prices lower than those of his competitors, he can be prosecuted for "unfair competition" or "restraint of trade"; and if he charges the same prices as his competitors, he can be prosecuted for "collusion" or "conspiracy." There is only one difference in the legal treatment accorded to a criminal or to a businessman: the criminal's rights are protected much more securely and objectively than the businessman's.

["Choose Your Issues," *TON*, Jan. 1962, 1.]

The alleged purpose of the Antitrust laws was to protect competition; that purpose was based on the socialistic fallacy that a free, unregulated market will inevitably lead to the establishment of coercive monopolies. But, in fact, no coercive monopoly has ever been or ever can be established by means of free trade on a free market. Every coercive monopoly was created by government intervention into the economy: by special privileges, such as franchises or subsidies, which closed the entry of competitors into a given field, by legislative action. (For a full demonstration of this fact, I refer you to the works of the best economists.) The Antitrust laws were the classic example of a moral inversion prevalent in the history of capitalism: an example of the victims, the businessmen, taking the blame for the evils caused by the government, and the government using its own guilt as a justification for acquiring wider powers, on the pretext of "correcting" the evils.

"*Free* competition *enforced* by law" is a grotesque contradiction in terms.

["Antitrust: The Rule of Unreason," *TON*, Feb. 1962, 1.]

[There is only one] meaning and purpose these laws could have, whether their authors intended it or not: the penalizing of ability for being ability, the penalizing of success for being success, and the sacrifice of productive genius to the demands of envious mediocrity.

["America's Persecuted Minority: Big Business," *CUI*, 57.]

See also CAPITALISM; COMPETITION; ECONOMIC POWER vs. POLITICAL POWER; FREE MARKET; LAW, OBJECTIVE AND NON-OBJECTIVE; MONOPOLY; PROPERTY RIGHTS.

Appeasement. Do not confuse appeasement with tactfulness or generosity. Appeasement is not consideration for the feelings of others, it is *consideration for and compliance with the unjust, irrational and evil feelings of others*. It is a policy of exempting the emotions of others from moral judgment, and of willingness to sacrifice innocent, virtuous victims to the evil malice of such emotions.

["The Age of Envy," *NL*, 160.]

The truly and deliberately evil men are a very small minority; it is the appeaser who unleashes them on mankind; it is the appeaser's intellectual abdication that invites them to take over. When a culture's dominant trend is geared to irrationality, the thugs win over the appeasers. When intellectual leaders fail to foster the best in the mixed, unformed, vacillating character of people at large, the thugs are sure to bring out the worst. When the ablest men turn into cowards, the average men turn into brutes.

["Altruism as Appeasement," *TO*, Jan. 1966, 6.]

It is understandable that men might seek to hide their vices from the eyes of people whose judgment they respect. But there are men who hide their virtues from the eyes of monsters. There are men who apologize for their own achievements, deride their own values, debase their own character—for the sake of pleasing those they know to be stupid, corrupt, malicious, evil.

["The Age of Envy," *NL*, 158.]

[Intellectual appeasement] is an attempt to apologize for his intellectual concerns and to escape from the loneliness of a thinker by professing that his thinking is dedicated to some social-altruistic goal. It is an attempt that amounts to the wordless equivalent of the plea: "I'm not an outsider! I'm your friend! Please forgive me for using my mind— I'm using it only in order to serve *you!*" . . . An intellectual appeaser surrenders morality, the realm of values, *in order to be permitted to use his mind.*

["Altruism as Appeasement," *TO*, Jan. 1966, 2.]

See also COMPROMISE; EVIL; INTEGRITY; MORAL COWARDICE; MORAL JUDGMENT; TACTFULNESS.

"A Priori."   The failure to recognize that logic is man's method of cognition, has produced a brood of artificial splits and dichotomies which represent restatements of the analytic-synthetic dichotomy from various aspects. Three in particular are prevalent today: logical truth vs. factual truth; the logically possible vs. the empirically possible; and the a priori vs. the a posteriori.

[Leonard Peikoff, "The Analytic-Synthetic Dichotomy," *ITOE*, 152.]

Any theory that propounds an opposition between the logical and the empirical, represents a failure to grasp the nature of logic and its role in human cognition. Man's knowledge is not acquired by logic apart from experience or by experience apart from logic, but *by the application of logic to experience.* All truths are the product of a logical identification of the facts of experience.

[Ibid., 151.]

See also ANALYTIC-SYNTHETIC DICHOTOMY; LOGIC; TRUTH.

Arbitrary.   "Arbitrary" means a claim put forth in the absence of evidence of any sort, perceptual or conceptual; its basis is neither direct observation nor any kind of theoretical argument. [An arbitrary idea is] a sheer assertion with no attempt to validate it or connect it to reality.

If a man asserts such an idea, whether he does so by error or ignorance or corruption, his idea is thereby epistemologically invalidated. It has no relation to reality or to human cognition.

Remember that man's consciousness is not automatic, and not automatically correct. So if man is to be able to claim any proposition as true, or even as possible, he must follow definite epistemological rules, rules designed to guide his mental processes and keep his conclusions in correspondence to reality. In sum, if man is to achieve knowledge, he must adhere to objective validating methods—i.e., he must shun the arbitrary. . . .

Since an arbitrary statement has no connection to man's means of knowledge or his grasp of reality, cognitively speaking such a statement must be treated as though nothing had been said.

Let me elaborate this point. An arbitrary claim has no cognitive status whatever. According to Objectivism, such a claim is not to be regarded as true or as false. If it is arbitrary, it is entitled to no epistemological assessment at all; it is simply to be dismissed as though it hadn't come up. . . . The truth is established by reference to a body of evidence and within a context; the false is pronounced false because it contradicts the evidence. The arbitrary, however, has *no* relation to evidence, facts, or context. It is the human equivalent of [noises produced by] a parrot . . . sounds without any tie to reality, without content or significance.

In a sense, therefore, the arbitrary is even worse than the false. The false at least has a relation (albeit a negative one) to reality; it has reached the field of human cognition, although it represents an error—but in that sense it is closer to reality than the brazenly arbitrary.

I want to note here parenthetically that the *words* expressing an arbitrary claim may perhaps be judged as true or false in some other cognitive context (if and when they are no longer put forth as arbitrary), but this is irrelevant to the present issue, because it changes the epistemological situation. For instance, if a savage utters "Two plus two equals four" as a memorized lesson which he doesn't understand or see any reason for, then in that context it is arbitrary and the savage did not utter truth or falsehood (it's just like the parrot example). In this sort of situation, the utterance is only sounds; in a cognitive context, when the speaker does know the meaning and the reasons, the same sounds may be used to utter a true proposition. It is inexact to describe this situation by saying, "The same idea is arbitrary in one case and true in another." The exact description would be: in the one case the verbiage does not express an idea at all, it is merely noise unconnected to reality; to the rational man, the words do express an idea: they are conceptual symbols denoting facts.

It is not your responsibility to refute someone's arbitrary assertion— to try to find or imagine arguments that will show that his assertion is false. It is a fundamental error on your part even to try to do this. The rational procedure in regard to an arbitrary assertion is to dismiss it out of hand, merely identifying it as arbitrary, and as such inadmissible and undiscussable.

[Leonard Peikoff, "The Philosophy of Objectivism" lecture series (1976), Lecture 6.]

There is no escape from the law of identity, neither in the universe with which [one] deals nor in the working of his own consciousness, and if he is to acquire knowledge of the first, he must discover the proper method of using the second; . . . there is no room for the *arbitrary* in any activity of man, least of all in his method of cognition—and just as he has learned to be guided by objective criteria in making his physical tools, so he must be guided by objective criteria in forming his tools of cognition: his concepts.

[*ITOE*, 110.]

See also AGNOSTICISM; CERTAINTY; OBJECTIVITY; POSSIBLE; PROOF; SKEPTICISM; TRUTH.

Argument from Intimidation.   There is a certain type of argument which, in fact, is not an argument, but a means of forestalling debate and extorting an opponent's agreement with one's undiscussed notions. It is a method of bypassing logic by means of psychological pressure. . . . [It] consists of threatening to impeach an opponent's character by means of his argument, thus impeaching the argument without debate. Example: "Only the immoral can fail to see that Candidate X's argument is false." . . . The falsehood of his argument is asserted arbitrarily and offered as proof of his immorality.

In today's epistemological jungle, that second method is used more frequently than any other type of irrational argument. It should be classified as a logical fallacy and may be designated as "The Argument from Intimidation."

The essential characteristic of the Argument from Intimidation is its appeal to moral self-doubt and its reliance on the fear, guilt or ignorance of the victim. It is used in the form of an ultimatum demanding that the victim renounce a given idea without discussion, under threat of being considered morally unworthy. The pattern is always: "Only those who are evil (dishonest, heartless, insensitive, ignorant, etc.) can hold such an idea."

["The Argument from Intimidation," *VOS*, 191; pb 139.]

The Argument from Intimidation dominates today's discussions in two forms. In public speeches and print, it flourishes in the form of long, involved, elaborate structures of unintelligible verbiage, which convey nothing clearly except a moral threat. ("Only the primitive-minded can fail to realize that clarity is oversimplification.") But in private, day-by-day experience, it comes up wordlessly, between the lines, in the form of inarticulate sounds conveying unstated implications. It relies, not on *what* is said, but on *how* it is said—not on content, but on tone of voice.

The tone is usually one of scornful or belligerent incredulity. "Surely you are not an advocate of capitalism, are you?" And if this does not intimidate the prospective victim—who answers, properly: "I am,"—the ensuing dialogue goes something like this: "Oh, you couldn't be! Not *really!*" "Really." "But *everybody* knows that capitalism is outdated!" "I don't." "Oh, come now!" "Since I don't know it, will you please tell me the reasons for thinking that capitalism is outdated?" "Oh, don't be ridiculous!" "Will you tell me the reasons?" "Well, really, if you don't know, I couldn't possibly tell you!"

All this is accompanied by raised eyebrows, wide-eyed stares, shrugs, grunts, snickers and the entire arsenal of nonverbal signals communicating ominous innuendoes and emotional vibrations of a single kind: *disapproval.*

If those vibrations fail, if such debaters are challenged, one finds that they have no arguments, no evidence, no proof, no reasons, no ground to stand on—that their noisy aggressiveness serves to hide a vacuum—that the Argument from Intimidation is a confession of intellectual impotence.

[Ibid., 193; pb 140.]

Let me emphasize that the Argument from Intimidation does *not* consist of introducing moral judgment into intellectual issues, but of *substituting* moral judgment for intellectual argument. Moral evaluations are implicit in most intellectual issues; it is not merely permissible, but *mandatory* to pass moral judgment when and where appropriate; to suppress such judgment is an act of moral cowardice. But a moral judgment must always *follow*, not *precede* (or supersede), the reasons on which it is based.

[Ibid., 197; pb 143.]

How does one resist that Argument? There is only one weapon against it: moral certainty.

When one enters any intellectual battle, big or small, public or private, one cannot seek, desire or expect the enemy's sanction. Truth or falsehood must be one's sole concern and sole criterion of judgment—not anyone's approval or disapproval; and, above all, *not* the approval of those whose standards are the opposite of one's own.

[Ibid.]

The most illustrious example of the proper answer to the Argument from Intimidation was given in American history by the man who, rejecting the enemy's moral standards and with full certainty of his own rectitude, said:

"If this be treason, make the most of it."

[Ibid., 198; pb 144.]

See also CERTAINTY; LOGIC; MORAL COWARDICE; "PSYCHOLOGIZ-ING."

Aristotle. If there is a philosophical Atlas who carries the whole of Western civilization on his shoulders, it is Aristotle. He has been opposed, misinterpreted, misrepresented, and—like an axiom—used by his enemies in the very act of denying him. Whatever intellectual progress men have achieved rests on his achievements.

Aristotle may be regarded as the cultural barometer of Western history. Whenever his influence dominated the scene, it paved the way for one of history's brilliant eras; whenever it fell, so did mankind. The Aristotelian revival of the thirteenth century brought men to the Renaissance. The intellectual counter-revolution turned them back toward the cave of his antipode: Plato.

There is only one fundamental issue in philosophy: the cognitive efficacy of man's mind. The conflict of Aristotle versus Plato is the conflict of reason versus mysticism. It was Plato who formulated most of philosophy's basic questions—and doubts. It was Aristotle who laid the foundation for most of the answers. Thereafter, the record of their duel is the record of man's long struggle to deny and surrender or to uphold and assert the validity of his particular mode of consciousness.

[Review of J.H. Randall's *Aristotle, TON*, May 1963, 18.]

Aristotle's philosophy was the intellect's Declaration of Independence. Aristotle, the father of logic, should be given the title of the world's first *intellectual*, in the purest and noblest sense of that word. No matter what remnants of Platonism did exist in Aristotle's system, his incomparable achievement lay in the fact that he defined the *basic* principles of a rational view of existence and of man's consciousness: that there is only *one* reality, the one which man perceives—that it exists as an *objective* absolute (which means: independently of the consciousness, the wishes or the feelings of any perceiver)—that the task of man's consciousness is to *perceive*, not to create, reality—that abstractions are man's method of integrating his sensory material—that man's mind is his only tool of knowledge—that A is A.

If we consider the fact that to this day everything that makes us civilized beings, every rational value that we possess—including the birth of science, the industrial revolution, the creation of the United States, even the structure of our language—is the result of Aristotle's influence, of the degree to which, explicitly or implicitly, men accepted his epistemological principles, we would have to say: never have so many owed so much to one man.

["For the New Intellectual," *FNI*, 20; pb 22.]

Aristotle is the champion of this world, the champion of nature, as against the supernaturalism of Plato. Denying Plato's World of Forms, Aristotle maintains that there is only one reality: the world of particulars in which we live, the world men perceive by means of their physical senses. Universals, he holds, are merely aspects of existing entities, isolated in thought by a process of selective attention; they have no existence apart from particulars. Reality is comprised, not of Platonic abstractions, but of concrete, individual entities, each with a definite nature, each obeying the laws inherent in its nature. Aristotle's universe is the universe of science. The physical world, in his view, is not a shadowy projection controlled by a divine dimension, but an autonomous, self-sufficient realm. It is an orderly, intelligible, *natural* realm, open to the mind of man.

In such a universe, knowledge cannot be acquired by special revelations from another dimension; there is no place for ineffable intuitions of the beyond. Repudiating the mystical elements in Plato's epistemology, Aristotle is the father of logic and the champion of *reason* as man's only means of knowledge. Knowledge, he holds, must be based on and derived from the data of sense experience; it must be formulated in terms of objectively defined concepts; it must be validated by a process of logic.

[Leonard Peikoff, *OP,* 21; pb 29.]

Indicating that the early scientists had discarded Aristotle in rebellion against his religious interpreters, Professor Randall points out that their scientific achievements had, in fact, an unacknowledged Aristotelian base and were carrying out the implications of Aristotle's theories.

[Review of J.H. Randall's *Aristotle, TON,* May 1963, 18.]

Let us note . . . the radical difference between Aristotle's view of concepts and the Objectivist view, particularly in regard to the issue of essential characteristics.

It is Aristotle who first formulated the principles of correct definition. It is Aristotle who identified the fact that only concretes exist. But Aristotle held that definitions refer to metaphysical *essences,* which exist *in* concretes as a special element or formative power, and he held that the process of concept-formation depends on a kind of direct intuition by which man's mind grasps these essences and forms concepts accordingly.

Aristotle regarded "essence" as metaphysical; Objectivism regards it as *epistemological*.

[*ITOE*, 68.]

For Aristotle, the good life is one of personal self-fulfillment. Man should enjoy the values of this world. Using his mind to the fullest, each man should work to achieve his own happiness here on earth. And in the process he should be conscious of his *own* value. Pride, writes Aristotle—a rational pride in oneself and in one's moral character—is, when it is earned, the "crown of the virtues."

A proud man does not negate his own identity. He does not sink selflessly into the community. He is not a promising subject for the Platonic state.

Although Aristotle's writings do include a polemic against the more extreme features of Plato's collectivism, Aristotle himself is not a consistent advocate of political individualism. His own politics is a mixture of statist and antistatist elements. But the primary significance of Aristotle, or of any philosopher, does not lie in his politics. It lies in the fundamentals of his system: his metaphysics and epistemology.

[Leonard Peikoff, *OP*, 21; pb 30.]

Throughout history the influence of Aristotle's philosophy (particularly of his epistemology) has led in the direction of individual freedom, of man's liberation from the power of the state . . . Aristotle (via John Locke) was the philosophical father of the Constitution of the United States and thus of *capitalism* . . . it is Plato and Hegel, not Aristotle, who have been the philosophical ancestors of all totalitarian and welfare states, whether Bismarck's, Lenin's or Hitler's.

[Review of J.H. Randall's *Aristotle*, *TON*, May 1963, 19.]

There is no future for the world except through a rebirth of the Aristotelian approach to philosophy. This would require an Aristotelian affirmation of the reality of existence, of the sovereignty of reason, of life on earth—and of the splendor of man.

Aristotle and Objectivism agree on fundamentals and, as a result, on this last point, also. Both hold that man *can* deal with reality, can achieve values, can live *non*-tragically. Neither believes in man the worm or man the monster; each upholds man the thinker and therefore man the hero. Aristotle calls him "the great-souled man." Ayn Rand calls him Howard Roark, or John Galt.

[Leonard Peikoff, *OP*, 337; pb 311.]

See also ANCIENT GREECE; DEFINITIONS; IDENTITY; LOGIC; OB-
JECTIVISM; PRIDE; RENAISSANCE; ROMANTICISM; SCIENCE;
TABULA RASA.

Art. Art is a selective re-creation of reality according to an artist's
metaphysical value-judgments. Man's profound need of art lies in the
fact that his cognitive faculty is conceptual, i.e., that he acquires knowledge by means of abstractions, and needs the power to bring his widest
metaphysical abstractions into his immediate, perceptual awareness. Art
fulfills this need: by means of a selective re-creation, it concretizes man's
fundamental view of himself and of existence. It tells man, in effect,
which aspects of his experience are to be regarded as essential, significant, important. In this sense, art teaches man how to use his consciousness. It conditions or stylizes man's consciousness by conveying to him a
certain way of looking at existence.

["Art and Cognition," *RM*, pb 45.]

By a selective re-creation, art isolates and integrates those aspects of
reality which represent man's fundamental view of himself and of existence. Out of the countless number of concretes—of single, disorga-
nized and (seemingly) contradictory attributes, actions and entities—an
artist isolates the things which he regards as metaphysically essential
and integrates them into a single new concrete that represents an embodied abstraction.

For instance, consider two statues of man: one as a Greek god, the
other as a deformed medieval monstrosity. Both are metaphysical estimates of man; both are projections of the artist's view of man's nature;
both are concretized representations of the philosophy of their respective cultures.

Art is a concretization of metaphysics. *Art brings man's concepts to the
perceptual level of his consciousness and allows him to grasp them directly, as if
they were percepts.*

This is the psycho-epistemological function of art and the reason of its
importance in man's life (and the crux of the Objectivist esthetics).

["The Psycho-Epistemology of Art," *RM*, 23; pb 19.]

Is the universe intelligible to man, or unintelligible and unknowable?
Can man find happiness on earth, or is he doomed to frustration and
despair? Does man have the power of *choice*, the power to choose his
goals and to achieve them, the power to direct the course of his life—or
is he the helpless plaything of forces beyond his control, which determine his fate? Is man, by nature, to be valued as good, or to be despised

as evil? These are *metaphysical* questions, but the answers to them determine the kind of *ethics* men will accept and practice; the answers are the
link between metaphysics and ethics. And although metaphysics as such
is not a normative science, the answers to this category of questions
assume, in man's mind, the function of metaphysical value-judgments,
since they form the foundation of all of his moral values.

Consciously or subconsciously, explicitly or implicitly, man knows
that he needs a comprehensive view of existence to integrate his
values, to choose his goals, to plan his future, to maintain the unity and
coherence of his life—and that his metaphysical value-judgments are
involved in every moment of his life, in his every choice, decision and
action.

Metaphysics—the science that deals with the fundamental nature of
reality—involves man's widest abstractions. It includes every concrete
he has ever perceived, it involves such a vast sum of knowledge and
such a long chain of concepts that no man could hold it all in the focus
of his immediate conscious awareness. Yet he needs that sum and that
awareness to guide him—he needs the power to summon them into full,
conscious focus.

That power is given to him by art.

[Ibid., 21; pb 19.]

It is not journalistic information or scientific education or moral guidance that man seeks from a work of art (though these may be involved
as secondary consequences), but the fulfillment of a more profound
need: a confirmation of his view of existence—a confirmation, not in
the sense of resolving cognitive doubts, but in the sense of permitting
him to contemplate his abstractions outside his own mind, in the form
of existential concretes.

["Art and Sense of Life," *RM*, 48; pb 38.]

As to the role of emotions in art and the subconscious mechanism
that serves as the integrating factor both in artistic creation and in man's
response to art, they involve a psychological phenomenon which we call
a *sense of life*. A sense of life is a pre-conceptual equivalent of metaphysics, an emotional, subconsciously integrated appraisal of man and of
existence.

["The Psycho-Epistemology of Art," *RM*, 28; pb 24.]

The emotion involved in art is not an emotion in the ordinary meaning of the term. It is experienced more as a "sense" or a "feel," but it
has two characteristics pertaining to emotions: it is automatically immediate and it has an intense, profoundly personal (yet undefined) value-

meaning to the individual experiencing it. The value involved is life, and the words naming the emotion are: "*This* is what life means to *me*."

["Art and Sense of Life," *RM*, 44; pb 35.]

Since man lives by reshaping his physical background to serve his purpose, since he must first define and then create his values—a rational man needs a concretized projection of these values, an image in whose likeness he will re-shape the world and himself. Art gives him that image; it gives him the experience of seeing the full, immediate, concrete reality of his distant goals.

Since a rational man's ambition is unlimited, since his pursuit and achievement of values is a lifelong process—and the higher the values, the harder the struggle—he needs a moment, an hour or some period of time in which he can experience the sense of his completed task, the sense of living in a universe where his values have been successfully achieved. It is like a moment of rest, a moment to gain fuel to move farther. Art gives him that fuel; the pleasure of contemplating the objectified reality of one's own sense of life is the pleasure of feeling what it would be like to live in one's ideal world.

[Ibid., 48; pb 38.]

The importance of that experience is not in *what* he learns from it, but in *that* he experiences it. The fuel is not a theoretical principle, not a didactic "message," but the life-giving fact of experiencing a moment of *metaphysical* joy—a moment of love for existence.

["The Goal of My Writing," *RM*, 171; pb 170.]

Art is man's metaphysical mirror; what a rational man seeks to see in that mirror is a salute; what an irrational man seeks to see is a justification—even if only a justification of his depravity, as a last convulsion of his betrayed self-esteem.

Between these two extremes, there lies the immense continuum of men of mixed premises—whose sense of life holds unresolved, precariously balanced or openly contradictory elements of reason and unreason—and works of art that reflect these mixtures. Since art is the product of philosophy (and mankind's philosophy is tragically mixed), most of the world's art, including some of its greatest examples, falls into this category.

["Art and Sense of Life," *RM*, 49; pb 39.]

Art is the indispensable medium for the communication of a moral ideal. . . .

This does not mean that art is a substitute for philosophical thought: without a conceptual theory of ethics, an artist would not be able successfully to concretize an image of the ideal. But without the assistance of art, ethics remains in the position of theoretical engineering: art is the model-builder. . . .

It is important to stress, however, that even though moral values are inextricably involved in art, they are involved only as a consequence, *not* as a causal determinant: the primary focus of art is metaphysical, not ethical. Art is not the "handmaiden" of morality, its *basic* purpose is not to educate, to reform or to advocate anything. The concretization of a moral ideal is not a textbook on how to become one. The basic purpose of art is *not* to teach, but to *show*—to hold up to man a concretized image of his nature and his place in the universe.

Any metaphysical issue will necessarily have an enormous influence on man's conduct and, therefore, on his ethics; and, since every art work has a theme, it will necessarily convey some conclusion, some "message," to its audience. But that influence and that "message" are only secondary consequences. *Art is not the means to any didactic end.* This is the difference between a work of art and a morality play or a propaganda poster. The greater a work of art, the more profoundly universal its theme. *Art is not the means of literal transcription.* This is the difference between a work of art and a news story or a photograph.

["The Psycho-Epistemology of Art," *RM*, 25; pb 21.]

As a re-creation of reality, a work of art has to be representational; its freedom of stylization is limited by the requirement of intelligibility; if it does not present an intelligible subject, it ceases to be art.

["Art and Cognition," *RM*, pb 75.]

What are the valid forms of art—and why these? . . . The proper forms of art present a selective re-creation of reality in terms needed by man's *cognitive faculty*, which includes his entity-perceiving senses, and thus assist the integration of the various elements of a *conceptual* consciousness. Literature deals with concepts, the visual arts with sight and touch, music with hearing. Each art fulfills the function of bringing man's concepts to the perceptual level of his consciousness and allowing him to grasp them directly, as if they were percepts. (The performing arts are a means of further concretization.) The different branches of art serve to unify man's consciousness and offer him a coherent view of existence. Whether that view is true or false is not an esthetic matter. The crucially esthetic matter is psycho-epistemological: *the integration of a conceptual consciousness.*

[Ibid., 73.]

Art (including literature) is the barometer of a culture. It reflects the sum of a society's deepest philosophical values: not its professed notions and slogans, but its actual view of man and of existence.

["Bootleg Romanticism," *RM*, 121; pb 129.]

See Conceptual Index: Esthetics.

Artistic Creation. As to the role of emotions in art and the subconscious mechanism that serves as the integrating factor both in artistic creation and in man's response to art, they involve a psychological phenomenon which we call a *sense of life*. A sense of life is a pre-conceptual equivalent of metaphysics, an emotional, subconsciously integrated appraisal of man and of existence.

["The Psycho-Epistemology of Art," *RM*, 28; pb 24.]

It is the artist's sense of life that controls and integrates his work, directing the innumerable choices he has to make, from the choice of subject to the subtlest details of style. It is the viewer's or reader's sense of life that responds to a work of art by a complex, yet automatic reaction of acceptance and approval, or rejection and condemnation.

["Art and Sense of Life," *RM*, 43; pb 34.]

The psycho-epistemological process of communication between an artist and a viewer or reader goes as follows: the artist starts with a broad abstraction which he has to concretize, to bring into reality by means of the appropriate particulars; the viewer perceives the particulars, integrates them and grasps the abstraction from which they came, thus completing the circle. Speaking metaphorically, the creative process resembles a process of deduction; the viewing process resembles a process of induction.

This does not mean that communication is the primary purpose of an artist: his primary purpose is to bring his view of man and of existence into reality; but to be brought into reality, it has to be translated into objective (therefore, communicable) terms.

[Ibid., 44; pb 35.]

An artist does not fake reality—he *stylizes* it. He selects those aspects of existence which he regards as metaphysically significant—and by isolating and stressing them, by omitting the insignificant and accidental, he presents *his* view of existence. His concepts are not divorced from the facts of reality—they are concepts which integrate the facts *and* his metaphysical evaluation of the facts. His selection constitutes his evaluation: everything included in a work of art—from theme to subject to brushstroke or adjective—acquires metaphysical significance by the mere fact of being included, of being *important* enough to include.

An artist (as, for instance, the sculptors of Ancient Greece) who presents man as a god-like figure is aware of the fact that men may be crippled or diseased or helpless; but he regards these conditions as accidental, as irrelevant to the essential nature of man—and he presents a figure embodying strength, beauty, intelligence, self-confidence, as man's proper, natural state.

[Ibid., 46; pb 36.]

See also ART; CREATION; EMOTIONS; PSYCHO-EPISTEMOLOGY; SENSE of LIFE; STYLIZATION.

Associations. *See Cooperation.*

Atheism.
Every argument for God and every attribute ascribed to Him rests on a false metaphysical premise. None can survive for a moment on a correct metaphysics. . . .

Existence exists, and only existence exists. Existence is a primary: it is uncreated, indestructible, eternal. So if you are to postulate something beyond existence—some supernatural realm—you must do it by openly denying reason, dispensing with definitions, proofs, arguments, and saying flatly, "To Hell with argument, I have faith." That, of course, is a willful rejection of reason.

Objectivism advocates reason as man's sole means of knowledge, and therefore, for the reasons I have already given, it is atheist. It denies any supernatural dimension presented as a contradiction of nature, of existence. This applies not only to God, but also to every variant of the supernatural ever advocated or to be advocated. In other words, we accept reality, and that's all.

[Leonard Peikoff, "The Philosophy of Objectivism" lecture series (1976), Lecture 2.]

See also AGNOSTICISM; EXISTENCE; GOD; MIRACLES; NATURE; RELIGION; SUPERNATURALISM.

Automatization.
All learning involves a process of automatizing, i.e., of first acquiring knowledge by fully conscious, focused attention and observation, then of establishing mental connections which make that knowledge automatic (instantly available as a context), thus freeing man's mind to pursue further, more complex knowledge.

[*ITOE*, 86.]

The function of psychological integrations is to make certain connections automatic, so that they work as a unit and do not require a conscious process of thought every time they are evoked.

["Art and Sense of Life," *RM*, 45; pb 36.]

A mind's cognitive development involves a continual process of automatization. For example, you cannot perceive a table as an infant perceives it—as a mysterious object with four legs. You perceive it as a table, i.e., a man-made piece of furniture, serving a certain purpose belonging to a human habitation, etc.; you cannot separate these attributes from your sight of the table, you experience it as a single, indivisible percept—yet all you see is a four-legged object; the rest is an automatized integration of a vast amount of conceptual knowledge which, at one time, you had to learn bit by bit. The same is true of everything you perceive or experience; as an adult, you cannot perceive or experience in a vacuum, you do it in a certain automatized *context*—and the efficiency of your mental operations depends on the kind of context your subconscious has automatized.

["The Comprachicos," *NL*, 192.]

The status of automatized knowledge in his mind is experienced by man as if it had the direct, effortless, self-evident quality (and certainty) of perceptual awareness. But it is *conceptual* knowledge—and its validity depends on the precision of his concepts, which require as strict a precision of meaning (i.e., as strict a knowledge of what specific referents they subsume) as the definitions of mathematical terms. (It is obvious what disasters will follow if one automatizes errors, contradictions and undefined approximations.)

[*ITOE*, 86.]

See also INTEGRATION (MENTAL); LEARNING; PSYCHO-EPISTE-MOLOGY; SUBCONSCIOUS.

Awareness. *See Consciousness.*

Axiomatic Concepts. Axioms are usually considered to be propositions identifying a fundamental, self-evident truth. But explicit propositions as such are not primaries: they are made of concepts. The base of man's knowledge—of all other concepts, all axioms, propositions and thought—consists of axiomatic concepts.

An axiomatic concept is the identification of a primary fact of reality, which cannot be analyzed, i.e., reduced to other facts or broken into component parts. It is implicit in all facts and in all knowledge. It is the fundamentally given and directly perceived or experienced, which requires no proof or explanation, but on which all proofs and explanations rest.

The first and primary axiomatic concepts are "existence," "identity" (which is a corollary of "existence") and "consciousness." One can study what exists and how consciousness functions; but one cannot analyze (or "prove") existence as such, or consciousness as such. These are irreducible primaries. (An attempt to "prove" them is self-contradictory: it is an attempt to "prove" existence by means of non-existence, and consciousness by means of unconsciousness.)

[*ITOE,* 73.]

[The] underscoring of primary facts is one of the crucial epistemological functions of axiomatic concepts. It is also the reason why they can be translated into a statement only in the form of a repetition (as a base and a reminder): Existence exists—Consciousness is conscious—A is A. (This converts axiomatic concepts into formal axioms.)

[Ibid., 78.]

Epistemologically, the formation of axiomatic concepts is an act of abstraction, a selective focusing on and mental isolation of metaphysical fundamentals; but metaphysically, it is an act of integration—*the widest integration possible to man:* it unites and embraces the total of his experience.

The units of the concepts "existence" and "identity" are every entity, attribute, action, event or phenomenon (including consciousness) that exists, has ever existed or will ever exist. The units of the concept "consciousness" are every state or process of awareness that one experiences, has ever experienced or will ever experience (as well as similar units, a similar faculty, which one infers in other living entities).

[Ibid., 74.]

Since axiomatic concepts refer to facts of reality and are not a matter of "faith" or of man's arbitrary choice, there is a way to ascertain whether a given concept is axiomatic or not: one ascertains it by observing the fact that an axiomatic concept cannot be escaped, that it is implicit in all knowledge, that it has to be accepted and used even in the process of any attempt to deny it.

For instance, when modern philosophers declare that axioms are a matter of arbitrary choice, and proceed to choose complex, derivative concepts as the alleged axioms of their alleged reasoning, one can observe that their statements imply and depend on "existence," "consciousness," "identity," which they profess to negate, but which are smuggled into their arguments in the form of unacknowledged, "stolen" concepts.

It is worth noting, at this point, that what the enemies of reason seem to know, but its alleged defenders have not discovered, is the fact that *axiomatic concepts are the guardians of man's mind and the foundation of reason* —the keystone, touchstone and hallmark of reason—and if reason is to be destroyed, it is axiomatic concepts that have to be destroyed.

[Ibid., 79.]

It is only conceptual awareness that can grasp and hold the total of its experience—extrospectively, the continuity of existence; introspectively, the continuity of consciousness—and thus enable its possessor to project his course long-range. It is by means of axiomatic concepts that man grasps and holds this continuity, bringing it into his conscious awareness and *knowledge*. It is axiomatic concepts that identify the precondition of knowledge: the distinction between existence and consciousness, between reality and the awareness of reality, between the object and the subject of cognition. Axiomatic concepts are the foundation of *objectivity*.

[Ibid., 75.]

It is only man's consciousness, a consciousness capable of conceptual errors, that needs a special identification of the directly given, to embrace and delimit the entire field of its awareness—to delimit it from the void of unreality to which conceptual errors can lead. Axiomatic concepts are epistemological guidelines. They sum up the essence of all human cognition: something *exists* of which I am *conscious;* I must discover its *identity*.

[Ibid., 78.]

Since axiomatic concepts are identifications of irreducible primaries, the only way to define one is by means of an ostensive definition—e.g., to define "existence," one would have to sweep one's arm around and say: "I mean *this*."

[Ibid., 53.]

See also AXIOMS; CONCEPTS; CONSCIOUSNESS; COROLLARIES; EXISTENCE; HIERARCHY *of* KNOWLEDGE; IDENTITY; IMPLICIT KNOWLEDGE; IRREDUCIBLE PRIMARIES; OBJECTIVITY; PRIMACY *of* EXISTENCE *vs.* PRIMACY *of* CONSCIOUSNESS; "STOLEN CONCEPT," FALLACY *of*.

Axioms. An axiom is a statement that identifies the base of knowledge and of any further statement pertaining to that knowledge, a statement necessarily contained in all others, whether any particular speaker chooses to identify it or not. An axiom is a proposition that defeats its opponents by the fact that they have to accept it and use it in the process of any attempt to deny it.

[GS, *FNI*, 193; pb 155.]

Existence exists—and the act of grasping that statement implies two corollary axioms: that something exists which one perceives and that one exists possessing consciousness, consciousness being the faculty of perceiving that which exists.

If nothing exists, there can be no consciousness: a consciousness with nothing to be conscious of is a contradiction in terms. A consciousness conscious of nothing but itself is a contradiction in terms: before it could identify itself as consciousness, it had to be conscious of something. If that which you claim to perceive does not exist, what you possess is not consciousness.

Whatever the degree of your knowledge, these two—existence and consciousness—are axioms you cannot escape, these two are the irreducible primaries implied in any action you undertake, in any part of your knowledge and in its sum, from the first ray of light you perceive at the start of your life to the widest erudition you might acquire at its end. Whether you know the shape of a pebble or the structure of a solar system, the axioms remain the same: that *it* exists and that you *know* it.

To exist is to be something, as distinguished from the nothing of non-existence, it is to be an entity of a specific nature made of specific attributes. Centuries ago, the man who was—no matter what his errors —the greatest of your philosophers, has stated the formula defining the concept of existence and the rule of all knowledge: *A is A.* A thing is itself. You have never grasped the meaning of his statement. I am here to complete it: Existence is Identity, Consciousness is Identification.

[Ibid., 152; pb 124.]

"You cannot *prove* that you exist or that you're conscious," they chatter, blanking out the fact that *proof* presupposes existence, consciousness and a complex chain of knowledge: the existence of something to know, of a consciousness able to know it, and of a knowledge that has learned to distinguish between such concepts as the proved and the unproved.

When a savage who has not learned to speak declares that existence must be proved, he is asking you to prove it by means of non-existence —when he declares that your consciousness must be proved, he is asking you to prove it by means of unconsciousness—he is asking you to step into a void outside of existence and consciousness to give him proof of both—he is asking you to become a zero gaining knowledge about a zero.

When he declares that an axiom is a matter of arbitrary choice and he doesn't choose to accept the axiom that he exists, he blanks out the fact that he has accepted it by uttering that sentence, that the only way to reject it is to shut one's mouth, expound no theories and die.

[Ibid., 192; pb 154.]

See also AXIOMATIC CONCEPTS; CONSCIOUSNESS; COROLLARIES; EXISTENCE; HIERARCHY *of* KNOWLEDGE; IDENTITY; IMPLICIT KNOWLEDGE; OBJECTIVITY; PRIMACY *of* EXISTENCE *vs.* PRIMACY *of* CONSCIOUSNESS; SELF-EVIDENT; "STOLEN CONCEPT," FALLACY *of.*

B

Ballet. The keynote of the stylization achieved in ballet is: weightlessness. Paradoxically, ballet presents man as almost disembodied: it does not distort man's body, it selects the kinds of movements that are normally possible to man (such as walking on tiptoe) and exaggerates them, stressing their beauty—and defying the law of gravitation. A gracefully effortless floating, flowing and flying are the essentials of the ballet's image of man. It projects a fragile kind of strength and a certain inflexible precision, but it is man with a fine steel skeleton and without flesh, man the spirit, not controlling, but transcending this earth. . . .

Strong passions or negative emotions cannot be projected in ballet, regardless of its librettos; it cannot express tragedy or fear—or sexuality; it is a perfect medium for the expression of spiritual love.

[*"Art and Cognition," RM*, pb 68.]

See also ART; CHOREOGRAPHER; DANCE; MUSIC; PERFORMING ARTS.

Beauty. Beauty is a sense of harmony. Whether it's an image, a human face, a body, or a sunset, take the object which you call beautiful, as a unit [and ask yourself]: what parts is it made up of, what are its constituent elements, and are they all harmonious? If they are, the result is beautiful. If there are contradictions and clashes, the result is marred or positively ugly.

For instance, the simplest example would be a human face. You know what features belong in a human face. Well, if the face is lopsided, [with a] very indefinite jawline, very small eyes, beautiful mouth, and a long nose, you would have to say that's *not* a beautiful face. But if all these features are harmoniously integrated, if they all fit your view of the importance of all these features on a human face, then that face is beautiful.

In this respect, a good example would be the beauty of different races of people. For instance, the black face, or an Oriental face, is built on a different standard, and therefore what would be beautiful on a white face will not be beautiful for them (or vice-versa), because there is a certain racial standard of features by which you judge which features, which face, in *that* classification is harmonious or distorted.

That's in regard to human beauty. In regard to a sunset, for instance, or a landscape, you will regard it as beautiful if all the colors complement each other, or go well together, or are dramatic together. And you will call it ugly if it is a bad rainy afternoon, and the sky isn't exactly pink nor exactly gray, but sort of "modern."

Now since this is an *objective* definition of beauty, there of course can be universal standards of beauty—provided you define the terms of what objects you are going to classify as beautiful and what you take as the ideal harmonious relationship of the elements of that particular object. To say, "It's in the eyes of the beholder"—that, of course, would be pure subjectivism, if taken literally. It isn't [a matter of] what you, for unknown reasons, decide to regard as beautiful. It is true, of course, that if there were no valuers, then nothing could be valued as beautiful or ugly, because values are created by the observing consciousness—but they are created by a standard based on reality. So here the issue is: values, including beauty, have to be judged as objective, not subjective or intrinsic.

[Ayn Rand, question period following Lecture 11
of Leonard Peikoff's series "The Philosophy of Objectivism" (1976).]

See also ART; ESTHETICS; INTEGRATION (MENTAL); OBJECTIVITY.

Behaviorism.   Many psychologists are envious of the prestige—and the achievements—of the physical sciences, which they try not to emulate, but to imitate. [B.F.] Skinner is archetypical in this respect: he is passionately intent on being accepted as a "scientist" and complains that only [the concept of] "Autonomous Man" stands in the way of such acceptance (which, I am sure, is true). Mr. Skinner points out scornfully that primitive men, who were unable to see the difference between living beings and inanimate objects, ascribed the objects' motions to conscious gods or demons, and that science could not begin until this belief was discarded. In the name of science, Mr. Skinner switches defiantly to the other side of the same basic coin: accepting the belief that consciousness is supernatural, he refuses to accept the existence of man's mind.

["The Stimulus and the Response," *PWNI*, 169; pb 140.]

Apparently to appease man's defenders, Mr. Skinner offers the following: "In shifting control from autonomous man to the observable environment we do not leave an empty organism. A great deal goes on inside the skin, and physiology will eventually tell us more about it" [*Beyond Freedom and Dignity*, p. 195]. This means: No, man is not empty, he is a solid piece of meat.

[Ibid., 175; pb 144.]

Behaviorists define psychology as the study of "observable behavior" (their term for action) and claim that man's behavior is controlled by the environment. In *Beyond Freedom and Dignity*, Skinner states that "a person does not act upon the world, the world acts upon him." Thoughts do not cause actions, according to Skinner, but are simply another type of behavior: "covert behavior." Learning is not defined cognitively (as the acquisition of knowledge) but as a change in behavior, caused by the environment. Behaviorism dispenses with such concepts as the self or personality, emotion, and mental illness, and replaces them with behaviorally defined notions such as response repertoire, bodily reaction, and abnormal behavior.

[Edwin A. Locke, "Behaviorism and Psychoanalysis," *TOF*, Feb. 1980, 10.]

Behaviorism's substitute for the mind is certain entities in the environment called "reinforcers." A "reinforcer," say the Behaviorists, is an event which follows a response and makes subsequent responses of the same type more likely. "What type of events change the probability of responding?" we ask. "Reinforcing events," we are told. "What is a reinforcing event?" we inquire. "One which modifies response probability," they reply. "Why does a reinforcer reinforce?" we ask. "That's not a relevant question," they answer. . . . To understand *why* a "reinforcer" reinforces, Behaviorists would have to make reference to the individual's mental contents and processes—i.e., they would have to abandon Behaviorism.

[Ibid., 14.]

See also CONSCIOUSNESS; DETERMINISM; FREE WILL; FREUD; MAN; PSYCHOLOGY.

Benevolent Universe Premise.

There is a fundamental conviction which some people never acquire, some hold only in their youth, and a few hold to the end of their days—the conviction that *ideas matter.* . . . That ideas matter means that knowledge matters, that truth matters, that one's mind matters. . . .

Its consequence is the inability to believe in the power or the triumph of evil. No matter what corruption one observes in one's immediate background, one is unable to accept it as normal, permanent or *metaphysically* right. One feels: "This injustice (or terror or falsehood or frustration or pain or agony) is the exception in life, not the rule." One feels certain that somewhere on earth—even if not anywhere in one's surroundings or within one's reach—a proper, human way of life is possible to human beings, and justice matters.

["The Inexplicable Personal Alchemy," *NL*, 118.]

Although accidents and failures are possible, they are not, according to Objectivism, the essence of human life. On the contrary, the achievement of values is the norm—speaking now for the moral man, moral by the Objectivist definition. Success and happiness are the metaphysically to-be-expected. In other words, Objectivism rejects the view that human fulfillment is impossible, that man is doomed to misery, that the universe is malevolent. We advocate the "benevolent universe" premise.

The "benevolent universe" does not mean that the universe feels kindly to man or that it is out to help him achieve his goals. No, the universe is neutral; it simply is; it is indifferent to you. You must care about and adapt to it, not the other way around. But reality is "benevolent" in the sense that if you *do* adapt to it—i.e., if you do think, value, and act rationally, then you can (and barring accidents you will) achieve your values. You will, because those values are based on reality.

Pain, suffering, failure do not have metaphysical significance—they do not reveal the nature of reality. Ayn Rand's heroes, accordingly, refuse to take pain seriously, i.e., metaphysically. You remember when Dagny asks Ragnar in the valley how his wife can live through the months he is away at sea, and he answers (I quote just part of this passage):

"We do not think that tragedy is our natural state. We do not live in chronic dread of disaster. We do not expect disaster until we have specific reason to expect it, and when we encounter it, we are free to fight it. It is not happiness, but suffering, that we consider unnatural. It is not success but calamity that we regard as the abnormal exception in human life."

This is why Ayn Rand's heroes respond to disaster, when it does strike, with a single instantaneous response: action—what can they *do?* If there's any chance at all, they refuse to accept defeat. They do what they can to counter the danger, because they are on the premise that success, not failure, is the to-be-expected.

[Leonard Peikoff, "The Philosophy of Objectivism" lecture series (1976), Lecture 8.]

See also EVIL; MALEVOLENT UNIVERSE PREMISE; METAPHYSICAL VALUE-JUDGMENTS; SENSE of LIFE; SUFFERING.

Birth Control. The capacity to procreate is merely a potential which man is not obligated to actualize. The choice to have children or not is morally optional. Nature endows man with a variety of potentials —and it is his *mind* that must decide which capacities he chooses to exercise, according to his own hierarchy of rational goals and values.

The mere fact that man has the capacity to kill, does not mean that it is his duty to become a murderer; in the same way, the mere fact that man has the capacity to procreate, does not mean that it is his duty to commit spiritual suicide by making procreation his primary goal and turning himself into a stud-farm animal. . . .

To an animal, the rearing of its young is a matter of temporary cycles. To man, it is a lifelong responsibility—a grave responsibility that must not be undertaken causelessly, thoughtlessly or accidentally.

In regard to the moral aspects of birth control, the primary right involved is not the "right" of an unborn child, nor of the family, nor of society, nor of God. The primary right is one which—in today's public clamor on the subject—few, if any, voices have had the courage to uphold: *the right of man and woman to their own life and happiness*—the right not to be regarded as the means to any end.

["Of Living Death," *TO*, Oct. 1968, 3.]

See also ABORTION; LIFE; MAN; RELIGION; SEX.

Blanking Out. *See Evasion.*

Businessmen. The professional businessman is the field agent of the army whose lieutenant-commander-in-chief is the *scientist*. The businessman carries scientific discoveries from the laboratory of the inventor to industrial plants, and transforms them into material products that fill men's physical needs and expand the comfort of men's existence. By creating a mass market, he makes these products available to every income level of society. By using machines, he increases the productivity of human labor, thus raising labor's economic rewards. By organizing human effort into productive enterprises, he creates employment for men of countless professions. *He* is the great liberator who, in the short span of a century and a half, has released men from bondage to their physical needs, has released them from the terrible drudgery of an eighteen-hour workday of manual labor for their barest subsistence, has released them from famines, from pestilences, from the stagnant hopelessness and terror in which most of mankind had lived in all the pre-capitalist centuries—and in which most of it still lives, in non-capitalist countries.

["For the New Intellectual," *FNI*, 26; pb 27.]

America's industrial progress, in the short span of a century and a half, has acquired the character of a legend: it has never been equaled anywhere on earth, in any period of history. The American businessmen, as a class, have demonstrated the greatest productive genius and the most spectacular achievements ever recorded in the economic history of mankind. What reward did they receive from our culture and its intellectuals? The position of a hated, persecuted minority. The position of a scapegoat for the evils of the bureaucrats.

["America's Persecuted Minority: Big Business," *CUI*, 48.]

If a small group of men were always regarded as guilty, in any clash with any other group, regardless of the issues or circumstances involved, would you call it persecution? If this group were always made to pay for the sins, errors, or failures of any other group, would you call *that* persecution? If this group had to live under a silent reign of terror, under special laws, from which all other people were immune, laws which the accused could not grasp or define in advance and which the accuser could interpret in any way he pleased—would you call *that* persecution? If this group were penalized, not for its faults, but for its virtues, not for its incompetence, but for its ability, not for its failures, but for its achievements, and the greater the achievement, the greater the penalty—would you call *that* persecution?

If your answer is "yes"—then ask yourself what sort of monstrous injustice you are condoning, supporting, or perpetrating. That group is the American businessmen. . . .

Every ugly, brutal aspect of injustice toward racial or religious minorities is being practiced toward businessmen. . . . Every movement that seeks to enslave a country, every dictatorship or potential dictatorship, needs some minority group as a scapegoat which it can blame for the nation's troubles and use as a justification of its own demands for dictatorial powers. In Soviet Russia, the scapegoat was the bourgeoisie; in Nazi Germany, it was the Jewish people; in America, it is the businessmen.

[Ibid., 44.]

The legal treatment accorded to actual criminals is much superior to that accorded to businessmen. The criminal's rights are protected by objective laws, objective procedures, objective rules of evidence. A criminal is presumed to be innocent until he is proved guilty. Only businessmen—the producers, the providers, the supporters, the Atlases who carry our whole economy on their shoulders—are regarded as guilty by nature and are required to prove their innocence, without any definable criteria of innocence or proof, and are left at the mercy of the whim, the favor, or the malice of any publicity-seeking politician, any scheming statist, any envious mediocrity who might chance to work his way into a bureaucratic job and who feels a yen to do some trust-busting.

[Ibid., 51.]

All the evils, abuses, and iniquities, popularly ascribed to businessmen and to capitalism, were not caused by an unregulated economy or by a free market, but by government intervention into the economy. The giants of American industry—such as James Jerome Hill or Commodore Vanderbilt or Andrew Carnegie or J. P. Morgan—were self-made men who earned their fortunes by personal ability, by free trade on a free market. But there existed another kind of businessmen, the products of a mixed economy, the men with political pull, who made fortunes by means of special privileges granted to them by the government, such men as the Big Four of the Central Pacific Railroad. It was the political power behind their activities—the power of forced, unearned, economically unjustified privileges—that caused dislocations in the country's economy, hardships, depressions, and mounting public protests. But it was the free market and the free businessmen that took the blame.

[*Ibid.*, 48.]

As a group, businessmen have been withdrawing for decades from the ideological battlefield, disarmed by the deadly combination of altruism and Pragmatism. Their public policy has consisted in appeasing, compromising and apologizing: appeasing their crudest, loudest antagonists; compromising with any attack, any lie, any insult; apologizing for their own existence. Abandoning the field of ideas to their enemies, they have been relying on lobbying, i.e., on private manipulations, on pull, on seeking momentary favors from government officials. Today, the last group one can expect to fight for capitalism is the capitalists.

["The Moratorium on Brains," *ARL*, I, 3, 2.]

Businessmen are the one group that distinguishes capitalism and the American way of life from the totalitarian statism that is swallowing the rest of the world. All the other social groups—workers, farmers, professional men, scientists, soldiers—exist under dictatorships, even though they exist in chains, in terror, in misery, and in progressive self-destruction. *But there is no such group as businessmen under a dictatorship.* Their place is taken by armed thugs: by bureaucrats and commissars. Businessmen are the symbol of a free society—the symbol of America. If and when they perish, civilization will perish. But if you wish to fight for freedom, you must begin by fighting for its unrewarded, unrecognized, unacknowledged, yet best representatives—the American businessmen.

["America's Persecuted Minority: Big Business," *CUI*, 62.]

See also ANTITRUST LAWS; BUSINESSMEN vs. BUREAUCRATS;
CAPITALISM; COMPETITION; CREATORS; LAW, OBJECTIVE and
NON-OBJECTIVE; MANAGERIAL WORK; PRAGMATISM; RETRO-
ACTIVE LAW.

Businessmen vs. Bureaucrats.   A businessman's success depends on his intelligence, his knowledge, his productive ability, his economic judgment—and on the voluntary agreement of all those he deals
with: his customers, his suppliers, his employees, his creditors or inves-
tors. A bureaucrat's success depends on his political pull. A businessman
cannot force you to buy his product; if he makes a mistake, *he* suffers
the consequences; if he fails, *he* takes the loss. A bureaucrat forces you
to obey his decisions, whether you agree with him or not—and the more
advanced the stage of a country's statism, the wider and more discre-
tionary the powers wielded by a bureaucrat. If he makes a mistake, *you*
suffer the consequences; if he fails, he passes the loss on to *you*, in the
form of heavier taxes.

A businessman cannot force you to work for him or to accept the
wages he offers; you are free to seek employment elsewhere and to
accept a better offer, if you can find it. (Remember, in this context, that
jobs do not exist "in nature," that they do not grow on trees, that someone has to *create* the job you need, and that that someone, the businessman, will go out of business if he pays you more than the market permits
him to pay you.) A bureaucrat *can* force you to work for him, when he
achieves the totalitarian power he seeks; he can force you to accept any
payment he offers—or none, as witness the forced labor camps in the
countries of full statism.

["From My 'Future File,' " *ARL*, III, 26, 5.]

The businessman's tool is *values;* the bureaucrat's tool is *fear*.
["America's Persecuted Minority: Big Business," *CUI*, 48.]

See also BUSINESSMEN; CAPITALISM; ECONOMIC POWER vs. PO-
LITICAL POWER; PHYSICAL FORCE.

Byronic View of Existence.   There are Romanticists whose basic
premise, in effect, is that man possesses volition *in regard to consciousness,
but not to existence,* i.e., in regard to his own character and choice of
values, but not in regard to the possibility of achieving his goals in the
physical world. The distinguishing characteristics of such writers are
grand-scale themes and characters, no plots and an overwhelming sense
of tragedy, the sense of a "malevolent universe." The chief exponents
of this category were poets. The leading one is Byron, whose name has

been attached to this particular, "Byronic," view of existence: its essence is the belief that man must lead a heroic life and fight for his values even though he is doomed to defeat by a malevolent fate over which he has no control.

["What Is Romanticism?" *RM*, 94; pb 109.]

See also ART; FREE WILL; MALEVOLENT UNIVERSE PREMISE; RO-MANTICISM; SENSE of LIFE.

C

Capitalism.

Theory

Capitalism is a social system based on the recognition of individual rights, including property rights, in which all property is privately owned.

The recognition of individual rights entails the banishment of physical force from human relationships: basically, rights can be violated only by means of force. In a capitalist society, no man or group may *initiate* the use of physical force against others. The only function of the government, in such a society, is the task of protecting man's rights, i.e., the task of protecting him from physical force; the government acts as the agent of man's right of self-defense, and may use force only in retaliation and only against those who initiate its use; thus the government is the means of placing the retaliatory use of force under *objective control*.

["What Is Capitalism?" *CUI*, 19.]

When I say "capitalism," I mean a full, pure, uncontrolled, unregulated laissez-faire capitalism—with a separation of state and economics, in the same way and for the same reasons as the separation of state and church.

["The Objectivist Ethics," *VOS*, 32; pb 33.]

The *moral* justification of capitalism does not lie in the altruist claim that it represents the best way to achieve "the common good." It is true that capitalism does—if that catch-phrase has any meaning—but this is merely a secondary consequence. The moral justification of capitalism lies in the fact that it is the only system consonant with man's rational nature, that it protects man's survival *qua* man, and that its ruling principle is: *justice*.

["What Is Capitalism?" *CUI*, 20.]

The action required to sustain human life is primarily intellectual: everything man needs has to be discovered by his mind and produced by his effort. Production is the application of reason to the problem of survival. . . .

Since knowledge, thinking, and rational action are properties of the individual, since the choice to exercise his rational faculty or not depends on the individual, man's survival requires that those who think be free of the interference of those who don't. Since men are neither omniscient nor infallible, they must be free to agree or disagree, to cooperate or to pursue their own independent course, each according to his own rational judgment. Freedom is the fundamental requirement of man's mind.

[Ibid., 17.]

It is the basic, metaphysical fact of man's nature—the connection between his survival and his use of reason—that capitalism recognizes and protects.

In a capitalist society, all human relationships are *voluntary*. Men are free to cooperate or not, to deal with one another or not, as their own individual judgments, convictions, and interests dictate. They can deal with one another only in terms of and by means of reason, i.e., by means of discussion, persuasion, and *contractual* agreement, by voluntary choice to mutual benefit. The right to agree with others is not a problem in any society; it is *the right to disagree* that is crucial. It is the institution of private property that protects and implements the right to disagree—and thus keeps the road open to man's most valuable attribute (valuable personally, socially, and *objectively*): the creative mind.

[Ibid., 19.]

It is . . . by reference to philosophy that the character of a social system has to be defined and evaluated. Corresponding to the four branches of philosophy, the four keystones of capitalism are: metaphysically, the requirements of man's nature and survival—epistemologically, reason—ethically, individual rights, politically, freedom.

[Ibid., 20.]

Capitalism demands the best of every man—his rationality—and rewards him accordingly. It leaves every man free to choose the work he likes, to specialize in it, to trade his product for the products of others, and to go as far on the road of achievement as his ability and ambition will carry him. His success depends on the *objective* value of his work and on the rationality of those who recognize that value. When men are free to trade, with reason and reality as their only arbiter, when no man may use physical force to extort the consent of another, it is the best product and the best judgment that win in every field of human endeavor, and raise the standard of living—and of thought—ever higher for all those who take part in mankind's productive activity.

["For the New Intellectual," *FNI*, 24; pb 25.]

The economic value of a man's work is determined, on a free market, by a single principle: by the voluntary consent of those who are willing to trade him their work or products in return. This is the moral meaning of the law of supply and demand.

["What Is Capitalism?" *CUI*, 26.]

The essence of capitalism's foreign policy is *free trade*—i.e., the abolition of trade barriers, of protective tariffs, of special privileges—the opening of the world's trade routes to free international exchange and competition among the private citizens of all countries dealing directly with one another.

["The Roots of War," *CUI*, 39.]

Laissez-faire capitalism is the only social system based on the recognition of individual rights and, therefore, the only system that bans force from social relationships. By the nature of its basic principles and interests, it is the only system fundamentally opposed to war.

[Ibid., 38.]

History

The flood of misinformation, misrepresentation, distortion, and outright falsehood about capitalism is such that the young people of today have no idea (and virtually no way of discovering any idea) of its actual nature. While archeologists are rummaging through the ruins of millennia for scraps of pottery and bits of bones, from which to reconstruct some information about prehistorical existence—the events of less than a century ago are hidden under a mound more impenetrable than the geological debris of winds, floods, and earthquakes: a mound of silence.

["Introduction," *CUI*, vii.]

The nineteenth century was the ultimate product and expression of the intellectual trend of the Renaissance and the Age of Reason, which means: of a predominantly Aristotelian philosophy. And, for the first time in history, it created a new economic system, the necessary corollary of political freedom, a system of free trade on a free market: *capitalism.*

No, it was not a full, perfect, unregulated, totally laissez-faire capitalism—as it should have been. Various degrees of government interference and control still remained, even in America—and *this* is what led to the eventual destruction of capitalism. But the extent to which certain countries were free was the exact extent of their economic progress. America, the freest, achieved the most.

Never mind the low wages and the harsh living conditions of the early years of capitalism. They were all that the national economies of the time could afford. Capitalism did not create poverty—it inherited it. Compared to the centuries of precapitalist starvation, the living conditions of the poor in the early years of capitalism were the first chance the poor had ever had to survive. As proof—the enormous growth of the European population during the nineteenth century, a growth of over 300 per cent, as compared to the previous growth of something like 3 per cent per century.

["Faith and Force: The Destroyers of the Modern World," *PWNI*, 80; pb 66.]

Capitalism has created the highest standard of living ever known on earth. The evidence is incontrovertible. The contrast between West and East Berlin is the latest demonstration, like a laboratory experiment for all to see. Yet those who are loudest in proclaiming their desire to eliminate poverty are loudest in denouncing capitalism. Man's well-being is not their goal.

["Theory and Practice," *CUI*, 136.]

If a detailed, factual study were made of all those instances in the history of American industry which have been used by the statists as an indictment of free enterprise and as an argument in favor of a government-controlled economy, it would be found that the actions blamed on businessmen were caused, necessitated, and made possible *only* by government intervention in business. The evils, popularly ascribed to big industrialists, were not the result of an unregulated industry, but of government power over industry. The villain in the picture was not the businessman, but the legislator, not free enterprise, but government controls.

["Notes on the History of American Free Enterprise," *CUI*, 102.]

Capitalism cannot work with slave labor. It was the agrarian, feudal South that maintained slavery. It was the industrial, capitalistic North that wiped it out—as capitalism wiped out slavery and serfdom in the whole civilized world of the nineteenth century.

What greater virtue can one ascribe to a social system than the fact that it leaves no possibility for any man to serve his own interests by enslaving other men? What nobler system could be desired by anyone whose goal is man's well-being?

["Theory and Practice," *CUI*, 136.]

Let those who are actually concerned with peace observe that *capitalism gave mankind the longest period of peace in history*—a period during which there were no wars involving the entire civilized world—from the end of the Napoleonic wars in 1815 to the outbreak of World War I in 1914.

It must be remembered that the political systems of the nineteenth century were not pure capitalism, but mixed economies. The element of freedom, however, was dominant; it was as close to a century of capitalism as mankind has come. But the element of statism kept growing throughout the nineteenth century, and by the time it blasted the world in 1914, the governments involved were dominated by statist policies.

Just as, in domestic affairs, all the evils caused by statism and government controls were blamed on capitalism and the free market—so, in foreign affairs, all the evils of statist policies were blamed on and ascribed to capitalism. Such myths as "capitalistic imperialism," "war-profiteering," or the notion that capitalism has to win "markets" by military conquest are examples of the superficiality or the unscrupulousness of statist commentators and historians.

["The Roots of War," *CUI*, 38.]

Observe the paradoxes built up about capitalism. It has been called a system of selfishness (which, in *my* sense of the term, it *is*)—yet it is the only system that drew men to unite on a large scale into great countries, and peacefully to cooperate across national boundaries, while all the collectivist, internationalist, One-World systems are splitting the world into Balkanized tribes.

Capitalism has been called a system of greed—yet it is the system that raised the standard of living of its poorest citizens to heights no collectivist system has ever begun to equal, and no tribal gang can conceive of.

Capitalism has been called nationalistic—yet it is the only system that banished ethnicity, and made it possible, in the United States, for men of various, formerly antagonistic nationalities to live together in peace.

Capitalism has been called cruel—yet it brought such hope, progress and general good will that the young people of today, who have not seen it, find it hard to believe.

As to pride, dignity, self-confidence, self-esteem—these are characteristics that mark a man for martyrdom in a tribal society and under any social system except capitalism.

["Global Balkanization," pamphlet, 15.]

It is often asked: Why was capitalism destroyed in spite of its incomparably beneficent record? The answer lies in the fact that the lifeline feeding any social system is a culture's dominant philosophy and that capitalism never had a philosophical base. It was the last and (theoretically) incomplete product of an Aristotelian influence. As a resurgent tide of mysticism engulfed philosophy in the nineteenth century, capitalism was left in an intellectual vacuum, its lifeline cut. Neither its moral nature nor even its political principles had ever been fully understood or defined. Its alleged defenders regarded it as compatible with government controls (i.e., government interference into the economy), ignoring the meaning and implications of the concept of laissez-faire. Thus, what existed in practice, in the nineteenth century, was not pure capitalism, but variously mixed economies. Since controls necessitate and breed further controls, it was the statist element of the mixtures that wrecked them; it was the free, capitalist element that took the blame.

Capitalism could not survive in a culture dominated by mysticism and altruism, by the soul-body dichotomy and the tribal premise. No social system (and no human institution or activity of any kind) can survive without a moral base. On the basis of the altruist morality, capitalism had to be—and was—damned from the start.

[*"What Is Capitalism?" CUI*, 30.]

If the good, the virtuous, the morally ideal is suffering and self-sacrifice—then, by that standard, capitalism had to be damned as evil. Capitalism does not tell men to suffer, but to pursue enjoyment and achievement, here, on earth—capitalism does not tell men to serve and sacrifice, but to produce and profit—capitalism does not preach passivity, humility, resignation, but independence, self-confidence, self-reliance—and, above all, capitalism does not permit anyone to expect or demand, to give or to take the *unearned*. In all human relationships—private or public, spiritual or material, social or political or economic or *moral*—capitalism requires that men be guided by a principle which is the antithesis of altruism: the principle of *justice*.

[*"*The Intellectual Bankruptcy of Our Age," pamphlet, 9.]

See also AMERICA; "CONSERVATIVES"; FREE MARKET; FREEDOM; INDIVIDUAL RIGHTS; INDIVIDUALISM; INTERVENTIONISM (ECONOMIC); JUSTICE; MIXED ECONOMY; NINETEENTH CENTURY; PHYSICAL FORCE; POLITICS; PROPERTY RIGHTS; TRADER PRINCIPLE; TRIBAL PREMISE (in ECONOMICS); STATISM; TAXATION; WELFARE STATE.

Career. In order to be in control of your life, you have to have a purpose—a productive purpose. . . . A central purpose serves to integrate all the other concerns of a man's life. It establishes the hierarchy, the relative importance, of his values, it saves him from pointless inner conflicts, it permits him to enjoy life on a wide scale and to carry that enjoyment into any area open to his mind; whereas a man without a purpose is lost in chaos. He does not know what his values are. He does not know how to judge. He cannot tell what is or is not important to him, and, therefore, he drifts helplessly at the mercy of any chance stimulus or any whim of the moment. He can enjoy nothing. He spends his life searching for some value which he will never find.

["*Playboy*'s Interview with Ayn Rand,"
March 1964, pamphlet, 6.]

"Productive work" does not mean the blind performance of the motions of some job. It means the conscious, rational pursuit of a *productive career*. In popular usage, the term "career" is applied only to the more ambitious types of work; but, in fact, it applies to *all* work: it denotes a man's attitude toward his work.

The difference between a career-man and a job-holder is as follows: a career-man regards his work as constant progress, as a constant upward motion from one achievement to another, higher one, driven by the constant expansion of his mind, his knowledge, his ability, his creative ingenuity, never stopping to stagnate on any level. A job-holder regards his work as a punishment imposed on him by the incomprehensible malevolence of reality or of society, which, somehow, does not let him exist without effort; so his policy is to go through the least amount of motions demanded of him by somebody and to stay put in any job or drift off to another, wherever chance, circumstances or relatives might happen to push him.

In this sense, a man of limited ability who rises by his own purposeful effort from unskilled laborer to shop-foreman, is a career-man in the proper, ethical meaning of the word—while an intelligent man who stagnates in the role of a company president, using one-tenth of his potential ability, is a mere job-holder. And so is a parasite posturing in a job too big for his ability. It is not the degree of a man's ability that is ethically relevant in this issue, but the full, purposeful use of his ability.

["From My 'Future File,' " *ARL*, III, 26, 3.]

A career requires the ability to sustain a purpose over a long period of time, through many separate steps, choices, decisions, adding up to a steady progression toward a goal. . . . In the course of a career, every achievement is an end in itself and, simultaneously, a step toward further achievements. . . . In a career, there is no such thing as achieving too much: the more one does, the more one loves one's work.

["Why I Like Stamp Collecting," *Minkus Stamp Journal*,
v. 6 (1971), no. 2, 2.]

PLAYBOY: Do you believe that women as well as men should organize their lives around work—and if so, what kind of work?

RAND: Of course. I believe that women are human beings. What is proper for a man is proper for a woman. The basic principles are the same. I would not attempt to prescribe what kind of work a man should do, and I would not attempt it in regard to women. There is no particular work which is specifically feminine. Women can choose their work according to their own purpose and premises in the same manner as men do.

PLAYBOY: In your opinion, is a woman immoral who chooses to devote herself to home and family instead of a career?

RAND: Not immoral—I would say she is impractical, because a home cannot be a full-time occupation, except when her children are young. However, if she wants a family and wants to make that her career, at least for a while, it would be proper—if she approaches it as a career, that is, if she studies the subject, if she defines the rules and principles by which she wants to bring up her children, if she approaches her task in an intellectual manner. It is a very responsible task and a very important one, but only when treated as a science, not as a mere emotional indulgence.

[*"Playboy*'s Interview with Ayn Rand," pamphlet, 7.]

See also AMBITION; PRODUCTIVENESS; PURPOSE.

Causality.   The law of causality is the law of identity applied to action. All actions are caused by entities. The nature of an action is caused and determined by the nature of the entities that act; a thing cannot act in contradiction to its nature. . . . The law of identity does not permit you to have your cake and eat it, too. The law of causality does not permit you to eat your cake *before* you have it.

[GS, *FNI*, 188; pb 151.]

To grasp the axiom that existence exists, means to grasp the fact that nature, i.e., the universe as a whole, cannot be created or annihilated, that it cannot come into or go out of existence. Whether its basic constituent elements are atoms, or subatomic particles, or some yet undiscovered forms of energy, it is not ruled by a consciousness or by will or by chance, but by the law of identity. All the countless forms, motions, combinations and dissolutions of elements within the universe—from a floating speck of dust to the formation of a galaxy to the emergence of life—are caused and determined by the identities of the elements involved.

["The Metaphysical vs. the Man-Made," *PWNI*, 30; pb 25.]

Since things are what they are, since everything that exists possesses a specific identity, nothing in reality can occur causelessly or by chance.

[Leonard Peikoff, "The Analytic-Synthetic Dichotomy," *ITOE*, 147.]

Choice . . . is not chance. Volition is not an exception to the Law of Causality; it is a type of causation.

[Ibid., 149.]

See also CHANGE; FINAL CAUSATION; FREE WILL; IDENTITY; MIR-ACLES; NECESSITY.

Censorship. "Censorship" is a term pertaining only to governmental action. No private action is censorship. No private individual or agency can silence a man or suppress a publication; only the government can do so. The freedom of speech of private individuals includes the right not to agree, not to listen and not to finance one's own antagonists.

["Man's Rights," *VOS*, 132; pb 98.]

Censorship, in its old-fashioned meaning, is a government edict that forbids the discussion of some specific subjects or ideas—such, for instance, as sex, religion or criticism of government officials—an edict enforced by the government's scrutiny of all forms of communication prior to their public release. But for stifling the freedom of men's minds the modern method is much more potent; it rests on the power of non-objective law; it neither forbids nor permits anything; it never defines or specifies; it merely delivers men's lives, fortunes, careers, ambitions into the arbitrary power of a bureaucrat who can reward or punish at whim. It spares the bureaucrat the troublesome necessity of committing himself to rigid rules—and it places upon the victims the burden of discovering how to please him, with a fluid unknowable as their only guide.

No, a federal commissioner may never utter a single word for or against any program. But what do you suppose will happen if and when, with or without his knowledge, a third-assistant or a second cousin or just a nameless friend from Washington whispers to a television executive that the commissioner does not like producer X or does not approve of writer Y or takes a great interest in the career of starlet Z or is anxious to advance the cause of the United Nations?

["Have Gun, Will Nudge," *TON*, March 1962, 9.]

For years, the collectivists have been propagating the notion that a private individual's refusal to finance an opponent is a violation of the opponent's right of free speech and an act of "censorship."

It is "censorship," they claim, if a newspaper refuses to employ or publish writers whose ideas are diametrically opposed to its policy.

It is "censorship," they claim, if businessmen refuse to advertise in a magazine that denounces, insults and smears them. . . .

And then there is Newton N. Minow [then chairman of the Federal Communications Commission] who declares: "There is censorship by ratings, by advertisers, by networks, by affiliates which reject programming offered to their areas." It is the same Mr. Minow who threatens to revoke the license of any station that does not comply with his views on programming—and who claims that *that* is not censorship. . . .

[This collectivist notion] means that the ability to provide the material tools for the expression of ideas deprives a man of the right to hold any ideas. It means that a publisher has to publish books he considers worthless, false or evil—that a TV sponsor has to finance commentators who choose to affront his convictions—that the owner of a newspaper must turn his editorial pages over to any young hooligan who clamors for the enslavement of the press. It means that one group of men acquires the "right" to unlimited license—while another group is reduced to helpless irresponsibility.

["Man's Rights," *VOS*, 131; pb 98.]

See also "CONSERVATIVES" vs. "LIBERALS"; DICTATORSHIP; FREE SPEECH; GOVERNMENT; GOVERNMENT GRANTS and SCHOLARSHIPS; PROPERTY RIGHTS.

Certainty. "Certain" represents an assessment of the evidence for a conclusion; it is usually contrasted with two other broad types of assessment: "possible" and "probable." . . .

Idea X is "certain" if, in a given context of knowledge, the evidence for X is *conclusive*. In such a context, all the evidence supports X and there is no evidence to support any alternative. . . .

You cannot challenge a claim to certainty by means of an *arbitrary* declaration of a counter-possibility, . . . you cannot manufacture possibilities without evidence. . . .

All the main attacks on certainty depend on evading its *contextual* character. . . .

The alternative is not to feign omniscience, erecting every discovery into an out-of-context absolute, or to embrace skepticism and claim that knowledge is impossible. Both these policies accept omniscience as the standard: the dogmatists pretend to have it, the skeptics bemoan their lack of it. The rational policy is to discard the very notion of omnisci-ence. Knowledge is contextual—it is knowledge, it is valid, *contextually*.

[Leonard Peikoff, "The Philosophy of Objectivism"
lecture series (1976), Lecture 6.]

Infallibility is not a precondition of knowing what one does know, of firmness in one's convictions, and of loyalty to one's values.

["The Shanghai Gesture," *ARL*, I, 14, 3.]

"Don't be so sure—nobody can be certain of anything." Bertrand Russell's gibberish to the contrary notwithstanding, that pronounce-ment includes itself; therefore, one cannot be sure that one cannot be sure of anything. The pronouncement means that no knowledge of any kind is possible to man, i.e., that man is not conscious. Furthermore, if one tried to accept that catch phrase, one would find that its second part contradicts its first: if nobody can be certain of anything, then everybody can be certain of everything he pleases—since it cannot be refuted, and he can claim he is not certain he is certain (which is the purpose of that notion).

["Philosophical Detection," *PWNI*, 17; pb 14.]

See also ABSOLUTES; AGNOSTICISM; ARBITRARY; AXIOMS; CON-TEXT; KNOWLEDGE; "OPEN MIND" and "CLOSED MIND"; POS-SIBLE; REASON.

Chance. Since things are what they are, since everything that exists possesses a specific identity, nothing in reality can occur causelessly or by chance.

[Leonard Peikoff, "The Analytic-Synthetic Dichotomy," *ITOE*, 147.]

Choice, however, is not chance. Volition is not an exception to the Law of Causality; it is a type of causation.

[Ibid., 149.]

See also CAUSALITY; FREE WILL; IDENTITY; POSSIBLE.

Change. They proclaim that there is no law of identity, that nothing exists but change, and blank out the fact that *change* presupposes the concepts of what changes, from what and to what, that without the law of identity no such concept as "change" is possible.

[GS, *FNI*, 192; pb 154.]

See also CAUSALITY; ENTITY; IDENTITY; MOTION; "STOLEN CON-CEPT," FALLACY of.

Character. "Character" means a man's nature or identity insofar as this is shaped by the moral values he accepts and automatizes. By "moral values" I mean values which are volitionally chosen, and which are fundamental, i.e., shape the whole course of a man's action, not merely a specialized, delimited area of his life. . . . So a man's character is, in effect, his moral essence—his self-made identity as expressed in the principles he lives by.

[Leonard Peikoff, "The Philosophy of Objectivism" lecture series (1976), question period, Lecture 2.]

We have only two sources of information about the character of the people around us: we judge them by what they do and by what they say (particularly the first).

["Basic Principles of Literature," *RM*, 66; pb 87.]

As man is a being of self-made wealth, so he is a being of self-made soul.

[GS, *FNI*, 160; pb 131.]

Just as man's physical survival depends on his own effort, so does his psychological survival. Man faces two corollary, interdependent fields of action in which a constant exercise of choice and a constant creative process are demanded of him: the world around him and his own soul (by "soul," I mean his consciousness). Just as he has to produce the material values he needs to sustain his life, so he has to acquire the values of character that enable him to sustain it and that make his life worth living. He is born without the knowledge of either. He has to discover both—and translate them into reality—and survive by shaping the world and himself in the image of his values.

["The Goal of My Writing," *RM*, 169; pb 169.]

See also AUTOMATIZATION; FREE WILL; IDENTITY; MORALITY; VALUES.

Characterization. Characterization is the portrayal of those essential traits which form the unique, distinctive personality of an individual human being.

Characterization requires an extreme degree of selectivity. A human being is the most complex entity on earth; a writer's task is to select the essentials out of that enormous complexity, then proceed to create an individual figure, endowing it with all the appropriate details down to the telling small touches needed to give it full reality. That figure has to be an abstraction, yet look like a concrete; it has to have the universality of an abstraction and, simultaneously, the unrepeatable uniqueness of a *person*.

In real life, we have only two sources of information about the character of the people around us: we judge them by what they do and by what they say (particularly the first). Similarly, characterization in a novel can be achieved only by two major means: *action* and *dialogue*. Descriptive passages dealing with a character's appearance, manner, etc. can contribute to a characterization; so can introspective passages dealing with a character's thoughts and feelings; so can the comments of other characters. But all these are merely auxiliary means, which are of no value without the two pillars: action and dialogue. To re-create the reality of a character, one must show what he does and what he says.

["Basic Principles of Literature," *RM*, 66; pb 87.]

See also CHARACTER; LITERATURE; MOTIVATION.

Charity.   My views on charity are very simple. I do not consider it a major virtue and, above all, I do not consider it a moral duty. There is nothing wrong in helping other people, if and when they are worthy of the help and you can afford to help them. I regard charity as a marginal issue. What I am fighting is the idea that charity is a moral duty and a primary virtue.

["*Playboy*'s Interview with Ayn Rand," pamphlet, 10.]

The fact that a man has no claim on others (i.e., that it is not their moral duty to help him and that he cannot demand their help as his right) does not preclude or prohibit good will among men and does not make it immoral to offer or to accept voluntary, non-sacrificial assistance.

It is altruism that has corrupted and perverted human benevolence by regarding the giver as an object of immolation, and the receiver as a helplessly miserable object of pity who holds a mortgage on the lives of others—a doctrine which is extremely offensive to both parties, leaving men no choice but the roles of sacrificial victim or moral cannibal. . . .

To view the question in its proper perspective, one must begin by rejecting altruism's terms and all of its ugly emotional aftertaste—then take a fresh look at human relationships. It is morally proper to accept help, when it is offered, not as a moral duty, but as an act of good will and generosity, when the giver can afford it (i.e., when it does not involve self-sacrifice on his part), and when it is offered in response to the receiver's virtues, *not* in response to his flaws, weaknesses or moral failures, and *not* on the ground of his need as such.

["The Question of Scholarships," *TO*, June 1966, 11.]

The proper method of judging when or whether one should help another person is by reference to one's own rational self-interest and one's own hierarchy of values: the time, money or effort one gives or the risk one takes should be proportionate to the value of the person in relation to one's own happiness.

To illustrate this on the altruists' favorite example: the issue of saving a drowning person. If the person to be saved is a stranger, it is morally proper to save him only when the danger to one's own life is minimal; when the danger is great, it would be immoral to attempt it: only a lack of self-esteem could permit one to value one's life no higher than that of any random stranger. (And, conversely, if one is drowning, one cannot expect a stranger to risk his life for one's sake, remembering that one's life cannot be as valuable to him as his own.)

If the person to be saved is not a stranger, then the risk one should be willing to take is greater in proportion to the greatness of that person's value to oneself. If it is the man or woman one loves, then one can be willing to give one's own life to save him or her—for the selfish reason that life without the loved person could be unbearable.

["The Ethics of Emergencies," *VOS*, 50; pb 45.]

The small minority of adults who are *unable* rather than unwilling to work, have to rely on voluntary charity; misfortune is not a claim to slave labor; there is no such thing as the *right* to consume, control, and destroy those without whom one would be unable to survive.

["What Is Capitalism?" *CUI*, 26.]

See also ALTRUISM; "DUTY"; EMERGENCIES; POVERTY; SACRIFICE; SELFISHNESS; VIRTUE; WELFARE STATE.

Choreographer.   Dancers are performing artists; music is the primary work they perform—with the help of an important intermediary: the choreographer. His creative task is similar to that of a stage director, but carries a more demanding responsibility: a stage director translates a primary work, a play, into physical action—a choreographer has to translate a primary work, a composition of sounds, into another medium, into a composition of movements, and create a structured, integrated work: a dance.

This task is so difficult and its esthetically qualified practitioners so rare that the dance has always been slow in its development and extremely vulnerable. Today, it is all but extinct.

[Art and Cognition," *RM*, pb 70.]

See also ART; BALLET; DANCE; DIRECTOR; PERFORMING ARTS.

Christmas. [In answer to the question of whether it is appropriate for an atheist to celebrate Christmas:]

Yes, of course. A national holiday, in this country, cannot have an exclusively religious meaning. The secular meaning of the Christmas holiday is wider than the tenets of any particular religion: it is good will toward men—a frame of mind which is not the exclusive property (though it is supposed to be part, but is a largely unobserved part) of the Christian religion.

The charming aspect of Christmas is the fact that it expresses good will in a cheerful, happy, benevolent, *non-sacrificial* way. One says: "Merry Christmas"—not "Weep and Repent." And the good will is expressed in a material, *earthly* form—by giving presents to one's friends, or by sending them cards in token of remembrance. . . .

The best aspect of Christmas is the aspect usually decried by the mystics: the fact that Christmas has been *commercialized*. The gift-buying . . . stimulates an enormous outpouring of ingenuity in the creation of products devoted to a single purpose: to give men pleasure. And the street decorations put up by department stores and other institutions— the Christmas trees, the winking lights, the glittering colors—provide the city with a spectacular display, which only "commercial greed" could afford to give us. One would have to be terribly depressed to resist the wonderful gaiety of that spectacle.

[*The Objectivist Calendar*, Dec. 1976.]

See also AMERICA; ATHEISM; MYSTICISM; RELIGION; THANKS-GIVING.

Civil Disobedience. Civil disobedience may be justifiable, in some cases, when and if an individual disobeys a law in order to bring an issue to court, as a test case. Such an action involves respect for legality and a protest directed only at a particular law which the individual seeks an opportunity to prove to be unjust. The same is true of a group of individuals when and if the risks involved are their own.

But there is no justification, in a civilized society, for the kind of mass civil disobedience that involves the violation of the rights of others— regardless of whether the demonstrators' goal is good or evil. The end does *not* justify the means. No one's rights can be secured by the violation of the rights of others. Mass disobedience is an assault on the concept of rights: it is a mob's defiance of legality as such.

The forcible occupation of another man's property or the obstruction of a public thoroughfare is so blatant a violation of rights that an attempt to justify it becomes an abrogation of morality. An individual has no right to do a "sit-in" in the home or office of a person he disagrees with—and he does not acquire such a right by joining a gang. Rights are not a matter of numbers—and there can be no such thing, in law or in morality, as actions forbidden to an individual, but permitted to a mob.

The only power of a mob, as against an individual, is greater muscular strength—i.e., plain, brute physical force. The attempt to solve social problems by means of physical force is what a civilized society is established to prevent. The advocates of mass civil disobedience admit that their purpose is intimidation. A society that tolerates intimidation as a means of settling disputes—the *physical* intimidation of some men or groups by others—loses its moral right to exist as a social system, and its collapse does not take long to follow.

Politically, mass civil disobedience is appropriate only as a prelude to civil war—as the declaration of a total break with a country's political institutions.

["The Cashing-In: The Student 'Rebellion,' " *CUI*, 256.]

See also INDIVIDUAL RIGHTS; LAW, OBJECTIVE and NON-OBJECTIVE; NEW LEFT; PHYSICAL FORCE.

Civilization. Civilization is the progress toward a society of privacy. The savage's whole existence is public, ruled by the laws of his tribe. Civilization is the process of setting man free from men.

["The Soul of an Individualist," *FNI*, 98; pb 84.]

The precondition of a civilized society is the barring of physical force from social relationships—thus establishing the principle that if men wish to deal with one another, they may do so only by means of *reason:* by discussion, persuasion and voluntary, uncoerced agreement.

The necessary consequence of man's right to life is his right to self-defense. In a civilized society, force may be used only in retaliation and only against those who initiate its use.

["The Nature of Government," *VOS*, 146; pb 108.]

See also CULTURE; FREEDOM; INDIVIDUAL RIGHTS; PHYSICAL FORCE.

Classicism. Classicism . . . was a school that had devised a set of arbitrary, *concretely* detailed rules purporting to represent the final and absolute criteria of esthetic value. In literature, these rules consisted of specific edicts, loosely derived from the Greek (and French) tragedies, which prescribed every formal aspect of a play (such as the unity of time, place and action) down to the number of acts and the number of verses permitted to a character in every act. Some of that stuff was based on Aristotle's esthetics and can serve as an example of what happens when concrete-bound mentalities, seeking to by-pass the responsibility of thought, attempt to transform abstract principles into concrete prescriptions and to replace creation with imitation. (For an example of Classicism that survived well into the twentieth century, I refer you to the architectural dogmas represented by Howard Roark's antagonists in *The Fountainhead.*)

Even though the Classicists had no answer to *why* their rules were to be accepted as valid (except the usual appeal to tradition, to scholarship and to the prestige of antiquity), this school was regarded as the representative of reason.(!)

["What Is Romanticism?" *RM*, 87; pb 104.]

See also ABSTRACTIONS *and* CONCRETES; *ART; NATURALISM; PRINCIPLES; ROMANTICISM.*

Coercion. *See Physical Force.*

"Collective Rights." Since only an individual man can possess rights, the expression "individual rights" is a redundancy (which one has to use for purposes of clarification in today's intellectual chaos). But the expression "collective rights" is a contradiction in terms.

Any group or "collective," large or small, is only a number of individuals. A group can have no rights other than the rights of its individual members.

["Collectivized 'Rights,' " *VOS*, 136; pb 101.]

A group, as such, has no rights. A man can neither acquire new rights by joining a group nor lose the rights which he does possess. The principle of individual rights is the only moral base of all groups or associations.

Any group that does not recognize this principle is not an association, but a gang or a mob. . . .

The notion of "collective rights" (the notion that rights belong to groups, not to individuals) means that "rights" belong to some men, but not to others—that some men have the "right" to dispose of others in any manner they please—and that the criterion of such privileged position consists of numerical superiority.

[Ibid., 137; pb 102.]

The notion that "Anything society does is right because *society* chose to do it," is not a moral principle, but a negation of moral principles and the banishment of morality from social issues.

[Ibid., 136; pb 101.]

See also COLLECTIVISM; FOREIGN POLICY; INDIVIDUAL RIGHTS; MORALITY; NATIONAL RIGHTS; SELF-DETERMINATION of NATIONS.

Collectivism.

Collectivism means the subjugation of the individual to a group—whether to a race, class or state does not matter. Collectivism holds that man must be chained to collective action and collective thought for the sake of what is called "the common good."

["The Only Path to Tomorrow," *Reader's Digest*, Jan. 1944, 8.]

Collectivism holds that, in human affairs, the collective—society, the community, the nation, the proletariat, the race, etc.—is *the unit of reality and the standard of value.* On this view, the individual has reality only as part of the group, and value only insofar as he serves it.

[Leonard Peikoff, *OP*, 7; pb 17.]

Collectivism holds that the individual has no rights, that his life and work belong to the group . . . and that the group may sacrifice him at its own whim to its own interests. The only way to implement a doctrine of that kind is by means of brute force—and *statism* has always been the political corollary of collectivism.

["Racism," *VOS*, 175; pb 128.]

Fascism and communism are not two opposites, but two rival gangs fighting over the same territory . . . both are variants of statism, based on the collectivist principle that man is the rightless slave of the state.

[" 'Extremism,' or the Art of Smearing," *CUI*, 180.]

Modern collectivists . . . see society as a super-organism, as some supernatural entity apart from and superior to the sum of its individual members.

["Collectivized 'Rights,' " *VOS*, 138; pb 103.]

The philosophy of collectivism upholds the existence of a mystic (and unperceivable) social organism, while denying the reality of perceived individuals—a view which implies that man's senses are not a valid instrument for perceiving reality. Collectivism maintains that an elite endowed with special mystic insight should rule men—which implies the existence of an elite source of knowledge, a fund of revelations inaccessible to logic and transcending the mind. Collectivism denies that men should deal with one another by voluntary means, settling their disputes by a process of rational persuasion; it declares that men should live under the reign of physical force (as wielded by the dictator of the omnipotent state)—a position which jettisons reason as the guide and arbiter of human relationships.

From every aspect, the theory of collectivism points to the same conclusion: collectivism and the advocacy of reason are philosophically antithetical; it is one or the other.

[Leonard Peikoff, "Nazism vs. Reason," *TO*, Oct. 1969, 1.]

The political philosophy of collectivism is based on a view of man as a congenital incompetent, a helpless, mindless creature who must be fooled and ruled by a special elite with some unspecified claim to superior wisdom and a lust for power.

["Who Will Protect Us from Our Protectors?" *TON*, May 1962, 17.]

What subjectivism is in the realm of ethics, collectivism is in the realm of politics. Just as the notion that "Anything I do is right because *I* chose to do it," is not a moral principle, but a negation of morality—so the notion that "Anything society does is right because *society* chose to do it," is not a moral principle, but a negation of moral principles and the banishment of morality from social issues.

["Collectivized 'Rights,' " *VOS*, 135; pb 101.]

As a cultural-intellectual power and a moral ideal, collectivism died in World War II. If we are still rolling in its direction, it is only by the inertia of a void and the momentum of disintegration. A social movement that began with the ponderous, brain-cracking, dialectical constructs of Hegel and Marx, and ends up with a horde of morally unwashed children stamping their foot and shrieking: "I want it *now!*" —is through.

["The Cashing-In: The Student 'Rebellion,' " *CUI*, 266.]

Collectivism has lost the two crucial weapons that raised it to world power and made all of its victories possible: intellectuality and idealism, or reason and morality. It had to lose them precisely at the height of its success, since its claim to both was a fraud: the full, actual reality of socialist-communist-fascist states has demonstrated the brute irrationality of collectivist systems and the inhumanity of altruism as a moral code.

[Ibid., 269.]

Collectivism does not preach sacrifice as a temporary means to some desirable end. Sacrifice is its end—sacrifice as a way of life. It is man's independence, success, prosperity, and happiness that collectivists wish to destroy.

Observe the snarling, hysterical hatred with which they greet any suggestion that sacrifice is not necessary, that a non-sacrificial society is possible to men, that it is the only society able to achieve man's well-being.

["Theory and Practice," *CUI*, 137.]

The advocates of collectivism are motivated not by a desire for men's happiness, but by hatred for man . . . hatred of the good for being the good; . . . the focus of that hatred, the target of its passionate fury, is the man of ability.

["An Untitled Letter," *PWNI*, 123; pb 102.]

See also ALTRUISM; "COLLECTIVE RIGHTS"; "COMMON GOOD"; DICTATORSHIP; INDIVIDUAL RIGHTS; INDIVIDUALISM; SELFISH-NESS; SOCIAL SYSTEM; SOCIETY; STATISM; TRIBALISM; TRIBAL PREMISE (in ECONOMICS).

"Common Good." The tribal notion of "the common good" has served as the moral justification of most social systems—and of all tyrannies—in history. The degree of a society's enslavement or freedom corresponded to the degree to which that tribal slogan was invoked or ignored.

"The common good" (or "the public interest") is an undefined and undefinable concept: there is no such entity as "the tribe" or "the public"; the tribe (or the public or society) is only a number of individual men. Nothing can be good for the tribe as such; "good" and "value" pertain *only* to a living organism—to an individual living organism—not to a disembodied aggregate of relationships.

"The common good" is a meaningless concept, unless taken literally, in which case its only possible meaning is: the sum of the good of *all* the individual men involved. But in that case, the concept is meaningless as a moral criterion: it leaves open the question of what *is* the good of individual men and how does one determine it?

It is not, however, in its literal meaning that that concept is generally used. It is accepted precisely for its elastic, undefinable, mystical character which serves, not as a moral guide, but as an escape from morality. Since the good is not applicable to the disembodied, it becomes a moral blank check for those who attempt to embody it.

When "the common good" of a society is regarded as something apart from and superior to the individual good of its members, it means that the good of *some* men takes precedence over the good of others, with those others consigned to the status of sacrificial animals. It is tacitly assumed, in such cases, that "the common good" means "the good of the *majority*" as against the minority or the individual. Observe the significant fact that that assumption is *tacit:* even the most collectivized mentalities seem to sense the impossibility of justifying it morally. But "the good of the majority," too, is only a pretense and a delusion: since, in fact, the violation of an individual's rights means the abrogation of all rights, it delivers the helpless majority into the power of any gang that proclaims itself to be "the voice of society" and proceeds to rule by means of physical force, until deposed by another gang employing the same means.

If one begins by defining the good of individual men, one will accept as proper only a society in which that good is achieved and *achievable.* But if one begins by accepting "the common good" as an axiom and regarding individual good as its possible but not necessary consequence (not necessary in any particular case), one ends up with such a gruesome absurdity as Soviet Russia, a country professedly dedicated to "the common good," where, with the exception of a minuscule clique of rulers, the entire population has existed in subhuman misery for over two generations.

["What Is Capitalism?" *CUI*, 20.]

Only on the basis of individual rights can any good—private or public —be defined and achieved. Only when each man is free to exist for his own sake—neither sacrificing others to himself nor being sacrificed to others—only then is every man free to work for the greatest good he can achieve for himself by his own choice and by his own effort. And the sum total of such individual efforts is the only kind of general, social good possible.

["Textbook of Americanism," pamphlet, 11.]

See also ALTRUISM; COLLECTIVISM; DEMOCRACY; INDIVIDUAL RIGHTS; MINORITY RIGHTS; "PUBLIC INTEREST," the; SOVIET RUSSIA; TRIBALISM.

Common Sense.   Common sense is a simple and non-self-conscious use of logic.

[Ayn Rand, question period following Lecture 11 of Leonard Peikoff's series "The Philosophy of Objectivism" (1976).]

That which today is called "common sense" is the remnant of an Aristotelian influence.

["For the New Intellectual," *FNI*, 45; pb 41.]

Americans are the most reality-oriented people on earth. Their outstanding characteristic is the childhood form of reasoning: common sense. It is their only protection. But common sense is not enough where theoretical knowledge is required: it can make simple, concrete-bound connections—it cannot integrate complex issues, or deal with wide abstractions, or forecast the future.

["Don't Let It Go," *PWNI*, 257; pb 211.]

See also AMERICA; ARISTOTLE; LOGIC.

Communication. Reason is the only means of communication among men, and an objectively perceivable reality is their only common frame of reference; when these are invalidated (i.e., held to be irrelevant) in the field of morality, force becomes men's only way of dealing with one another.

["What Is Capitalism?" *CUI*, 22.]

Concepts and, therefore, language are *primarily* a tool of cognition— *not* of communication, as is usually assumed. Communication is merely the consequence, not the cause nor the primary purpose of concept-formation—a crucial consequence, of invaluable importance to men, but still only a consequence. *Cognition precedes communication;* the necessary precondition of communication is that one have something to communicate. (This is true even of communication among animals, or of communication by grunts and growls among inarticulate men, let alone of communication by means of so complex and exacting a tool as language.)

[*ITOE*, 92.]

See also CONCEPTS; LANGUAGE; PHYSICAL FORCE; REASON.

Communism. When, at the age of twelve, at the time of the Russian revolution, I first heard the Communist principle that Man must exist for the sake of the State, I perceived that this was the essential issue, that this principle was evil, and that it could lead to nothing but evil, regardless of any methods, details, decrees, policies, promises and pious platitudes. This was the reason for my opposition to Communism then —and it is my reason now. I am still a little astonished, at times, that too many adult Americans do not understand the nature of the fight against Communism as clearly as I understood it at the age of twelve: they continue to believe that only Communist methods are evil, while Communist ideals are noble. All the victories of Communism since the year 1917 are due to that particular belief among the men who are still free.

["Foreword," *WTL*, vii.]

Communists, like all materialists, are neo-mystics: it does not matter whether one rejects the mind in favor of revelations or in favor of conditioned reflexes. The basic premise and the results are the same.

["Faith and Force: The Destroyers of the Modern World," *PWNI*, 85; pb 70.]

The Communists' chief purpose is to destroy every form of independence—independent work, independent action, independent property, independent thought, an independent mind, or an independent man. Conformity, alikeness, servility, submission and obedience are necessary to establish a Communist slave-state.

["Screen Guide for Americans," *Plain Talk*, Nov. 1947, 41.]

It is the Communists' intention to make people think that personal success is somehow achieved at the expense of others and that every successful man has hurt somebody by becoming successful. It is the Communists' aim to discourage all personal effort and to drive men into a hopeless, dispirited, gray herd of robots who have lost all personal ambition, who are easy to rule, willing to obey and willing to exist in selfless servitude to the State.

[Ibid., 39.]

If America perishes, it will perish by intellectual default. There is no diabolical conspiracy to destroy it: no conspiracy could be big enough and strong enough. . . . As to the communist conspirators in the service of Soviet Russia, they are the best illustration of victory by default: their successes are handed to them by the concessions of their victims.

["For the New Intellectual," *FNI*, 52; pb 46.]

When men share the same basic premise, it is the most consistent ones who win. So long as men accept the altruist morality, they will not be able to stop the advance of communism. The altruist morality is Soviet Russia's best and *only* weapon.

["Conservatism: An Obituary," *CUI*, 196.]

See also COLLECTIVISM; DICTATORSHIP; EGALITARIANISM; FAS-CISM and COMMUNISM/SOCIALISM; HUMAN RIGHTS and PROP-ERTY RIGHTS; "McCARTHYISM"; POLYLOGISM; PROPERTY RIGHTS; SOCIALISM; SOVIET RUSSIA; STATISM.

Compassion.
I regard compassion as proper *only* toward those who are innocent victims, but not toward those who are morally guilty. If one feels compassion for the victims of a concentration camp, one can-

not feel it for the torturers. If one does feel compassion for the torturers, it is an act of moral treason toward the victims.

[*"Playboy*'s Interview with Ayn Rand," pamphlet, 10.]

See also ALTRUISM; JUSTICE; MERCY; PITY.

Competition.
Competition is a by-product of productive work, *not* its goal. A creative man is motivated by the desire to achieve, *not* by the desire to beat others.

["The Moratorium on Brains," *ARL*, I,2,4.]

A competition presupposes some basic principles held in common by all the competitors, such as the rules of the game in athletics, or the functions of the free market in business.

["Apollo 11," *TO*, Sept. 1969, 9.]

The only actual factor required for the existence of free competition is: the unhampered, unobstructed operation of the mechanism of a free market. The only action which a government can take to protect free competition is: *Laissez-faire!*—which, in free translation, means: *Hands off!* But the antitrust laws established exactly opposite conditions—and achieved the exact opposite of the results they had been intended to achieve.

There is no way to legislate competition; there are no standards by which one could define who should compete with whom, how many competitors should exist in any given field, what should be their relative strength or their so-called "relevant markets," what prices they should charge, what methods of competition are "fair" or "unfair." None of these can be answered, because *these* precisely are the questions that can be answered only by the mechanism of a free market.

["America's Persecuted Minority: Big Business," *CUI*, 54.]

The concept of *free* competition *enforced* by law is a grotesque contradiction in terms. It means: forcing people to be free at the point of a gun. It means: protecting people's freedom by the arbitrary rule of unanswerable bureaucratic edicts.

[Ibid., 52.]

Competition, properly so-called, rests on the activity of separate, independent individuals owning and exchanging private property in the pursuit of their self-interest. It arises when two or more such individuals become rivals for the same trade.

[George Reisman, "Platonic Competition," *TO*, Aug. 1968, 9.]

The competition which takes place under capitalism acts to regulate prices simply in accordance with the full costs of production and with the requirements of earning a rate of profit. It does not act to drive prices to the level of "marginal costs" or to the point where they reflect a "scarcity" of capacity.

[Ibid., 11.]

The competitor who cuts his price is fully aware of the impact on other competitors and that they will try to match his price. He acts in the knowledge that some of them will not be able to afford the cut, while he is, and that he will eventually pick up their business. He is able to afford the cut when and if his productive efficiency is greater than theirs, which lowers his costs to a level they cannot match. . . . Thus price competition, under capitalism, is the result of a contest of efficiency, competence, ability.

[Ibid., Sept. 1968, 9.]

"Competition" is an active, not a passive, noun. It applies to the entire sphere of economic activity, not merely to production, but also to trade; it implies the necessity of taking action to affect the conditions of the market in one's own favor.

The error of the nineteenth-century observers was that they restricted a wide abstraction—competition—to a narrow set of particulars, to the "passive" competition projected by their own interpretation of classical economics. As a result, they concluded that the alleged "failure" of this fictitious "passive competition" negated the entire theoretical structure of classical economics, including the demonstration of the fact that laissez-faire is the most efficient and productive of all possible economic systems. They concluded that a free market, by its nature, leads to its own destruction—and they came to the grotesque contradiction of attempting to preserve the freedom of the market by government controls, i.e., to preserve the benefits of laissez-faire by abrogating it.

[Alan Greenspan, "Antitrust," *CUI*, 67.]

See also ANTITRUST LAWS; CAPITALISM; COMPROMISE; FREE MARKET; FREEDOM; MONOPOLY; PRODUCTIVENESS.

Compromise. A compromise is an adjustment of conflicting claims by mutual concessions. This means that both parties to a compromise have some valid claim and some value to offer each other. And *this* means that both parties agree upon some fundamental principle which serves as a base for their deal.

["Doesn't Life Require Compromise?" *VOS*, 85; pb 68.]

There can be no compromise on basic principles. There can be no compromise on moral issues. There can be no compromise on matters of knowledge, of truth, of rational conviction.

[" 'Extremism,' or The Art of Smearing," *CUI*, 182.]

It is only in regard to concretes or particulars, implementing a mutually accepted basic principle, that one may compromise. For instance, one may bargain with a buyer over the price one wants to receive for one's product, and agree on a sum somewhere between one's demand and his offer. The mutually accepted basic principle, in such case, is the principle of trade, namely: that the buyer must pay the seller for his product. But if one wanted to be paid and the alleged buyer wanted to obtain one's product for nothing, no compromise, agreement or discussion would be possible, only the total surrender of one or the other.

There can be no compromise between a property owner and a burglar; offering the burglar a single teaspoon of one's silverware would not be a compromise, but a total surrender—the recognition of his *right* to one's property.

["Doesn't Life Require Compromise?" *VOS*, 85; pb 68.]

Contrary to the fanatical belief of its advocates, compromise [on basic principles] does not satisfy, but *dissatisfies* everybody; it does not lead to general fulfillment, but to general frustration; those who try to be all things to all men, end up by not being anything to anyone. And more: the partial victory of an unjust claim, encourages the claimant to try further; the partial defeat of a just claim, discourages and paralyzes the victim.

["The Cashing-In: The Student 'Rebellion,' " *CUI*, 255.]

There are two sides to every issue: one side is right and the other is wrong, but the middle is always evil. The man who is wrong still retains some respect for truth, if only by accepting the responsibility of choice. But the man in the middle is the knave who blanks out the truth in order to pretend that no choice or values exist, who is willing to sit out the course of any battle, willing to cash in on the blood of the innocent or to crawl on his belly to the guilty, who dispenses justice by condemning both the robber and the robbed to jail, who solves conflicts by ordering the thinker and the fool to meet each other halfway. In any compromise between food and poison, it is only death that can win. In any compromise between good and evil, it is only evil that can profit. In that transfusion of blood which drains the good to feed the evil, the compromiser is the transmitting rubber tube. . . .

When men reduce their virtues to the approximate, then evil acquires the force of an absolute, when loyalty to an unyielding purpose is dropped by the virtuous, it's picked up by scoundrels—and you get the indecent spectacle of a cringing, bargaining, traitorous good and a self-righteously uncompromising evil.

[GS, *FNI*, 217; pb 173.]

The three rules listed below are by no means exhaustive; they are merely the first leads to the understanding of a vast subject.

1. In any *conflict* between two men (or two groups) who hold the *same* basic principles, it is the more consistent one who wins.

2. In any *collaboration* between two men (or two groups) who hold *different* basic principles, it is the more evil or irrational one who wins.

3. When opposite basic principles are clearly and openly defined, it works to the advantage of the rational side; when they are *not* clearly defined, but are hidden or evaded, it works to the advantage of the irrational side.

["The Anatomy of Compromise," *CUI*, 145.]

See also ABSOLUTES; APPEASEMENT; COOPERATION; INTEGRITY; JUSTICE; MORAL COWARDICE; MORAL JUDGMENT; PRAGMATISM; PRINCIPLES.

Concept-Formation.

According to Objectivism, concepts "represent classifications of observed existents according to their relationships to other observed existents." (Ayn Rand, *Introduction to Objectivist Epistemology;* all further quotations in this section, unless otherwise identified, are from this work.) To form a concept, one mentally *isolates* a group of concretes (of distinct perceptual units), on the basis of observed similarities which distinguish them from all other known concretes (similarity is "the relationship between two or more existents which possess the same characteristic(s), but in different measure or degree"); then, by a process of omitting the particular measurements of these concretes, one *integrates* them into a single new mental unit: the concept, which subsumes all concretes of this kind (a potentially unlimited number). The integration is completed and retained by the selection of a perceptual symbol (a word) to designate it. "A concept is a mental integration of two or more units possessing the same distinguishing characteristic(s), with their particular measurements omitted."

[Leonard Peikoff, "The Analytic-Synthetic Dichotomy," *ITOE*, 131.]

Bear firmly in mind that the term "measurements omitted" does not mean, in this context, that measurements are regarded as non-existent; it means that *measurements exist, but are not specified.* That measurements *must* exist is an essential part of the process. The principle is: the relevant measurements must exist in *some* quantity, but may exist in *any* quantity.

[ITOE, 14.]

Let us now examine the process of forming the simplest concept, the concept of a single attribute (chronologically, this is not the first concept that a child would grasp; but it is the simplest one epistemologically)—for instance, the concept *"length."* If a child considers a match, a pencil and a stick, he observes that length is the attribute they have in common, but their specific lengths differ. The *difference is one of measurement.* In order to form the concept "length," the child's mind retains the attribute and omits its particular measurements. Or, more precisely, if the process were identified in words, it would consist of the following: "Length must exist in *some* quantity, but may exist in *any* quantity. I shall identify as 'length' that attribute of any existent possessing it which can be quantitatively related to a unit of length, without specifying the quantity."

The child does not think in such words (he has, as yet, no knowledge of words), but *that* is the nature of the process which his mind performs wordlessly. And that is the principle which his mind follows, when, having grasped the concept "length" by observing the three objects, he uses it to identify the attribute of length in a piece of string, a ribbon, a belt, a corridor or a street.

The same principle directs the process of forming concepts of entities —for instance, the concept *"table."* The child's mind isolates two or more tables from other objects, by focusing on their distinctive characteristic: their shape. He observes that their shapes vary, but have one characteristic in common: a flat, level surface and support(s). He forms the concept "table" by retaining that characteristic and omitting *all* particular measurements, not only the measurements of the shape, but of all the other characteristics of tables (many of which he is not aware of at the time).

[Ibid., 12.]

Observe the multiple role of measurements in the process of concept-formation, in both of its two essential parts: differentiation and integration. Concepts cannot be formed at random. All concepts are formed by first differentiating two or more existents from other existents. All conceptual differentiations are made in terms of *commensurable characteristics* (i.e., characteristics possessing a common unit of measurement). No concept could be formed, for instance, by attempting to distinguish long objects from green objects. Incommensurable characteristics cannot be integrated into one unit.

Tables, for instance, are first differentiated from chairs, beds and other objects by means of the characteristic of *shape*, which is an attribute possessed by all the objects involved. Then, their particular kind of shape is set as the distinguishing characteristic of tables—i.e., a certain category of geometrical measurements of shape is specified. Then, within that category, the particular measurements of individual table-shapes are omitted.

Please note the fact that a given shape represents a certain category or set of geometrical measurements. Shape is an attribute; differences of shape—whether cubes, spheres, cones or any complex combinations—are a matter of differing measurements; any shape can be reduced to or expressed by a set of figures in terms of *linear measurement*. When, in the process of concept-formation, man observes that shape is a commensurable characteristic of certain objects, he does not have to measure all the shapes involved *nor even to know how to measure them;* he merely has to observe the element of *similarity*.

Similarity is grasped *perceptually;* in observing it, man is not and does not have to be aware of the fact that it involves a matter of measurement. It is the task of philosophy and of science to identify that fact.

[Ibid., 16.]

A commensurable characteristic (such as shape in the case of tables, or hue in the case of colors) is an essential element in the process of concept-formation. I shall designate it as the "Conceptual Common Denominator" and define it as "The characteristic(s) reducible to a unit of measurement, by means of which man differentiates two or more existents from other existents possessing it."

The distinguishing characteristic(s) of a concept represents a specified category of measurements within the "Conceptual Common Denominator" involved.

New concepts can be formed by integrating earlier-formed concepts into wider categories, or by subdividing them into narrower categories (a process which we shall discuss later). But all concepts are ultimately reducible to their base in perceptual entities, which are the base (the given) of man's cognitive development.

[Ibid., 18.]

When concepts are integrated into a wider one, the new concept includes *all* the characteristics of its constituent units; but their distinguishing characteristics are regarded as omitted measurements, and one of their common characteristics determines the distinguishing characteristic of the new concept: the one representing their "Conceptual Common Denominator" with the existents from which they are being differentiated.

When a concept is subdivided into narrower ones, its distinguishing characteristic is taken as their "Conceptual Common Denominator"—and is given a narrower range of specified measurements or is combined with an additional characteristic(s), to form the individual distinguishing characteristics of the new concepts.

[Ibid., 30.]

The formation of introspective concepts follows the same principles as the formation of extrospective concepts. A concept pertaining to consciousness is a mental integration of two or more instances of a psychological process possessing the same distinguishing characteristics, with the particular contents and the measurements of the action's intensity omitted—on the principle that these omitted measurements must exist in *some* quantity, but may exist in *any* quantity (i.e., a given psychological process must possess *some* content and *some* degree of intensity, but may possess *any* content or degree of the appropriate category).

[Ibid., 40.]

Concepts are not and cannot be formed in a vacuum; they are formed in a context; the process of conceptualization consists of observing the differences and similarities of the existents *within the field of one's awareness* (and organizing them into concepts accordingly). From a child's grasp of the simplest concept integrating a group of perceptually given concretes, to a scientist's grasp of the most complex abstractions integrating long conceptual chains—all conceptualization is a contextual process; the context is the entire field of a mind's awareness or knowledge at any level of its cognitive development.

This does not mean that conceptualization is a subjective process or that the content of concepts depends on an individual's subjective (i.e., arbitrary) choice. The only issue open to an individual's choice in this matter is how much knowledge he will seek to acquire and, consequently, what conceptual complexity he will be able to reach. But so long as and to the extent that his mind deals with concepts (as distinguished from memorized sounds and floating abstractions), the content of his concepts is determined and dictated by the cognitive content of his mind, i.e., by his grasp of the facts of reality.

[Ibid., 55.]

Objectivity begins with the realization that man (including his every attribute and faculty, including his consciousness) is an entity of a specific nature who must act accordingly; that there is no escape from the law of identity, neither in the universe with which he deals nor in the working of his own consciousness, and if he is to acquire knowledge of the first, he must discover the proper method of using the second; that there is no room for the *arbitrary* in any activity of man, least of all in his method of cognition—and just as he has learned to be guided by objective criteria in making his physical tools, so he must be guided by objective criteria in forming his tools of cognition: his concepts.

Just as man's physical existence was liberated when he grasped the principle that "nature, to be commanded, must be obeyed," so his consciousness will be liberated when he grasps that *nature, to be apprehended, must be obeyed*—that the rules of cognition must be derived from the nature of existence and the nature, the *identity*, of his cognitive faculty.

[Ibid., 110.]

Man's sense organs function automatically; man's brain integrates his sense data into percepts automatically; but the process of integrating percepts into concepts—the process of abstraction and of concept-formation—is *not* automatic.

The process of concept-formation does not consist merely of grasping a few simple abstractions, such as "chair," "table," "hot," "cold," and of learning to speak. It consists of a method of using one's consciousness, best designated by the term "conceptualizing." It is not a passive state of registering random impressions. It is an actively sustained process of identifying one's impressions in conceptual terms, of integrating every event and every observation into a conceptual context, of grasping relationships, differences, similarities in one's perceptual material and of abstracting them into new concepts, of drawing inferences, of making deductions, of reaching conclusions, of asking new questions and discovering new answers and expanding one's knowledge into an ever-growing sum. The faculty that directs this process, the faculty that works by means of concepts, is: *reason.* The process is *thinking.*

["The Objectivist Ethics," *VOS*, 12; pb 20.]

See also ABSTRACTION (PROCESS of); ABSTRACTIONS and CON-CRETES; CONCEPTUAL COMMON DENOMINATOR; CONCEPTS; DEFINITIONS; GENUS and SPECIES; INTEGRATION (MENTAL); LANGUAGE; MEASUREMENT; UNIT; WORDS.

Concepts. A *concept* is a mental integration of two or more units which are isolated by a process of abstraction and united by a specific definition. By organizing his perceptual material into concepts, and his concepts into wider and still wider concepts, man is able to grasp and retain, to identify and integrate an unlimited amount of knowledge, a knowledge extending beyond the immediate concretes of any given, immediate moment.

In any given moment, concepts enable man to hold in the focus of his conscious awareness much more than his purely perceptual capacity would permit. The range of man's perceptual awareness—the number of percepts he can deal with at any one time—is limited. He may be able to visualize four or five units—as, for instance, five trees. He cannot visualize a hundred trees or a distance of ten light-years. It is only his conceptual faculty that makes it possible for him to deal with knowledge of that kind.

Man retains his concepts by means of language. With the exception of proper names, every word we use is a concept that stands for an unlimited number of concretes of a certain kind. A concept is like a mathematical series of *specifically defined units,* going off in both directions, open at both ends and including *all* units of that particular kind. For instance, the concept "man" includes all men who live at present, who have ever lived or will ever live—a number of men so great that one would not be able to perceive them all visually, let alone to study them or discover anything about them.

["The Psycho-Epistemology of Art," *RM,* 19; pb 17.]

To what precisely do we refer when we designate three persons as "men"? We refer to the fact that they are living beings who possess the *same* characteristic distinguishing them from all other living species: a rational faculty—though the specific measurements of their distinguishing characteristic *qua* men, as well as of all their other characteristics *qua* living beings, are different. (As living beings of a certain kind, they possess innumerable characteristics in common: the same shape, the same range of size, the same facial features, the same vital organs, the same fingerprints, etc., and all these characteristics differ only in their measurements.)

[*ITOE,* 21.]

A concept is a mental integration of two or more units possessing the same distinguishing characteristic(s), with their particular measurements omitted.

[Ibid., 15.]

The basic principle of concept-formation (which states that the omitted measurements must exist in *some* quantity, but may exist in *any* quantity) is the equivalent of the basic principle of algebra, which states that algebraic symbols must be given *some* numerical value, but may be given *any* value. In this sense and respect, perceptual awareness is the arithmetic, but *conceptual awareness is the algebra of cognition.*

[Ibid., 22.]

None of [the traditional theories of concepts] regards concepts as *objective*, i.e., as neither revealed nor invented, but as produced by man's consciousness in accordance with the facts of reality, as mental integrations of factual data computed by man—as the products of a cognitive method of classification whose processes must be performed by man, but whose content is dictated by reality.

[Ibid., 71.]

Concepts represent condensations of knowledge, which make further study and the division of cognitive labor possible.

[Ibid., 87.]

Conceptualization is a method of expanding man's consciousness by reducing the number of its content's units—a systematic means to an unlimited integration of cognitive data.

[Ibid., 85.]

It is crucially important to grasp the fact that a concept is an "open-end" classification which includes the yet-to-be-discovered characteristics of a given group of existents. All of man's knowledge rests on that fact.

[Ibid., 87.]

Concepts and, therefore, language are *primarily* a tool of cognition—*not* of communication, as is usually assumed. Communication is merely the consequence, not the cause nor the primary purpose of concept-formation—a crucial consequence, of invaluable importance to men, but still only a consequence. *Cognition precedes communication;* the necessary precondition of communication is that one have something to communicate....

The primary purpose of concepts and of language is to provide man with a system of cognitive classification and organization, which enables him to acquire knowledge on an unlimited scale; this means: to keep order in man's mind and enable him to think.

[Ibid., 92.]

Abstract ideas are conceptual integrations which subsume an incalculable number of concretes—and ... without abstract ideas you would not be able to deal with concrete, particular, real-life problems. You would be in the position of a newborn infant, to whom every object is a unique, unprecedented phenomenon. The difference between his mental state and yours lies in the number of conceptual integrations your mind has performed.

["Philosophy: Who Needs It," *PWNI*, 6; pb 5.]

Conceptual awareness is the only type of awareness capable of integrating past, present and future. Sensations are merely an awareness of the present and cannot be retained beyond the immediate moment; percepts are retained and, through automatic memory, provide a certain rudimentary link to the past, but cannot project the future. It is only conceptual awareness that can grasp and hold the total of its experience—extrospectively, the continuity of existence; introspectively, the continuity of consciousness—and thus enable its possessor to project his course long-range.

[*ITOE*, 75.]

There are many special or "cross-filed" chains of abstractions (of interconnected concepts) in man's mind. Cognitive abstractions are the fundamental chain, on which all the others depend. Such chains are mental integrations, serving a special purpose and formed accordingly by a special criterion.

Cognitive abstractions are formed by the criterion of: what is *essential?* (epistemologically essential to distinguish one class of existents from all others). *Normative* abstractions are formed by the criterion of: what is *good? Esthetic* abstractions are formed by the criterion of: what is *important?*

["Art and Sense of Life," *RM*, 45; pb 36.]

See also "ANTI-CONCEPTS"; *ANTI-CONCEPTUAL MENTALITY; AXIOMATIC CONCEPTS; COMMUNICATION; DEFINITIONS; ESTHETIC ABSTRACTIONS; "FROZEN ABSTRACTION," FALLACY of; INTEGRATION (MENTAL); INVALID CONCEPTS; LANGUAGE; MATERIALS, CONCEPTS of; MEANING (of CONCEPTS); METHOD, CONCEPTS of; NORMATIVE ABSTRACTIONS; "PACKAGE-DEALING," FALLACY of; PERCEPTION; PLATONIC REALISM; "RAND'S RAZOR"; REASON; "STOLEN CONCEPT," FALLACY of; UNIT; UNIT-ECONOMY; WORDS.*

Conceptual Common Denominator.

A commensurable characteristic (such as shape in the case of tables, or hue in the case of colors) is an essential element in the process of concept-formation. I shall designate it as the "Conceptual Common Denominator" and define it as "The characteristic(s) reducible to a unit of measurement, by means of which man differentiates two or more existents from other existents possessing it."

The distinguishing characteristic(s) of a concept represents a specified category of measurements within the "Conceptual Common Denominator" involved.

[*ITOE*, 18.]

Two fundamental attributes are involved in every state, aspect or function of man's consciousness: content and action—the content of awareness, and the action of consciousness in regard to that content. These two attributes are the fundamental Conceptual Common Denominator of all concepts pertaining to consciousness.

[Ibid., 38.]

When concepts are integrated into a wider one, the new concept includes *all* the characteristics of its constituent units; but their distinguishing characteristics are regarded as omitted measurements, and one of their common characteristics determines the distinguishing characteristic of the new concept: the one representing their "Conceptual Common Denominator" with the existents from which they are being differentiated.

When a concept is subdivided into narrower ones, its distinguishing characteristic is taken as their "Conceptual Common Denominator"—and is given a narrower range of specified measurements or is combined with an additional characteristic(s), to form the individual distinguishing characteristics of the new concepts.

[Ibid., 30.]

The rules of correct definition are derived from the process of concept-formation. The units of a concept were differentiated—by means of a distinguishing characteristic(s)—from other existents possessing a commensurable characteristic, a Conceptual Common Denominator. A definition follows the same principle: it specifies the distinguishing characteristic(s) of the units, and indicates the category of existents from which they were differentiated.

The distinguishing characteristic(s) of the units becomes the *differentia* of the concept's definition; the existents possessing a Conceptual Common Denominator become the *genus*.

[Ibid., 53.]

Since axiomatic concepts are not formed by differentiating one group of existents from others, but represent an integration of all existents, they have no Conceptual Common Denominator with anything else. They have no contraries, no alternatives.

[Ibid., 77.]

See also AXIOMATIC CONCEPTS; CONCEPT-FORMATION; DEFINITIONS; GENUS and SPECIES; MEASUREMENT; UNIT.

Concretes.   *See Abstractions and Concretes.*

Confidence. *See Courage and Confidence; Self-Esteem.*

Consciousness. Existence exists—and the act of grasping that statement implies two corollary axioms: that something exists which one perceives and that one exists possessing consciousness, consciousness being the faculty of perceiving that which exists.

If nothing exists, there can be no consciousness: a consciousness with nothing to be conscious of is a contradiction in terms. A consciousness conscious of nothing but itself is a contradiction in terms: before it could identify itself as consciousness, it had to be conscious of something. If that which you claim to perceive does not exist, what you possess is not consciousness.

Whatever the degree of your knowledge, these two—existence and consciousness—are axioms you cannot escape, these two are the irreducible primaries implied in any action you undertake, in any part of your knowledge and in its sum, from the first ray of light you perceive at the start of your life to the widest erudition you might acquire at its end. Whether you know the shape of a pebble or the structure of a solar system, the axioms remain the same: that *it* exists and that you *know* it. . . . Existence is Identity, Consciousness is Identification.

[GS, *FNI*, 152; pb 124.]

Consciousness is the faculty of awareness—the faculty of perceiving that which exists.

Awareness is not a passive state, but an active process. On the lower levels of awareness, a complex neurological process is required to enable man to experience a sensation and to integrate sensations into percepts; that process is automatic and non-volitional: man is aware of its results, but not of the process itself. On the higher, conceptual level, the process is psychological, conscious and volitional. In either case, awareness is achieved and maintained by continuous *action.*

Directly or indirectly, every phenomenon of consciousness is derived from one's awareness of the external world. Some object, i.e., some *content*, is involved in every state of awareness. Extrospection is a process of cognition directed outward—a process of apprehending some existent(s) of the external world. Introspection is a process of cognition directed inward—a process of apprehending one's own psychological actions in regard to some existent(s) of the external world, such actions as thinking, feeling, reminiscing, etc. It is only in relation to the external world that the various actions of a consciousness can be experienced, grasped, defined or communicated. Awareness is awareness of something. A content-less state of consciousness is a contradiction in terms.

[*ITOE*, 37.]

The first and primary axiomatic concepts are "existence," "identity" (which is a corollary of "existence") and "consciousness." One can study what exists and how consciousness functions; but one cannot analyze (or "prove") existence as such, or consciousness as such. These are irreducible primaries. (An attempt to "prove" them is self-contradictory: it is an attempt to "prove" existence by means of non-existence, and consciousness by means of unconsciousness.)

[Ibid., 73.]

Consciousness—for those living organisms which possess it—is the basic means of survival.

["The Objectivist Ethics," *VOS*, 9; pb 18.]

Man's consciousness is his least known and most abused vital organ. Most people believe that consciousness as such is some sort of indeterminate faculty which has no *nature*, no specific identity and, therefore, no requirements, no needs, no rules for being properly or improperly used. The simplest example of this belief is people's willingness to lie or cheat, to fake reality on the premise that "I'm the only one who'll know" or "It's only in my mind"—without any concern for what this does to one's mind, what complex, untraceable, disastrous impairments it produces, what crippling damage may result.

The loss of control over one's consciousness is the most terrifying of human experiences: a consciousness that doubts its own efficacy is in a monstrously intolerable state. Yet men abuse, subvert and starve their consciousness in a manner they would not dream of applying to their hair, toenails or stomachs. They know that these things have a specific identity and specific requirements, and, if one wishes to preserve them, one must comb one's hair, trim one's toenails and refrain from swallowing rat poison. But one's mind? Aw, it needs nothing and can swallow anything. Or so most people believe. And they go on believing it while they toss in agony on a psychologist's couch, screaming that their mind keeps them in a state of chronic terror for no reason whatever. . . .

The fact [is] that man's consciousness possesses a specific nature with specific *cognitive* needs, that it is *not* infinitely malleable and cannot be twisted, like a piece of putty, to fit any private evasions or any public "conditioning."

["Our Cultural Value-Deprivation," *TO*, April 1966, 1.]

Just as man's physical existence was liberated when he grasped the principle that "nature, to be commanded, must be obeyed," so his consciousness will be liberated when he grasps that *nature, to be apprehended, must be obeyed*—that the rules of cognition must be derived from the nature of existence and the nature, the *identity*, of his cognitive faculty.

[*ITOE*, 110.]

The hallmark of a mystic is the savagely stubborn refusal to accept the fact that consciousness, like any other existent, possesses identity, that it is a faculty of a specific nature, functioning through specific means. While the advance of civilization has been eliminating one area of magic after another, the last stand of the believers in the miraculous consists of their frantic attempts to regard *identity* as the *disqualifying* element of consciousness.

The implicit, but unadmitted premise of the neo-mystics of modern philosophy, is the notion that only an ineffable consciousness can acquire a valid knowledge of reality, that "true" knowledge has to be causeless, i.e., acquired without any means of cognition.

[Ibid., 106.]

Two fundamental attributes are involved in every state, aspect or function of man's consciousness: content and action—the content of awareness, and the action of consciousness in regard to that content.

These two attributes are the fundamental Conceptual Common Denominator of all concepts pertaining to consciousness. . . .

To form concepts of consciousness, one must isolate the action from the content of a given state of consciousness, by a process of abstraction. Just as, extrospectively, man can abstract attributes from entities—so, introspectively, he can abstract the actions of his consciousness from its contents, and observe the *differences* among these various actions.

For instance (on the adult level), when a man sees a woman walking down the street, the action of his consciousness is *perception;* when he notes that she is beautiful, the action of his consciousness is *evaluation;* when he experiences an inner state of pleasure and approval, of admiration, the action of his consciousness is *emotion;* when he stops to watch her and draws conclusions, from the evidence, about her character, age, social position, etc., the action of his consciousness is *thought;* when, later, he recalls the incident, the action of his consciousness is *reminiscence;* when he projects that her appearance would be improved if her hair were blond rather than brown, and her dress were blue rather than red, the action of his consciousness is *imagination.*

[Ibid., 38.]

In the realm of introspection, the concretes, the *units* which are integrated into a single concept, are the specific instances of a given psychological process. The measurable attributes of a psychological process are its object or *content* and its *intensity*.

The content is some aspect of the external world (or is derived from some aspect of the external world) and is measurable by the various methods of measurement applicable to the external world. The intensity of a psychological process is the automatically summed up result of many factors: of its scope, its clarity, its cognitive and motivational context, the degree of mental energy or effort required, etc.

There is no exact method of measuring the intensity of all psychological processes, but—as in the case of forming concepts of colors—conceptualization does not require the knowledge of exact measurements. Degrees of intensity can be and are measured approximately, on a comparative scale. For instance, the intensity of the emotion of joy in response to certain facts varies according to the importance of these facts in one's *hierarchy* of values; it varies in such cases as buying a new suit, or getting a raise in pay, or marrying the person one loves. The intensity of a process of thought and of the intellectual effort required varies according to the *scope* of its content; it varies when one grasps the concept "table" or the concept "justice," when one grasps that $2 + 2 = 4$ or that $e = mc^2$.

[Ibid., 39.]

See also AXIOMATIC CONCEPTS; EMOTIONS; FOCUS; FREE WILL; INTROSPECTION; PERCEPTION; PRIMACY of EXISTENCE vs. PRIMACY of CONSCIOUSNESS; PRIOR CERTAINTY of CONSCIOUSNESS; PSYCHOLOGY; REASON; SELF; SENSATIONS; SOUL-BODY DICHOTOMY; SUBCONSCIOUS; TABULA RASA; UNDERSTANDING.

"Conservatives." Objectivists are *not* "conservatives." We are *radicals for capitalism;* we are fighting for that philosophical base which capitalism did not have and without which it was doomed to perish. . . .

Politics is based on three other philosophical disciplines: metaphysics, epistemology and ethics—on a theory of man's nature and of man's relationship to existence. It is only on such a base that one can formulate a consistent political theory and achieve it in practice. When, however, men attempt to rush into politics without such a base, the result is that embarrassing conglomeration of impotence, futility, inconsistency and superficiality which is loosely designated today as "conservatism." . . .

Today's culture is dominated by the philosophy of mysticism (irrationalism)—altruism—collectivism, the base from which only *statism* can be derived; the statists (of any brand: communist, fascist or welfare) are merely cashing in on it—while the "conservatives" are scurrying to ride on the enemy's premises and, somehow, to achieve political freedom by stealth. It can't be done.

["Choose Your Issues," *TON*, Jan. 1962, 1.]

What are the "conservatives"? What is it that they are seeking to "conserve"?

It is generally understood that those who support the "conservatives," expect them to uphold the system which has been camouflaged by the loose term of "the *American* way of life." The moral treason of the "conservative" leaders lies in the fact that they are hiding behind that camouflage: they do not have the courage to admit that the *American* way of life was *capitalism*, that *that* was the politico-economic system born and established in the United States, the system which, in one brief century, achieved a level of freedom, of progress, of prosperity, of human happiness, unmatched in all the other systems and centuries combined—and that *that* is the system which they are now allowing to perish by silent default.

If the "conservatives" do not stand for capitalism, they stand for and are nothing; they have no goal, no direction, no political principles, no social ideals, no intellectual values, no leadership to offer anyone.

Yet capitalism is what the "conservatives" dare not advocate or defend. They are paralyzed by the profound conflict between capitalism and the moral code which dominates our culture: the morality of altruism. . . . Capitalism and altruism are incompatible; they are philosophical opposites; they cannot co-exist in the same man or in the same society.

["Conservatism: An Obituary," *CUI*, 194.]

What is the moral stature of those who are afraid to proclaim that they are the champions of freedom? What is the integrity of those who outdo their enemies in smearing, misrepresenting, spitting at, and apologizing for their own ideal? What is the rationality of those who expect to trick people into freedom, cheat them into justice, fool them into progress, con them into preserving their rights, and, while indoctrinating them with statism, put one over on them and let them wake up in a perfect capitalist society some morning?

These are the "conservatives"—or most of their intellectual spokesmen.

[Ibid.]

There are three interrelated arguments used by today's "conservatives" to justify capitalism, which can best be designated as: the argument from *faith*—the argument from *tradition*—the argument from *depravity.*

Sensing their need of a moral base, many "conservatives" decided to choose *religion* as their moral justification; they claim that America and capitalism are based on faith in God. Politically, such a claim contradicts the fundamental principles of the United States: in America, religion is a private matter which cannot and must not be brought into political issues.

Intellectually, to rest one's case on *faith* means to concede that reason is on the side of one's enemies—that one has no rational arguments to offer. The "conservatives' " claim that their case rests on faith, means that there are no rational arguments to support the American system, no rational justification for freedom, justice, property, individual rights, that these rest on a mystic revelation and can be accepted only *on faith* —that in reason and logic the enemy is right, but men must hold faith as superior to reason.

Consider the implications of that theory. While the communists claim that they are the representatives of reason and science, the "conservatives" concede it and retreat into the realm of mysticism, of faith, of the supernatural, into another world, surrendering *this* world to communism. It is the kind of victory that the communists' irrational ideology could never have won on its own merits. . . .

Now consider the second argument: the attempt to justify capitalism on the ground of *tradition.* Certain groups are trying to switch the word "conservative" into the exact opposite of its modern American usage, to switch it back to its nineteenth-century meaning, and to put this over on the public. These groups declare that to be a "conservative" means to uphold the *status quo,* the given, the established, regardless of what it might be, regardless of whether it is good or bad, right or wrong, defensible or indefensible. They declare that we must defend the American political system not because it is *right,* but because our ancestors chose it, not because it is *good,* but because it is *old.* . . .

The argument that we must respect "tradition" as such, respect it *merely* because it is a "tradition," means that we must accept the values other men have chosen, *merely* because other men have chosen them— with the necessary implication of: who are *we* to change them? The affront to a man's self-esteem, in such an argument, and the profound contempt for man's nature are obvious.

This leads us to the third—and the worst—argument, used by some "conservatives": the attempt to defend capitalism on the ground of *man's depravity.*

This argument runs as follows: since men are weak, fallible, non-omniscient and innately depraved, no man may be entrusted with the responsibility of being a dictator and of ruling everybody else; therefore, a free society is the proper way of life for imperfect creatures. Please grasp fully the implications of this argument: since men are depraved, they are *not good enough for a dictatorship;* freedom is all that they deserve; if they were perfect, they would be worthy of a totalitarian state.

Dictatorship—this theory asserts—believe it or not, is the result of *faith in man* and in man's goodness; if people believed that man is depraved by nature, they would not entrust a dictator with power. This means that a belief in human depravity protects human freedom—that it is wrong to enslave the depraved, but would be right to enslave the virtuous. And more: dictatorships—this theory declares—and all the other disasters of the modern world are man's punishment for the sin of relying on his intellect and of attempting to improve his life on earth by seeking to devise a perfect political system and to establish a *rational* society. This means that humility, passivity, lethargic resignation and a belief in Original Sin are the bulwarks of capitalism. One could not go farther than this in historical, political, and psychological ignorance or subversion. This is truly the voice of the Dark Ages rising again—in the midst of our industrial civilization.

The cynical, man-hating advocates of this theory sneer at all ideals, scoff at all human aspirations and deride all attempts to improve men's existence. "You can't change human nature," is their stock answer to the socialists. Thus they concede that socialism *is* the ideal, but human nature is unworthy of it; after which, they invite men to crusade for capitalism—a crusade one would have to start by spitting in one's own face. Who will fight and die to defend his status as a miserable sinner? If, as a result of such theories, people become contemptuous of "conservatism," do not wonder and do not ascribe it to the cleverness of the socialists.

[Ibid., 196.]

Today's "conservatives" are futile, impotent and, culturally, dead. They have nothing to offer and can achieve nothing. They can only help to destroy intellectual standards, to disintegrate thought, to discredit capitalism, and to accelerate this country's uncontested collapse into despair and dictatorship.

[Ibid., 199.]

The most immoral contradiction—in the chaos of today's anti-ideological groups—is that of the so-called "conservatives," who posture as defenders of individual rights, particularly *property* rights, but uphold and advocate the draft. By what infernal evasion can they hope to justify the proposition that creatures who have no right to life, have the right to a bank account?

["The Wreckage of the Consensus," CUI, 227.]

The Antitrust laws—an unenforceable, uncompliable, unjudicable mess of contradictions—have for decades kept American businessmen under a silent, growing reign of terror. Yet these laws were created and, to this day, are upheld by the "conservatives," as a grim monument to their lack of political philosophy, of economic knowledge and of any concern with principles.

["Choose Your Issues," TON, Jan. 1962, 1.]

It was the so-called "conservatives" . . . who ran to the government for regulations and controls [over the broadcasting industry], and who cheered the notion of "public property" and service to the "public interest."

["The Property Status of the Airwaves," CUI, 126.]

Escalation of controls has been the policy of conservatives in regard to antitrust laws, labor legislation, the military draft, taxation, the "negative income tax," etc.

["Ideas v. Men," ARL, III, 15, 4.]

If the religionist wing of conservatism is futile, the secular one is, perhaps, worse. The religionists preach the morality of altruism, knowing that the liberals and the extreme left are its much more consistent practitioners, but hoping—since consistency is a requirement of reason, not of faith—that a miracle will wipe out that fact. The secular conservatives solve the contradiction by discarding morality altogether, by surrendering it to the enemy and declaring that social-political-economic problems are *amoral*.

["Moral Inflation," ARL, III, 12, 2.]

Capitalism is not the system of the past; it is the system of the future —if mankind is to have a future. Those who wish to fight for it, must discard the title of "conservatives." "Conservatism" has always been a misleading name, inappropriate to America. Today, there is nothing left to "conserve": the established political philosophy, the intellectual orthodoxy, and the *status quo* are *collectivism*. Those who reject all the basic premises of collectivism are *radicals* in the proper sense of the word: "radical" means "fundamental." Today, the fighters for capitalism have to be, not bankrupt "conservatives," but new radicals, new intellectuals and, above all, new, dedicated moralists.

["Conservatism: An Obituary," CUI, 201.]

See also ALTRUISM; CAPITALISM; COMPROMISE; "CONSERVA-TIVES" vs. "LIBERALS"; FAITH; INDIVIDUAL RIGHTS; "LIBERALS"; "LIBERTARIANS"; ORIGINAL SIN; RELIGION; STATISM; TRADI-TION.

"Conservatives" vs. "Liberals." Both [conservatives and liberals] hold the same premise—*the mind-body dichotomy*—but choose opposite sides of this lethal fallacy.

The conservatives want freedom to act in the material realm; they tend to oppose government control of production, of industry, of trade, of business, of physical goods, of material wealth. But they advocate government control of man's spirit, i.e., man's consciousness; they advocate the State's right to impose censorship, to determine moral values, to create and enforce a governmental establishment of morality, to rule the intellect. The liberals want freedom to act in the spiritual realm; they oppose censorship, they oppose government control of ideas, of the arts, of the press, of education (note their concern with "academic freedom"). But they advocate government control of material production, of business, of employment, of wages, of profits, of all physical property—they advocate it all the way down to total expropriation.

The conservatives see man as a body freely roaming the earth, building sand piles or factories—with an electronic computer inside his skull, controlled from Washington. The liberals see man as a soul freewheeling to the farthest reaches of the universe—but wearing chains from nose to toes when he crosses the street to buy a loaf of bread.

Yet it is the conservatives who are predominantly religionists, who proclaim the superiority of the soul over the body, who represent what I call the "mystics of spirit." And it is the liberals who are predominantly materialists, who regard man as an aggregate of meat, and who represent what I call the "mystics of muscle."

This is merely a paradox, not a contradiction: *each camp wants to control the realm it regards as metaphysically important; each grants freedom only to the activities it despises.* Observe that the conservatives insult and demean the rich or those who succeed in material production, regarding them as morally inferior—and that the liberals treat ideas as a cynical con game. "Control," to both camps, means the power to rule by physical force. Neither camp holds freedom as a value. The conservatives want to rule man's consciousness; the liberals, his body.

["Censorship: Local and Express," *PWNI*, 228; pb 186.]

See also CENSORSHIP; "CONSERVATIVES"; FREEDOM; "LIBERALS"; MYSTICS of SPIRIT and MUSCLE; PROPERTY RIGHTS; RELIGION; RIGHTISTS and LEFTISTS; SOUL-BODY DICHOTOMY; "WINDOW-DRESSING."

Constitution.   Today, when a concerted effort is made to obliterate this point, it cannot be repeated too often that the Constitution is a limitation on the government, not on private individuals—that it does not prescribe the conduct of private individuals, only the conduct of the government—that it is not a charter *for* government power, but a charter of the citizens' protection *against* the government.

["The Nature of Government," *VOS*, 154; pb 114.]

Ours was the first government based on and strictly limited by a written document—the Constitution—which specifically forbids it to violate individual rights or to act on whim. The history of the atrocities perpetrated by all the other kinds of governments—unrestricted governments acting on unprovable assumptions—demonstrates the value and validity of the original political theory on which this country was built.

["Censorship: Local and Express," *PWNI*, 221; pb 181.]

A complex legal system, based on *objectively* valid principles, is required to make a society free and *to keep it free*—a system that does not depend on the motives, the moral character or the intentions of any given official, a system that leaves no opportunity, no legal loophole for the development of tyranny.

The American system of checks and balances was just such an achievement. And although certain contradictions in the Constitution did leave a loophole for the growth of statism, the incomparable achievement was the concept of a constitution as a means of limiting and restricting the power of the government.

["The Nature of Government," *VOS*, 154; pb 113.]

The clause giving Congress the power to regulate interstate commerce is one of the major errors in the Constitution. That clause, more than any other, was the crack in the Constitution's foundation, the entering wedge of statism, which permitted the gradual establishment of the welfare state. But I would venture to say that the framers of the Constitution could not have conceived of what that clause has now become. If, in writing it, one of their goals was to facilitate the flow of trade and prevent the establishment of trade barriers among the states, that clause has reached the opposite destination.

["Censorship: Local and Express," *PWNI*, 225; pb 184.]

See also AMERICA; FOUNDING FATHERS; GOVERNMENT; INDIVID-UAL RIGHTS; LAW, OBJECTIVE and NON-OBJECTIVE; PHYSICAL FORCE.

"Consumerism." No "anti-concept" launched by the "liberals" goes so far so crudely as the [conservatives'] tag "consumerism." It implies loudly and clearly that the status of "consumer" is separate from and superior to the status of "producer"; it suggests a social system dedicated to the service of a new aristocracy which is distinguished by the ability to "consume" and vested with a special claim on the caste of serfs marked by the ability to produce.

["The Obliteration of Capitalism," *CUI*, 185.]

There is no such thing as "consumers' rights," just as there can be no "rights" belonging to some special group or race and to no others. There are only *the rights of man*—rights possessed by every individual man and by *all* men as individuals. The right to be protected from physical injury or fraud belongs to *all* men, not merely to "consumers," and does not require any special protection other than that provided by *the criminal law.* . . .

If a businessman—or any other citizen—willfully and knowingly cheats or injures others ("consumers" or otherwise), it is a matter to be *proved* and punished in a criminal court. But the precedent which [the "consumer protection" movement] is here attempting to establish is the legal hallmark of a dictatorship: *preventive law*—the concept that a man is guilty until he is proved innocent by the permissive rubber stamp of a commissar or a Gauleiter.

What protects us from any private citizen who may choose to turn criminal and injure or defraud us? *That*, precisely, is the proper duty of a government. But if the government assumes a totalitarian power and its officials are not subject to any law, then *who will protect us from our protectors?* What will be our recourse against the dishonesty, vindictiveness, cupidity or stupidity of a bureaucrat?

If matters such as *science* are to be placed into the unanswerable power of a single bureau, what will guarantee the superior wisdom, justice and integrity of the bureaucrats? Why, the vote of the people, a statist would answer—of the people who choose the ruler who then appoints the bureaucrats—of the same people whom [he] does not consider competent to choose electric toasters, credit contracts, face lotions, laxative tablets or canned vegetables.

["Who Will Protect Us from Our Protectors?" *TON*, May 1962, 20.]

You propose to establish a social order based on the following tenets: that you're incompetent to run your own life, but competent to run the lives of others—that you're unfit to exist in freedom, but fit to become an omnipotent ruler—that you're unable to earn your living by the use of your own intelligence, but able to judge politicians and to vote them into jobs of total power over arts you have never seen, over sciences you have never studied, over achievements of which you have no knowledge, over the gigantic industries where you, by your own definition of your capacity, would be unable successfully to fill the job of assistant greaser.

[GS, *FNI*, 208; pb 167.]

See also "ANTI-CONCEPTS"; CONSUMPTION; FRAUD; GOVERNMENT; INDIVIDUAL RIGHTS; PRODUCTION; SERVICE; TRIBAL PREMISE (in ECONOMICS).

Consumption.

Consumption is the *final*, not the *efficient*, cause of production. The efficient cause is savings, which can be said to represent the opposite of consumption: they represent *unconsumed* goods. Consumption is the end of production, and a *dead end*, as far as the productive process is concerned. The worker who produces so little that he consumes everything he earns, carries his own weight economically, but contributes nothing to future production. The worker who has a modest savings account, and the millionaire who invests a fortune (and all the men in between), are those who finance the future. The man who consumes without producing is a parasite, whether he is a welfare recipient or a rich playboy.

["Egalitarianism and Inflation," *PWNI*, 160; pb 132.]

Trained in college to believe that to look beyond the immediate moment—to look for causes or to foresee consequences—is impossible, modern men have developed context-dropping as their normal method of cognition. Observing a bad, small-town shopkeeper, the kind who is doomed to fail, they believe—as he does—that lack of customers is his only problem; and that the question of the goods he sells, or *where these goods come from*, has nothing to do with it. The goods, they believe, are here and will always be here. Therefore, they conclude, the consumer —not the producer—is the motor of an economy. Let us extend credit, i.e., our savings, to the consumers—they advise—in order to expand the market for our goods.

But, in fact, consumers *qua consumers* are not part of anyone's market; qua consumers, they are *irrelevant* to economics. Nature does not grant anyone an innate title of "consumer"; it is a title that has to be earned— by production. Only *producers* constitute a market—only men who trade products or services for products or services. In the role of producers, they represent a market's "supply"; in the role of consumers, they represent a market's "demand." The law of supply and demand has an implicit subclause: that it involves the same people in both capacities.

When this subclause is forgotten, ignored or evaded—you get the economic situation of today.

[Ibid., 157; pb 130.]

See also "CONSUMERISM"; FINAL CAUSATION; INVESTMENT; PRODUCTION; PURCHASING POWER; SAVINGS.

Context. Knowledge is contextual. . . . By "context" we mean the sum of cognitive elements conditioning the acquisition, validity or application of any item of human knowledge. Knowledge is an organization or integration of interconnected elements, each relevant to the others. . . . Knowledge is not a mosaic of independent pieces each of which stands apart from the rest. . . .

In regard to any concept, idea, proposal, theory, or item of knowledge, never forget or ignore the context on which it depends and which conditions its validity and use.

[Leonard Peikoff, "The Philosophy of Objectivism" lecture series (1976), Lecture 5.]

Concepts are not and cannot be formed in a vacuum; they are formed in a context; the process of conceptualization consists of observing the differences and similarities of the existents *within the field of one's awareness* (and organizing them into concepts accordingly). From a child's grasp of the simplest concept integrating a group of perceptually given concretes, to a scientist's grasp of the most complex abstractions integrating long conceptual chains—all conceptualization is a contextual process; the context is the entire field of a mind's awareness or knowledge at any level of its cognitive development.

This does not mean that conceptualization is a subjective process or that the content of concepts depends on an individual's subjective (i.e., arbitrary) choice. The only issue open to an individual's choice in this matter is how much knowledge he will seek to acquire and, consequently, what conceptual complexity he will be able to reach. But so long as and to the extent that his mind deals with concepts (as distinguished from memorized sounds and floating abstractions), the content of his concepts is determined and dictated by the cognitive content of his mind, i.e., by his grasp of the facts of reality. If his grasp is noncontradictory, then even if the scope of his knowledge is modest and the content of his concepts is primitive, *it will not contradict the content of the same concepts in the mind of the most advanced scientists.*

The same is true of definitions. *All definitions are contextual,* and a primitive definition *does not contradict* a more advanced one: the latter merely expands the former.

[ITOE, 55.]

No concept man forms is valid unless he integrates it without contradiction into the total sum of his knowledge.

[GS, *FNI*, 154; pb 126.]

One must never make any decisions, form any convictions or seek any values out of context, i.e., apart from or against the total, integrated sum of one's knowledge.

["The Objectivist Ethics," *VOS*, 21; pb 26.]

See also CERTAINTY; CONTEXT-DROPPING; CONTRADICTIONS; DEFINITIONS; HIERARCHY of KNOWLEDGE; INTEGRATION (MENTAL); KNOWLEDGE; PRINCIPLES.

Context-Dropping.

Context-dropping is one of the chief psychological tools of evasion. In regard to one's desires, there are two major ways of context-dropping: the issues of *range* and of *means*.

A rational man sees his interests in terms of a lifetime and selects his goals accordingly. This does not mean that he has to be omniscient, infallible or clairvoyant. It means that he does not live his life short-range and does not drift like a bum pushed by the spur of the moment. It means that he does not regard any moment as cut off from the context of the rest of his life, and that he allows no conflicts or contradictions between his short-range and long-range interests. He does not become his own destroyer by pursuing a desire today which wipes out all his values tomorrow.

A rational man does not indulge in wistful longings for ends divorced from means. He does not hold a desire without knowing (or learning) and considering the means by which it is to be achieved.

["The 'Conflicts' of Men's Interests," *VOS*, 60; pb 51.]

Whenever you tear an idea from its context and treat it as though it were a self-sufficient, independent item, you invalidate the thought process involved. If you omit the context, or even a crucial aspect of it, then no matter what you say it will not be valid. . . .

A context-dropper forgets or evades any wider context. He stares at only one element, and he thinks, "I can change just this one point, and everything else will remain the same." In fact, everything is interconnected. That one element involves a whole context, and to assess a change in one element, you must see what it means in the whole context.

[Leonard Peikoff, "The Philosophy of Objectivism" lecture series (1976), Lecture 5.]

See also CONTEXT; EVASION; SELF-INTEREST.

"Contingent Truth." *See Analytic-Synthetic Dichotomy.*

Contracts.   In a free society, men are not forced to deal with one another. They do so only by voluntary agreement and, when a time element is involved, by *contract.* If a contract is broken by the arbitrary decision of one man, it may cause a disastrous financial injury to the other.... This leads to one of the most important and most complex functions of the government: to the function of an arbiter who settles disputes among men according to objective laws.

["The Nature of Government," *VOS*, 149; pb 110.]

A unilateral breach of contract involves an indirect use of physical force: it consists, in essence, of one man receiving the material values, goods or services of another, then refusing to pay for them and thus keeping them by force (by mere physical possession), not by right—i.e., keeping them without the consent of the owner.

[Ibid., 150; pb 111.]

In a free society, the "rights" of any group are derived from the rights of its members through their voluntary, individual choice and *contractual* agreement, and are merely the application of these individual rights to a specific undertaking. Every legitimate group undertaking is based on the participants' right of free association and free trade. (By "legitimate," I mean: noncriminal and freely formed, that is, a group which no one was *forced* to join.)

For instance, the right of an industrial concern to engage in business is derived from the right of its owners to invest their money in a productive venture—from their right to hire employees—from the right of the employees to sell their services—from the right of all those involved to produce and to sell their products—from the right of the customers to buy (or not to buy) those products. Every link of this complex chain of contractual relationships rests on individual rights, individual choices, individual agreements. Every agreement is delimited, specified and subject to certain conditions, that is, dependent upon a mutual trade to mutual benefit.

["Collectivized 'Rights,' " *VOS*, 136; pb 102.]

See also COOPERATION; GOVERNMENT; INDIVIDUAL RIGHTS; PHYSICAL FORCE; PROPERTY RIGHTS.

Contradictions.   A contradiction cannot exist. An atom is itself, and so is the universe; neither can contradict its own identity; nor can a part contradict the whole. No concept man forms is valid unless he integrates it without contradiction into the total sum of his knowledge. To arrive at a contradiction is to confess an error in one's thinking; to maintain a contradiction is to abdicate one's mind and to evict oneself from the realm of reality.

[GS, *FNI*, 154; pb 126.]

[Objectivism agrees with Aristotle's formulation of the Law of Non-Contradiction]: These truths hold good for everything that is, and not for some special genus apart from others. And all men use them, because they are true of being *qua* being. . . . For a principle which everyone must have who understands anything that is, is not a hypothesis. . . . Evidently then such a principle is the most certain of all; which principle this is, let us proceed to say. It is, that the same attribute cannot at the same time belong and not belong to the same subject and in the same respect.

[Aristotle, *Metaphysics*, IV, 3 (W. D. Ross, trans.).]

The Law of Identity (A is A) is a rational man's paramount consideration in the process of determining his interests. He knows that the contradictory is the impossible, that a contradiction cannot be achieved in reality and that the attempt to achieve it can lead only to disaster and destruction. Therefore, he does not permit himself to hold contradictory values, to pursue contradictory goals, or to imagine that the pursuit of a contradiction can ever be to his interest.

["The 'Conflicts' of Men's Interests," *VOS*, 58; pb 51.]

See also ARISTOTLE; AXIOMATIC CONCEPTS; AXIOMS; CAUSALITY; EXISTENCE; IDENTITY; INTEGRATION (MENTAL); LOGIC.

Cooperation.
Cooperation is the free association of men who work together by voluntary agreement, each deriving from it his own personal benefit.

["Screen Guide for Americans," *Plain Talk*, Nov. 1947, 40.]

A proper association is united by ideas, not by men, and its members are loyal to the ideas, not to the group. It is eminently reasonable that men should seek to associate with those who share their convictions and values. It is impossible to deal or even to communicate with men whose ideas are fundamentally opposed to one's own (and one should be free not to deal with them). All proper associations are formed or joined by individual choice and on conscious, intellectual grounds (philosophical, political, professional, etc.)—not by the physiological or geographical accident of birth, and not on the ground of tradition. When men are united by ideas, i.e., by explicit principles, there is no room for favors, whims, or arbitrary power: the principles serve as an *objective* criterion for determining actions and for *judging* men, whether leaders or members.

This requires a high degree of conceptual development and independence. . . . But this is the only way men can work together justly, benevolently and safely.

["The Missing Link," *PWNI*, 54; pb 45.]

The principle of individual rights is the only moral base of all groups or associations. Any group that does not recognize this principle is not an association, but a gang or a mob.

["Collectivized 'Rights,' " *VOS*, 137; pb 102.]

See also INDEPENDENCE; INDIVIDUAL RIGHTS; INDIVIDUALISM; TRIBALISM.

Copyrights. *See Patents and Copyrights.*

Corollaries. A corollary is a self-evident implication of already established knowledge.

[Leonard Peikoff, "The Philosophy of Objectivism"
lecture series (1976), Lecture 2.]

Many of the most important truths in philosophy are neither primary axioms nor theorems susceptible of discursive proof; rather, they are corollaries—most often, corollaries of axioms.

[Ibid.]

See also AXIOMS; LOGIC; PROOF; SELF-EVIDENT; VALIDATION.

Corporations. A corporation is a union of human beings in a voluntary, cooperative endeavor. It exemplifies the principle of free association, which is an expression of the right to freedom. Any attributes which corporations have are attributes (or rights) which the individuals have—including the right to combine in a certain way, offer products under certain terms, and deal with others according to certain rules, for instance, limited liability.

An individual can say to a storekeeper, "I would like to have credit, but I put you on notice that if I can't pay, you can't attach my home—take it or leave it." The storekeeper is free to accept those terms, or not. A corporation is a cooperative productive endeavor which gives a similar warning explicitly. It has no mystical attributes, no attributes that don't go back to the rights of individuals, including their right of free association.

[Leonard Peikoff, "The Philosophy of Objectivism"
lecture series (1976), question period, Lecture 9.]

See also BUSINESSMEN; CONTRACTS; COOPERATION; FREEDOM; INDIVIDUAL RIGHTS.

Courage and Confidence.   Courage and confidence are practical necessities . . . courage is the practical form of being true to existence, of being true to truth, and confidence is the practical form of being true to one's own consciousness.

[GS, *FNI*, 158; pb 129.]

See also INTEGRITY; MORALITY; RATIONALITY; TRUTH; VIRTUE.

Creation.   The power to rearrange the combinations of natural elements is the only creative power man possesses. It is an enormous and glorious power—and it is the only meaning of the concept "creative." "Creation" does not (and metaphysically cannot) mean the power to bring something into existence out of nothing. "Creation" means the power to bring into existence an arrangement (or combination or integration) of natural elements that had not existed before. (This is true of any human product, scientific or esthetic: man's imagination is nothing more than the ability to rearrange the things he has observed in reality.) The best and briefest identification of man's power in regard to nature is Francis Bacon's "Nature, to be commanded, must be obeyed." In this context, "to be commanded" means to be made to serve man's purposes; "to be obeyed" means that they cannot be served unless man discovers the properties of natural elements and uses them accordingly.

["The Metaphysical Versus the Man-Made," *PWNI*, 31; pb 25.]

See also ARTISTIC CREATION; EXISTENCE; IMAGINATION; MATTER; METAPHYSICAL vs. MAN-MADE.

Creators.   Throughout the centuries there were men who took first steps down new roads armed with nothing but their own vision. Their goals differed, but they all had this in common: that the step was first, the road new, the vision unborrowed, and the response they received— hatred. The great creators—the thinkers, the artists, the scientists, the inventors—stood alone against the men of their time. Every great new thought was opposed. Every great new invention was denounced. The first motor was considered foolish. The airplane was considered impossible. The power loom was considered vicious. Anesthesia was considered sinful. But the men of unborrowed vision went ahead. They fought, they suffered and they paid. But they won.

No creator was prompted by a desire to serve his brothers, for his brothers rejected the gift he offered and that gift destroyed the slothful routine of their lives. His truth was his only motive. His own truth, and his own work to achieve it in his own way. A symphony, a book, an engine, a philosophy, an airplane or a building—that was his goal and his life. Not those who heard, read, operated, believed, flew or inhabited the thing he had created. The creation, not its users. The creation, not the benefits others derived from it. The creation which gave form to his truth. He held his truth above all things and against all men.

His vision, his strength, his courage came from his own spirit. A man's spirit, however, is his self. That entity which is his consciousness. To think, to feel, to judge, to act are functions of the ego.

The creators were not selfless. It is the whole secret of their power—that it was self-sufficient, self-motivated, self-generated. A first cause, a fount of energy, a life force, a Prime Mover. The creator served nothing and no one. He lived for himself.

And only by living for himself was he able to achieve the things which are the glory of mankind. Such is the nature of achievement.

["The Soul of an Individualist," *FNI*, 90; pb 77.]

We inherit the products of the thought of other men. We inherit the wheel. We make a cart. The cart becomes an automobile. The automobile becomes an airplane. But all through the process what we receive from others is only the end product of their thinking. The moving force is the creative faculty which takes this product as material, uses it and originates the next step. This creative faculty cannot be given or received, shared or borrowed. It belongs to single, individual men. That which it creates is the property of the creator. Men learn from one another. But all learning is only the exchange of material. No man can give another the capacity to think. Yet that capacity is our only means of survival.

[Ibid., 92; pb 79.]

The basic need of the creator is independence. The reasoning mind cannot work under any form of compulsion. It cannot be curbed, sacrificed or surbordinated to any consideration whatsoever. It demands total independence in function and in motive. To a creator, all relations with men are secondary.

[Ibid.]

Men have been taught that the highest virtue is not to achieve, but to give. Yet one cannot give that which has not been created. Creation comes before distribution—or there will be nothing to distribute. The need of the creator comes before the need of any possible beneficiary. Yet we are taught to admire the second-hander who dispenses gifts he has not produced above the man who made the gifts possible. We praise an act of charity. We shrug at an act of achievement.

[Ibid., 93; pb 80.]

Men have been taught that it is a virtue to agree with others. But the creator is the man who disagrees. Men have been taught that it is a virtue to swim with the current. But the creator is the man who goes against the current. Men have been taught that it is a virtue to stand together. But the creator is the man who stands alone.

Men have been taught that the ego is the synonym of evil, and self-lessness the ideal of virtue. But the creator is the egoist in the absolute sense, and the selfless man is the one who does not think, feel, judge or act. These are functions of the self.

[Ibid., 94; pb 80.]

See also ALTRUISM; COOPERATION; INDEPENDENCE; INDIVID-UALISM; INTELLIGENCE; PRODUCTIVENESS; PYRAMID *of* ABIL-ITY; SECOND-HANDERS; SELFISHNESS.

Credit. In all its countless variations and applications, "credit" means money, i.e., *unconsumed goods,* loaned by one productive person (or group) to another, to be repaid out of future production. Even the credit extended for a consumption purpose, such as the purchase of an automobile, is based on the productive record and prospects of the borrower. Credit is not . . . a magic piece of paper that reverses cause and effect, and transforms consumption into a source of production.

["Egalitarianism and Inflation," *PWNI,* 160; pb 132.]

All credit transactions are *contractual agreements.* A credit transaction is any exchange which involves a passage of time between the payment and the receipt of goods or services. This includes the vast majority of economic transactions in a complex industrial society.

["Government Financing in a Free Society," *VOS,* 158; pb 117.]

See also CONSUMPTION; DEFICIT FINANCING; INTEREST *(on* LOANS); INVESTMENT; MONEY; PURCHASING POWER; SAVINGS.

Crime. A crime is a violation of the right(s) of other men by force (or fraud). It is only the initiation of physical force against others—i.e., the recourse to violence—that can be classified as a crime in a free society (as distinguished from a civil wrong). Ideas, in a free society, are not a crime—and neither can they serve as the justification of a crime.

[" 'Political' Crimes," *NL,* 99.]

There can be no such thing as a *political* crime under the American system of law. Since an individual has the right to hold and to propagate any ideas he chooses (obviously including political ideas), the government may not infringe his right; it may neither penalize nor reward him for his ideas; it may not take any judicial cognizance whatever of his ideology.

By the same principle, the government may not give special leniency to the perpetrator of a crime, on the grounds of the nature of his ideas.

[Ibid.]

All actions defined as criminal in a free society are actions involving force—and only such actions are answered by force.

Do not be misled by sloppy expressions such as "A murderer commits a crime against society." It is not society that a murderer murders, but an individual man. It is not a social right that he breaks, but an individual right. He is not punished for hurting a collective—he has not hurt a whole collective—he has hurt one man. If a criminal robs ten men— it is still not "society" that he has robbed, but ten individuals. There are no "crimes against society"—all crimes are committed against specific men, against individuals. And it is precisely the duty of a proper social system and of a proper government to protect an individual against criminal attack—against force.

["Textbook of Americanism," pamphlet, 7.]

See also FRAUD; INDIVIDUAL RIGHTS; PHYSICAL FORCE; RETRO-ACTIVE LAW; RIGHTS of the ACCUSED; SOCIETY.

"Crow Epistemology." *See Unit-Economy.*

Culture. Just as there is no such thing as a collective or racial mind, so there is no such thing as a collective or racial achievement. There are only individual minds and individual achievements—and a *culture* is not the anonymous product of undifferentiated masses, but the sum of the intellectual achievements of individual men.

["Racism," *VOS,* 174; pb 127.]

A nation's culture is the sum of the intellectual achievements of individual men, which their fellow-citizens have accepted in whole or in part, and which have influenced the nation's way of life. Since a culture is a complex battleground of different ideas and influences, to speak of a "culture" is to speak only of the *dominant* ideas, always allowing for the existence of dissenters and exceptions.

["Don't Let It Go," *PWNI,* 250; pb 205.]

The acceptance of the achievements of an individual by other individuals does not represent "ethnicity": it represents a cultural division of labor in a free market; it represents a conscious, individual choice on the part of all the men involved; the achievements may be scientific or technological or industrial or intellectual or esthetic—and the sum of such accepted achievements constitutes a free, civilized nation's *culture*. Tradition has nothing to do with it; tradition is being challenged and blasted daily in a free, civilized society: its citizens accept ideas and products because they are true and/or good—*not* because they are old *nor* because their ancestors accepted them. In such a society, concretes change, but what remains immutable—by individual conviction, not by tradition—are those philosophical principles which correspond to reality, i.e., which are true.

["Global Balkanization," pamphlet, 6.]

See also CIVILIZATION; COLLECTIVISM; "ETHNICITY"; INDIVID-UALISM; TRADITION.

Cynicism.   There is nothing so naive as cynicism. A cynic is one who believes that men are innately depraved, that irrationality and cowardice are their basic characteristics, that fear is the most potent of human incentives—and, therefore, that the most practical method of dealing with men is to count on their stupidity, appeal to their knavery, and keep them in constant terror.

In private life, this belief creates a criminal; in politics, it creates a statist. But, contrary to the cynic's belief, crime and statism do not pay.

A criminal might thrive on human vices, but is reduced to impotence when he comes up against the fact that "you can't cheat an honest man." A statist might ride to power by dispensing promises, threats and handouts to the seekers of the unearned—but he finds himself impotent in a national emergency, because the language, methods and policies which were successful with parasites, do not work when the country needs producers.

["From My 'Future File,' " *ARL*, III, 26, 3.]

When one discards ideals, the fact that a given policy (such as government controls) is evil, does not constitute a reason for rejecting it. On the contrary, such an estimate serves as an incentive to adopt and expand that policy: to a cynic's mind, that which is evil, is potent and practical.

["Ideas v. Goods," *ARL*, III, 11, 4.]

See also AMORALISM; APPEASEMENT; BENEVOLENT UNIVERSE PREMISE; HONOR; MALEVOLENT UNIVERSE PREMISE; MORAL COWARDICE; MORAL-PRACTICAL DICHOTOMY; MORALITY; VALUES; VIRTUE.

D

Dance. Among the performing arts, dancing requires a special discussion. Is there an abstract meaning in dancing? What does dancing express?

The dance is the silent partner of music and participates in a division of labor: music presents a stylized version of man's consciousness in action—the dance presents a stylized version of man's body in action. "Stylized" means condensed to essential characteristics, which are chosen according to an artist's view of man.

Music presents an abstraction of man's emotions in the context of his cognitive processes—the dance presents an abstraction of man's emotions in the context of his physical movements. The task of the dance is not the projection of single, momentary emotions, *not* a pantomime version of joy or sorrow or fear, etc., but a more profound issue: the projection of metaphysical value-judgments, the stylization of man's movements by the continuous power of a fundamental emotional state —and thus the use of man's body to express his sense of life.

Every strong emotion has a kinesthetic element, experienced as an impulse to leap or cringe or stamp one's foot, etc. Just as a man's sense of life is part of all his emotions, so it is part of all his movements and determines his manner of using his body: his posture, his gestures, his way of walking, etc. We can observe a different sense of life in a man who characteristically stands straight, walks fast, gestures decisively— and in a man who characteristically slumps, shuffles heavily, gestures limply. This particular element—the overall manner of moving—constitutes the material, the special province of the dance. The dance stylizes it into *a system of motion* expressing a metaphysical view of man.

A *system* of motion is the essential element, the pre-condition of the dance as an art. An indulgence in random movements, such as those of children romping in a meadow, may be a pleasant game, but it is not art. The creation of a consistently stylized, metaphysically expressive system is so rare an achievement that there are very few distinctive forms of dancing to qualify as art. Most dance performances are conglomerations of elements from different systems and of random contortions, arbitrarily thrown together, signifying nothing. A male or a female skipping, jumping or rolling over a stage is no more artistic than the children in the meadow, only more pretentious.

["Art and Cognition," *RM*, pb 66.]

Within each system, specific emotions may be projected or faintly suggested, but only as the basic style permits. Strong passions or negative emotions cannot be projected in ballet, regardless of its librettos; it cannot express tragedy or fear—or sexuality; it is a perfect medium for the expression of spiritual love. The Hindu dance can project passions, but not positive emotions; it cannot express joy or triumph, it is eloquent in expressing fear, doom—and a physicalistic kind of sexuality.

[Ibid., 68.]

Music is an independent, primary art; the dance is not. In view of their division of labor, the dance is entirely dependent on music. With the emotional assistance of music, it expresses an abstract meaning; without music, it becomes meaningless gymnastics. It is music, the voice of man's consciousness, that integrates the dance to man and to art. Music sets the terms; the task of the dance is to follow, as closely, obediently and expressively as possible. The tighter the integration of a given dance to its music—in rhythm, in mood, in style, in theme—the greater its esthetic value.

A clash between dance and music is worse than a clash between actor and play: it is an obliteration of the entire performance. It permits neither the music nor the dance to be integrated into an esthetic entity in the viewer's mind—and it becomes a series of jumbled motions superimposed on a series of jumbled sounds.

[Ibid., 69.]

See also ART; BALLET; CHOREOGRAPHER; MUSIC; PERFORMING ARTS; STYLIZATION.

Dark Ages.　The infamous times you call the Dark Ages were an era of intelligence on strike, when men of ability went underground and lived undiscovered, studying in secret, and died, destroying the works of their mind, when only a few of the bravest martyrs remained to keep the human race alive. Every period ruled by mystics was an era of stagnation and want, when most men were on strike against existence, working for less than their barest survival, leaving nothing but scraps for their rulers to loot, refusing to think, to venture, to produce, when the ultimate collector of their profits and the final authority on truth or error was the whim of some gilded degenerate sanctioned as superior to reason by divine right and by grace of a club.

[GS, FNI, 211; pb 169.]

In the history of Western civilization, the period known as the Dark Ages, after the fall of the Roman Empire, was a period when Western

Europe existed without any social organization beyond chance local groupings clustered around small villages, large castles, and remnants of various traditions—swept periodically by massive barbarian invasions, warring robber bands, and sundry local looters. It was as close to a state of pure anarchy as men could come.

["A Nation's Unity," *ARL*, II, 2, 2.]

See also HISTORY; MIDDLE AGES; MYSTICISM; PHILOSOPHY; REASON; RENAISSANCE.

Decorative Arts. The task of the decorative arts is to ornament utilitarian objects, such as rugs, textiles, lighting fixtures, etc. This is a valuable task, often performed by talented artists, but it is not an art in the esthetic-philosophical meaning of the term. The psycho-epistemological base of the decorative arts is not conceptual, but purely sensory: their standard of value is appeal to the senses of sight and/or touch. Their material is colors and shapes in nonrepresentational combinations conveying no meaning other than visual harmony; the meaning or purpose is concrete and lies in the specific object which they decorate.

As a re-creation of reality, a work of art has to be representational; its freedom of stylization is limited by the requirement of intelligibility; if it does not present an intelligible subject, it ceases to be art. On the other hand, a representational element is a detriment in the decorative arts: it is an irrelevant distraction, a clash of intentions. And although designs of little human figures or landscapes or flowers are often used to decorate textiles or wallpaper, they are artistically inferior to the nonrepresentational designs. When recognizable objects are subordinated to and treated as a mere pattern of colors and shapes, they become incongruous.

["Art and Cognition," *RM*, pb 74.]

See also: ART; BEAUTY; ESTHETICS; PSYCHO-EPISTEMOLOGY; VISUAL ARTS.

Deficit Financing. The government has no source of revenue, except the taxes paid by the producers. To free itself—for a while—from the limits set by reality, the government initiates a credit con game on a scale which the private manipulator could not dream of. It borrows money from you today, which is to be repaid with money it will borrow from you tomorrow, which is to be repaid with money it will borrow from you day after tomorrow, and so on. This is known as "deficit financing." It is made possible by the fact that the government cuts the connection between goods and money. It issues paper money, which is used as a claim check on actually existing goods—but that money is not backed by any goods, it is not backed by gold, it is backed by nothing. It is a promissory note issued to you in exchange for your goods, to be paid by you (in the form of taxes) out of your future production.

["Egalitarianism and Inflation," *PWNI*, 161; pb 133.]

See also CREDIT; GOLD STANDARD; GOVERNMENT; INFLATION; MONEY; TAXATION; WELFARE STATE.

Definitions.   A definition is a statement that identifies the nature of the units subsumed under a concept.

It is often said that definitions state the meaning of words. This is true, but it is not exact. A word is merely a visual-auditory symbol used to represent a concept; a word has no meaning other than that of the concept it symbolizes, and the meaning of a concept consists of its units. It is not words, but concepts that man defines—by specifying their referents.

The purpose of a definition is to distinguish a concept from all other concepts and thus to keep its units differentiated from all other existents.

Since the definition of a concept is formulated in terms of other concepts, it enables man, not only to identify and *retain* a concept, but also to establish the relationships, the hierarchy, the *integration* of all his concepts and thus the integration of his knowledge. Definitions preserve, not the chronological order in which a given man may have learned concepts, but the *logical* order of their hierarchical interdependence.

With certain significant exceptions, every concept can be defined and communicated in terms of other concepts. The exceptions are concepts referring to sensations, and metaphysical axioms.

[*ITOE*, 52.]

The rules of correct definition are derived from the process of concept-formation. The units of a concept were differentiated—by means of a distinguishing characteristic(s)—from other existents possessing a commensurable characteristic, a Conceptual Common Denominator. A definition follows the same principle: it specifies the distinguishing characteristic(s) of the units, and indicates the category of existents from which they were differentiated.

The distinguishing characteristic(s) of the units becomes the *differentia* of the concept's definition; the existents possessing a Conceptual Common Denominator become the *genus*.

Thus a definition complies with the two essential functions of consciousness: differentiation and integration. The differentia isolates the units of a concept from all other existents; the genus indicates their connection to a wider group of existents.

For instance, in the definition of table ("An item of furniture, consisting of a flat, level surface and supports, intended to support other, smaller objects"), the specified shape is the differentia, which distinguishes tables from the other entities belonging to the same genus: furniture. In the definition of man ("A rational animal"), "rational" is the differentia, "animal" is the genus.

[Ibid., 53.]

A definition must identify the *nature* of the units, i.e., the *essential* characteristics without which the units would not be the kind of existents they are.

[Ibid., 55.]

It is the principle of unit-economy that necessitates the definition of concepts in terms of *essential* characteristics. If, when in doubt, a man recalls a concept's definition, the essential characteristic(s) will give him an instantaneous grasp of the concept's meaning, i.e., of the nature of its referents. For example, if he is considering some social theory and recalls that "man is a rational animal," he will evaluate the validity of the theory accordingly; but if, instead, he recalls that "man is an animal possessing a thumb," his evaluation and conclusion will be quite different.

[Ibid., 86.]

Now observe . . . the process of determining an essential characteristic: the rule of *fundamentality*. When a given group of existents has more than one characteristic distinguishing it from other existents, man must observe the relationships among these various characteristics and discover the one on which all the others (or the greatest number of others) depend, i.e., the fundamental characteristic without which the others would not be possible. This fundamental characteristic is the *essential* distinguishing characteristic of the existents involved, and the proper *defining* characteristic of the concept.

Metaphysically, a fundamental characteristic is that distinctive characteristic which makes the greatest number of others possible; epistemologically, it is the one that explains the greatest number of others.

[Ibid., 59.]

All definitions are contextual, and a primitive definition *does not contradict* a more advanced one: the latter merely expands the former.

[Ibid., 56.]

Since man is not omniscient, a definition cannot be changelessly absolute, because it cannot establish the relationship of a given group of existents to everything else in the universe, including the undiscovered and unknown. And for the very same reasons, a definition is false and worthless if it is not *contextually* absolute—if it does not specify the known relationships among existents (in terms of the known *essential* characteristics) or if it contradicts the known (by omission or evasion).

[Ibid., 62.]

An objective definition, valid for all men, is one that designates the *essential* distinguishing characteristic(s) and genus of the existents subsumed under a given concept—according to all the relevant knowledge available at that stage of mankind's development.

[Ibid., 61.]

Truth is the product of the recognition (i.e., identification) of the facts of reality. Man identifies and integrates the facts of reality by means of concepts. He retains concepts in his mind by means of definitions. He organizes concepts into propositions—and the truth or falsehood of his propositions rests, not only on their relation to the facts he asserts, but also on the truth or falsehood of the definitions of the concepts he uses to assert them, which rests on the truth or falsehood of his designations of *essential* characteristics.

[Ibid., 63.]

The truth or falsehood of all of man's conclusions, inferences, thought and knowledge rests on the truth or falsehood of his definitions.

[Ibid., 65.]

Definitions are the guardians of rationality, the first line of defense against the chaos of mental disintegration.

["Art and Cognition," *RM*, pb 77.]

To know the exact meaning of the concepts one is using, one must know their correct definitions, one must be able to retrace the specific (logical, not chronological) steps by which they were formed, and one must be able to demonstrate their connection to their base in perceptual reality.

When in doubt about the meaning or the definition of a concept, the best method of clarification is to look for its referents—i.e., to ask oneself: What fact or facts of reality gave rise to this concept? What distinguishes it from all other concepts?

[*ITOE*, 67.]

Let us note, at this point, the radical difference between Aristotle's view of concepts and the Objectivist view, particularly in regard to the issue of essential characteristics.

It is Aristotle who first formulated the principles of correct definition. It is Aristotle who identified the fact that only concretes exist. But Aristotle held that definitions refer to metaphysical *essences*, which exist *in* concretes as a special element or formative power, and he held that the process of concept-formation depends on a kind of direct intuition by which man's mind grasps these essences and forms concepts accordingly.

Aristotle regarded "essence" as metaphysical; Objectivism regards it as *epistemological*.

Objectivism holds that the essence of a concept is that fundamental characteristic(s) of its units on which the greatest number of other characteristics depend, and which distinguishes these units from all other existents within the field of a man's knowledge. Thus the essence of a concept is determined *contextually* and may be altered with the growth of man's knowledge. The metaphysical referent of man's concepts is not a special, separate metaphysical essence, but the *total* of the facts of reality he has observed, and this total determines which characteristics of a given group of existents he designates as *essential*. An essential characteristic is factual, in the sense that it does exist, does determine other characteristics and does distinguish a group of existents from all others; it is *epistemological* in the sense that the classification of "essential characteristic" is a device of man's method of cognition—a means of classifying, condensing and integrating an ever-growing body of knowledge.

[Ibid., 68.]

It is important to remember that a definition implies *all* the characteristics of the units, since it identifies their *essential*, not their *exhaustive*, characteristics; since it designates *existents*, not their isolated aspects; and since it is a condensation of, not a substitute for, a wider knowledge of the existents involved.

[Ibid., 55.]

When "rational animal" is selected as the definition of "man," this does not mean that the concept "man" becomes a shorthand tag for "anything whatever that has rationality and animality." It does not mean that the concept "man" is interchangeable with the phrase "rational animal," and that all of man's other characteristics are excluded from the concept. It means: A certain type of entity, including all its characteristics, is, in the present context of knowledge, most fundamentally distinguished from all other entities by the fact that it is a rational animal. All the presently available knowledge of man's *other* characteristics is required to validate this definition, and is implied by it. All these other characteristics remain part of the content of the concept "man."

[Leonard Peikoff, "The Analytic-Synthetic Dichotomy," *ITOE*, 139.]

See also ANALYTIC-SYNTHETIC DICHOTOMY; ARISTOTLE; COMMUNICATION; CONCEPTS; CONCEPTUAL COMMON DENOMINATOR; CONTEXT; GENUS and SPECIES; HIERARCHY of KNOWLEDGE; LANGUAGE; OSTENSIVE DEFINITION; SENSATIONS; UNIT; UNIT-ECONOMY; WORDS.

Democracy. "Democratic" in its original meaning [refers to] unlimited majority rule . . . a social system in which one's work, one's property, one's mind, and one's life are at the mercy of any gang that may muster the vote of a majority at any moment for any purpose.

["How to Read (and Not to Write)," *ARL*, I, 26, 4.]

If we discard morality and substitute for it the Collectivist doctrine of unlimited majority rule, if we accept the idea that a majority may do anything it pleases, and that anything done by a majority is right *because* it's done by a majority (this being the only standard of right and wrong) —how are men to apply this in practice to their actual lives? Who is the majority? In relation to each particular man, all other men are potential members of that majority which may destroy him at its pleasure at any moment. Then each man and all men become enemies; each has to fear and suspect all; each must try to rob and murder first, before he is robbed and murdered.

["Textbook of Americanism," pamphlet, 9.]

The American system is *not* a democracy. It is a constitutional republic. A democracy, if you attach meaning to terms, is a system of unlimited majority rule; the classic example is ancient Athens. And the symbol of it is the fate of Socrates, who was put to death legally, because the majority didn't like what he was saying, although he had initiated no force and had violated no one's rights.

Democracy, in short, is a form of collectivism, which denies individual rights: the majority can do whatever it wants with no restrictions. In principle, the democratic government is all-powerful. Democracy is a totalitarian manifestation; it is not a form of freedom. . . .

The American system is a constitutionally limited republic, restricted to the protection of individual rights. In such a system, majority rule is

applicable only to lesser details, such as the selection of certain personnel. But the majority has no say over the *basic* principles governing the
government. It has no power to ask for or gain the infringement of
individual rights.

> [Leonard Peikoff, "The Philosophy of Objectivism"
> lecture series (1976), Lecture 9.]

*See also COLLECTIVISM; DICTATORSHIP; FREEDOM; GOVERN-
MENT; INDIVIDUAL RIGHTS; MINORITY RIGHTS; REPRE-
SENTATIVE GOVERNMENT; REPUBLIC; SOCIALISM; STATISM;
TYRANNY; VOTING.*

Deontological Theory of Ethics. *See "Duty."*

Determinism.   Determinism is the theory that everything that happens in the universe—including every thought, feeling, and action of
man—is necessitated by previous factors, so that nothing could ever
have happened differently from the way it did, and everything in the
future is already pre-set and inevitable. Every aspect of man's life and
character, on this view, is merely a product of factors that are ultimately
outside his control. Objectivism rejects this theory.

> [Leonard Peikoff, "The Philosophy of Objectivism"
> lecture series, Lecture 1.]

Dictatorship and determinism are reciprocally reinforcing corollaries:
if one seeks to enslave men, one has to destroy their reliance on the
validity of their own judgments and choices—if one believes that reason
and volition are impotent, one has to accept the rule of force.

> ["Representation Without Authorization," *ARL*, I, 21, 1.]

*See also AXIOMS; CAUSALITY; DICTATORSHIP; EMOTIONS; FREE
WILL; METAPHYSICAL vs. MAN-MADE; NATURALISM; NECESSITY.*

Dictator.   A mystic is driven by the urge to impress, to cheat, to
flatter, to deceive, *to force* that omnipotent consciousness of others.
"They" are his only key to reality, he feels that he cannot exist save by
harnessing their mysterious power and extorting their unaccountable
consent. *"They"* are his only means of perception and, like a blind man
who depends on the sight of a dog, he feels he must leash them in order
to live. To control the consciousness of others becomes his only passion;
power-lust is a weed that grows only in the vacant lots of an abandoned
mind.

Every dictator is a mystic, and every mystic is a potential dictator. A mystic craves obedience from men, not their agreement. He wants them to surrender their consciousness to his assertions, his edicts, his wishes, his whims—as *his* consciousness is surrendered to theirs. He wants to deal with men by means of faith and force—he finds no satisfaction in their consent if he must earn it by means of facts and reason. Reason is the enemy he dreads and, simultaneously, considers precarious; reason, to him, is a means of deception; he *feels* that men possess some power more potent than reason—and only their causeless belief or their forced obedience can give him a sense of security, a proof that he has gained control of the mystic endowment he lacked. His lust is to command, not to convince: conviction requires an act of independence and rests on the absolute of an objective reality. What he seeks is power over reality and over men's means of perceiving it, their mind, the power to interpose his will between existence and consciousness, as if, by agreeing to fake the reality he orders them to fake, men would, in fact, create it.

[GS, *FNI*, 201; pb 161.]

Destruction is the only end that the mystics' creed has ever achieved, as it is the only end that you see them achieving today, and if the ravages wrought by their acts have not made them question their doctrines, if they profess to be moved by love, yet are not deterred by piles of human corpses, it is because the truth about their souls is worse than the obscene excuse you have allowed them, the excuse that the end justifies the means and that the horrors they practice are means to nobler ends. The truth is that those horrors are their ends.

You who're depraved enough to believe that you could adjust yourself to a mystic's dictatorship and could please him by obeying his orders—there is no way to please him; when you obey, he will reverse his orders; he seeks obedience for the sake of obedience and destruction for the sake of destruction. You who are craven enough to believe that you can make terms with a mystic by giving in to his extortions—there is no way to buy him off, the bribe he wants is your life, as slowly or as fast as you are willing to give it in—and the monster he seeks to bribe is the hidden blank-out in his mind, which drives him to kill in order not to learn that the death he desires is his own.

[Ibid., 203; pb 162.]

Perhaps the most craven attitude of all is the one expressed by the injunction "don't be certain." As stated explicitly by many intellectuals, it is the suggestion that if nobody is certain of anything, if nobody holds any firm convictions, if everybody is willing to give in to everybody else, no dictator will rise among us and we will escape the destruction sweeping the rest of the world. This is the secret voice of the Witch Doctor confessing that he sees a dictator, an Attila, as a man of confident strength and uncompromising conviction. Nothing but a psycho-epistemological panic can blind such intellectuals to the fact that a dictator, like any thug, runs from the first sign of confident resistance; that he can rise *only* in a society of precisely such uncertain, compliant, shaking compromisers as they advocate, a society that invites a thug to take over; and that the task of resisting an Attila can be accomplished only by men of intransigent conviction and moral certainty.

["For the New Intellectual," *FNI*, 51; pb 45.]

See also COMPROMISE; DICTATORSHIP; MYSTICISM; PHYSICAL FORCE; SECOND-HANDERS; STATISM; TYRANNY.

Dictatorship. A dictatorship is a country that does not recognize individual rights, whose government holds total, unlimited power over men.

["*Playboy's* Interview with Ayn Rand," pamphlet, 15.]

There are four characteristics which brand a country unmistakably as a dictatorship: one-party rule—executions without trial or with a mock trial, for political offenses—the nationalization or expropriation of private property—and censorship. A country guilty of these outrages forfeits any moral prerogatives, any claim to national rights or sovereignty, and becomes an outlaw.

["Collectivized 'Rights,' " *VOS*, 141; pb 105.]

Volumes can be and have been written about the issue of freedom versus dictatorship, but, in essence, it comes down to a single question: do you consider it moral to treat men as sacrificial animals and to rule them by physical force?

["Foreword," *WTL*, viii.]

The right of a nation to determine its own form of government does not include the right to establish a slave society (that is, to legalize the enslavement of some men by others). *There is no such thing as "the right to enslave."* A nation *can* do it, just as a man *can* become a criminal—but neither can do it *by right*.

It does not matter, in this context, whether a nation was enslaved by force, like Soviet Russia, or by vote, like Nazi Germany. Individual rights are not subject to a public vote; a majority has no right to vote away the rights of a minority; the political function of rights is precisely to protect minorities from oppression by majorities (and the smallest minority on earth is the individual). Whether a slave society was conquered or *chose* to be enslaved, it can claim no national rights and no recognition of such "rights" by civilized countries. . . .

Dictatorship nations are outlaws. Any free nation had the *right* to invade Nazi Germany and, today, has the *right* to invade Soviet Russia, Cuba or any other slave pen. Whether a free nation chooses to do so or not is a matter of its own self-interest, *not* of respect for the non-existent "rights" of gang rulers. It is not a free nation's *duty* to liberate other nations at the price of self-sacrifice, but a free nation has the right to do it, when and if it so chooses.

This right, however, is conditional. Just as the suppression of crimes does not give a policeman the right to engage in criminal activities, so the invasion and destruction of a dictatorship does not give the invader the right to establish another variant of a slave society in the conquered country.

["Collectivized 'Rights,' " *VOS*, 139; pb 104.]

Dictatorship and determinism are reciprocally reinforcing corollaries: if one seeks to enslave men, one has to destroy their reliance on the validity of their own judgments and choices—if one believes that reason and volition are impotent, one has to accept the rule of force.

["Representation Without Authorization," *ARL*, I, 21, 1.]

It is a grave error to suppose that a dictatorship rules a nation by means of strict, rigid laws which are obeyed and enforced with rigorous, military precision. Such a rule would be evil, but almost bearable; men could endure the harshest edicts, provided these edicts were known, specific and stable; it is not the known that breaks men's spirits, but the unpredictable. A dictatorship has to be capricious; it has to rule by means of the unexpected, the incomprehensible, the wantonly irrational; it has to deal not in death, but in *sudden* death; a state of chronic uncertainty is what men are psychologically unable to bear.

["Antitrust: The Rule of Unreason," *TON*, Feb. 1962, 5.]

The legal hallmark of a dictatorship [is] *preventive law*—the concept that a man is guilty until he is proved innocent by the permissive rubber stamp of a commissar or a Gauleiter.

["Who Will Protect Us from Our Protectors?" *TON*, May 1962, 20.]

A dictatorship has to promulgate some sort of distant goals and moral ideals in order to justify its rule and the people's immolation; the extent to which it succeeds in convincing its victims, is the extent of its own danger; sooner or later, its contradictions are thrown in its face by the best of its subjects: the ablest, the most intelligent, the *most honest*. Thus a dictatorship is forced to destroy and to keep on destroying the best of its "human resources." And be it fifty years or five centuries later, ambitious thugs and lethargic drones are all a dictatorship will have left to exploit and rule; the rest will die young, physically or spiritually.

["The 'Inexplicable Personal Alchemy,'" *NL*, 119.]

Every movement that seeks to enslave a country, every dictatorship or potential dictatorship, needs some minority group as a scapegoat which it can blame for the nation's troubles and use as a justification of its own demands for dictatorial powers. In Soviet Russia, the scapegoat was the bourgeoisie; in Nazi Germany, it was the Jewish people; in America, it is the businessmen.

["America's Persecuted Minority: Big Business," *CUI*, 45.]

It makes no difference whether government controls allegedly favor the interests of labor or business, of the poor or the rich, of a special class or a special race: the results are the same. The notion that a dictatorship can benefit any one social group at the expense of others is a worn remnant of the Marxist mythology of class warfare, refuted by half a century of factual evidence. All men are victims and losers under a dictatorship; nobody wins—except the ruling clique.

["The Fascist New Frontier," pamphlet, 13.]

See also COLLECTIVISM; COMMUNISM; DETERMINISM; DICTATOR; FASCISM/NAZISM; FASCISM and COMMUNISM/SOCIALISM; FOREIGN POLICY; FREEDOM; GOVERNMENT; INDIVIDUAL RIGHTS; SOVIET RUSSIA; SELF-DETERMINATION of NATIONS; STATISM; TYRANNY.

Director.   In all the arts that involve more than one performer, a crucially important artist is the *director*. (In music, his counterpart is the conductor.) The director is the link between the performing and the primary arts. He is a performer in relation to the primary work, in the sense that his task is the means to the end set by the work—he is a primary artist in relation to the cast, the set designer, the cameraman, etc., in the sense that they are the means to his end, which is the translation of the work into physical action as a meaningful, stylized, integrated whole. In the dramatic arts, the director is the esthetic *integrator*.

This task requires a first-hand understanding of all the arts, combined with an unusual power of abstract thought and of creative imagination. Great directors are extremely rare. An average director alternates between the twin pitfalls of abdication and usurpation. Either he rides on the talents of others and merely puts the actors through random motions signifying nothing, which results in a hodgepodge of clashing intentions—or he hogs the show, putting everyone through senseless tricks unrelated to or obliterating the play (if any), on the inverted premise that the play is the means to the end of exhibiting *his* skill, thus placing himself in the category of circus acrobats, except that he is much less skillful and much less entertaining.

["Art and Cognition," *RM*, pb 71.]

See also ART; CHOREOGRAPHER; INTEGRATION (MENTAL); MO-TION PICTURES; PERFORMING ARTS.

Distinguishing Characteristic. *See Concept-Formation.*

Dogma. A dogma is a set of beliefs accepted on faith; that is, without rational justification or against rational evidence. A dogma is a matter of blind faith.

["*Playboy's* Interview with Ayn Rand," pamphlet, 9.]

PLAYBOY: If widely accepted, couldn't Objectivism harden into a dogma?
RAND: No. I have found that Objectivism is its own protection against people who might attempt to use it as a dogma. Since Objectivism requires the use of one's mind, those who attempt to take broad principles and apply them unthinkingly and indiscriminately to the concretes of their own existence find that it cannot be done. They are then compelled either to reject Objectivism or to apply it. When I say apply, I mean that they have to use their own mind, their own thinking, in order to know how to apply Objectivist principles to the specific problems of their own lives.

[Ibid.]

See also FAITH; LOGIC; MYSTICISM; OBJECTIVISM; PROOF; REA-SON; RELIGION.

Draft. Of all the statist violations of individual rights in a mixed economy, the military draft is the worst. It is an abrogation of rights. It negates man's fundamental right—the right to life—and establishes the fundamental principle of statism: that a man's life belongs to the state, and the state may claim it by compelling him to sacrifice it in battle. Once that principle is accepted, the rest is only a matter of time.

If the state may force a man to risk death or hideous maiming and crippling, in a war declared at the state's discretion, for a cause he may neither approve of nor even understand, if his consent is not required to send him into unspeakable martyrdom—then, in principle, *all* rights are negated in that state, and its government is not man's protector any longer. What else is there left to protect?

The most immoral contradiction—in the chaos of today's anti-ideological groups—is that of the so-called "conservatives," who posture as defenders of individual rights, particularly *property* rights, but uphold and advocate the draft. By what infernal evasion can they hope to justify the proposition that creatures who have no right to life, have the right to a bank account? A slightly higher—though not much higher—rung of hell should be reserved for those "liberals" who claim that man has the "right" to economic security, public housing, medical care, education, recreation, but no right to life, or: that man has the right to *livelihood*, but not to *life*.

One of the notions used by all sides to justify the draft, is that "rights impose obligations." Obligations, to whom?—and imposed, by whom? Ideologically, that notion is worse than the evil it attempts to justify: it implies that rights are a gift from the state, and that a man has to buy them by offering something (his life) in return. Logically, that notion is a contradiction: since the only proper function of a government is to protect man's rights, it cannot claim title to his life in exchange for that protection.

The only "obligation" involved in individual rights is an obligation imposed, not by the state, but by the nature of reality (i.e., by the law of identity): *consistency*, which, in this case, means the obligation to respect the rights of others, if one wishes one's own rights to be recognized and protected.

Politically, the draft is clearly unconstitutional. No amount of rationalization, neither by the Supreme Court nor by private individuals, can alter the fact that it represents "involuntary servitude."

A *volunteer* army is the only proper, moral—and practical—way to defend a free country. Should a man volunteer to fight, if his country is attacked? Yes—if he values his own rights and freedom. A free (or even semi-free) country has never lacked volunteers in the face of foreign aggression. Many military authorities have testified that a volunteer army—an army of men who know what they are fighting for and why —is the best, most effective army, and that a drafted one is the least effective.

It is often asked: "But what if a country cannot find a sufficient number of volunteers?" Even so, this would not give the rest of the population a right to the lives of the country's young men. But, in fact, the lack of volunteers occurs for one of two reasons: (1) If a country is demoralized by a corrupt, authoritarian government, its citizens will not volunteer to defend it. But neither will they fight for long, if drafted. For example, observe the literal disintegration of the Czarist Russian army in World War I. (2) If a country's government undertakes to fight a war for some reason other than self-defense, for a purpose which the citizens neither share nor understand, it will not find many volunteers. Thus a volunteer army is one of the best protectors of peace, not only against foreign aggression, but also against any warlike ideologies or projects on the part of a country's own government.

Not many men would volunteer for such wars as Korea or Vietnam. Without the power to draft, the makers of our foreign policy would not be able to embark on adventures of that kind. This is one of the best practical reasons for the abolition of the draft.

["The Wreckage of the Consensus," *CUI*, 226.]

The years from about fifteen to twenty-five are the crucial formative years of a man's life. This is the time when he confirms his impressions of the world, of other men, of the society in which he is to live, when he acquires conscious convictions, defines his moral values, chooses his goals, and plans his future, developing or renouncing ambition. These are the years that mark him for life. And it is *these* years that an allegedly humanitarian society forces him to spend in terror—the terror of knowing that he can plan nothing and count on nothing, that any road he takes can be blocked at any moment by an unpredictable power, that, barring his vision of the future, there stands the gray shape of the barracks, and, perhaps, beyond it, death for some unknown reason in some alien jungle.

[Ibid., 229.]

Once in a while, I receive letters from young men asking me for personal advice on problems connected with the draft. Morally, no one can give advice in any issue where choices and decisions are not voluntary: "Morality ends where a gun begins." As to the practical alternatives available, the best thing to do is to consult a good lawyer.

There is, however, one moral aspect of the issue that needs clarification. Some young men seem to labor under the misapprehension that since the draft is a violation of their rights, compliance with the draft law would constitute a moral sanction of that violation. This is a serious error. A forced compliance is not a sanction. All of us are forced to comply with many laws that violate our rights, but so long as we advocate the repeal of such laws, our compliance does not constitute a sanction. Unjust laws have to be fought ideologically; they cannot be fought or corrected by means of mere disobedience and futile martyrdom. To quote from an editorial on this subject in the April 1967 issue of *Persuasion:* "One does not stop the juggernaut by throwing oneself in front of it. . . ."

[Ibid., 235.]

See also COLLECTIVISM; "DUTY"; FREEDOM; INDIVIDUAL RIGHTS; LIFE, RIGHT to; RESPONSIBILITY/OBLIGATION; WAR.

"Duty." One of the most destructive anti-concepts in the history of moral philosophy is the term "duty."

An anti-concept is an artificial, unnecessary and rationally unusable term designed to replace and obliterate some legitimate concept. The term "duty" obliterates more than single concepts; it is a metaphysical and psychological killer: it negates all the essentials of a rational view of life and makes them inapplicable to man's actions. . . .

The meaning of the term "duty" is: the moral necessity to perform certain actions for no reason other than obedience to some higher authority, without regard to any personal goal, motive, desire or interest.

It is obvious that that anti-concept is a product of mysticism, not an abstraction derived from reality. In a mystic theory of ethics, "duty" stands for the notion that man *must* obey the dictates of a supernatural authority. Even though the anti-concept has been secularized, and the authority of God's will has been ascribed to earthly entities, such as parents, country, State, mankind, etc., their alleged supremacy still rests on nothing but a mystic edict. Who in hell can have the right to claim that sort of submission or obedience? This is the only proper form— and locality—for the question, because nothing and no one can have such a right or claim here on earth.

The arch-advocate of "duty" is Immanuel Kant; he went so much farther than other theorists that they seem innocently benevolent by comparison. "Duty," he holds, is the only standard of virtue; but virtue is not its own reward: if a reward is involved, it is no longer virtue. The only moral motivation, he holds, is devotion to duty for duty's sake; only an action motivated exclusively by such devotion is a moral action. . . .

If one were to accept it, the anti-concept "duty" destroys the concept of reality: an unaccountable, supernatural power takes precedence over facts and dictates one's actions regardless of context or consequences.

"Duty" destroys reason: it supersedes one's knowledge and judgment, making the process of thinking and judging irrelevant to one's actions.

"Duty" destroys values: it demands that one betray or sacrifice one's highest values for the sake of an inexplicable command—and it transforms values into a threat to one's moral worth, since the experience of pleasure or desire casts doubt on the moral purity of one's motives.

"Duty" destroys love: who could want to be loved not from "inclination," but from "duty"?

"Duty" destroys self-esteem: it leaves no self to be esteemed.

If one accepts that nightmare in the name of morality, the infernal irony is that "duty" destroys morality. A deontological (duty-centered) theory of ethics confines moral principles to a list of prescribed "duties" and leaves the rest of man's life without any moral guidance, cutting morality off from any application to the actual problems and concerns of man's existence. Such matters as work, career, ambition, love, friendship, pleasure, happiness, values (insofar as they are not pursued as duties) are regarded by these theories as *amoral*, i.e., outside the province of morality. If so, then by what standard is a man to make his daily choices, or direct the course of his life?

In a deontological theory, all personal desires are banished from the realm of morality; a personal desire has no moral significance, be it a desire to create or a desire to kill. For example, if a man is not supporting his life from duty, such a morality makes no distinction between supporting it by honest labor or by robbery. If a man *wants* to be honest, he deserves no moral credit; as Kant would put it, such honesty is "praiseworthy," but without "moral import." Only a vicious represser, who feels a profound desire to lie, cheat and steal, but forces himself to act honestly for the sake of "duty," would receive a recognition of moral worth from Kant and his ilk.

This is the sort of theory that gives morality a bad name.

[*"Causality Versus Duty," PWNI*, 114; pb 95.]

In reality and in the Objectivist ethics, there is no such thing as "duty." There is only choice and the full, clear recognition of a principle obscured by the notion of "duty": *the law of causality.* . . .

In order to make the choices required to achieve his goals, a man needs the constant, automatized awareness of the principle which the anti-concept "duty" has all but obliterated in his mind: the principle of causality—specifically, of Aristotelian *final causation* (which, in fact, applies only to a conscious being), i.e., the process by which an end determines the means, i.e., the process of choosing a goal and taking the actions necessary to achieve it.

In a rational ethics, it is causality—not "duty"—that serves as the guiding principle in considering, evaluating and choosing one's actions, particularly those necessary to achieve a long-range goal. Following this principle, a man does not act without knowing the purpose of his action. In choosing a goal, he considers the means required to achieve it, he weighs the value of the goal against the difficulties of the means and against the full, hierarchical context of all his other values and goals. He does not demand the impossible of himself, and he does not decide too easily which things are impossible. He never drops the context of the knowledge available to him, and never evades reality, realizing fully that his goal will not be granted to him by any power other than his own action, and, should he evade, it is not some Kantian authority that he would be cheating, but himself.

[Ibid., 118; pb 98.]

A Kantian or even a semi-Kantian cannot permit himself to value anything profoundly, since an inexplicable "duty" may demand the sacrifice of his values at any moment, wiping out any long-range plan or struggle he might have undertaken to achieve them. . . .

The notion of "duty" is intrinsically anti-causal. In its origin, a "duty" defies the principle of efficient causation—since it is causeless (or supernatural); in its effects, it defies the principle of final causation—since it must be performed regardless of consequences.

[Ibid., 120; pb 100.]

The acceptance of full responsibility for one's own choices and actions (and their consequences) is such a demanding moral discipline that many men seek to escape it by surrendering to what they believe is the easy, automatic, unthinking safety of a morality of "duty." They learn better, often when it is too late.

The disciple of causation faces life without inexplicable chains, unchosen burdens, impossible demands or supernatural threats. His metaphysical attitude and guiding moral principle can best be summed up by an old Spanish proverb: "God said: 'Take what you want and pay for it.' " But to know one's own desires, their meaning and their costs requires the highest human virtue: rationality.

[Ibid., 121; pb 101.]

See also ALTRUISM; "ANTI-CONCEPTS"; FREE WILL; KANT, IMMANUEL; MORALITY; MYSTICAL ETHICS; RATIONALITY; RELIGION; RESPONSIBILITY/OBLIGATION; SACRIFICE; SELF-ESTEEM; SELF-INTEREST; SELFISHNESS; SELFLESSNESS.

E

Ecology/Environmental Movement.   Ecology as a social principle . . . condemns cities, culture, industry, technology, the intellect,
and advocates men's return to "nature," to the state of grunting suban-
imals digging the soil with their bare hands.

["The Lessons of Vietnam," *ARL*, III, 25, 1.]

An Asian peasant who labors through all of his waking hours, with
tools created in Biblical times—a South American aborigine who is de-
voured by piranha in a jungle stream—an African who is bitten by the
tsetse fly—an Arab whose teeth are green with decay in his mouth—
these do live with their "natural environment," but are scarcely able to
appreciate its beauty. Try to tell a Chinese mother, whose child is dying
of cholera: "Should one do everything one can? Of course not." Try to
tell a Russian housewife, who trudges miles on foot in sub-zero weather
in order to spend hours standing in line at a state store dispensing food
rations, that America is defiled by shopping centers, expressways and
family cars.   ["The Left: Old and New," *NL*, 88.]

In Western Europe, in the preindustrial Middle Ages, man's life expectancy was 30 years. In the nineteenth century, Europe's population
grew by 300 percent—which is the best proof of the fact that for the
first time in human history, industry gave the great masses of people a
chance to survive.
If it were true that a heavy concentration of industry is destructive to
human life, one would find life expectancy declining in the more advanced countries. But it has been rising steadily. Here are the figures
on life expectancy in the United States (from the Metropolitan Life
Insurance Company):
         1900—47.3 years
         1920—53 years
         1940—60 years
         1968—70.2 years (the latest figures compiled)
Anyone over 30 years of age today, give a silent "Thank you" to the
nearest, grimiest, sootiest smokestacks you can find.

["The Anti-Industrial Revolution," *NL*, 137.]

The dinosaur and its fellow-creatures vanished from this earth long
before there were any industrialists or any men. . . . But this did not

end life on earth. Contrary to the ecologists, nature does not stand still and does not maintain the kind of "equilibrium" that guarantees the survival of any particular species—least of all the survival of her greatest and most fragile product: man.

[Ibid., 134.]

Now observe that in all the propaganda of the ecologists—amidst all their appeals to nature and pleas for "harmony with nature"—there is no discussion of *man's* needs and the requirements of *his* survival. Man is treated as if he were an *unnatural* phenomenon. Man cannot survive in the kind of state of nature that the ecologists envision—i.e., on the level of sea urchins or polar bears. . . .

In order to survive, man has to discover and produce everything he needs, which means that he has to *alter* his background and adapt it to his needs. Nature has not equipped him for adapting himself to his background in the manner of animals. From the most primitive cultures to the most advanced civilizations, man has had to *manufacture* things; his well-being depends on his success at production. The lowest human tribe cannot survive without that alleged source of pollution: fire. It is not merely symbolic that fire was the property of the gods which Prometheus brought to man. The ecologists are the new vultures swarming to extinguish that fire.

[Ibid., 136.]

Without machines and technology, the task of mere survival is a terrible, mind-and-body-wrecking ordeal. In "nature," the struggle for food, clothing and shelter consumes all of a man's energy and spirit; it is a losing struggle—the winner is any flood, earthquake or swarm of locusts. (Consider the 500,000 bodies left in the wake of a single flood in Pakistan; they had been men who lived without technology.) To work only for bare necessities is a *luxury* that mankind cannot afford.

[Ibid., 149.]

It has been reported in the press many times that the issue of pollution is to be the next big crusade of the New Left activists, after the war in Vietnam peters out. And just as peace was not their goal or motive in that crusade, so clean air is not their goal or motive in this one.

["The Left: Old and New," *NL*, 89.]

The immediate goal is obvious: the destruction of the remnants of capitalism in today's mixed economy, and the establishment of a global dictatorship. This goal does not have to be inferred—many speeches and books on the subject state explicitly that the ecological crusade is a means to that end.

["The Anti-Industrial Revolution," *NL*, 140.]

If, after the failure of such accusations as "Capitalism leads you to the poorhouse" and "Capitalism leads you to war," the New Left is left with nothing better than: "Capitalism defiles the beauty of your countryside," one may justifiably conclude that, as an intellectual power, the collectivist movement is through.

["The Left: Old and New," *NL*, 93.]

City smog and filthy rivers are not good for men (though they are not the kind of danger that the ecological panic-mongers proclaim them to be). This is a scientific, *technological* problem—not a political one—and it can be solved *only* by technology. Even if smog were a risk to human life, we must remember that life in nature, without technology, is wholesale death.

["The Anti-Industrial Revolution," *NL*, 142.]

See also CAPITALISM; MAN; NEW LEFT; POLLUTION; PRODUCTION; SCIENCE; TECHNOLOGY.

Economic Good.   In order for a thing to become a *good*, three conditions must be fulfilled. Not only must it satisfy a human need, but also one must *know* that it satisfies one's need, and one must have *disposal* over it.

[George Reisman, "The Revolt Against Affluence: Galbraith's Neo-Feudalism," pamphlet, 6.]

See also MARKET VALUE; PROPERTY RIGHTS.

Economic Growth.   "Economic growth" means the rise of an economy's productivity, due to the discovery of new products, new techniques, which means: due to the achievements of men's productive ability.

["Promises to Parasites Fail to Bring Results," *Los Angeles Times*, June 24, 1962.]

Nothing can raise a country's productivity except technology, and technology is the final product of a complex of sciences (including philosophy), each of them kept alive and moving by the achievements of a few independent minds.

["The Moratorium on Brains," *ARL*, I, 3, 5.]

See also CAPITALISM; ECOLOGY/ENVIRONMENTAL MOVEMENT; NEW LEFT; PRODUCTION; TECHNOLOGY.

Economic Power vs. Political Power.

A disastrous intellectual package-deal, put over on us by the theoreticians of statism, is the equation of *economic* power with *political* power. You have heard it expressed in such bromides as: "A hungry man is not free," or "It makes no difference to a worker whether he takes orders from a businessman or from a bureaucrat." Most people accept these equivocations—and yet they know that the poorest laborer in America is freer and more secure than the richest commissar in Soviet Russia. What is the basic, the essential, the crucial principle that differentiates freedom from slavery? It is the principle of voluntary action *versus* physical coercion or compulsion.

The difference between political power and any other kind of social "power," between a government and any private organization, is the fact that *a government holds a legal monopoly on the use of physical force.*

["America's Persecuted Minority: Big Business," *CUI*, 46.]

What is economic power? It is the power to produce and to trade what one has produced. In a free economy, where no man or group of men can use physical coercion against anyone, economic power can be achieved only by *voluntary* means: by the voluntary choice and agreement of all those who participate in the process of production and trade. In a free market, all prices, wages, and profits are determined—not by the arbitrary whim of the rich or of the poor, not by anyone's "greed" or by anyone's need—but by the law of supply and demand. The mechanism of a free market reflects and sums up all the economic choices and decisions made by all the participants. Men trade their goods or services by mutual consent to mutual advantage, according to their own independent, uncoerced judgment. A man can grow rich only if he is able to offer better *values*—better products or services, at a lower price —than others are able to offer.

Wealth, in a free market, is achieved by a free, general, "democratic" vote—by the sales and the purchases of every individual who takes part in the economic life of the country. Whenever you buy one product rather than another, you are voting for the success of some manufacturer. And, in this type of voting, every man votes only on those matters which he is qualified to judge: on his own preferences, interests, and needs. No one has the power to decide for others or to substitute *his* judgment for theirs; no one has the power to appoint himself "the voice of the public" and to leave the public voiceless and disfranchised.

Now let me define the difference between economic power and political power: economic power is exercised by means of a *positive*, by offering men a reward, an incentive, a payment, a value; political power is exercised by means of a *negative*, by the threat of punishment, injury, imprisonment, destruction. The businessman's tool is *values;* the bureaucrat's tool is fear.

[Ibid., 47.]

Evading the difference between production and looting, they called the businessman a robber. Evading the difference between freedom and compulsion, they called him a slave driver. Evading the difference between reward and terror, they called him an exploiter. Evading the difference between pay checks and guns, they called him an autocrat. Evading the difference between trade and force, they called him a tyrant. The most crucial issue they had to evade was the difference between the *earned* and the *unearned.*

["For the New Intellectual," *FNI*, 44; pb 40.]

You had said that you saw no difference between economic and political power, between the power of money and the power of guns—no difference between reward and punishment, no difference between purchase and plunder, no difference between pleasure and fear, no difference between life and death. You are learning the difference now.

[GS, *FNI*, 236; pb 187.]

See also BUSINESSMEN vs. BUREAUCRATS; CAPITALISM; FREE MARKET; FREEDOM; GOVERNMENT; INDIVIDUAL RIGHTS; MONEY; MOTIVATION by LOVE vs. by FEAR; "PACKAGE-DEALING," FALLACY of; PHYSICAL FORCE; STATISM.

Education.   The only purpose of education is to teach a student how to live his life—by developing his mind and equipping him to deal with reality. The training he needs is theoretical, i.e., *conceptual.* He has to be taught to think, to understand, to integrate, to prove. He has to be taught the essentials of the knowledge discovered in the past—and he has to be equipped to acquire further knowledge by his own effort.

["The Comprachicos," *NL*, 231.]

The academia-jet set coalition is attempting to tame the American character by the deliberate breeding of helplessness and resignation—in those incubators of lethargy known as "Progressive" schools, which are dedicated to the task of crippling a child's mind by arresting his cognitive development. (See "The Comprachicos" in my book *The New Left: The Anti-Industrial Revolution.*) It appears, however, that the "progressive" rich will be the first victims of their own social theories: it is the children of the well-to-do who emerge from expensive nursery schools and colleges as hippies, and destroy the remnants of their paralyzed brains by means of drugs.

The middle class has created an antidote which is perhaps the most helpful movement of recent years: the spontaneous, unorganized, grass-roots revival of the Montessori system of education—a system aimed at the development of a child's cognitive, i.e., rational, faculty.

["Don't Let It Go," *PWNI*, 261; pb 214.]

See also CONCEPTS; INTEGRATION (MENTAL); LEARNING; UNDERSTANDING.

Egalitarianism. Egalitarianism means the belief in the equality of all men. If the word "equality" is to be taken in any serious or rational sense, the crusade for this belief is dated by about a century or more: the United States of America has made it an anachronism—by establishing a system based on the principle of individual rights. "Equality," in a human context, is a political term: it means equality before the law, the equality of fundamental, inalienable rights which every man possesses by virtue of his birth as a human being, and which may not be infringed or abrogated by man-made institutions, such as titles of nobility or the division of men into castes established by law, with special privileges granted to some and denied to others. The rise of capitalism swept away all castes, including the institutions of aristocracy and of slavery or serfdom.

But this is not the meaning that the altruists ascribe to the word "equality."

They turn the word into an anti-concept: they use it to mean, not *political*, but *metaphysical* equality—the equality of personal attributes and virtues, regardless of natural endowment or individual choice, performance and character. It is not man-made institutions, but nature, i.e., *reality*, that they propose to fight—by means of man-made institutions.

Since nature does not endow all men with equal beauty or equal intelligence, and the faculty of volition leads men to make different choices, the egalitarians propose to abolish the "unfairness" of nature and of volition, and to establish universal equality *in fact*—in defiance of facts. Since the Law of Identity is impervious to human manipulation, it is the Law of Causality that they struggle to abrogate. Since personal attributes or virtues cannot be "redistributed," they seek to deprive men of their consequences—of the rewards, the benefits, the achievements created by personal attributes and virtues.

It is not equality before the law that they seek, but *inequality:* the establishment of an inverted social pyramid, with a new aristocracy on top—*the aristocracy of non-value.*

["The Age of Envy," *NL,* 164.]

To understand the meaning and motives of egalitarianism, project it into the field of medicine. Suppose a doctor is called to help a man with a broken leg and, instead of setting it, proceeds to break the legs of ten other men, explaining that this would make the patient feel better; when all these men become crippled for life, the doctor advocates the passage of a law compelling everyone to walk on crutches—in order to make the cripples feel better and equalize the "unfairness" of nature.

If this is unspeakable, how does it acquire an aura of morality—or even the benefit of a moral doubt—when practiced in regard to man's mind?

[Ibid., 170.]

Of special significance to the present discussion is the egalitarians' defiance of the Law of Causality: their demand for equal results from unequal causes—or equal rewards for unequal performance.

["Egalitarianism and Inflation," *PWNI,* 146; pb 121.]

The new "theory of justice" [of John Rawls] demands that men counteract the "injustice" of nature by instituting the most obscenely unthinkable injustice among men: deprive "those favored by nature" (i.e., the talented, the intelligent, the creative) of the right to the rewards they produce (i.e., the right to life)—and grant to the incompetent, the stupid, the slothful a right to the effortless enjoyment of the rewards they could not produce, could not imagine, and would not know what to do with.

["An Untitled Letter," *PWNI,* 132; pb 110.]

Observe that . . . the egalitarians' view of man is literally the view of a children's fairy tale—the notion that man, before birth, is some sort of indeterminate thing, an entity without identity, something like a shapeless chunk of human clay, and that fairy godmothers proceed to grant or deny him various attributes ("favors"): intelligence, talent, beauty, rich parents, etc. These attributes are handed out "arbitrarily" (this word is preposterously inapplicable to the processes of nature), it is a "lottery" among pre-embryonic non-entities, and—the supposedly adult mentalities conclude—since a winner could not possibly have "deserved" his "good fortune," a man does not deserve or earn anything after birth, as a human being, because he acts by means of "undeserved," "unmerited," "unearned" attributes. Implication: to earn something means to choose and earn your personal attributes *before* you exist.

[Ibid., 133; pb 111.]

If there were such a thing as a passion for equality (not equality *de jure*, but *de facto*), it would be obvious to its exponents that there are only two ways to achieve it: either by raising all men to the mountaintop—or by razing the mountains. The first method is impossible because it is the faculty of volition that determines a man's stature and actions; but the nearest approach to it was demonstrated by the United States and capitalism, which protected the freedom, the rewards and the incentives for every individual's achievement, each to the extent of his ability and ambition, thus raising the intellectual, moral and economic state of the whole society. The second method is impossible because, if mankind were leveled down to the common denominator of its least competent members, it would not be able to survive (and its best would not choose to survive on such terms). Yet it is the second method that the altruist-egalitarians are pursuing. The greater the evidence of their policy's consequences, i.e., the greater the spread of misery, of injustice, of vicious inequality throughout the world, the more frantic their pursuit —which is one demonstration of the fact that there is no such thing as a benevolent passion for equality and that the claim to it is only a rationalization to cover a passionate hatred of the good for being the good.

["The Age of Envy," *NL*, 169.]

See also ALTRUISM; ENVY/HATRED of the GOOD for BEING the GOOD; FREE WILL; JUSTICE; METAPHYSICAL vs. MAN-MADE; STATISM.

Egoism. *See Selfishness.*

Emergencies. It is important to differentiate between the rules of conduct in an emergency situation and the rules of conduct in the normal conditions of human existence. This does not mean a double standard of morality: the standard and the basic principles remain the same, but their application to either case requires precise definitions.

An emergency is an unchosen, unexpected event, limited in time, that creates conditions under which human survival is impossible—such as a flood, an earthquake, a fire, a shipwreck. In an emergency situation, men's primary goal is to combat the disaster, escape the danger and restore normal conditions (to reach dry land, to put out the fire, etc.).

By "normal" conditions I mean *metaphysically* normal, normal in the nature of things, and appropriate to human existence. Men can live on land, but not in water or in a raging fire. Since men are not omnipotent, it is metaphysically possible for unforeseeable disasters to strike them, in which case their only task is to return to those conditions under which their lives can continue. By its nature, an emergency situation is temporary; if it were to last, men would perish.

It is only in emergency situations that one should volunteer to help strangers, if it is in one's power. For instance, a man who values human life and is caught in a shipwreck, should help to save his fellow passengers (though not at the expense of his own life). But this does not mean that after they all reach shore, he should devote his efforts to saving his fellow passengers from poverty, ignorance, neurosis or whatever other troubles they might have. Nor does it mean that he should spend his life sailing the seven seas in search of shipwreck victims to save. . . .

The principle that one should help men in an emergency cannot be extended to regard all human suffering as an emergency and to turn the misfortune of some into a first mortgage on the lives of others.

[“The Ethics of Emergencies,” *VOS*, 53; pb 47.]

See also BENEVOLENT UNIVERSE PREMISE; CHARITY; POVERTY; SELFISHNESS; SUFFERING.

Emotions. Just as the pleasure-pain mechanism of man's body is an automatic indicator of his body's welfare or injury, a barometer of its basic alternative, life or death—so the emotional mechanism of man's consciousness is geared to perform the same function, as a barometer that registers the same alternative by means of two basic emotions: joy or suffering. Emotions are the automatic results of man's value judgments integrated by his subconscious; emotions are estimates of that which furthers man's values or threatens them, that which is *for* him or *against* him—lightning calculators giving him the sum of his profit or loss.

But while the standard of value operating the physical pleasure-pain mechanism of man's body is automatic and innate, determined by the nature of his body—the standard of value operating his emotional mechanism, is *not*. Since man has no automatic knowledge, he can have no automatic values; since he has no innate ideas, he can have no innate value judgments.

Man is born with an emotional mechanism, just as he is born with a cognitive mechanism; but, at birth, *both* are “tabula rasa.” It is man's cognitive faculty, his mind, that determines the *content* of both. Man's emotional mechanism is like an electronic computer, which his mind has to program—and the programming consists of the values his mind chooses.

But since the work of man's mind is not automatic, his values, like all his premises, are the product either of his thinking or of his evasions: man chooses his values by a conscious process of thought—or accepts them by default, by subconscious associations, on faith, on someone's authority, by some form of social osmosis or blind imitation. Emotions are produced by man's premises, held consciously or subconsciously, explicitly or implicitly.

["The Objectivist Ethics," *VOS*, 23; pb 27.]

Your subconscious is like a computer—more complex a computer than men can build—and its main function is the integration of your ideas. Who programs it? Your conscious mind. If you default, if you don't reach any firm convictions, your subconscious is programmed by chance—and you deliver yourself into the power of ideas you do not know you have accepted. But one way or the other, your computer gives you print-outs, daily and hourly, in the form of *emotions*—which are lightning-like estimates of the things around you, calculated according to your values.

["Philosophy: Who Needs It," *PWNI*, 7; pb 5.]

An emotion is an automatic response, an automatic effect of man's value premises. An effect, not a cause. There is no necessary clash, no dichotomy between man's reason and his emotions—provided he observes their proper relationship. A rational man knows—or makes it a point to discover—the source of his emotions, the basic premises from which they come; if his premises are wrong, he corrects them. He never acts on emotions for which he cannot account, the meaning of which he does not understand. In appraising a situation, he knows why he reacts as he does and whether he is right. He has no inner conflicts, his mind and his emotions are integrated, his consciousness is in perfect harmony. His emotions are not his enemies, they are his means of enjoying life. But they are not his guide; the guide is his mind. This relationship cannot be reversed, however. If a man takes his emotions as the cause and his mind as their passive effect, if he is guided by his emotions and uses his mind only to rationalize or justify them somehow—*then* he is acting immorally, he is condemning himself to misery, failure, defeat, and he will achieve nothing but destruction—his own and that of others.

["*Playboy's* Interview with Ayn Rand," pamphlet, 6.]

An emotion as such tells you nothing about reality, beyond the fact that something makes you feel something. Without a ruthlessly honest commitment to introspection—to the conceptual identification of your inner states—you will not discover what you feel, what arouses the feeling, and whether your feeling is an appropriate response to the facts of reality, or a mistaken response, or a vicious illusion produced by years of self-deception. . . .

In the field of introspection, the two guiding questions are: *"What* do I feel?" and *"Why* do I feel it?"

[*"Philosophical Detection,"* *PWNI*, 20; pb 17.]

There can be no causeless love or any sort of causeless emotion. An emotion is a response to a fact of reality, an estimate dictated by your standards.

[GS, *FNI*, 182; pb 147.]

Man has no choice about his capacity to feel that something is good for him or evil, but *what* he will consider good or evil, what will give him joy or pain, what he will love or hate, desire or fear, depends on his standard of value. If he chooses irrational values, he switches his emotional mechanism from the role of his guardian to the role of his destroyer. The irrational is the impossible; it is that which contradicts the facts of reality; facts cannot be altered by a wish, but they *can* destroy the wisher. If a man desires and pursues contradictions—if he wants to have his cake and eat it, too—he disintegrates his consciousness; he turns his inner life into a civil war of blind forces engaged in dark, incoherent, pointless, meaningless conflicts (which, incidentally, is the inner state of most people today).

[*"The Objectivist Ethics,"* *VOS*, 24; pb 28.]

An emotion that clashes with your reason, an emotion that you cannot explain or control, is only the carcass of that stale thinking which you forbade your mind to revise.

[GS, *FNI*, 187; pb 151.]

The quality of a computer's output is determined by the quality of its input. If your subconscious is programmed by chance, its output will have a corresponding character. You have probably heard the computer operators' eloquent term "gigo"—which means: "Garbage in, garbage out." The same formula applies to the relationship between a man's thinking and his emotions.

A man who is run by emotions is like a man who is run by a computer whose print-outs he cannot read. He does not know whether its programming is true or false, right or wrong, whether it's set to lead him to success or destruction, whether it serves his goals or those of some evil, unknowable power. He is blind on two fronts: blind to the world around him and to his own inner world, unable to grasp reality or his own motives, and he is in chronic terror of both.

[*"Philosophy: Who Needs It,"* *PWNI*, 7; pb 6.]

Emotions are not tools of cognition ... one must differentiate between one's thoughts and one's emotions with full clarity and precision. One does not have to be omniscient in order to possess knowledge; one merely has to know that which one does know, and distinguish it from that which one feels. Nor does one need a full system of philosophical epistemology in order to distinguish one's own considered judgment from one's feelings, wishes, hopes or fears.

["For the New Intellectual," *FNI*, 64; pb 55.]

The concept "emotion" is formed by retaining the distinguishing characteristics of the psychological action (an automatic response proceeding from an evaluation of an existent) and by omitting the particular contents (the existents) as well as the degree of emotional intensity.

[*ITOE*, 41.]

See also AUTOMATIZATION; ENVY/HATRED of the GOOD for BEING the GOOD; FREUD; HAPPINESS; HOSTILITY; INTROSPECTION; LONELINESS; LOVE; MOTIVATION; MOTIVATION by LOVE vs. by FEAR; PLEASURE and PAIN; PSYCHO-EPISTEMOLOGY; RATIONALITY; RATIONALIZATION; REASON; SENSE of LIFE; SOUL-BODY DICHOTOMY; SUBCONSCIOUS; VALUES; WHIMS/WHIM-WORSHIP.

End in Itself. *See Ultimate Value.*

Enlightenment, Age of. The development from Aquinas through Locke and Newton represents more than four hundred years of stumbling, tortuous, prodigious effort to secularize the Western mind, i.e., to liberate man from the medieval shackles. It was the buildup toward a climax: the eighteenth century, the *Age of Enlightenment*. For the first time in modern history, an authentic respect for reason became the mark of an entire culture; the trend that had been implicit in the centuries-long crusade of a handful of innovators now swept the West explicitly, reaching and inspiring educated men in every field. Reason, for so long the wave of the future, had become the animating force of the present.

[Leonard Peikoff, *OP*, 102; pb 101.]

Confidence in the power of man replaced dependence on the grace of God—and that rare intellectual orientation emerged, the key to the Enlightenment approach in every branch of philosophy: *secularism without skepticism*.

In metaphysics, this meant a fundamental change in emphasis: from God to this world, the world of particulars in which men live, the realm of *nature*. ... Men's operative conviction was that nature is an autonomous realm—solid, eternal, *real* in its own right. For centuries, nature had been regarded as a realm of miracles manipulated by a personal deity, a realm whose significance lay in the clues it offered to the purposes of its author. Now the operative conviction was that nature is a realm governed by scientific laws, which permit no miracles and which are intelligible without reference to the supernatural.

[Ibid., 107; pb 106.]

Just as there are no limits to man's knowledge, many [Enlightenment era] thinkers held, so there are no limits to man's moral improvement. If man is not yet perfect, they held, he is at least perfectible. Just as there are objective, natural laws in science, so there are objective, natural laws in ethics; and man is capable of discovering such laws and of acting in accordance with them. He is capable not only of developing his intellect, but also of *living* by its guidance. (This, at least, was the Enlightenment's ethical program and promise.)

Whatever the vacillations or doubts of particular thinkers, the dominant trend represented a new vision and estimate of man: man as a self-sufficient, rational being and, therefore, as basically good, as potentially noble, as a *value*.

[Ibid., 109; pb 107.]

The father of this new world was a single philosopher: Aristotle. On countless issues, Aristotle's views differ from those of the Enlightenment. But, in terms of broad fundamentals, the philosophy of Aristotle *is* the philosophy of the Enlightenment.

[Ibid., 111; pb 109.]

In epistemology, the European champions of the intellect had been unable to formulate a tenable view of the nature of reason or, therefore, to validate their proclaimed confidence in its power. As a result, from the beginning of the eighteenth century (and even earlier), the philosophy advocating reason was in the process of gradual, but accelerating, disintegration.

[Ibid., 115; pb 113.]

See also AMERICA; ARISTOTLE; DARK AGES; FOUNDING FATHERS; HISTORY; MIDDLE AGES; NATURE; REASON; RELIGION; RENAISSANCE; SKEPTICISM.

Entity. To exist is to be something, as distinguished from the nothing of non-existence, it is to be an entity of a specific nature made of specific attributes.

[GS, *FNI*, 152; pb 125.]

The development of human cognition starts with the ability to perceive *things*, i.e., *entities*. Of man's five cognitive senses, only two provide him with a direct awareness of entities: sight and touch. The other three senses—hearing, taste and smell—give him an awareness of some of an entity's attributes (or of the consequences produced by an entity): they tell him that something makes sounds, or something tastes sweet, or something smells fresh; but in order to perceive this something, he needs sight and/or touch.

The concept "entity" is (implicitly) the start of man's conceptual development and the building-block of his entire conceptual structure. It is by perceiving entities that man perceives the universe.

["Art and Cognition," *RM*, pb 46.]

The first concepts man forms are concepts of entities—since entities are the only primary existents. (Attributes cannot exist by themselves, they are merely the characteristics of entities; motions are motions of entities; relationships are relationships among entities.)

[*ITOE*, 18.]

This term [entity] may be used in several senses. If you speak in the primary sense, "entity" has to be defined ostensively—that is to say, by pointing. I can, however, give you three descriptive characteristics essential to the primary, philosophic use of the term, according to Objectivism. This is not a definition, because I'd have to rely ultimately on pointing to make these points clear, but it will give you certain criteria for the application of the term in the primary sense. . . .

1. An entity means a self-sufficient form of existence—as against a quality, an action, a relationship, etc., which are simply aspects of an entity that we separate out by specialized focus. An entity is a *thing*.

2. An entity, in the primary sense, is a solid thing with a definite boundary—as against a fluid, such as air. In the literal sense, air is not an entity. There are contexts, such as when the wind moves as one mass, when you can call it that, by analogy, but in the primary sense, fluids are not entities.

3. An entity is perceptual in scale, in size. In other words it is a "this" which you can point to and grasp by human perception. In an extended sense you can call molecules—or the universe as a whole—"entities," because they are self-sufficient things. But in the primary sense when we say that entities are what is given in sense perception, we mean solid things which we can directly perceive.

[Leonard Peikoff, "The Philosophy of Objectivism"
lecture series (1976), question period, Lecture 3.]

An entity is a solid thing open to human perception and capable of independent action.

[Ibid., question period, Lecture 2.]

See also CAUSALITY; CHANGE; EXISTENCE; EXISTENT; IDENTITY; MOTION; UNIVERSE.

Environmentalism.   *See Ecology/Environmental Movement.*

Envy/Hatred of the Good for Being the Good.   Today, we live in the Age of Envy.

"Envy" is not the emotion I have in mind, but it is the clearest manifestation of an emotion that has remained nameless; it is the only element of a complex emotional sum that men have permitted themselves to identify.

Envy is regarded by most people as a petty, superficial emotion and, therefore, it serves as a semihuman cover for so inhuman an emotion that those who feel it seldom dare admit it even to themselves. . . . That emotion is: *hatred of the good for being the good.*

This hatred is not resentment against some prescribed view of the good with which one does not agree. . . . Hatred of the good for being the good means hatred of that which one regards as good by one's own (conscious or subconscious) judgment. It means hatred of a person for possessing a value or virtue one regards as desirable.

If a child wants to get good grades in school, but is unable or unwilling to achieve them and begins to hate the children who do, *that* is hatred of the good. If a man regards intelligence as a value, but is troubled by self-doubt and begins to hate the men *he* judges to be intelligent, *that* is hatred of the good.

The nature of the particular values a man chooses to hold is not the primary factor in this issue (although irrational values may contribute a great deal to the formation of that emotion). The primary factor and distinguishing characteristic is an emotional mechanism set in reverse: a response of hatred, not toward human vices, but toward human virtues.

To be exact, the emotional mechanism is not set in reverse, but is set one way: its exponents do not experience love for evil men; their emotional range is limited to hatred or indifference. It is impossible to experience love, which is a response to values, when one's automatized response to values is hatred.

["The Age of Envy," *NL,* 152.]

Consider the full meaning of this attitude. Values are that which one acts to gain and/or keep. Values are a necessity of man's survival, and wider: of any living organism's survival. Life is a process of self-sustaining and self-generated action, and the successful pursuit of values is a precondition of remaining alive. Since nature does not provide man with an automatic knowledge of the code of values he requires, there are differences in the codes which men accept and the goals they pursue. But consider the abstraction "value," apart from the particular content of any given code, and ask yourself: What is the nature of a creature in which the sight of a value arouses hatred and the desire to destroy? In the most profound sense of the term, such a creature is a killer, not a physical, but a metaphysical one—it is not an enemy of *your* values, but of *all* values, it is an enemy of anything that enables men to survive, it is an enemy of life as such and of everything living.

[Ibid., 157.]

They do not want to own your fortune, they want you to lose it; they do not want to succeed, they want you to fail; they do not want to live, they want you to die; they desire nothing, they hate existence, and they keep running, each trying not to learn that the object of his hatred is himself. . . . *They* are the essence of evil, they, those anti-living objects who seek, by devouring the world, to fill the *selfless* zero of their soul. It is not your wealth that they're after. Theirs is a conspiracy against the mind, which means: against life and man.

[GS, *FNI*, 203; pb 163.]

See also AMORALISM; ANTI-CONCEPTUAL MENTALITY; APPEASEMENT; EMOTIONS; EVIL; GOOD, the; HOSTILITY; VALUES.

Epistemology.   Epistemology is a science devoted to the discovery of the proper methods of acquiring and validating knowledge.

[*ITOE*, 47.]

Since man is not omniscient or infallible, you have to discover what you can claim as knowledge and how to *prove* the validity of your conclusions. Does man acquire knowledge by a process of reason—or by sudden revelation from a supernatural power? Is reason a faculty that identifies and integrates the material provided by man's senses—or is it fed by innate ideas, implanted in man's mind before he was born? Is reason competent to perceive reality—or does man possess some other cognitive faculty which is superior to reason? Can man achieve certainty—or is he doomed to perpetual doubt? The extent of your self-confidence—and of your success—will be different, according to which set of answers you accept.

["Philosophy: Who Needs It," *PWNI*, 3; pb 3.]

Man is neither infallible nor omniscient; if he were, a discipline such as epistemology—the theory of knowledge—would not be necessary nor possible: his knowledge would be automatic, unquestionable and total. But such is not man's nature. Man is a being of volitional consciousness: beyond the level of percepts—a level inadequate to the cognitive requirements of his survival—man has to acquire knowledge by his own effort, which he may exercise or not, and by a process of reason, which he may apply correctly or not. Nature gives him no automatic guarantee of his mental efficacy; he is capable of error, of evasion, of psychological distortion. He needs a *method* of cognition, which he himself has to discover: he must discover how to use his rational faculty, how to validate his conclusions, how to distinguish truth from falsehood, how to set the criteria of *what* he may accept as knowledge. Two questions are involved in his every conclusion, conviction, decision, choice or claim: *What* do I know?—and: *How* do I know it?

It is the task of epistemology to provide the answer to the "How?"—which then enables the special sciences to provide the answers to the "What?"

In the history of philosophy—with some very rare exceptions—epistemological theories have consisted of attempts to escape one or the other of the two fundamental questions which cannot be escaped. Men have been taught either that knowledge is impossible (skepticism) or that it is available without effort (mysticism). These two positions appear to be antagonists, but are, in fact, two variants on the same theme, two sides of the same fraudulent coin: the attempt to escape the responsibility of rational cognition and the absolutism of reality—the attempt to assert the primacy of consciousness over existence.

[*ITOE*, 104.]

See Conceptual Index: Epistemology.

Equality (Social-Political). *See Egalitarianism.*

Errors of Knowledge vs. Breaches of Morality.
Learn to distinguish the difference between errors of knowledge and breaches of morality. An error of knowledge is not a moral flaw, provided you are willing to correct it; only a mystic would judge human beings by the standard of an impossible, automatic omniscience. But a breach of morality is the conscious choice of an action you know to be evil, or a willful evasion of knowledge, a suspension of sight and of thought. That which you do not know, is not a moral charge against you; but that which you refuse to know, is an account of infamy growing in your soul. Make every allowance for errors of knowledge; do not forgive or accept any

breach of morality. Give the benefit of the doubt to those who seek to know; but treat as potential killers those specimens of insolent depravity who make demands upon you, announcing that they have and seek no reasons, proclaiming, as a license, that they "just feel it"—or those who reject an irrefutable argument by saying: "It's only logic," which means: "It's only reality." The only realm opposed to reality is the realm and premise of death.

[GS, *FNI*, 224; pb 179.]

See also EVASION; EVIL; FREE WILL; GOOD, the; IRRATIONALITY; KNOWLEDGE; MORALITY; STANDARD of VALUE.

Essence/Essential Characteristic. *See Definitions.*

Esthetic Abstractions.

There are many special or "cross-filed" chains of abstractions (of interconnected concepts) in man's mind. Cognitive abstractions are the fundamental chain, on which all the others depend. Such chains are mental integrations, serving a special purpose and formed accordingly by a special criterion.

Cognitive abstractions are formed by the criterion of: what is *essential?* (epistemologically essential to distinguish one class of existents from all others). *Normative* abstractions are formed by the criterion of: what is *good? Esthetic* abstractions are formed by the criterion of: what is *important?*

An artist does not fake reality—he *stylizes* it. He selects those aspects of existence which he regards as metaphysically significant—and by isolating and stressing them, by omitting the insignificant and accidental, he presents *his* view of existence. His concepts are not divorced from the facts of reality—they are concepts which integrate the facts *and* his metaphysical evaluation of the facts. His selection constitutes his evaluation: everything included in a work of art—from theme to subject to brushstroke or adjective—acquires metaphysical significance by the mere fact of being included, of being *important* enough to include.

An artist (as, for instance, the sculptors of Ancient Greece) who presents man as a god-like figure is aware of the fact that men may be crippled or diseased or helpless; but he regards these conditions as accidental, as irrelevant to the essential nature of man—and he presents a figure embodying strength, beauty, intelligence, self-confidence, as man's proper, natural state.

An artist (as, for instance, the sculptors of the Middle Ages) who presents man as a deformed monstrosity is aware of the fact that there are men who are healthy, happy or confident; but he regards *these* conditions as accidental or illusory, as irrelevant to man's essential nature—and he presents a tortured figure embodying pain, ugliness, terror, as man's proper, natural state.

["Art and Sense of Life," *RM*, 45; pb 36.]

See also ABSTRACTIONS and CONCRETES; ART; CONCEPTS; ESTHETICS; METAPHYSICAL VALUE-JUDGMENTS; NORMATIVE ABSTRACTIONS; SENSE of LIFE.

Esthetic Judgment. Now a word of warning about the criteria of esthetic judgment. A sense of life is the source of art, but it is *not* the sole qualification of an artist or of an esthetician, and it is *not* a criterion of esthetic judgment. Emotions are not tools of cognition. Esthetics is a branch of philosophy—and just as a philosopher does not approach any other branch of his science with his feelings or emotions as his criterion of judgment, so he cannot do it in the field of esthetics. A sense of life is not sufficient professional equipment. An esthetician—as well as any man who attempts to evaluate art works—must be guided by more than an emotion.

The fact that one agrees or disagrees with an artist's philosophy is irrelevant to an *esthetic* appraisal of his work *qua* art. One does not have to agree with an artist (nor even to enjoy him) in order to evaluate his work. In essence, an objective evaluation requires that one identify the artist's theme, the abstract meaning of his work (exclusively by identifying the evidence contained in the work and allowing no other, outside considerations), then evaluate the means by which he conveys it—i.e., taking *his* theme as criterion, evaluate the purely esthetic elements of the work, the technical mastery (or lack of it) with which he projects (or fails to project) *his* view of life. . . .

Since art is a philosophical composite, it is not a contradiction to say: "This is a great work of art, but I don't like it," provided one defines the exact meaning of that statement: the first part refers to a purely esthetic appraisal, the second to a deeper philosophical level which includes more than esthetic values.

["Art and Sense of Life," *RM*, 53; pb 42.]

See also ART; ESTHETICS; MORAL JUDGMENT; SENSE of LIFE.

Esthetics. The fifth and last branch of philosophy is *esthetics*, the study of art, which is based on metaphysics, epistemology and ethics.

["Philosophy: Who Needs It," *PWNI*, 4; pb 4.]

The esthetic principles which apply to all art, regardless of an individual artist's philosophy, and which must guide an objective evaluation

. . . are defined by the science of esthetics—a task at which modern philosophy has failed dismally.

["Art and Sense of Life," *RM*, 54; pb 42.]

The position of art in the scale of human knowledge is, perhaps, the most eloquent symptom of the gulf between man's progress in the physical sciences and his stagnation (or, today, his retrogression) in the humanities. . . .

While, in other fields of knowledge, men have outgrown the practice of seeking the guidance of mystic oracles whose qualification for the job was unintelligibility, in the field of esthetics this practice has remained in full force and is becoming more crudely obvious today. Just as savages took the phenomena of nature for granted, as an irreducible primary not to be questioned or analyzed, as the exclusive domain of unknowable demons—so today's epistemological savages take art for granted, as an irreducible primary not to be questioned or analyzed, as the exclusive domain of a special kind of unknowable demons: their emotions. The only difference is that the prehistorical savages' error was innocent.

["The Psycho-Epistemology of Art," *RM*, 17; pb 15.]

See Conceptual Index: Esthetics

Ethics. *See Morality.*

"Ethnicity." "Ethnicity" is an anti-concept, used as a disguise for the word "racism"—and it has no clearly definable meaning. . . . The term "ethnicity" stresses the traditional, rather than the physiological characteristics of a group, such as language—but physiology, i.e., *race,* is involved. . . . So the advocacy of "ethnicity," means *racism plus tradition* —i.e., racism plus conformity—i.e., racism plus staleness.

["Global Balkanization," pamphlet, 6.]

Ethnicity is not a valid consideration, morally or politically, and does not endow anyone with any special rights.

[Ibid., 14.]

See also "ANTI-CONCEPTS"; COLLECTIVISM; CULTURE; RACISM; TRADITION; TRIBALISM.

Evasion. Thinking is man's only basic virtue, from which all the others proceed. And his basic vice, the source of all his evils, is that nameless act which all of you practice, but struggle never to admit: the act of blanking out, the willful suspension of one's consciousness, the refusal to think—not blindness, but the refusal to see; not ignorance, but the refusal to know. It is the act of unfocusing your mind and inducing an inner fog to escape the responsibility of judgment—on the unstated premise that a thing will not exist if only you refuse to identify it, that A will not be A so long as you do not pronounce the verdict "It *is*." Non-thinking is an act of annihilation, a wish to negate existence, an attempt to wipe out reality. But existence exists; reality is not to be wiped out, it will merely wipe out the wiper. By refusing to say "It is," you are refusing to say "I am." By suspending your judgment, you are negating your person. When a man declares: "Who am I to know?" he is declaring: "Who am I to live?"

[GS, *FNI*, 155; pb 127.]

Dropping below the level of a savage, who believes that the magic words he utters have the power to alter reality, they believe that reality can be altered by the power of the words they do *not* utter—and their magic tool is the blank-out, the pretense that nothing can come into existence past the voodoo of their refusal to identify it.

[Ibid., 191; pb 154.]

It is not any crime you have ever committed that infects your soul with permanent guilt, it is none of your failures, errors or flaws, but the *blank-out* by which you attempt to evade them—it is not any sort of Original Sin or unknown prenatal deficiency, but the knowledge and fact of your basic default, of suspending your mind, of refusing to think. Fear and guilt are your chronic emotions, they are real and you do deserve them, but they don't come from the superficial reasons you invent to disguise their cause, not from your "selfishness," weakness or ignorance, but from a real and basic threat to your existence: *fear*, because you have abandoned your weapon of survival, *guilt*, because you know you have done it volitionally.

[Ibid., 221; pb 176.]

See also CONTEXT-DROPPING; EVIL; FOCUS; FREE WILL; IRRATIONALITY; PRIMACY of EXISTENCE vs. PRIMACY of CONSCIOUSNESS; RATIONALITY; RATIONALIZATION; SUBJECTIVISM.

Evil. The standard of value of the Objectivist ethics—the standard by which one judges what is good or evil—is *man's life*, or: that which is required for man's survival *qua* man.

Since reason is man's basic means of survival, that which is proper to the life of a rational being is the good; that which negates, opposes or destroys it is the evil.

["The Objectivist Ethics," *VOS*, 16; pb 23.]

Thinking is man's only basic virtue, from which all the others proceed. And his basic vice, the source of all his evils, is that nameless act which all of you practice, but struggle never to admit: the act of blanking out, the willful suspension of one's consciousness, the refusal to think— not blindness, but the refusal to see; not ignorance, but the refusal to know. It is the act of unfocusing your mind and inducing an inner fog to escape the responsibility of judgment—on the unstated premise that a thing will not exist if only you refuse to identify it, that A will not be A so long as you do not pronounce the verdict "It *is*."

[*GS, FNI,* 155; pb 127.]

Evil, not value, is an absence and a negation, evil is impotent and has no power but that which we let it extort from us.

[Ibid., 167; pb 135.]

I saw that evil was impotent—that evil was the irrational, the blind, the anti-real—and that the only weapon of its triumph was the willingness of the good to serve it.

[Ibid., 206; pb 165.]

The spread of evil is the symptom of a vacuum. Whenever evil wins, it is only by default: by the moral failure of those who evade the fact that there can be no compromise on basic principles.

["The Anatomy of Compromise," *CUI,* 149.]

In any compromise between food and poison, it is only death that can win. In any compromise between good and evil, it is only evil that can profit.

[*GS, FNI,* 217; pb 173.]

The truly and deliberately evil men are a very small minority; it is the appeaser who unleashes them on mankind; it is the appeaser's intellectual abdication that invites them to take over. When a culture's dominant trend is geared to irrationality, the thugs win over the appeasers. When intellectual leaders fail to foster the best in the mixed, unformed, vacillating character of people at large, the thugs are sure to bring out the worst. When the ablest men turn into cowards, the average men turn into brutes.

["Altruism as Appeasement," *TO,* Jan. 1966, 6.]

When men reduce their virtues to the approximate, then evil acquires the force of an absolute, when loyalty to an unyielding purpose is dropped by the virtuous, it's picked up by scoundrels—and you get the indecent spectacle of a cringing, bargaining, traitorous good and a self-righteously uncompromising evil.

[GS, *FNI*, 217; pb 173.]

As a being of volitional consciousness, [man] knows that he must know his own value in order to maintain his own life. He knows that he has to be *right;* to be wrong in action means danger to his life; to be wrong in person, to be *evil,* means to be unfit for existence. . . . No man can survive the moment of pronouncing himself irredeemably evil; should he do it, his next moment is insanity or suicide.

[Ibid., 221; pb 176.]

See also ABSOLUTES; AMORALISM; APPEASEMENT; COMPROMISE; CYNICISM; ENVY/HATRED of the GOOD for BEING the GOOD; ERRORS of KNOWLEDGE vs. BREACHES of MORALITY; EVASION; FREE WILL; GOOD, the; IRRATIONALITY; MORAL COWARDICE; MORAL JUDGMENT; MORALITY; ORIGINAL SIN; STANDARD of VALUE; VIRTUE.

Existence.

Existence exists—and the act of grasping that statement implies two corollary axioms: that something exists which one perceives and that one exists possessing consciousness, consciousness being the faculty of perceiving that which exists.

If nothing exists, there can be no consciousness: a consciousness with nothing to be conscious of is a contradiction in terms. A consciousness conscious of nothing but itself is a contradiction in terms: before it could identify itself as consciousness, it had to be conscious of something. If that which you claim to perceive does not exist, what you possess is not consciousness.

Whatever the degree of your knowledge, these two—existence and consciousness—are axioms you cannot escape, these two are the irreducible primaries implied in any action you undertake, in any part of your knowledge and in its sum, from the first ray of light you perceive at the start of your life to the widest erudition you might acquire at its end. Whether you know the shape of a pebble or the structure of a solar system, the axioms remain the same: that *it* exists and that you *know* it.

To exist is to be something, as distinguished from the nothing of non-existence, it is to be an entity of a specific nature made of specific attributes. Centuries ago, the man who was—no matter what his errors —the greatest of your philosophers, has stated the formula defining the concept of existence and the rule of all knowledge: *A is A.* A thing is itself. You have never grasped the meaning of his statement. I am here to complete it: Existence is Identity, Consciousness is Identification.

[GS, *FNI*, 152; pb 124.]

Reality is that which exists; the unreal does not exist; the unreal is merely that negation of existence which is the content of a human consciousness when it attempts to abandon reason.

[Ibid., 154; pb 126.]

Existence is a self-sufficient primary. It is not a product of a supernatural dimension, or of anything else. There is nothing antecedent to existence, nothing apart from it—*and no alternative to it.* Existence exists—and only existence exists. Its existence and its nature are irreducible and unalterable.

[Leonard Peikoff, "The Analytic-Synthetic Dichotomy," *ITOE*, 148.]

The first and primary axiomatic concepts are "existence," "identity" (which is a corollary of "existence") and "consciousness."

[*ITOE*, 73.]

An axomatic concept is the identification of a primary fact of reality, which cannot be analyzed, i.e., reduced to other facts or broken into component parts. It is implicit in all facts and in all knowledge. It is the fundamentally given and directly perceived or experienced, which requires no proof or explanation, but on which all proofs and explanations rest.

[Ibid.]

One can study what exists and how consciousness functions; but one cannot analyze (or "prove") existence as such, or consciousness as such. These are irreducible primaries. (An attempt to "prove" them is self-contradictory: it is an attempt to "prove" existence by means of non-existence, and consciousness by means of unconsciousness.)

[Ibid.]

Existence and identity are *not attributes* of existents, they *are* the existents. . . . The units of the concepts "existence" and "identity" are every entity, attribute, action, event or phenomenon (including consciousness) that exists, has ever existed or will ever exist.

[Ibid., 74.]

See also ABSOLUTES; ABSTRACTIONS and CONCRETES; ATHEISM; AXIOMATIC CONCEPTS; AXIOMS; EXISTENT; IDENTITY; INFINITY; METAPHYSICS; METAPHYSICAL; NATURE; PRIMACY of EXISTENCE vs. PRIMACY of CONSCIOUSNESS; SPACE; TIME; UNIVERSE; ZERO, REIFICATION of.

Existent. The building-block of man's knowledge is the concept of an *"existent"*—of something that exists, be it a thing, an attribute or an action. Since it is a concept, man cannot grasp it *explicitly* until he has reached the conceptual stage. But it is implicit in every percept (to perceive a thing is to perceive that it exists) and man grasps it *implicitly* on the perceptual level—i.e., he grasps the constituents of the concept "existent," the data which are later to be integrated by that concept. It is this implicit knowledge that permits his consciousness to develop further.

(It may be supposed that the concept "existent" is implicit even on the level of sensations—if and to the extent that a consciousness is able to discriminate on that level. A sensation is a sensation of *something,* as distinguished from the *nothing* of the preceding and succeeding moments. A sensation does not tell man *what* exists, but only *that* it exists.)

The (implicit) concept "existent" undergoes three stages of development in man's mind. The first stage is a child's awareness of objects, of things—which represents the (implicit) concept *"entity."* The second and closely allied stage is the awareness of specific, particular things which he can recognize and distinguish from the rest of his perceptual field— which represents the (implicit) concept *"identity."*

The third stage consists of grasping relationships among these entities by grasping the similarities and differences of their identities. This requires the transformation of the (implicit) concept "entity" into the (implicit) concept *"unit."*

[*ITOE*, 6.]

See also CONCEPT-FORMATION; ENTITY; EXISTENCE; IDENTITY; IMPLICIT KNOWLEDGE; SENSATIONS; UNIT.

F

Faith "Faith" designates blind acceptance of a certain ideational content, acceptance induced by feeling in the absence of evidence or proof.

[Leonard Peikoff, *OP*, 48; pb 54.]

Do not say that you're afraid to trust your mind because you know so little. Are you safer in surrendering to mystics and discarding the little that you know? Live and act within the limit of your knowledge and keep expanding it to the limit of life. Redeem your mind from the hockshops of authority. Accept the fact that you are not omniscient, but playing a zombie will not give you omniscience—that your mind is fallible, but becoming mindless will not make you infallible—that an error made on your own is safer than ten truths accepted on faith, because the first leaves you the means to correct it, but the second destroys your capacity to distinguish truth from error.

[GS, *FNI*, 223; pb 178.]

The alleged short-cut to knowledge, which is faith, is only a short-circuit destroying the mind.

[Ibid., 157; pb 128.]

Faith in the supernatural begins as faith in the superiority of others.

[Ibid., 200; pb 161.]

Faith and *force* . . . are corollaries: every period of history dominated by mysticism, was a period of statism, of dictatorship, of tyranny.

["Faith and Force: The Destroyers of the Modern World," *PWNI*, 80; pb 66.]

See also *ATHEISM; DOGMA; GOD; KNOWLEDGE; LOGIC; MYSTICISM; PHYSICAL FORCE; REASON; RELIGION; STATISM; SUPERNATURALISM.*

Falsehood. "True" and "false" are assessments within the field of human cognition: they designate a relationship [of] correspondence or contradiction between an idea and reality. . . . The false is established as false by reference to a body of evidence and within a context, and is pronounced false because it contradicts the evidence.

[Leonard Peikoff, "The Philosophy of Objectivism" lecture series (1976), Lecture 6.]

All falsehoods are self-contradictions.

When making a statement about an existent, one has, ultimately, only two alternatives: "X (which means X, the existent, including all its characteristics) *is* what it is"—or: "X *is not* what it is." The choice between truth and falsehood is the choice between "tautology" (in the sense explained) and self-contradiction.

[Leonard Peikoff, "The Analytic-Synthetic Dichotomy," *ITOE*, 136.]

See also ANALYTIC-SYNTHETIC DICHOTOMY; ARBITRARY; CONTRADICTIONS; IDENTITY; TRUTH.

Fascism/Nazism.

The difference between [socialism and fascism] is superficial and purely formal, but it is significant psychologically: it brings the authoritarian nature of a planned economy crudely into the open.

The main characteristic of socialism (and of communism) is public ownership of the means of production, and, therefore, the abolition of private property. The right to property is the right of use and disposal. Under fascism, men retain the semblance or pretense of private property, but the government holds total power over its use and disposal.

The dictionary definition of *fascism* is: "a governmental system with strong centralized power, permitting no opposition or criticism, controlling all affairs of the nation (industrial, commercial, etc.), emphasizing an aggressive nationalism . . ." [*The American College Dictionary*, New York: Random House, 1957.]

Under fascism, citizens retain the responsibilities of owning property, without freedom to act and without any of the advantages of ownership. Under socialism, government officials acquire all the advantages of ownership, without any of the responsibilities, since they do not hold title to the property, but merely the right to use it—at least until the next purge. In either case, the government officials hold the economic, political and legal power of life or death over the citizens.

Needless to say, under either system, the inequalities of income and standard of living are greater than anything possible under a free economy—and a man's position is determined, not by his productive ability and achievement, but by political pull and force.

Under both systems, sacrifice is invoked as a magic, omnipotent solution in any crisis—and "the public good" is the altar on which victims are immolated. But there are stylistic differences of emphasis. The socialist-communist axis keeps promising to achieve abundance, material comfort and security for its victims, in some indeterminate future. The fascist-Nazi axis scorns material comfort and security, and keeps extolling some undefined sort of spiritual duty, service and conquest. The socialist-communist axis offers its victims an alleged social ideal. The fascist-Nazi axis offers nothing but loose talk about some unspecified form of *racial* or *national* "greatness." The socialist-communist axis proclaims some grandiose economic plan, which keeps receding year by year. The fascist-Nazi axis merely extols leadership—leadership without purpose, program or direction—and power for power's sake.

["The Fascist New Frontier," pamphlet, 5]

If the term "statism" designates concentration of power in the state at the expense of individual liberty, then Nazism in politics was a form of statism. In principle, it did not represent a new approach to government; it was a continuation of the political absolutism—the absolute monarchies, the oligarchies, the theocracies, the random tyrannies— which has characterized most of human history.

In degree, however, the total state does differ from its predecessors: it represents statism pressed to its limits, in theory and in practice, devouring the last remnants of the individual. Although previous dictators (and many today, e.g., in Latin America) often preached the unlimited power of the state, they were on the whole unable to enforce such power. As a rule, citizens of such countries had a kind of partial "freedom," not a freedom-on-principle, but at least a freedom-by-default.

Even the latter was effectively absent in Nazi Germany. The efficiency of the government in dominating its subjects, the all-encompassing character of its coercion, the complete mass regimentation on a scale involving millions of men—and, one might add, the enormity of the slaughter, the planned, systematic mass slaughter, in peacetime, initiated by a government against its own citizens—these are the insignia of twentieth-century totalitarianism (Nazi *and* communist), which are without parallel in recorded history. In the totalitarian regimes, as the Germans found out after only a few months of Hitler's rule, every detail of life is prescribed, or proscribed. There is no longer any distinction between private matters and public matters. "There are to be no more private Germans," said Friedrich Sieburg, a Nazi writer; "each is to attain significance only by his service to the state, and to find complete self-fulfillment in this service." "The only person who is still a private individual in Germany," boasted Robert Ley, a member of the Nazi hierarchy, after several years of Nazi rule, "is somebody who is asleep."

In place of the despised "private individuals," the Germans heard daily or hourly about a different kind of entity, a supreme entity, whose will, it was said, is what determines the course and actions of the state: the nation, the whole, the *group*. Over and over, the Germans heard the idea that underlies the advocacy of omnipotent government, the idea that totalitarians of every kind stress as the justification of their total states: *collectivism*.

Collectivism is the theory that the group (the collective) has primacy over the individual. Collectivism holds that, in human affairs, the collective—society, the community, the nation, the proletariat, the race, etc.—is *the unit of reality and the standard of value*. On this view, the individual has reality only as part of the group, and value only insofar as he serves it; on his own he has no political rights; he is to be sacrificed for the group whenever it—or its representative, the state—deems this desirable.

[Leonard Peikoff, *OP*, 6; pb 16.]

Contrary to the Marxists, the Nazis did not advocate public ownership of the means of production. They did demand that the government oversee and run the nation's economy. The issue of legal ownership, they explained, is secondary; what counts is the issue of *control*. Private citizens, therefore, may continue to hold titles to property—so long as the state reserves to itself the unqualified right to regulate the use of their property.

If "ownership" means the right to determine the use and disposal of material goods, then Nazism endowed the state with every real prerogative of ownership. What the individual retained was merely a formal deed, a contentless deed, which conferred no rights on its holder. Under communism, there is collective ownership of property *de jure*. Under Nazism, there is the same collective ownership *de facto*.

[Ibid., 9; pb 18.]

It took centuries and a brain-stopping chain of falsehoods to bring a whole people to the state of Hitler-worship. Modern German culture, including its Nazi climax, is the result of a complex development in the history of philosophy, involving dozens of figures stretching back to the beginnings of Western thought. The same figures helped to shape every Western nation; but in other countries, to varying extents, the results were mixed, because there was also an opposite influence or antidote at work. In Germany, by the turn of our century, the cultural atmosphere was unmixed; the traces of the antidote had long since disappeared, and the intellectual establishment was monolithic.

If we view the West's philosophic development in terms of essentials, three fateful turning points stand out, three major philosophers who, above all others, are responsible for generating the disease of collectivism and transmitting it to the dictators of our century.

The three are: Plato—Kant—Hegel. (The antidote to them is: Aristotle.)

[Ibid., 17; pb 26.]

No weird cultural aberration produced Nazism. No intellectual lunatic fringe miraculously overwhelmed a civilized country. It is modern philosophy—not some peripheral aspect of it, but the most central of its mainstreams—which turned the Germans into a nation of killers.

The land of poets and philosophers was brought down by its poets and philosophers.

Twice in our century Germany fought to rule and impose its culture on the rest of the world. It lost both wars. But on a deeper level it is achieving its goal nevertheless. It is on the verge of winning the *philosophical* war against the West, with everything this implies.

[Ibid., 98; pb 98.]

I have stated repeatedly that the trend in this country is toward a fascist system with communist slogans. But what all of today's pressure groups are busy evading is the fact that neither business nor labor nor anyone else, except the ruling clique, gains anything under fascism or communism or any form of statism—that all become victims of an impartial, egalitarian destruction.

["The Moratorium on Brains," *ARL,* I, 3, 3.]

See also ALTRUISM; CAPITALISM; COLLECTIVISM; DICTATORSHIP; FASCISM and COMMUNISM/SOCIALISM; HUMAN RIGHTS and PROPERTY RIGHTS; INDIVIDUAL RIGHTS; INDIVIDUALISM; PROPERTY RIGHTS; RACISM; RIGHTISTS vs. LEFTISTS; STATISM; TYRANNY; WAR.

Fascism and Communism/Socialism.

For many decades, the leftists have been propagating the false dichotomy that the choice confronting the world is only: communism or fascism—a dictatorship of the left or of an alleged right—with the possibility of a free society, of *capitalism,* dismissed and obliterated, as if it had never existed.

["The Presidential Candidates 1968," *TO,* June 1968, 5.]

[Some "moderates" are trying to] revive that old saw of pre–World War II vintage, the notion that the two political opposites confronting us, the two *"extremes,"* are: fascism versus communism.

The political origin of that notion is more shameful than the "moderates" would care publicly to admit. Mussolini came to power by claim-

ing that that was the only choice confronting Italy. Hitler came to power
by claiming that that was the only choice confronting Germany. It is a
matter of record that in the German election of 1933, the Communist
Party was ordered by its leaders to vote for the Nazis—with the explanation that they could later fight the Nazis for power, but first they had
to help destroy their common enemy: capitalism and its parliamentary
form of government.

It is obvious what the fraudulent issue of fascism versus communism
accomplishes: it sets up, as opposites, two variants of the same political
system; it eliminates the possibility of considering capitalism; it switches
the choice of "Freedom or dictatorship?" into "Which kind of dictatorship?"—thus establishing dictatorship as an inevitable fact and offering
only a choice of rulers. The choice—according to the proponents of
that fraud—is: a dictatorship of the rich (fascism) or a dictatorship of
the poor (communism).

That fraud collapsed in the 1940's, in the aftermath of World War II.
It is too obvious, too easily demonstrable that fascism and communism
are not two opposites, but two rival gangs fighting over the same territory—that both are variants of statism, based on the collectivist principle
that man is the rightless slave of the state—that both are socialistic, in
theory, in practice, and in the explicit statements of their leaders—that
under both systems, the poor are enslaved and the rich are expropriated
in favor of a ruling clique—that fascism is not the product of the political "right," but of the "left"—that the basic issue is not "rich versus
poor," but man versus the state, or: individual rights versus totalitarian
government—which means: capitalism versus socialism.

[" 'Extremism,' or The Art of Smearing," *CUI*, 180.]

The main characteristic of socialism (and of communism) is public
ownership of the means of production, and, therefore, the abolition of
private property. The right to property is the right of use and disposal.
Under fascism, men retain the semblance or pretense of private property, but the government holds total power over its use and disposal. . . .

Under fascism, citizens retain the responsibilities of owning property,
without freedom to act and without any of the advantages of ownership.
Under socialism, government officials acquire all the advantages of ownership, without any of the responsibilities, since they do not hold title to
the property, but merely the right to use it—at least until the next
purge. In either case, the government officials hold the economic, political and legal power of life or death over the citizens. . . .

Under both systems, sacrifice is invoked as a magic, omnipotent solution in any crisis—and "the public good" is the altar on which victims
are immolated. But there are stylistic differences of emphasis. The so-

cialist-communist axis keeps promising to achieve abundance, material comfort and security for its victims, in some indeterminate future. The fascist-Nazi axis scorns material comfort and security, and keeps extolling some undefined sort of spiritual duty, service and conquest. The socialist-communist axis offers its victims an alleged social ideal. The fascist-Nazi axis offers nothing but loose talk about some unspecified form of *racial* or *national* "greatness." The socialist-communist axis proclaims some grandiose economic plan, which keeps receding year by year. The fascist-Nazi axis merely extols leadership—leadership without purpose, program or direction—and power for power's sake.

["The Fascist New Frontier," pamphlet, 5.]

Look at Europe.... Can't you see past the guff and recognize the essence? One country is dedicated to the proposition that man has no rights, that the collective is all. The individual held as evil, the mass—as God. No motive and no virtue permitted—except that of service to the proletariat. That's one version [communism]. Here's another. A country dedicated to the proposition that man has no rights, that the State is all. The individual held as evil, the race—as God. No motive and no virtue permitted—except that of service to the race [fascism]. Am I raving or is this the cold reality of two continents already? Watch the pincer movement. If you're sick of one version, we push you into the other. We get you coming and going. We've closed the doors. We've fixed the coin. Heads—collectivism, and tails—collectivism. Fight the doctrine which slaughters the individual with a doctrine which slaughters the individual. Give up your soul to a council—or give it up to a leader. But give it up, give it up, give it up. My technique.... Offer poison as food and poison as antidote.

["The Soul of a Collectivist," *FNI*, 88; pb 76.]

[Adolf Hitler on Nazism and socialism:] "Each activity and each need of the individual will thereby be regulated by the party as the representative of the general good. There will be no license, no free space, in which the individual belongs to himself. This is Socialism—not such trifles as the private possession of the means of production. Of what importance is that if I range men firmly within a discipline they cannot escape? Let them then own land or factories as much as they please. The decisive factor is that the State, through the party, is supreme over them, regardless whether they are owners or workers. All that, you see, is unessential. Our Socialism goes far deeper....

"[T]he people about us are unaware of what is really happening to them. They gaze fascinated at one or two familiar superficialities, such as possessions and income and rank and other outworn conceptions. As long as these are kept intact, they are quite satisfied. But in the meantime they have entered a new relation; a powerful social force has caught them up. They themselves are changed. What are ownership and income to that? Why need we trouble to socialize banks and factories? We socialize human beings."

> [Adolf Hitler to Hermann Rauschning, quoted in
> Leonard Peikoff, *OP*, 248; pb 231.]

Through the agency of three new guilds (the Food Estate, the Estate of Trade and Industry, and the Labor Front), the government assumed control of every group of producers and consumers in the country. In accordance with the method of "German socialism," the facade of a market economy was retained. All prices, wages, and interest rates, however, were "fixed by the central authority. They [were] prices, wages, and interest rates in appearance only; in reality they [were] merely determinations of quantity relations in the government's orders. . . . This is socialism in the outward guise of capitalism."

The nation's businessmen retained the responsibility to produce and suffered the losses attendant on failure. The state determined the purpose and conditions of their production, and reaped the benefits; directly or indirectly, it expropriated all profits. "The time is past," explained the Nazi Minister of Economics, "when the notion of economic self-seeking and unrestricted use of profits made can be allowed to dominate. . . . The economic system must serve the nation."

"What a dummkopf I was!" cried steel baron Fritz Thyssen, an early Nazi supporter, who fled the country. . . .

As to Hitler's pledges to the poorer groups: the Republic's social insurance budgets were greatly increased, and a variety of welfare funds, programs, agencies, and policies were introduced or expanded, including special provisions for such items as unemployment relief, workmen's compensation, health insurance, pensions, Winter Help campaigns for the destitute, the Reich Mothers' Service for indigent mothers and children, and the National Socialist People's Welfare organization.

> [Leonard Peikoff, *OP*, 246; pb 230.]

During the Hitler years—in order to finance the party's programs, including the war expenditures—every social group in Germany was mercilessly exploited and drained. White-collar salaries and the earnings of small businessmen were deliberately held down by government controls, freezes, taxes. Big business was bled by taxes and "special contributions" of every kind, and strangled by the bureaucracy. . . . At the same time the income of the farmers was held down, and there was a desperate flight to the cities—where the middle class, especially the small tradesmen, were soon in desperate straits, and where the workers were forced to labor at low wages for increasingly longer hours (up to 60 or more per week).

But the Nazis defended their policies, and the country did not rebel; it accepted the Nazi argument. Selfish individuals may be unhappy, the Nazis said, but what we have established in Germany is the ideal system, *socialism.* In its Nazi usage this term is not restricted to a theory of economics; it is to be understood in a fundamental sense. "Socialism" for the Nazis denotes the principle of collectivism as such and its corollary, statism—in every field of human action, including but not limited to economics.

"To be a socialist," says Goebbels, "is to submit the I to the thou; socialism is sacrificing the individual to the whole."

By this definition, the Nazis practiced what they preached. They practiced it at home and then abroad. No one can claim that they did not sacrifice enough individuals.

[Ibid., 9; pb 19.]

See also ALTRUISM; CAPITALISM; COLLECTIVISM; COMMUNISM; DICTATORSHIP; FASCISM/NAZISM; MYSTICS OF SPIRIT and of MUSCLE; POLYLOGISM; RIGHTISTS vs. LEFTISTS; SOCIALISM; SOVIET RUSSIA; STATISM.

Femininity. For a woman *qua* woman, the essence of femininity is hero-worship—the desire to look up to man. "To look up" does not mean dependence, obedience or anything implying inferiority. It means an intense kind of admiration; and admiration is an emotion that can be experienced only by a person of strong character and independent value-judgments. A "clinging vine" type of woman is not an admirer, but an exploiter of men. Hero-worship is a demanding virtue: a woman has to be worthy of it and of the hero she worships. Intellectually and morally, i.e., as a human being, she has to be his equal; then the object of her worship is specifically his *masculinity,* not any human virtue she might lack.

This does not mean that a feminine woman feels or projects hero-worship for any and every individual man; as human beings, many of them may, in fact, be her inferiors. Her worship is an abstract emotion for the *metaphysical* concept of masculinity as such—which she experiences fully and concretely only for the man she loves, but which colors her attitude toward all men. This does not mean that there is a romantic or sexual intention in her attitude toward all men; quite the contrary: the higher her view of masculinity, the more severely demanding her standards. It means that she never loses the awareness of her own sexual identity and theirs. It means that a properly feminine woman does not treat men as if she were their pal, sister, mother—or leader.

["An Answer to Readers (About a Woman President)," *TO*, Dec. 1968, 1.]

See also CAREER; INDEPENDENCE; LOVE; SEX; VIRTUE.

Final Causation. In order to make the choices required to achieve his goals, a man needs the constant, automatized awareness of the principle which the anti-concept "duty" has all but obliterated in his mind: the principle of causality—specifically, of Aristotelian *final causation* (which, in fact, applies only to a conscious being), i.e., the process by which an end determines the means, i.e., the process of choosing a goal and taking the actions necessary to achieve it.

In a rational ethics, it is causality—not "duty"—that serves as the guiding principle in considering, evaluating and choosing one's actions, particularly those necessary to achieve a long-range goal. Following this principle, a man does not act without knowing the purpose of his action. In choosing a goal, he considers the means required to achieve it, he weighs the value of the goal against the difficulties of the means and against the full, hierarchical context of all his other values and goals. He does not demand the impossible of himself, and he does not decide too easily which things are impossible. He never drops the context of the knowledge available to him, and never evades reality, realizing fully that his goal will not be granted to him by any power other than his own action, and, should he evade, it is not some Kantian authority that he would be cheating, but himself.

["Causality Versus Duty," *PWNI*, 119; pb 99.]

Only a process of final causation—i.e., the process of choosing a goal, then taking the steps to achieve it—can give logical continuity, coherence and meaning to a man's actions.

["Basic Principles of Literature," *RM*, 60; pb 82.]

See also "ANTI-CONCEPTS"; CONTEXT-DROPPING; "DUTY"; GOAL-DIRECTED ACTION; KANT, IMMANUEL; PURPOSE; STANDARD of VALUE; TELEOLOGICAL MEASUREMENT.

Focus. In any hour and issue of his life, man is free to think or to evade that effort. Thinking requires a state of full, focused awareness. The act of focusing one's consciousness is volitional. Man can focus his mind to a full, active, purposefully directed awareness of reality—or he can unfocus it and let himself drift in a semiconscious daze, merely reacting to any chance stimulus of the immediate moment, at the mercy of his undirected sensory-perceptual mechanism and of any random, associational connections it might happen to make.

When man unfocuses his mind, he may be said to be conscious in a subhuman sense of the word, since he experiences sensations and perceptions. But in the sense of the word applicable to man—in the sense of a consciousness which is aware of reality and able to deal with it, a consciousness able to direct the actions and provide for the survival of a human being—an unfocused mind is *not* conscious.

Psychologically, the choice "to think or not" is the choice "to focus or not." Existentially, the choice "to focus or not" is the choice "to be conscious or not." Metaphysically, the choice "to be conscious or not" is the choice of life or death.

["The Objectivist Ethics," *VOS*, 13; pb 20.]

"Focus" designates a quality of one's mental state, a quality of active alertness. "Focus" means the state of a goal-directed mind committed to attaining full awareness of reality. It's the state of a mind committed to seeing, to grasping, to understanding, to knowing.

"Full awareness" does not mean omniscience. It means: commitment to grasp *all* the facts relevant to one's concern and activity at any given time . . . as against a splintered grasp, a grasp of some facts while others which you know to be relevant are left in fog. By "full" I include also the commitment to grasp the relevant facts *clearly*, with the fullest clarity and precision one is capable of.

"Focus" is not synonymous with "thinking," in the sense of step-by-step problem-solving or the drawing of new conclusions. You may be walking down the street, merely contemplating the sights, but you can do it in focus or out of focus. "In focus" would mean you have some purpose directing your mental activity—in this case, a simple one: to observe the sights. But this is still a purpose, and it implies that you know what you are doing mentally, that you have set yourself a goal and are carrying it out, that you have assumed the responsibility of taking control of your consciousness and directing it. . . .

The process of focus is not the same as the process of thought; it is the precondition of thought. . . . Just as you must first focus your eyes, and then, if you choose, you can turn your gaze systematically to the objects on the table in front of you and inventory them, so first you must focus your mind, and then, when you choose, you can direct that focus to the step-by-step resolution of a specific problem—which latter is *thinking*.

[Leonard Peikoff, "The Philosophy of Objectivism" lecture series (1976), Lecture 3.]

[In answer to the question "What is the difference between concentration and focus?"]

Briefly: concentration means undivided attention on some particular task or object. . . . It is an attention, an activity, devoted to a particular subject. Now, focus is more fundamental than that. You need to be in focus in order to concentrate, but focus is the particular "set" of your consciousness which is not delimited by the particular task, object, or action that you are concentrating on. You do have to focus on something, but focus is not [limited to] the continuing task that you are performing. The concept "focus" isn't tied to the concrete . . . it remains the same no matter what you are focused on. It is the "set" of your mind.

[Ayn Rand, question period following Lecture 6 of Leonard
Peikoff's series "The Philosophy of Objectivism" (1976).]

See also CONSCIOUSNESS; EVASION; FREE WILL; MORALITY; RATIONALITY; THOUGHT/THINKING.

Foreign Policy.

We do need a policy based on long-range principles, i.e., an *ideology*. But a revision of our foreign policy, from its basic premises on up, is what today's anti-ideologists dare not contemplate. The worse its results, the louder our public leaders proclaim that our foreign policy is *bipartisan*.

A proper solution would be to elect statesmen—if such appeared—with a radically different foreign policy, a policy explicitly and proudly dedicated to the defense of America's rights and national self-interests, repudiating foreign aid and all forms of international self-immolation.

["The Wreckage of the Consensus," *CUI*, 226.]

The essence of capitalism's foreign policy is *free trade*—i.e., the abolition of trade barriers, of protective tariffs, of special privileges—the opening of the world's trade routes to free international exchange and competition among the private citizens of all countries dealing directly with one another. During the nineteenth century, it was free trade that liberated the world, undercutting and wrecking the remnants of feudalism and the statist tyranny of absolute monarchies.

["The Roots of War," *CUI*, 39.]

PLAYBOY: What about force in foreign policy? You have said that any free nation had the right to invade Nazi Germany during World War II . . .

RAND: Certainly.

PLAYBOY: . . . And that any free nation today has the moral right—though not the duty—to invade Soviet Russia, Cuba, or any other "slave pen." Correct?

RAND: Correct. A dictatorship—a country that violates the rights of its own citizens—is an outlaw and can claim no rights.

PLAYBOY: Would you actively advocate that the United States invade Cuba or the Soviet Union?

RAND: Not at present. I don't think it's necessary. I would advocate that which the Soviet Union fears above all else: economic boycott, I would advocate a blockade of Cuba and an economic boycott of Soviet Russia; and you would see both of those regimes collapse without the loss of a single American life.

PLAYBOY: Would you favor U.S. withdrawal from the United Nations?

RAND: Yes. I do not sanction the grotesque pretense of an organization allegedly devoted to world peace and human rights, which includes Soviet Russia, the worst aggressor and bloodiest butcher in history, as one of its members. The notion of protecting rights, with Soviet Russia among the protectors, is an insult to the concept of rights and to the intelligence of any man who is asked to endorse or sanction such an organization. I do not believe that an individual should cooperate with criminals, and, for all the same reasons, I do not believe that free countries should cooperate with dictatorships.

PLAYBOY: Would you advocate severing diplomatic relations with Russia?

RAND: Yes.

[*"Playboy's* Interview with Ayn Rand," pamphlet, 11.]

Russia, like Nazi Germany, like any bully, feeds on appeasement and will retreat placatingly at the first sound of firm opposition.

["U.S. Position on Cuba Endangered by U.N.,"
Los Angeles Times, Nov. 11, 1962.]

When certain statist groups, counting, apparently, on a total collapse of American self-esteem, dare go so far as to urge America's surrender into slavery without a fight, under the slogan *"Better Red Than Dead"*—the "conservatives" rush to proclaim that they prefer to be dead, thus helping to spread the idea that our only alternative is communism or destruction, forgetting that the only proper answer to an ultimatum of that kind is: *"Better See The Reds Dead."*

["Choose Your Issues," *TON*, Jan. 1962, 1.]

See also "COLLECTIVE RIGHTS"; COMMUNISM; DICTATORSHIP; DRAFT; FREEDOM; GOVERNMENT; IDEOLOGY; "ISOLATIONISM"; NATIONAL RIGHTS; PACIFISM; PEACE MOVEMENTS; SELF-DEFENSE; SELF-DETERMINATION of NATIONS; SOVIET RUSSIA; UNITED NATIONS; WAR.

Founding Fathers. The basic premise of the Founding Fathers was man's right to his own life, to his own liberty, to the pursuit of his own happiness—which means: man's right to exist for his own sake, neither sacrificing himself to others nor sacrificing others to himself; and that the political implementation of this right is a society where men deal with one another as *traders,* by voluntary exchange to mutual benefit.

["For the New Intellectual," *FNI,* 62; pb 53.]

The Founding Fathers were neither passive, death-worshipping mystics nor mindless, power-seeking looters; as a political group, they were a phenomenon unprecedented in history: they were *thinkers* who were also men of action. They had rejected the soul-body dichotomy, with its two corollaries: the impotence of man's mind and the damnation of this earth; they had rejected the doctrine of suffering as man's metaphysical fate, they proclaimed man's right to the pursuit of happiness and were determined to establish on earth the conditions required for man's proper existence, by the "unaided" power of their intellect.

[Ibid., 23; pb 25.]

In the modern world, under the influence of the pervasive new climate, a succession of thinkers developed a new conception of the nature of government. The most important of these men and the one with the greatest influence on America was John Locke. The political philosophy Locke bequeathed to the Founding Fathers is what gave rise to the new nation's distinctive institutions. That political philosophy is the social implementation of the Aristotelian spirit.

Throughout history the state had been regarded, implicitly or explicitly, as the ruler of the individual—as a sovereign authority (with or without supernatural mandate), an authority logically antecedent to the citizen and to which he must submit. The Founding Fathers challenged this primordial notion. They started with the premise of the *primacy and sovereignty of the individual.* The individual, they held, logically precedes the group or the institution of government. Whether or not any social organization exists, each man possesses certain *individual rights.* And "among these are Life, Liberty and the pursuit of Happiness"—or, in the words of a New Hampshire state document, "among which are the enjoying and defending life and liberty; acquiring, possessing, and protecting property; and in a word, of seeking and obtaining happiness."

[Leonard Peikoff, *OP,* 111; pb 109.]

The genius of the Founding Fathers was their ability not only to grasp the revolutionary ideas of the period, but to devise a means of implementing those ideas in practice, a means of translating them from the realm of philosophic abstraction into that of sociopolitical reality. By defining in detail the division of powers within the government and the ruling procedures, including the brilliant mechanism of checks and balances, they established a system whose operation and integrity were independent, so far as possible, of the moral character of any of its temporary officials—a system impervious, so far as possible, to subversion by an aspiring dictator or by the public mood of the moment.

The heroism of the Founding Fathers was that they recognized an unprecedented opportunity, the chance to create a country of individual liberty for the first time in history—and that they staked everything on their judgment: the new nation and their own "lives, fortunes, and sacred honor."

[Ibid., 114; pb 112.]

"I have sworn upon the altar of God, eternal hostility against every form of tyranny over the mind of man."

Jefferson—and the other Founding Fathers—meant it. They did not confine their efforts to the battle against theocracy and monarchy; they fought, on the same grounds, invoking the same principle of individual rights—against *democracy,* i.e., the system of unlimited majority rule. They recognized that the cause of freedom is not advanced by the multiplication of despots, and they did not propose to substitute the tyranny of a mob for that of a handful of autocrats. . . .

When the framers of the American republic spoke of "the people," they did not mean a collectivist organism one part of which was authorized to consume the rest. They meant a sum of individuals, each of whom—whether strong or weak, rich or poor—retains his inviolate guarantee of individual rights.

[Ibid., 113; pb 111.]

The political philosophy of America's Founding Fathers is so thoroughly buried under decades of statist misrepresentations on one side and empty lip-service on the other, that it has to be *re-discovered,* not ritualistically repeated. It has to be rescued from the shameful barnacles of platitudes now hiding it. It has to be *expanded*—because it was only a magnificent beginning, not a completed job, it was only a *political* philosophy without a full philosophical and *moral* foundation, which the "conservatives" cannot provide.

["It Is Earlier Than You Think," *TON,* Dec. 1964, 52.]

See also AMERICA; ARISTOTLE; CONSTITUTION; ENLIGHTEN-MENT, AGE of; FREEDOM; INDIVIDUALISM; INDIVIDUAL RIGHTS;

LIFE, RIGHT to; PURSUIT of HAPPINESS, RIGHT to; RELIGION; RE-PUBLIC; SOUL-BODY DICHOTOMY.

Fraud. A unilateral breach of contract involves an indirect use of physical force: it consists, in essence, of one man receiving the material values, goods or services of another, then refusing to pay for them and thus keeping them by force (by mere physical possession), not by right —i.e., keeping them without the consent of their owner. Fraud involves a similarly indirect use of force: it consists of obtaining material values without their owner's consent, under false pretenses or false promises.

["The Nature of Government," *VOS*, 150; pb 111.]

See also CONTRACTS; PHYSICAL FORCE.

Free Market. In a free economy, where no man or group of men can use physical coercion against anyone, economic power can be achieved only by *voluntary* means: by the voluntary choice and agreement of all those who participate in the process of production and trade. In a free market, all prices, wages, and profits are determined—not by the arbitrary whim of the rich or of the poor, not by anyone's "greed" or by anyone's need—but by the law of supply and demand. The mechanism of a free market reflects and sums up all the economic choices and decisions made by all the participants. Men trade their goods or services by mutual consent to mutual advantage, according to their own independent, uncoerced judgment. A man can grow rich only if he is able to offer better *values*—better products or services, at a lower price —than others are able to offer.

Wealth, in a free market, is achieved by a free, general, "democratic" vote—by the sales and the purchases of every individual who takes part in the economic life of the country. Whenever you buy one product rather than another, you are voting for the success of some manufacturer. And, in this type of voting, every man votes only on those matters which he is qualified to judge: on his own preferences, interests, and needs. No one has the power to decide for others or to substitute *his* judgment for theirs; no one has the power to appoint himself "the voice of the public" and to leave the public voiceless and disfranchised.

["America's Persecuted Minority: Big Business," *CUI*, 47.]

Intellectual freedom cannot exist without *political* freedom; political freedom cannot exist without *economic* freedom; *a free mind and a free market are corollaries.*

["For the New Intellectual," *FNI*, 23; pb 25.]

The free market represents the *social* application of an objective theory of values. Since values are to be discovered by man's mind, men must be free to discover them—to think, to study, to translate their knowledge into physical form, to offer their products for trade, to judge them, and to choose, be it material goods or ideas, a loaf of bread or a philosophical treatise. Since values are established contextually, every man must judge for himself, in the context of his own knowledge, goals, and interests. Since values are determined by the nature of reality, it is reality that serves as men's ultimate arbiter: if a man's judgment is right, the rewards are his; if it is wrong, he is his only victim.

["What Is Capitalism?" *CUI*, 24.]

Now observe that a free market does not level men down to some common denominator—that the intellectual criteria of the majority do not rule a free market or a free society—and that the exceptional men, the innovators, the intellectual giants, are not held down by the majority. In fact, it is the members of this exceptional minority who lift the whole of a free society to the level of their own achievements, while rising further and ever further.

A free market is a *continuous process* that cannot be held still, an upward process that demands the best (the most rational) of every man and rewards him accordingly. While the majority have barely assimilated the value of the automobile, the creative minority introduces the airplane. The majority learn by demonstration, the minority is free to demonstrate. The "philosophically objective" value of a new product serves as the teacher for those who are willing to exercise their rational faculty, each to the extent of his ability. Those who are unwilling remain unrewarded—as well as those who aspire to more than their ability produces. The stagnant, the irrational, the subjectivist have no power to stop their betters. . . .

The mental parasites—the imitators who attempt to cater to what they think is the public's known taste—are constantly being beaten by the innovators whose products raise the public's knowledge and taste to ever higher levels. It is in this sense that the free market is ruled, not by the consumers, but by the producers. The most successful ones are those who discover new fields of production, fields which had not been known to exist.

A given product may not be appreciated at once, particularly if it is too radical an innovation; but, barring irrelevant accidents, it wins in the long run. It is in this sense that the free market is not ruled by the intellectual criteria of the majority, which prevail only at and for any given moment; the free market is ruled by those who are able to see and plan long-range—and the better the mind, the longer the range.

[Ibid., 25.]

All the evils, abuses, and iniquities, popularly ascribed to businessmen and to capitalism, were not caused by an unregulated economy or by a free market, but by government intervention into the economy.

["America's Persecuted Minority: Big Business," *CUI*, 48.]

See also CAPITALISM; INTERVENTIONISM (ECONOMIC); MARKET VALUE.

Free Speech. Freedom of speech means freedom from interference, suppression or punitive action by the government—and nothing else. It does not mean the right to demand the financial support or the material means to express your views at the expense of other men who may not wish to support you. Freedom of speech includes the freedom not to agree, not to listen and not to support one's own antagonists. A "right" does not include the material implementation of that right by other men; it includes only the freedom to earn that implementation by one's own effort. Private citizens cannot use physical force or coercion; they cannot *censor* or *suppress* anyone's views or publications. Only the government can do so. And *censorship* is a concept that pertains *only* to governmental action.

["The Fascist New Frontier," pamphlet, 10.]

While people are clamoring about "economic rights," the concept of political rights is vanishing. It is forgotten that the right of free speech means the freedom to advocate one's views and to bear the possible consequences, including disagreement with others, opposition, unpopularity and lack of support. The political function of "the right of free speech" is to protect dissenters and unpopular minorities from forcible suppression—*not* to guarantee them the support, advantages and rewards of a popularity they have not gained.

The Bill of Rights reads: "Congress shall make no law . . . abridging the freedom of speech, or of the press . . ." It does not demand that private citizens provide a microphone for the man who advocates their destruction, or a passkey for the burglar who seeks to rob them, or a knife for the murderer who wants to cut their throats.

["Man's Rights," *VOS*, 133; pb 99.]

The communists and the Nazis are merely two variants of the same evil notion: collectivism. But both should be free to speak—evil ideas are dangerous only by default of men advocating better ideas.

[*The Objectivist Calendar,* June 1978.]

The difference between an exchange of ideas and an exchange of blows is self-evident. The line of demarcation between freedom of speech and freedom of action is established by the ban on the initiation of physical force.

[*"The Cashing-In: The Student 'Rebellion,' " CUI*, 258.]

[In regard to the lawsuit to prevent a Nazi group from marching in Skokie, Illinois:]

What I challenge (and not only because of that particular case) is the interpretation of demonstrations and of other *actions* as so-called "symbolic speech." When you lose the distinction between action and speech, you lose, eventually, the freedom of both. The Skokie case is a good illustration of that principle. There is no such thing as "symbolic speech." You do not have the right to parade through the public streets or to obstruct public thoroughfares. You have the right of assembly, yes, on your own property, and on the property of your adherents or your friends. But nobody has the "right" to clog the streets. The streets are only for passage. The hippies, in the 60s, should have been forbidden to lie down on city pavements. (They used to lie down across a street and cause dreadful traffic snarls, in order to display their views, to attract attention, to register a protest.) If they were permitted to do it, the Nazis should be permitted as well. Properly, both should have been forbidden. They may speak, yes. They may not take action at whim on public property.

[*The Objectivist Calendar*, June 1978.]

I want to state, for the record, my own view of what is called "hard-core" pornography. I regard it as unspeakably disgusting. I have not read any of the books or seen any of the current movies belonging to that category, and I do not intend ever to read or see them. The descriptions provided in legal cases, as well as the "modern" touches in "soft-core" productions, are sufficient grounds on which to form an opinion. The reason of my opinion is the opposite of the usual one: I do *not* regard sex as evil—I regard it as *good*, as one of the most important aspects of human life, too important to be made the subject of public *anatomical* display. But the issue here is not one's view of sex. The issue is freedom of speech and of the press—i.e., the right to hold *any* view and to express it.

It is not very inspiring to fight for the freedom of the purveyors of pornography or their customers. But in the transition to statism, every infringement of human rights has begun with the suppression of a given right's least attractive practitioners. In this case, the disgusting nature of the offenders makes it a good test of one's loyalty to a principle.

[*"Censorship: Local and Express," PWNI*, 211; pb 173.]

Only one aspect of sex is a legitimate field for legislation: the protection of minors and of unconsenting adults. Apart from criminal actions (such as rape), this aspect includes the need to protect people from being confronted with sights they regard as loathsome. (A corollary of the freedom to see and hear, is the freedom not to look or listen.) Legal restraints on certain types of public displays, such as posters or window displays, are proper—but this is an issue of procedure, of *etiquette*, not of morality. . . .

The rights of those who seek pornography would not be infringed by rules protecting the rights of those who find pornography offensive—e.g., sexually explicit posters may properly be forbidden in public places; warning signs, such as "For Adults Only," may properly be required of private places which are open to the public. This protects the unconsenting, and has nothing to do with censorship, i.e., with prohibiting thought or speech.

["Thought Control," *ARL*, III, 2, 2.]

See also CENSORSHIP; HUMAN RIGHTS and PROPERTY RIGHTS; INDIVIDUAL RIGHTS; PROPERTY RIGHTS.

Free Will.   That which you call your soul or spirit is your consciousness, and that which you call "free will" is your mind's freedom to think or not, the only will you have, your only freedom, the choice that controls all the choices you make and determines your life and your character.

[GS, *FNI*, 155; pb 127.]

To think is an act of choice. The key to what you so recklessly call "human nature," the open secret you live with, yet dread to name, is the fact that *man is a being of volitional consciousness.* Reason does not work automatically; thinking is not a mechanical process; the connections of logic are not made by instinct. The function of your stomach, lungs or heart is automatic; the function of your mind is not. In any hour and issue of your life, you are free to think or to evade that effort. But you are not free to escape from your nature, from the fact that *reason* is your means of survival—so that for *you*, who are a human being, the question "to be or not to be" is the question "to think or not to think." "A being of volitional consciousness has no automatic course of behavior. He needs a code of values to guide his actions.

[Ibid., 146; pb 120.]

Man's consciousness shares with animals the first two stages of its development: sensations and perceptions; but it is the third state, *con-*

ceptions, that makes him man. Sensations are integrated into perceptions automatically, by the brain of a man or of an animal. But to integrate perceptions into conceptions by a process of abstraction, is a feat that man alone has the power to perform—and he has to perform it *by choice.* The process of abstraction, and of concept-formation is a process of reason, of *thought;* it is not automatic nor instinctive nor involuntary nor infallible. Man has to initiate it, to sustain it and to bear responsibility for its results. The pre-conceptual level of consciousness is nonvolitional; volition begins with the first syllogism. Man has the choice to think or to evade—to maintain a state of full awareness or to drift from moment to moment, in a semi-conscious daze, at the mercy of whatever associational whims the unfocused mechanism of his consciousness produces.

["For the New Intellectual," *FNI*, 9; pb 14.]

Reason is the faculty that identifies and integrates the material provided by man's senses. It is a faculty that man has to exercise *by choice.* Thinking is not an automatic function. In any hour and issue of his life, man is free to think or to evade that effort. Thinking requires a state of full, focused awareness. The act of focusing one's consciousness is volitional. Man can focus his mind to a full, active, purposefully directed awareness of reality—or he can unfocus it and let himself drift in a semiconscious daze, merely reacting to any chance stimulus of the immediate moment, at the mercy of his undirected sensory-perceptual mechanism and of any random, associational connections it might happen to make.

When man unfocuses his mind, he may be said to be conscious in a subhuman sense of the word, since he experiences sensations and perceptions. But in the sense of the word applicable to man—in the sense of a consciousness which is aware of reality and able to deal with it, a consciousness able to direct the actions and provide for the survival of a human being—an unfocused mind is *not* conscious.

Psychologically, the choice "to think or not" is the choice "to focus or not." Existentially, the choice "to focus or not" is the choice "to be conscious or not." Metaphysically, the choice "to be conscious or not" is the choice of life or death. . . .

A process of thought is not automatic nor "instinctive" nor involuntary—nor *infallible.* Man has to initiate it, to sustain it and to bear responsibility for its results. He has to discover how to tell what is true or false and how to correct his own errors; he has to discover how to validate his concepts, his conclusions, his knowledge; he has to discover the rules of thought, *the laws of logic,* to direct his thinking. Nature gives him no automatic guarantee of the efficacy of his mental effort.

Nothing is given to man on earth except a potential and the material on which to actualize it. The potential is a superlative machine: his consciousness; but it is a machine without a spark plug, a machine of which his own will has to be the spark plug, the self-starter and the driver; *he* has to discover how to use it and *he* has to keep it in constant action. The material is the whole of the universe, with no limits set to the knowledge he can acquire and to the enjoyment of life he can achieve. But everything he needs or desires has to be learned, discovered and produced by *him*—by his own choice, by his own effort, by his own mind. . . .

That which [man's] survival requires is set by his nature and is not open to his choice. What *is* open to his choice is only whether he will discover it or not, whether he will choose the right goals and *values* or not. He is free to make the wrong choice, but not free to succeed with it. He is free to evade reality, he is free to unfocus his mind and stumble blindly down any road he pleases, but not free to avoid the abyss he refuses to see. Knowledge, for any conscious organism, is the means of survival; to a living consciousness, every *"is"* implies an *"ought."* Man is free to choose not to be conscious, but not free to escape the penalty of unconsciousness: destruction. Man is the only living species that has the power to act as his own destroyer—and that is the way he has acted through most of his history.

["The Objectivist Ethics," *VOS*, 13; pb 21.]

The faculty of volition operates in regard to the two fundamental aspects of man's life: consciousness and existence, i.e., his psychological action and his existential action, i.e., the formation of his own character and the course of action he pursues in the physical world.

["What Is Romanticism?" *RM*, 82; pb 100.]

A social environment can neither force a man to think nor prevent him from thinking. But a social environment can offer incentives or impediments; it can make the exercise of one's rational faculty easier or harder; it can encourage thinking and penalize evasion or vice versa.

["Our Cultural Value-Deprivation," *TO*, April 1966, 2.]

A man's volition is outside the power of other men. What the unalterable basic constituents are to nature, the attribute of a volitional consciousness is to the entity "man." Nothing can force a man to think. Others may offer him incentives or impediments, rewards or punishments, they may destroy his brain by drugs or by the blow of a club, but they cannot order his mind to function: *this* is in his exclusive, sovereign power. Man is neither to be obeyed nor to be commanded.

[The Metaphysical Versus the Man-Made," *PWNI*, 38; pb 31.]

Because man has free will, no human choice—and no phenomenon which is a product of human choice—is metaphysically necessary. In regard to any man-made fact, it is valid to claim that man *has* chosen thus, but it was not inherent in the nature of existence for him to have done so: he could have chosen otherwise.

Choice, however, is not chance. Volition is not an exception to the Law of Causality; it is a type of causation.

[Leonard Peikoff, "The Analytic-Synthetic Dichotomy," *ITOE*, 149.]

Man exists and his mind exists. Both are part of nature, both possess a specific identity. The attribute of volition does not contradict the fact of identity, just as the existence of living organisms does not contradict the existence of inanimate matter. Living organisms possess the power of self-initiated motion, which inanimate matter does not possess; man's consciousness possesses the power of self-initiated motion in the realm of cognition (thinking), which the consciousnesses of other living species do not possess. But just as animals are able to move only in accordance with the nature of their bodies, so man is able to initiate and direct his mental action only in accordance with the nature (the *identity*) of his consciousness. His volition is limited to his cognitive processes; he has the power to identify (and to conceive of rearranging) the elements of reality, but not the power to alter them. He has the power to use his cognitive faculty as its nature requires, but not the power to alter it nor to escape the consequences of its misuse. He has the power to suspend, evade, corrupt or subvert his perception of reality, but not the power to escape the existential and psychological disasters that follow. (The use or misuse of his cognitive faculty determines a man's choice of values, which determine his emotions and his character. It is in this sense that man is a being of self-made soul.)

["The Metaphysical Versus the Man-Made," *PWNI*, 32; pb 26.]

See also CAUSALITY; CONSCIOUSNESS; DETERMINISM; EVASION; FOCUS; METAPHYSICAL vs. MAN-MADE; MORALITY; PERCEPTION; ROMANTICISM; REASON; THOUGHT/THINKING; SENSATIONS; STANDARD of VALUE; VOLITIONAL.

Freedom. What is the basic, the essential, the crucial principle that differentiates freedom from slavery? It is the principle of voluntary action *versus* physical coercion or compulsion.

["America's Persecuted Minority: Big Business," *CUI*, 46.]

Freedom, in a political context, has only one meaning: *the absence of physical coercion.*

[Ibid.]

Since knowledge, thinking, and rational action are properties of the individual, since the choice to exercise his rational faculty or not depends on the individual, man's survival requires that those who think be free of the interference of those who don't. Since men are neither omniscient nor infallible, they must be free to agree or disagree, to cooperate or to pursue their own independent course, each according to his own rational judgment. Freedom is the fundamental requirement of man's mind.

A rational mind does not work under compulsion; it does not subordinate its grasp of reality to anyone's orders, directives, or controls; it does not sacrifice its knowledge, its view of the truth, to anyone's opinions, threats, wishes, plans, or "welfare." Such a mind may be hampered by others, it may be silenced, proscribed, imprisoned, or destroyed; it cannot be forced; a gun is not an argument. (An example and symbol of this attitude is Galileo.)

It is from the work and the inviolate integrity of such minds—from the intransigent innovators—that all of mankind's knowledge and achievements have come. (See *The Fountainhead.*) It is to such minds that mankind owes its survival. (See *Atlas Shrugged.*)

["What Is Capitalism?" *CUI,* 17.]

Foggy metaphors, sloppy images, unfocused poetry, and equivocations—such as "A hungry man is not free"—do not alter the fact that *only* political power is the power of physical coercion.

["America's Persecuted Minority: Big Business," *CUI,* 46.]

Freedom, in a political context, means freedom from government coercion. It does *not* mean freedom from the landlord, or freedom from the employer, or freedom from the laws of nature which do not provide men with automatic prosperity. It means freedom from the coercive power of the state—and nothing else.

["Conservatism: An Obituary," *CUI,* 192.]

The issue is *not* slavery for a "good" cause versus slavery for a "bad" cause; the issue is *not* dictatorship by a "good" gang versus dictatorship by a "bad" gang. The issue is freedom versus dictatorship.

[Ibid., 193.]

A "right" is a moral principle defining and sanctioning a man's freedom of action in a social context.

["Man's Rights," *VOS*, 124; pb 93.]

If one upholds freedom, one must uphold man's individual rights; if one upholds man's individual rights, one must uphold his right to his own life, to his own liberty, to the pursuit of his own happiness—which means: one must uphold a political system that guarantees and protects these rights—which means: the politico-economic system of *capitalism*.

["Conservatism: An Obituary," *CUI*, 193.]

During the nineteenth century, mankind came close to economic freedom, for the first and only time in history. Observe the results. Observe also that the degree of a country's freedom from government control, was the degree of its progress. America was the freest and achieved the most.

["The Intellectual Bankruptcy of Our Age," pamphlet, 7.]

Intellectual freedom cannot exist without *political* freedom; political freedom cannot exist without *economic* freedom; *a free mind and a free market are corollaries.*

["For the New Intellectual," *FNI*, 23; pb 25.]

These two—reason and freedom—are corollaries, and their relationship is reciprocal: when men are rational, freedom wins; when men are free, reason wins.

["Faith and Force: The Destroyers of the
Modern World," *PWNI*, 80; pb 66.]

Do not be misled . . . by an old collectivist trick which goes like this: there is no absolute freedom anyway, since you are not free to murder; society limits your freedom when it does not permit you to kill; therefore, society holds the right to limit your freedom in any manner it sees fit; therefore, drop the delusion of freedom—freedom is whatever society decides it is.

It is *not* society, nor any social right, that forbids you to kill—but the inalienable *individual* right of another man to live. This is not a "compromise" between two rights—but a line of division that preserves both rights untouched. The division is not derived from an edict of society—but from your own inalienable individual right. The definition of this limit is not set arbitrarily by society—but is implicit in the definition of your own right.

Within the sphere of your own rights, your freedom *is* absolute.

["Textbook of Americanism," pamphlet, 6.]

*See also CAPITALISM; DICTATORSHIP; ECONOMIC POWER vs. PO-
LITICAL POWER; FREE MARKET; GOVERNMENT; MIXED ECON-
OMY; PHYSICAL FORCE; RETALIATORY FORCE; STATISM.*

Freud. According to [Freud's] theory, the prime mover in human
nature is an unperceivable entity with a will and purpose of its own, the
unconscious—which is basically an "id," i.e., a contradictory, amoral "it"
seething with innate, bestial, primevally inherited, imperiously insistent
cravings or "instincts." In deadly combat with this element is man's
conscience or "superego," which consists essentially, not of reasoned
moral convictions, but of primitive, illogical, largely unconscious taboos
or categorical imperatives, representing the mores of the child's parents
(and ultimately of society), whose random injunctions every individual
unquestioningly "introjects" and cowers before. Caught in the middle
between these forces—between a psychopathic hippie screaming: satisfaction now! and a jungle chieftain intoning: tribal obedience!—sentenced by nature to ineradicable conflict, guilt, anxiety, and neurosis is
man, i.e., man's mind, his reason or "ego," the faculty which is able to
grasp reality, and which exists primarily to mediate between the clashing
demands of the psyche's two irrational masters.

As this theory makes eloquently clear, Freud's view of reason is fundamentally Kantian. Both men hold that human thought is ultimately
governed, not by a man's awareness of external fact, but by inner mental
elements independent of such fact. Both see the basic task of the mind
not as perception, but as creation, the creation of a subjective world in
compliance with the requirements of innate (or "introjected") mental
structures. . . .

The real root of the outrage his own doctrines provoked, Freud says
with a certain pride, is their assault on "the self-love of humanity."
Whatever the "wounds" that men have suffered from earlier scientific
theories, he explains, the "blow" of psychoanalysis "is probably the most
wounding." The blow, he states, is the idea that man is not "supreme in
his own soul," "that *the ego is not master in its own house.*" . . .

Freud offers to the world not man the dutiful, decorous nonperceiver
(as in Kant); not man the defeated plaything of grand-scale forces, such
as a malevolent reality or God or society or a "tragic flaw" (as in the
works of countless traditional cynics and pessimists); but man the defeated plaything of the gutter; man the smutty pawn shaped by sexual
aberrations and toilet training, itching to rape his mother, castrate his
father, hoard his excrement; man the sordid cheat who pursues science

because he is a frustrated voyeur, practices surgery because he is a sublimating sadist, and creates the *David* because he craves, secretly, to mold his own feces.

Man as a loathsomely small, ordure-strewn pervert: such is the sort of "wound" that Freud inflicted on the being who had once been defined, in a radiantly different age, as the "rational animal."

[Leonard Peikoff, *OP*, 211; pb 198.]

See also BEHAVIORISM; EMOTIONS; KANT, IMMANUEL; MAN; PSYCHOLOGY; RATIONALIZATION; SELF; SUBCONSCIOUS.

"Frozen Abstraction," Fallacy of.

A fallacy which may be termed "the fallacy of the frozen abstraction" . . . consists of substituting some one particular concrete for the wider abstract class to which it belongs—[e.g.,] substituting a specific ethics (altruism) for the wider abstraction of "ethics." Thus, a man may reject the theory of altruism and assert that he has accepted a rational code—but, failing to integrate his ideas, he continues unthinkingly to approach ethical questions in terms established by altruism.

["Collectivized Ethics," *VOS*, 104; pb 81.]

See also ABSTRACTIONS and CONCRETES; ALTRUISM; MORALITY; PRINCIPLES.

Fundamentality, Rule of.

Now observe, on the above example [the definition of "man"], the process of determining an essential characteristic: the rule of *fundamentality*. When a given group of existents has more than one characteristic distinguishing it from other existents, man must observe the relationships among these various characteristics and discover the one on which all the others (or the greatest number of others) depend, i.e., the fundamental characteristic without which the others would not be possible. This fundamental characteristic is the *essential* distinguishing characteristic of the existents involved, and the proper *defining* characteristic of the concept.

Metaphysically, a fundamental characteristic is that distinctive characteristic which makes the greatest number of others possible; epistemologically, it is the one that explains the greatest number of others.

For instance, one could observe that man is the only animal who speaks English, wears wristwatches, flies airplanes, manufactures lipstick, studies geometry, reads newspapers, writes poems, darns socks, etc. None of these is an essential characteristic: none of them explains the others; none of them applies to all men; omit any or all of them, assume a man who has never done any of these things, and he will still be a *man*. But observe that all these activities (and innumerable others) require a *conceptual grasp* of reality, that an animal would not be able to understand them, that they are the expressions and consequences of man's rational faculty, that an organism without that faculty would *not* be a man—and you will know why man's rational faculty is his *essential* distinguishing and defining characteristic.

[*ITOE*, 59.]

See also CONCEPTS; DEFINITIONS; IDENTITY.

G

Genocide. There is no principle by which genocide—a crime against a group of men—can be regarded as *morally* different from (or worse than) a crime against an individual: the difference is only quantitative, not moral. It can be easily demonstrated that Communism means and requires the extermination—the genocide, if you wish—of a particular human species: the men of ability.

[*The Objectivist Calendar*, June 1978.]

See also CRIME; INDIVIDUALISM; LIFE, RIGHT to; WAR.

Genus and Species. Just as a concept becomes a unit when integrated with others into a wider concept, so a genus becomes a single unit, a *species*, when integrated with others into a wider genus. For instance, "table" is a species of the genus "furniture," which is a species of the genus "household goods," which is a species of the genus "man-made objects." "Man" is a species of the genus "animal," which is a species of the genus "organism," which is a species of the genus "entity."

[*ITOE*, 54.]

See also CONCEPT-FORMATION; DEFINITIONS.

Goal-Directed Action. Only a *living* entity can have goals or can originate them. And it is only a living organism that has the capacity for self-generated, goal-directed action. On the *physical* level, the functions of all living organisms, from the simplest to the most complex—from the nutritive function in the single cell of an amoeba to the blood circulation in the body of a man—are actions generated by the organism itself and directed to a single goal: the maintenance of the organism's *life*.

When applied to physical phenomena, such as the automatic functions of an organism, the term "goal-directed" is not to be taken to mean "purposive" (a concept applicable only to the actions of a consciousness) and is not to imply the existence of any teleological principle operating in insentient nature. I use the term "goal-directed," in this context, to designate the fact that the automatic functions of living organisms are actions whose nature is such that they *result* in the preservation of an organism's life.

["The Objectivist Ethics," *VOS*, 6; pb 16.]

See also LIFE; ULTIMATE VALUE; VALUES.

God.   They claim that they perceive a mode of being superior to your existence on this earth. The mystics of spirit call it "another dimension," which consists of denying dimensions. The mystics of muscle call it "the future," which consists of denying the present. To exist is to possess identity. What identity are they able to give to their superior realm? They keep telling you what it is *not*, but never tell you what it *is*. All their identifications consist of negating: God is that which no human mind can know, they say—and proceed to demand that you consider it knowledge—God is non-man, heaven is non-earth, soul is non-body, virtue is non-profit, A is non-A, perception is non-sensory, knowledge is non-reason. Their definitions are not acts of defining, but of wiping out.

[GS, *FNI*, 184; pb 148.]

Every argument for God and every attribute ascribed to Him rests on a false metaphysical premise. None can survive for a moment on a correct metaphysics.

For instance, God is infinite. Nothing can be infinite, according to the Law of Identity. Everything is what it is, and nothing else. It is limited in its qualities and in its *quantity*: it is *this* much, and no more. "Infinite" as applied to quantity does not mean "very large": it means "larger than any specific quantity." That means: no specific quantity—i.e., a quantity without identity. This is prohibited by the Law of Identity.

Is God the creator of the universe? There can be no creation of something out of nothing. There is no nothing.

Is God omnipotent? Can he do *anything*? Entities can act only in accordance with their natures; nothing can make them violate their natures. . . .

"God" as traditionally defined is a systematic contradiction of every valid metaphysical principle. The point is wider than just the Judeo-Christian concept of God. No argument will get you from this world to a supernatural world. No reason will lead you to a world contradicting this one. No method of inference will enable you to leap from existence to a "super-existence."

[Leonard Peikoff, "The Philosophy of Objectivism"
lecture series (1976), Lecture 2.]

See also AGNOSTICISM; ATHEISM; FAITH; IDENTITY; MYSTICISM; MYSTICS of SPIRIT and of MUSCLE; NATURE; REASON; RELIGION; SUPERNATURALISM; UNIVERSE.

Gold Standard. Gold and economic freedom are inseparable, . . . the gold standard is an instrument of laissez-faire and . . . each implies and requires the other.

What medium of exchange will be acceptable to all participants in an economy is not determined arbitrarily. Where store-of-value considerations are important, as they are in richer, more civilized societies, the medium of exchange must be a durable commodity, usually a metal. A metal is generally chosen because it is homogeneous and divisible: every unit is the same as every other and it can be blended or formed in any quantity. Precious jewels, for example, are neither homogeneous nor divisible.

More important, the commodity chosen as a medium must be a luxury. Human desires for luxuries are unlimited and, therefore, luxury goods are always in demand and will always be acceptable. . . .

The term "luxury good" implies scarcity and high unit value. Having a high unit value, such a good is easily portable; for instance, an ounce of gold is worth a half-ton of pig iron. . . .

Under the gold standard, a free banking system stands as the protector of an economy's stability and balanced growth.

In the absence of the gold standard, there is no way to protect savings from confiscation through inflation. There is no safe store of value. If there were, the government would have to make its holding illegal, as was done in the case of gold. . . .

The financial policy of the welfare state requires that there be no way for the owners of wealth to protect themselves.

This is the shabby secret of the welfare statists' tirades against gold. Deficit spending is simply a scheme for the "hidden" confiscation of wealth. Gold stands in the way of this insidious process. It stands as a protector of property rights. If one grasps this, one has no difficulty in understanding the statists' antagonism toward the gold standard.

[Alan Greenspan, "Gold and Economic Freedom," *CUI*, 96.]

See also DEFICIT FINANCING; FREEDOM; INFLATION; MONEY; PROPERTY RIGHTS; SAVINGS; WELFARE STATE.

Good, the. All that which is proper to the life of a rational being is the good; all that which destroys it is the evil.

[GS, *FNI*, 149; pb 122.]

For centuries, the battle of morality was fought between those who claimed that your life belongs to God and those who claimed that it belongs to your neighbors—between those who preached that the good is self-sacrifice for the sake of ghosts in heaven and those who preached that the good is self-sacrifice for the sake of incompetents on earth. And no one came to say that your life belongs to you and that the good is to live it.

[Ibid., 145; pb 120.]

There are, in essence, three schools of thought on the nature of the good: the intrinsic, the subjective, and the objective. The *intrinsic* theory holds that the good is inherent in certain things or actions as such, regardless of their context and consequences, regardless of any benefit or injury they may cause to the actors and subjects involved. It is a theory that divorces the concept of "good" from beneficiaries, and the concept of "value" from valuer and purpose—claiming that the good is good in, by, and of itself.

The *subjectivist* theory holds that the good bears no relation to the facts of reality, that it is the product of a man's consciousness, created by his feelings, desires, "intuitions," or whims, and that it is merely an "arbitrary postulate" or an "emotional commitment."

The intrinsic theory holds that the good resides in some sort of reality, independent of man's consciousness; the subjectivist theory holds that the good resides in man's consciousness, independent of reality.

The *objective* theory holds that the good is neither an attribute of "things in themselves" nor of man's emotional states, but *an evaluation* of the facts of reality by man's consciousness according to a rational standard of value. (Rational, in this context, means: derived from the facts of reality and validated by a process of reason.) The objective theory holds that *the good is an aspect of reality in relation to man*—and that it must be discovered, not invented, by man. Fundamental to an objective theory of values is the question: Of value to whom and for what? An objective theory does not permit context-dropping or "concept-stealing"; it does not permit the separation of "value" from "purpose," of the good from beneficiaries, and of man's actions from reason.

["What Is Capitalism?" *CUI*, 21.]

See also EVIL; INTRINSIC THEORY of ETHICS; LIFE; MORALITY; MYSTICAL ETHICS; SOCIAL THEORY of ETHICS; STANDARD of VALUE; SUBJECTIVISM.

Government.   A government is an institution that holds the exclusive power to *enforce* certain rules of social conduct in a given geographical area.

["The Nature of Government," *VOS*, 144; pb 107.]

If physical force is to be barred from social relationships, men need an institution charged with the task of protecting their rights under an *objective* code of rules.

This is the task of a government—of a *proper* government—its basic task, its only moral justification and the reason why men do need a government.

A government is the means of placing the retaliatory use of physical force under objective control—i.e., under objectively defined laws.

[Ibid., 147; pb 109.]

The only proper purpose of a government is to protect man's rights, which means: to protect him from physical violence. A proper government is only a policeman, acting as an agent of man's self-defense, and, as such, may resort to force *only* against those who *start* the use of force. The only proper functions of a government are: the police, to protect you from criminals; the army, to protect you from foreign invaders; and the courts, to protect your property and contracts from breach or fraud by others, to settle disputes by rational rules, according to *objective* law. But a government that *initiates* the employment of force against men who had forced no one, the employment of armed compulsion against disarmed victims, is a nightmare infernal machine designed to annihilate morality: such a government reverses its only moral purpose and switches from the role of protector to the role of man's deadliest enemy, from the role of policeman to the role of a criminal vested with the right to the wielding of violence against victims deprived of the right of self-defense. Such a government substitutes for morality the following rule of social conduct: you may do whatever you please to your neighbor, provided your gang is bigger than his.

[GS, *FNI*, 231; pb 183.]

The source of the government's authority is "the consent of the governed." This means that the government is not the *ruler,* but the servant or *agent* of the citizens; it means that the government as such has no rights except the rights *delegated* to it by the citizens for a specific purpose.

["The Nature of Government," *VOS*, 149; pb 110.]

The difference between political power and any other kind of social "power," between a government and any private organization, is the fact that *a government holds a legal monopoly on the use of physical force.* This distinction is so important and so seldom recognized today that I must urge you to keep it in mind. Let me repeat it: *a government holds a legal monopoly on the use of physical force.*

No individual or private group or private organization has the legal power to initiate the use of physical force against other individuals or groups and to compel them to act against their own voluntary choice. Only a government holds that power. The nature of governmental action is: *coercive* action. The nature of political power is: the power to force obedience under threat of physical injury—the threat of property expropriation, imprisonment, or death.

["America's Persecuted Minority: Big Business," *CUI*, 46.]

The fundamental difference between private action and governmental action—a difference thoroughly ignored and evaded today—lies in the fact that a government holds a monopoly on the legal use of physical force. It has to hold such a monopoly, since it is the agent of restraining and combating the use of force; and for that very same reason, its actions have to be rigidly defined, delimited and circumscribed; no touch of whim or caprice should be permitted in its performance; it should be an impersonal robot, with the laws as its only motive power. If a society is to be free, its government has to be controlled.

Under a proper social system, a private individual is legally free to take any action he pleases (so long as he does not violate the rights of others), while a government official is bound by law in his every official act. A private individual may do anything except that which is legally *forbidden;* a government official may do nothing except that which is legally *permitted.*

This is the means of subordinating "might" to "right." This is the American concept of "a government of laws and not of men."

["The Nature of Government," *VOS*, 148; pb 109.]

See also ANARCHISM; CAPITALISM; CONSTITUTION; DICTATOR-SHIP; ECONOMIC POWER vs. POLITICAL POWER; FREEDOM; INDIVIDUAL RIGHTS; LAW, OBJECTIVE and NON-OBJECTIVE; PACIFISM; PHYSICAL FORCE; PROPERTY RIGHTS; RETALIATORY FORCE; SELF-DEFENSE; STATISM; WAR.

Government Grants and Scholarships.

The fundamental evil of government grants is the fact that men are forced to pay for the support of ideas diametrically opposed to their own. This is a profound violation of an individual's integrity and conscience. It is viciously wrong to take the money of rational men for the support of B.F. Skinner—or vice versa. The Constitution forbids a governmental establishment of religion, properly regarding it as a violation of individual rights. Since a man's beliefs are protected from the intrusion of force, the same

principle should protect his reasoned convictions and forbid governmental establishments in the field of thought.

["The Establishing of an Establishment," *PWNI*, 204; pb 168.]

How would Washington bureaucrats—or Congressmen, for that matter—know which scientist to encourage, particularly in so controversial
a field as social science? The safest method is to choose men who have
achieved some sort of reputation. Whether their reputation is deserved
or not, whether their achievements are valid or not, whether they rose
by merit, pull, publicity or accident, are questions which the awarders
do not and cannot consider. When personal judgment is inoperative (or
forbidden), men's first concern is not how to choose, but how to justify
their choice. This will necessarily prompt committee members, bureaucrats and politicians to gravitate toward "prestigious names." The result
is to help establish those already established—i.e., to entrench the status
quo.

The worst part of it is the fact that this method of selection is not
confined to the cowardly or the corrupt, that the *honest* official is obliged
to use it. The method is forced on him by the terms of the situation. To
pass an informed, independent judgment on the value of every appli-
cant or project in every field of science, an official would have to be a
universal scholar. If he consults "experts" in the field, the dilemma
remains: either he has to be a scholar who knows which experts to
consult—or he has to surrender his judgment to men trained by the
very professors he is supposed to judge. The awarding of grants to
famous "leaders," therefore, appears to him as the only fair policy—on
the premise that "somebody made them famous, somebody knows, even
if I don't."

(If the officials attempted to by-pass the "leaders" and give grants to
promising beginners, the injustice and irrationality of the situation
would be so much worse that most of them have the good sense not to
attempt it. If universal scholarship is required to judge the value of the
actual in every field, nothing short of omniscience would be required to
judge the value of the potential—as various privately sponsored contests
to discover future talent, even in limited fields, have amply demonstrated.)

Furthermore, the terms of the situation actually forbid an honest
official to use his own judgment. He is supposed to be "impartial" and
"fair"—while considering awards in the social sciences. An official who
does not have some knowledge and some convictions in *this* field, has no
moral right to be a public official. Yet the kind of "fairness" demanded
of him means that he must suspend, ignore or evade his own convictions
(these would be challenged as "prejudices" or "censorship") and pro-

ceed to dispose of large sums of public money, with incalculable consequences for the future of the country—without judging the nature of the recipients' ideas, i.e., without using any judgment whatever.

The awarders may hide behind the notion that, in choosing recognized "leaders," they are acting "democratically" and rewarding men chosen by the public. But there is no "democracy" in this field. Science and the mind do not work by vote or by consensus. The best-known is not necessarily the best (nor is the least-known, for that matter). Since no rational standards are applicable, the awarders' method leads to concern with personalities, not ideas; pull, not merit; "prestige," not truth. The result is: rule by press agents.

[Ibid., 202; pb 166.]

Many students of Objectivism are troubled by a certain kind of moral dilemma confronting them in today's society. We are frequently asked the questions: "Is it morally proper to accept scholarships, private or public?" and: "Is it morally proper for an advocate of capitalism to accept a government research grant or a government job?"

I shall hasten to answer: *"Yes"*—then proceed to explain and qualify it. There are many confusions on these issues, created by the influence and implications of the altruist morality.

There is nothing wrong in accepting *private* scholarships. The fact that a man has no claim on others (i.e., that it is not their moral duty to help him and that he cannot demand their help as his right) does not preclude or prohibit good will among men and does not make it immoral to offer or to accept voluntary, non-sacrificial assistance.

A different principle and different considerations are involved in the case of public (i.e., governmental) scholarships. The right to accept them rests on the right of the victims to the property (or some part of it) which was taken from them by force.

The recipient of a public scholarship is morally justified *only so long as he regards it as restitution and opposes all forms of welfare statism.* Those who advocate public scholarships, have no right to them; those who oppose them, have. If this sounds like a paradox, the fault lies in the moral contradictions of welfare statism, not in its victims.

Since there is no such thing as the right of some men to vote away the rights of others, and no such thing as the right of the government to seize the property of some men for the unearned benefit of others—the advocates and supporters of the welfare state are morally guilty of robbing their opponents, and the fact that the robbery is legalized makes it morally worse, not better. The victims do not have to add self-inflicted martyrdom to the injury done to them by others; they do not have to let the looters profit doubly, by letting them distribute the money exclusively to the parasites who clamored for it. Whenever the welfare-state laws offer them some small restitution, *the victims should take it.* . . .

The same moral principles and considerations apply to the issue of accepting social security, unemployment insurance or other payments of that kind. It is obvious, in such cases, that a man receives his own money which was taken from him by force, directly and specifically, without his consent, against his own choice. Those who advocated such laws are morally guilty, since they assumed the "right" to force employers and unwilling co-workers. But the victims, who opposed such laws, have a clear right to any refund of their own money—and they would not advance the cause of freedom if they left their money, unclaimed, for the benefit of the welfare-state administration.

The same moral principles and considerations apply to the issue of government research grants.

The growth of the welfare state is approaching the stage where virtually the only money available for scientific research will be government money. (The disastrous effects of this situation and the disgraceful state of government-sponsored science are apparent already, but that is a different subject. We are concerned here only with the moral dilemma of scientists.) Taxation is destroying private resources, while government money is flooding and taking over the field of research.

In these conditions, a scientist is morally justified in accepting government grants—*so long as he opposes all forms of welfare statism.* As in the case of scholarship-recipients, a scientist does not have to add self-martyrdom to the injustices he suffers.

["The Question of Scholarships," *TO,* June 1966, 11.]

See also ALTRUISM; CENSORSHIP; CHARITY; FREE SPEECH; WELFARE STATE.

Grammar. Grammar is a science dealing with the formulation of the proper methods of verbal expression and communication, i.e., the methods of organizing words (concepts) into sentences. Grammar pertains to the actions of consciousness, and involves a number of special concepts—such as conjunctions, which are concepts denoting relationships among thoughts ("and," "but," "or," etc.). These concepts are formed by retaining the distinguishing characteristics of the relationship and omitting the particular thoughts involved.

[*ITOE,* 48.]

Adverbs are concepts of the characteristics of motion (or action); they are formed by specifying a characteristic and omitting the measurements of the motion and of the entities involved—e.g., "rapidly," which may be applied to "walking" or "swimming" or "speaking," etc., with the measurement of what is "rapid" left open and depending, in any given case, on the type of motion involved.

Prepositions are concepts of relationships, predominantly of spatial or temporal relationships, among existents; they are formed by specifying the relationship and omitting the measurements of the existents and of the space or time involved—e.g., "on," "in," "above," "after," etc.

Adjectives are concepts of attributes or of characteristics. *Pronouns* belong to the category of concepts of entities. *Conjunctions* are concepts of relationships among thoughts, and belong to the category of concepts of consciousness.

[Ibid., 20.]

The purpose of conjunctions is verbal economy: they serve to integrate and/or condense the content of certain thoughts.

For instance, the word "and" serves to integrate a number of facts into one thought. If one says: "Smith, Jones and Brown are walking," the "and" indicates that the observation "are walking" applies to the three individuals named. Is there an object in reality corresponding to the word "and"? No. Is there a fact in reality corresponding to the word "and"? Yes. The fact is that three men are walking—and that the word "and" integrates into one thought a fact which otherwise would have to be expressed by: "Smith is walking. Jones is walking. Brown is walking."

The word "but" serves to indicate an exception to or a contradiction of the possible implications of a given thought. If one says: "She is beautiful, but dumb," the "but" serves to condense the following thoughts: "This girl is beautiful. Beauty is a positive attribute, a value. Before you conclude that this girl is valuable, you must consider also her negative attribute: she is dumb." If one says: "I work every day, but not on Sunday," the "but" indicates an exception and condenses the following: "I work on Monday. I work on Tuesday. (And so on, four more times.) My activity on Sunday is different: I do not work on Sunday."

(These examples are for the benefit of those victims of modern philosophy who are taught by Linguistic Analysis that there is no way to derive conjunctions from experience, i.e., from the facts of reality.)

[Ibid., 48.]

See also COMMUNICATION; CONCEPTS; LANGUAGE; LINGUISTIC ANALYSIS; PROPOSITIONS; WORDS.

Greece. *See Ancient Greece.*

Guild Socialism.   The particular form of economic organization, which is becoming more and more apparent in this country, as an outgrowth of the power of pressure groups, is one of the worst variants of statism: *guild socialism.* Guild socialism robs the talented young of their future—by freezing men into professional castes under rigid rules. It represents an open embodiment of the basic motive of most statists, though they usually prefer not to confess it: the entrenchment and protection of mediocrity from abler competitors, the shackling of the men of superior ability down to the mean average of their professions. That theory is not too popular among socialists (though it has its advocates)—but the most famous instance of its large-scale practice was Fascist Italy.

In the 1930's, a few perceptive men said that Roosevelt's New Deal was a form of guild socialism and that it was closer to Mussolini's system than to any other. They were ignored. Today, the evidence is unmistakable.

It was also said that if fascism ever came to the United States, it would come disguised as socialism.

["The New Fascism: Rule by Consensus," *CUI,* 218.]

The [student] rebels' notion that universities should be run by students and faculties was an open, explicit assault on the right attacked implicitly by all their other notions: the right of private property. And of all the various statist-collectivist systems, the one they chose as their goal is, politico-economically, the least practical; intellectually, the least defensible; morally, the most shameful: *guild socialism.*

Guild socialism is a system that abolishes the exercise of individual ability by chaining men into groups according to their line of work, and delivering the work into the group's power, as its exclusive domain, with the group dictating the rules, standards, and practices of how the work is to be done and who shall or shall not do it.

Guild socialism is the concrete-bound, routine-bound mentality of a savage, elevated into a social theory. Just as a tribe of savages seizes a piece of jungle territory and claims it as a monopoly by reason of the fact of being there—so guild socialism grants a monopoly, not on a jungle forest or waterhole, but on a factory or a university—not by reason of a man's ability, achievement, or even "public service," but by reason of the fact that he is there.

Just as savages have no concept of causes or consequences, of past or future, and no concept of efficacy beyond the muscular power of their tribe—so guild socialists, finding themselves in the midst of an industrial civilization, regard its institutions as phenomena of nature and see no reason why the gang should not seize them.

If there is any one proof of a man's incompetence, it is the stagnant mentality of a worker (or of a professor) who, doing some small, routine job in a vast undertaking, does not care to look beyond the lever of a machine (or the lectern of a classroom), does not choose to know how the machine (or the classroom) got there or what makes his job possible, and proclaims that the management of the undertaking is parasitical and unnecessary. Managerial work—the organization and integration of human effort into purposeful, large-scale, long-range activities—is, in the realm of action, what man's conceptual faculty is in the realm of cognition. It is beyond the grasp and, therefore, is the first target of the self-arrested, sensory-perceptual mentality.

If there is any one way to confess one's own mediocrity, it is the willingness to place one's work in the absolute power of a group, particularly a group of one's *professional colleagues.* Of any forms of tyranny, this is the worst; it is directed against a single human attribute: the mind —and against a single enemy: the innovator. The innovator, by definition, is the man who challenges the established practices of his profession. To grant a professional monopoly to any group, is to sacrifice human ability and abolish progress; to advocate such a monopoly, is to confess that one has nothing to sacrifice.

Guild socialism is the rule of, by, and for mediocrity. Its cause is a society's intellectual collapse; its consequence is a quagmire of stagnation; its historical example is the guild system of the Middle Ages (or, in modern times, the fascist system of Italy under Mussolini).

[*"The Cashing-in: The Student 'Rebellion,' "* CUI, 261.]

What makes guild socialism cruder than (but not different from) most statist-collectivist theories is the fact that it represents the other, the usually unmentioned, side of altruism: it is the voice, not of the givers, but of the receivers. While most altruistic theorists proclaim "the common good" as their justification, advocate self-sacrificial service to the "community," and keep silent about the exact nature or identity of the recipients of sacrifices—guild socialists brazenly declare themselves to be the recipients and present their claims to the community, demanding its services. If they want a monopoly on a given profession, they claim, the rest of the community must give up the right to practice it. If they want a university, they claim, the community must provide it.

[Ibid., 263.]

See also ALTRUISM; COLLECTIVISM; FASCISM/NAZISM; MEDIOC-RITY; NEW LEFT; SOCIALISM; STATISM.

H

Happiness. Happiness is the successful state of life, pain is an agent of death. Happiness is that state of consciousness which proceeds from the achievement of one's values. A morality that dares to tell you to find happiness in the renunciation of your happiness—to value the failure of your values—is an insolent negation of morality. A doctrine that gives you, as an ideal, the role of a sacrificial animal seeking slaughter on the altars of others, is giving you *death* as your standard. By the grace of reality and the nature of life, man—every man—is an end in himself, he exists for his own sake, and the achievement of his own happiness is his highest moral purpose.

But neither life nor happiness can be achieved by the pursuit of irrational whims. Just as man is free to attempt to survive in any random manner, but will perish unless he lives as his nature requires, so he is free to seek his happiness in any mindless fraud, but the torture of frustration is all he will find, unless he seeks the happiness proper to man. The purpose of morality is to teach you, not to suffer and die, but to enjoy yourself and live.

[GS, *FNI*, 150; pb 123.]

Happiness is not to be achieved at the command of emotional whims. Happiness is not the satisfaction of whatever irrational wishes you might blindly attempt to indulge. Happiness is a state of non-contradictory joy —a joy without penalty or guilt, a joy that does not clash with any of your values and does not work for your own destruction, not the joy of escaping from your mind, but of using your mind's fullest power, not the joy of faking reality, but of achieving values that are real, not the joy of a drunkard, but of a producer. Happiness is possible only to a rational man, the man who desires nothing but rational goals, seeks nothing but rational values and finds his joy in nothing but rational actions.

Just as I support my life, neither by robbery nor alms, but by my own effort, so I do not seek to derive my happiness from the injury or the favor of others, but earn it by my own achievement. Just as I do not consider the pleasure of others as the goal of my life, so I do not consider my pleasure as the goal of the lives of others. Just as there are no contradictions in my values and no conflicts among my desires—so there are no victims and no conflicts of interest among rational men,

men who do not desire the unearned and do not view one another with a cannibal's lust, men who neither make sacrifices nor accept them.

[Ibid., 162; pb 132.]

In psychological terms, the issue of man's survival does not confront his consciousness as an issue of "life or death," but as an issue of "happiness or suffering." Happiness is the successful state of life, suffering is the warning signal of failure, of death. Just as the pleasure-pain mechanism of man's body is an automatic indicator of his body's welfare or injury, a barometer of its basic alternative, life or death—so the emotional mechanism of man's consciousness is geared to perform the same function, as a barometer that registers the same alternative by means of two basic emotions: joy or suffering. Emotions are the automatic results of man's value judgments integrated by his subconscious; emotions are estimates of that which furthers man's values or threatens them, that which is *for* him or *against* him—lightning calculators giving him the sum of his profit or loss.

But while the standard of value operating the physical pleasure-pain mechanism of man's body is automatic and innate, determined by the nature of his body—the standard of value operating his emotional mechanism, is *not*. Since man has no automatic knowledge, he can have no automatic values; since he has no innate ideas, he can have no innate value judgments.

["The Objectivist Ethics," *VOS*, 23; pb 27.]

Happiness is that state of consciousness which proceeds from the achievement of one's values. If a man values productive work, his happiness is the measure of his success in the service of his life. But if a man values destruction, like a sadist—or self-torture, like a masochist— or life beyond the grave, like a mystic—or mindless "kicks," like the driver of a hotrod car—*his* alleged happiness is the measure of his success in the service of his own destruction. It must be added that the emotional state of all those irrationalists cannot be properly designated as happiness or even as pleasure: it is merely a moment's *relief* from their chronic state of terror.

Neither life nor happiness can be achieved by the pursuit of irrational whims. Just as man is free to attempt to survive by any random means, as a parasite, a moocher or a looter, but not free to succeed at it beyond the range of the moment—so he is free to seek his happiness in any irrational fraud, any whim, any delusion, any mindless escape from reality, but not free to succeed at it beyond the range of the moment nor to escape the consequences.

[Ibid., 24; pb 28.]

The maintenance of life and the pursuit of happiness are not two separate issues. To hold one's own life as one's ultimate value, and one's own happiness as one's highest purpose are two aspects of the same achievement. Existentially, the activity of pursuing rational goals is the activity of maintaining one's life; psychologically, its result, reward and concomitant is an emotional state of happiness. It is by experiencing happiness that one lives one's life, in any hour, year or the whole of it. And when one experiences the kind of pure happiness that is an end in itself—the kind that makes one think: "*This* is worth living for"—what one is greeting and affirming in emotional terms is the metaphysical fact that *life* is an end in itself.

But the relationship of cause to effect cannot be reversed. It is only by accepting "man's life" as one's primary and by pursuing the rational values it requires that one can achieve happiness—*not* by taking "happiness" as some undefined, irreducible primary and then attempting to live by its guidance. If you achieve that which is the good by a rational standard of value, it will necessarily make you happy; but that which makes you happy, by some undefined emotional standard, is not necessarily the good. To take "whatever makes one happy" as a guide to action means: to be guided by nothing but one's emotional whims. Emotions are not tools of cognition; to be guided by whims—by desires whose source, nature and meaning one does not know—is to turn oneself into a blind robot, operated by unknowable demons (by one's stale evasions), a robot knocking its stagnant brains out against the walls of reality which it refuses to see.

[Ibid., 25; pb 29.]

See also BENEVOLENT UNIVERSE PREMISE; EMOTIONS; HEDONISM; LIFE; PLEASURE AND PAIN; SUFFERING; ULTIMATE VALUE; VALUES; WHIMS/WHIM-WORSHIP.

Hatred of the Good for Being the Good. *See Envy/Hatred of the Good for Being the Good.*

Hedonism.

I am profoundly opposed to the philosophy of hedonism. Hedonism is the doctrine which holds that the good is whatever gives you pleasure and, therefore, pleasure is the standard of morality. Objectivism holds that the good must be defined by a rational standard of value, that pleasure is not a first cause, but only a consequence, that only the pleasure which proceeds from a rational value judgment can be regarded as moral, that pleasure, as such, is not a guide to action nor a standard of morality. To say that pleasure should be the standard of morality simply means that whichever values you happen to have chosen, consciously or subconsciously, rationally or irrationally, are right and moral. This means that you are to be guided by chance feelings, emotions and whims, not by your mind. My philosophy is the opposite of hedonism. I hold that one cannot achieve happiness by random, arbitrary or subjective means. One can achieve happiness only on the basis of rational values. By rational values, I do not mean anything that a man may arbitrarily or blindly declare to be rational. It is the province of morality, of the science of ethics, to define for men what is a rational standard and what are the rational values to pursue.

["*Playboy*'s Interview with Ayn Rand," pamphlet, 8.]

This is the fallacy inherent in *hedonism*—in any variant of ethical hedonism, personal or social, individual or collective. "Happiness" can properly be the *purpose* of ethics, but *not* the *standard*. The task of ethics is to define man's proper code of values and thus to give him the means of achieving happiness. To declare, as the ethical hedonists do, that "the proper value is whatever gives you pleasure" is to declare that "the proper value is whatever you happen to value"—which is an act of intellectual and philosophical abdication, an act which merely proclaims the futility of ethics and invites all men to play it deuces wild.

["The Objectivist Ethics," *VOS*, 26; pb 29.]

In practice, men have no way of obeying the tenets of hedonism, except by taking *their already formed feelings*—their desires and aversions, their loves and fears—as *the given*, as irreducible primaries the satisfaction of which is the purpose of morality, regardless of whether the value-judgments that caused these feelings are rational or irrational, consistent or contradictory, consonant with reality or in flagrant defiance of it.

Objectivism holds that such a policy is suicidal; that if man is to survive, he needs the guidance of an *objective* and *rational* morality, a code of values based on and derived from man's nature as a specific type of living organism, and the nature of the universe in which he lives. Objectivism rejects any subjectivist ethics that begins, not with facts, but with: "I (we, they) *wish* . . ." Which means: it rejects hedonism of any variety.

[Leonard Peikoff, "Ethical Hedonism," *TON*, Feb. 1962, 7.]

See also EMOTIONS; HAPPINESS; PLEASURE *and* PAIN; UTILITAR-IANISM; STANDARD *of* VALUE; SUBJECTIVISM.

Hierarchy of Knowledge. Concepts have a hierarchical structure, i.e., . . . the higher, more complex abstractions are derived from the simpler, basic ones (starting with the concepts of perceptually given concretes).

[*ITOE*, 41.]

[There is a] long conceptual chain that starts from simple, ostensive definitions and rises to higher and still higher concepts, forming a hierarchical structure of knowledge so complex that no electronic computer could approach it. It is by means of such chains that man has to acquire and retain his knowledge of reality.

["The Psycho-Epistemology of Art," *RM*, 20; pb 18.]

Starting from the base of conceptual development—from the concepts that identify perceptual concretes—the process of cognition moves in two interacting directions: toward more extensive and more intensive knowledge, toward wider integrations and more precise differentiations. Following the process and *in accordance with cognitive evidence*, earlier-formed concepts are integrated into wider ones or subdivided into narrower ones.

[*ITOE*, 24.]

Observe that the concept "furniture" is an abstraction one step further removed from perceptual reality than any of its constituent concepts. "Table" is an abstraction, since it designates *any* table, but its meaning can be conveyed simply by pointing to one or two perceptual objects. There is no such perceptual object as "furniture"; there are only tables, chairs, beds, etc. The meaning of "furniture" cannot be grasped unless one has first grasped the meaning of its constituent concepts; these are its link to reality. (On the lower levels of an unlimited conceptual chain, this is an illustration of the hierarchical structure of concepts.)

[Ibid., 28.]

The first concepts man forms are concepts of entities—since entities are the only primary existents. (Attributes cannot exist by themselves, they are merely the characteristics of entities; motions are motions of entities; relationships are relationships among entities.)

[Ibid., 18.]

Since the definition of a concept is formulated in terms of other concepts, it enables man, not only to identify and *retain* a concept, but also to establish the relationships, the hierarchy, the *integration* of all his concepts and thus the integration of his knowledge. Definitions preserve, not the chronological order in which a given man may have learned concepts, but the *logical* order of their hierarchical interdependence.

[Ibid., 52.]

To know the exact meaning of the concepts one is using, one must know their correct definitions, one must be able to retrace the specific (logical, not chronological) steps by which they were formed, and one must be able to demonstrate their connection to their base in perceptual reality.

[Ibid., 67.]

See also AXIOMATIC CONCEPTS; AXIOMS; GENUS *and* SPECIES; IRREDUCIBLE PRIMARIES; KNOWLEDGE; LOGIC; PERCEPTION; "STOLEN CONCEPT," FALLACY *of;* TABULA RASA.

History.

Contrary to the prevalent views of today's alleged scholars, history is *not* an unintelligible chaos ruled by chance and whim—historical trends *can* be predicted, and changed—men are *not* helpless, blind, doomed creatures carried to destruction by incomprehensible forces beyond their control.

There is only one power that determines the course of history, just as it determines the course of every individual life: the power of man's rational faculty—*the power of ideas.* If you know a man's convictions, you can predict his actions. If you understand the dominant philosophy of a society, you can predict its course. But convictions and philosophy are matters open to man's choice.

There is no fatalistic, predetermined historical necessity. *Atlas Shrugged* is not a prophecy of our unavoidable destruction, but a manifesto of our power to avoid it, if we choose to change our course.

It is the philosophy of the mysticism-altruism-collectivism axis that has brought us to our present state and is carrying us toward a finale such as that of the society presented in *Atlas Shrugged.* It is only the philosophy of the reason-individualism-capitalism axis that can save us and carry us, instead, toward the Atlantis projected in the last two pages of my novel.

["Is Atlas Shrugging?" *CUI*, 165.]

Just as a man's actions are preceded and determined by some form of idea in his mind, so a society's existential conditions are preceded and determined by the ascendancy of a certain philosophy among those whose job is to deal with ideas. The events of any given period of history are the result of the thinking of the preceding period. The nineteenth century—with its political freedom, science, industry, business, trade, all the necessary conditions of material progress—was the result and the last achievement of the intellectual power released by the Renaissance. The men engaged in those activities were still riding on the remnants of an Aristotelian influence in philosophy, particularly on an Aristotelian epistemology (more implicitly than explicitly).

["For the New Intellectual," *FNI*, 27; pb 28.]

History is made by minorities—or, more precisely, history is made by intellectual movements, which are created by minorities. Who belongs to these minorities? Anyone who is able and willing actively to concern himself with intellectual issues. Here, it is not quantity, but *quality* that counts (the quality—and consistency—of the ideas one is advocating).

["What Can One Do?" *PWNI*, 245; pb 200.]

The battle of human history is fought and determined by those who are predominantly consistent, those who, for good or evil, are committed to and motivated by their chosen psycho-epistemology and its corollary view of existence.

["For the New Intellectual," *FNI*, 18; pb 21.]

See also ANCIENT GREECE; CIVILIZATION; CULTURE; DARK AGES; ENLIGHTENMENT, AGE of; INTELLECTUALS; MIDDLE AGES; NINETEENTH CENTURY; PHILOSOPHY; RENAISSANCE; TRADITION.

Honesty. Honesty is the recognition of the fact that the unreal is unreal and can have no value, that neither love nor fame nor cash is a value if obtained by fraud—that an attempt to gain a value by deceiving the mind of others is an act of raising your victims to a position higher than reality, where you become a pawn of their blindness, a slave of their non-thinking and their evasions, while their intelligence, their rationality, their perceptiveness becomes the enemies you have to dread and flee—that you do not care to live as a dependent, least of all a dependent on the stupidity of others, or as a fool whose source of values is the fools he succeeds in fooling—that honesty is not a social duty, not a sacrifice for the sake of others, but the most profoundly selfish virtue man can practice: his refusal to sacrifice the reality of his own existence to the deluded consciousness of others.

[GS, *FNI*, 158; pb 129.]

Self-esteem is reliance on one's power to think. It cannot be replaced by one's power to deceive. The self-confidence of a scientist and the self-confidence of a con man are not interchangeable states, and do not come from the same psychological universe. The success of a man who deals with reality augments his self-confidence. The success of a con man augments his panic.

The intellectual con man has only one defense against panic: the momentary relief he finds by succeeding at further and further frauds.

["The Comprachicos," *NL*, 181.]

The mark of an honest man . . . is that he means what he says and knows what he means.

["Textbook of Americanism," 12.]

Intellectual honesty consists in taking ideas seriously. To take ideas seriously means that you intend to live by, to *practice*, any idea you accept as true.

["Philosophical Detection," *PWNI*, 19; pb 16.]

Intellectual honesty [involves] knowing what one does know, constantly expanding one's knowledge, and *never* evading or failing to correct a contradiction. This means: the development of an *active* mind as a permanent attribute.

["What Can One Do?" *PWNI*, 247; pb 201.]

See also EVASION; INDEPENDENCE; INTEGRITY; MORALITY; RATIONALITY; TRUTH; VIRTUE.

Honor.   Honor is self-esteem made visible in action.

["Philosophy: Who Needs It," *PWNI*, 12; pb 10.]

See also MORALITY; PRIDE; SELF-ESTEEM; VALUES.

Hostility.   Caused by a profound self-doubt, self-condemnation and fear, hostility is a type of projection that directs toward other people the hatred which the hostile person feels toward himself. Blaming the evil of others for his own shortcomings, he feels a chronic need to justify himself by demonstrating their evil, by seeking it, by hunting for it— and by inventing it.

["The Psychology of Psychologizing," *TO*, March 1971, 3.]

See also AMORALISM; EMOTIONS; ENVY/HATRED of the GOOD for BEING the GOOD; EVASION.

Human Rights and Property Rights.   The modern mystics of muscle who offer you the fraudulent alternative of "human rights" versus "property rights," as if one could exist without the other, are making a last, grotesque attempt to revive the doctrine of soul versus body. Only a ghost can exist without material property; only a slave can work with no right to the product of his effort. The doctrine that "human rights" are superior to "property rights" simply means that some human beings have the right to make property out of others; since the competent have nothing to gain from the incompetent, it means the right of the incompetent to own their betters and to use them as productive cattle. Whoever regards this as human and right, has no right to the title of "human."

[GS, *FNI*, 230; pb 183.]

There is no such dichotomy as "human rights" versus "property rights." No human rights can exist without property rights. Since material goods are produced by the mind and effort of individual men, and are needed to sustain their lives, if the producer does not own the result of his effort, he does not own his life. To deny property rights means to turn men into property owned by the state. Whoever claims the "right" to "redistribute" the wealth produced by others is claiming the "right" to treat human beings as chattel.

["The Monument Builders," *VOS*, 120; pb 91.]

See also FASCISM and COMMUNISM/SOCIALISM; FREEDOM; INDIVIDUAL RIGHTS; PROPERTY RIGHTS; SOUL-BODY DICHOTOMY.

Humility.   There is no more despicable coward than the man who deserted the battle for his joy, fearing to assert his right to existence, lacking the courage and the loyalty to life of a bird or a flower reaching for the sun. Discard the protective rags of that vice which you call a virtue: humility—learn to value yourself, which means: to fight for your happiness—and when you learn that *pride* is the sum of all virtues, you will learn to live like a man.

[GS, *FNI*, 225; pb 179.]

Humility and presumptuousness are always two sides of the same premise, and always share the task of filling the space vacated by self-esteem in a collectivized mentality. The man who is willing to serve as the means to the ends of others, will necessarily regard others as the means to *his* ends.

["Collectivized Ethics," *VOS*, 105; pb 81.]

Self-abasement is the antithesis of morality. If a man has acted immorally, but regrets it and wants to atone for it, it is not self-abasement that prompts him, but some remnant of love for moral values—and it is not self-abasement that he expresses, but a longing to regain his self-esteem. Humility is not a recognition of one's failings, but a rejection of morality. "I am no good" is a statement that may be uttered only in the past tense. To say: "I am no good" is to declare: "—and I never intend to be any better."

["Moral Inflation," *ARL,* III, 13, 1.]

See also ALTRUISM; MORALITY; PRIDE; SACRIFICE; SELF-ESTEEM.

Humor. Humor is the denial of metaphysical importance to that which you laugh at. The classic example: you see a very snooty, very well dressed dowager walking down the street, and then she slips on a banana peel. . . . What's funny about it? It's the contrast of the woman's pretensions to reality. She acted very grand, but reality undercut it with a plain banana peel. That's the denial of the metaphysical validity or importance of the pretensions of that woman.

Therefore, humor is a destructive element—which is quite all right, but its value and its morality depend on what it is that you are laughing at. If what you are laughing at is the evil in the world (provided that you take it seriously, but occasionally you permit yourself to laugh at it), that's fine. [To] laugh at that which is good, at heroes, at values, and above all at *yourself* [is] monstrous. . . . The worst evil that you can do, psychologically, is to laugh at yourself. That means spitting in your own face.

[Ayn Rand, question period following Lecture 11 of Leonard Peikoff's series "The Philosophy of Objectivism" (1976).]

Humor is not an unconditional virtue; its moral character depends on its object. To laugh at the contemptible, is a virtue; to laugh at the good, is a hideous vice. Too often, humor is used as the camouflage of moral cowardice.

["Bootleg Romanticism," *RM,* 126; pb 133.]

See also METAPHYSICAL; MORAL COWARDICE; SELF-ESTEEM; VIR-TUE.

I

Identity. To exist is to be something, as distinguished from the nothing of non-existence, it is to be an entity of a specific nature made of specific attributes. Centuries ago, the man who was—no matter what his errors—the greatest of your philosophers, has stated the formula defining the concept of existence and the rule of all knowledge: *A is A.* A thing is itself. You have never grasped the meaning of his statement. I am here to complete it: Existence is Identity, Consciousness is Identification.

Whatever you choose to consider, be it an object, an attribute or an action, the law of identity remains the same. A leaf cannot be a stone at the same time, it cannot be all red and all green at the same time, it cannot freeze and burn at the same time. A is A. Or, if you wish it stated in simpler language: You cannot have your cake and eat it, too.

Are you seeking to know what is wrong with the world? All the disasters that have wrecked your world, came from your leaders' attempt to evade the fact that A is A. All the secret evil you dread to face within you and all the pain you have ever endured, came from your own attempt to evade the fact that A is A. The purpose of those who taught you to evade it, was to make you forget that Man is Man.

[GS, *FNI*, 152; pb 125.]

A thing is—what it is; its characteristics constitute its identity. An existent apart from its characteristics, would be an existent apart from its identity, which means: a nothing, a non-existent.

[Leonard Peikoff, "The Analytic-Synthetic Dichotomy," *ITOE*, 142.]

No matter how eagerly you claim that the goal of your mystic wishing is a higher mode of life, the rebellion against identity is the wish for non-existence. The desire not to be anything is the desire not to be.

[GS, *FNI*, 187; pb 150.]

A characteristic is an aspect of an existent. It is not a disembodied, Platonic universal. Just as a concept cannot mean existents apart from their identity, so it cannot mean identities apart from that which exists. Existence *is* Identity.

[Leonard Peikoff, "The Analytic-Synthetic Dichotomy," *ITOE*, 143.]

208

The concept "identity" does not indicate the particular natures of the existents it subsumes; it merely underscores the primary fact that *they are what they are.*

[*ITOE*, 78.]

The law of identity does not permit you to have your cake and eat it, too. The law of causality does not permit you to eat your cake *before* you have it. . . .

The law of causality is the law of identity applied to action. All actions are caused by entities. The nature of an action is caused and determined by the nature of the entities that act; a thing cannot act in contradiction to its nature.

[GS, *FNI*, 188; pb 152.]

The (implicit) concept "existent" undergoes three stages of development in man's mind. The first stage is a child's awareness of objects, of things—which represents the (implicit) concept *"entity."* The second and closely allied stage is the awareness of specific, particular things which he can recognize and distinguish from the rest of his perceptual field—which represents the (implicit) concept *"identity."*

[*ITOE*, 6.]

They proclaim that there is no law of identity, that nothing exists but change, and blank out the fact that *change* presupposes the concepts of what changes, from what and to what, that without the law of identity no such concept as "change" is possible.

[GS, *FNI*, 192; pb 154.]

See also ARISTOTLE; AXIOMATIC CONCEPTS; AXIOMS; CAUSALITY; CHARACTER; ENTITY; EXISTENCE; IMPLICIT KNOWLEDGE; IN-FINITY; LOGIC; SUBJECTIVISM; ZERO, REIFICATION of.

Ideology. A political ideology is a set of principles aimed at establishing or maintaining a certain social system; it is a program of long-range action, with the principles serving to unify and integrate particular steps into a consistent course. It is only by means of principles that men can project the future and choose their actions accordingly.

Anti-ideology consists of the attempts to shrink men's minds down to the range of the immediate moment, without regard to past or future, without context or memory—above all, without memory, so that contradictions cannot be detected, and errors or disasters can be blamed on the victims.

In anti-ideological practice, principles are used implicitly and are relied upon to disarm the opposition, but are never acknowledged, and are switched at will, when it suits the purpose of the moment. Whose purpose? The gang's. Thus men's moral criterion becomes, not "my view of the good—or of the right—or of the truth," but "my *gang*, right or wrong."

["The Wreckage of the Consensus," *CUI*, 222.]

A majority without an ideology is a helpless mob, to be taken over by anyone. . . . Political freedom requires much more than the people's wish. It requires an enormously complex knowledge of political theory and of how to implement it in practice.

["Theory and Practice," *CUI*, 138.]

See also POLITICS; PHILOSOPHY; PRINCIPLES; REVOLUTION vs. PUTSCH.

Imagination.   Man's imagination is nothing more than the ability to rearrange the things he has observed in reality.

["The Metaphysical Versus the Man-Made," *PWNI*, 31; pb 25.]

Imagination is not a faculty for escaping reality, but a faculty for *rearranging* the elements of reality to achieve human values; it requires and presupposes some knowledge of the elements one chooses to rearrange. An imagination divorced from knowledge has only one product: a nightmare. . . . An imagination that replaces cognition is one of the surest ways to create neurosis.

[Ayn Rand, quoted in "The Montessori Method," *TO*, July 1970, 7.]

See also CONSCIOUSNESS; CREATION; KNOWLEDGE; MENTAL HEALTH.

Immorality.   *See Evil.*

Implicit Knowledge.   Axiomatic concepts identify explicitly what is merely implicit in the consciousness of an infant or of an animal. (Implicit knowledge is passively held material which, to be grasped, requires a special focus and process of consciousness—a process which an infant learns to perform eventually, but which an animal's consciousness is unable to perform.)

[*ITOE*, 76.]

Man grasps [the concept of "existent"] *implicitly* on the perceptual level—i.e., he grasps the constituents of the concept "existent," the data which are later to be integrated by that concept. It is this implicit knowledge that permits his consciousness to develop further.

[Ibid., 6.]

That which is merely implicit is not in men's conscious control; they can lose it by means of other implications, without knowing what it is that they are losing or when or why.

["For the New Intellectual," *FNI*, 62; pb 53.]

See also CONCEPTS; EXISTENT; KNOWLEDGE; PERCEPTION; UNIT.

Important. *See Metaphysical Value-Judgments.*

Inalienability.   When we say that we hold individual rights to be *inalienable*, we must mean *just that*. *Inalienable* means that which we may not take away, suspend, infringe, restrict or violate—not ever, not at any time, not for any purpose whatsoever.

You cannot say that "man has inalienable rights except in cold weather and on every second Tuesday," just as you cannot say that "man has inalienable rights except in an emergency," or "man's rights cannot be violated except for a good purpose."

Either man's rights are inalienable, or they are not. You cannot say a thing such as "semi-inalienable" and consider yourself either honest or sane. When you begin making conditions, reservations and exceptions, you admit that there is something or someone above man's rights, who may violate them at his discretion. Who? Why, society—that is, the Collective. For what reason? For the good of the Collective. Who decides when rights should be violated? The Collective. If this is what you believe, move over to the side where you belong and admit that you are a Collectivist.

["Textbook of Americanism," pamphlet, 12.]

See also ABSOLUTES; COLLECTIVISM; COMPROMISE; INDIVIDUAL RIGHTS; PRINCIPLES.

Independence.   Independence is the recognition of the fact that yours is the responsibility of judgment and nothing can help you escape it—that no substitute can do your thinking, as no pinch-hitter can live your life—that the vilest form of self-abasement and self-destruction is the subordination of your mind to the mind of another, the acceptance of an authority over your brain, the acceptance of his assertions as facts, his say-so as truth, his edicts as middle-man between your consciousness and your existence.

[GS, *FNI*, 157; pb 128.]

No matter how vast your knowledge or how modest, it is your own mind that has to acquire it. It is only with your own knowledge that you can deal. It is only your own knowledge that you can claim to possess or ask others to consider. Your mind is your only judge of truth—and if others dissent from your verdict, reality is the court of final appeal. Nothing but a man's mind can perform that complex, delicate, crucial process of identification which is thinking. Nothing can direct the process but his own judgment. Nothing can direct his judgment but his moral integrity.

[Ibid., 134; pb 126.]

Live and act within the limit of your knowledge and keep expanding it to the limit of your life. Redeem your mind from the hockshops of authority. Accept the fact that you are not omniscient, but playing a zombie will not give you omniscience—that your mind is fallible, but becoming mindless will not make you infallible—that an error made on your own is safer than ten truths accepted on faith, because the first leaves you the means to correct it, but the second destroys your capacity to distinguish truth from error. In place of your dream of an omniscient automaton, accept the fact that any knowledge man acquires is acquired by his own will and effort, and that *that* is his distinction in the universe, *that* is his nature, his morality, his glory.

[Ibid., 224; pb 178.]

[An] error is committed by the man who declares that since man must be guided by his own independent judgment, any action he chooses to take is moral if *he* chooses it. One's own independent judgment is the *means* by which one must choose one's actions, but it is not a moral criterion nor a moral validation: only reference to a demonstrable principle can validate one's choices.

["Introduction," *VOS*, xiv; pb x.]

See also CREATORS; INTEGRITY; RATIONALITY; SECOND-HANDERS; SELFISHNESS; VIRTUE.

Individual Rights. A "right" is a moral principle defining and sanctioning a man's freedom of action in a social context. There is only *one* fundamental right (all the others are its consequences or corollaries): a man's right to his own life. Life is a process of self-sustaining and self-generated action; the right to life means the right to engage in self-sustaining and self-generated action—which means: the freedom to take all the actions required by the nature of a rational being for the support, the furtherance, the fulfillment and the enjoyment of his own life. (Such is the meaning of the right to life, liberty and the pursuit of happiness.)

The concept of a "right" pertains only to action—specifically, to freedom of action. It means freedom from physical compulsion, coercion or interference by other men.

Thus, for every individual, a right is the moral sanction of a *positive*—of his freedom to act on his own judgment, for his own goals, by his own *voluntary, uncoerced* choice. As to his neighbors, his rights impose no obligations on them except of a *negative* kind: to abstain from violating his rights.

The right to life is the source of all rights—and the right to property is their only implementation. Without property rights, no other rights are possible. Since man has to sustain his life by his own effort, the man who has no right to the product of his effort has no means to sustain his life. The man who produces while others dispose of his product, is a slave.

Bear in mind that the right to property is a right to action, like all the others: it is not the right *to an object*, but to the action and the consequences of producing or earning that object. It is not a guarantee that a man *will* earn any property, but only a guarantee that he will own it if he earns it. It is the right to gain, to keep, to use and to dispose of material values.

["Man's Rights," *VOS*, 124; pb 93.]

"Rights" are a moral concept—the concept that provides a logical transition from the principles guiding an individual's actions to the principles guiding his relationship with others—the concept that preserves and protects individual morality in a social context—the link between the moral code of a man and the legal code of a society, between ethics and politics. *Individual rights are the means of subordinating society to moral law.*

[Ibid., 122; pb 92.]

Man holds these rights, not *from* the Collective nor *for* the Collective, but *against* the Collective—as a barrier which the Collective cannot cross; . . . these rights are man's protection against all other men.

["Textbook of Americanism," pamphlet, 5.]

The source of man's rights is not divine law or congressional law, but the law of identity. A is A—and Man is Man. *Rights* are conditions of existence required by man's nature for his proper survival. If man is to live on earth, it is *right* for him to use his mind, it is *right* to act on his own free judgment, it is *right* to work for his values and to keep the product of his work. If life on earth is his purpose, he has a *right* to live as a rational being: nature forbids him the irrational. Any group, any gang, any nation that attempts to negate man's rights, is *wrong*, which means: is evil, which means: is anti-life.

[GS, *FNI*, 229; pb 182.]

Since knowledge, thinking, and rational action are properties of the individual, since the choice to exercise his rational faculty or not depends on the individual, man's survival requires that those who think be free of the interference of those who don't. Since men are neither omniscient nor infallible, they must be free to agree or disagree, to cooperate or to pursue their own independent course, each according to his own rational judgment. Freedom is the fundamental requirement of man's mind.

["What Is Capitalism?" *CUI*, 17.]

Individual rights is the only proper principle of human coexistence, because it rests on man's nature, i.e., the nature and requirements of a conceptual consciousness. Man gains enormous values from dealing with other men; living in a human society is his proper way of life—but only on certain conditions. Man is not a lone wolf and he is not a social animal. He is a *contractual* animal. He has to plan his life long-range, make his own choices, and deal with other men by voluntary agreement (and he has to be able to rely on their observance of the agreements they entered).

["A Nation's Unity," *ARL*, II, 2, 3.]

A right is the sanction of independent action. A right is that which can be exercised without anyone's permission.

If you exist only because society permits you to exist—you have no *right* to your own life. A permission can be revoked at any time.

If, before undertaking some action, you must obtain the permission of society—you are not free, whether such permission is granted to you or not. Only a slave acts on permission. A permission is not a right.

Do not make the mistake, at this point, of thinking that a worker is a slave and that he holds his job by his employer's permission. He does not hold it by permission—but *by contract,* that is, by a voluntary mutual agreement. A worker can quit his job. A slave cannot.

["Textbook of Americanism," pamphlet, 5.]

The Right to the Pursuit of Happiness means man's right to live for himself, to choose what constitutes his own private, personal, individual happiness and to work for its achievement, so long as he respects the same right in others. It means that Man cannot be forced to devote his life to the happiness of another man nor of any number of other men. It means that the collective cannot decide what is to be the purpose of a man's existence nor prescribe his choice of happiness.

[Ibid.,]

Since Man has inalienable individual rights, this means that the same rights are held, individually, by every man, by all men, at all times. Therefore, the rights of one man cannot and must not violate the rights of another.

For instance: a man has the right to live, but he has no right to take the life of another. He has the right to be free, but no right to enslave another. He has the right to choose his own happiness, but no right to decide that his happiness lies in the misery (or murder or robbery or enslavement) of another. The very right upon which he acts defines the same right of another man, and serves as a guide to tell him what he may or may not do.

[Ibid., 6.]

It is *not* society, nor any social right, that forbids you to kill—but the inalienable *individual* right of another man to live. This is not a "compromise" between two rights—but a line of division that preserves both rights untouched. The division is not derived from an edict of society—but from your own inalienable individual right. The definition of this limit is not set arbitrarily by society—but is implicit in the definition of your own right.

Within the sphere of your own rights, your freedom *is* absolute.

[Ibid., 7.]

A right cannot be violated except by physical force. One man cannot deprive another of his life, nor enslave him, nor forbid him to pursue his happiness, except by using force against him. Whenever a man is made to act without his own free, personal, individual, *voluntary* consent —his right has been violated.

Therefore, we can draw a clear-cut division between the rights of one man and those of another. It is an *objective* division—not subject to differences of opinion, nor to majority decision, nor to the arbitrary decree of society. *No man has the right to initiate the use of physical force against another man.*

[Ibid., 6.]

There is no such thing as "a right to a job"—there is only the right of free trade, that is: a man's right to take a job if another man chooses to hire him. There is no "right to a home," only the right of free trade: the right to build a home or to buy it. There are no "rights to a 'fair' wage or a 'fair' price" if no one chooses to pay it, to hire a man or to buy his product. There are no "rights of consumers" to milk, shoes, movies or champagne if no producers choose to manufacture such items (there is only the right to manufacture them oneself). There are no "rights" of special groups, there are no "rights of farmers, of workers, of business-men, of employees, of employers, of the old, of the young, of the un-born." There are only *the Rights of Man*—rights possessed by every individual man and by *all* men as individuals.

["Man's Rights," *VOS*, 130; pb 97.]

If some men are entitled *by right* to the products of the work of others, it means that those others are deprived of rights and condemned to slave labor.

Any alleged "right" of one man, which necessitates the violation of the rights of another, is not and cannot be a right.

No man can have a right to impose an unchosen obligation, an unre-warded duty or an involuntary servitude on another man. There can be no such thing as *"the right to enslave."*

[Ibid., 129; pb 96.]

The end does *not* justify the means. No one's rights can be secured by the violation of the rights of others.

["The Cashing-In: The Student 'Rebellion,' " *CUI*, 256.]

Since only an individual man can possess rights, the expression "in-dividual rights" is a redundancy (which one has to use for purposes of clarification in today's intellectual chaos). But the expression "collective rights" is a contradiction in terms.

["Collectivized 'Rights,' " *VOS*, 136; pb 101.]

A group, as such, has no rights. A man can neither acquire new rights by joining a group nor lose the rights which he does possess. The prin-ciple of individual rights is the only moral base of all groups or associa-tions.

[Ibid., 137; pb 102.]

Individual rights are not subject to a public vote; a majority has no right to vote away the rights of a minority; the political function of rights is precisely to protect minorities from oppression by majorities (and the smallest minority on earth is the individual).

[Ibid., 140; pb 104.]

When individual rights are abrogated, there is no way to determine who is entitled to what; there is no way to determine the justice of anyone's claims, desires, or interests. The criterion, therefore, reverts to the tribal concept of: one's wishes are limited only by the power of one's gang. In order to survive under such a system, men have no choice but to fear, hate, and destroy one another; it is a system of underground plotting, of secret conspiracies, of deals, favors, betrayals, and sudden, bloody coups.

["The Roots of War," *CUI*, 37.]

One of the notions used by all sides to justify the draft, is that "rights impose obligations." Obligations, to whom?—and imposed, by whom? Ideologically, that notion is worse than the evil it attempts to justify: it implies that rights are a gift from the state, and that a man has to buy them by offering something (his life) in return. Logically, that notion is a contradiction: since the only proper function of a government is to protect man's rights, it cannot claim title to his life in exchange for that protection.

The only "obligation" involved in individual rights is an obligation imposed, not by the state, but by the nature of reality (i.e., by the law of identity): *consistency*, which, in this case, means the obligation to respect the rights of others, if one wishes one's own rights to be recognized and protected.

["The Wreckage of the Consensus," *CUI*, 227.]

An embryo *has no rights*. Rights do not pertain to a *potential*, only to an *actual* being. A child cannot acquire any rights until it is born. The living take precedence over the not-yet-living (or the unborn).

["Of Living Death," *TO*, Oct. 1968, 6.]

The concept of individual rights is so prodigious a feat of political thinking that few men grasp it fully—and two hundred years have not been enough for other countries to understand it. But this is the concept to which we owe our lives—the concept which made it possible for us to bring into reality everything of value that any of us did or will achieve or experience.

["A Nation's Unity," *ARL*, II, 2, 3.]

See also AMERICA; CAPITALISM; COLLECTIVISM; DICTATORSHIP; FREEDOM; HUMAN RIGHTS and PROPERTY RIGHTS; INALIENABILITY; INDIVIDUALISM; LIFE, RIGHT to; PERMISSION (vs. RIGHTS); PHYSICAL FORCE; POLITICS; PRINCIPLES; PROPERTY RIGHTS; PURSUIT of HAPPINESS, RIGHT to; RETALIATORY FORCE; SELF-DEFENSE; STATISM; TYRANNY.

Individualism. Individualism regards man—every man—as an independent, sovereign entity who possesses an inalienable right to his own life, a right derived from his nature as a rational being. Individualism holds that a civilized society, or any form of association, cooperation or peaceful coexistence among men, can be achieved only on the basis of the recognition of individual rights—and that a group, as such, has no rights other than the individual rights of its members.

["Racism," *VOS*, 176; pb 129.]

Do not make the mistake of the ignorant who think that an individualist is a man who says: "I'll do as I please at everybody else's expense." An individualist is a man who recognizes the inalienable individual rights of man—his own and those of others.

An individualist is a man who says: "I will not run anyone's life—nor let anyone run mine. I will not rule nor be ruled. I will not be a master nor a slave. I will not sacrifice myself to anyone—nor sacrifice anyone to myself."

["Textbook of Americanism," pamphlet, 6.]

The mind is an attribute of the individual. There is no such thing as a collective brain. There is no such thing as a collective thought. An agreement reached by a group of men is only a compromise or an average drawn upon many individual thoughts. It is a secondary consequence. The primary act—the process of reason—must be performed by each man alone. We can divide a meal among many men. We cannot digest it in a collective stomach. No man can use his lungs to breathe for another man. No man can use his brain to think for another. All the functions of body and spirit are private. They cannot be shared or transferred.

We inherit the products of the thought of other men. We inherit the wheel. We make a cart. The cart becomes an automobile. The automobile becomes an airplane. But all through the process what we receive from others is only the end product of their thinking. The moving force is the creative faculty which takes this product as material, uses it and originates the next step. This creative faculty cannot be given or received, shared or borrowed. It belongs to single, individual men. That which it creates is the property of the creator. Men learn from one another. But all learning is only the exchange of material. No man can give another the capacity to think. Yet that capacity is our only means of survival.

["The Soul of an Individualist," *FNI*, 91; pb 78.]

Mankind is not an entity, an organism, or a coral bush. The entity involved in production and trade is *man*. It is with the study of man—

not of the loose aggregate known as a "community"—that any science of the humanities has to begin. . . .

A great deal may be learned about society by studying man; but this process cannot be reversed: nothing can be learned about man by studying society—by studying the inter-relationships of entities one has never identified or defined.

["What Is Capitalism?" *CUI*, 15.]

See also CAPITALISM; COLLECTIVISM; "COMMON GOOD"; COOPERATION; FREE WILL; FREEDOM; INDEPENDENCE; INDIVIDUAL RIGHTS; NIETZSCHE, FRIEDRICH; REASON; SACRIFICE; SELFISHNESS; SOCIAL SYSTEM; SOCIETY.

Induction and Deduction.   The process of forming and applying concepts contains the essential pattern of two fundamental methods of cognition: *induction* and *deduction.*

The process of observing the facts of reality and of integrating them into concepts is, in essence, a process of induction. The process of subsuming new instances under a known concept is, in essence, a process of deduction.

[*ITOE*, 36.]

See also CONCEPT-FORMATION; LOGIC; PROPOSITIONS; RATIONALISM vs. EMPIRICISM.

Infinity.   There is a use of [the concept] "infinity" which is valid, as Aristotle observed, and that is the mathematical use. It is valid only when used to indicate a potentiality, never an actuality. Take the number series as an example. You can say it is infinite in the sense that, no matter how many numbers you count, there is always another number. You can always keep on counting; there's no end. In that sense it is infinite—as a potential. But notice that, actually, however many numbers you count, wherever you stop, you only reached that point, you only got so far. . . . That's Aristotle's point that the actual is always finite. Infinity exists only in the form of the ability of certain series to be extended indefinitely; but however much they are extended, in actual fact, wherever you stop it is finite.

[Leonard Peikoff, "The Philosophy of Objectivism" lecture series (1976), question period, Lecture 3.]

An arithmetical sequence extends into infinity, without implying that infinity actually exists; such extension means only that whatever number of units does exist, it is to be included in the same sequence.

[*ITOE*, 22.]

Every unit of length, no matter how small, has some specific extension; every unit of time, no matter how small, has some specific duration. The idea of an *infinitely* small amount of length or temporal duration has validity only as a mathematical device useful for making certain calculations, *not* as a description of components of reality. Reality does not contain either points or instants (in the mathematical sense). By analogy: the average family has 2.2 children, but no actual family has 2.2 children; the "average family" exists only as a mathematical device.

[Harry Binswanger, "Q & A Department: Identity and Motion," *TOF*, Dec. 1981, 13.]

See also IDENTITY; MATHEMATICS; NUMBERS; UNIVERSE.

Inflation. "Inflation" is defined in the dictionary as "undue expansion or increase of the currency of a country, esp. by the issuing of paper money not redeemable in specie" (*Random House Dictionary*). It is interesting to note that the word "inflated" is defined as "distended with air or gas; swollen."

This last is not a coincidence: in regard to social issues, "inflation" does not mean growth, enlargement or expansion, it means an "undue" —or improper or fraudulent—expansion. The expansion of a country's currency (which, incidentally, cannot be perpetrated by private citizens, only by the government) consists in palming off, as values, a stream of paper backed by nothing but promises (or hot air) and getting actual values, the citizens' goods or services, in return—until the country's wealth is drained. A similar activity, in private performance, is the passing of checks on a non-existent bank account. But, in private performance, this is regarded as a crime—and most people understand why such an activity cannot last for long.

Today, people are beginning to understand that the government's account is overdrawn, that a piece of paper is not the equivalent of a gold coin, or an automobile, or a loaf of bread—and that if you attempt to falsify monetary values, you do not achieve abundance, you merely debase the currency and go bankrupt.

["Moral Inflation," *ARL*, III, 12, 1.]

Inflation is not caused by the actions of private citizens, but *by the government:* by an artificial expansion of the money supply required to support deficit spending. No private embezzlers or bank robbers in history have ever plundered people's savings on a scale comparable to the plunder perpetrated by the fiscal policies of statist governments.

["Who Will Protect Us from Our Protectors?" *TON*, May 1962, 18.]

The law of supply and demand is not to be conned. As the supply of money (of claims) increases relative to the supply of tangible assets in the economy, prices must eventually rise. Thus the earnings saved by the productive members of the society lose value in terms of goods. When the economy's books are finally balanced, one finds that this loss in value represents the goods purchased by the government for welfare or other purposes with the money proceeds of the government bonds financed by bank credit expansion.

In the absence of the gold standard, there is no way to protect savings from confiscation through inflation. There is no safe store of value. If there were, the government would have to make its holding illegal, as was done in the case of gold.

[Alan Greenspan, "Gold and Economic Freedom," *CUI*, 101.]

There is only one institution that can arrogate to itself the power legally to trade by means of rubber checks: the government. And it is the only institution that can mortgage your future without your knowledge or consent: government securities (and paper money) are promissory notes on future tax receipts, i.e., on your future production.

["Egalitarianism and Inflation," *PWNI*, 156; pb 128.]

The "wage-price spiral," which is merely a consequence of inflation, is being blamed as its cause, thus deflecting the blame from the real culprit: the government. But the government's guilt is hidden by the esoteric intricacies of the national budget and of international finance —which the public cannot be expected to understand—while the disaster of nationwide strikes is directly perceivable by everyone and gives plausibility to the public's growing resentment of labor unions.

["The Moratorium on Brains," *ARL*, I, 3, 3.]

You have heard economists say that they are puzzled by the nature of today's problem: they are unable to understand why inflation is accompanied by recession—which is contrary to their Keynesian doctrines; and they have coined a ridiculous name for it: "stagflation." Their theories ignore the fact that money can function only so long as it represents actual goods—and that at a certain stage of inflating the money supply, the government begins to consume a nation's investment capital, thus making production impossible.

["Egalitarianism and Inflation," *PWNI*, 163; pb 134.]

See also CAPITALISM; DEFICIT FINANCING; GOLD STANDARD; MONEY; SAVINGS.

Innate Ideas. *See Tabula Rasa.*

"Instinct."   An *instinct* of self-preservation is precisely what man does not possess. An "instinct" is an unerring and automatic form of knowledge. A desire is not an instinct. A desire to live does not give you the knowledge required for living. And even man's desire to live is not automatic. . . . Your fear of death is not a love for life and will not give you the knowledge needed to keep it. Man must obtain his knowledge and choose his actions by a process of thinking, which nature will not force him to perform. Man has the power to act as his own destroyer— and that is the way he has acted through most of his history.

[GS, *FNI*, 148; pb 121.]

[Man] is born naked and unarmed, without fangs, claws, horns or "instinctual" knowledge.

["The Anti-Industrial Revolution," *NL*, 136.]

Man has no automatic code of survival. He has no automatic course of action, no automatic set of values. His senses do not tell him automatically what is good for him or evil, what will benefit his life or endanger it, what goals he should pursue and what means will achieve them, what *values* his life depends on, what course of action it requires. His own consciousness has to discover the answers to all these questions— but his consciousness will not function *automatically*.

["The Objectivist Ethics," *VOS*, 11; pb 19.]

Since man has no automatic knowledge, he can have no automatic values; since he has no innate ideas, he can have no innate value judgments.

Man is born with an emotional mechanism, just as he is born with a cognitive mechanism; but, at birth, *both* are "tabula rasa."

[Ibid., 23; pb 27.]

See also EMOTIONS; FREE WILL; FREUD; GOAL-DIRECTED ACTION; TABULA RASA.

Integration (Mental).   Consciousness, as a state of awareness, is not a passive state, but an active process that consists of two essentials: differentiation and integration.

[*ITOE*, 5.]

Integration is a cardinal function of man's consciousness on all the levels of his cognitive development. First, his brain brings order into his sensory chaos by integrating sense data into percepts; this integration is performed automatically; it requires effort, but no conscious volition.

His next step is the integration of percepts into concepts, as he learns to speak. Thereafter, his cognitive development consists in integrating concepts into wider and ever wider concepts, expanding the range of his mind. This stage is fully volitional and demands an unremitting effort.

["Art and Cognition," *RM*, pb 57.]

A *concept* is a mental integration of two or more units which are isolated according to a specific characteristic(s) and united by a specific definition. . . . [In concept-formation], the uniting involved is not a mere sum, but an *integration*, i.e., a blending of the units into a *single*, new *mental* entity which is used thereafter as a single unit of thought (but which can be broken into its component units whenever required).

[*ITOE*, 11.]

[The] enemies of reason seem to know that *integration* is the psycho-epistemological key to reason . . . and that if reason is to be destroyed, it is man's integrating capacity that has to be destroyed.

["Art and Cognition," *RM*, pb 77.]

Integration is the essential part of understanding.

["The Comprachicos," *NL*, 208.]

See also CONCEPT-FORMATION; CONCEPTS; CONSCIOUSNESS; LEARNING; PSYCHO-EPISTEMOLOGY; SENSATIONS; UNDER-STANDING.

Integrity.   Integrity is the recognition of the fact that you cannot fake your consciousness, just as honesty is the recognition of the fact that you cannot fake existence—that man is an indivisible entity, an integrated unit of two attributes: of matter and consciousness, and that he may permit no breach between body and mind, between action and thought, between his life and his convictions—that, like a judge impervious to public opinion, he may not sacrifice his convictions to the wishes of others, be it the whole of mankind shouting pleas or threats against him—that courage and confidence are practical necessities, that courage is the practical form of being true to existence, of being true to truth, and confidence is the practical form of being true to one's own consciousness.

[GS, *FNI*, 157; pb 128.]

The virtue involved in helping those one loves is not "selflessness" or "sacrifice," but *integrity*. Integrity is loyalty to one's convictions and values; it is the policy of acting in accordance with one's values, of expressing, upholding and translating them into practical reality. If a man professes to love a woman, yet his actions are indifferent, inimical or damaging to her, it is his lack of integrity that makes him immoral.

["The Ethics of Emergencies," *VOS*, 51; pb 46.]

Integrity does not consist of loyalty to one's subjective whims, but of loyalty to rational principles.

["Doesn't Life Require Compromise?" *VOS*, 87; pb 69.]

See also COMPROMISE; HONESTY; RATIONALITY; SUBJECTIVISM; SACRIFICE; VIRTUE; WHIMS/WHIM-WORSHIP.

Intellectuals. The professional intellectual is the field agent of the army whose commander-in-chief is the *philosopher*. The intellectual carries the application of philosophical principles to every field of human endeavor. He sets a society's course by transmitting ideas from the "ivory tower" of the philosopher to the university professor—to the writer—to the artist—to the newspaperman—to the politician—to the movie maker—to the night-club singer—to the man in the street. The intellectual's specific professions are in the field of the sciences that study man, the so-called "humanities," but for that very reason his influence extends to all other professions. Those who deal with the sciences studying nature have to rely on the intellectual for philosophical guidance and information: for moral values, for social theories, for political premises, for psychological tenets and, above all, for the principles of epistemology, that crucial branch of philosophy which studies man's means of knowledge and makes all other sciences possible. The intellectual is the eyes, ears and voice of a free society: it is *his* job to observe the events of the world, to evaluate their meaning and to inform the men in all the other fields.

["For the New Intellectual," *FNI*, 25; pb 27.]

[The intellectuals] are a group that holds a unique prerogative: the potential of being either the most productive or the most parasitical of all social groups.

The intellectuals serve as guides, as trend-setters, as the transmission belts or middlemen between philosophy and the culture. If they adopt a philosophy of reason—if their goal is the development of man's rational faculty and the pursuit of knowledge—they are a society's most productive and most powerful group, because their work provides the base and the integration of all other human activities. If the intellectuals are dominated by a philosophy of irrationalism, they become a society's unemployed and unemployable.

From the early nineteenth century on, American intellectuals—with very rare exceptions—were the humbly obedient followers of European philosophy, which had entered its age of decadence. Accepting its fundamentals, they were unable to deal with or even to grasp the nature of this country.

["A Preview," *ARL*, I, 24, 1.]

Historically, the professional intellectual is a very recent phenomenon: he dates only from the industrial revolution. There are no professional intellectuals in primitive, savage societies, there are only witch doctors. There were no professional intellectuals in the Middle Ages, there were only monks in monasteries. In the post-Renaissance era, prior to the birth of capitalism, the men of the intellect—the philosophers, the teachers, the writers, the early scientists—were men without a profession, that is: without a socially recognized position, without a market, without a means of earning a livelihood. Intellectual pursuits had to depend on the accident of inherited wealth or on the favor and financial support of some wealthy protector. And wealth was not earned on an open market, either; wealth was acquired by conquest, by force, by political power, or by the favor of those who held political power. Tradesmen were more vulnerably and precariously dependent on favor than the intellectuals.

The professional businessman and the professional intellectual came into existence together, as brothers born of the industrial revolution. Both are the sons of capitalism—and if they perish, they will perish together. The tragic irony will be that they will have destroyed each other; and the major share of the guilt will belong to the intellectual.

["For the New Intellectual," *FNI*, 6; pb 12.]

See also BUSINESSMEN; CULTURE; HISTORY; PHILOSOPHY.

Intelligence.   Intelligence is the ability to deal with a broad range of abstractions. Whatever a child's natural endowment, the use of intelligence is an acquired skill. It has to be acquired by a child's own effort and automatized by his own mind, but adults can help or hinder him in this crucial process.

["The Comprachicos," *NL*, 195.]

[Man] survives by means of man-made products, and . . . the source of man-made products is man's *intelligence*. Intelligence is the ability to grasp the facts of reality and to deal with them long-range (i.e., conceptually). On the axiom of the primacy of existence, intelligence is man's most precious attribute. But it has no place in a society ruled by the primacy of consciousness: it is such a society's deadliest enemy.

Today, intelligence is neither recognized nor rewarded, but is being systematically extinguished in a growing flood of brazenly flaunted irrationality.

["The Metaphysical Versus the Man-Made," *PWNI*, 40; pb 32.]

Intelligence is not an exclusive monopoly of genius; it is an attribute of all men, and the differences are only a matter of degree. If conditions of existence are destructive to genius, they are destructive to every man, each in proportion to his intelligence. If genius is penalized, so is the faculty of intelligence in every other man. There is only this difference: the average man does not possess the genius's power of self-confident resistance, and will break much faster; he will give up his mind, in hopeless bewilderment, under the first touch of pressure.

["Requiem for Man," *CUI*, 306.]

See also ABSTRACTIONS and CONCRETES; AUTOMATIZATION; CONCEPTS; INTEGRATION (MENTAL); PRIMACY of EXISTENCE vs. PRIMACY of CONSCIOUSNESS; REASON; UNDERSTANDING.

Interest (on loans).   If you have wondered how one can start producing, when nature requires time paid in advance, this is the beneficent process that enables men to do it: a successful man lends his goods to a promising beginner (or to any reputable producer)—in exchange for the payment of interest. The payment is for the risk he is taking: nature does not guarantee man's success, neither on a farm nor in a factory. If the venture fails, it means that the goods have been consumed without a productive return, so the investor loses his money; if the venture succeeds, the producer pays the interest out of the new goods, the *profits*, which the investment enabled him to make.

["Egalitarianism and Inflation," *PWNI*, 159; pb 131.]

See also CREDIT; INVESTMENT; MONEY; SAVINGS.

Interventionism (economic).   A "mixed economy" is a society in the process of committing suicide.

If a nation cannot survive half-slave, half-free, consider the condition of a nation in which every social group becomes both the slave and the enslaver of every other group. Ask yourself how long such a condition can last and what is its inevitable outcome.

When government controls are introduced into a free economy, they create economic dislocations, hardships, and problems which, if the controls are not repealed, necessitate still further controls, which necessitate still further controls, etc. Thus a chain reaction is set up: the victimized groups seek redress by imposing controls on the profiteering groups, who retaliate in the same manner, on an ever widening scale.

["Statism Is the Only Victor in Cold Civil War,"
Los Angeles Times, July 22, 1962.]

Every government interference in the economy consists of giving an unearned benefit, extorted by force, to some men at the expense of others. By what criterion of justice is a consensus-government to be guided? By the size of the victim's gang.

["The New Fascism: Rule by Consensus," *CUI,* 205.]

If parasitism, favoritism, corruption, and greed for the unearned did not exist, a mixed economy would bring them into existence.

Since there is no rational justification for the sacrifice of some men to others, there is no objective criterion by which such a sacrifice can be guided in practice. All "public interest" legislation (and any distribution of money taken by force from some men for the unearned benefit of others) comes down ultimately to the grant of an undefined, undefinable, non-objective, arbitrary power to some government officials.

The worst aspect of it is not that such a power can be used dishonestly, but that *it cannot be used honestly.*

["The Pull Peddlers," *CUI,* 170.]

See also CAPITALISM; FREE MARKET; GOVERNMENT; LOBBYING; MIXED ECONOMY; "PUBLIC INTEREST," the; WELFARE STATE.

Intrinsic Theory of Values.   There are, in essence, three schools of thought on the nature of the good: the intrinsic, the subjective, and the objective. The *intrinsic* theory holds that the good is inherent in certain things or actions as such, regardless of their context and consequences, regardless of any benefit or injury they may cause to the actors and subjects involved. It is a theory that divorces the concept of "good" from beneficiaries, and the concept of "value" from valuer and purpose —claiming that the good is good in, by, and of itself.

["What Is Capitalism?" *CUI,* 21.]

The intrinsic theory holds that the good resides in some sort of reality, independent of man's consciousness.

[Ibid., 22.]

If a man believes that the good is intrinsic in certain actions, he will not hesitate to force others to perform them. If he believes that the human benefit or injury caused by such actions is of no significance, he will regard a sea of blood as of no significance. If he believes that the beneficiaries of such actions are irrelevant (or interchangeable), he will regard wholesale slaughter as his moral duty in the service of a "higher" good. It is the intrinsic theory of values that produces a Robespierre, a Lenin, a Stalin, or a Hitler. It is not an accident that Eichmann was a Kantian.

[Ibid.]

See also GOOD, the; MORALITY; MYSTICAL ETHICS; OBJECTIVE THE-ORY OF VALUES; OBJECTIVITY; PHYSICAL FORCE; SOCIAL THE-ORY OF ETHICS; SUBJECTIVISM.

Introspection.   Extrospection is a process of cognition directed outward—a process of apprehending some existent(s) of the external world. Introspection is a process of cognition directed inward—a process of apprehending one's own psychological actions in regard to some existent(s) of the external world, such actions as thinking, feeling, reminiscing, etc. It is only in relation to the external world that the various actions of a consciousness can be experienced, grasped, defined or communicated.

[*ITOE*, 37.]

A major source of men's *earned* guilt in regard to philosophy—as well as in regard to their own minds and lives—is failure of introspection. Specifically, it is the failure to identify the nature and causes of their emotions.

An emotion as such tells you nothing about reality, beyond the fact that something makes you feel something. Without a ruthlessly honest commitment to introspection—to the conceptual identification of your inner states—you will not discover what you feel, what arouses the feeling, and whether your feeling is an appropriate response to the facts of reality, or a mistaken response, or a vicious illusion produced by years of self-deception. The men who scorn or dread introspection take their inner states for granted, as an irreducible and irresistible primary, and let their emotions determine their actions. This means that they choose to act without knowing the context (reality), the causes (motives), and the consequences (goals) of their actions.

The field of extrospection is based on two cardinal questions: "What do I know?" and "How do I know it?" In the field of introspection, the two guiding questions are: "*What* do I feel?" and "*Why* do I feel it?"

["Philosophical Detection," *PWNI*, 20; pb 17.]

In regard to one's own feelings, only a rigorously conscientious habit of introspection can enable one to be certain of the nature and causes of one's emotional responses.

["The Age of Envy," *NL*, 154.]

The formation of introspective concepts follows the same principles as the formation of extrospective concepts. A concept pertaining to consciousness is a mental integration of two or more instances of a psychological process possessing the same distinguishing characteristics, with the particular contents and the measurements of the action's intensity omitted—on the principle that these omitted measurements must exist in *some* quantity, but may exist in *any* quantity (i.e., a given psychological process must possess *some* content and *some* degree of intensity, but may possess *any* content or degree of the appropriate category).

[*ITOE*, 40.]

See also BEHAVIORISM; CONCEPTS; CONSCIOUSNESS; EMOTIONS; PSYCHOLOGY; RATIONALIZATION; VALUES.

Invalid Concepts.   There are such things as invalid concepts, i.e., words that represent attempts to integrate errors, contradictions or false propositions, such as concepts originating in mysticism—or words without specific definitions, without referents, which can mean anything to anyone, such as modern "anti-concepts." Invalid concepts appear occasionally in men's languages, but are usually—though not necessarily—short-lived, since they lead to cognitive dead-ends. An invalid concept invalidates every proposition or process of thought in which it is used as a cognitive assertion.

[*ITOE*, 65.]

No concept man forms is valid unless he integrates it without contradiction into the total sum of his knowledge.

[GS, *FNI*, 154; pb 126.]

See also "ANTI-CONCEPTS"; CONCEPTS; INTEGRATION (MENTAL); MYSTICISM; "STOLEN CONCEPT," FALLACY of.

Investment.   If a man does not consume his goods at once, but saves them for the future, whether he wants to enlarge his production or to live on his savings (which he holds in the form of money)—in either case, he is counting on the fact that he will be able to exchange his money for the things he needs, when and as he needs them. This means that he is relying on a continuous process of production—which requires an uninterrupted flow of goods saved to fuel further and further production. This flow is "investment capital," the stock seed of industry. When a rich man lends money to others, what he lends to them is the goods which he has not consumed.

This is the meaning of the concept "investment." If you have wondered how one can start producing, when nature requires time paid in advance, this is the beneficent process that enables men to do it: a successful man lends his goods to a promising beginner (or to any reputable producer)—in exchange for the payment of interest. The payment is for the risk he is taking: nature does not guarantee man's success, neither on a farm nor in a factory. If the venture fails, it means that the goods have been consumed without a productive return, so the investor loses his money; if the venture succeeds, the producer pays the interest out of the new goods, the *profits*, which the investment enabled him to make.

Observe, and bear in mind above all else, that this process applies *only* to financing the needs of production, *not* of consumption—and that its success rests on the investor's judgment of men's productive ability, *not* on his compassion for their feelings, hopes or dreams.

["Egalitarianism and Inflation," *PWNI*, 159; pb 131.]

See also CONSUMPTION; CREDIT; PRODUCTION; SAVINGS.

Irrationalism. Reason is the faculty that identifies, in conceptual terms, the material provided by man's senses. "Irrationalism" is the doctrine that reason is not a valid means of knowledge or a proper guide to action.

[Leonard Peikoff, *OP*, 41; pb 47.]

See also IRRATIONALITY; MYSTICISM; REASON; SKEPTICISM.

Irrationality. Man's basic vice, the source of all his evils, is the act of unfocusing his mind, the suspension of his consciousness, which is not blindness, but the refusal to see, not ignorance, but the refusal to know. Irrationality is the rejection of man's means of survival and, therefore, a commitment to a course of blind destruction; that which is anti-mind, is anti-life.

["The Objectivist Ethics," *VOS*, 20; pb 25.]

To the extent to which a man is rational, life is the premise directing his actions. To the extent to which he is irrational, the premise directing his actions is death.

[GS, *FNI*, 156; pb 127.]

The irrational is the impossible; it is that which contradicts the facts of reality; facts cannot be altered by a wish, but they *can* destroy the wisher.

["The Objectivist Ethics," *VOS*, 24; pb 28.]

Irrationality is a state of default, the state of an unachieved human stature. When men do not choose to reach the conceptual level, their consciousness has no recourse but to its automatic, perceptual, semi-animal functions.

["For the New Intellectual," *FNI*, 19; pb 21.]

See also CONTRADICTIONS; EMOTIONS; EVASION; EVIL; FOCUS; RATIONALITY; REASON; WHIMS/WHIM-WORSHIP.

Irreducible Primaries. An irreducible primary is a fact which cannot be analyzed (i.e., broken into components) or derived from antecedent facts.

["Philosophical Detection," *PWNI*, 15; pb 13.]

See also AXIOMATIC CONCEPTS; AXIOMS; COROLLARIES; HIER-ARCHY *of* KNOWLEDGE; OSTENSIVE DEFINITION; SELF-EVIDENT.

"Is"-"Ought" Dichotomy. It is only an ultimate goal, and *end in itself*, that makes the existence of values possible. Metaphysically, *life* is the only phenomenon that is an end in itself: a value gained and kept by a constant process of action. Epistemologically, the concept of "value" is genetically dependent upon and derived from the antecedent concept of "life." To speak of "value" as apart from "life" is worse than a contradiction in terms. "It is only the concept of 'Life' that makes the concept of 'Value' possible."

In answer to those philosophers who claim that no relation can be established between ultimate ends or values and the facts of reality, let me stress that the fact that living entities exist and function necessitates the existence of values and of an ultimate value which for any given living entity is its own life. Thus the validation of value judgments is to be achieved by reference to the facts of reality. The fact that a living entity *is*, determines what it *ought* to do. So much for the issue of the relation between "*is*" and "*ought*."

["The Objectivist Ethics," *VOS*, 7; pb 17.]

See also GOAL-DIRECTED ACTION; GOOD, the; LIFE; MORALITY; STANDARD *of* VALUE; ULTIMATE VALUE; VALUES.

"Isolationism."   A large-scale instance [of political smear-tactics], in the 1930's, was the introduction of the word *"isolationism"* into our political vocabulary. It was a derogatory term, suggesting something evil, and it had no clear, explicit definition. It was used to convey two meanings: one alleged, the other real—and to damn both.

The alleged meaning was defined approximately like this: "Isolationism is the attitude of a person who is interested only in his own country and is not concerned with the rest of the world." The real meaning was: "Patriotism and national self-interest."

What, exactly, is *"concern* with the rest of the world"? Since nobody did or could maintain the position that the state of the world is of no *concern* to this country, the term "isolationism" was a straw man used to misrepresent the position of those who were concerned with this country's interests. The concept of patriotism was replaced by the term "isolationism" and vanished from public discussion.

The number of distinguished patriotic leaders smeared, silenced, and eliminated by that tag would be hard to compute. Then, by a gradual, imperceptible process, the real purpose of the tag took over: the concept of "concern" was switched into *"selfless* concern." The ultimate result was a view of foreign policy which is wrecking the United States to this day: the suicidal view that our foreign policy must be guided, not by considerations of national self-interest, but by concern for the interests and welfare of the world, that is, of all countries except our own.

[" 'Extremism,' or The Art of Smearing," *CUI*, 175.]

Observe the double-standard switch of the anti-concept of "isolationism." The same intellectual groups (and even some of the same aging individuals) who coined that anti-concept in World War II—and used it to denounce any patriotic opponent of America's self-immolation— the same groups who screamed that it was our duty to save the world (when the enemy was Germany or Italy or fascism), are now rabid isolationists who denounce any U.S. concern with countries fighting for freedom, when the enemy is communism and Soviet Russia.

["The Lessons of Vietnam," *ARL*, III, 24, 4.]

See also "ANTI-CONCEPTS"; COMMUNISM; FOREIGN POLICY; SOVIET RUSSIA.

J

Judgment. See Moral Judgment.

Justice. Justice is the recognition of the fact that you cannot fake the character of men as you cannot fake the character of nature, that you must judge all men as conscientiously as you judge inanimate objects, with the same respect for truth, with the same incorruptible vision, by as pure and as *rational* a process of identification—that every man must be judged for what he *is* and treated accordingly, that just as you do not pay a higher price for a rusty chunk of scrap than for a piece of shining metal, so you do not value a rotter above a hero—that your moral appraisal is the coin paying men for their virtues or vices, and this payment demands of you as scrupulous an honor as you bring to financial transactions—that to withhold your contempt from men's vices is an act of moral counterfeiting, and to withhold your admiration from their virtues is an act of moral embezzlement—that to place any other concern higher than justice is to devaluate your moral currency and defraud the good in favor of the evil, since only the good can lose by a default of justice and only the evil can profit—and that the bottom of the pit at the end of that road, the act of moral bankruptcy, is to punish men for their virtues and reward them for their vices, that that is the collapse to full depravity, the Black Mass of the worship of death, the dedication of your consciousness to the destruction of existence.

[GS, *FNI*, 158; pb 129.]

What fact of reality gave rise to the concept "justice"? The fact that man must draw conclusions about the things, people and events around him, i.e., must judge and evaluate them. Is his judgment automatically right? No. What causes his judgment to be wrong? The lack of sufficient evidence, or his evasion of the evidence, or his inclusion of considerations other than the facts of the case. How, then, is he to arrive at the right judgment? By basing it exclusively on the factual evidence and by considering all the relevant evidence available. But isn't this a description of "objectivity"? Yes, "objective judgment" is one of the wider categories to which the concept "justice" belongs. What distinguishes "justice" from other instances of objective judgment? When one evaluates the nature or actions of inanimate objects, the criterion of judgment is determined by the particular purpose for which one evaluates them. But how does one determine a criterion for evaluating the character and actions of men, in view of the fact that men possess the faculty of volition? What science can provide an objective criterion of evaluation in regard to volitional matters? Ethics. Now, do I need a concept to designate the act of judging a man's character and/or actions exclusively on the basis of all the factual evidence available, and of evaluating it by means of an objective moral criterion? Yes. That concept is "justice."

[*ITOE*, 67.]

It is not justice or equal treatment that you grant to men when you abstain equally from praising men's virtues and from condemning men's vices. When your impartial attitude declares, in effect, that neither the good nor the evil may expect anything from you—whom do you betray and whom do you encourage?

["How Does One Lead a Rational Life
in an Irrational Society," *VOS*, 89; pb 71.]

Since men are born *tabula rasa,* both cognitively and morally, a rational man regards strangers as innocent until proved guilty, and grants them that initial good will in the name of their human potential. After that, he judges them according to the moral character they have actualized. If he finds them guilty of major evils, his good will is replaced by contempt and moral condemnation. (If one values human life, one cannot value its destroyers.) If he finds them to be virtuous, he grants them personal, individual value and appreciation, in proportion to their virtues.

["The Ethics of Emergencies," *VOS*, 52; pb 47.]

The new "theory of justice" [of John Rawls] demands that men counteract the "injustice" of nature by instituting the most obscenely unthinkable injustice among men: deprive "those favored by nature" (i.e., the talented, the intelligent, the creative) of the right to the rewards they produce (i.e., the right to life)—and grant to the incompetent, the stupid, the slothful a right to the effortless enjoyment of the rewards they could not produce, could not imagine, and would not know what to do with.

["An Untitled Letter," *PWNI*, 132; pb 110.]

See also CAPITALISM; COMPASSION; EGALITARIANISM; HONESTY; MERCY; MORAL JUDGMENT; MORALITY; OBJECTIVITY; RATIONALITY; TRADER PRINCIPLE; VIRTUE.

K

Kant, Immanuel.

On every fundamental issue, Kant's philosophy is the exact opposite of Objectivism.

["Brief Summary," *TO*, Sept. 1971, 4.]

Metaphysics and Epistemology

The man who . . . closed the door of philosophy to reason, was Immanuel Kant. . . .

Kant's expressly stated purpose was to save the morality of self-abnegation and self-sacrifice. He knew that it could not survive without a mystic base—and what it had to be saved from was *reason*.

Attila's share of Kant's universe includes this earth, physical reality, man's senses, perceptions, reason and science, all of it labeled the "phenomenal" world. The Witch Doctor's share is another, "higher," reality, labeled the "noumenal" world, and a special manifestation, labeled the "categorical imperative," which dictates to man the rules of morality and which makes itself known by means of a *feeling*, as a special sense of duty.

The "phenomenal" world, said Kant, is not real: reality, as perceived by man's mind, is a distortion. The distorting mechanism is man's conceptual faculty: man's basic concepts (such as time, space, existence) are not derived from experience or reality, but come from an automatic system of filters in his consciousness (labeled "categories" and "forms of perception") which impose their own design on his perception of the external world and make him incapable of perceiving it in any manner other than the one in which he does perceive it. This proves, said Kant, that man's concepts are only a delusion, but a *collective* delusion which no one has the power to escape. Thus reason and science are "limited," said Kant; they are valid only so long as they deal with this world, with a permanent, pre-determined collective delusion (and thus the criterion of reason's validity was switched from the *objective* to the *collective*), but they are impotent to deal with the fundamental, metaphysical issues of existence, which belong to the "noumenal" world. The "noumenal" world is unknowable; it is the world of "real" reality, "superior" truth and "things in themselves" or "things as they are"—which means: things as they are *not* perceived by man.

Even apart from the fact that Kant's theory of the "categories" as the source of man's concepts was a preposterous invention, his argument

235

amounted to a negation, not only of man's consciousness, but of *any* consciousness, of consciousness as such. His argument, in essence, ran as follows: man is *limited* to a consciousness of a specific nature, which perceives by specific means and no others, therefore, his consciousness is not valid; man is blind, because he has eyes—deaf, because he has ears—deluded, because he has a mind—and the things he perceives do not exist, *because* he perceives them.

["For the New Intellectual," *FNI*, 31; pb 30.]

The motive of all the attacks on man's rational faculty—from any quarter, in any of the endless variations, under the verbal dust of all the murky volumes—is a single, hidden premise: the desire to exempt consciousness from the law of identity. The hallmark of a mystic is the savagely stubborn refusal to accept the fact that consciousness, like any other existent, possesses identity, that it is a faculty of a specific nature, functioning through specific means. While the advance of civilization has been eliminating one area of magic after another, the last stand of the believers in the miraculous consists of their frantic attempts to regard *identity* as the *disqualifying* element of consciousness.

The implicit, but unadmitted premise of the neo-mystics of modern philosophy, is the notion that only an ineffable consciousness can acquire a valid knowledge of reality, that "true" knowledge has to be causeless, i.e., acquired without any means of cognition.

The entire apparatus of Kant's system, like a hippopotamus engaged in belly-dancing, goes through its gyrations while resting on a single point: that man's knowledge is not valid because his consciousness possesses identity. . . .

This is a negation, not only of man's consciousness, but of *any* consciousness, of consciousness as such, whether man's, insect's or God's. (If one supposed the existence of God, the negation would still apply: either God perceives through no means whatever, in which case he possesses no identity—or he perceives by some divine means and no others, in which case his perception is not valid.) As Berkeley negated existence by claiming that "to be, is to be perceived," so Kant negates consciousness by implying that to be perceived, is not to be. . . .

From primordial mysticism to this, its climax, the attack on man's consciousness and particularly on his conceptual faculty has rested on the unchallenged premise that any knowledge acquired by a *process* of consciousness is necessarily subjective and cannot correspond to the facts of reality, since it is "*processed* knowledge."

Make no mistake about the actual meaning of that premise: it is a revolt, not only against being conscious, but against being alive—since in fact, in reality, on earth, every aspect of being alive involves a process of self-sustaining and self-generated action. (This is an example of the fact that the revolt against identity is a revolt against existence. "The desire not to be anything, is the desire not to be." *Atlas Shrugged*.)

All knowledge *is* processed knowledge—whether on the sensory, perceptual or conceptual level. An "unprocessed" knowledge would be a knowledge acquired without means of cognition. Consciousness . . . is not a passive state, but an active process. And more: the satisfaction of every need of a living organism requires an act of *processing* by that organism, be it the need of air, of food or of knowledge.

[*ITOE*, 106.]

A "straw man" is an odd metaphor to apply to such an enormous, cumbersome, ponderous construction as Kant's system of epistemology. Nevertheless, a straw man is what it was—and the doubts, the uncertainty, the skepticism that followed, skepticism about man's ability ever to know anything, were not, in fact, applicable to human consciousness, because it was not a human consciousness that Kant's robot represented. But philosophers accepted it as such. And while they cried that reason had been invalidated, they did not notice that reason had been pushed off the philosophical scene altogether and that the faculty they were arguing about was *not* reason.

No, Kant did not destroy reason; he merely did as thorough a job of undercutting as anyone could ever do.

If you trace the roots of all our current philosophies—such as pragmatism, logical positivism, and all the rest of the neo-mystics who announce happily that you cannot *prove* that you exist—you will find that they all grew out of Kant.

["Faith and Force: The Destroyers of the Modern World," *PWNI*, 77; pb 64.]

One of Kant's major goals was to save religion (including the essence of religious morality) from the onslaughts of science. His system represents a massive effort to raise the principles of Platonism, in a somewhat altered form, once again to a position of commanding authority over Western culture.

[Leonard Peikoff, *OP*, 23; pb 31.]

Plato was more than a Platonist; despite his mysticism, he was also a pagan Greek. As such he exhibited a certain authentic respect for reason, a respect which was implicit in Greek philosophy no matter how explicitly irrational it became. The Kantian mysticism, however, suffers from no such pagan restraints. It flows forth triumphantly, sweeping the prostrate human mind before it. Since man can never escape the distorting agents inherent in the structure of his consciousness, says

Kant, "things in themselves" are in principle unknowable. Reason is impotent to discover anything about reality; if it tries, it can only bog down in impenetrable contradictions. Logic is merely a subjective human device, devoid of reference to or basis in reality. Science, while useful as a means of ordering the data of the world of appearances, is limited to describing a surface world of man's own creation and says nothing about things as they really are.

Must men then resign themselves to a total skepticism? No, says Kant, there is one means of piercing the barrier between man and existence. Since reason, logic, and science are denied access to reality, the door is now open for men to approach reality by a different, *nonrational* method. The door is now open to *faith*. Taking their cue from their needs, men can properly *believe* (for instance, in God and in an afterlife), even though they cannot prove the truth of their beliefs. . . . "I have," writes Kant, "therefore found it necessary to deny *knowledge*, in order to make room for *faith*."

[Ibid., 24; pb 32.]

There are two different kinds of subjectivism, distinguished by their answers to the question: *whose* consciousness creates reality? Kant rejected the older of these two, which was the view that each man's feelings create a private universe for him. Instead, Kant ushered in the era of *social* subjectivism—the view that it is not the consciousness of individuals, but of *groups*, that creates reality. In Kant's system, mankind as a whole is the decisive group; what creates the phenomenal world is not the idiosyncrasies of particular individuals, but the mental structure common to all men.

Later philosophers accepted Kant's fundamental approach, but carried it a step further. If, many claimed, the mind's structure is a brute given, which cannot be explained—as Kant had said—then there is no reason why all men should have the same mental structure. There is no reason why mankind should not be splintered into *competing* groups, each defined by its own distinctive type of consciousness, each vying with the others to capture and control reality.

The first world movement thus to pluralize the Kantian position was Marxism, which propounded a social subjectivism in terms of competing economic classes. On this issue, as on many others, the Nazis follow the Marxists, but substitute race for class.

[Ibid., 59; pb 63.]

A man's self, [Kant] maintains, like everything else, is a part of reality —it, too, is something in itself—and if reality is unknowable, then *so is a man's self*. A man is able, Kant concludes, to know only his phenomenal ego, his self as it appears to him (in introspection); he cannot know his noumenal ego, his "ego as it is in itself."

Man is, therefore, a creature in metaphysical conflict. He is so to speak a metaphysical biped, with one (unreal) foot in the phenomenal world and one (unknowable) foot in the noumenal world.

[Ibid., 75; pb 77.]

Ethics

As to Kant's version of morality, it was appropriate to the kind of zombies that would inhabit that kind of [Kantian] universe: it consisted of total, abject *selflessness*. An action is moral, said Kant, only if one has no desire to perform it, but performs it out of a sense of *duty* and derives no benefit from it of any sort, neither material nor spiritual; a benefit destroys the moral value of an action. (Thus, if one has no desire to be evil, one cannot be good; if one has, one can.)

Those who accept any part of Kant's philosophy—metaphysical, epistemological or moral—deserve it.

["For the New Intellectual," *FNI*, 33; pb 32.]

The arch-advocate of "duty" is Immanuel Kant; he went so much farther than other theorists that they seem innocently benevolent by comparison. "Duty," he holds, is the only standard of virtue; but virtue is not its own reward: if a reward is involved, it is no longer virtue. The only moral motivation, he holds, is devotion to duty for duty's sake; only an action motivated exclusively by such devotion is a moral action (i.e., an action performed without any concern for "inclination" [desire] or self-interest).

"It is a duty to preserve one's life, and moreover everyone has a direct inclination to do so. But for that reason the often anxious care which most men take of it has no intrinsic worth, and the maxim of doing so has no moral import. They preserve their lives according to duty, but not from duty. But if adversities and hopeless sorrow completely take away the relish for life, if an unfortunate man, strong in soul, is indignant rather than despondent or dejected over his fate and wishes for death, and yet preserves his life without loving it and from neither inclination nor fear but from duty—then his maxim has a moral import" (Immanuel Kant, *Foundations of the Metaphysics of Morals*, ed. R. P. Wolff, New York, Bobbs-Merrill, 1969, pp. 16–17).

["Causality Versus Duty," *PWNI*, 115; pb 96.]

His view of morality is propagated by men who have never heard of him—he merely gave them a formal, academic status. A Kantian sense of "duty" is inculcated by parents whenever they declare that a child *must* do something because he *must*. A child brought up under the constant battering of causeless, arbitrary, contradictory, inexplicable "musts" loses (or never acquires) the ability to grasp the distinction between realistic necessity and human whims—and spends his life abjectly, dutifully obeying the second and defying the first. In the full meaning of the term, he grows up without a clear grasp of reality.

[Ibid., 118; pb 98.]

In a deontological [duty-centered] theory, all personal desires are banished from the realm of morality; a personal desire has no moral significance, be it a desire to create or a desire to kill. For example, if a man is not supporting his life from duty, such a morality makes no distinction between supporting it by honest labor or by robbery. If a man *wants* to be honest, he deserves no moral credit; as Kant would put it, such honesty is "praiseworthy," but without "moral import." Only a vicious represser, who feels a profound desire to lie, cheat and steal, but forces himself to act honestly for the sake of "duty," would receive a recognition of moral worth from Kant and his ilk.

This is the sort of theory that gives morality a bad name.

The widespread fear and/or resentment of morality—the feeling that morality is an enemy, a musty realm of suffering and senseless boredom —is not the product of mystic, ascetic or Christian codes as such, but a monument to the ugliest repository of hatred for life, man and reason: the soul of Immanuel Kant.

[Ibid., 117; pb 97.]

In theory, Kant states, a man deserves moral credit for an action done from duty, even if his inclinations also favor it—but only insofar as the latter are incidental and play no role in his motivation. But in practice, Kant maintains, whenever the two coincide no one can *know* that he has escaped the influence of inclination. For all practical purposes, therefore, a moral man must have no private stake in the outcome of his actions, no personal motive, no expectation of profit or gain of any kind.

Even then, however, he cannot be sure that no fragment of desire is "secretly" moving him. The far clearer case, the one case in which a man can at least come close to knowing that he is moral, occurs when the man's desires *clash* with his duty and he acts in defiance of his desires.

[Leonard Peikoff, *OP*, 73; pb 75.]

Kant is the first philosopher of self-sacrifice to advance this ethics as a matter of philosophic *principle*, explicit, self-conscious, uncompromised—essentially uncontradicted by any remnants of the Greek, pro-self viewpoint.

Thus, although he believed that the dutiful man would be rewarded with happiness after death (and that this is proper), Kant holds that the man who is motivated by such a consideration is nonmoral (since he is still acting from inclination, albeit a supernaturally oriented one). Nor will Kant permit the dutiful man to be motivated even by the desire to feel a sense of moral self-approval.

The main line of pre-Kantian moralists had urged man to perform certain actions in order to reach a goal of some kind. They had urged man to love the object which is the good (however it was conceived) and strive to gain it, even if most transferred the quest to the next life. They had asked man to practice a code of virtues as a means to the attainment of *values*. Kant dissociates virtue from the pursuit of any goal. He dissociates it from man's love of or even interest in any object. Which means: *he dissociates morality from values, any values, values as such.*

[Ibid., 76; pb 78.]

It is not inner peace that Kant holds out to man, not otherworldly serenity or ethereal tranquillity, but war, a bloody, unremitting war against passionate, indomitable temptation. It is the lot of the moral man to struggle against undutiful feelings inherent in his nature, and the more intensely he feels and the more desperately he struggles, the greater his claim to virtue. It is the lot of the moral man to burn with desire and then, on principle—the principle of duty—to thwart it. The hallmark of the moral man is to suffer.

[Ibid., 80; pb 82.]

If men lived the sort of life Kant demands, who or what would gain from it? Nothing and no one. The concept of "gain" has been expunged from morality. For Kant, it is the dutiful sacrifice as such that constitutes a man's claim to virtue; the welfare of any recipient is morally incidental. Virtue, for Kant, is not the service of an interest—neither of the self nor of God nor of others. (A man can claim moral credit for service to others in this view, not because *they* benefit, but only insofar as *he* loses.)

Here is the essence and climax of the ethics of self-sacrifice, finally, after two thousand years, come to full, philosophic expression in the Western world: your interests—of whatever kind, including the interest in being moral—are a mark of moral imperfection *because* they are interests. Your desires, regardless of their content, deserve no respect *because* they are desires. Do your duty, which is yours *because* you have desires, and which is sublime *because*, unadulterated by the stigma of any gain, it shines forth unsullied, in loss, pain, conflict, torture. Sacrifice the thing you want, without beneficiaries, supernatural or social; sacrifice your values, your self-interest, your happiness, your self, *because* they are your values, your self-interest, your happiness, your self; sacrifice them to morality, i.e., to the noumenal dimension, i.e., to nothing knowable or conceivable to man, i.e., as far as man living on this earth is concerned, to *nothing*.

The moral commandment is: thou shalt sacrifice, sacrifice everything, sacrifice for the sake of sacrifice, *as an end in itself*.

[Ibid., 82; pb 83.]

Sacrifice is the surrender of that which you value in favor of that which you don't. . . . It is not a sacrifice to renounce the unwanted. It is not a sacrifice to give your life to others, if death is your personal desire. To achieve the virtue of sacrifice, you must want to live, you must love it, you must burn with passion for this earth and for all the splendor it can give you—you must feel the twist of every knife as it slashes your desires away from your reach and drains your love out of your body. It is not mere death that the morality of sacrifice holds out to you as an ideal, but death by slow torture.

[GS, *FNI*, 172; pb 140.]

You may also find it hard to believe that anyone could advocate the things Kant is advocating. If you doubt it, I suggest that you look up the references given and read the original works. Do not seek to escape the subject by thinking: "Oh, Kant didn't mean it!" He did. . . .

Kant is the most evil man in mankind's history.

["Brief Summary," *TO*, Sept. 1971, 4.]

Psychological Techniques

Kant originated the technique required to sell irrational notions to the men of a skeptical, cynical age who have formally rejected mysticism without grasping the rudiments of rationality. The technique is as follows: if you want to propagate an outrageously evil idea (based on traditionally accepted doctrines), your conclusion must be brazenly clear, but your proof unintelligible. Your proof must be so tangled a mess that it will paralyze a reader's critical faculty—a mess of evasions, equivocations, obfuscations, circumlocutions, non sequiturs, endless sentences leading nowhere, irrelevant side issues, clauses, sub-clauses and sub-sub-clauses, a meticulously lengthy proving of the obvious, and big chunks of the arbitrary thrown in as self-evident, erudite references to sciences, to pseudo-sciences, to the never-to-be-sciences, to the un-

traceable and the unprovable—all of it resting on a zero: the *absence* of definitions. I offer in evidence the *Critique of Pure Reason.*
["An Untitled Letter," *PWNI*, 141; pb 116.]

If "genius" denotes extraordinary ability, then Kant may be called a genius in his capacity to sense, play on and perpetuate human fears, irrationalities and, above all, ignorance. His influence rests not on philosophical but on *psychological* factors.
["Causality Versus Duty," *PWNI*, 117; pb 98.]

The philosophy of Kant is a systematic rationalization of every major psychological vice. The metaphysical inferiority of this world (as a "phenomenal" world of mere "appearances"), is a rationalization for the hatred of reality. The notion that reason is unable to perceive reality and deals only with "appearances," is a rationalization for the hatred of reason; it is also a rationalization for a profound kind of epistemological egalitarianism which reduces reason to equality with the futile puttering of "idealistic" dreamers. The metaphysical superiority of the "noumenal" world, is a rationalization for the supremacy of emotions, which are thus given the power to know the unknowable by ineffable means.

The complaint that man can perceive things only through his own consciousness, not through any other kinds of consciousnesses, is a rationalization for the most profound type of second-handedness ever confessed in print: it is the whine of a man tortured by perpetual concern with what others think and by inability to decide which others he should conform to. The wish to perceive "things in themselves" unprocessed by any consciousness, is a rationalization for the wish to escape the effort and responsibility of cognition—by means of the automatic omniscience a whim-worshiper ascribes to his emotions. The moral imperative of the duty to sacrifice oneself to duty, a sacrifice without beneficiaries, is a gross rationalization for the image (and soul) of an austere, ascetic monk who winks at you with an obscenely sadistic pleasure—the pleasure of breaking man's spirit, ambition, success, self-esteem, and enjoyment of life on earth. Et cetera. These are just some of the highlights.
["Philosophical Detection," *PWNI*, 22; pb 19.]

See also ALTRUISM; CONCEPTS; "DUTY"; FAITH; IDENTITY; KNOWLEDGE; LINGUISTIC ANALYSIS; LOGIC; LOGICAL POSITIVISM; MODERN ART; MYSTICISM; OBJECTIVITY; PRAGMATISM; PRIMACY of EXISTENCE vs. PRIMACY of CONSCIOUSNESS; RATIONALIZATION; REASON; RELIGION; SACRIFICE; SELF; SELFISHNESS; SELFLESSNESS; SUBJECTIVISM.

Knowledge. "Knowledge" is . . . a mental grasp of a fact(s) of reality, reached either by perceptual observation or by a process of reason based on perceptual observation.

[*ITOE*, 45.]

See also CERTAINTY; EPISTEMOLOGY; LOGIC; PERCEPTION; REASON.

L

Language. In order to be used as a single unit, the enormous sum integrated by a concept has to be given the form of a single, specific, *perceptual* concrete, which will differentiate it from all other concretes and from all other concepts. This is the function performed by language. Language is a code of visual-auditory symbols that serves the psycho-epistemological function of converting concepts into the mental equivalent of concretes. Language is the exclusive domain and tool of concepts. Every word we use (with the exception of proper names) is a symbol that denotes a concept, i.e., that stands for an unlimited number of concretes of a certain kind.

(Proper names are used in order to identify and include particular entities in a conceptual method of cognition. Observe that even proper names, in advanced civilizations, follow the definitional principles of *genus* and *differentia:* e.g., John Smith, with "Smith" serving as *genus* and "John" as *differentia*—or New York, U.S.A.)

[*ITOE*, 11.]

Concepts represent a system of mental filing and cross-filing, so complex that the largest electronic computer is a child's toy by comparison. This system serves as the context, the frame-of-reference, by means of which man grasps and classifies (and studies further) every existent he encounters and every aspect of reality. Language is the physical (visual-audible) implementation of this system.

Concepts and, therefore, language are *primarily* a tool of cognition—*not* of communication, as is usually assumed. Communication is merely the consequence, not the cause nor the primary purpose of concept-formation—a crucial consequence, of invaluable importance to men, but still only a consequence. *Cognition precedes communication;* the necessary pre-condition of communication is that one have something to communicate. (This is true even of communication among animals, or of communication by grunts and growls among inarticulate men, let alone of communication by means of so complex and exacting a tool as language.) The primary purpose of concepts and of language is to provide man with a system of cognitive classification and organization, which enables him to acquire knowledge on an unlimited scale; this means: to keep order in man's mind and enable him to think.

[Ibid., 91.]

The first words a child learns are words denoting visual objects, and he retains his first concepts *visually*. Observe that the visual form he gives them is reduced to those *essentials* which distinguish the particular kind of entities from all others—for instance, the universal type of a child's drawing of man in the form of an oval for the torso, a circle for the head, four sticks for extremities, etc. Such drawings are a visual record of the process of abstraction and concept-formation in a mind's transition from the perceptual level to the full vocabulary of the conceptual level.

There is evidence to suppose that written language originated in the form of drawings—as the pictographic writing of the Oriental peoples seems to indicate. With the growth of man's knowledge and of his power of abstraction, a pictorial representation of concepts could no longer be adequate to his conceptual range, and was replaced by a fully symbolic code.

[*Ibid.*, 15.]

Language is a conceptual tool—a code of visual-auditory symbols that denote concepts. To a person who understands the function of language, it makes no difference what sounds are chosen to name things, provided these sounds refer to clearly defined aspects of reality. But to a tribalist, language is a mystic heritage, a string of sounds handed down from his ancestors and memorized, not understood. To him, the importance lies in the perceptual concrete, the *sound* of a word, not its meaning. . . .

The learning of another language expands one's abstract capacity and vision. Personally, I speak four—or rather three-and-a-half—languages: English, French, Russian and the half is German, which I can read, but not speak. I found this knowledge extremely helpful when I began writing: it gave me a wider range and choice of concepts, it showed me four different styles of expression, it made me grasp the nature of language as such, apart from any set of concretes.

(Speaking of concretes, I would say that every civilized language has its own inimitable power and beauty, but the one I love is English—the language of my choice, not of my birth. English is the most eloquent, the most precise, the most economical and, therefore, the most powerful. English fits me best—but I would be able to express *my* identity in any Western language.)

["Global Balkanization," pamphlet, 8.]

The Miracle Worker by William Gibson . . . tells the story of how Annie Sullivan brought Helen Keller to grasp the nature of *language*. . . .

I suggest that you read *The Miracle Worker* and study its implications. . . . this particular play is an invaluable lesson in the fundamentals of a rational epistemology.

I suggest that you consider Annie Sullivan's titanic struggle to arouse a child's conceptual faculty by means of a single sense, the sense of touch, then evaluate the meaning, motive and moral status of the notion that man's conceptual faculty does not require any sensory experience.

I suggest that you consider what an enormous intellectual feat Helen Keller had to perform in order to develop a full conceptual range (including a college education, which required more in her day than it does now), then judge those normal people who learn their first, perceptual-level abstractions without any difficulty and freeze on that level, and keep the higher ranges of their conceptual development in a chaotic fog of swimming, indeterminate approximations, playing a game of signals without referents, as Helen Keller did at first, but without her excuse. Then check on whether *you* respect and how carefully *you* employ your priceless possession: language.

And, lastly, I suggest that you try to project what would have happened if, instead of Annie Sullivan, a sadist had taken charge of Helen Keller's education. A sadist would spell "water" into Helen's palm, while making her touch water, stones, flowers and dogs interchangeably; he would teach her that water is called "water" today, but "milk" tomorrow; he would endeavor to convey to her that there is no necessary connection between names and things, that the signals in her palm are a game of arbitrary conventions and that she'd better obey him without trying to understand.

If this projection is too monstrous to hold in one's mind for long, remember that *this* is what today's academic philosophers are doing to the young—to minds as confused, as plastic and almost as helpless (on the higher conceptual levels) as Helen Keller's mind was at her start.

["Kant Versus Sullivan," *PWNI*, 109; pb 90.]

See also COMMUNICATION; CONCEPT-FORMATION; CONCEPTS; GRAMMAR; LINGUISTIC ANALYSIS; PERCEPTION; PSYCHO-EPISTEMOLOGY; REASON; WORDS.

Law, Objective and Non-Objective.

All laws must be *objective* (and objectively justifiable): men must know clearly, and in advance of taking an action, what the law forbids them to do (and why), what constitutes a crime and what penalty they will incur if they commit it.

["The Nature of Government," *VOS*, 149; pb 110.]

The retaliatory use of force requires *objective* rules of evidence to establish that a crime has been committed and to *prove* who committed it, as well as *objective* rules to define punishments and enforcement procedures. Men who attempt to prosecute crimes, without such rules, are a lynch mob. If a society left the retaliatory use of force in the hands of individual citizens, it would degenerate into mob rule, lynch law and an endless series of bloody private feuds or vendettas.

If physical force is to be barred from social relationships, men need an institution charged with the task of protecting their rights under an *objective* code of rules.

This is the task of a government—of a *proper* government—its basic task, its only moral justification and the reason why men do need a government.

A government is the means of placing the retaliatory use of physical force under objective control—i.e., under objectively defined laws.

[Ibid., 147; pb 109.]

When men are caught in the trap of non-objective law, when their work, future and livelihood are at the mercy of a bureaucrat's whim, when they have no way of knowing what unknown "influence" will crack down on them for which unspecified offense, *fear* becomes their basic motive, if they remain in the industry at all—and compromise, conformity, staleness, dullness, the dismal grayness of the middle-of-the-road are all that can be expected of them. Independent thinking does not submit to bureaucratic edicts, originality does not follow "public policies," integrity does not petition for a license, heroism is not fostered by fear, creative genius is not summoned forth at the point of a gun.

Non-objective law is the most effective weapon of human enslavement: its victims become its enforcers and enslave themselves.

["Vast Quicksands," *TON*, July 1963, 25.]

That which cannot be formulated into an objective law, cannot be made the subject of legislation—not in a free country, not if we are to have "a government of laws and not of men." An undefineable law is not a law, but merely a license for some men to rule others.

[Ibid., 28.]

It is a grave error to suppose that a dictatorship rules a nation by means of strict, rigid laws which are obeyed and enforced with rigorous, military precision. Such a rule would be evil, but almost bearable; men could endure the harshest edicts, provided these edicts were known, specific and stable; it is not the known that breaks men's spirits, but the unpredictable. A dictatorship has to be capricious; it has to rule by means of the unexpected, the incomprehensible, the wantonly irrational; it has to deal not in death, but in *sudden* death; a state of chronic uncertainty is what men are psychologically unable to bear.

["Antitrust: The Rule of Unreason," *TON*, Feb. 1962, 5.]

An *objective* law protects a country's freedom; only a *non-objective* law can give a statist the chance he seeks: a chance to impose *his* arbitrary will—*his* policies, *his* decisions, *his* interpretations, *his* enforcement, *his* punishment or favor—on disarmed, defenseless victims.

[Ibid., 5.]

The threat of sudden destruction, of unpredictable retaliation for unnamed offenses, is a much more potent means of enslavement than explicit dictatorial laws. It demands more than mere obedience; it leaves men no policy save one: *to please* the authorities; to please—blindly, uncritically, without standards or principles; to please—in any issue, matter or circumstance, for fear of an unknowable, unprovable vengeance.

[Ibid., 8.]

See also ANARCHISM; ANTITRUST LAWS; CONSTITUTION; CRIME; DICTATORSHIP; GOVERNMENT; INDIVIDUAL RIGHTS; RETALIA-TORY FORCE; RETROACTIVE LAW; STATISM.

Learning. Men can learn from one another, but learning requires a process of thought on the part of every individual student. Men can cooperate in the discovery of new knowledge, but such cooperation requires the independent exercise of his rational faculty by every individual scientist. Man is the only living species that can transmit and expand his store of knowledge from generation to generation; but such transmission requires a process of thought on the part of the individual recipients.

["What Is Capitalism?" *CUI*, 16.]

All learning involves a process of automatizing, i.e., of first acquiring knowledge by fully conscious, focused attention and observation, then of establishing mental connections which make that knowledge automatic (instantly available as a context), thus freeing man's mind to pursue further, more complex knowledge.

[*ITOE*, 86.]

There are two different methods of learning: by memorizing and by understanding. The first belongs primarily to the perceptual level of a human consciousness, the second to the conceptual.

The first is achieved by means of repetition and concrete-bound association (a process in which one sensory concrete leads automatically to another, with no regard to content or meaning). The best illustration of this process is a song which was popular some twenty years ago, called "Mairzy Doats." Try to recall some poem you had to memorize in grade school; you will find that you can recall it only if you recite the sounds automatically, by the "Mairzy Doats" method; if you focus on the meaning, the memory vanishes. This form of learning is shared with man by the higher animals: all animal training consists of making the animal memorize a series of actions by repetition and association.

The second method of learning—by a process of understanding—is possible only to man. To understand means to focus on the content of a given subject (as against the sensory—visual or auditory—form in which it is communicated), to isolate its essentials, to establish its relationship to the previously known, and to integrate it with the appropriate categories of other subjects. Integration is the essential part of understanding.

The predominance of memorizing is proper only in the first few years of a child's education, while he is observing and gathering perceptual material. From the time he reaches the conceptual level (i.e., from the time he learns to speak), his education requires a progressively larger scale of understanding and progressively smaller amounts of memorizing.

["The Comprachicos," *NL,* 207.]

Learning is a conceptual process; an educational method devised to ignore, by-pass and contradict the requirements of conceptual development, cannot arouse any interest in learning. The "adjusted" are bored because they are unable actively to absorb knowledge. The independent are bored because they seek *knowledge,* not games of "class projects" or group "discussions." The first are unable to digest their lessons; the second are starved.

[Ibid., 216.]

The process of forming, integrating and using concepts is not an automatic, but a volitional process—i.e., a process which uses both new and automatized material, but which is directed volitionally. It is not an innate, but an acquired skill; it has to be *learned*—it is the most crucially important part of learning—and all of man's other capacities depend on how well or how badly he learns it.

This skill does not pertain to the particular *content* of a man's knowledge at any given age, but to the *method* by which he acquires and organizes knowledge—the method by which his mind deals with its content. The method *programs* his subconscious computer, determining how efficiently, lamely or disastrously his cognitive processes will function.

[Ibid., 193.]

See also AUTOMATIZATION; CONCEPTS; EDUCATION; INTEGRATION (MENTAL); SUBCONSCIOUS; UNDERSTANDING.

Leftists. *See Rightists vs. Leftists.*

"Liberals." The basic and crucial political issue of our age is: *capitalism versus socialism,* or freedom versus statism. For decades, this issue has been silenced, suppressed, evaded, and hidden under the foggy, undefined rubber-terms of "conservatism" and "liberalism" which had lost their original meaning and could be stretched to mean all things to all men.

The goal of the "liberals"—as it emerges from the record of the past decades—was to smuggle this country into welfare statism by means of single, concrete, specific measures, enlarging the power of the government a step at a time, never permitting these steps to be summed up into principles, never permitting their direction to be identified or the basic issue to be named. Thus statism was to come, not by vote or by violence, but by slow rot—by a long process of evasion and epistemological corruption, leading to a *fait accompli.* (The goal of the "conservatives" was only to retard that process.)

[" 'Extremism,' or The Art of Smearing," *CUI,* 178.]

The most timid, frightened, conservative defenders of the status quo —of the *intellectual* status quo—are today's liberals (the leaders of the conservatives never ventured into the realm of the intellect). What they dread to discover is the fact that the intellectual status quo they inherited is bankrupt, that they have no ideological base to stand on and no capacity to construct one. Brought up on the philosophy of Pragmatism, they have been taught that principles are unprovable, impractical or non-existent—which has destroyed their ability to integrate ideas, to deal with abstractions, and to see beyond the range of the immediate moment. Abstractions, they claim, are "simplistic" (another anti-concept); myopia is sophisticated. "Don't polarize!" and "Don't rock the boat!" are expressions of the same kind of panic.

["Credibility and Polarization," *ARL,* I, 1, 2.]

In the 1930's, the "liberals" had a program of broad social reforms and a crusading spirit, they advocated a planned society, they talked in

terms of abstract principles, they propounded theories of a predominantly socialistic nature—and most of them were touchy about the accusation that they were enlarging the government's power; most of
them were assuring their opponents that government power was only a
temporary means to an end—a "noble end," the liberation of the individual from his bondage to material needs.

Today, nobody talks of a planned society in the "liberal" camp; long-
range programs, theories, principles, abstractions, and "noble ends" are
not fashionable any longer. Modern "liberals" deride any political concern with such large-scale matters as an entire society or an economy as
a whole; they concern themselves with single, concrete-bound, range-
of-the-moment projects and demands, without regard to cost, context,
or consequences. "Pragmatic"—*not* "idealistic"—is their favorite adjective when they are called upon to justify their "stance," as they call it,
not "stand." They are militantly opposed to political philosophy; they
denounce political concepts as "tags," "labels," "myths," "illusions"—and
resist any attempt to "label"—i.e., to *identify*—their own views. They
are belligerently anti-theoretical and—with a faded mantle of intellectuality still clinging to their shoulders—they are anti-intellectual. The
only remnant of their former "idealism" is a tired, cynical, ritualistic
quoting of shopworn "humanitarian" slogans, when the occasion demands it.

Cynicism, uncertainty, and fear are the insignia of the culture which
they are still dominating by default. And the only thing that has not
rusted in their ideological equipment, but has grown savagely brighter
and clearer through the years, is their lust for power—for an autocratic,
statist, totalitarian government power. It is not a crusading brightness,
it is not the lust of a fanatic with a mission—it is more like the glassy-
eyed brightness of a somnambulist whose stuporous despair has long
since swallowed the memory of his purpose, but who still clings to his
mystic weapon in the stubborn belief that "there ought to be a law," that
everything will be all right if only somebody will pass a law, that every
problem can be solved by the magic power of brute force.

["The New Fascism: Rule by Consensus," *CUI*, 209.]

The majority of those who are loosely identified by the term "liberals"
are afraid to let *themselves* discover that what they advocate *is* statism.
They do not want to accept the full meaning of their goal; they want to
keep all the advantages and effects of capitalism, while destroying the
cause, and they want to establish statism without its necessary effects.
They do not want to know or to admit that they are the champions of
dictatorship and slavery.

["Conservatism: An Obituary," *CUI*, 194.]

For more than fifty years, the West's liberal intellectuals have proclaimed their love for mankind, while being bored by the rivers of blood pouring out of the Soviet Union. Professing their compassion for human suffering, they have none for the victims in Russia. Unable or unwilling to give up their faith in collectivism, they evade the existence of Soviet atrocities, of terror, secret police and concentration camps— and publish glowing tributes to Soviet technology, production and art. Posturing as humanitarians, they man the barricades to fight the "injustice," "exploitation," "repression," and "persecution" they claim to find *in America;* as to the full reality of such things in Russia, they keep silent.

[Susan Ludel, review of Anatoly Marchenko's
My Testimony, TO, July 1970, 15.]

See also CAPITALISM; COLLECTIVISM; COMPROMISE; "CONSERVATIVES"; "CONSERVATIVES" vs. "LIBERALS"; CYNICISM; INDIVIDUAL RIGHTS; MIXED ECONOMY; NEW LEFT; PRAGMATISM; SOCIALISM; SOVIET RUSSIA; STATISM; WELFARE STATE.

"Libertarians." For the record, I shall repeat what I have said many times before: I do not join or endorse any political group or movement. More specifically, I disapprove of, disagree with, and have no connection with, the latest aberration of some conservatives, the so-called "hippies of the right," who attempt to snare the younger or more careless ones of my readers by claiming simultanteously to be followers of my philosophy and advocates of anarchism. Anyone offering such a combination confesses his inability to understand either. Anarchism is the most irrational, anti-intellectual notion ever spun by the concrete-bound, context-dropping, whim-worshiping fringe of the collectivist movement, where it properly belongs.

["Brief Summary," *TO,* Sept. 1971, 1.]

Above all, do not join the wrong *ideological* groups or movements, in order to "do something." By "ideological" (in this context), I mean groups or movements proclaiming some vaguely generalized, undefined (and, usually, contradictory) *political* goals. (E.g., the Conservative Party, which subordinates reason to faith, and substitutes theocracy for capitalism; or the "libertarian" hippies, who subordinate reason to whims, and substitute anarchism for capitalism.) To join such groups means to reverse the philosophical hierarchy and to sell out fundamental principles for the sake of some superficial political action which is bound to fail. It means that you help the defeat of *your* ideas and the victory of your enemies. (For a discussion of the reasons, see

"The Anatomy of Compromise" in my book *Capitalism: The Unknown Ideal.*)

["What Can One Do?" *PWNI*, 248; pb 202.]

The "libertarians" . . . plagiarize Ayn Rand's principle that no man may initiate the use of physical force, and treat it as a mystically revealed, out-of-context absolute. . . .

In the philosophical battle for a free society, the one crucial connection to be upheld is that between capitalism and reason. The religious conservatives are seeking to tie capitalism to mysticism; the "libertarians" are tying capitalism to the whim-worshipping subjectivism and chaos of anarchy. To cooperate with either group is to betray capitalism, reason, and one's own future.

[Harry Binswanger, "Q & A Department: Anarchism," *TOF*, Aug. 1981, 12.]

See also ANARCHISM; COMPROMISE; CONTEXT-DROPPING; GOVERNMENT; PHYSICAL FORCE; SUBJECTIVISM; WHIMS/WHIM-WORSHIP.

Life.   There is only one fundamental alternative in the universe: existence or non-existence—and it pertains to a single class of entities: to living organisms. The existence of inanimate matter is unconditional, the existence of life is not: it depends on a specific course of action. Matter is indestructible, it changes its forms, but it cannot cease to exist. It is only a living organism that faces a constant alternative: the issue of life or death. Life is a process of self-sustaining and self-generated action. If an organism fails in that action, it dies; its chemical elements remain, but its life goes out of existence. It is only the concept of "Life" that makes the concept of "Value" possible. It is only to a living entity that things can be good or evil.

[GS, *FNI*, 147; pb 121.]

Only a *living* entity can have goals or can originate them. And it is only a living organism that has the capacity for self-generated, goal-directed action. On the *physical* level, the functions of all living organisms, from the simplest to the most complex—from the nutritive function in the single cell of an amoeba to the blood circulation in the body of a man—are actions generated by the organism itself and directed to a single goal: the maintenance of the organism's *life*.

An organism's life depends on two factors: the material or fuel which it needs from the outside, from its physical background, and the action of its own body, the action of using that fuel *properly*. What standard determines what is *proper* in this context? The standard is the organism's life, or: that which is required for the organism's survival.

["The Objectivist Ethics," *VOS*, 6; pb 16.]

When applied to physical phenomena, such as the automatic functions of an organism, the term "goal-directed" is not to be taken to mean "purposive" (a concept applicable only to the actions of a consciousness) and is not to imply the existence of any teleological principle operating in insentient nature. I use the term "goal-directed," in this context, to designate the fact that the automatic functions of living organisms are actions whose nature is such that they *result* in the preservation of an organism's life.

[Ibid.]

In a fundamental sense, stillness is the antithesis of life. Life can be kept in existence only by a constant process of self-sustaining action. The goal of that action, the ultimate *value* which, to be kept, must be gained through its every moment, is the organism's *life*.

[Ibid., 7; pb 16.]

See also HAPPINESS; LIFE, RIGHT to; MAN; MORALITY; STANDARD of VALUE; ULTIMATE VALUE; VALUES.

Life, Right to. A "right" is a moral principle defining and sanctioning a man's freedom of action in a social context. There is only *one* fundamental right (all the others are its consequences or corollaries): a man's right to his own life. Life is a process of self-sustaining and self-generated action; the right to life means the right to engage in self-sustaining and self-generated action—which means: the freedom to take all the actions required by the nature of a rational being for the support, the furtherance, the fulfillment and the enjoyment of his own life. (Such is the meaning of the right to life, liberty and the pursuit of happiness.)

["Man's Rights," *VOS*, 124; pb 93.]

The right to life means that a man has the right to support his life by his own work (on any economic level, as high as his ability will carry him); it does *not* mean that others must provide him with the necessities of life.

[Ibid., 129; pb 97.]

The Right of Life means that Man cannot be deprived of his life for the benefit of another man nor of any number of other men.

["Textbook of Americanism," pamphlet, 5.]

See also INDIVIDUAL RIGHTS; LIFE.

Linguistic Analysis. There is an element of grim irony in the emergence of Linguistic Analysis on the philosophical scene. The assault on man's conceptual faculty has been accelerating since Kant, widening the breach between man's mind and reality. The cognitive function of concepts was undercut by a series of grotesque devices—such, for instance, as the "analytic-synthetic" dichotomy which, by a route of tortuous circumlocutions and equivocations, leads to the dogma that a "necessarily" true proposition cannot be factual, and a factual proposition cannot be "necessarily" true. The crass skepticism and epistemological cynicism of Kant's influence have been seeping from the universities to the arts, the sciences, the industries, the legislatures, saturating our culture, decomposing language and thought. If ever there was a need for a Herculean philosophical effort to clean up the Kantian stables—particularly, to redeem language by establishing objective criteria of meaning and definition, which average men could not attempt —the time was *now*. As if sensing that need, Linguistic Analysis came on the scene for the avowed purpose of "clarifying" language—and proceeded to declare that the meaning of concepts is determined in the minds of average men, and that the job of philosophers consists of observing and reporting on how people use words.

The *reductio ad absurdum* of a long line of mini-Kantians, such as pragmatists and positivists, Linguistic Analysis holds that words are an arbitrary social product immune from any principles or standards, an irreducible primary not subject to inquiry about its origin or purpose— and that we can "dissolve" all philosophical problems by "clarifying" the use of these arbitrary, causeless, meaningless sounds which hold ultimate power over reality. . . .

Proceeding from the premise that words (concepts) are created by whim, Linguistic Analysis offers us a choice of whims: individual or collective. It declares that there are two kinds of definitions: "stipulative," which may be anything anyone chooses, and "reportive," which are ascertained by polls of popular use.

As reporters, linguistic analysts were accurate: Wittgenstein's theory that a concept refers to a conglomeration of things vaguely tied together by a "family resemblance" is a perfect description of the state of a mind out of focus.

[*ITOE*, 102.]

Linguistic Analysis declares that the ultimate reality is not even percepts, but words, and that words have no specific referents, but mean whatever people want them to mean. . . . Linguistic Analysis is vehemently opposed to . . . any kinds of principles or broad generalizations —i.e., to consistency. It is opposed to basic axioms (as "analytic" and "redundant")—i.e., to the necessity of any grounds for one's assertions. It is opposed to the hierarchical structure of concepts (i.e., to the process of abstraction) and regards any word as an isolated primary (i.e., as a perceptually given concrete). It is opposed to "system-building"—i.e., to the integration of knowledge.

["The Comprachicos," *NL*, 225.]

Through decades of promulgating such doctrines as Pragmatism, Logical Positivism, Linguistic Analysis, [philosophers] refused to consider the fact that these doctrines would disarm and paralyze the best among men, those who take philosophy seriously, and that they would unleash the worst, those who, scorning philosophy, reason, justice, morality, would have no trouble brushing the disarmed out of the way. . . . To what sort of problems had [today's philosophers] been giving priority over the problems of politics? Among the papers to be read at that [1969 American Philosophical Association (Eastern Division)] convention were: "Pronouns and Proper Names"—"Can Grammar Be Thought?"—"Propositions as the Only Realities."

["The Chickens' Homecoming," *NL*, 112.]

It is the claim of Linguistic Analysis that its purpose is not the communication of any particular philosophic content, but the *training* of a student's mind. This is true—in the terrible, butchering sense of a comprachico operation. The detailed discussions of inconsequential minutiae—the discourses on trivia picked at random and in midstream, without base, context or conclusion—the shocks of self-doubt at the professor's sudden revelations of some such fact as the student's inability to define the word "but," which, he claims, proves that they do not understand their own statements—the countering of the question: "What is the meaning of philosophy?" with: "Which sense of 'meaning' do you mean?" followed by a discourse on twelve possible uses of the word "meaning," by which time the question is lost—and, above all, the necessity to shrink one's focus to the range of a flea's, and to keep it there—will cripple the best of minds, if it attempts to comply.

"Mind-training" pertains to psycho-epistemology; it consists in making a mind automatize certain processes, turning them into permanent habits. What habits does Linguistic Analysis inculcate? Context-dropping, "concept-stealing," disintegration, purposelessness, the inability to grasp, retain or deal with abstractions. Linguistic Analysis is not a philosophy, it is a method of eliminating the *capacity* for philosophical thought—it is a course in brain-destruction, a systematic attempt to turn a rational animal into an animal unable to reason.

["The Comprachicos," *NL*, 226.]

See also ANALYTIC-SYNTHETIC DICHOTOMY; GRAMMAR; INTE-GRATION (MENTAL); KANT, IMMANUEL; LANGUAGE; LOGICAL POSITIVISM; MEANING (of CONCEPTS); PHILOSOPHY; PRAGMA-TISM; PRINCIPLES; "STOLEN CONCEPT," FALLACY of; WORDS.

Literature. Art is a selective re-creation of reality according to an artist's metaphysical value-judgments. Man's profound need of art lies in the fact that his cognitive faculty is conceptual, i.e., that he acquires knowledge by means of abstractions, and needs the power to bring his widest metaphysical abstractions into his immediate, perceptual awareness. . . .

Literature re-creates reality by means of language. . . . The relation of literature to man's cognitive faculty is obvious: literature re-creates reality by means of words, i.e., *concepts*. But in order to re-create reality, it is the sensory-perceptual level of man's awareness that literature has to convey conceptually: the reality of concrete, individual men and events, of specific sights, sounds, textures, etc.

All these arts are *conceptual* in essence, all are products of and addressed to the conceptual level of man's consciousness, and they differ only in their means. Literature starts with concepts and integrates them to percepts—painting, sculpture and architecture start with percepts and integrate them to concepts. The ultimate psycho-epistemological function is the same: a process that integrates man's forms of cognition, unifies his consciousness and clarifies his grasp of reality.

["Art and Cognition," *RM*, pb 45.]

The most important principle of the esthetics of literature was formulated by Aristotle, who said that fiction is of greater philosophical importance than history, because "history represents things as they are, while fiction represents them as they might be and ought to be."

This applies to all forms of literature and most particularly to a form that did not come into existence until twenty-three centuries later: the novel.

A novel is a long, fictional story about human beings and the events of their lives. The four essential attributes of a novel are: Theme—Plot—Characterization—Style.

These are *attributes*, not separable parts. They can be isolated conceptually for purposes of study, but one must always remember that they are interrelated and that a novel is their sum. (If it is a good novel, it is an indivisible sum.)

These four attributes pertain to all forms of literature, i.e., of fiction, with one exception. They pertain to novels, plays, scenarios, librettos, short stories. The single exception is poems. A poem does not have to tell a story; its basic attributes are theme and style.

A novel is *the* major literary form—in respect to its scope, its inexhaustible potentiality, its almost unlimited freedom (including the freedom from physical limitations of the kind that restrict a stage play) and, most importantly, in respect to the fact that a novel is a purely *literary* form of art which does not require the intermediary of the performing arts to achieve its ultimate effect.

["Basic Principles of Literature," *RM*, 57; pb 80.]

An artist recreates those aspects of reality which represent his fundamental view of man and of existence. In forming a view of man's nature, a fundamental question one must answer is whether man possesses the faculty of volition—because one's conclusions and evaluations in regard to all the characteristics, requirements and actions of man depend on the answer.

Their opposite answers to this question constitute the respective basic premises of two broad categories of art: Romanticism, which recognizes the existence of man's volition—and Naturalism, which denies it.

["What Is Romanticism?" *RM*, 81; pb 99.]

Prior to the nineteenth century, literature presented man as a helpless being whose life and actions were determined by forces beyond his control: either by fate and the gods, as in the Greek tragedies, or by an innate weakness, "a tragic flaw," as in the plays of Shakespeare. Writers regarded man as metaphysically impotent; their basic premise was *determinism*. On that premise, one could not project what might happen to men; one could only record what *did* happen—and chronicles were the appropriate literary form of such recording.

Man as a being who possesses the faculty of volition did not appear in literature until the nineteenth century. The *novel* was his proper literary form—and Romanticism was the great new movement in art. Romanticism saw man as a being able to choose his values, to achieve his goals, to control his own existence. The Romantic writers did not record the events that *had* happened, but projected the events that *should* happen; they did not record the choices men *had* made, but projected the choices men *ought to make*.

With the resurgence of mysticism and collectivism, in the later part of the nineteenth century, the Romantic novel and the Romantic movement vanished gradually from the cultural scene.

Man's new enemy, in art, was Naturalism. Naturalism rejected the concept of volition and went back to a view of man as a helpless creature determined by forces beyond his control; only now the new ruler of man's destiny was held to be *society*. The Naturalists proclaimed that values have no power and no place, neither in human life nor in literature, that writers must present men "as they are," which meant: must record whatever they happen to see around them—that they must not pronounce value-judgments nor project abstractions, but must content themselves with a faithful transcription, a carbon copy, of any existing concretes.

[*"The Esthetic Vacuum of Our Age," RM*, 113; pb 123.]

[The] basic premises of Romanticism and Naturalism (the volition or anti-volition premise) affect all the other aspects of a literary work, such as the choice of theme and the quality of the style, but it is the nature of the story structure—the attribute of plot or plotlessness—that represents the most important difference between them and serves as the main distinguishing characteristic for classifying a given work in one category or the other.

[*"What Is Romanticism?" RM*, 83; pb 101.]

The theme of a novel can be conveyed only through the events of the plot, the events of the plot depend on the characterization of the men who enact them—and the characterization cannot be achieved except through the events of the plot, and the plot cannot be constructed without a theme.

This is the kind of integration required by the nature of a novel. And this is why a good novel is an indivisible sum: every scene, sequence and passage of a good novel has to involve, contribute to and advance all three of its major attributes: theme, plot, characterization.

[*"Basic Principles of Literature," RM*, 74; pb 93.]

A cardinal principle of good fiction [is]: *the theme and the plot of a novel must be integrated*—as thoroughly integrated as mind and body or thought and action in a rational view of man.

[*"Basic Principles of Literature," RM*, 63; pb 85.]

In art, and in literature, the end and the means, or the subject and the style, must be worthy of each other.

That which is not worth contemplating in life, is not worth re-creating in art.

[*"The Goal of My Writing," RM*, 166; pb 166.]

The writer who develops a beautiful style, but has nothing to say, represents a kind of arrested esthetic development; he is like a pianist who acquires a brilliant technique by playing finger-exercises, but never gives a concert.

The typical literary product of such writers—and of their imitators, who possess no style—are so-called "mood-studies," popular among today's literati, which are little pieces conveying nothing but a certain mood. Such pieces are not an art-form, they are merely finger-exercises that never develop into art.

["Basic Principles of Literature," *RM*, 78; pb 96.]

Now take a look at modern literature.

Man—the nature of man, the metaphysically significant, important, essential in man—is now represented by dipsomaniacs, drug addicts, sexual perverts, homicidal maniacs and psychotics. The subjects of modern literature are such themes as: the hopeless love of a bearded lady for a mongoloid pinhead in a circus side show—or: the problem of a married couple whose child was born with six fingers on her left hand —or: the tragedy of a gentle young man who just can't help murdering strangers in the park, for kicks.

All this is still presented to us under the Naturalistic heading of "a slice of life" or "*real* life"—but the old slogans have worn thin. The obvious question, to which the heirs of statistical Naturalism have no answer, is: if heroes and geniuses are not to be regarded as representative of mankind, by reason of their numerical rarity, why are freaks and monsters to be regarded as representative? Why are the problems of a bearded lady of greater universal significance than the problems of a genius? Why is the soul of a murderer worth studying, but not the soul of a hero?

["The Esthetic Vacuum of Our Age," *RM*, 115; pb 125.]

If you wonder what is the ultimate destination toward which modern philosophy and modern art are leading you, you may observe its advance symptoms all around us. Observe that literature is returning to the art form of the pre-industrial ages, to the *chronicle*—that fictionalized biographies of "real" people, of politicians, baseball players or Chicago gangsters, are given preference over works of imaginative fiction, in the theater, in the movies, in television—and that a favored literary form is *the documentary*.

["The Esthetic Vacuum of Our Age," *RM*, 118; pb 127.]

Except for the exceptions, there is no literature (and no art) today— in the sense of a broad, vital cultural movement and influence. There are only bewildered imitators with nothing to imitate—and charlatans who rise to split-second notoriety, as they always did in periods of cultural collapse.

Some remnants of Romanticism may still be found in the popular media—but in such a mangled, disfigured form that they achieve the opposite of Romanticism's original purpose.

["What Is Romanticism?" *RM*, 108; pb 119.]

See also ARISTOTLE; ART; CHARACTERIZATION; CLASSICISM; CONCEPTS; DETERMINISM; MODERN ART; NATURALISM; NOVEL; PLOT; PLOT-THEME; POPULAR LITERATURE; PSYCHO-EPISTEMOLOGY; ROMANTICISM; SENSE of LIFE; STYLE; THEME (LITERARY); THRILLERS.

Lobbying. "Lobbying" is the activity of attempting to influence legislation by privately influencing the legislators. It is the result and creation of a mixed economy—of government by pressure groups. Its methods range from mere social courtesies and cocktail-party or luncheon "friendships" to favors, threats, bribes, blackmail.

["The Pull Peddlers," *CUI*, 168.]

See also INTERVENTIONISM (ECONOMIC); MIXED ECONOMY; WELFARE STATE.

Logic. All thinking is a process of identification and integration. Man perceives a blob of color; by integrating the evidence of his sight and his touch, he learns to identify it as a solid object; he learns to identify the object as a table; he learns that the table is made of wood; he learns that the wood consists of cells, that the cells consist of molecules, that the molecules consist of atoms. All through this process, the work of his mind consists of answers to a single question: *What* is it? His means to establish the truth of his answers is logic, and logic rests on the axiom that existence exists. Logic is the art of *non-contradictory identification*. A contradiction cannot exist. An atom is itself, and so is the universe; neither can contradict its own identity; nor can a part contradict the whole. No concept man forms is valid unless he integrates it without contradiction into the total sum of his knowledge. To arrive at a contradiction is to confess an error in one's thinking; to maintain a contradiction is to abdicate one's mind and to evict oneself from the realm of reality.

[GS, *FNI*, 153; pb 125.]

The fundamental concept of method, the one on which all the others depend, is *logic*. The distinguishing characteristic of logic (the art of non-contradictory identification) indicates the nature of the actions (actions of consciousness required to achieve a correct identification) and their goal (knowledge)—while omitting the length, complexity or specific steps of the process of logical inference, as well as the nature of the particular cognitive problem involved in any given instance of using logic.

[*ITOE*, 46.]

"It's logical, but logic has nothing to do with reality." Logic is the art or skill of non-contradictory identification. Logic has a single law, the Law of Identity, and its various corollaries. If logic has nothing to do with reality, it means that the Law of Identity is inapplicable to reality. If so, then: a. things are not what they are; b. things can be and not be at the same time, in the same respect, i.e., reality is made up of contradictions. If so, by what means did anyone discover it? By illogical means. (This last is for sure.) The purpose of that notion is crudely obvious. Its actual meaning is not: "Logic has nothing to do with reality," but: "I, the speaker, have nothing to do with logic (or with reality)." When people use that catch phrase, they mean either: "It's logical, but I don't choose to be logical" or: "It's logical, but people are not logical, they don't think—and I intend to pander to their irrationality."

["Philosophical Detection," *PWNI*, 17; pb 15.]

Logic is man's method of reaching conclusions *objectively* by deriving them without contradiction from the facts of reality—ultimately, from the evidence provided by man's senses. If men reject logic, then the tie between their mental processes and reality is severed; all cognitive standards are repudiated, and anything goes; any contradiction, on any subject, may be endorsed (and simultaneously rejected) by anyone, as and when he feels like it.

[Leonard Peikoff, "Nazism and Subjectivism," *TO*, Feb. 1971, 12.]

Any theory that propounds an opposition between the logical and the empirical, represents a failure to grasp the nature of logic and its role in human cognition. Man's knowledge is not acquired by logic apart from experience or by experience apart from logic, but *by the application of logic to experience*. All truths are the product of a logical identification of the facts of experience.

Man is born *tabula rasa;* all his knowledge is based on and derived from the evidence of his senses. To reach the distinctively human level of cognition, man must conceptualize his perceptual data—and conceptualization is a process which is neither automatic nor infallible. Man needs to discover a method to guide this process, if it is to yield conclusions which correspond to the facts of reality—i.e., which represent knowledge. The principle at the base of the proper method is the fundamental principle of metaphysics: the Law of Identity. In reality, contradictions cannot exist; in a cognitive process, a contradiction is the proof of an error. Hence the method man must follow: to identify the facts he observes, in a non-contradictory manner. This method is logic —"the art of non-contradictory identification." *(Atlas Shrugged.)* Logic must be employed at every step of a man's conceptual development, from the formation of his first concepts to the discovery of the most complex scientific laws and theories. Only when a conclusion is based on a non-contradictory identification and integration of all the evidence available at a given time, can it qualify as knowledge.

The failure to recognize that logic is man's method of cognition, has produced a brood of artificial splits and dichotomies which represent restatements of the analytic-synthetic dichotomy from various aspects. Three in particular are prevalent today: logical truth vs. factual truth; the logically possible vs. the empirically possible; and the a priori vs. the a posteriori.

The logical-factual dichotomy opposes truths which are validated "merely" by the use of logic (the analytic ones), and truths which describe the facts of experience (the synthetic ones). Implicit in this dichotomy is the view that logic is a subjective game, a method of manipulating arbitrary symbols, not a method of acquiring knowledge.

It is the use of logic that enables man to determine what is and what is not a fact. To introduce an opposition between the "logical" and the "factual" is to create a split between consciousness and existence, between truths in accordance with man's method of cognition and truths in accordance with the facts of reality. The result of such a dichotomy is that logic is divorced from reality ("Logical truths are empty and conventional")—and reality becomes unknowable ("Factual truths are contingent and uncertain"). This amounts to the claim that man has no method of cognition, i.e., no way of acquiring knowledge.

[Leonard Peikoff, "The Analytic-Synthetic Dichotomy," *ITOE*, 151.]

See also ANALYTIC-SYNTHETIC DICHOTOMY; ARISTOTLE; AXIOMS; CONTRADICTIONS; EPISTEMOLOGY; IDENTITY; INDUCTION and DEDUCTION; METHOD, CONCEPTS of; MYSTICISM; OBJECTIVITY; PROOF; REASON; VALIDATION.

Logical Positivism. As a defense against the Witch-doctory of Hegel, who claimed universal omniscience, the scientist was offered the combined neo-mystic Witch-doctory and Attila-ism of the Logical Positivists. They assured him that such concepts as metaphysics or existence or reality or thing or matter or mind are meaningless—let the mystics care whether they exist or not, a scientist does not have to know it; the task of theoretical science is the manipulation of symbols, and scientists are the special elite whose symbols have the magic power of making reality conform to their will ("matter is that which fits mathematical equations"). Knowledge, they said, consists, not of facts, but of *words*, words unrelated to objects, words of an arbitrary social convention, as an irreducible primary; thus knowledge is merely a matter of manipulating language. The job of scientists, they said, is not the study of reality, but the creation of arbitrary constructs by means of arbitrary sounds, and any construct is as valid as another, since the criterion of validity is only "convenience" and the definition of science is "that which the scientists do." But this omnipotent power, surpassing the dreams of ancient numerologists or of medieval alchemists, was granted to the scientist by philosophical Attila-ism on two conditions: *a.* that he never claim certainty for his knowledge, since certainty is unknown to man, and that he claim, instead, "percentages of probability," not troubling himself with such questions as how one calculates percentages of the unknowable; *b.* that he claim as absolute knowledge the proposition that all values lie outside the sphere of science, that reason is impotent to deal with morality, that moral values are a matter of subjective choice, dictated by one's feelings, not one's mind.

["For the New Intellectual," *FNI*, 36; pb 34.]

Ever since Kant divorced reason from reality, his intellectual descendants have been diligently widening the breach. In the name of reason, Pragmatism established a range-of-the-moment view as an enlightened perspective on life, context-dropping as a rule of epistemology, expediency as a principle of morality, and collective subjectivism as a substitute for metaphysics. Logical Positivism carried it farther and, in the name of reason, elevated the immemorial psycho-epistemology of shyster-lawyers to the status of a scientific epistemological system—by proclaiming that knowledge consists of linguistic manipulations.

["The Cashing-in: The Student 'Rebellion,' " *CUI*, 246.]

If [the student "rebels"] "seem unable to formulate or sustain a systematized political theory of society," yet shriek with moral righteousness that they propose to achieve their social goals by physical force—hasn't Logical Positivism taught them that ethical propositions have no cognitive meaning and are merely a report on one's feelings or the equivalent of emotional ejaculations? If they are savagely blind to everything but the immediate moment—hasn't Logical Positivism taught them that nothing else can be claimed with certainty to exist?

[Ibid., 248.]

Logical Positivism declares that "reality," "identity," "existence," "mind" are meaningless terms, that man can be certain of nothing but the sensory perceptions of the immediate moment . . . it declares that the meaning of the proposition: "Napoleon lost the battle of Waterloo" is your walk to the library where you read it in a book.

["The Comprachicos," *NL*, 225.]

See also ANALYTIC-SYNTHETIC DICHOTOMY; BEHAVIORISM; CER-TAINTY; KANT, IMMANUEL; MEANING (of CONCEPTS); PHILOSO-PHY; PRAGMATISM; SCIENCE; SUBJECTIVISM; WORDS.

Loneliness. The thinking child is not antisocial (he is, in fact, the only type of child fit for social relationships). When he develops his first values and conscious convictions, particularly as he approaches adolescence, he feels an intense desire to share them with a friend who would understand him; if frustrated, he feels an acute sense of loneliness. (Loneliness is specifically the experience of this type of child—or adult; it is the experience of those who have something to offer. The emotion that drives conformists to "belong," is not loneliness, but fear—the fear of intellectual independence and responsibility. The thinking child seeks equals; the conformist seeks protectors.)

["The Comprachicos," *NL*, 213.]

See also EMOTIONS; INDEPENDENCE; RATIONALITY; SECOND-HANDERS.

Love. Love, friendship, respect, admiration are the emotional response of one man to the virtues of another, the spiritual *payment* given in exchange for the personal, selfish pleasure which one man derives from the virtues of another man's character. Only a brute or an altruist would claim that the appreciation of another person's virtues is an act of selflessness, that as far as one's own selfish interest and pleasure are concerned, it makes no difference whether one deals with a genius or a fool, whether one meets a hero or a thug, whether one marries an ideal woman or a slut.

["The Objectivist Ethics," *VOS*, 29; pb 31.]

Romantic love, in the full sense of the term, is an emotion possible only to the man (or woman) of unbreached self-esteem: it is his response to his own highest values in the person of another—an integrated response of mind and body, of love and sexual desire. Such a man (or woman) is incapable of experiencing a sexual desire divorced from spiritual values.

["Of Living Death," *TO*, Oct. 1968, 2.]

Man is an end in himself. Romantic love—the profound, exalted, life-long *passion* that unites his mind and body in the sexual act—is the living testimony to that principle.

[Ibid., 3.]

There are two aspects of man's existence which are the special province and expression of his sense of life: love and art.

I am referring here to romantic love, in the serious meaning of that term—as distinguished from the superficial infatuations of those whose sense of life is devoid of any consistent values, i.e., of any lasting emotions other than fear. Love is a response to values. It is with a person's sense of life that one falls in love—with that essential sum, that fundamental stand or way of facing existence, which is the essence of a personality. One falls in love with the embodiment of the values that formed a person's character, which are reflected in his widest goals or smallest gestures, which create the *style* of his soul—the individual style of a unique, unrepeatable, irreplaceable consciousness. It is one's own sense of life that acts as the selector, and responds to what it recognizes as one's own basic values in the person of another. It is not a matter of professed convictions (though these are not irrelevant); it is a matter of much more profound, conscious *and subconscious* harmony.

Many errors and tragic disillusionments are possible in this process of emotional recognition, since a sense of life, by itself, is not a reliable cognitive guide. And if there are degrees of evil, then one of the most evil consequences of mysticism—in terms of human suffering—is the belief that love is a matter of "the heart," not the mind, that love is an emotion independent of reason, that love is blind and impervious to the power of philosophy. Love is *the expression of philosophy*—of a subconscious philosophical sum—and, perhaps, no other aspect of human existence needs the *conscious* power of philosophy quite so desperately. When that power is called upon to verify and support an emotional appraisal, when love is a conscious integration of reason and emotion, of mind and values, then—and only then—it is the greatest reward of man's life.

["Philosophy and Sense of Life," *RM*, 40; pb 32.]

To love is to value. Only a rationally selfish man, a man of *self-esteem*, is capable of love—because he is the only man capable of holding firm, consistent, uncompromising, unbetrayed values. The man who does not value himself, cannot value anything or anyone.

["The Objectivist Ethics," *VOS*, 29; pb 32.]

[In *The Fountainhead*] the hero utters a line that has often been quoted by readers: "To say 'I love you' one must know first how to say the 'I.' "

["*Playboy's* Interview with Ayn Rand," pamphlet, 7.]

[Selfless love] would have to mean that you derive no personal pleasure or happiness from the company and the existence of the person you love, and that you are motivated only by self-sacrificial pity for that person's need of you. I don't have to point out to you that no one would be flattered by, nor would accept, a concept of that kind. Love is not self-sacrifice, but the most profound assertion of your own needs and values. It is for your *own* happiness that you need the person you love, and that is the greatest compliment, the greatest tribute you can pay to that person.

[Ibid.]

One gains a profoundly personal, selfish joy from the mere existence of the person one loves. It is one's own personal, selfish happiness that one seeks, earns and derives from love.

A "selfless," "disinterested" love is a contradiction in terms: it means that one is indifferent to that which one values.

Concern for the welfare of those one loves is a rational part of one's selfish interests. If a man who is passionately in love with his wife spends a fortune to cure her of a dangerous illness, it would be absurd to claim that he does it as a "sacrifice" for *her* sake, not his own, and that it makes no difference to *him,* personally and selfishly, whether she lives or dies.

["The Ethics of Emergencies," *VOS,* 48; pb 44.]

The practical implementation of friendship, affection and love consists of incorporating the welfare (the *rational* welfare) of the person involved into one's own hierarchy of values, then acting accordingly.

[Ibid., 51; pb 46.]

To love is to *value.* The man who tells you that it is possible to value without values, to love those whom you appraise as worthless, is the man who tells you that it is possible to grow rich by consuming without producing and that paper money is as valuable as gold. . . . When it comes to love, the highest of emotions, you permit them to shriek at you accusingly that you are a moral delinquent if you're incapable of feeling causeless love. When a man feels fear without reason, you call him to the attention of a psychiatrist; you are not so careful to protect the meaning, the nature and the dignity of love.

Love is the expression of one's values, the greatest reward you can earn for the moral qualities you have achieved in your character and person, the emotional price paid by one man for the joy he receives from the virtues of another. Your morality demands that you divorce your love from values and hand it down to any vagrant, not as response to his worth, but as response to his *need*, not as reward, but as alms, not as a payment for virtues, but as a blank check on vices. Your morality tells you that the purpose of love is to set you free of the bonds of morality, that love is superior to moral judgment, that true love transcends, forgives and survives every manner of evil in its object, and the greater the love the greater the depravity it permits to the loved. To love a man for his virtues is paltry and human, it tells you; to love him for his flaws is divine. To love those who are worthy of it is self-interest; to love the unworthy is sacrifice. You owe your love to those who don't deserve it, and the less they deserve it, the more love you owe them—the more loathsome the object, the nobler your love—the more unfastidious your love, the greater your virtue—and if you can bring your soul to the state of a dump heap that welcomes anything on equal terms, if you can cease to value moral values, you have achieved the state of moral perfection.

[GS, *FNI*, 182; pb 147.]

Like any other value, love is not a static quantity to be divided, but an unlimited response to be earned. The love for one friend is not a threat to the love for another, and neither is the love for the various members of one's family, assuming they have earned it. The most exclusive form —romantic love—is not an issue of competition. If two men are in love with the same woman, what she feels for either of them is not determined by what she feels for the other and is not taken away from him. If she chooses one of them, the "loser" could not have had what the "winner" has earned.

It is only among the irrational, emotion-motivated persons, whose love is divorced from any standards of value, that chance rivalries, accidental conflicts and blind choices prevail. But then, whoever wins does not win much. Among the emotion-driven, neither love nor any other emotion has any meaning.

["The 'Conflicts' of Men's Interests," *VOS*, 65; pb 55.]

Let us answer the question: "Can you measure love?"

The concept "love" is formed by isolating two or more instances of the appropriate psychological process, then retaining its distinguishing characteristics (an emotion proceeding from the evaluation of an existent as a positive value and as a source of pleasure) and omitting the object and the measurements of the process's intensity.

The object may be a thing, an event, an activity, a condition or a person. The intensity varies according to one's evaluation of the object, as, for instance, in such cases as one's love for ice cream, or for parties, or for reading, or for freedom, or for the person one marries. The concept "love" subsumes a vast range of values and, consequently, of intensity: it extends from the lower levels (designated by the subcategory "liking") to the higher level (designated by the subcategory "affection," which is applicable only in regard to persons) to the highest level, which includes romantic love.

If one wants to measure the intensity of a particular instance of love, one does so by reference to the hierarchy of values of the person experiencing it. A man may love a woman, yet may rate the neurotic satisfactions of sexual promiscuity higher than her value to him. Another man may love a woman, but may give her up, rating his fear of the disapproval of others (of his family, his friends or any random strangers) higher than her value. Still another man may risk his life to save the woman he loves, because all his other values would lose meaning without her. The emotions in these examples are not emotions of the same intensity or dimension. Do not let a James Taggart type of mystic tell you that love is immeasurable.

[*ITOE*, 44.]

See also ALTRUISM; CHARACTER; EMOTIONS; FEMININITY; MARRIAGE; PHILOSOPHY; SACRIFICE; SELF-ESTEEM; SELFISHNESS; SELFLESSNESS; SENSE of LIFE; SEX; TELEOLOGICAL MEASUREMENT; VALUES; VIRTUE.

M

Malevolent Universe Premise.

The altruist ethics is based on a "malevolent universe" metaphysics, on the theory that man, by his very nature, is helpless and doomed—that success, happiness, achievement are impossible to him—that emergencies, disasters, catastrophes are the norm of his life and that his primary goal is to combat them.

As the simplest empirical refutation of that metaphysics—as evidence of the fact that the material universe is not inimical to man and that catastrophes are the exception, not the rule of his existence—observe the fortunes made by insurance companies.

["The Ethics of Emergencies," *VOS*, 55; pb 48.]

If you hold the wrong ideas on any fundamental philosophic issue, that will undercut or destroy the benevolent universe premise.... For example, any departure in metaphysics from the view that this world in which we live is reality, the full, final, absolute reality—any such departure will necessarily undercut a man's confidence in his ability to deal with the world, and thus will inject the malevolent-universe element. The same applies in epistemology: if you conclude in any form that reason is not valid, then man has no tool of achieving values; so defeat and tragedy are unavoidable.

This is true also of ethics. If men hold values incompatible with life— such as self-sacrifice and altruism—obviously they can't achieve such values; they will soon come to feel that evil is potent, whereas they are doomed to misery, suffering, failure. It is irrational codes of ethics above all else that feed the malevolent-universe attitude in people and lead to the syndrome eloquently expressed by the philosopher Schopenhauer: "Whatever one may say, the happiest moment of the happy man is the moment of his falling asleep, and the unhappiest moment of the unhappy that of his waking. Human life must be some kind of mistake."

Now there is certainly "some kind of mistake" here. But it's not life. It's the kind of philosophies used to wreck man—to make him incapable of living—philosophies, I may say, which are perfectly exemplified by the ideas of Schopenhauer.

[Leonard Peikoff, "The Philosophy of Objectivism" lecture series (1976), Lecture 8.]

See also ALTRUISM; BENEVOLENT UNIVERSE PREMISE; EVIL; HAPPINESS; MAN; METAPHYSICAL VALUE-JUDGMENTS; SENSE of LIFE; SUFFERING.

Man.   Man's distinctive characteristic is his type of consciousness—a consciousness able to abstract, to form concepts, to apprehend reality by a process of reason . . . [The] valid definition of man, within the context of his knowledge and of all of mankind's knowledge to-date [is]: "*A rational animal.*"

("Rational," in this context, does not mean "acting invariably in accordance with reason"; it means "possessing the faculty of reason." A full biological definition of man would include many subcategories of "animal," but the general category and the ultimate definition remain the same.)

[ITOE, 58.]

Man's life, as required by his nature, is not the life of a mindless brute, of a looting thug or a mooching mystic, but the life of a thinking being—not life by means of force or fraud, but life by means of achievement—not survival at any price, since there's only one price that pays for man's survival: reason.

[GS, *FNI*, 149; pb 122.]

Man has been called a rational being, but rationality is a matter of choice—and the alternative his nature offers him is: rational being or suicidal animal. Man has to be man—by choice; he has to hold his life as a value—by choice; he has to learn to sustain it—by choice; he has to discover the values it requires and practice his virtues—by choice.

[Ibid.]

The key to what you so recklessly call "human nature," the open secret you live with, yet dread to name, is the fact that *man is a being of volitional consciousness.*

[Ibid., 146; pb 120.]

Man has no automatic code of survival. His particular distinction from all other living species is the necessity to act in the face of alternatives by means of *volitional choice.* He has no automatic knowledge of what is good for him or evil, what values his life depends on, what course of action it requires. Are you prattling about an instinct of self-preservation? An *instinct* of self-preservation is precisely what man does not possess. An "instinct" is an unerring and automatic form of knowledge. A desire is not an instinct. A desire to live does not give you the knowledge required for living. And even man's desire to live is not automatic: your secret evil today is that *that* is the desire you do not hold. Your fear of death is not a love for life and will not give you the knowledge needed to keep it.

[Ibid., 148; pb 121.]

Man cannot survive on the perceptual level of *his* consciousness; his senses do not provide him with an automatic guidance, they do not give him the knowledge he needs, only the *material* of knowledge, which his mind has to integrate. Man is the only living species who has to perceive reality—which means: to be *conscious*—by choice. But he shares with other species the penalty of unconsciousness: destruction. For an animal, the question of survival is primarily physical; for man, primarily epistemological.

Man's unique reward, however, is that while animals survive by adjusting themselves to their background, man survives by adjusting his background to himself. If a drought strikes them, animals perish—man builds irrigation canals; if a flood strikes them, animals perish—man builds dams; if a carnivorous pack attacks them animals perish—man writes the Constitution of the United States. But one does not obtain food, safety or freedom—by instinct.

["For the New Intellectual," *FNI*, 10; pb 15.]

Consciousness—for those living organisms which possess it—is the basic means of survival. For man, the basic means of survival is *reason*. Man cannot survive, as animals do, by the guidance of mere percepts. A sensation of hunger will tell him that he needs food (if he has learned to identify it as "hunger"), but it will not tell him how to obtain his food and it will not tell him what food is good for him or poisonous. He cannot provide for his simplest physical needs without a process of thought. He needs a process of thought to discover how to plant and grow his food or how to make weapons for hunting. His percepts might lead him to a cave, if one is available—but to build the simplest shelter, he needs a process of thought. No percepts and no "instincts" will tell him how to light a fire, how to weave cloth, how to forge tools, how to make a wheel, how to make an airplane, how to perform an appendectomy, how to produce an electric light bulb or an electronic tube or a cyclotron or a box of matches. Yet his life depends on such knowledge—and only a volitional act of his consciousness, a process of thought, can provide it.

["The Objectivist Ethics," *VOS*, 13; pb 21.]

To the extent that a man is guided by his rational judgment, he acts in accordance with the requirements of his nature and, to that extent, succeeds in achieving a human form of survival and well-being; to the extent that he acts irrationally, he acts as his own destroyer.

["What Is Capitalism?" *CUI*, 21.]

If some men do not choose to think, they can survive only by imitating and repeating a routine of work discovered by others—but those others had to discover it, or none would have survived. If some men do not choose to think or to work, they can survive (temporarily) only by looting the goods produced by others—but those others had to produce them, or none would have survived. Regardless of what choice is made, in this issue, by any man or by any number of men, regardless of what blind, irrational, or evil course they may choose to pursue—the fact remains that reason is man's means of survival and that men prosper or fail, survive or perish in proportion to the degree of their rationality.

[Ibid.]

Nothing is given to man on earth except a potential and the material on which to actualize it. The potential is a superlative machine: his consciousness; but it is a machine without a spark plug, a machine of which his own will has to be the spark plug, the self-starter and the driver; *he* has to discover how to use it and *he* has to keep it in constant action. The material is the whole of the universe, with no limits set to the knowledge he can acquire and to the enjoyment of life he can achieve. But everything he needs or desires has to be learned, discovered and produced by *him*—by his own choice, by his own effort, by his own mind.

A being who does not know automatically what is true or false, cannot know automatically what is right or wrong, what is good for him or evil. Yet he needs that knowledge in order to live. He is not exempt from the laws of reality, he is a specific organism of a specific nature that requires specific actions to sustain his life. He cannot achieve his survival by arbitrary means nor by random motions nor by blind urges nor by chance nor by whim. That which his survival requires is set by his nature and is not open to his choice. What *is* open to his choice is only whether he will discover it or not, whether he will choose the right goals and *values* or not.

["The Objectivist Ethics," *VOS*, 14; pb 22.]

The faculty of volition gives man a special status in two crucial respects: 1. unlike the metaphysically given, man's products, whether material or intellectual, are not to be accepted uncritically—and 2. by *its metaphysically given nature*, a man's volition is outside the power of other men. What the unalterable basic constituents are to nature, the attribute of a volitional consciousness is to the entity "man." Nothing can force a man to think. Others may offer him incentives or impediments, rewards or punishments, they may destroy his brain by drugs or by the blow of a club, but they cannot order his mind to function: *this* is in his exclusive, sovereign power. Man is neither to be obeyed nor to be commanded.

["The Metaphysical Versus the Man-Made," *PWNI*, 38; pb 31.]

To deal with men by force is as impractical as to deal with nature by persuasion.

[Ibid., 39; pb 32.]

An animal's life consists of a series of separate cycles, repeated over and over again, such as the cycle of breeding its young, or of storing food for the winter; an animal's consciousness cannot integrate its entire lifespan; it can carry just so far, then the animal has to begin the cycle all over again, with no connection to the past. *Man's* life is a continuous whole: for good or evil, every day, year and decade of his life holds the sum of all the days behind him.

["The Objectivist Ethics," *VOS*, 18; pb 24.]

Man is the only living species that can transmit and expand his store of knowledge from generation to generation; but such transmission requires a process of thought on the part of the individual recipients. As witness, the breakdowns of civilization, the dark ages in the history of mankind's progress, when the accumulated knowledge of centuries vanished from the lives of men who were unable, unwilling, or forbidden to think.

["What Is Capitalism?" *CUI*, 16.]

Man gains enormous values from dealing with other men; living in a human society is his proper way of life—but only on certain conditions. Man is not a lone wolf and he is not a social animal. He is a *contractual* animal. He has to plan his life long-range, make his own choices, and deal with other men by voluntary agreement (and he has to be able to rely on their observance of the agreements they entered).

["A Nation's Unity," *ARL*, II, 2, 3.]

A living entity that regarded its means of survival as evil, would not survive. A plant that struggled to mangle its roots, a bird that fought to break its wings would not remain for long in the existence they affronted. But the history of man has been a struggle to deny and to destroy his mind.

[GS, *FNI*, 148; pb 122.]

Almost unanimously, man is regarded as an *unnatural* phenomenon: either as a *supernatural* entity, whose mystic (divine) endowment, the mind ("soul"), is above nature—or as a *subnatural* entity, whose mystic (demoniacal) endowment, the mind, is an enemy of nature ("ecology"). The purpose of all such theories is to exempt man from the law of identity.

But man exists and his mind exists. Both are part of nature, both possess a specific identity. The attribute of volition does not contradict the fact of identity, just as the existence of living organisms does not contradict the existence of inanimate matter. Living organisms possess the power of self-initiated motion, which inanimate matter does not possess; man's consciousness possesses the power of self-initiated motion in the realm of cognition (thinking), which the consciousnesses of other living species do not possess. But just as animals are able to move only in accordance with the nature of their bodies, so man is able to initiate and direct his mental action only in accordance with the nature (the *identity*) of his consciousness. His volition is limited to his cognitive processes; he has the power to identify (and to conceive of rearranging) the elements of reality, but not the power to alter them. He has the power to use his cognitive faculty as its nature requires, but not the power to alter it nor to escape the consequences of its misuse. He has the power to suspend, evade, corrupt or subvert his perception of reality, but not the power to escape the existential and psychological disasters that follow. (The use or misuse of his cognitive faculty determines a man's choice of values, which determine his emotions and his character. It is in this sense that man is a being of self-made soul.)

["The Metaphysical Versus the Man-Made," *PWNI*, 32; pb 26.]

Whatever he was—that robot in the Garden of Eden, who existed without mind, without values, without labor, without love—he was not man.

[GS, *FNI*, 169; pb 137.]

They have cut man in two, setting one half against the other. They have taught him that his body and his consciousness are two enemies engaged in deadly conflict, two antagonists of opposite natures, contradictory claims, incompatible needs, that to benefit one is to injure the other, that his soul belongs to a supernatural realm, but his body is an evil prison holding it in bondage to this earth—and that the good is to defeat his body, to undermine it by years of patient struggle, digging his way to that glorious jail-break which leads into the freedom of the grave.

They have taught man that he is a hopeless misfit made of two elements, both symbols of death. A body without a soul is a corpse, a soul without a body is a ghost—yet such is their image of man's nature: the battleground of a struggle between a corpse and a ghost, a corpse endowed with some evil volition of its own and a ghost endowed with the knowledge that everything known to man is non-existent, that only the unknowable exists.

Do you observe what human faculty that doctrine was designed to ignore? It was man's mind that had to be negated in order to make him fall apart. Once he surrendered reason, he was left at the mercy of two monsters whom he could not fathom or control: of a body moved by unaccountable instincts and a soul moved by mystic revelations—he was left as the passively ravaged victim of a battle between a robot and a dictaphone.

[Ibid., 170; pb 138.]

Man is an indivisible entity, an integrated unit of two attributes: of matter and consciousness, and . . . he may permit no breach between body and mind, between action and thought, between his life and his convictions.

[Ibid., 157; pb 129.]

Man cannot survive in the kind of state of nature that the ecologists envision—i.e., on the level of sea urchins or polar bears. In that sense, man is the weakest of animals: he is born naked and unarmed, without fangs, claws, horns or "instinctual" knowledge. Physically, he would fall an easy prey, not only to the higher animals, but also to the lowest bacteria: he is the most complex organism and, in a contest of brute force, extremely fragile and vulnerable. His only weapon—his basic means of survival—is his mind.

In order to survive, man has to discover and produce everything he needs, which means that he has to *alter* his background and adapt it to his needs. Nature has not equipped him for adapting himself to his background in the manner of animals. From the most primitive cultures to the most advanced civilizations, man has had to *manufacture* things; his well-being depends on his success at production. The lowest human tribe cannot survive without that alleged source of pollution: fire. It is not merely symbolic that fire was the property of the gods which Prometheus brought to man. The ecologists are the new vultures swarming to extinguish that fire.

["The Anti-Industrial Revolution," *NL*, 136.]

"It's only human," you cry in defense of any depravity, reaching the stage of self-abasement where you seek to make the concept *"human"* mean the weakling, the fool, the rotter, the liar, the failure, the coward, the fraud, and to exile from the human race the hero, the thinker, the producer, the inventor, the strong, the purposeful, the pure—as if "to feel" were human, but to think were not, as if to fail were human, but to succeed were not, as if corruption were human, but virtue were not

—as if the premise of *death* were proper to man, but the premise of *life* were not.

[GS, *FNI*, 209; pb 167.]

In the name of the values that keep you alive, do not let your vision of man be distorted by the ugly, the cowardly, the mindless in those who have never achieved his title. Do not lose your knowledge that man's proper estate is an upright posture, an intransigent mind and a step that travels unlimited roads.

[Ibid., 241; pb 191.]

See also CONCEPTS; EMOTIONS; FREE WILL; HISTORY; MAN-WORSHIP; METAPHYSICAL vs. MAN-MADE; MORALITY; OBJECTIVISM; PERCEPTION; PHYSICAL FORCE; PRODUCTION; REASON; SOUL-BODY DICHOTOMY; THOUGHT/THINKING.

Man-Worship.

Just as religion has pre-empted the field of ethics, turning morality *against* man, so it has usurped the highest moral concepts of our language, placing them outside this earth and beyond man's reach. "Exaltation" is usually taken to mean an emotional state evoked by contemplating the supernatural. "Worship" means the emotional experience of loyalty and dedication to something higher than man. "Reverence" means the emotion of a sacred respect, to be experienced on one's knees. "Sacred" means superior to and not-to-be-touched-by any concerns of man or of this earth. Etc.

But such concepts do name actual emotions, even though no supernatural dimension exists; and these emotions are experienced as uplifting or ennobling, without the self-abasement required by religious definitions. What, then, is their source or referent in reality? It is the entire emotional realm of man's dedication to a moral ideal. Yet apart from the man-degrading aspects introduced by religion, that emotional realm is left unidentified, without concepts, words or recognition.

It is this highest level of man's emotions that has to be redeemed from the murk of mysticism and redirected at its proper object: man.

It is in this sense, with this meaning and intention, that I would identify the sense of life dramatized in *The Fountainhead* as *man worship.*

It is an emotion that a few—a very few—men experience consistently; some men experience it in rare, single sparks that flash and die without consequences; some do not know what I am talking about; some do and spend their lives as frantically virulent spark-extinguishers.

Do not confuse "man worship" with the many attempts, not to emancipate morality from religion and bring it into the realm of reason, but to substitute a secular meaning for the worst, the most profoundly irrational elements of religion. For instance, there are all the variants of modern collectivism (communist, fascist, Nazi, etc.), which preserve the religious-altruist ethics in full and merely substitute "society" for God as the beneficiary of man's self-immolation. There are the various schools of modern philosophy which, rejecting the law of identity, proclaim that reality is an indeterminate flux ruled by miracles and shaped by whims—not God's whims, but man's or "society's." These neomystics are not man-worshipers; they are merely the secularizers of as profound a hatred for man as that of their avowedly mystic predecessors.

A cruder variant of the same hatred is represented by those concrete-bound, "statistical" mentalities who—unable to grasp the meaning of man's volition—declare that man cannot be an object of worship, since they have never encountered any specimens of humanity who deserved it.

The man-worshipers, in my sense of the term, are those who see man's highest potential and strive to actualize it. . . . [Man-worshipers are] those dedicated to the *exaltation* of man's self-esteem and the *sacredness* of his happiness on earth.

["Introduction to *The Fountainhead*," *TO*, March 1968, 4.]

This view of man has rarely been expressed in human history. Today, it is virtually non-existent. Yet this is the view with which—in various degrees of longing, wistfulness, passion and agonized confusion—the best of mankind's youth start out in life. It is not even a view, for most of them, but a foggy, groping, undefined sense made of raw pain and incommunicable happiness. It is a sense of enormous expectation, the sense that one's life is important, that great achievements are within one's capacity, and that great things lie ahead.

It is not in the nature of man—nor of any living entity—to start out by giving up, by spitting in one's own face and damning existence; that requires a process of corruption, whose rapidity differs from man to man. Some give up at the first touch of pressure; some sell out; some run down by imperceptible degrees and lose their fire, never knowing when or how they lost it. Then all of these vanish in the vast swamp of their elders who tell them persistently that maturity consists of abandoning one's mind; security, of abandoning one's values; practicality, of losing self-esteem. Yet a few hold on and move on, knowing that that fire is not to be betrayed, learning how to give it shape, purpose and reality. But whatever their future, at the dawn of their lives, men seek a noble vision of man's nature and of life's potential.

[Ibid., 6.]

See also FEMININITY; MAN; HAPPINESS; RELIGION; SACRED; SELF-ESTEEM; SENSE of LIFE.

Managerial Work.   Managerial work—the organization and integration of human effort into purposeful, large-scale, long-range activities—is, in the realm of action, what man's conceptual faculty is in the realm of cognition.

["The Cashing-in: The Student 'Rebellion,' " *CUI*, 262.]

If there is any one proof of a man's incompetence, it is the stagnant mentality of a worker (or of a professor) who, doing some small, routine job in a vast undertaking, does not care to look beyond the lever of a machine (or the lectern of a classroom), does not choose to know how the machine (or the classroom) got there or what makes his job possible, and proclaims that the management of the undertaking is parasitical and unnecessary.

[Ibid.]

See also BUSINESSMEN; CAREER.

Market Value.   It is in regard to a free market that the distinction between an intrinsic, subjective, and objective view of values is particularly important to understand. The market value of a product is *not* an intrinsic value, not a "value in itself" hanging in a vacuum. A free market never loses sight of the question: Of value *to whom?* And, within the broad field of objectivity, the market value of a product does not reflect its *philosophically objective* value, but only its *socially objective* value.

By "philosophically objective," I mean a value estimated from the standpoint of the best possible to man, i.e., by the criterion of the most rational mind possessing the greatest knowledge, in a given category, in a given period, and in a defined context (nothing can be estimated in an undefined context). For instance, it can be rationally proved that the airplane is *objectively* of immeasurably greater value to man (to *man at his best*) than the bicycle—and that the works of Victor Hugo are *objectively* of immeasurably greater value than true-confession magazines. But if a given man's intellectual potential can barely manage to enjoy true confessions, there is no reason why his meager earnings, the product of *his* effort, should be spent on books he cannot read—or on subsidizing the airplane industry, if his own transportation needs do not extend beyond the range of a bicycle. (Nor is there any reason why the rest of mankind should be held down to the level of his literary taste, his engineering capacity, and his income. Values are not determined by fiat nor by majority vote.)

Just as the number of its adherents is not a proof of an idea's truth or falsehood, of an art work's merit or demerit, of a product's efficacy or inefficacy—so the free-market value of goods or services does not necessarily represent their philosophically objective value, but only their *socially objective* value, i.e., the sum of the individual judgments of all the men involved in trade at a given time, the sum of what *they* valued, each in the context of his own life.

Thus, a manufacturer of lipstick may well make a greater fortune than a manufacturer of microscopes—even though it can be rationally demonstrated that microscopes are scientifically more valuable than lipstick. But—valuable *to whom?*

A microscope is of no value to a little stenographer struggling to make a living; a lipstick is; a lipstick, to her, may mean the difference between self-confidence and self-doubt, between glamour and drudgery.

This does not mean, however, that the values ruling a free market are *subjective.* If the stenographer spends all her money on cosmetics and has none left to pay for the use of a microscope (for a visit to the doctor) *when she needs it,* she learns a better method of budgeting her income; the free market serves as her teacher: she has no way to penalize others for her mistakes. If she budgets rationally, the microscope is always available to serve her own specific needs *and no more,* as far as she is concerned: she is not taxed to support an entire hospital, a research laboratory, or a space ship's journey to the moon. Within her own productive power, she does pay a part of the cost of scientific achievements, *when and as she needs them.*

["What Is Capitalism?" *CUI,* 24.]

Within every category of goods and services offered on a free market, it is the purveyor of the best product at the cheapest price who wins the greatest financial rewards *in that field*—not automatically nor immediately nor by fiat, but by virtue of the free market, which teaches every participant to look for the *objective* best within the category of his own competence, and penalizes those who act on irrational considerations.

[Ibid., 25.]

The "philosophically objective" value of a new product serves as the teacher for those who are willing to exercise their rational faculty, each to the extent of his ability. Those who are unwilling remain unrewarded—as well as those who aspire to more than their ability produces. . . .

A given product may not be appreciated at once, particularly if it is too radical an innovation; but, barring irrelevant accidents, it wins in the long run. It is in this sense that the free market is not ruled by the intellectual criteria of the majority, which prevail only at and for any given moment; the free market is ruled by those who are able to see and plan long-range—and the better the mind, the longer the range.

The economic value of a man's work is determined, on a free market, by a single principle: by the voluntary consent of those who are willing to trade him their work or products in return.

[Ibid., 26.]

[An] objection is usually expressed by a question such as: "Why should Elvis Presley make more money than Einstein?" The answer is: Because men work in order to support and enjoy their own lives—and if many men find value in Elvis Presley, they are entitled to spend their money on their own pleasure. Presley's fortune is not taken from those who do not care for his work (I am one of them) nor from Einstein—nor does he stand in Einstein's way—nor does Einstein lack proper recognition and support in a free society, on an appropriate intellectual level.

[Ibid., 27.]

See also CAPITALISM; COMPETITION; FREE MARKET; MONEY; PURCHASING POWER; TRADER PRINCIPLE.

Marriage.   I consider marriage a very important institution, but it is important *when* and *if* two people have found the person with whom they wish to spend the rest of their lives—a question of which no man or woman can be automatically certain. When one is certain that one's choice is final, then marriage is, of course, a desirable state. But this does *not* mean that any relationship based on less than total certainty is improper. I think the question of an affair or a marriage depends on the knowledge and the position of the two persons involved and should be left up to them. Either is moral, provided only that both parties take the relationship seriously and that it is based on values.

["*Playboy's* Interview with Ayn Rand," pamphlet, 8.]

See also LOVE; SEX.

Materials, Concepts of.   Concepts of *materials* are formed by observing the differences in the constituent materials of entities. (Materials exist only in the form of specific entities, such as a nugget of gold, a plank of wood, a drop or an ocean of water.) The concept of "gold," for instance, is formed by isolating gold objects from all others, then abstracting and retaining the material, the gold, and omitting the measurements of the objects (or of the alloys) in which gold may exist. Thus, the material is the same in all the concrete instances subsumed under the concept, and differs only in quantity.

[*ITOE*, 19.]

See also CONCEPT-FORMATION; CONCEPTS; MATTER.

Mathematics.   Mathematics is a science of *method* (the science of measurement, i.e., of establishing quantitative relationships), a cognitive method that enables man to perform an unlimited series of integrations. Mathematics indicates the pattern of the cognitive role of concepts and the *psycho-epistemological* need they fulfill.

[*ITOE*, 85.]

With the grasp of the (implicit) concept "unit," man reaches the conceptual level of cognition which consists of two interrelated fields: the *conceptual* and the *mathematical*. The process of concept-formation is, in large part, a mathematical process.

[Ibid., 8.]

A vast part of higher mathematics, from geometry on up, is devoted to the task of discovering methods by which various shapes can be measured—complex methods which consist of reducing the problem to the terms of a simple, primitive method, the only one available to man in this field: linear measurement. (Integral calculus, used to measure the area of circles, is just one example.)

In this respect, concept-formation and applied mathematics have a similar task, just as philosophical epistemology and theoretical mathematics have a similar goal: the goal and task of bringing the universe within the range of man's knowledge—by identifying relationships to perceptual data.

[Ibid., 17.]

See also EPISTEMOLOGY; MEASUREMENT; METHOD, CONCEPTS of; NUMBERS; PSYCHO-EPISTEMOLOGY; SCIENCE; UNIT; UNIT-ECONOMY.

Matter.   Matter is indestructible, it changes its forms, but it cannot cease to exist.

[GS, *FNI*, 147; pb 121.]

The day when [one] grasps that matter has no volition is the day when he grasps that *he* has—and this is his birth as a *human* being.

[Ibid., 194; pb 156.]

To grasp the axiom that existence exists, means to grasp the fact that nature, i.e., the universe as a whole, cannot be created or annihilated, that it cannot come into or go out of existence. Whether its basic constituent elements are atoms, or subatomic particles, or some yet undiscovered forms of energy, it is not ruled by a consciousness or by will or by chance, but by the Law of Identity. All the countless forms, motions, combinations and dissolutions of elements within the universe—from a floating speck of dust to the formation of a galaxy to the emergence of life—are caused and determined by the identities of the elements involved. Nature is the *metaphysically given*—i.e., the nature of nature is outside the power of any volition.

["The Metaphysical Versus the Man-Made," *PWNI*, 30; pb 25.]

See also EXISTENCE; FREE WILL; LIFE; MATERIALS, CONCEPTS of; UNIVERSE.

"McCarthyism." In the late 1940's, another newly coined term was shot into our cultural arteries: *"McCarthyism."* Again, it was a derogatory term, suggesting some insidious evil, and without any clear definition. Its alleged meaning was: "Unjust accusations, persecutions, and character assassinations of innocent victims." Its real meaning was: "Anti-communism."

Senator McCarthy was never proved guilty of those allegations, but the effect of that term was to intimidate and silence public discussions. Any uncompromising denunciation of communism or communists was —and still is—smeared as "McCarthyism." As a consequence, opposition to and exposés of communist penetration have all but vanished from our intellectual scene. (I must mention that I am not an admirer of Senator McCarthy, but *not* for the reasons implied in that smear.)

[" 'Extremism,' or The Art of Smearing," *CUI*, 176.]

See also "ANTI-CONCEPTS"; COMMUNISM; SOVIET RUSSIA.

Meaning (of Concepts). A word has no meaning other than that of the concept it symbolizes, and the meaning of a concept consists of its units.

[*ITOE*, 52.]

A widespread error, in this context, holds that the wider the concept, the less its cognitive content—on the ground that its distinguishing characteristic is more generalized than the distinguishing characteristics of its constituent concepts. The error lies in assuming that a concept consists of nothing but its distinguishing characteristic. But the fact is that in the process of abstracting from abstractions, one cannot know *what* is a distinguishing characteristic unless one has observed other characteristics of the units involved and of the existents from which they are differentiated.

Just as the concept "man" does not consist merely of "rational faculty" (if it did, the two would be equivalent and interchangeable, which they are not), but includes *all* the characteristics of "man," with "rational faculty" serving as the distinguishing characteristic—so, in the case of wider concepts, the concept "animal" does not consist merely of "consciousness and locomotion," but subsumes *all* the characteristics of all the animal species, with "consciousness and locomotion" serving as the distinguishing characteristic.

[Ibid., 34.]

To know the exact meaning of the concepts one is using, one must know their correct definitions, one must be able to retrace the specific (logical, not chronological) steps by which they were formed, and one must be able to demonstrate their connection to their base in perceptual reality.

When in doubt about the meaning or the definition of a concept, the best method of clarification is to look for its referents—i.e., to ask oneself: What fact or facts of reality gave rise to this concept? What distinguishes it from all other concepts?

For instance: what fact of reality gave rise to the concept "justice"? The fact that man must draw conclusions about the things, people and events around him, i.e., must judge and evaluate them. Is his judgment automatically right? No. What causes his judgment to be wrong? The lack of sufficient evidence, or his evasion of the evidence, or his inclusion of considerations other than the facts of the case. How, then, is he to arrive at the right judgment? By basing it exclusively on the factual evidence and by considering all the relevant evidence available. But isn't this a description of "objectivity"? Yes, "objective judgment" is one of the wider categories to which the concept "justice" belongs. What distinguishes "justice" from other instances of objective judgment? When one evaluates the nature or actions of inanimate objects, the criterion of judgment is determined by the particular purpose for which one evaluates them. But how does one determine a criterion for evaluating the character and actions of men, in view of the fact that men possess the faculty of volition? What science can provide an objective criterion of evaluation in regard to volitional matters? Ethics. Now, do I need a concept to designate the act of judging a man's character and/or actions exclusively on the basis of all the factual evidence available, and of evaluating it by means of an objective moral criterion? Yes. That concept is "justice."

[Ibid., 67.]

Since a word is a symbol for a concept, it has no meaning apart from the content of the concept it symbolizes. And since a concept is an integration of units, *it* has no content or meaning apart from its units.

The meaning of a concept consists of the units—the existents—which it integrates, including all the characteristics of these units.

Observe that concepts mean *existents*, not arbitrarily selected portions of existents. There is no basis whatever—neither metaphysical nor epistemological, neither in the nature of reality nor of a conceptual consciousness—for a division of the characteristics of a concept's units into two groups, one of which is excluded from the concept's meaning.

[Leonard Peikoff, "The Analytic-Synthetic Dichotomy," *ITOE*, 132.]

What, then, is the meaning of the concept "man"? "Man" means a certain type of entity, a rational animal, including *all* the characteristics of this entity (anatomical, physiological, psychological, etc., as well as the relations of these characteristics to those of other entities)—all the characteristics already known, and all those ever to be discovered. Whatever is true of the entity, is meant by the concept.

It follows that there are no grounds on which to distinguish "analytic" from "synthetic" propositions. Whether one states that "A man is a rational animal," or that "A man has only two eyes"—in both cases, the predicated characteristics are true of man and are, therefore, included in the concept "man." The meaning of the first statement is: "A certain type of entity, including all its characteristics (among which are rationality and animality) is: a rational animal." The meaning of the second is: "A certain type of entity, including all its characteristics (among which is the possession of only two eyes) has: only two eyes." Each of these statements is an instance of the Law of Identity; each is a "tautology"; to deny either is to contradict the meaning of the concept "man," and thus to endorse a self-contradiction.

A similar type of analysis is applicable to *every* true statement. Every truth about a given existent(s) reduces, in basic pattern, to: "X is: one or more of the things which it is." The predicate in such a case states some characteristic(s) of the subject; but since it *is* a characteristic of the subject, the *concept(s)* designating the subject in fact includes the predicate from the outset.

[Ibid., 135.]

See also ANALYTIC-SYNTHETIC DICHOTOMY; CONCEPTS; UNIT; WORDS.

Measurement. Measurement is the identification of a relationship—a quantitative relationship established by means of a standard that serves as a unit. Entities (and their actions) are measured by their attributes (length, weight, velocity, etc.) and the standard of measurement is a concretely specified unit representing the appropriate attribute.

Thus, one measures length in inches, feet and miles—weight in pounds —velocity by means of a given distance traversed in a given time, etc.

It is important to note that while the choice of a given standard is optional, the mathematical rules of using it are not. It makes no difference whether one measures length in terms of feet or meters; the standard provides only the form of notation, not the substance nor the result of the process of measuring. The facts established by measurement will be the same, regardless of the particular standard used; the standard can neither alter nor affect them. The requirements of a standard of measurement are: that it represent the appropriate attribute, that it be easily perceivable by man and that, once chosen, it remain immutable and absolute whenever used. (Please remember this; we will have reason to recall it.)

Now what is the purpose of measurement? Observe that measurement consists of relating an easily perceivable unit to larger or smaller quantities, then to infinitely larger or infinitely smaller quantities, which are not directly perceivable to man. (The word "infinitely" is used here as a mathematical, not a metaphysical, term.) The purpose of measurement is to expand the range of man's consciousness, of his knowledge, beyond the perceptual level: beyond the direct power of his senses and the immediate concretes of any given moment. Man can perceive the length of one foot directly; he cannot perceive ten miles. By establishing the relationship of feet to miles, he can grasp and know any distance on earth; by establishing the relationship of miles to light-years, he can know the distances of galaxies.

The process of measurement is a process of integrating an unlimited scale of knowledge to man's limited perceptual experience—a process of making the universe knowable by bringing it within the range of man's consciousness, by establishing its relationship to man. It is not an accident that man's earliest attempts at measurement (the evidence of which survives to this day) consisted of relating things to *himself*—as, for instance, taking the length of his foot as a standard of length, or adopting the decimal system, which is supposed to have its origin in man's ten fingers as units of counting.

It is here that Protagoras' old dictum may be given a new meaning, the opposite of the one he intended: "Man is the measure of all things." Man *is* the measure, epistemologically—*not* metaphysically. In regard to human knowledge, man has to be the measure, since he has to bring all things into the realm of the humanly knowable. But, far from leading to subjectivism, the methods which he has to employ require the most rigorous mathematical precision, the most rigorous compliance with objective rules and facts—if the end product is to be *knowledge*.

[*ITOE*, 8.]

Observe the multiple role of measurements in the process of concept-formation, in both of its two essential parts: differentiation and integration. Concepts cannot be formed at random. All concepts are formed by first differentiating two or more existents from other existents. All conceptual differentiations are made in terms of *commensurable characteristics* (i.e., characteristics possessing a common unit of measurement). No concept could be formed, for instance, by attempting to distinguish long objects from green objects. Incommensurable characteristics cannot be integrated into one unit.

Tables, for instance, are first differentiated from chairs, beds and other objects by means of the characteristic of *shape,* which is an attribute possessed by all the objects involved. Then, their particular kind of shape is set as the distinguishing characteristic of tables—i.e., a certain category of geometrical measurements of shape is specified. Then, within that category, the particular measurements of individual table-shapes are omitted.

Please note the fact that a given shape represents a certain category or set of geometrical measurements. Shape is an attribute; differences of shape—whether cubes, spheres, cones or any complex combinations —are a matter of differing measurements; any shape can be reduced to or expressed by a set of figures in terms of *linear measurement.* When, in the process of concept-formation, man observes that shape is a commensurable characteristic of certain objects, he does not have to measure all the shapes involved *nor even to know how to measure them;* he merely has to observe the element of *similarity.*

Similarity is grasped *perceptually;* in observing it, man is not and does not have to be aware of the fact that it involves a matter of measurement. It is the task of philosophy and of science to identify that fact.

As to the actual process of measuring shapes, a vast part of higher mathematics, from geometry on up, is devoted to the task of discovering methods by which various shapes can be measured—complex methods which consist of reducing the problem to the terms of a simple, primitive method, the only one available to man in this field: linear measurement. (Integral calculus, used to measure the area of circles, is just one example.)

[Ibid., 16.]

There is no exact method of measuring the intensity of all psychological processes, but—as in the case of forming concepts of colors—conceptualization does not require the knowledge of exact measurements. Degrees of intensity can be and are measured approximately, on a comparative scale. For instance, the intensity of the emotion of joy in response to certain facts varies according to the importance of these facts in one's *hierarchy* of values; it varies in such cases as buying a new suit, or getting a raise in pay, or marrying the person one loves. The intensity of a process of thought and of the intellectual effort required varies according to the *scope* of its content; it varies when one grasps the concept "table" or the concept "justice," when one grasps that $2 + 2 = 4$ or that $e = mc^2$.

[Ibid., 40.]

Observe that the attacks on the conceptual level of man's consciousness, i.e., on reason, come from the same ideological quarters as the attacks on *measurement*. When discussing man's consciousness, particularly his emotions, some persons use the word "measurement" as a pejorative term—as if an attempt to apply it to the phenomena of consciousness were a gross, insulting, "materialistic" impropriety. The question "Can you measure love?" is an example and a symptom of that attitude.

As in many other issues, the two allegedly opposite camps are merely two variants growing out of the same basic premises. The old-fashioned mystics proclaim that you cannot measure love in pounds, inches or dollars. They are aided and abetted by the neo-mystics who—punch-drunk with undigested concepts of measurement, proclaiming measurement to be the sole tool of science—proceed to measure knee-jerks, statistical questionnaires, and the learning time of rats, as indices to the human psyche.

Both camps fail to observe that *measurement requires an appropriate standard,* and that in the physical sciences—which one camp passionately hates, and the other passionately envies—one does not measure length in pounds, or weight in inches.

Measurement is the identification of a relationship in numerical terms —and the complexity of the science of measurement indicates the complexity of the relationships which exist in the universe and which man has barely begun to investigate. They exist, even if the appropriate standards and methods of measurement are not always as easily apparent nor the degree of achievable precision as great as in the case of measuring the basic, perceptually given attributes of matter. If anything were actually "immeasurable," it would bear no relationship of any kind to the rest of the universe, it would not affect nor be affected by anything else in any manner whatever, it would enact no causes and bear no consequences—in short, it would not exist.

The motive of the anti-measurement attitude is obvious: it is the desire to preserve a sanctuary of the indeterminate for the benefit of the irrational—the desire, epistemologically, to escape from the responsibility of cognitive precision and wide-scale integration; and, metaphysically, the desire to escape from the absolutism of existence, of facts, of reality and, above all, of *identity*.

[Ibid., 49.]

See also IDENTITY; MATHEMATICS; TELEOLOGICAL MEASUREMENT; UNIT.

Mediocrity. "Mediocrity" does not mean an average intelligence; it means an average intelligence that resents and envies its betters.

["The Comprachicos," *NL*, 213.]

See also GUILD SOCIALISM; INTELLIGENCE; PYRAMID of ABILITY.

Mental Health. Psychology does not regard its subject morally, but medically—i.e., from the aspect of health or malfunction (with cognitive competence as the proper standard of health).

["The Psychology of 'Psychologizing,' " *TO*, March 1971, 5.]

See also BEHAVIORISM; EVASION; FREUD; IMAGINATION; NEUROSIS vs. PSYCHOSIS; PSYCHO-EPISTEMOLOGY; PSYCHOLOGY; SELF-ESTEEM; SUBCONSCIOUS.

Mercy. "Mercy" means an unearned forgiveness.

[Leonard Peikoff, "The Philosophy of Objectivism" lecture series (1976), question period, Lecture 8.]

See also JUSTICE; MORAL JUDGMENT.

"Meritocracy." "Meritocracy" is an old anti-concept and one of the most contemptible package deals. By means of nothing more than its last five letters, that word obliterates the difference between mind and force: it equates the men of ability with *political* rulers, and the power of their creative achievements with *political* power. There is no difference, the word suggests, between freedom and tyranny: an "aristocracy" is tyranny by a politically established elite, a "democracy" is tyranny by the majority—and when a government protects individual rights, the result is tyranny by talent or "merit" (and since "to merit" means "to deserve," a free society is ruled by the tyranny of justice).

["An Untitled Letter," *PWNI*, 126; pb 105.]

See also "ANTI-CONCEPTS"; DEMOCRACY; ECONOMIC POWER vs. POLITICAL POWER; FREEDOM; INDIVIDUAL RIGHTS; JUSTICE; "PACKAGE-DEALING," FALLACY of; TYRANNY.

Metaphysical. I use the word "metaphysical" to mean: that which pertains to reality, to the nature of things, to existence.

["The Objectivist Ethics," *VOS*, 2; pb 14.]

See also EXISTENCE; METAPHYSICAL VALUE-JUDGMENTS; META-PHYSICAL vs. MAN-MADE; METAPHYSICS.

Metaphysical Value-Judgments. The key concept, in the formation of a sense of life, is the term *"important."* It is a concept that belongs to the realm of values, since it implies an answer to the question: Important—to whom? Yet its meaning is different from that of moral values. "Important" does not necessarily mean "good." It means "a quality, character or standing such as to entitle to attention or consideration" (*The American College Dictionary*). What, in a fundamental sense, is entitled to one's attention or consideration? Reality.

"Important"—in its essential meaning, as distinguished from its more limited and superficial uses—is a *metaphysical* term. It pertains to that aspect of metaphysics which serves as a bridge between metaphysics and ethics: to a fundamental view of man's nature. That view involves the answers to such questions as whether the universe is knowable or not, whether man has the power of choice or not, whether he can achieve his goals in life or not. The answers to such questions are "metaphysical value-judgments," since they form the base of ethics.

It is only those values which he regards or grows to regard as "important," those which represent his implicit view of reality, that remain in a man's subconscious and form his sense of life.

"It is important to understand things"—"It is important to obey my parents"—"It is important to act on my own"—"It is important to please other people"—"It is important to fight for what I want"—"It is important not to make enemies"—"My life is important"—"Who am I to stick my neck out?" Man is a being of self-made soul—and it is of such conclusions that the stuff of his soul is made. (By "soul" I mean "consciousness.")

["Philosophy and Sense of Life," *RM*, 34; pb 28.]

Is the universe intelligible to man, or unintelligible and unknowable? Can man find happiness on earth, or is he doomed to frustration and despair? Does man have the power of *choice*, the power to choose his goals and to achieve them, the power to direct the course of his life—or is he the helpless plaything of forces beyond his control, which determine his fate? Is man, by nature, to be valued as good, or to be despised as evil? These are *metaphysical* questions, but the answers to them determine the kind of *ethics* men will accept and practice; the answers are the link between metaphysics and ethics. And although metaphysics as such is not a normative science, the answers to this category of questions assume, in man's mind, the function of metaphysical value-judgments, since they form the foundation of all of his moral values.

Consciously or subconsciously, explicitly or implicitly, man knows that he needs a comprehensive view of existence to integrate his values, to choose his goals, to plan his future, to maintain the unity and coherence of his life—and that his metaphysical value-judgments are involved in every moment of his life, in his every choice, decision and action.

["The Psycho-Epistemology of Art," *RM*, 21; pb 19.]

See also ART; BENEVOLENT UNIVERSE PREMISE; MALEVOLENT UNIVERSE PREMISE; METAPHYSICS; MORALITY; PHILOSOPHY; SENSE of LIFE; SUBCONSCIOUS.

Metaphysical vs. Man-Made. Any natural phenomenon, i.e., any event which occurs without human participation, is the metaphysically given, and could not have occurred differently or failed to occur; any phenomenon involving human action is the man-made, and could have been different. For example, a flood occurring in an uninhabited land, is the metaphysically given; a dam built to contain the flood water, is the man-made; if the builders miscalculate and the dam breaks, the disaster is metaphysical in its origin, but intensified by man in its consequences. To correct the situation, men must obey nature by studying the causes and potentialities of the flood, then command nature by building better flood controls.

["The Metaphysical Versus the Man-Made," *PWNI*, 33; pb 27.]

Things of human origin (whether physical or psychological) may be designated as "man-made facts"—as distinguished from the metaphysically given facts. A skyscraper is a man-made fact, a mountain is a metaphysically given fact. One can alter a skyscraper or blow it up (just as one can alter or blow up a mountain), but so long as it exists, one cannot pretend that it is not there or that it is not what it is.

[Ibid., 37; pb 31.]

Nature, i.e., the universe as a whole, cannot be created or annihilated . . . it cannot come into or go out of existence. Whether its basic constituent elements are atoms, or subatomic particles, or some yet undiscovered forms of energy, it is not ruled by a consciousness or by will or by chance, but by the law of identity. All the countless forms, motions, combinations and dissolutions of elements within the universe—from a floating speck of dust to the formation of a galaxy to the emergence of life—are caused and determined by the identities of the elements involved. Nature is the *metaphysically given*—i.e., the nature of nature is outside the power of any volition.

[Ibid., 30; pb 25.]

Man's faculty of volition as such is not a contradiction of nature, but it opens the way for a host of contradictions—when and if men do not grasp *the crucial difference between the metaphysically given and any object, institution, procedure, or rule of conduct made by man.*

It is the metaphysically given that must be accepted: it cannot be changed. It is the man-made that must never be accepted uncritically: it must be judged, then accepted or rejected and changed when necessary. Man is not omniscient or infallible: he can make innocent errors through lack of knowledge, or he can lie, cheat and fake. The man-made may be a product of genius, perceptiveness, ingenuity—or it may be a product of stupidity, deception, malice, evil. One man may be right and everyone else wrong, or vice versa (or any numerical division in between). Nature does not give man any automatic guarantee of the truth of his judgments (and *this* is a metaphysically given fact, which must be accepted). Who, then, is to judge? Each man, to the best of his ability and honesty. What is his standard of judgment? *The metaphysically given.*

The metaphysically given cannot be true or false, it simply *is*—and man determines the truth or falsehood of his judgments by whether they correspond to or contradict the facts of reality. The metaphysically given cannot be right or wrong—it is the standard of right or wrong, by which a (rational) man judges his goals, his values, his choices. The metaphysically given is, was, will be, and had to be. Nothing made by man *had to be:* it was made by choice.

[Ibid., 32; pb 27.]

A man-made product did not have to exist, but, once made, it *does* exist. A man's actions did not have to be performed, but, once performed, they are *facts* of reality. The same is true of a man's character: he did not have to make the choices he made, but, once he has formed his character, it is a *fact*, and it is his personal *identity*. (Man's volition gives him great, but not unlimited, latitude to change his character; if he does, the change becomes a *fact*.)

[Ibid., 37; pb 31.]

[One must] distinguish *metaphysical* facts from *man-made* facts—i.e., facts which are inherent in the identities of that which exists, from facts which depend upon the exercise of human volition. Because man has free will, no human choice—and no phenomenon which is a product of human choice—is metaphysically necessary. In regard to any man-made fact, it is valid to claim that man *has* chosen thus, but it was not inherent in the nature of existence for him to have done so; he could have chosen otherwise. For instance, the U.S. did not have to consist of 50 states; men could have subdivided the larger ones, or consolidated the smaller ones, etc.

Choice, however, is not chance. Volition is not an exception to the Law of Causality; it is a type of causation. . . . Further, metaphysical facts are unalterable by man, and limit the alternatives open to his choice. Man can rearrange the materials that exist in reality, but he cannot violate their identity; he cannot escape the laws of nature. "Nature, to be commanded, must be obeyed."

[Leonard Peikoff, "The Analytic-Synthetic Dichotomy," *ITOE*, 149.]

In regard to nature, "to accept what I cannot change" means to accept the metaphysically given; "to change what I can" means to strive to rearrange the given by acquiring knowledge—as science and technology (e.g., medicine) are doing; "to know the difference" means to know that one cannot rebel against nature and, when no action is possible, one must accept nature serenely. . . . What one must accept is the fact that the minds of other men are not in one's power, as one's own mind is not in theirs; one must accept their right to make their own choices, and one must agree or disagree, accept or reject, join or oppose them, as one's mind dictates. The only means of "changing" men is the same as the means of "changing" nature: knowledge—which, in regard to men, is to be used as a process of *persuasion,* when and if their minds are active; when they are not, one must leave them to the consequences of their own errors. . . .

To deal with men by force is as impractical as to deal with nature by persuasion.

["The Metaphysical Versus the Man-Made," *PWNI,* 39; pb 32.]

See also ABSOLUTES; CHARACTER; CREATION; FREE WILL; IDENTITY; MORAL JUDGMENT; NATURE; NECESSITY; PHYSICAL FORCE; UNIVERSE.

Metaphysics.

Are you in a universe which is ruled by natural laws and, therefore, is stable, firm, absolute—and knowable? Or are you in an incomprehensible chaos, a realm of inexplicable miracles, an unpredictable, unknowable flux, which your mind is impotent to grasp? Are the things you see around you real—or are they only an illusion? Do they exist independent of any observer—or are they created by the observer? Are they the object or the subject of man's consciousness? Are they *what they are*—or can they be changed by a mere act of your consciousness, such as a wish?

The nature of your actions—and of your ambition—will be different, according to which set of answers you come to accept. These answers are the province of *metaphysics*—the study of existence as such or, in Aristotle's words, of "being qua being"—the basic branch of philosophy.

["Philosophy: Who Needs It," *PWNI*, 3; pb 2.]

The branch of philosophy that studies existence is *metaphysics*. Metaphysics identifies the nature of the universe as a whole. It tells men what kind of world they live in, and whether there is a supernatural dimension beyond it. It tells men whether they live in a world of solid entities, natural laws, absolute facts, or in a world of illusory fragments, unpredictable miracles, and ceaseless flux. It tells men whether the things they perceive by their senses and mind form a comprehensible reality, with which they can deal, or some kind of unreal appearance, which leaves them staring and helpless.

[Leonard Peikoff, *OP*, 14; pb 23.]

See also ABSOLUTES; ABSTRACTIONS and CONCRETES; CAUSALITY; CONSCIOUSNESS; EXISTENCE; IDENTITY; METAPHYSICAL VALUE-JUDGMENTS; METAPHYSICAL vs. MAN-MADE; PRIMACY of EXISTENCE vs. PRIMACY of CONSCIOUSNESS; SUBJECTIVISM.

Method, Concepts of.   A special subcategory of concepts pertaining to the products of consciousness, is reserved for concepts of *method*. Concepts of method designate systematic courses of action devised by men for the purpose of achieving certain goals. The course of action may be purely psychological (such as a method of using one's consciousness) or it may involve a combination of psychological and physical actions (such as a method of drilling for oil), according to the goal to be achieved.

Concepts of method are formed by retaining the distinguishing characteristics of the purposive course of action and of its goal, while omitting the particular measurements of both.

For instance, *the* fundamental concept of method, the one on which all the others depend, is *logic*. The distinguishing characteristic of logic (the art of non-contradictory identification) indicates the nature of the actions (actions of consciousness required to achieve a correct identification) and their goal (knowledge)—while omitting the length, complexity or specific steps of the process of logical inference, as well as the nature of the particular cognitive problem involved in any given instance of using logic.

Concepts of method represent a large part of man's conceptual equipment. Epistemology is a science devoted to the discovery of the proper methods of acquiring and validating knowledge. Ethics is a science devoted to the discovery of the proper methods of living one's life. Medicine is a science devoted to the discovery of the proper methods of curing disease. All the applied sciences (i.e., technology) are sciences devoted to the discovery of methods.

[*ITOE*, 46.]

See also CONCEPT-FORMATION; CONCEPTS; CONSCIOUSNESS; EPISTEMOLOGY; LOGIC; MATHEMATICS.

Middle Ages. The Middle Ages were an era of mysticism, ruled by blind faith and blind obedience to the dogma that faith is superior to reason.

["The Left: Old and New," *NL*, 83.]

In the history of Western civilization, the period known as the Dark Ages, after the fall of the Roman Empire, was a period when Western Europe existed without any social organization beyond chance local groupings clustered around small villages, large castles, and remnants of various traditions—swept periodically by massive barbarian invasions, warring robber bands, and sundry local looters. It was as close to a state of pure anarchy as men could come. The feudal system grew out of the need for organized protection. The system, in essence, consisted in the peasants swearing allegiance to a lord, who claimed ownership of the land and a percentage of their harvest in exchange for his duty to protect them against military attacks.

This system brought some semblance of order, but no protection and no peace. Disarmed men were left in the total power of an armed ruler, who had his own military gang and who robbed them as ruthlessly as, but more systematically than, any foreign invader. The history of the Middle Ages is a series of internal and external wars: there were various lords struggling to enlarge their domains, foreign lords struggling to subjugate neighboring lands, and bloody, hopeless uprisings of desperate peasants, bloodily suppressed. It was also the longest period of stagnation—intellectually and productively—in Europe's history.

["A Nation's Unity," *ARL*, II, 2, 2.]

The medieval period, under the sway of such philosophers as Plotinus and Augustine, was an era dominated by Platonism. During much of this period Aristotle's philosophy was almost unknown in the West.

[Leonard Peikoff, *OP*, 22; pb 30.]

For centuries, nature had been regarded as a realm of miracles manipulated by a personal deity, a realm whose significance lay in the clues it offered to the purposes of its author.

[Ibid., 107; pb 106.]

The dominant moralists had said that man must not seek his ultimate fulfillment on earth; that he must renounce the pleasures of this life, whether as a flesh-mortifying ascetic or as an abstemious toiler, for the sake of God, salvation, and the life to come. . . . Whatever their concern with the individual soul, the medievals had derogated or failed to discover the *individual man*. In philosophy, the Platonists had denied his reality; in practice, the feudal system had (by implication) treated the group—the caste, the guild, etc.—as the operative social unit.

[Ibid., 110; pb 108.]

An entirely different view of man dominated the medieval Christian civilization. Man, according to Augustine, is "crooked and sordid, bespotted and ulcerous." Medieval mystics regarded man as an evil creature whose body is loathsome because it is material, and whose mind is impotent because it is human. Hating man's body, they said that pleasure is evil, and virtue consists of renunciation. Hating this earth, they said that it is a prison where man is doomed to pain, misery, calamity. Hating life, they said that death and escape into some other dimension is all that man could—and should—hope for.

Man as a helpless and depraved creature, was the basic theme of medieval sculpture until the Gothic period, whether he was shown being pushed into Hell or accepted into Heaven.

[Mary Ann Sures, "Metaphysics in Marble," *TO*, Feb. 1969, 14.]

The supernatural doctrines of the Middle Ages, . . . kept men huddling on the mud floors of their hovels, in terror that the devil might steal the soup they had worked eighteen hours to earn.

[GS, *FNI*, 199; pb 160.]

See also ARISTOTLE; DARK AGES; FAITH; HISTORY; INDIVIDUAL-ISM; MIRACLES; MYSTICISM; RELIGION; RENAISSANCE.

Middle Class.   A nation's productive—and moral, and intellectual —top is *the middle class*. It is a broad reservoir of energy, it is a country's motor and lifeblood, which feeds the rest. The common denominator of its members, on their various levels of ability, is: independence. The upper classes are merely a nation's past; the middle class is its future.

["The Dead End," *ARL*, I, 20, 3.]

The middle class is the heart, the lifeblood, the energy source of a free, industrial economy, i.e., of capitalism; it did not and cannot exist under any other system; it is the product of upward mobility, incompatible with frozen social castes. Do not ask, therefore, for whom the bell of inflation is tolling; it tolls for *you*. It is not at the destruction of a handful of the rich that inflation is aimed (the rich are mostly in the vanguard of the destroyers), but at the middle class.

["The Inverted Moral Priorities," *ARL*, III, 21, 2.]

See also CAPITALISM; INFLATION.

Military Conscription. *See Draft.*

Mill, John Stuart.
Religious influences are not the only villain behind the censorship legislation; there is another one: the social school of morality, exemplified by John Stuart Mill. Mill rejected the concept of individual rights and replaced it with the notion that the "public good" is the sole justification of individual freedom. (Society, he argued, has the power to enslave or destroy its exceptional men, but it should *permit* them to be free, because it benefits from their efforts.) Among the many defaults of the conservatives in the past hundred years, the most shameful one, perhaps, is the fact that they accepted John Stuart Mill as a defender of capitalism.

["Thought Control," *ARL*, III, 2, 2.]

The terrible aspect of Mill's influence is the fact that his followers become unable to consider great values—such as truth, science, morality, art—apart from and without the permission of "the people's desires."

[Ibid., 3.]

[Mill's] *On Liberty* is the most pernicious piece of collectivism ever adopted by suicidal defenders of liberty.

["An Untitled Letter," *PWNI*, 138; pb 114.]

A weary agnostic on most of the fundamental issues of philosophy, Mill bases his defense of capitalism on the ethics of *Utilitarianism*.

Utilitarianism is a union of hedonism and Christianity. The first teaches man to love pleasure; the second, to love his neighbor. The union consists in teaching man to love his neighbor's pleasure. To be exact, the Utilitarians teach that an action is moral if its result is to maximize pleasure among men in general. This theory holds that man's duty is to serve—according to a purely quantitative standard of value.

He is to serve not the well-being of the nation or of the economic class, but "the greatest happiness of the greatest number," regardless of who comprise it in any given issue. As to one's *own* happiness, says Mill, the individual must be "disinterested" and "strictly impartial"; he must remember that he is only one unit out of the dozens, or millions, of men affected by his actions. "All honor to those who can abnegate for themselves the personal enjoyment of life," says Mill, "when by such renunciation they contribute worthily to increase the amount of happiness in the world. . . ."

Capitalism, Mill acknowledges, is not based on any desire for abnegation or renunciation; it is based on the desire for selfish profit. Nevertheless, he says, the capitalist system ensures that, most of the time, the actual result of individual profit-seeking is the happiness of society as a whole. Hence the individual should be left free of government regulation. He should be left free not as an absolute (there are no absolutes, says Mill), but under the present circumstances—not on the ground of inalienable rights (there are no such rights, Mill holds), but of social utility.

Under capitalism, concluded one American economist of the period with evident moral relief, "the Lord maketh the selfishness of man to work for the material welfare of his kind." As one commentator observes, the essence of this argument is the claim that capitalism is justified by its ability to convert "man's baseness" to "noble ends." "Baseness" here means *egoism;* "nobility" means *altruism.* And the justification of individual freedom in terms of its contribution to the welfare of society means *collectivism.*

Mill (along with Smith, Say, and the rest of the classical economists) was trying to defend an individualist system by accepting the fundamental moral ideas of its opponents. It did not take Mill long to grasp this contradiction in some terms and amend his political views accordingly. He ended his life as a self-proclaimed "qualified socialist."

[Leonard Peikoff, *OP,* 122; pb 119.]

See also AGNOSTICISM; ALTRUISM; CAPITALISM; COLLECTIVISM; "CONSERVATIVES"; FREE SPEECH; HAPPINESS; HEDONISM; INDIVIDUAL RIGHTS; PLEASURE and PAIN; "PUBLIC INTEREST," the; UTILITARIANISM; VALUES.

Mind-Body Dichotomy. *See Soul-Body Dichotomy.*

Minority Rights. The smallest minority on earth is the individual. Those who deny individual rights, cannot claim to be defenders of minorities.

["America's Persecuted Minority: Big Business," *CUI,* 61.]

The defense of minority rights is acclaimed today, virtually by everyone, as a moral principle of a high order. But this principle, which forbids discrimination, is applied by most of the "liberal" intellectuals in a *discriminatory* manner: it is applied only to racial or religious minorities. It is not applied to that small, exploited, denounced, defenseless minority which consists of businessmen.

Yet every ugly, brutal aspect of injustice toward racial or religious minorities is being practiced toward businessmen.

[Ibid., 44.]

See also BUSINESSMEN; DEMOCRACY; "ETHNICITY"; INDIVIDUAL RIGHTS; RACISM.

Miracles. The enemy you seek to defeat is the law of causality: it permits you no miracles.

[GS, *FNI*, 188; pb 151.]

See also CAUSALITY; GOD; MYSTICISM; RELIGION; SUPERNATU-RALISM.

Mixed Economy. We are not a capitalist system any longer: we are a mixed economy, i.e., a mixture of capitalism and statism, of freedom and controls. A mixed economy is a country in the process of disintegration, a civil war of pressure-groups looting and devouring one another.

["The Obliteration of Capitalism," *CUI*, 185.]

A mixed economy is a mixture of freedom and controls—with no principles, rules, or theories to define either. Since the introduction of controls necessitates and leads to further controls, it is an unstable, explosive mixture which, ultimately, has to repeal the controls or collapse into dictatorship. A mixed economy has no principles to define its policies, its goals, its laws—no principles to limit the power of its government. The *only* principle of a mixed economy—which, necessarily, has to remain unnamed and unacknowledged—is that no one's interests are safe, everyone's interests are on a public auction block, and anything goes for anyone who can get away with it. Such a system—or, more precisely, anti-system—breaks up a country into an ever-growing number of enemy camps, into economic groups fighting one another for self preservation in an indeterminate mixture of *defense* and *offense*, as the nature of such a jungle demands. While, *politically*, a mixed economy preserves the semblance of an organized society with a semblance of law and order, *economically* it is the equivalent of the chaos that had ruled China for centuries: a chaos of robber gangs looting—and draining—the productive elements of the country.

A mixed economy is rule by pressure groups. It is an amoral, institutionalized civil war of special interests and lobbies, all fighting to seize a momentary control of the legislative machinery, to extort some special privilege at one another's expense by an act of government—i.e., by force. In the absence of individual rights, in the absence of any moral or legal principles, a mixed economy's only hope to preserve its precarious semblance of order, to restrain the savage, desperately rapacious groups it itself has created, and to prevent the legalized plunder from running over into plain, unlegalized looting of all by all—is *compromise;* compromise on everything and in every realm—material, spiritual, intellectual—so that no group would step over the line by demanding too much and topple the whole rotted structure. If the game is to continue, nothing can be permitted to remain firm, solid, absolute, untouchable; everything (and everyone) has to be fluid, flexible, indeterminate, approximate. By what standard are anyone's actions to be guided? By the expediency of any immediate moment.

The only danger, to a mixed economy, is any not-to-be-compromised value, virtue, or idea. The only threat is any uncompromising person, group, or movement. The only enemy is integrity.

["The New Fascism: Rule by Consensus," *CUI*, 206.]

There can be no compromise between freedom and government controls; to accept "just a few controls" is to surrender the principle of inalienable individual rights and to substitute for it the principle of the government's unlimited, arbitrary power, thus delivering oneself into gradual enslavement. As an example of this process, observe the present domestic policy of the United States.

["Doesn't Life Require Compromise?" *VOS*, 86; pb 68.]

You have seen, within the span of the last few years, that controls breed more controls, and that the proliferation of controls breeds the proliferation of pressure groups. Today, you see political manipulators setting up new conflicts, such as ethnic minorities against the majority, the young against the old, the old against the middle, women against men, even welfare-recipients against the self-supporting. Openly and cynically, these new groups clamor for "a bigger slice of the pie" (which you have to bake).

["The Principals and the Principles," *ARL*, II, 21, 3.]

In a controlled (or mixed) economy, a legislator's job consists in sacrificing some men to others. No matter what choice he makes, no choice of this kind can be morally justified (and never has been). Proceeding from an immoral base, no decision of his can be honest or dishonest, just or unjust—these concepts are inapplicable. He becomes, therefore, an easy target for the promptings of any pressure group, any lobbyist, any influence-peddler, any manipulator—he has no standards by which to judge or to resist them. You do not know what hidden powers drive him or what he is doing. Neither does he.

[Ibid., 4.]

If parasitism, favoritism, corruption, and greed for the unearned did not exist, a mixed economy would bring them into existence.

["The Pull Peddlers," *CUI*, 170.]

A mixed economy has to reach the day when it faces a final crossroad: either the private sector regains its freedom and starts rebuilding—or it gives up and lets the absolute state take over the shambles.

["A Preview," *ARL*, I, 23, 4.]

See also CAPITALISM; COMPROMISE; FREEDOM; GOVERNMENT; INDIVIDUAL RIGHTS; INTERVENTIONISM (ECONOMIC); LOBBYING; PHYSICAL FORCE; STATISM.

Modern Art. As a re-creation of reality, a work of art has to be representational; its freedom of stylization is limited by the requirement of intelligibility; if it does not present an intelligible subject, it ceases to be art.

["Art and Cognition," *RM*, pb 75.]

Decomposition is the postscript to the death of a human body; disintegration is the preface to the death of a human mind. Disintegration is the keynote and goal of modern art—the disintegration of man's conceptual faculty, and the retrogression of an adult mind to the state of a mewling infant.

To reduce man's consciousness to the level of sensations, with no capacity to integrate them, is the intention behind the reducing of language to grunts, of literature to "moods," of painting to smears, of sculpture to slabs, of music to noise.

But there is a philosophically and psychopathologically instructive element in the spectacle of that gutter. It demonstrates—by the negative means of an absence—the relationships of art to philosophy, of reason to man's survival, of hatred for reason to hatred for existence. After centuries of the philosophers' war against reason, they have succeeded —by the method of vivisection—in producing exponents of what man is like when deprived of his rational faculty, and these in turn are giving us images of what existence is like to a being with an empty skull.

While the alleged advocates of reason oppose "system-building" and haggle apologetically over concrete-bound words or mystically floating abstractions, its enemies seem to know that *integration* is the psycho-epistemological key to reason, that art is man's psycho-epistemological conditioner, and that if reason is to be destroyed, it is man's integrating capacity that has to be destroyed.

It is highly doubtful that the practitioners and admirers of modern art have the intellectual capacity to understand its philosophical meaning; all they need to do is indulge the worst of their subconscious premises. But their leaders do understand the issue consciously: the father of modern art is Immanuel Kant (see his *Critique of Judgment*).

I do not know which is worse: to practice modern art as a colossal fraud or to do it sincerely.

Those who do not wish to be the passive, silent victims of frauds of this kind, can learn from modern art the *practical* importance of philosophy, and the consequences of philosophical default. Specifically, it is the destruction of logic that disarmed the victims, and, more specifically, the destruction of definitions. Definitions are the guardians of rationality, the first line of defense against the chaos of mental disintegration.

Works of art—like everything else in the universe—are entities of a specific nature: the concept requires a definition by their essential characteristics, which distinguish them from all other existing entities. The *genus* of art works is: man-made objects which present a selective re-creation of reality according to the artist's metaphysical value-judgments, by means of a specific material medium. The *species* are the works of the various branches of art, defined by the particular media which they employ and which indicate their relation to the various elements of man's cognitive faculty.

Man's need of precise definitions rests on the Law of Identity: A is A, a thing is itself. A work of art is a specific entity which possesses a specific nature. If it does not, it is not a work of art. If it is merely a material object, it belongs to some category of material objects—and if it does not belong to any particular category, it belongs to the one reserved for such phenomena: junk.

"Something made by an artist" is *not* a definition of art. A beard and a vacant stare are *not* the defining characteristics of an artist.

"Something in a frame hung on a wall" is *not* a definition of painting.

"Something with a number of pages in a binding" is *not* a definition of literature.

"Something piled together" is *not* a definition of sculpture.

"Something made of sounds produced by anything" is *not* a definition of music.

"Something glued on a flat surface" is *not* a definition of any art.

There is no art that uses glue as a medium. Blades of grass glued on a sheet of paper to represent grass might be good occupational therapy for retarded children—though I doubt it—but it is *not* art.

"Because I felt like it" is *not* a definition or validation of anything.

There is no place for *whim* in any human activity—if it is to be regarded as human. There is no place for the unknowable, the unintelligible, the undefinable, the non-objective in any human product. This side of an insane asylum, the actions of a human being are motivated by a conscious purpose; when they are not, they are of no interest to anyone outside a psychotherapist's office. And when the practitioners of modern art declare that they don't know what they are doing or what makes them do it, we should take their word for it and give them no further consideration.

["Art and Cognition," *RM*, pb 76.]

As an example of an entire field of activity based on nothing but the Argument from Intimidation, I give you modern art—where, in order to prove that they *do* possess the special insight possessed only by the mystic "elite," the populace are trying to surpass one another in loud exclamations on the splendor of some bare (but smudged) piece of canvas.

["The Argument from Intimidation," *VOS*, 193; pb 140.]

Just as modern philosophy is dominated by the attempt to destroy the conceptual level of man's consciousness and even the perceptual level, reducing man's awareness to mere sensations—so modern art and literature are dominated by the attempt to disintegrate man's consciousness and reduce it to mere sensations, to the "enjoyment" of meaningless colors, noises and moods.

The art of any given period or culture is a faithful mirror of that culture's philosophy. If you see obscene, dismembered monstrosities leering at you from today's esthetic mirrors—the aborted creations of mediocrity, irrationality and panic—you are seeing the embodied, *concretized* reality of the philosophical premises that dominate today's culture. Only in this sense can those manifestations be called "art"—not by the intention or accomplishment of their perpetrators.

["Basic Principles of Literature," *RM*, 79; pb 97.]

The composite picture of man that emerges from the art of our time is the gigantic figure of an aborted embryo whose limbs suggest a vaguely anthropoid shape, who twists his upper extremity in a frantic quest for a light that cannot penetrate its empty sockets, who emits inarticulate sounds resembling snarls and moans, who crawls through a bloody muck, red froth dripping from his jaws, and struggles to throw the froth at his own non-existent face, who pauses periodically and, lifting the stumps of his arms, screams in abysmal terror at the universe at large.

Engendered by generations of anti-rational philosophy, three emotions dominate the sense of life of modern man: fear, guilt and pity (more precisely, self-pity). Fear, as the appropriate emotion of a creature deprived of his means of survival, his mind; guilt, as the appropriate emotion of a creature devoid of moral values; pity, as the means of escape from these two, as the only response such a creature could beg for. A sensitive, discriminating man, who has absorbed that sense of life, but retained some vestige of self-esteem, will avoid so revealing a profession as art. But this does not stop the others.

Fear, guilt and the quest for pity combine to set the trend of art in the same direction, in order to express, justify and rationalize the artists' own feelings. To justify a chronic fear, one has to portray existence as evil; to escape from guilt and arouse pity, one has to portray man as impotent and innately loathsome. Hence the competition among modern artists to find ever lower levels of depravity and ever higher degrees of mawkishness—a competition to shock the public out of its wits and jerk its tears. Hence the frantic search for misery, the descent from compassionate studies of alcoholism and sexual perversion to dope, incest, psychosis, murder, cannibalism.

["Bootleg Romanticism," *RM*, 122; pb 130.]

See also ARGUMENT from INTIMIDATION; ART; DEFINITIONS; GENUS and SPECIES; INTEGRATION (MENTAL); OBJECTIVITY; PERCEPTION; PHILOSOPHY; REASON; SENSATIONS; SUBJECTIVISM; WHIMS/WHIM-WORSHIP.

Money.   Money is the tool of men who have reached a high level of productivity and a long-range control over their lives. Money is not merely a tool of exchange: much more importantly, it is *a tool of saving*, which permits delayed consumption and buys time for future production. To fulfill this requirement, money has to be some material commodity which is imperishable, rare, homogeneous, easily stored, not subject to wide fluctuations of value, and always in demand among those you trade with. This leads you to the decision to use gold as money. Gold money is a tangible value in itself and a token of wealth actually produced. When you accept a gold coin in payment for your goods, you actually deliver the goods to the buyer; the transaction is as safe as simple barter. When you store your savings in the form of gold coins, they represent the goods which you have actually produced and which have gone to buy time for other producers, who will keep the productive process going, so that you'll be able to trade your coins for goods any time you wish.

["Egalitarianism and Inflation," *PWNI,* 154; pb 127.]

Money cannot function as money, i.e., as a medium of exchange, unless it is backed by actual, *unconsumed* goods.

["Hunger and Freedom," *ARL,* III, 22, 3.]

So you think that money is the root of all evil? . . . Have you ever asked what is the root of money? Money is a tool of exchange, which can't exist unless there are goods produced and men able to produce them. Money is the material shape of the principle that men who wish to deal with one another must deal by trade and give value for value. Money is not the tool of the moochers, who claim your product by tears, or of the looters, who take it from you by force. Money is made possible only by the men who produce. Is this what you consider evil?

When you accept money in payment for your effort, you do so only on the conviction that you will exchange it for the product of the effort of others. It is not the moochers or the looters who give value to money. Not an ocean of tears nor all the guns in the world can transform those pieces of paper in your wallet into the bread you will need to survive tomorrow. Those pieces of paper, which should have been gold, are a token of honor—your claim upon the energy of the men who produce. Your wallet is your statement of hope that somewhere in the world around you there are men who will not default on that moral principle which is the root of money. Is this what you consider evil?

Have you ever looked for the root of production? Take a look at an electric generator and dare tell yourself that it was created by the muscular effort of unthinking brutes. Try to grow a seed of wheat without the knowledge left to you by men who had to discover it for the first time. Try to obtain your food by means of nothing but physical motions—and you'll learn that man's mind is the root of all the goods produced and of all the wealth that has ever existed on earth.

But you say that money is made by the strong at the expense of the weak? What strength do you mean? It is not the strength of guns or muscles. Wealth is the product of man's capacity to think. Then is money made by the man who invents a motor at the expense of those who did not invent it? Is money made by the intelligent at the expense of the fools? By the able at the expense of the incompetent? By the ambitious at the expense of the lazy? Money is *made*—before it can be looted or mooched—made by the effort of every honest man, each to the extent of his ability. An honest man is one who knows that he can't consume more than he has produced.

["The Meaning of Money," *FNI*, 104; pb 88.]

Money rests on the axiom that every man is the owner of his mind and his effort. Money allows no power to prescribe the value of your effort except the voluntary choice of the man who is willing to trade you his effort in return. Money permits you to obtain for your goods and your labor that which they are worth to the men who buy them, but no more. Money permits no deals except those to mutual benefit by the unforced judgment of the traders.

[Ibid., 105; pb 89.]

So long as men live together on earth and need means to deal with one another—their only substitute, if they abandon money, is the muzzle of a gun.

[Ibid., 108; pb 91.]

Most people lump together into the same category all men who become rich, refusing to consider the essential question: the *source* of the riches, the means by which the wealth was acquired.

Money is a tool of exchange; it represents wealth only so long as it can be traded for material goods and services. Wealth does not grow in nature; it has to be produced by men. Nature gives us only the raw materials, but it is man's mind that has to discover the knowledge of how to use them. It is man's thinking and labor that transform the materials into food, clothing, shelter or television sets—into all the goods that men require for their survival, comfort and pleasure.

Behind every step of humanity's long climb from the cave to New York City, there is the man who took that step for the first time—the man who discovered how to make a fire or a wheel or an airplane or an electric light.

When people refuse to consider the source of wealth, what they refuse to recognize is the fact that *wealth is the product of man's intellect*, of his creative ability, fully as much as is art, science, philosophy or any other human value.

["The Money-Making Personality," *TOF*, Feb. 1983, 2.]

Money is a great power—because, in a free or even a semi-free society, it is a frozen form of productive energy. And, therefore, the spending of money is a grave responsibility. Contrary to the altruists and the advocates of the so-called "academic freedom," it is a moral crime to give money to support ideas with which you disagree; it means: ideas which you consider wrong, false, evil. It is a moral crime to give money to support your own destroyers.

["The Sanction of the Victims," *TOF*, April 1982, 7.]

See also CONSUMPTION; CREDIT; GOLD STANDARD; INFLATION; MARKET VALUE; OBJECTIVE THEORY of VALUES; PHYSICAL FORCE; PRODUCTION; PURCHASING POWER; SANCTION of the VICTIM; SAVINGS; SELFISHNESS; TRADER PRINCIPLE.

Monopoly. The alleged purpose of the Antitrust laws was to protect competition; that purpose was based on the socialistic fallacy that a free, unregulated market will inevitably lead to the establishment of coercive monopolies. But, in fact, no coercive monopoly has ever been or ever can be established by means of free trade on a free market. Every coercive monopoly was created by government intervention into the economy: by special privileges, such as franchises or subsidies, which closed the entry of competitors into a given field, by legislative action. (For a full demonstration of this fact, I refer you to the works of the best economists.)

["Antitrust: The Rule of Unreason," *TON*, Feb. 1962, 5.]

A "coercive monopoly" is a business concern that can set its prices and production policies independent of the market, with immunity from competition, from the law of supply and demand. An economy dominated by such monopolies would be rigid and stagnant.

The necessary precondition of a coercive monopoly is closed entry— the barring of all competing producers from a given field. This can be accomplished only by an act of government intervention, in the form of special regulations, subsidies, or franchises. Without government assistance, it is impossible for a would-be monopolist to set and maintain his prices and production policies independent of the rest of the economy. For if he attempted to set his prices and production at a level that would yield profits to new entrants significantly above those available in other fields, competitors would be sure to invade his industry.

[Alan Greenspan, "Antitrust," *CUI*, 68.]

See also ANTITRUST LAWS; COMPETITION; ECONOMIC POWER vs. POLITICAL POWER; FREE MARKET; INTERVENTIONISM (ECONOMIC).

Moral Cowardice. Moral cowardice is fear of upholding the good *because* it is good, and fear of opposing the evil *because* it is evil.

["Altruism as Appeasement," *TO*, Jan. 1966, 5.]

Moral cowardice is the necessary consequence of discarding morality as inconsequential. It is the common symptom of all intellectual appeasers. The image of the brute is the symbol of an appeaser's belief in the supremacy of evil, which means—not in conscious terms, but in terms of his quaking, cringing, blinding panic—that when his mind judges a thing to be evil, his emotions proclaim its power, and the more evil, the more powerful.

[Ibid., 4.]

See also *APPEASEMENT; COMPROMISE; COURAGE and CONFIDENCE; EVIL; MORAL JUDGMENT; MORALITY.*

Moral Judgment.   *One must never fail to pronounce moral judgment.*
Nothing can corrupt and disintegrate a culture or a man's character as thoroughly as does the precept of *moral agnosticism,* the idea that one must never pass moral judgment on others, that one must be morally tolerant of anything, that the good consists of never distinguishing good from evil.

It is obvious who profits and who loses by such a precept. It is not justice or equal treatment that you grant to men when you abstain equally from praising men's virtues and from condemning men's vices. When your impartial attitude declares, in effect, that neither the good nor the evil may expect anything from you—whom do you betray and whom do you encourage?

But to pronounce moral judgment is an enormous responsibility. To be a judge, one must possess an unimpeachable character; one need not be omniscient or infallible, and it is not an issue of errors of knowledge; one needs an unbreached integrity, that is, the absence of any indulgence in conscious, willful evil. Just as a judge in a court of law may err, when the evidence is inconclusive, but may not evade the evidence available, nor accept bribes, nor allow any personal feeling, emotion, desire or fear to obstruct his mind's judgment of the facts of reality—so every rational person must maintain an equally strict and solemn integrity in the courtroom within his own mind, where the responsibility is more awesome than in a public tribunal, because *he,* the judge, is the only one to know when he has been impeached.

["How Does One Lead a Rational Life in an Irrational Society?" *VOS,* 89; pb 71.]

If people did not indulge in such abject evasions as the claim that some contemptible liar "means well"—that a mooching bum "can't help it"—that a juvenile delinquent "needs love"—that a criminal "doesn't know any better"—that a power-seeking politician is moved by patriotic concern for "the public good"—that communists are merely "agrarian reformers"—the history of the past few decades, or centuries, would have been different.

[Ibid., 93; pb 73.]

The precept: "Judge not, that ye be not judged" . . . is an abdication of moral responsibility: it is a moral blank check one gives to others in exchange for a moral blank check one expects for oneself.

There is no escape from the fact that men have to make choices; so long as men have to make choices, there is no escape from moral values; so long as moral values are at stake, no moral neutrality is possible. To abstain from condemning a torturer, is to become an accessory to the torture and murder of his victims.

The moral principle to adopt in this issue, is: *"Judge, and be prepared to be judged."*

The opposite of moral neutrality is not a blind, arbitrary, self-righteous condemnation of any idea, action or person that does not fit one's mood, one's memorized slogans or one's snap judgment of the moment. Indiscriminate tolerance and indiscriminate condemnation are not two opposites: they are two variants of the same evasion. To declare that "everybody is white" or "everybody is black" or "everybody is neither white nor black, but gray," is not a moral judgment, but an escape from the responsibility of moral judgment.

To judge means: to evaluate a given concrete by reference to an abstract principle or standard. It is not an easy task; it is not a task that can be performed automatically by one's feelings, "instincts" or hunches. It is a task that requires the most precise, the most exacting, the most ruthlessly objective and *rational* process of thought. It is fairly easy to grasp abstract moral principles; it can be very difficult to apply them to a given situation, particularly when it involves the moral character of another person. When one pronounces moral judgment, whether in praise or in blame, one must be prepared to answer "Why?" and to prove one's case—to oneself and to any rational inquirer.

[Ibid., 91; pb 72.]

The man who refuses to judge, who neither agrees nor disagrees, who declares that there are no absolutes and believes that he escapes responsibility, is the man responsible for all the blood that is now spilled in the world. Reality is an absolute, existence is an absolute, a speck of dust is an absolute and so is a human life. . . .

There are two sides to every issue: one side is right and the other is wrong, but the middle is always evil. The man who is wrong still retains some respect for truth, if only by accepting the responsibility of choice.

But the man in the middle is the knave who blanks out the truth in order to pretend that no choice or values exist.

[GS, *FNI*, 216; pb 173.]

Morality is the province of philosophical judgment, not of psychological diagnosis. Moral judgment must be objective, i.e., based on perceivable, demonstrable facts. *A man's moral character must be judged on the basis of his actions, his statements and his conscious convictions*—not on the basis of inferences (usually, spurious) about his subconscious.

A man is not to be condemned or excused on the grounds of the state of his subconscious. His psychological problems are his private concern which is not to be paraded in public and not to be made a burden on innocent victims or a hunting ground for poaching psychologizers. Morality demands that one treat and judge men as responsible adults.

This means that one grants a man the respect of assuming that he is conscious of what he says and does, and one judges his statements and actions *philosophically*, i.e., as what they *are*—not *psychologically*, i.e., as leads or clues to some secret, hidden, unconscious meaning. One neither speaks nor listens to people in code.

["The Psychology of 'Psychologizing,' " *TO*, March 1971, 5.]

It is not man's subconscious, but his *conscious* mind that is subject to his direct control—and to moral judgment. It is a specific individual's *conscious* mind that one judges (on the basis of objective evidence) in order to judge his moral character.

. . . The alternative is not: rash, indiscriminate moralizing or cowardly, evasive moral neutrality—i.e., condemnation without knowledge or the refusal to know, in order not to condemn. These are two interchangeable variants of the same motive: escape from the responsibility of cognition and of moral judgment.

[Ibid., 6.]

See also ABSOLUTES; CHARACTER; COMPROMISE; ERRORS of KNOWLEDGE vs. BREACHES of MORALITY; EVASION; EVIL; JUSTICE; MORALITY; MORAL COWARDICE; "PSYCHOLOGIZING"; RATIONALITY; STANDARD of VALUE; VIRTUE.

Moral-Practical Dichotomy.

Your impracticable creed . . . [inculcates a] lethal tenet: the belief that the moral and the practical are opposites. Since childhood, you have been running from the terror of a choice you have never dared fully to identify: If the *practical*, whatever you must practice to exist, whatever works, succeeds, achieves your purpose, whatever brings you food and joy, whatever profits you, is evil—

and if the good, the moral, is the *impractical*, whatever fails, destroys, frustrates, whatever injures you and brings you loss or pain—then your choice is to be moral or to live.

The sole result of that murderous doctrine was to remove morality from life. You grew up to believe that moral laws bear no relation to the job of living, except as an impediment and threat, that man's existence is an amoral jungle where anything goes and anything works. And in that fog of switching definitions which descends upon a frozen mind, you have forgotten that the evils damned by your creed were the virtues required for living, and you have come to believe that actual evils are the *practical* means of existence. Forgetting that the impractical "good" was self-sacrifice, you believe that self-esteem is impractical; forgetting that the practical "evil" was production, you believe that robbery is practical.

Swinging like a helpless branch in the wind of an uncharted moral wilderness, you dare not fully to be evil or fully to live. When you are honest, you feel the resentment of a sucker; when you cheat, you feel terror and shame. When you are happy, your joy is diluted by guilt; when you suffer, your pain is augmented by the feeling that pain is your natural state. You pity the men you admire, you believe they are doomed to fail; you envy the men you hate, you believe they are the masters of existence. You feel disarmed when you come up against a scoundrel: you believe that evil is bound to win, since the moral is the impotent, the *impractical*.

Morality, to you, is a phantom scarecrow made of duty, of boredom, of punishment, of pain, a cross-breed between the first schoolteacher of your past and the tax collector of your present, a scarecrow standing in a barren field, waving a stick to chase away your pleasures—and *pleasure*, to you, is a liquor-soggy brain, a mindless slut, the stupor of a moron who stakes his cash on some animal's race, since pleasure cannot be moral.

If you identify your actual belief, you will find a triple damnation— of yourself, of life, of virtue—in the grotesque conclusion you have reached: you believe that morality is a necessary evil.

[GS, *FNI*, 214; pb 171.]

See also ALTRUISM; "DUTY"; EVIL; GOOD, the; MORALITY; ORIGINAL SIN; PLEASURE and PAIN; RATIONALITY; SACRIFICE; SELFISHNESS; STANDARD of VALUE.

Morality.   What is morality, or ethics? It is a code of values to guide man's choices and actions—the choices and actions that determine the purpose and the course of his life. Ethics, as a science, deals with discovering and defining such a code.

The first question that has to be answered, as a precondition of any attempt to define, to judge or to accept any specific system of ethics, is: *Why* does man need a code of values?

Let me stress this. The first question is not: What particular code of values should man accept? The first question is: Does man need values at all—and why?

[*"The Objectivist Ethics," VOS*, 2; pb 13.]

Ethics is an *objective, metaphysical necessity of man's survival.* . . .

I quote from Galt's speech: "Man has been called a rational being, but rationality is a matter of choice—and the alternative his nature offers him is: rational being or suicidal animal. Man has to be man—by choice; he has to hold his life as a value—by choice; he has to learn to sustain it —by choice; he has to discover the values it requires and practice his virtues—by choice. A code of values accepted by choice is a code of morality."

The standard of value of the Objectivist ethics—the standard by which one judges what is good or evil—is *man's life*, or: that which is required for man's survival *qua* man.

Since reason is man's basic means of survival, that which is proper to the life of a rational being is the good; that which negates, opposes or destroys it is the evil.

Since everything man needs has to be discovered by his own mind and produced by his own effort, the two essentials of the method of survival proper to a rational being are: thinking and productive work.

[Ibid., 16; pb 23.]

Man must choose his actions, values and goals by the standard of that which is proper to man—in order to achieve, maintain, fulfill and enjoy that ultimate value, that end in itself, which is his own life.

[Ibid., 19; pb 25.]

Life or death is man's only fundamental alternative. To live is his basic act of choice. If he chooses to live, a rational ethics will tell him what principles of action are required to implement his choice. If he does not choose to live, nature will take its course.

[*"Causality Versus Duty," PWNI*, 118; pb 99.]

The purpose of morality is to teach you, not to suffer and die, but to enjoy yourself and live.

[*GS, FNI*, 150; pb 123.]

Sweep aside those parasites of subsidized classrooms, who live on the profits of the mind of others and proclaim that man needs no morality, no values, no code of behavior. They, who pose as scientists and claim that man is only an animal, do not grant him inclusion in the law of existence they have granted to the lowest of insects. They recognize that every living species has a way of survival demanded by its nature, they do not claim that a fish can live out of water or that a dog can live without its sense of smell—but man, they claim, the most complex of beings, man can survive in any way whatever, man has no identity, no nature, and there's no practical reason why he cannot live with his means of survival destroyed, with his mind throttled and placed at the disposal of any orders *they* might care to issue.

Sweep aside those hatred-eaten mystics, who pose as friends of humanity and preach that the highest virtue man can practice is to hold his own life as of no value. Do they tell you that the purpose of morality is to curb man's instinct of self-preservation? It is for the purpose of self-preservation that man needs a code of morality. The only man who desires to be moral is the man who desires to live.

[Ibid.]

If I were to speak your kind of language, I would say that man's only moral commandment is: Thou shalt think. But a "moral commandment" is a contradiction in terms. The moral is the chosen, not the forced; the understood, not the obeyed. The moral is the rational, and reason accepts no commandments.

My morality, the morality of reason, is contained in a single axiom: existence exists—and in a single choice: to live. The rest proceeds from these. To live, man must hold three things as the supreme and ruling values of his life: Reason—Purpose—Self-esteem. Reason, as his only tool of knowledge—Purpose, as his choice of the happiness which that tool must proceed to achieve—Self-esteem, as his inviolate certainty that his mind is competent to think and his person is worthy of happiness, which means: is worthy of living. These three values imply and require all of man's virtues, and all his virtues pertain to the relation of existence and consciousness: rationality, independence, integrity, honesty, justice, productiveness, pride.

[Ibid., 156; pb 128.]

You who prattle that morality is social and that man would need no morality on a desert island—it is on a desert island that he would need it most. Let him try to claim, when there are no victims to pay for it, that a rock is a house, that sand is clothing, that food will drop into his mouth without cause or effort, that he will collect a harvest tomorrow by devouring his stock seed today—and reality will wipe him out, as he deserves; reality will show him that life is a value to be bought and that thinking is the only coin noble enough to buy it.

[Ibid., 156; pb 127.]

A moral code is a system of teleological measurement which grades the choices and actions open to man, according to the degree to which they achieve or frustrate the code's standard of value. The standard is the end, to which man's actions are the means.

A moral code is a set of abstract principles; to practice it, an individual must translate it into the appropriate concretes—he must choose the particular goals and values which he is to pursue. This requires that he define his particular hierarchy of values, in the order of their importance, and that he act accordingly.

[*ITOE*, 42.]

Morality pertains only to the sphere of man's free will—only to those actions which are open to his choice.

["*Playboy's* Interview with Ayn Rand," pamphlet, 4.]

A sin without volition is a slap at morality and an insolent contradiction in terms: that which is outside the possibility of choice is outside the province of morality. If man is evil by birth, he has no will, no power to change it; if he has no will, he can be neither good nor evil; a robot is amoral. To hold, as man's sin, a fact not open to his choice is a mockery of morality.

[GS, *FNI*, 168; pb 136.]

In spite of all their irrationalities, inconsistencies, hypocrisies and evasions, the majority of men will not act, in major issues, without a sense of being *morally right* and will not oppose the morality they have accepted. They will break it, they will cheat on it, but they will not oppose it; and when they break it, they take the blame on themselves. The power of morality is the greatest of all intellectual powers—and mankind's tragedy lies in the fact that the vicious moral code men have accepted destroys them by means of the best within them.

["Faith and Force: The Destroyers of the Modern World," *PWNI*, 81; pb 67.]

See Conceptual Index: Ethics.

Motion. They proclaim that there are no entities, that nothing exists but motion, and blank out the fact that *motion* presupposes the thing which moves, that without the concept of entity, there can be no such concept as "motion."

[GS, *FNI*, 191; pb 154.]

Motions are motions of entities; . . . a child is aware of motion *perceptually*, but cannot conceptualize "motion" until he has formed some concepts of that which moves, i.e., of entities.

[*ITOE*, 18.]

Concepts of *motion* are formed by specifying the distinctive nature of the motion and of the entities performing it, and/or of the medium in which it is performed—and omitting the particular measurements of any given instance of such motion and of the entities involved. For instance, the concept "walking" denotes a certain kind of motion performed by living entities possessing legs, and does not apply to the motion of a snake or of an automobile. The concept "swimming" denotes the motion of any living entity propelling itself through water, and does not apply to the motion of a boat. The concept "flying" denotes the motion of any entity propelling itself through the air, whether a bird or an airplane.

[Ibid., 20.]

The concept of "location" arises in the context of entities which are at rest relative to each other. A thing's location is the place where it is situated. But a moving object is not at any one place—it is in motion. One can locate a moving object only in the sense of specifying the location of the larger fixed region through which it is moving during a given period of time. For instance: "Between 4:00 and 4:05 p.m., the car was moving through New York City." One can narrow down the time period and, correspondingly, the region; but one cannot narrow down the time to nothing in the contradictory attempt to locate the moving car at a single, fixed position. If it is moving, it is not at a fixed position.

The law of identity does not attempt to freeze reality. Change exists; it is a fact of reality. When a thing is changing, that is what it is doing, that is its identity for that period. What is still is still. What is in process is in process. A is A.

[Harry Binswanger, "Q & A Department: Identity and Motion," *TOF*, Dec. 1981, 14.]

See also CHANGE; ENTITY; HIERARCHY of KNOWLEDGE; "STOLEN CONCEPT," FALLACY of.

Motion Pictures.   In motion pictures or television, literature is *the* ruler and term-setter, with music serving only as an incidental, background accompaniment. Screen and television plays are subcategories of the drama, and in the dramatic arts *"the play is the thing."* The play is that which makes it art; the play provides the end, to which all the rest is the means.

["Art and Cognition," *RM*, pb 71.]

Visual art is an intrinsic part of films in a much deeper sense than the mere selection of sets and camera angles . . . a "motion picture" is literally *that*, and has to be a stylized visual composition in motion. . . .

Potentially, motion pictures are a great art, but that potential has not as yet been actualized, except in single instances and random moments. An art that requires the synchronization of so many esthetic elements and so many different talents cannot develop in a period of philosophical-cultural disintegration such as the present. Its development requires the creative cooperation of men who are united, not necessarily by their formal philosophical convictions, but by their fundamental view of man, i.e., by their sense of life.

[Ibid., 72.]

The movies are still in the position of a retarded child: born into a collapsing family, i.e., a deteriorating culture, an art that demanded Romanticism was left to struggle blindly in the midst of a value-desert. It produced a few rare, almost accidental sparks of true greatness, displaying its untouched potential, then was swallowed again in a growing tide of mediocrity.

[Frank O'Connor, review of Lillian Gish's *The Movies, Mr. Griffith, and Me, TO*, Nov. 1969, 8.]

Today, the movies have gone all the way back to the pre-Griffith days; or rather, they have accepted, on a broad scale, the error that destroyed D. W. Griffith: the belief that a movie is primarily a director's art, that content, story, and cast do not matter—i.e., that it is an art concerned only with the "how," not the "what"—i.e., that it is an art of means, without ends—i.e., that it is the field of trick photographers, not of artists.

[Ibid., 15.]

See also ART; DIRECTOR; LITERATURE; ROMANTICISM; SENSE of LIFE.

Motivation.   Motivation is a key-concept in psychology and in fiction. It is a man's basic premises and values that form his character and move him to action—and in order to understand a man's character, it is the motivation behind his actions that we must understand. To know "what makes a man tick," we must ask: "What is he after?"

To re-create the reality of his characters, to make both their nature and their actions intelligible, it is their motivation that a writer has to reveal. He may do it gradually, revealing it bit by bit, building up the evidence as the story progresses, but at the end of the novel the reader must know *why* the characters did the things they did.

["Basic Principles of Literature," *RM*, 67; pb 88.]

See also ART; FREE WILL; LITERATURE; MOTIVATION by LOVE vs. by FEAR; PSYCHOLOGY; VALUES.

Motivation by Love vs. by Fear.
Achieving life is not the equivalent of avoiding death. Joy is not the absence of pain.

[GS, *FNI*, 166; pb 135.]

You seek escape from pain. We seek the achievement of happiness. You exist for the sake of avoiding punishment. We exist for the sake of earning rewards. Threats will not make us function; fear is not our incentive. It is not death that we wish to avoid, but life that we wish to live.

You, who have lost the concept of the difference, you who claim that fear and joy are incentives of equal power—and secretly add that fear is the more "practical"—you do not wish to live, and only fear of death still holds you to the existence you have damned.

[Ibid., 167; pb 135.]

See also MOTIVATION; HAPPINESS; PLEASURE and PAIN; SUFFERING; VALUES; ZERO, REIFICATION of.

Music.
Music employs the sounds produced by the *periodic* vibrations of a sonorous body, and evokes man's sense-of-life emotions.

["Art and Cognition," *RM*, pb 46.]

The fundamental difference between music and the other arts lies in the fact that music is experienced as if it reversed man's normal psycho-epistemological process.

The other arts create a physical object (i.e., an object perceived by man's senses, be it a book or a painting) and the psycho-epistemological process goes from the perception of the object to the conceptual grasp of its meaning, to an appraisal in terms of one's basic values, to a consequent emotion. The pattern is: from perception—to conceptual understanding—to appraisal—to emotion.

The pattern of the process involved in music is: from perception—to emotion—to appraisal—to conceptual understanding.

Music is experienced as if it had the power to reach man's emotions directly.

[Ibid., 50.]

Psycho-epistemologically, the pattern of the response to music seems to be as follows: one perceives the music, one grasps the suggestion of a certain emotional state and, with one's sense of life serving as the criterion, one appraises this state as enjoyable or painful, desirable or undesirable, significant or negligible, according to whether it corresponds to or contradicts one's fundamental feeling about life.

[Ibid., 53.]

It is in terms of his fundamental emotions—i.e., the emotions produced by his own metaphysical value-judgments—that man responds to music.

Music cannot tell a story, it cannot deal with concretes, it cannot convey a specific existential phenomenon, such as a peaceful countryside or a stormy sea. The theme of a composition entitled "Spring Song" is not spring, but the *emotions* which spring evoked in the composer. Even concepts which, intellectually, belong to a complex level of abstraction, such as "peace," "revolution," "religion," are too specific, too *concrete* to be expressed in music. All that music can do with such themes is convey the emotions of serenity, or defiance, or exaltation. Liszt's "St. Francis Walking on the Waters" was inspired by a specific legend, but what it conveys is a passionately dedicated struggle and triumph—by whom and in the name of what, is for each individual listener to supply.

Music communicates emotions, which one grasps, but does not actually feel; what one feels is a suggestion, a kind of distant, dissociated, depersonalized emotion—until and unless it unites with one's own sense of life. But since the music's emotional content is not communicated conceptually or evoked existentially, one does feel it in some peculiar, subterranean way.

Music conveys the same categories of emotions to listeners who hold widely divergent views of life. As a rule, men agree on whether a given piece of music is gay or sad or violent or solemn. But even though, in a generalized way, they experience the same emotions in response to the same music, there are radical differences in how they *appraise* this experience—i.e., how they feel about these feelings.

[Ibid., 52.]

The formulation of a common vocabulary of music . . . would require: a translation of the musical experience, the inner experience, into *conceptual* terms; an explanation of why certain sounds strike us a certain way; a definition of the axioms of musical perception, from which the appropriate esthetic principles could be derived, which would serve as a base for the objective validation of esthetic judgments. . . .

Until a conceptual vocabulary is discovered and defined, *no objectively valid criterion of esthetic judgment is possible in the field of music.* . . .

No one, therefore, can claim the *objective* superiority of his choices over the choices of others. Where no objective proof is available, it's every man for himself—and *only* for himself.

The nature of musical perception has not been discovered because the key to the secret of music is *physiological*—it lies in the nature of the process by which man perceives sounds—and the answer would require the joint effort of a physiologist, a psychologist and a philosopher (an esthetician).

The start of a scientific approach to this problem and the lead to an answer were provided by Helmholtz, the great physiologist of the nineteenth century.

[Ibid., 55.]

From the standpoint of psycho-epistemology, I can offer a hypothesis on the nature of man's response to music, but I urge the reader to remember that it is only a hypothesis. . . .

One may listen to noise for an hour, a day or a year, and it remains just noise. But musical tones heard in a certain kind of succession produce a different result—the human ear and brain *integrate* them into a new cognitive experience, into what may be called an auditory entity: a melody. The integration is a physiological process; it is performed unconsciously and automatically. Man is aware of the process only by means of its results.

Helmholtz has demonstrated that the essence of musical perception is mathematical: the consonance or dissonance of harmonies depends on the ratios of the frequencies of their tones. The brain can integrate a ratio of one to two, for instance, but not of eight to nine. . . .

The psycho-epistemological meaning of a given composition lies in the kind of work it demands of a listener's ear and brain.

A composition may demand the active alertness needed to resolve complex mathematical relationships—or it may deaden the brain by means of monotonous simplicity. It may demand a process of building an integrated sum—or it may break up the process of integration into an arbitrary series of random bits—or it may obliterate the process by a jumble of sounds mathematically-physiologically impossible to integrate, and thus turn into noise.

The listener becomes aware of this process in the form of a sense of efficacy, or of strain, or of boredom, or of frustration. His reaction is determined by his *psycho-epistemological* sense of life—i.e., by the level of cognitive functioning on which he feels at home.

[Ibid., 57.]

Music gives man's consciousness the same experience as the other arts: a concretization of his sense of life. But the abstraction being concretized is primarily epistemological, rather than metaphysical; the abstraction is man's consciousness, i.e., his method of cognitive functioning, which he experiences in the concrete form of hearing a specific piece of music. A man's acceptance or rejection of that music depends on whether it calls upon or clashes with, confirms or contradicts, his mind's way of working. The metaphysical aspect of the experience is the sense of a world which he is able to grasp, to which his mind's working is appropriate.

Music is the only phenomenon that permits an adult to experience the process of dealing with pure sense data. Single musical tones are not percepts, but pure sensations; they become percepts only when integrated. Sensations are man's first contact with reality; when integrated into percepts, they are the given, the self-evident, the not-to-be-doubted. Music offers man the singular opportunity to reenact, on the adult level, the primary process of his method of cognition: the automatic integration of sense data into an intelligible, meaningful entity. To a conceptual consciousness, it is a unique form of rest and reward.

[Ibid., 59.]

See also ART; BALLET; CONCEPT-FORMATION; DANCE; EMOTIONS; PSYCHO-EPISTEMOLOGY; OPERA and OPERETTA; PERFORMING ARTS; SENSATIONS; SENSE of LIFE.

Mystical Ethics.   The mystic theory of ethics is explicitly based on the premise that the standard of value of man's ethics is set beyond the grave, by the laws or requirements of another, supernatural dimension, that ethics is impossible for man to practice, that it is unsuited for and opposed to man's life on earth, and that man must take the blame for it and suffer through the whole of his earthly existence, to atone for the guilt of being unable to practice the impracticable. The Dark Ages and the Middle Ages are the existential monument to *this* theory of ethics.

["The Objectivist Ethics," *VOS*, 33; pb 34.]

A mystic code of morality demanding self-sacrifice cannot be promulgated or propagated without a supreme ruler that becomes the collector of the sacrificing. Traditionally, there have been two such collectors: either God or society. The collector had to be inaccessible to mankind at large, and his authority had to be revealed only through an elite of special intermediaries, variously called "high priests," "commissars," "Gauleiters," etc.

["The Stimulus and the Response," *PWNI*, 177; pb 146.]

See also GOD; INTRINSIC THEORY of VALUES; MORALITY; RELIGION; SACRIFICE; STANDARD of VALUE; SUPERNATURALISM; VALUES.

Mysticism. What is mysticism? Mysticism is the acceptance of allegations without evidence or proof, either apart from or *against* the evidence of one's senses and one's reason. Mysticism is the claim to some non-sensory, non-rational, non-definable, non-identifiable means of knowledge, such as "instinct," "intuition," "revelation," or any form of "just knowing."

Reason is the perception of reality, and rests on a single axiom: the Law of Identity.

Mysticism is the claim to the perception of some other reality—other than the one in which we live—whose definition is only that it is *not* natural, it is supernatural, and is to be perceived by some form of unnatural or supernatural means.

["Faith and Force: The Destroyers of the Modern World," *PWNI*, 75; pb 62.]

The damnation of this earth as a realm where nothing is possible to man but pain, disaster and defeat, a realm inferior to another, "higher," reality; the damnation of all values, enjoyment, achievement and success on earth as a proof of depravity; the damnation of man's mind as a source of *pride,* and the damnation of reason as a "limited," deceptive, unreliable, impotent faculty, incapable of perceiving the "real" reality and the "true" truth; the split of man in two, setting his consciousness (his soul) against his body, and his moral values against his own interest; the damnation of man's nature, body and *self* as evil; the commandment of self-sacrifice, renunciation, suffering, obedience, humility and faith, as the good; the damnation of life and the worship of death, with the promise of rewards beyond the grave—*these* are the necessary tenets of the [mystic's] view of existence, as they have been in every variant of [mystical] philosophy throughout the course of mankind's history.

["For the New Intellectual," *FNI*, 14; pb 18.]

To the [mystic], as to an animal, the irreducible primary is the automatic phenomena of his own consciousness.

An animal has no critical faculty; he has no control over the function of his brain and no power to question its content. To an animal, whatever strikes his awareness is an absolute that corresponds to reality—or rather, it is a distinction he is incapable of making: reality, to him, is whatever he senses or feels. And *this* is the [mystic's] epistemological ideal, the mode of consciousness he strives to induce in himself. To the [mystic], emotions are tools of cognition, and wishes take precedence over facts. He seeks to escape the risks of a quest for knowledge by obliterating the distinction between consciousness and reality, between the perceiver and the perceived, hoping that an automatic certainty and an infallible knowledge of the universe will be granted to him by the blind, unfocused stare of his eyes turned inward, contemplating the sensations, the feelings, the urgings, the muggy associational twistings projected by the rudderless mechanism of his undirected consciousness. Whatever his mechanism produces is an absolute not to be questioned; and whenever it clashes with reality, it is reality that he ignores.

Since the clash is constant, the [mystic's] solution is to believe that what he perceives is another, "higher" reality—where his wishes are omnipotent, where contradictions are possible and A is non-A, where his assertions, which are false on earth, become true and acquire the status of a "superior" truth which *he* perceives by means of a special faculty denied to other, "inferior," beings. The only validation of his consciousness he can obtain on earth is the belief and the obedience of others, when they accept his "truth" as superior to their own perception of reality.

[Ibid., 12; pb 17.]

A mystic is a man who surrendered his mind at its first encounter with the minds of others. Somewhere in the distant reaches of his childhood, when his own understanding of reality clashed with the assertions of others, with their arbitrary orders and contradictory demands, he gave in to so craven a fear of independence that he renounced his rational faculty. At the crossroads of the choice between "I know" and "They say," he chose the authority of others, he chose to submit rather than to understand, to *believe* rather than to think. Faith in the supernatural begins as faith in the superiority of others. His surrender took the form of the feeling that he must hide his lack of understanding, that others possess some mysterious knowledge of which he alone is deprived, that reality is whatever they want it to be, through some means forever denied to him.

From then on, afraid to think, he is left at the mercy of unidentified feelings. His feelings become his only guide, his only remnant of personal identity, he clings to them with ferocious possessiveness—and whatever thinking he does is devoted to the struggle of hiding from himself that the nature of his feelings is terror.

When a mystic declares that he *feels* the existence of a power superior to reason, he feels it all right, but that power is not an omniscient super-spirit of the universe, it is the consciousness of any passer-by to whom he has surrendered his own. A mystic is driven by the urge to impress, to cheat, to flatter, to deceive, *to force* that omnipotent consciousness of others. *"They"* are his only key to reality, he feels that he cannot exist save by harnessing their mysterious power and extorting their unac-countable consent. *"They"* are his only means of perception and, like a blind man who depends on the sight of a dog, he feels he must leash them in order to live. To control the consciousness of others becomes his only passion; power-lust is a weed that grows only in the vacant lots of an abandoned mind.

[GS, *FNI*, 200; pb 160.]

The motive of all the attacks on man's rational faculty—from any quarter, in any of the endless variations, under the verbal dust of all the murky volumes—is a single, hidden premise: the desire to exempt con-sciousness from the law of identity. The hallmark of a mystic is the savagely stubborn refusal to accept the fact that consciousness, like any other existent, possesses identity, that it is a faculty of a specific nature, functioning through specific means. While the advance of civilization has been eliminating one area of magic after another, the last stand of the believers in the miraculous consists of their frantic attempts to re-gard *identity* as the *disqualifying* element of consciousness.

The implicit, but unadmitted premise of the neo-mystics of modern philosophy, is the notion that only an ineffable consciousness can ac-quire a valid knowledge of reality, that "true" knowledge has to be causeless, i.e., acquired without any means of cognition.

[*ITOE*, 106.]

Mysticism requires the notion of the unknowable, which is revealed to some and withheld from others; this divides men into those who feel guilt and those who cash in on it. The two groups are interchangeable, according to circumstances. When being judged, a mystic cries: "I couldn't help it!" When judging others, he declares: "You can't know, but *I* can."

["The Psychology of 'Psychologizing,'" *TO*, March 1971, 1.]

There is only one state that fulfills the mystic's longing for infinity, non-causality, non-identity: *death*. No matter what unintelligible causes he ascribes to his incommunicable feelings, whoever rejects reality re-jects existence—and the feelings that move him from then on are hatred for all the values of man's life, and lust for all the evils that destroy it.

[GS, *FNI*, 202; pb 162.]

The advocates of mysticism are motivated not by a quest for truth, but by hatred for man's mind.

["An Untitled Letter," *PWNI*, 123; pb 102.]

For centuries, the mystics of spirit had existed by running a protection racket—by making life on earth unbearable, then charging you for consolation and relief, by forbidding all the virtues that make existence possible, then riding on the shoulders of your guilt, by declaring production and joy to be sins, then collecting blackmail from the sinners.

[GS, *FNI*, 190; pb 153.]

I have said that faith and force are corollaries, and that mysticism will always lead to the rule of brutality. The cause of it is contained in the very nature of mysticism. *Reason* is the only *objective* means of communication and of understanding among men; when men deal with one another by means of reason, reality is their *objective* standard and frame of reference. But when men claim to possess supernatural means of knowledge, no persuasion, communication or understanding are possible. Why do we kill wild animals in the jungle? Because no other way of dealing with them is open to us. And *that* is the state to which mysticism reduces mankind—a state where, in case of disagreement, men have no recourse except to physical violence. And more: no man or mystical elite can hold a whole society subjugated to their arbitrary assertions, edicts and whims, without the use of force. Anyone who resorts to the formula: "It's so, because I say so," will have to reach for a gun, sooner or later. Communists, like all materialists, are neo-mystics: it does not matter whether one rejects the mind in favor of revelations or in favor of conditioned reflexes. The basic premise and the results are the same.

["Faith and Force: The Destroyers of the Modern World," *PWNI*, 85; pb 70.]

Men have been taught either that knowledge is impossible (skepticism) or that it is available without effort (mysticism). These two positions appear to be antagonists, but are, in fact, two variants on the same theme, two sides of the same fraudulent coin: the attempt to escape the responsibility of rational cognition and the absolutism of reality—the attempt to assert the primacy of consciousness over existence.

Although skepticism and mysticism are ultimately interchangeable, and the dominance of one always leads to the resurgence of the other, they differ in the form of their inner contradiction—the contradiction, in both cases, between their philosophical doctrine and their psychological motivation. Philosophically, the mystic is usually an exponent of the *intrinsic* (revealed) school of epistemology; the skeptic is usually an advocate of epistemological *subjectivism*. But, psychologically, the mystic is a subjectivist who uses intrinsicism as a means to claim the primacy of *his* consciousness over that of others. The skeptic is a disillusioned intrinsicist who, having failed to find automatic supernatural guidance, seeks a substitute in the collective subjectivism of others.

[*ITOE*, 105.]

Only three brief periods of history were culturally dominated by a philosophy of reason: ancient Greece, the Renaissance, the nineteenth century. These three periods were the source of mankind's greatest progress in all fields of intellectual achievement—and the eras of greatest political freedom. The rest of human history was dominated by mysticism of one kind or another, that is: by the belief that man's mind is impotent, that reason is futile or evil or both, and that man must be guided by some irrational "instinct" or feeling or intuition or revelation, by some form of blind, unreasoning *faith*. All the centuries dominated by mysticism were the eras of political tyranny and slavery, of rule by brute force—from the primitive barbarism of the jungle—to the Pharaohs of Egypt—to the emperors of Rome—to the feudalism of the Dark and Middle Ages—to the absolute monarchies of Europe—to the modern dictatorships of Soviet Russia, Nazi Germany and all their lesser carbon copies.

["The Intellectual Bankruptcy of Our Age," pamphlet, 5.]

See also AXIOMS; CAUSALITY; CONSCIOUSNESS; DICTATOR; EMOTIONS; EPISTEMOLOGY; GOD; FAITH; KANT, IMMANUEL; KNOWLEDGE; LOGIC; MYSTICS of SPIRIT and of MUSCLE; OBJECTIVITY; PERCEPTION; PHYSICAL FORCE; PROOF; REASON; RELIGION; SECOND-HANDERS; SKEPTICISM; SUPERNATURALISM.

Mystics of Spirit and of Muscle.

As products of the split between man's soul and body, there are two kinds of teachers of the Morality of Death: the mystics of spirit and the mystics of muscle, whom you call the spiritualists and the materialists, those who believe in consciousness without existence and those who believe in existence without consciousness. Both demand the surrender of your mind, one to their revelations, the other to their reflexes. No matter how loudly they posture in the roles of irreconcilable antagonists, their moral codes are alike, and so are their aims: in matter—the enslavement of man's body, in spirit—the destruction of his mind.

The good, say the mystics of spirit, is God, a being whose only definition is that he is beyond man's power to conceive—a definition that invalidates man's consciousness and nullifies his concepts of existence. The good, say the mystics of muscle, is Society—a thing which they define as an organism that possesses no physical form, a super-being embodied in no one in particular and everyone in general except yourself. Man's mind, say the mystics of spirit, must be subordinated to the will of God. Man's mind, say the mystics of muscle, must be subordinated to the will of Society. Man's standard of value, say the mystics of spirit, is the pleasure of God, whose standards are beyond man's power of comprehension and must be accepted on faith. Man's standard of value, say the mystics of muscle, is the pleasure of Society, whose standards are beyond man's right of judgment and must be obeyed as a primary absolute. The purpose of man's life, say both, is to become an abject zombie who serves a purpose he does not know, for reasons he is not to question. His reward, say the mystics of spirit, will be given to him beyond the grave. His reward, say the mystics of muscle, will be given on earth—to his great-grandchildren.

Selfishness—say both—is man's evil. Man's good—say both—is to give up his personal desires, to deny himself, renounce himself, surrender; man's good is to negate the life he lives. *Sacrifice*—cry both—is the essence of morality, the highest virtue within man's reach.

[GS, *FNI*, 171; pb 138.]

The mystics of spirit declare that they possess an extra sense you lack: this special sixth sense consists of contradicting the whole of the knowledge of your five. The mystics of muscle do not bother to assert any claim to extrasensory perception: they merely declare that your senses are not valid, and that their wisdom consists of perceiving your blindness by some manner of unspecified means. Both kinds demand that you invalidate your own consciousness and surrender yourself into their power. They offer you, as proof of their superior knowledge, the fact that they assert the opposite of everything you know, and as proof of their superior ability to deal with existence, the fact that they lead you to misery, self-sacrifice, starvation, destruction.

They claim that they perceive a mode of being superior to your existence on this earth. The mystics of spirit call it "another dimension," which consists of denying dimensions. The mystics of muscle call it "the future," which consists of denying the present.

[Ibid., 184; pb 148.]

What is the nature of that superior world to which they sacrifice the world that exists? The mystics of spirit curse matter, the mystics of muscle curse profit. The first wish men to profit by renouncing the earth, the second wish men to inherit the earth by renouncing all profit.

Their non-material, non-profit worlds are realms where rivers run with milk and coffee, where wine spurts from rocks at their command, where pastry drops on them from clouds at the price of opening their mouth. On this material, profit-chasing earth, an enormous investment of virtue —of intelligence, integrity, energy, skill—is required to construct a railroad to carry them the distance of one mile; in their non-material, non-profit world, they travel from planet to planet at the cost of a wish. If an honest person asks them: "How?"—they answer with righteous scorn that a "how" is the concept of vulgar realists; the concept of superior spirits is "Somehow." On this earth restricted by matter and profit, rewards are achieved by thought; in a world set free of such restrictions rewards are achieved by wishing.

And *that* is the whole of their shabby secret. The secret of all their esoteric philosophies, of all their dialectics and super-senses, of their evasive eyes and snarling words, the secret for which they destroy civilization, language, industries and lives, the secret for which they pierce their own eyes and eardrums, grind out their senses, blank out their minds, the purpose for which they dissolve the absolutes of reason, logic, matter, existence, reality—is to erect upon that plastic fog a single holy absolute: their *Wish*.

[Ibid., 185; pb 149.]

For centuries, the mystics of spirit have proclaimed that faith is superior to reason, but have not dared deny the existence of reason. Their heirs and product, the mystics of muscle, have completed their job and achieved their dream: they proclaim that everything is faith, and call it a revolt against believing. As revolt against unproved assertions, they proclaim that nothing can be proved; as revolt against supernatural knowledge, they proclaim that no knowledge is possible; as revolt against the enemies of science, they proclaim that science is superstition; as revolt against the enslavement of the mind, they proclaim that there is no mind.

[Ibid., 196; pb 158.]

See also MYSTICISM.

N

National Rights. A nation, like any other group, is only a number of individuals and can have no rights other than the rights of its individual citizens. A free nation—a nation that recognizes, respects and protects the individual rights of its citizens—has a right to its territorial integrity, its social system and its form of government. The government of such a nation is not the ruler, but the servant or *agent* of its citizens and has no rights other than the rights *delegated* to it by the citizens for a specific, delimited task (the task of protecting them from physical force, derived from their right of self-defense). . . .

Such a nation has a right to its sovereignty (derived from the rights of its citizens) and a right to demand that its sovereignty be respected by all other nations.

["Collectivized 'Rights,' " *VOS*, 138; pb 103.]

Dictatorship nations are outlaws. Any free nation had the *right* to invade Nazi Germany and, today, has the *right* to invade Soviet Russia, Cuba or any other slave pen. Whether a free nation chooses to do so or not is a matter of its own self-interest, *not* of respect for the nonexistent "rights" of gang rulers. It is not a free nation's *duty* to liberate other nations at the price of self-sacrifice, but a free nation has the right to do it, when and if it so chooses.

[Ibid., 140; pb 104.]

See also COLLECTIVISM; DEMOCRACY; FOREIGN POLICY; FREE-DOM; INDIVIDUAL RIGHTS; SECESSION; SELF-DETERMINATION *of NATIONS.*

Naturalism. [Today we observe] two broad categories of art: Romanticism, which recognizes the existence of man's volition—and Naturalism, which denies it.

["What Is Romanticism?" *RM*, 81; pb 99.]

[The] basic premises of Romanticism and Naturalism (the volition or anti-volition premise) affect all the other aspects of a literary work, such as the choice of theme and the quality of the style, but it is the nature of the story structure—the attribute of plot or plotlessness—that represents the most important difference between them and serves as the main distinguishing characteristic for classifying a given work in one category or the other.

[Ibid., 83; pb 101.]

Instead of presenting a *metaphysical* view of man and of existence, the Naturalists presented a *journalistic* view. In answer to the question: "What is man?"—they said: "This is what the village grocers are, in the south of France, in the year 1887," or: "This is what the inhabitants of the slums are, in New York, in 1921," or: "These are the folks next door."

["The Esthetic Vacuum of Our Age," *RM*, 114; pb 124.]

The practitioners of the literary school diametrically opposed to mine —the school of Naturalism—claim that a writer must reproduce what they call "real life," allegedly "as it is," exercising no selectivity and no value-judgments. By "reproduce," they mean "photograph"; by "real life," they mean whatever given concretes they happen to observe; by "as it is," they mean "as it is lived by the people around them." But observe that these Naturalists—or the good writers among them—are extremely selective in regard to two attributes of literature: *style* and *characterization*. Without selectivity, it would be impossible to achieve any sort of characterization whatever, neither of an unusual man nor of an average one who is to be offered as statistically typical of a large segment of the population. Therefore, the Naturalists' opposition to selectivity applies to only one attribute of literature: the content or *subject*. It is in regard to his choice of subject that a novelist must exercise no choice, they claim.

Why?

The Naturalists have never given an answer to that question—not a rational, logical, noncontradictory answer. Why should a writer photograph his subjects indiscriminately and unselectively? Because they "really" happened? To record what really happened is the job of a reporter or of a historian, not of a novelist. To enlighten readers and educate them? That is the job of science, not of literature, of nonfiction writing, not of fiction. To improve men's lot by exposing their misery? But *that* is a value-judgment and a moral purpose and a didactic "message"—all of which are forbidden by the Naturalist doctrine. Besides, to improve anything one must know what constitutes an improvement —and to know that, one must know what is the good and how to achieve it—and to know that, one must have a whole system of value-judgments, a system of *ethics*, which is anathema to the Naturalists.

Thus, the Naturalists' position amounts to giving a novelist full esthetic freedom in regard to *means*, but not in regard to *ends*. He may exercise choice, creative imagination, value-judgments in regard to *how* he portrays things, but not in regard to *what* he portrays—in regard to style or characterization, but not in regard to *subject*. Man—the subject of literature—must not be viewed or portrayed selectively. Man must be accepted as the given, the unchangeable, the not-to-be-judged, the status quo. But since we observe that men do change, that they differ from one another, that they pursue different values, who, then, is to determine the human status quo? Naturalism's implicit answer is: everybody except the novelist.

The novelist—according to the Naturalist doctrine—must neither judge nor value. He is not a creator, but only a recording secretary whose master is the rest of mankind. Let others pronounce judgments, make decisions, select goals, fight over values and determine the course, the fate and the soul of man. The novelist is the only outcast and deserter of that battle. His is not to reason why—his is only to trot behind his master, notebook in hand, taking down whatever the master dictates, picking up such pearls or such swinishness as the master may choose to drop.

[*"The Goal of My Writing," RM*, 163; pb 164.]

The Naturalists object that a plot is an artificial contrivance, because in "real life" events do not fall into a logical pattern. That claim depends on the observer's viewpoint, in the literal sense of the word "viewpoint." A nearsighted man standing two feet away from the wall of a house and staring at it, would declare that the map of the city's streets is an artificial, invented contrivance. That is not what an airplane pilot would say, flying two thousand feet above the city. The events of men's lives follow the logic of men's premises and values—as one can observe if one looks past the range of the immediate moment, past the trivial irrelevancies, repetitions and routines of daily living, and sees the essentials, the turning points, the direction of a man's life.

[*"Basic Principles of Literature," RM*, 60; pb 83.]

The Naturalists object that the events of men's lives are inconclusive, diffuse and seldom fall into the clear-cut, dramatic situations required by a plot structure. This is predominantly true—and this is the chief esthetic argument *against* the Naturalist position. Art is a selective re-creation of reality, its means are evaluative abstractions, its task is the concretization of metaphysical essentials. To isolate and bring into clear focus, into a single issue or a single scene, the essence of a conflict which, in "real life," might be atomized and scattered over a lifetime in the form of meaningless clashes, to condense a long, steady drizzle of buckshot into the explosion of a blockbuster—*that* is the highest, hardest and most demanding function of art. To default on that function is to default on the essence of art and to engage in child's play along its periphery.

[Ibid., 61; pb 83.]

Although Naturalism is a product of the nineteenth century, its spiritual father, in modern history, was Shakespeare. The premise that man does not possess volition, that his destiny is determined by an innate "tragic flaw," is fundamental in Shakespeare's work. But, granted this false premise, his approach is metaphysical, not journalistic. His characters are not drawn from "real life," they are not copies of observed concretes nor statistical averages: they are grand-scale abstractions of the character traits which a determinist would regard as inherent in human nature: ambition, power-lust, jealousy, greed, etc.

["What Is Romanticism?" *RM*, 102; pb 115.]

No matter how concrete-bound their theories forced them to be, the writers of the Naturalist school still had to exercise their power of abstraction to a significant extent: in order to reproduce "real-life" characters, they had to select the characteristics they regarded as essential, differentiating them from the non-essential or accidental. Thus they were led to substitute statistics for values as a criterion of selectivity: that which is statistically prevalent among men, they held, is metaphysically significant and representative of man's nature; that which is rare or exceptional, is not. (See Chapter 7.)

At first, having rejected the element of plot and even of story, the Naturalists concentrated on the element of characterization—and psychological perceptiveness was the chief value that the best of them had to offer. With the growth of the statistical method, however, that value shrank and vanished: characterization was replaced by indiscriminate recording and buried under a catalogue of trivia, such as minute inventories of a character's apartment, clothing and meals. Naturalism lost the attempted universality of Shakespeare or Tolstoy, descending from metaphysics to photography with a rapidly shrinking lens directed at the range of the immediate moment—until the final remnants of Naturalism became a superficial, meaningless, "unserious" school that had nothing to say about human existence.

[Ibid., 104; pb 117.]

The obvious question, to which the heirs of statistical Naturalism have no answer, is: if heroes and geniuses are not to be regarded as representative of mankind, by reason of their numerical rarity, why are freaks and monsters to be regarded as representative? Why are the problems of a bearded lady of greater universal significance than the problems of a genius? Why is the soul of a murderer worth studying, but not the soul of a hero?

The answer lies in the basic metaphysical premise of Naturalism, whether its practitioners ever chose it consciously or not: as an outgrowth of modern philosophy, that basic premise is anti-man, anti-mind, anti-life; and, as an outgrowth of the altruist morality, Naturalism is a frantic escape from moral judgment—a long, wailing plea for pity, for tolerance, for the forgiveness of anything.

["The Esthetic Vacuum of Our Age," *RM*, 116; pb 125.]

See also ART; CHARACTERIZATION; DETERMINISM; FREE WILL; LITERATURE; PLOT; ROMANTICISM; SENSE of LIFE; STYLIZATION; VALUES.

Nature. What is nature? Nature is existence—the sum of that which is. It is usually called "nature" when we think of it as a system of interconnected, interacting entities governed by law. So "nature" really means the universe of entities acting and interacting in accordance with their identities.

[Leonard Peikoff, "The Philosophy of Objectivism"
lecture series (1976), Lecture 2.]

See also ATHEISM; CAUSALITY; EXISTENCE; SUPERNATURALISM; UNIVERSE.

Nazism. *See Fascism/Nazism.*

Necessity. As far as metaphysical reality is concerned (omitting human actions from consideration, for the moment), there are no "facts which happen to be but could have been otherwise" as against "facts which must be." There are only: facts which *are. . . .* Since things are what they are, since everything that exists possesses a specific identity, nothing in reality can occur causelessly or by chance. The nature of an entity determines what it can do and, in any given set of circumstances, dictates what it *will* do. The Law of Causality is entailed by the Law of Identity. Entities follow certain laws of action in consequence of their identity, and have no alternative to doing so. Metaphysically, all facts are inherent in the identities of the entities that exist; i.e., all facts are "necessary." In this sense, to be *is* to be "necessary." The concept of "necessity," in a metaphysical context, is superfluous.

[Leonard Peikoff, "The Analytic-Synthetic Dichotomy," *ITOE*, 146.]

A typical package-deal, used by professors of philosophy, runs as follows: to prove the assertion that there is no such thing as "necessity" in the universe, a professor declares that just as this country did not *have* to have fifty states, there could have been forty-eight or fifty-two— so the solar system did not *have to* have nine planets, there could have been seven or eleven. It is not sufficient, he declares, to prove that something *is*, one must also prove that it *had to be*—and since nothing had to be, nothing is certain and anything goes.

The technique of undercutting man's mind consists in palming off the man-made as if it were the metaphysically given, then ascribing to nature the concepts that refer only to men's lack of knowledge, such as "chance" or "contingency," then reversing the two elements of the package-deal. From the assertion: "Man is unpredictable, therefore nature is unpredictable," the argument goes to: "Nature possesses volition, man does not—nature is free, man is ruled by unknowable forces—nature is not to be conquered, man is."

["The Metaphysical Versus the Man-Made," *PWNI*, 34; pb 28.]

See also ANALYTIC-SYNTHETIC DICHOTOMY; CAUSALITY; IDENTITY; FREE WILL; METAPHYSICAL vs. MAN-MADE; "PACKAGE-DEALING," FALLACY of; PRIMACY of EXISTENCE vs. PRIMACY of CONSCIOUSNESS.

Neurosis vs. Psychosis. A man who has psychological problems is a conscious being; his cognitive faculty is hampered, burdened, slowed down, but not destroyed. A neurotic is not a psychotic. Only a psychotic is presumed to suffer from a total break with reality and to have no control over his actions or the operations of his consciousness (and even this is not always true). A neurotic retains the ability to perceive reality, and to control his consciousness and his actions (this control is merely more difficult for him than for a healthy person). So long as he is not psychotic, this is the control that a man *cannot* lose and *must not* abdicate.

["The Psychology of 'Psychologizing,' " *TO*, March 1971, 5.]

See also FREE WILL; MENTAL HEALTH; "PSYCHOLOGIZING"; PSYCHOLOGY; RATIONALITY.

New Left. Old-line Marxists claimed [falsely] that they were champions of *reason*, that socialism or communism was a *scientific* social system, that an advanced technology could not function in a capitalist society, but required a scientifically planned and organized human community to bring its maximum benefits to every man, in the form of material comforts and a higher standard of living. . . . [T]oday we see the spectacle of old Marxists blessing, aiding and abetting the young hoodlums [of the New Left] (who are their products and heirs) who proclaim the superiority of feelings over reason, of faith over knowledge, of leisure over production, of spiritual concerns over material comforts, of primitive nature over technology, of astrology over science, of drugs over consciousness.

["The Left: Old and New," *NL*, 90.]

If concern with poverty and human suffering were the collectivists' motive, they would have become champions of capitalism long ago; they would have discovered that it is the only political system capable of producing abundance. But they evaded the evidence as long as they could. When the issue became overwhelmingly clear to the whole world, the collectivists were faced with a choice: either turn to the right, in the name of humanity—or to the left, in the name of dictatorial power. They turned to the left—the New Left.

Instead of their old promises that collectivism would create universal abundance and their denunciations of capitalism for creating poverty, they are now denouncing capitalism *for creating abundance*. Instead of promising comfort and security for everyone, they are now denouncing people for being comfortable and secure.

["The Anti-Industrial Revolution," *NL*, 141.]

Intellectually, the activists of the New Left are the most docile conformists. They have accepted as dogma all the philosophical beliefs of their elders for generations: the notions that faith and feeling are superior to reason, that material concerns are evil, that love is the solution to all problems, that the merging of one's self with a tribe or a community is the noblest way to live. There is not a single basic principle of today's Establishment which they do not share. Far from being rebels, they embody the philosophic trend of the past 200 years (or longer): the mysticism-altruism-collectivism axis, which has dominated Western philosophy from Kant to Hegel to James and on down.

["From a Symposium," *NL*, 97.]

See also ALTRUISM; CAPITALISM; CIVIL DISOBEDIENCE; COLLECTIVISM; COMMUNISM; ECOLOGY/ENVIRONMENTAL MOVEMENT; ECONOMIC GROWTH; GUILD SOCIALISM; MYSTICISM; PHYSICAL FORCE; SOCIALISM.

Nietzsche, Friedrich. Philosophically, Nietzsche is a mystic and an irrationalist. His metaphysics consists of a somewhat "Byronic" and mystically "malevolent" universe; his epistemology subordinates reason to "will," or feeling or instinct or blood or innate virtues of character.

But, as a poet, he projects at times (not consistently) a magnificent feeling for man's greatness, expressed in emotional, *not* intellectual, terms.

["Introduction to *The Fountainhead*," *TO*, March 1968, 6.]

Nietzsche's rebellion against altruism consisted of replacing the sacrifice of oneself to others by the sacrifice of others to oneself. He proclaimed that the ideal man is moved, not by reason, but by his "blood," by his innate instincts, feelings and will to power—that he is predestined by birth to rule others and sacrifice them to himself, while *they* are predestined by birth to be his victims and slaves—that reason, logic, principles are futile and debilitating, that morality is useless, that the "superman" is "beyond good and evil," that he is a "beast of prey" whose ultimate standard is nothing but his own whim. Thus Nietzsche's rejection of the Witch Doctor consisted of elevating Attila into a moral ideal—which meant: a double surrender of morality to the Witch Doctor.

["For the New Intellectual," *FNI*, 39; pb 36.]

See also ALTRUISM; BYRONIC VIEW of EXISTENCE; COLLECTIV-
ISM; "INSTINCT"; IRRATIONALISM; MALEVOLENT UNIVERSE
PREMISE; PRINCIPLES; REASON; SELFISHNESS; WHIMS/WHIM-
WORSHIP.

Nineteenth Century. If you want to prove to yourself the power of ideas and, particularly, of morality—the intellectual history of the nineteenth century would be a good example to study. The greatest, unprecedented, undreamed of events and achievements were taking place before men's eyes—but men did not see them and did not understand their meaning, as they do not understand it to this day. I am speaking of the industrial revolution, of the United States and of capitalism. For the first time in history, men gained control over physical nature and threw off the control of men over men—that is: men discovered science and political freedom. The creative energy, the abundance, the wealth, the rising standard of living for *every* level of the population were such that the nineteenth century looks like a fiction-Utopia, like a blinding burst of sunlight, in the drab progression of most of human history. If life on earth is one's standard of value, then the nineteenth century moved mankind forward more than all the other centuries combined.

Did anyone appreciate it? Does anyone appreciate it now? Has anyone identified the causes of that historical miracle?

They did not and have not. What blinded them? The morality of altruism.

Let me explain this. There are, fundamentally, only two causes of the progress of the nineteenth century—the same two causes which you will find at the root of any happy, benevolent, progressive era in human history. One cause is psychological, the other existential—or: one pertains to man's consciousness, the other to the physical conditions of his existence. The first is *reason*, the second is *freedom*. And when I say *"freedom,"* I do not mean poetic sloppiness, such as "freedom from want" or "freedom from fear" or "freedom from the necessity of earning a living." I mean *"freedom from compulsion*—freedom from rule by *physical force*."* Which means: *political* freedom.

["Faith and Force: The Destroyers of the
Modern World," *PWNI*, 79; pb 65.]

See also AMERICA; CAPITALISM; FREEDOM; HISTORY; PHYSICAL
FORCE; WAR.

Nominalism. The "nominalists" . . . hold that all our ideas are only images of concretes, and that abstractions are merely "names" which we give to arbitrary groupings of concretes on the basis of vague resemblances. . . . (There is also the extreme nominalist position, the modern one, which consists of declaring that the problem [of universals] is a meaningless issue, that "reality" is a meaningless term, that we can never know whether our concepts correspond to anything or not, that our knowledge consists of words—and that words are an arbitrary social convention.)

[*ITOE*, 2.]

Denying that concepts have an objective basis in the facts of reality, nominalists declare that the source of concepts is a subjective human decision: men *arbitrarily* select certain characteristics to serve as the basis (the "essentials") for a classification; thereafter, they agree to apply the same term to any concretes that happen to exhibit these "essentials," no matter how diverse these concretes are in other respects. On this view, the concept (the term) means only those characteristics initially decreed to be "essential." The other characteristics of the subsumed concretes bear no necessary connection to the "essential" characteristics, and are excluded from the concept's meaning.

Observe that, while condemning Plato's *mystic* view of a concept's meaning, the nominalists embrace the same view in a *skeptic* version. Condemning the essence-accident dichotomy as implicitly arbitrary, they institute an *explicitly* arbitrary equivalent. Condemning Plato's "intuitive" selection of essences as a disguised subjectivism, they spurn the disguise and adopt subjectivism as their official theory—as though a concealed vice were heinous, but a brazenly flaunted one, rational. Condemning Plato's supernaturally-determined essences, they declare that essences are *socially*-determined, thus transferring to the province of *human whim* what had once been the prerogative of Plato's divine realm. The nominalists' "advance" over Plato consisted of *secularizing* his theory. To secularize an error is still to commit it.

Its form, however, changes. Nominalists do not say that a concept designates only an entity's "essence," excluding its "accidents." Their secularized version is: A concept is only a shorthand tag for the characteristics stated in its definition; a concept and its definition are interchangeable; *a concept means only its definition.*

It is the Platonic-nominalist approach to concept-formation, expressed in such views as these, that gives rise to the theory of the analytic-synthetic dichotomy.

[Leonard Peikoff, "The Analytic-Synthetic Dichotomy," *ITOE*, 129.]

The nominalist view that a concept is merely a shorthand tag for its definition, represents a profound failure to grasp the function of a definition in the process of concept-formation. The penalty for this failure is that the process of definition, in the hands of the nominalists, achieves the exact opposite of its actual purpose. The purpose of a definition is to keep a concept distinct from all others, *to keep it connected to a specific group of existents.* On the nominalist view, it is precisely this connection that is severed: as soon as a concept is defined, it ceases to designate *existents,* and designates instead only the defining characteristic.

And further: On a rational view of definitions, a definition organizes and condenses—and thus helps one to retain—a wealth of knowledge about the characteristics of a concept's units. On the nominalist view, it is precisely this knowledge that is *discarded* when one defines a concept: as soon as a defining characteristic is chosen, all the other characteristics of the units are banished from the concept, which shrivels to mean merely the definition. For instance, as long as a child's concept of "man" is retained ostensively, the child knows that man has a head, two eyes, two arms, etc.; on the nominalist view, as soon as the child defines "man," he discards all this knowledge; thereafter, "man" means to him only: "a thing with rationality and animality."

On the nominalist view, the process of defining a concept is a process of cutting the concept off from its referents, and of systematically evading what one knows about their characteristics. Definition, the very tool which is designed to promote conceptual integration, becomes an agent of its destruction, a means of *disintegration.*

[Ibid., 140.]

See also ABSTRACTIONS and CONCRETES; ANALYTIC-SYNTHETIC DICHOTOMY; ARBITRARY; CONCEPT-FORMATION; CONCEPTS; INTEGRATION (MENTAL); LANGUAGE; LINGUISTIC ANALYSIS; LOGICAL POSITIVISM; MEANING (of CONCEPTS); MYSTICISM; SKEPTICISM; WORDS.

Non-Contradiction. *See Contradictions.*

Non-Existence. Non-existence is not a fact, it is the *absence* of a fact, it is a derivative concept pertaining to a relationship, i.e., a concept which can be formed or grasped only in relation to some existent that has ceased to exist. (One can arrive at the concept "absence" starting from the concept "presence," in regard to some particular existent(s); one cannot arrive at the concept "presence" starting from the concept "absence," with the absence including everything.) Non-existence as such is a zero with no sequence of numbers to follow it, it is the nothing, the total blank.

[*ITOE*, 77.]

Achieving life is not the equivalent of avoiding death. Joy is not "the absence of pain," intelligence is not "the absence of stupidity," light is not "the absence of darkness," an entity is not "the absence of a nonentity." Building is not done by abstaining from demolition; centuries of sitting and waiting in such abstinence will not raise one single girder for you to abstain from demolishing. . . . Existence is not a negation of negatives.

[*GS*, *FNI*, 166; pb 135.]

See also EXISTENCE; ZERO, REIFICATION of.

Normative Abstractions. There are many special or "cross-filed" chains of abstractions (of interconnected concepts) in man's mind. Cognitive abstractions are the fundamental chain, on which all the others depend. Such chains are mental integrations, serving a special purpose and formed accordingly by a special criterion. *Cognitive* abstractions are formed by the criterion of: what is *essential*? (epistemologically essential to distinguish one class of existents from all others). *Normative* abstractions are formed by the criterion of: what is *good*?

["Art and Sense of Life," *RM*, 45; pb 36.]

Consider the long conceptual chain that starts from simple, ostensive definitions and rises to higher and still higher concepts, forming a hierarchical structure of knowledge so complex that no electronic computer could approach it. It is by means of such chains that man has to acquire and retain his knowledge of reality.

Yet this is the simpler part of his psycho-epistemological task. There is another part which is still more complex.

The other part consists of *applying* his knowledge—i.e., evaluating the facts of reality, choosing his goals and guiding his actions accordingly. To do that, man needs another chain of concepts, derived from and dependent on the first, yet separate and, in a sense, more complex: a chain of *normative* abstractions.

While cognitive abstractions identify the facts of reality, normative abstractions evaluate the facts, thus prescribing a choice of values and a course of action. Cognitive abstractions deal with that which *is*; normative abstractions deal with that which *ought to be* (in the realms open to man's choice).

[*"The Psycho-Epistemology of Art," RM*, 20; pb 18.]

The process of a child's development consists of acquiring knowledge, which requires the development of his capacity to grasp and deal with an ever-widening range of abstractions. This involves the growth of two interrelated but different chains of abstractions, two hierarchical structures of concepts, which should be integrated, but seldom are: the *cognitive* and the *normative*. The first deals with knowledge of the facts of reality—the second, with the evaluation of these facts. The first forms the epistemological foundation of science—the second, of morality and of art.

In today's culture, the development of a child's *cognitive* abstractions is assisted to some minimal extent, even if ineptly, half-heartedly, with many hampering, crippling obstacles (such as anti-rational doctrines and influences which, today, are growing worse). But the development of a child's *normative* abstractions is not merely left unaided, it is all but stifled and destroyed. The child whose valuing capacity survives the moral barbarism of his upbringing has to find his own way to preserve and develop his sense of values.

[*"Art and Moral Treason," RM*, 140; pb 145.]

See also ABSTRACTION (PROCESS of); ABSTRACTIONS and CONCRETES; CONCEPT-FORMATION; CONCEPTS; GOOD, the; LEARNING; MORALITY; VALUES.

Novel. A novel is a long, fictional story about human beings and the events of their lives. The four essential attributes of a novel are: Theme—Plot—Characterization—Style.

These are *attributes*, not separable parts. They can be isolated conceptually for purposes of study, but one must always remember that they are interrelated and that a novel is their sum. (If it is a good novel, it is an indivisible sum.) . . .

A novel is *the* major literary form—in respect to its scope, its inexhaustible potentiality, its almost unlimited freedom (including the freedom from physical limitations of the kind that restrict a stage play) and, most importantly, in respect to the fact that a novel is a purely *literary* form of art which does not require the intermediary of the performing arts to achieve its ultimate effect.

["Basic Principles of Literature," *RM*, 57; pb 80.]

A good novel is an indivisible sum: every scene, sequence and passage of a good novel has to involve, contribute to and advance all three of its major attributes: theme, plot, characterization.

[Ibid., 74; pb 93.]

Since the theme of a novel is an idea about or pertaining to human existence, it is in terms of its effects on or expression in human actions that that idea has to be presented.

This leads to *the* crucial attribute of a novel—the *plot.* . . .

To present a story in terms of action means: to present it in terms of events. A story in which nothing happens is not a story. A story whose events are haphazard and accidental is either an inept conglomeration or, at best, a chronicle, a memoir, a reportorial recording, *not* a novel.

[Ibid., 59; pb 82.]

See also ART; CHARACTERIZATION; LITERATURE; PLOT; POPULAR LITERATURE; STYLE; THEME (LITERARY); THRILLERS.

Numbers. A "number" is a mental symbol that integrates units into a single larger unit (or subdivides a unit into fractions) with reference to the basic number of "one," which is the basic mental symbol of "unit." Thus "5" stands for | | | | |. (Metaphysically, the referents of "5" are any five existents of a specified kind; epistemologically, they are represented by a single symbol.)

[*ITOE*, 84.]

See also CONCEPTS; MATHEMATICS; MEASUREMENT; UNIT; UNIT-ECONOMY.

O

Objective. *See Objectivity.*

Objective Theory of Values.   The intrinsic theory holds that the good resides in some sort of reality, independent of man's consciousness; the subjectivist theory holds that the good resides in man's consciousness, independent of reality.

The *objective* theory holds that the good is neither an attribute of "things in themselves" nor of man's emotional states, but *an evaluation* of the facts of reality by man's consciousness according to a rational standard of value. (Rational, in this context, means: derived from the facts of reality and validated by a process of reason.) The objective theory holds that *the good is an aspect of reality in relation to man*—and that it must be discovered, not invented, by man. Fundamental to an objective theory of values is the question: Of value to whom and for what? An objective theory does not permit context-dropping or "concept-stealing"; it does not permit the separation of "value" from "purpose," of the good from beneficiaries, and of man's actions from reason.

["What Is Capitalism?" *CUI*, 22.]

The objective theory of values is the only moral theory incompatible with rule by force. Capitalism is the only system based implicitly on an objective theory of values—and the historic tragedy is that this has never been made explicit.

If one knows that the good is *objective*—i.e., determined by the nature of reality, but to be discovered by man's mind—one knows that an attempt to achieve the good by physical force is a monstrous contradiction which negates morality at its root by destroying man's capacity to recognize the good, i.e., his capacity to value. Force invalidates and paralyzes a man's judgment, demanding that he act against it, thus rendering him morally impotent. A value which one is forced to accept at the price of surrendering one's mind, is not a value to anyone; the forcibly mindless can neither judge nor choose nor value. An attempt to achieve the good by force is like an attempt to provide a man with a picture gallery at the price of cutting out his eyes. Values cannot exist (cannot be valued) outside the full context of a man's life, needs, goals, and *knowledge*.

[Ibid., 23.]

The free market represents the *social* application of an objective theory of values. Since values are to be discovered by man's mind, men must be free to discover them—to think, to study, to translate their knowledge into physical form, to offer their products for trade, to judge them, and to choose, be it material goods or ideas, a loaf of bread or a philosophical treatise. Since values are established contextually, every man must judge for himself, in the context of his own knowledge, goals, and interests. Since values are determined by the nature of reality, it is reality that serves as men's ultimate arbiter: if a man's judgment is right, the rewards are his; if it is wrong, he is his only victim.

[Ibid., 24.]

See also CAPITALISM; CONTEXT-DROPPING; FREE MARKET; INTRINSIC THEORY of VALUES; MARKET VALUE; MYSTICAL ETHICS; OBJECTIVITY; PHYSICAL FORCE; REASON; SOCIAL THEORY of ETHICS; "STOLEN CONCEPT," FALLACY of; SUBJECTIVISM (IN ETHICS); VALUES.

Objectivism.   The name I have chosen for my philosophy is *Objectivism.*

["Preface," *FNI,* ii, pb viii.]

My philosophy, in essence, is the concept of man as a heroic being, with his own happiness as the moral purpose of his life, with productive achievement as his noblest activity, and reason as his only absolute.

["About the Author," Appendix to *Atlas Shrugged.*]

At a sales conference at Random House, preceding the publication of *Atlas Shrugged,* one of the book salesmen asked me whether I could present the essence of my philosophy while standing on one foot. I did, as follows:

1. *Metaphysics:* Objective Reality
2. *Epistemology:* Reason
3. *Ethics:* Self-interest
4. *Politics:* Capitalism

If you want this translated into simple language, it would read: 1. "Nature, to be commanded, must be obeyed" or "Wishing won't make it so." 2. "You can't eat your cake and have it, too." 3. "Man is an end in himself." 4. "Give me liberty or give me death."

If you held these concepts with total consistency, as the base of your convictions, you would have a full philosophical system to guide the course of your life. But to hold them with total consistency—to understand, to define, to prove and to apply them—requires volumes of thought. Which is why philosophy cannot be discussed while standing on one foot—nor while standing on two feet on both sides of every fence. This last is the predominant philosophical position today, particularly in the field of politics.

In the space of a column, I can give only the briefest summary of my position, as a frame-of-reference for all my future columns. My philosophy, Objectivism, holds that:

1. Reality exists as an objective absolute—facts are facts, independent of man's feelings, wishes, hopes or fears.

2. Reason (the faculty which identifies and integrates the material provided by man's senses) is man's only means of perceiving reality, his only source of knowledge, his only guide to action, and his basic means of survival.

3. Man—every man—is an end in himself, not the means to the ends of others. He must exist for his own sake, neither sacrificing himself to others nor sacrificing others to himself. The pursuit of his own *rational* self-interest and of his own happiness is the highest moral purpose of his life.

4. The ideal political-economic system is *laissez-faire* capitalism. It is a system where men deal with one another, not as victims and executioners, nor as masters and slaves, but as *traders,* by free, voluntary exchange to mutual benefit. It is a system where no man may obtain any values from others by resorting to physical force, and *no man may initiate the use of physical force against others.* The government acts only as a policeman that protects man's rights; it uses physical force *only* in retaliation and *only* against those who initiate its use, such as criminals or foreign invaders. In a system of full capitalism, there should be (but, historically, has not yet been) a complete separation of state and economics, in the same way and for the same reasons as the separation of state and church.

["Introducing Objectivism," *TON*, Aug. 1962, 35.]

I am not *primarily* an advocate of capitalism, but of egoism; and I am not *primarily* an advocate of egoism, but of reason. If one recognizes the supremacy of reason and applies it consistently, all the rest follows.

This—the supremacy of reason—was, is and will be the primary concern of my work, and the essence of Objectivism.

["Brief Summary," *TO*, Sept. 1971, 1.]

The only philosophical debt I can acknowledge is to Aristotle. I most emphatically disagree with a great many parts of his philosophy—but his definition of the laws of logic and of the means of human knowledge is so great an achievement that his errors are irrelevant by comparison.

["About the Author," Appendix to *Atlas Shrugged.*]

Objectivism is a philosophical movement; since politics is a branch of philosophy, Objectivism advocates certain political principles—specifically, those of laissez-faire capitalism—as the consequence and the ultimate practical application of its fundamental philosophical principles. It does not regard politics as a separate or primary goal, that is: as a goal that can be achieved without a wider ideological context.

Politics is based on three other philosophical disciplines: metaphysics, epistemology and ethics—on a theory of man's nature and of man's relationship to existence. It is only on such a base that one can formulate a consistent political theory and achieve it in practice. When, however, men attempt to rush into politics without such a base, the result is that embarrassing conglomeration of impotence, futility, inconsistency and superficiality which is loosely designated today as "conservatism." Objectivists are *not* "conservatives." We are *radicals for capitalism;* we are fighting for that philosophical base which capitalism did not have and without which it was doomed to perish.

["Choose Your Issues," *TON*, Jan. 1962, 1.]

I regard the spread of Objectivism through today's culture as an intellectual movement—i.e., a trend among independent individuals who share the same ideas—but *not* as an organized movement.

["A Statement of Policy," *TO*, June 1968, 7.]

Objectivity.   Objectivity is both a metaphysical and an epistemological concept. It pertains to the relationship of consciousness to existence. Metaphysically, it is the recognition of the fact that reality exists independent of any perceiver's consciousness. Epistemologically, it is the recognition of the fact that a perceiver's (man's) consciousness must acquire knowledge of reality by certain means (reason) in accordance with certain rules (logic). This means that although reality is immutable and, in any given context, only one answer is true, the truth is not automatically available to a human consciousness and can be obtained only by a certain mental process which is required of every man who seeks knowledge—that there is no substitute for this process, no escape from the responsibility for it, no shortcuts, no special revelations to privileged observers—and that there can be no such thing as a final "authority" in matters pertaining to human knowledge. Metaphysically, the only authority is reality; epistemologically—one's own mind. The first is the ultimate arbiter of the second.

The concept of objectivity contains the reason why the question "Who decides what is right or wrong?" is wrong. Nobody *"decides."* Nature does not *decide*—it merely *is;* man does not *decide*, in issues of knowledge, he merely *observes* that which is. When it comes to applying his knowledge, man decides what he chooses to do, according to what he has learned, remembering that the basic principle of rational action in *all* aspects of human existence, is: "Nature, to be commanded, must be obeyed." This means that man does not *create* reality and can achieve his values only by making his decisions consonant with the facts of reality.

["Who Is the Final Authority in Ethics?" *TON*, Feb. 1965, 7.]

Objectivity begins with the realization that man (including his every attribute and faculty, including his consciousness) is an entity of a specific nature who must act accordingly; that there is no escape from the law of identity, neither in the universe with which he deals nor in the working of his own consciousness, and if he is to acquire knowledge of the first, he must discover the proper method of using the second; that there is no room for the *arbitrary* in any activity of man, least of all in his method of cognition—and just as he has learned to be guided by objective criteria in making his physical tools, so he must be guided by objective criteria in forming his tools of cognition: his concepts.

[*ITOE*, 110.]

It is axiomatic concepts that identify the precondition of knowledge: the distinction between existence and consciousness, between reality and the awareness of reality, between the object and the subject of cognition. Axiomatic concepts are the foundation of *objectivity*.

[Ibid., 76.]

Most people . . . think that abstract thinking must be "impersonal"— which means that ideas must hold no personal meaning, value or importance to the thinker. This notion rests on the premise that a personal interest is an agent of distortion. But "personal" does not mean "non-objective"; it depends on the kind of person you are. If your thinking is determined by your emotions, then you will not be able to judge anything, personally or impersonally. But if you are the kind of person who knows that reality is not your enemy, that truth and knowledge are of crucial, personal, *selfish* importance to you and to your own life—then, the more passionately personal the thinking, the clearer and truer.

["Philosophical Detection," *PWNI*, 19; pb 16.]

See also AXIOMATIC CONCEPTS; AXIOMS; CONCEPTS; DEFINI-TIONS; EPISTEMOLOGY; IDENTITY; KANT, IMMANUEL; KNOWL-EDGE; LOGIC; METAPHYSICS; MORALITY; MYSTICISM; "OPEN MIND" and "CLOSED MIND"; PRIMARY of EXISTENCE vs. PRIMARY of CONSCIOUSNESS; PROOF; REASON; SUBJECTIVISM; TRUTH.

Obligation. *See Responsibility/Obligation.*

"Open Mind" and "Closed Mind."   [There is a] dangerous little catch phrase which advises you to keep an "open mind." This is a very ambiguous term—as demonstrated by a man who once accused a famous politician of having "a wide open mind." That term is an anti-concept: it is usually taken to mean an objective, unbiased approach to ideas, but it is used as a call for perpetual skepticism, for holding no firm convictions and granting plausibility to anything. A "closed mind" is usually taken to mean the attitude of a man impervious to ideas, arguments, facts and logic, who clings stubbornly to some mixture of unwarranted assumptions, fashionable catch phrases, tribal prejudices —and emotions. But this is not a "closed" mind, it is a *passive* one. It is a mind that has dispensed with (or never acquired) the practice of thinking or judging, and feels threatened by any request to consider anything.

What objectivity and the study of philosophy require is not an "open mind," but an *active mind*—a mind able and eagerly willing to examine ideas, but to examine them *critically*. An active mind does not grant equal status to truth and falsehood; it does not remain floating forever in a stagnant vacuum of neutrality and uncertainty; by assuming the responsibility of judgment, it reaches firm convictions and holds to them. Since it is able to prove its convictions, an active mind achieves an unassailable certainty in confrontations with assailants—a certainty untainted by spots of blind faith, approximation, evasion and fear.

["Philosophical Detection," *PWNI*, 25; pb 21.]

See also ABSOLUTES; AGNOSTICISM; "ANTI-CONCEPTS"; CER-TAINTY; OBJECTIVITY; PROOF; REASON; SKEPTICISM.

Opera and Operetta.   In operas and operettas, the esthetic base is music, with the libretto serving only to provide an appropriate emotional context or opportunity for the musical score, and an integrating line for the total performance. (In this respect, there are very few good librettos.)

["Art and Cognition," *RM*, pb 71.]

See also ART; MUSIC; PERFORMING ARTS.

Original Sin.   Your code begins by damning man as evil, then demands that he practice a good which it defines as impossible for him to practice. It demands, as his first proof of virtue, that he accept his own depravity without proof. It demands that he start, not with a standard of value, but with a standard of evil, which is himself, by means of which he is then to define the good: the good is that which he is not.

It does not matter who then becomes the profiteer on his renounced glory and tormented soul, a mystic God with some incomprehensible design or any passer-by whose rotting sores are held as some inexplicable claim upon him—it does not matter, the good is not for him to understand, his duty is to crawl through years of penance, atoning for the guilt of his existence to any stray collector of unintelligible debts, his only concept of a value is a zero: the good is that which is non-man.

The name of this monstrous absurdity is Original Sin.

A sin without volition is a slap at morality and an insolent contradiction in terms: that which is outside the possibility of choice is outside the province of morality. If man is evil by birth, he has no will, no power to change it; if he has no will, he can be neither good nor evil; a robot is amoral. To hold, as man's sin, a fact not open to his choice is a mockery of morality. To hold man's nature as his sin is a mockery of nature. To punish him for a crime he committed before he was born is a mockery of justice. To hold him guilty in a matter where no innocence exists is a mockery of reason. To destroy morality, nature, justice and reason by means of a single concept is a feat of evil hardly to be matched. Yet *that* is the root of your code.

Do not hide behind the cowardly evasion that man is born with free will, but with a "tendency" to evil. A free will saddled with a tendency is like a game with loaded dice. It forces man to struggle through the effort of playing, to bear responsibility and pay for the game, but the decision is weighted in favor of a tendency that he had no power to escape. If the tendency is of his choice, he cannot possess it at birth; if it is not of his choice, his will is not free.

What is the nature of the guilt that your teachers call his Original Sin? What are the evils man acquired when he fell from a state they consider perfection? Their myth declares that he ate the fruit of the tree of knowledge—he acquired a mind and became a rational being. It was the knowledge of good and evil—he became a moral being. He was sentenced to earn his bread by his labor—he became a productive being. He was sentenced to experience desire—he acquired the capacity of sexual enjoyment. The evils for which they damn him are reason, morality, creativeness, joy—all the cardinal values of his existence. It is not his vices that their myth of man's fall is designed to explain and condemn, it is not his errors that they hold as his guilt, but the essence of his nature as man. Whatever he was—that robot in the Garden of Eden, who existed without mind, without values, without labor, without love —he was not man.

Man's fall, according to your teachers, was that he gained the virtues required to live. These virtues, by their standard, are his Sin. His evil, they charge, is that he's man. His guilt, they charge, is that he lives.

They call it a morality of mercy and a doctrine of love for man.

[GS, *FNI*, 168; pb 136.]

Ostensive Definition.

With certain significant exceptions, every concept can be defined and communicated in terms of other concepts. The exceptions are concepts referring to sensations, and metaphysical axioms.

Sensations are the primary material of consciousness and, therefore, cannot be communicated by means of the material which is derived from them. The existential causes of sensations can be described and defined in conceptual terms (e.g., the wavelengths of light and the structure of the human eye, which produce the sensations of color), but one cannot communicate what color is like, to a person who is born blind. To define the meaning of the concept "blue," for instance, one must point to some blue objects to signify, in effect: "I mean *this*." Such an identification of a concept is known as an "ostensive definition."

Ostensive definitions are usually regarded as applicable only to conceptualized sensations. But they are applicable to axioms as well. Since axiomatic concepts are identifications of irreducible primaries, the only way to define one is by means of an ostensive definition—e.g., to define "existence," one would have to sweep one's arm around and say: "I mean *this*."

[*ITOE*, 52.]

P

Pacifism. The necessary consequence of man's right to life is his right to self-defense. In a civilized society, force may be used only in retaliation and only against those who initiate its use. All the reasons which make the initiation of physical force an evil, make the retaliatory use of physical force a moral imperative.

If some "pacifist" society renounced the retaliatory use of force, it would be left helplessly at the mercy of the first thug who decided to be immoral. Such a society would achieve the opposite of its intention: instead of abolishing evil, it would encourage and reward it.

["The Nature of Government," *VOS*, 146; pb 108.]

See also ANARCHISM; GOVERNMENT; PEACE MOVEMENTS; PHYSICAL FORCE; RETALIATORY FORCE; SELF-DEFENSE; WAR.

"Package-Dealing," Fallacy of. "Package-dealing" is the fallacy of failing to discriminate crucial differences. It consists of treating together, as parts of a single conceptual whole or "package," elements which differ essentially in nature, truth-status, importance or value.

[Leonard Peikoff, editor's footnote to Ayn Rand's "The Metaphysical Versus the Man-Made," *PWNI*, 30; pb 24.]

[Package-dealing employs] the shabby old gimmick of equating opposites by substituting nonessentials for their essential characteristics, obliterating differences.

["How to Read (and Not to Write)," *ARL*, I, 26, 3.]

A disastrous intellectual package-deal, put over on us by the theoreticians of statism, is the equation of *economic* power with *political* power. You have heard it expressed in such bromides as: "A hungry man is not free," or "It makes no difference to a worker whether he takes orders from a businessman or from a bureaucrat." Most people accept these equivocations—and yet they know that the poorest laborer in America is freer and more secure than the richest commissar in Soviet Russia. What is the basic, the essential, the crucial principle that differentiates freedom from slavery? It is the principle of voluntary action *versus* physical coercion or compulsion.

The difference between political power and any other kind of social "power," between a government and any private organization, is the fact that *a government holds a legal monopoly on the use of physical force.*

["America's Persecuted Minority: Big Business," *CUI*, 46.]

A typical package-deal, used by professors of philosophy, runs as follows: to prove the assertion that there is no such thing as "necessity" in the universe, a professor declares that just as this country did not *have* to have fifty states, there could have been forty-eight or fifty-two— so the solar system did not *have to* have nine planets, there could have been seven or eleven. It is not sufficient, he declares, to prove that something *is*, one must also prove that it *had to be*—and since nothing had to be, nothing is certain and anything goes.

["The Metaphysical Versus the Man-Made," *PWNI*, 34; pb 28.]

See also "ANTI-CONCEPTS"; DEFINITIONS; ECONOMIC POWER vs. POLITICAL POWER; FUNDAMENTALITY, RULE of; NECESSITY; "RAND'S RAZOR"; STATISM.

Painting.   *Painting* [re-creates reality] by means of color on a two-dimensional surface.

["Art and Cognition," *RM*, pb 46.]

The so-called visual arts (painting, sculpture, architecture) produce concrete, perceptually available entities and make them convey an abstract, conceptual meaning.

[Ibid., 47.]

The visual arts do not deal with the sensory field of awareness as such, but with *the sensory field as perceived by a conceptual consciousness.*

[Ibid.]

It is a common experience to observe that a particular painting—for example, a still life of apples—makes its subject "more real than it is in reality." The apples seem brighter and firmer, they seem to possess an almost self-assertive character, a kind of heightened reality which neither their real-life models nor any color photograph can match. Yet if one examines them closely, one sees that no real-life apple ever looked like that. What is it, then, that the artist has done? He has created a *visual abstraction.*

He has performed the process of concept-formation—of isolating and integrating—but in exclusively visual terms. He has isolated the *essential,* distinguishing characteristics of apples, and integrated them into a single visual unit. He has brought the conceptual method of functioning to the operations of a single sense organ, the organ of sight.

[Ibid.]

The closer an artist comes to a conceptual method of functioning visually, the greater his work. The greatest of all artists, Vermeer, devoted his paintings to a single theme: light itself. The guiding principle of his compositions is: the *contextual* nature of our perception of light (and of color). The physical objects in a Vermeer canvas are chosen and placed in such a way that their combined interrelationships feature, lead to and make possible the painting's brightest patches of light, sometimes blindingly bright, in a manner which no one has been able to render before or since.

(Compare the radiant austerity of Vermeer's work to the silliness of the dots-and-dashes Impressionists who allegedly intended to paint pure light. He raised perception to the conceptual level; they attempted to disintegrate perception into sense data.)

One might wish (and I do) that Vermeer had chosen better subjects to express his theme, but to him, apparently, the subjects were only the means to his end. What his *style* projects is a concretized image of an immense, nonvisual abstraction: the psycho-epistemology of a rational mind. It projects clarity, discipline, confidence, purpose, power—a universe open to man. When one feels, looking at a Vermeer painting: "This is *my* view of life," the feeling involves much more than mere visual perception.

[Ibid., 48.]

See also ABSTRACTIONS and CONCRETES; ART; BEAUTY; CONCEPTS; CONTEXT; ESTHETICS; MODERN ART; SENSE of LIFE; STYLE; SUBJECT (in ART); VISUAL ARTS.

Parts of Speech. *See Grammar.*

Patents and Copyrights. Patents and copyrights are the legal implementation of the base of all property rights: a man's right to the product of his mind.

["Patents and Copyrights," *CUI*, 130.]

What the patent and copyright laws acknowledge is the paramount role of mental effort in the production of material values; these laws protect the mind's contribution in its purest form: the origination of an *idea*. The subject of patents and copyrights is *intellectual* property.

An idea as such cannot be protected until it has been given a material form. An invention has to be embodied in a physical model before it can be patented; a story has to be written or printed. But what the patent or copyright protects is not the physical object as such, but the *idea* which it embodies. By forbidding an unauthorized reproduction of the object, the law declares, in effect, that the physical labor of copying is not the source of the object's value, that that value is created by the originator of the idea and may not be used without his consent; thus the law establishes the property right of a mind to that which it has brought into existence.

It is important to note, in this connection, that a *discovery* cannot be patented, only an *invention*. A scientific or philosophical discovery, which identifies a law of nature, a principle or a fact of reality not previously known, cannot be the exclusive property of the discoverer because: (a) he did not *create* it, and (b) if he cares to make his discovery public, claiming it to be true, he cannot demand that men continue to pursue or practice falsehoods except by his permission. He *can* copyright the book in which he presents his discovery and he *can* demand that his authorship of the discovery be acknowledged, that no other man appropriate or plagiarize the credit for it—but he cannot copyright *theoretical* knowledge. Patents and copyrights pertain only to the *practical* application of knowledge, to the creation of a specific object which did not exist in nature—an object which, in the case of patents, *may* never have existed without its particular originator; and in the case of copyrights, *would* never have existed.

The government does not "grant" a patent or copyright, in the sense of a gift, privilege, or favor; the government merely *secures* it—i.e., the government certifies the origination of an idea and protects its owner's exclusive right of use and disposal.

[Ibid.]

Since intellectual property rights cannot be exercised in perpetuity, the question of their time limit is an enormously complex issue. . . . In the case of copyrights, the most rational solution is Great Britain's Copyright Act of 1911, which established the copyright of books, paintings, movies, etc. for the lifetime of the author and fifty years thereafter.

[Ibid., 132.]

As an objection to the patent laws, some people cite the fact that two inventors may work independently for years on the same invention, but one will beat the other to the patent office by an hour or a day and will acquire an exclusive monopoly, while the loser's work will then be totally wasted. This type of objection is based on the error of equating the potential with the actual. The fact that a man *might* have been first, does not alter the fact that he *wasn't*. Since the issue is one of commercial rights, the loser in a case of that kind has to accept the fact that in seeking to trade with others he must face the possibility of a competitor winning the race, which is true of all types of competition.

[Ibid., 133.]

See also CREATION; GOVERNMENT; INDIVIDUAL RIGHTS; PROPERTY RIGHTS.

Peace Movements. Observe the nature of today's alleged peace movements. Professing love and concern for the survival of mankind, they keep screaming that the nuclear-weapons race should be stopped, that armed force should be abolished as a means of settling disputes among nations, and that war should be outlawed in the name of humanity. Yet these same peace movements do not oppose dictatorships; the political views of their members range through all shades of the statist spectrum, from welfare statism to socialism to fascism to communism. This means that they are opposed to the use of coercion by one nation against another, but not by the government of a nation against its own citizens; it means that they are opposed to the use of force against *armed* adversaries, but not against the *disarmed*.

Consider the plunder, the destruction, the starvation, the brutality, the slave-labor camps, the torture chambers, the wholesale slaughter perpetrated by dictatorships. Yet *this* is what today's alleged peace-lovers are willing to advocate or tolerate—in the name of love for humanity.

["The Roots of War," *CUI*, 35.]

It is capitalism that today's peace-lovers oppose and statism that they advocate—in the name of peace.

Laissez-faire capitalism is the only social system based on the recognition of individual rights and, therefore, the only system that bans force from social relationships. By the nature of its basic principles and interests, it is the only system fundamentally opposed to war.

[Ibid., 37.]

It is true that nuclear weapons have made wars too horrible to contemplate. But it makes no difference to a man whether he is killed by a nuclear bomb or a dynamite bomb or an old-fashioned club. Nor does the number of other victims or the scale of the destruction make any difference to him. And there is something obscene in the attitude of those who regard horror as a matter of numbers, who are willing to send a small group of youths to die for the tribe, but scream against the danger to the tribe itself—and more: who are willing to condone the slaughter of defenseless victims, but march in protest against wars between the well-armed. . . .

If nuclear weapons are a dreadful threat and mankind cannot afford war any longer, then *mankind cannot afford statism any longer.* Let no man of good will take it upon his conscience to advocate the rule of force—outside or *inside* his own country. Let all those who are actually concerned with peace—those who do love *man* and do care about his survival—realize that if war is ever to be outlawed, it is *the use of force* that has to be outlawed.

[Ibid., 42.]

See also CAPITALISM; DICTATORSHIP; FOREIGN POLICY; GENO-CIDE; PACIFISM; PHYSICAL FORCE; RETALIATORY FORCE; SELF-DEFENSE; SOVIET RUSSIA; STATISM; WAR.

Perception.   The higher organisms possess a much more potent form of consciousness: they possess the faculty of *retaining* sensations, which is the faculty of *perception.* A "perception" is a group of sensations automatically retained and integrated by the brain of a living organism, which gives it the ability to be aware, not of single stimuli, but of *entities,* of things. An animal is guided, not merely by immediate sensations, but by *percepts.* Its actions are not single, discrete responses to single, separate stimuli, but are directed by an integrated awareness of the *perceptual* reality confronting it. It is able to grasp the perceptual concretes immediately present and it is able to form automatic perceptual associations, but it can go no further.

["The Objectivist Ethics," *VOS,* 10; pb 19.]

Man's senses are his only direct cognitive contact with reality and, therefore, his only *source* of information. Without sensory evidence, there can be no concepts; without concepts, there can be no language; without language, there can be no knowledge and no science.

["Kant Versus Sullivan," *PWNI,* 108; pb 90.]

Although, chronologically, man's consciousness develops in three stages: the stage of sensations, the perceptual, the conceptual—epistemologically, the base of all of man's knowledge is the *perceptual* stage.

Sensations, as such, are not retained in man's memory, nor is man able to experience a pure isolated sensation. As far as can be ascertained, an infant's sensory experience is an undifferentiated chaos. Discriminated awareness begins on the level of percepts.

A percept is a group of sensations automatically retained and integrated by the brain of a living organism. It is in the form of percepts that man grasps the evidence of his senses and apprehends reality. When we speak of "direct perception" or "direct awareness," we mean the perceptual level. Percepts, not sensations, are the given, the self-evident. The knowledge of sensations as components of percepts is not direct, it is acquired by man much later: it is a scientific, *conceptual* discovery.

[*ITOE*, 5.]

[Man's] senses do not provide him with automatic knowledge in separate snatches independent of context, but only with the material of knowledge, which his mind must learn to integrate. . . . His senses cannot deceive him, . . . physical objects cannot act without causes, . . . his organs of perception are physical and have no volition, no power to invent or to distort . . . the evidence they give him is an absolute, but his mind must learn to understand it, his mind must discover the nature, the causes, the full context of his sensory material, his mind must identify the things that he perceives.

[GS, *FNI*, 194; pb 156.]

Let the witch doctor who does not choose to accept the validity of sensory perception, try to prove it without using the data he obtained by sensory perception.

[Ibid., 193; pb 155.]

The arguments of those who attack the senses are merely variants of the fallacy of the "stolen concept."

[*ITOE*, 4.]

As far as can be ascertained, the perceptual level of a child's awareness is similar to the awareness of the higher animals: the higher animals are able to perceive entities, motions, attributes, and certain numbers of entities. But what an animal cannot perform is the process of abstraction—of mentally separating attributes, motions or numbers from entities. It has been said that an animal can perceive two oranges or two potatoes, but cannot grasp the concept "two."

[Ibid., 19.]

The range of man's perceptual awareness—the number of percepts he can deal with at any one time—is limited. He may be able to visualize four or five units—as, for instance, five trees. He cannot visualize a hundred trees or a distance of ten light-years. It is only his conceptual faculty that makes it possible for him to deal with knowledge of that kind.

[*"The Psycho-Epistemology of Art," RM*, 20; pb 17.]

See also AXIOMS; CONCEPTS; CONSCIOUSNESS; ENTITY; EPISTE-MOLOGY; FREE WILL; HIERARCHY of KNOWLEDGE; INTEGRA-TION (MENTAL); OSTENSIVE DEFINITION; PRIMACY of EXIS-TENCE vs. PRIMACY of CONSCIOUSNESS; REASON; SELF-EVIDENT; SENSATIONS; "STOLEN CONCEPT," FALLACY of; UNIT-ECONOMY.

Performing Arts.   Let us turn now to the performing arts (acting, playing a musical instrument, singing, dancing).

In these arts, the medium employed is the person of the artist. His task is not to re-create reality, but to implement the re-creation made by one of the primary arts.

This does not mean that the performing arts are secondary in esthetic value or importance, but only that they are an extension of and dependent on the primary arts. Nor does it mean that performers are mere "interpreters": on the higher levels of his art, a performer contributes a creative element which the primary work could not convey by itself; he becomes a partner, almost a co-creator—if and when he is guided by the principle that *he* is the means to the end set by the work.

The basic principles which apply to all the other arts, apply to the performing artist as well, particularly stylization, i.e., selectivity: the choice and emphasis of essentials, the structuring of the progressive steps of a performance which lead to an ultimately meaningful sum. The performing artist's own metaphysical value-judgments are called upon to create and apply the kind of technique his performance requires. For instance, an actor's view of human grandeur or baseness or courage or timidity will determine how he projects these qualities on the stage. A work intended to be performed leaves a wide latitude of creative choice to the artist who will perform it. In an almost literal sense, he has to *embody* the soul created by the author of the work; a special kind of creativeness is required to bring that soul into full physical reality.

When the performance and the work (literary or musical) are perfectly integrated in meaning, style and intention, the result is a magnificent esthetic achievement and an unforgettable experience for the audience.

The psycho-epistemological role of the performing arts—their relationship to man's cognitive faculty—lies in the full concretization of the metaphysical abstractions projected by a work of the primary arts. The distinction of the performing arts lies in their immediacy—in the fact that they translate a work of art into existential *action,* into a concrete event open to direct awareness.

["Art and Cognition," *RM,* pb 64.]

Music and/or literature are the base of the performing arts and of the large-scale combinations of all the arts, such as opera or motion pictures. The base, in this context, means that primary art which provides the metaphysical element and enables the performance to become a concretization of an abstract view of man.

Without this base, a performance may be entertaining, in such fields as vaudeville or the circus, but it has nothing to do with art. The performance of an aerialist, for instance, demands an enormous physical skill —greater, perhaps, and harder to acquire than the skill demanded of a ballet dancer—but what it offers is merely an exhibition of that skill, with no further meaning, i.e., a concrete, not a concretization of anything.

[Ibid., 70.]

See also ART; BALLET; DANCE; ESTHETICS; INTEGRATION (MENTAL); METAPHYSICAL VALUE-JUDGMENTS; MUSIC; OPERA and OPERETTA; PSYCHO-EPISTEMOLOGY.

Permission (vs. Rights).

A right is the sanction of independent action. A right is that which can be exercised without anyone's permission.

If you exist only because society permits you to exist—you have no *right* to your own life. A permission can be revoked at any time.

If, before undertaking some action, you must obtain the permission of society—you are not free, whether such permission is granted to you or not. Only a slave acts on permission. A permission is not a right.

Do not make the mistake, at this point, of thinking that a worker is a slave and that he holds his job by his employer's permission. He does not hold it by permission—but *by contract,* that is, by a voluntary mutual agreement. A worker can quit his job. A slave cannot.

["Textbook of Americanism," pamphlet, 5.]

See also CONTRACTS; INALIENABILITY; INDIVIDUAL RIGHTS.

Philosophy.

Philosophy studies the *fundamental* nature of existence, of man, and of man's relationship to existence. As against the special sciences, which deal only with particular aspects, philosophy deals with those aspects of the universe which pertain to everything that exists. In the realm of cognition, the special sciences are the trees, but philosophy is the soil which makes the forest possible.

["Philosophy: Who Needs It," *PWNI*, 2; pb 2.]

Philosophy is the science that studies the fundamental aspects of the nature of existence. The task of philosophy is to provide man with a comprehensive view of life. This view serves as a base, a frame of reference, for all his actions, mental or physical, psychological or existential. This view tells him the nature of the universe with which he has to deal (metaphysics); the means by which he is to deal with it, i.e., the means of acquiring knowledge (epistemology); the standards by which he is to choose his goals and values, in regard to his own life and character (ethics)—and in regard to society (politics); the means of concretizing this view is given to him by esthetics.

["The Chickens' Homecoming," *NL*, 107.]

In order to live, man must act; in order to act, he must make choices; in order to make choices, he must define a code of values; in order to define a code of values, he must know *what* he is and *where* he is—i.e., he must know his own nature (including his means of knowledge) and the nature of the universe in which he acts—i.e., he needs metaphysics, epistemology, ethics, which means: *philosophy*. He cannot escape from this need; his only alternative is whether the philosophy guiding him is to be chosen by his mind or by chance.

["Philosophy and Sense of Life," *RM*, 37; pb 30.]

As a human being, you have no choice about the fact that you need a philosophy. Your only choice is whether you define your philosophy by a conscious, rational, disciplined process of thought and scrupulously logical deliberation—or let your subconscious accumulate a junk heap of unwarranted conclusions, false generalizations, undefined contradictions, undigested slogans, unidentified wishes, doubts and fears, thrown together by chance, but integrated by your subconscious into a kind of mongrel philosophy and fused into a single, solid weight: *self-doubt*, like a ball and chain in the place where your mind's wings should have grown.

["Philosophy: Who Needs It," *PWNI*, 6; pb 5.]

The men who are not interested in philosophy need it most urgently: they are most helplessly in its power.

The men who are not interested in philosophy absorb its principles from the cultural atmosphere around them—from schools, colleges, books, magazines, newspapers, movies, television, etc. Who sets the tone of a culture? A small handful of men: the philosophers. Others follow their lead, either by conviction or by default.

[Ibid., 8; pb 6.]

Philosophy is a necessity for a rational being: philosophy is the foundation of science, the organizer of man's mind, the integrator of his knowledge, the programmer of his subconscious, the selector of his values.

["From the Horse's Mouth," *PWNI*, 99; pb 82.]

Just as a man's actions are preceded and determined by some form of idea in his mind, so a society's existential conditions are preceded and determined by the ascendancy of a certain philosophy among those whose job is to deal with ideas. The events of any given period of history are the result of the thinking of the preceding period.

["For the New Intellectual," *FNI*, 27; pb 28.]

The power that determines the establishment, the changes, the evolution, and the destruction of social systems is philosophy. The role of chance, accident, or tradition, in this context, is the same as their role in the life of an individual: their power stands in inverse ratio to the power of a culture's (or an individual's) philosophical equipment, and grows as philosophy collapses. It is, therefore, by reference to philosophy that the character of a social system has to be defined and evaluated.

["What Is Capitalism?" *CUI*, 19.]

The present state of the world is not the proof of philosophy's impotence, but the proof of philosophy's power. It is philosophy that has brought men to this state—it is only philosophy that can lead them out.

["For the New Intellectual," *FNI*, 58; pb 50.]

In philosophy, the fundamentals are metaphysics and epistemology. On the basis of a knowable universe and of a rational faculty's competence to grasp it, you can define man's proper ethics, politics and esthetics. (And if you make an error, you retain the means and the frame of reference necessary to correct it.) But what will you accomplish if you advocate honesty in ethics, while telling men that there is no such thing as truth, fact or reality? What will you do if you advocate political freedom on the grounds that you *feel* it is good, and find yourself confronting an ambitious thug who declares that he feels quite differently?

The layman's error, in regard to philosophy, is the tendency to accept consequences while ignoring their causes—to take the end result of a long sequence of thought as the given and to regard it as "self-evident" or as an irreducible primary, while negating its preconditions.

["Philosophical Detection," *PWNI*, 14; pb 12.]

Philosophy provides man with a comprehensive view of life. In order to evaluate it properly, ask yourself what a given theory, if accepted, would do to a human life, starting with your own.

[Ibid., 19; pb 16.]

Man came into his own in Greece, some two-and-a-half thousand years ago. The birth of philosophy marked his adulthood; not the *content* of any particular system of philosophy, but deeper: the *concept* of philosophy—the realization that a comprehensive view of existence is to be reached by man's *mind*.

Philosophy is the goal toward which religion was only a helplessly blind groping. The grandeur, the reverence, the exalted purity, the austere dedication to the pursuit of truth, which are commonly associated with religion, should properly belong to the field of philosophy. Aristotle lived up to it and, in part, so did Plato, Aquinas, Spinoza—but how many others? It is earlier than we think.

If you observe that ever since Hume and Kant (mainly Kant, because Hume was merely the Bertrand Russell of his time) philosophy has been striving to prove that man's mind is impotent, that there's no such thing as reality and we wouldn't be able to perceive it if there were—you will realize the magnitude of the treason involved.

["The Chickens' Homecoming," *NL*, 107.]

The foundation of any culture, the source responsible for all of its manifestations, is its philosophy. What does modern philosophy offer us? Virtually the only point of agreement among today's leading philosophers is that there is no such thing as philosophy—and that this knowledge constitutes their claim to the title of philosophers. With a hysterical virulence, strange in advocates of skepticism, they insist that there can be no valid philosophical *systems* (i.e., there can be no integrated, consistent, comprehensive view of existence)—that there are no answers to fundamental questions—there is no such thing as truth—there is no such thing as reason, and the battle is only over what should replace it: "linguistic games" or unbridled feelings?

["Our Cultural Value-Deprivation," *TO*, April 1966, 4.]

If, in the course of philosophical detection, you find yourself, at times, stopped by the indignantly bewildered question: "How could anyone arrive at such nonsense?"—you will begin to understand it when you discover that *evil philosophies are systems of rationalization.*

["Philosophical Detection," *PWNI*, 22; pb 18.]

Even though philosophy is held in a (today) well-earned contempt by the other college departments, it is philosophy that determines the nature and direction of all the other courses, because it is philosophy that formulates the principles of epistemology, i.e., the rules by which men are to acquire knowledge. The influence of the dominant philosophic theories permeates every other department, including the physical sciences.

["The Comprachicos," *NL*, 224.]

Philosophy is the foundation of science; epistemology is the foundation of philosophy. It is with a new approach to epistemology that the rebirth of philosophy has to begin.

[*ITOE*, 99.]

See also ARISTOTLE; COMMON SENSE; CULTURE; EPISTEMOLOGY; ESTHETICS; HISTORY; IDEOLOGY; INTELLECTUALS; LINGUISTIC ANALYSIS; LOGICAL POSITIVISM; MAN; METAPHYSICS; MILL, JOHN STUART; MORALITY; NIETZSCHE, FRIEDRICH; OBJECTIVISM; POLITICS; PRAGMATISM; PRINCIPLES; RATIONALISM vs. EMPIRICISM; RATIONALIZATION; REASON; RELIGION; SCIENCE; SELF-EVIDENT.

Photography. A certain type of confusion about the relationship between scientific discoveries and art, leads to a frequently asked question: Is photography an art? The answer is: No. It is a technical, not a creative, skill. Art requires a selective re-creation. A camera cannot perform the basic task of painting: a visual conceptualization, i.e., the creation of a concrete in terms of abstract essentials. The selection of camera angles, lighting or lenses is merely a selection of the means to reproduce various aspects of the given, i.e., of an existing concrete. There is an artistic element in some photographs, which is the result of such selectivity as the photographer can exercise, and some of them can be very beautiful—but the same artistic element (purposeful selectivity) is present in many utilitarian products: in the better kinds of furniture, dress design, automobiles, packaging, etc. The commercial art work in ads (or posters or postage stamps) is frequently done by real artists and has greater esthetic value than many paintings, but utilitarian objects cannot be classified as works of art.

["Art and Cognition," *RM*, pb 74.]

See also ART; ESTHETICS.

Physical Force. Whatever may be open to disagreement, there is one act of evil that may not, the act that no man may commit against others and no man may sanction or forgive. So long as men desire to live together, no man may *initiate*—do you hear me? no man may *start* —the use of physical force against others.

To interpose the threat of physical destruction between a man and his perception of reality, is to negate and paralyze his means of survival; to force him to act against his own judgment, is like forcing him to act against his own sight. Whoever, to whatever purpose or extent, initiates the use of force, is a killer acting on the premise of death in a manner wider than murder: the premise of destroying man's capacity to live.

Do not open your mouth to tell me that your mind has convinced you of your right to force my mind. Force and mind are opposites; morality ends where a gun begins. When you declare that men are irrational animals and propose to treat them as such, you define thereby your own character and can no longer claim the sanction of reason—as no advocate of contradictions can claim it. There can be no "right" to destroy the source of rights, the only means of judging right and wrong: the mind.

To force a man to drop his own mind and to accept your will as a substitute, with a gun in place of a syllogism, with terror in place of proof, and death as the final argument—is to attempt to exist in defiance of reality. Reality demands of man that he act for his own rational interest; your gun demands of him that he act against it. Reality threatens man with death if he does not act on his rational judgment; you threaten him with death if he does. You place him in a world where the price of his life is the surrender of all the virtues required by life—and death by a process of gradual destruction is all that you and your system will achieve, when death is made to be the ruling power, the winning argument in a society of men.

Be it a highwayman who confronts a traveler with the ultimatum: "Your money or your life," or a politician who confronts a country with the ultimatum: "Your children's education or your life," the meaning of that ultimatum is: "Your mind or your life"—and neither is possible to man without the other.

[GS, *FNI*, 164; pb 133.]

The basic political principle of the Objectivist ethics is: no man may *initiate* the use of physical force against others. No man—or group or society or government—has the right to assume the role of a criminal and initiate the use of physical compulsion against any man. Men have the right to use physical force *only* in retaliation and *only* against those who initiate its use. The ethical principle involved is simple and clearcut: it is the difference between murder and self-defense. A holdup man seeks to gain a value, wealth, by killing his victim; the victim does not grow richer by killing a holdup man. The principle is: no man may obtain any values from others by resorting to physical force.

["The Objectivist Ethics," *VOS*, 31; pb 32.]

Man's rights can be violated only by the use of physical force. It is only by means of physical force that one man can deprive another of his life, or enslave him, or rob him, or prevent him from pursuing his own goals, or compel him to act against his own rational judgment.

The precondition of a civilized society is the barring of physical force from social relationships—thus establishing the principle that if men wish to deal with one another, they may do so only by means of *reason:* by discussion, persuasion and voluntary, uncoerced agreement.

["The Nature of Government," *VOS*, 146; pb 108.]

When men abandon reason, physical force becomes their only means of dealing with one another and of settling disagreements.

["The Comprachicos," *NL*, 234.]

A rational mind does not work under compulsion; it does not subordinate its grasp of reality to anyone's orders, directives, or controls; it does not sacrifice its knowledge, its view of the truth, to anyone's opinions, threats, wishes, plans, or "welfare." Such a mind may be hampered by others, it may be silenced, proscribed, imprisoned, or destroyed; it cannot be forced; a gun is not an argument. (An example and symbol of this attitude is Galileo.)

["What Is Capitalism?" *CUI*, 17.]

Force is the antonym and negation of thought. Understanding is not produced by a punch in the face; intellectual clarity does not flow from the muzzle of a gun; the weighing of evidence is not mediated by spasms of terror. The mind is a cognitive faculty; it cannot achieve knowledge or conviction apart from or against its perception of reality; it cannot be forced.

[Leonard Peikoff, *OP*, 336; pb 309.]

An attempt to achieve the good by physical force is a monstrous contradiction which negates morality at its root by destroying man's capacity to recognize the good, i.e., his capacity to value. Force invalidates and paralyzes a man's judgment, demanding that he act against it, thus rendering him morally impotent. A value which one is forced to accept at the price of surrendering one's mind, is not a value to anyone; the forcibly mindless can neither judge nor choose nor value. An attempt to achieve the good by force is like an attempt to provide a man with a picture gallery at the price of cutting out his eyes. Values cannot exist (cannot be valued) outside the full context of a man's life, needs, goals, and *knowledge*.

["What Is Capitalism?" *CUI*, 23.]

To deal with men by force is as impractical as to deal with nature by persuasion.

["The Metaphysical Versus the Man-Made," *PWNI*, 39; pb 32.]

If some men attempt to survive by means of brute force or fraud, by looting, robbing, cheating or enslaving the men who produce, it still remains true that their survival is made possible only by their victims, only by the men who choose to think and to produce the goods which they, the looters, are seizing. Such looters are parasites incapable of survival, who exist by destroying those who *are* capable, those who are pursuing a course of action proper to man.

The men who attempt to survive, not by means of reason, but by means of force, are attempting to survive by the method of animals. But just as animals would not be able to survive by attempting the method of plants, by rejecting locomotion and waiting for the soil to feed them —so men cannot survive by attempting the method of animals, by rejecting reason and counting on productive *men* to serve as their prey. Such looters may achieve their goals for the range of a moment, at the price of destruction: the destruction of their victims and their own. As evidence, I offer you any criminal or any dictatorship.

["What Is Capitalism?" *CUI*, 17.]

One does not and cannot "negotiate" with brutality, nor give it the benefit of the doubt. The moral absolute should be: if and when, in any dispute, one side *initiates* the use of physical force, *that side is wrong*— and no consideration or discussion of the issues is necessary or appropriate.

["Brief Comments," *TO*, March 1969, 1.]

When a society establishes criminals-by-right and looters-by-law— men who use force to seize the wealth of *disarmed* victims—then money becomes its creators' avenger. Such looters believe it safe to rob defenseless men, once they've passed a law to disarm them. But their loot becomes the magnet for other looters, who get it from them as they got it. Then the race goes, not to the ablest at production, but to those most ruthless at brutality. When force is the standard, the murderer wins over the pickpocket.

["The Meaning of Money," *FNI*, 109; pb 92.]

There are only two fundamental methods by which men can deal with one another: by reason or by force, by intellectual persuasion or by physical coercion, by directing to an opponent's brain an argument—or a bullet.

[Leonard Peikoff, *OP*, 90; pb 90.]

Those who declare, today, that force is the only way to deal with men (with the unstated footnote that they, the speakers, would be safe in the position of rulers), ought to take a careful look at the history of absolute monarchies—and of modern dictatorships as well. Under the rule of force, it is the rulers who are in greatest danger, who live—and die—in permanent terror. The court intrigues, the plots and counterplots, the coups d'état, the known executions and secret assassinations are a matter of record. So are the purges of Party leaders and their cliques, in Nazi Germany and Soviet Russia.

["A Nation's Unity," *ARL*, II, 2, 2.]

Altruism gives to the use of force a *moral sanction*, making it not only an unavoidable practical recourse, but also a positive virtue, an expression of militant righteousness.

A man is morally the property of others—of those others it is his duty to serve—argue Fichte, Hegel, and the rest, explicitly or by implication. As such, a man has no moral right to refuse to make the requisite sacrifices for others. If he attempts it, he is depriving men of what is properly theirs, he is violating men's rights, their right to his service—and it is, therefore, an assertion of morality if others intervene forcibly and compel him to fulfill his obligations. "Social justice" in this view not only allows but *demands* the use of force against the non-sacrificial individual.

[Leonard Peikoff, *OP*, 90; pb 91.]

The use of physical force—even its retaliatory use—cannot be left at the discretion of individual citizens. Peaceful coexistence is impossible if a man has to live under the constant threat of force to be unleashed against him by any of his neighbors at any moment. Whether his neighbors' intentions are good or bad, whether their judgment is rational or irrational, whether they are motivated by a sense of justice or by ignorance or by prejudice or by malice—the use of force against one man cannot be left to the arbitrary decision of another.

Visualize, for example, what would happen if a man missed his wallet, concluded that he had been robbed, broke into every house in the neighborhood to search it, and shot the first man who gave him a dirty look, taking the look to be a proof of guilt.

The retaliatory use of force requires *objective* rules of evidence to establish that a crime has been committed and to *prove* who committed it, as well as *objective* rules to define punishments and enforcement procedures. Men who attempt to prosecute crimes, without such rules, are a lynch mob. If a society left the retaliatory use of force in the hands of individual citizens, it would degenerate into mob rule, lynch law and an endless series of bloody private feuds or vendettas.

If physical force is to be barred from social relationships, men need an institution charged with the task of protecting their rights under an *objective* code of rules.

This is the task of a government—of a *proper* government—its basic task, its only moral justification and the reason why men do need a government.

A government is the means of placing the retaliatory use of physical force under objective control—i.e., under objectively defined laws.

["The Nature of Government," *VOS*, 146; pb 108.]

A unilateral breach of contract involves an indirect use of physical force: it consists, in essence, of one man receiving the material values, goods or services of another, then refusing to pay for them and thus keeping them by force (by mere physical possession), not by right—i.e., keeping them without the consent of their owner. Fraud involves a similarly indirect use of force: it consists of obtaining material values without their owner's consent, under false pretenses or false promises. Extortion is another variant of an indirect use of force: it consists of obtaining material values, not in exchange for values, but by the threat of force, violence or injury.

[Ibid., 150; pb 111.]

See also ALTRUISM; CRIME; DICTATORSHIP; ECONOMIC POWER *vs.* POLITICAL POWER; FRAUD; FREEDOM; GOVERNMENT; INDIVIDUAL RIGHTS; JUSTICE; LAW, OBJECTIVE *and* NON-OBJECTIVE; MORALITY; OBJECTIVE THEORY *of* VALUES; PRODUCTION; REASON; RETALIATORY FORCE; SELF-DEFENSE; SELFISHNESS; STATISM; WAR.

Pity.   Pity for the guilty is treason to the innocent.

["Bootleg Romanticism," *RM*, 123; pb 131.]

See also COMPASSION; COMPROMISE; MERCY; MORAL COWARD-
ICE; MORAL JUDGMENT.

Platonic Realism.   The "extreme realists" or Platonists, . . . hold
that abstractions exist as real entities or archetypes in another dimension
of reality and that the concretes we perceive are merely their imperfect
reflections, but the concretes evoke the abstractions in our mind. (According to Plato, they do so by evoking the memory of the archetypes
which we had known, before birth, in that other dimension.)

[*ITOE*, 2.]

The extreme realist (Platonist) and the moderate realist (Aristotelian)
schools of thought regard the referents of concepts as *intrinsic*, i.e., as
"universals" inherent in things (either as archetypes or as metaphysical
essences), as special existents unrelated to man's consciousness—to be
perceived by man directly, like any other kind of concrete existents, but
perceived by some non-sensory or extra-sensory means.

[Ibid., 70.]

The Platonist school begins by accepting the primacy of consciousness, by reversing the relationship of consciousness to existence, by
assuming that reality must conform to the content of consciousness, not
the other way around—on the premise that the presence of any notion
in man's mind proves the existence of a corresponding referent in
reality.

[Ibid., 71.]

The content of true reality, according to Plato, is a set of universals
or Forms—in effect, a set of disembodied abstractions representing that
which is in common among various groups of particulars in this world.
Thus for Plato abstractions are supernatural existents. They are non-
material entities in another dimension, independent of man's mind and
of any of their material embodiments. The Forms, Plato tells us repeatedly, are what is really real. The particulars they subsume—the concretes that make up this world—are not; they have only a shadowy,
dreamlike half-reality.

Momentous conclusions about man are implicit in this metaphysics
(and were later made explicit by a long line of Platonists): since individual men are merely particular instances of the universal "man," they are
not ultimately real. What is real about men is only the Form which they
share in common and reflect. To common sense, there appear to be
many separate, individual men, each independent of the others, each
fully real in his own right. To Platonism, this is a deception; all the

seemingly individual men are *really* the same one Form, in various reflections or manifestations. Thus, all men ultimately comprise one unity, and no earthly man is an autonomous entity—just as, if a man were reflected in a multifaceted mirror, the many reflections would not be autonomous entities.

[Leonard Peikoff, *OP*, 18; pb 27.]

See also ABSTRACTION (PROCESS of); ABSTRACTIONS and CONCRETES; ARISTOTLE; COLLECTIVISM; CONCEPT-FORMATION; CONCEPTS; OBJECTIVITY; PRIMACY of EXISTENCE vs. PRIMACY of CONSCIOUSNESS; RATIONALISM vs. EMPIRICISM; REASON.

Pleasure and Pain.   Now in what manner does a human being discover the concept of *"value"*? By what means does he first become aware of the issue of *"good or evil"* in its simplest form? By means of the physical sensations of *pleasure* or *pain*. Just as sensations are the first step of the development of a human consciousness in the realm of *cognition*, so they are its first step in the realm of *evaluation*.

The capacity to experience pleasure or pain is innate in a man's body; it is part of his *nature*, part of the kind of entity he *is*. He has no choice about it, and he has no choice about the standard that determines what will make him experience the physical sensation of pleasure or of pain. What is that standard? *His life.*

The pleasure-pain mechanism in the body of man—and in the bodies of all the living organisms that possess the faculty of consciousness—serves as an automatic guardian of the organism's life. The physical sensation of pleasure is a signal indicating that the organism is pursuing the *right* course of action. The physical sensation of pain is a warning signal of danger, indicating that the organism is pursuing the *wrong* course of action, that something is impairing the proper function of its body, which requires action to correct it. The best illustration of this can be seen in the rare, freak cases of children who are born without the capacity to experience physical pain; such children do not survive for long; they have no means of discovering what can injure them, no warning signals, and thus a minor cut can develop into a deadly infection, or a major illness can remain undetected until it is too late to fight it.

["The Objectivist Ethics," *VOS*, 8; pb 17.]

The form in which man experiences the reality of his values is *pleasure*. . . . A chronic lack of pleasure, of any enjoyable, rewarding or stimulating experiences, produces a slow, gradual, day-by-day erosion of man's emotional vitality, which he may ignore or repress, but which is recorded by the relentless computer of his subconscious mechanism that registers an ebbing flow, then a trickle, then a few last drops of fuel —until the day when his inner motor stops and he wonders desperately why he has no desire to go on, unable to find any definable cause of his hopeless, chronic sense of exhaustion.

["Our Cultural Value-Deprivation," *TO*, April 1966, 3.]

See also EMOTIONS; HAPPINESS; HEDONISM; LIFE; MILL, JOHN STUART; STANDARD of VALUE; SENSATIONS; SUBCON- SCIOUS; SUFFERING; UTILITARIANISM; VALUES; WHIMS/WHIM- WORSHIP.

Plot. A *plot* is a purposeful progression of logically connected events leading to the resolution of a climax.

The word "purposeful" in this definition has two applications: it ap- plies to the author and to the characters of a novel. It demands that the author devise a logical structure of events, a sequence in which every major event is connected with, determined by and proceeds from the preceding events of the story—a sequence in which nothing is irrele- vant, arbitrary or accidental, so that the logic of the events leads inevi- tably to a final resolution.

Such a sequence cannot be constructed unless the main characters of the novel are engaged in the pursuit of some purpose—unless they are motivated by some goals that direct their actions. In real life, only a process of final causation—i.e., the process of choosing a goal, then taking the steps to achieve it—can give logical continuity, coherence and meaning to a man's actions. Only men striving to achieve a purpose can move through a meaningful series of events.

Contrary to the prevalent literary doctrines of today, it is *realism* that demands a plot structure in a novel. All human actions are goal- directed, consciously or subconsciously; purposelessness is contrary to man's nature: it is a state of neurosis. Therefore, if one is to present man *as he is*—as he is metaphysically, by his nature, in reality—one has to present him in goal-directed action.

["Basic Principles of Literature," *RM*, 59; pb 82.]

To present a story in terms of action means: to present it in terms of events. A story in which nothing happens is not a story. A story whose events are haphazard and accidental is either an inept conglomeration or, at best, a chronicle, a memoir, a reportorial recording, *not* a novel.

A chronicle, real or invented, may possess certain values; but these values are primarily informative—historical or sociological or psycho- logical—not primarily esthetic or literary; they are only partly literary.

Since art is a selective re-creation and since events are the building blocks of a novel, a writer who fails to exercise selectivity in regard to events defaults on the most important aspect of his art.

[Ibid.]

Since a plot is the dramatization of goal-directed action, it has to be based on *conflict;* it may be one character's inner conflict or a conflict of goals and values between two or more characters. Since goals are not achieved automatically, the dramatization of a purposeful pursuit has to include obstacles; it has to involve a clash, a struggle—an action struggle, but not a purely physical one. Since art is a concretization of values, there are not many errors as bad esthetically—or as dull—as fist fights, chases, escapes and other forms of physical action, divorced from any psychological conflict or intellectual value-meaning. Physical action, as such, is not a plot nor a substitute for a plot—as many bad writers attempt to make it, particularly in today's television dramas.

This is the other side of the mind-body dichotomy that plagues literature. Ideas or psychological states divorced from action do not constitute a story—and neither does physical action divorced from ideas and values.

[Ibid., 65; pb 86.]

To isolate and bring into clear focus, into a single issue or a single scene, the essence of a conflict which, in "real life," might be atomized and scattered over a lifetime in the form of meaningless clashes, to condense a long, steady drizzle of buckshot into the explosion of a blockbuster—*that* is the highest, hardest and most demanding function of art.

[Ibid., 61; pb 84.]

The plot of a novel serves the same function as the steel skeleton of a skyscraper: it determines the use, placement and distribution of all the other elements. Matters such as number of characters, background, descriptions, conversations, introspective passages, etc. have to be determined by what the plot can carry, i.e., have to be integrated with the events and contribute to the progression of the story. Just as one cannot pile extraneous weight or ornamentation on a building without regard for the strength of its skeleton, so one cannot burden a novel with irrelevancies without regard for its plot. The penalty, in both cases, is the same: the collapse of the structure.

If the characters of a novel engage in lengthy abstract discussions of their ideas, but their ideas do not affect their actions or the events of the story, it is a bad novel. . . .

In judging a novel, one must take the events as expressing its *meaning*, because it is the events that present what the story is about. No amount of esoteric discussions on transcendental topics, attached to a novel in which nothing happens except "boy meets girl," will transform it into anything other than "boy meets girl."

This leads to a cardinal principle of good fiction: *the theme and the plot of a novel must be integrated*—as thoroughly integrated as mind and body or thought and action in a rational view of man.

[Ibid., 62; pb 84.]

See also ART; LITERATURE; MOTIVATION; NATURALISM; NOVEL; PLOT-THEME; ROMANTICISM; THEME (LITERARY); THRILLERS.

Plot-Theme. The link between the theme and the events of a novel is an element which I call the *plot-theme*. It is the first step of the translation of an abstract theme into a story, without which the construction of a plot would be impossible. A "plot-theme" is the central conflict or "situation" of a story—a conflict in terms of action, corresponding to the theme and complex enough to create a purposeful progression of events.

The *theme* of a novel is the core of its abstract meaning—the *plot-theme* is the core of its events.

For example, the theme of *Atlas Shrugged* is: "The role of the mind in man's existence." The plot-theme is: "The men of the mind going on strike against an altruist-collectivist society."

The theme of *Les Misérables* is: "The injustice of society toward its lower classes." The plot-theme is: "The life-long flight of an ex-convict from the pursuit of a ruthless representative of the law."

The theme of *Gone With the Wind* is: "The impact of the Civil War on Southern society." The plot-theme is: "The romantic conflict of a woman who loves a man representing the old order, and is loved by another man, representing the new."

["Basic Principles of Literature," *RM*, 63; pb 85.]

See also PLOT; THEME (LITERARY).

Political Power. *See Economic Power vs. Political Power.*

Politics. The answers given by ethics determine how man should treat other men, and this determines the fourth branch of philosophy: *politics*, which defines the principles of a proper social system. As an example of philosophy's function, political philosophy will not tell you how much rationed gas you should be given and on which day of the week—it will tell you whether the government has the right to impose any rationing on anything.

["Philosophy: Who Needs It," *PWNI*, 4; pb 4.]

The basic and crucial political issue of our age is: *capitalism versus socialism*, or freedom versus statism. For decades, this issue has been silenced, suppressed, evaded, and hidden under the foggy, undefined rubber-terms of "conservatism" and "liberalism" which had lost their original meaning and could be stretched to mean all things to all men.

[" 'Extremism,' or The Art of Smearing," *CUI*, 178.]

It is political philosophy that sets the goals and determines the course of a country's practical politics. But political philosophy means: abstract theory to identify, explain and evaluate the trend of events, to discover their causes, project their consequences, define the problems and offer the solutions.

["The Chickens' Homecoming," *NL*, 109.]

Politics is based on three other philosophical disciplines: metaphysics, epistemology and ethics—on a theory of man's nature and of man's relationship to existence. It is only on such a base that one can formulate a consistent political theory and achieve it in practice. When, however, men attempt to rush into politics without such a base, the result is that embarrassing conglomeration of impotence, futility, inconsistency and superficiality which is loosely designated today as "conservatism." Objectivists are *not* "conservatives." We are *radicals for capitalism;* we are fighting for that philosophical base which capitalism did not have and without which it was doomed to perish.

["Choose Your Issues," *TON*, Jan. 1962, 1.]

The basic political principle of the Objectivist ethics is: no man may *initiate* the use of physical force against others. No man—or group or society or government—has the right to assume the role of a criminal and initiate the use of physical compulsion against any man. Men have the right to use physical force *only* in retaliation and *only* against those who initiate its use.

["The Objectivist Ethics," *VOS*, 31; pb 32.]

See: Conceptual Index: Politics.

Pollution. The word "pollution" implies health hazards, such as smog or dirty waters.

["The Left: Old and New," *NL*, 87.]

As far as the issue of actual pollution is concerned, it is primarily a scientific, not a political, problem. In regard to the political principle involved: if a man creates a physical danger or harm to others, which extends beyond the line of his own property, such as unsanitary conditions or even loud noise, and if this is *proved*, the law can and does hold him responsible. If the condition is collective, such as in an overcrowded city, appropriate and *objective* laws can be defined, protecting the rights of all those involved—as was done in the case of oil rights, air-space rights, etc. But such laws cannot demand the impossible, must not be aimed at a single scapegoat, i.e., the industrialists, and must take into consideration the whole context of the problem, i.e., the absolute necessity of the continued existence of industry—if the preservation of human life is the standard.

It has been reported in the press many times that the issue of pollution is to be the next big crusade of the New Left activists, after the war in Vietnam peters out. And just as peace was not their goal or motive in that crusade, so clean air is not their goal or motive in this one.

[Ibid., 89.]

See also ECOLOGY/ENVIRONMENTAL MOVEMENT; ECONOMIC GROWTH; LAW, OBJECTIVE AND NON-OBJECTIVE; NEW LEFT; TECHNOLOGY.

Polylogism. Polylogism is the doctrine that there is not *one* correct logic, one correct method of reasoning necessarily binding on all men, but that there are many logics, each valid for some men and invalid for the others. The polylogist divides men into groups, and holds that each group has by nature (or creates for itself by choice) its own distinctive method of inference based on its own distinctive logical laws, so that the inferences that are entirely logical for one group are entirely illogical for the others. . . .

On the polylogist view, there is no common or universal logic to serve as the objective standard and arbiter when men disagree. There is no way for members of opposing groups, with opposing views, to resolve their disputes; it is useless to appeal to facts or to evidence for this purpose, since the minds which engage in the process of reasoning obey different rules of thinking.

In the Nazi version of polylogism, . . . there is Aryan logic, British logic, Jewish logic, etc., and these give rise respectively to Aryan truth, British truth, Jewish truth, etc. . . . The movement that first launched the doctrine of polylogism in a culturally influential form [is] Marxism. Aware of the fact that communism cannot be defended by reason, the Marxists proceeded to turn the fallacy of *ad hominem* into a formal philosophic doctrine, claiming that logic varies with men's economic class, and that objections to communist doctrine may be dismissed as expressions of "bourgeois logic." Thus, vilification of an opponent replaces analysis of his argument. . . . Kant [is] the real father of polylogism, the first among the major philosophers officially to sever logic from reality. . . . In terms of fundamentals, Nazi polylogism, like Nazi subjectivism, is simply a pluralizing and racializing of the Kantian view.

Actually, polylogism is not a theory of logic—it is a denial of logic. The polylogist invests "logic" with the character of a mystic revelation, and turns logic into its antithesis: instead of being the means of validating objectively men's claims to knowledge, logic becomes a subjective device to be used to "justify" anything anyone wishes.

[Leonard Peikoff, "Nazi Politics," *TO*, Feb. 1971, 12.]

See also COMMUNISM; FASCISM/NAZISM; KANT, IMMANUEL; LOGIC; OBJECTIVITY; RACISM.

Popular Literature. Popular literature is fiction that does not deal with abstract problems; it takes moral principles as the given, accepting certain generalized, *common-sense* ideas and values as its base. (Common-sense values and conventional values are not the same thing; the first can be justified rationally, the second cannot. Even though the second may include some of the first, they are justified, not on the ground of reason, but on the ground of social conformity.)

Popular fiction does not raise or answer abstract questions; it assumes that man knows what he needs to know in order to live, and it proceeds to show his adventures in living (which is one of the reasons for its popularity among all types of readers, including the problem-laden intellectuals). The distinctive characteristic of popular fiction is the absence of an *explicitly* ideational element, of the intent to convey intellectual information (or misinformation).

["What Is Romanticism?" *RM*, 95; pb 110.]

See also LITERATURE; ROMANTICISM; THRILLERS.

Possible. "X is possible" means: in the present context of knowledge, there is some, but not much, evidence in favor of X and nothing known that contradicts X.

[Leonard Peikoff, "The Philosophy of Objectivism"
lecture series (1976), Lecture 6.]

When you say "maybe," you are saying there is at least some evidence, some reason to suspect X. This is a claim that must be justified. There are many fantasies that are outrightly impossible, because they contradict already known facts. And there are other fantasies that are mere arbitrary inventions; even if you cannot specify facts which contradict these inventions, you have absolutely no basis to hypothesize them.

[Ibid.]

It is possible, the skeptic argument declares, *for* man to be in error; therefore, it is possible *that* every individual is in error on every question. This argument is a non sequitur; it is an equivocation on the term "possible."

What is possible to a species under some circumstances, is not necessarily possible to every individual member of that species under every set of circumstances. Thus, it is possible for a human being to run the mile in less than four minutes; and it is possible for a human being to be pregnant. I cannot, however, go over to a crippled gentleman in his wheelchair and say: "Perhaps you'll give birth to a son next week, after you've run the mile to the hospital in 3.9 minutes—after all, you're human, and it is possible for human beings to do these things."

The same principle applies to the possibility of error.

[Leonard Peikoff, " 'Maybe You're Wrong,' " *TOF*, April 1981, 10.]

See also AGNOSTICISM; ARBITRARY; CERTAINTY; CHANCE; CONTEXT; KNOWLEDGE; SKEPTICISM.

Poverty. If concern for human poverty and suffering were one's primary motive, one would seek to discover their cause. One would not fail to ask: Why did some nations develop, while others did not? Why have some nations achieved material abundance, while others have remained stagnant in subhuman misery? History and, specifically, the unprecedented prosperity-explosion of the nineteenth century, would give an immediate answer: capitalism is the only system that enables men to produce abundance—and the key to capitalism is individual freedom.

["Requiem for Man," *CUI*, 308.]

Poverty is not a mortgage on the labor of others—misfortune is not a mortgage on achievement—failure is not a mortgage on success—suffering is not a claim check, and its relief is not the goal of existence—man is not a sacrificial animal on anyone's altar nor for anyone's cause—life is not one huge hospital.

["Apollo 11," *TO*, Sept. 1969, 13.]

See also ALTRUISM; CAPITALISM; CHARITY; FREEDOM; NINETEENTH CENTURY; SACRIFICE; SELFISHNESS.

Pragmatism. [The Pragmatists] declared that philosophy must be *practical* and that practicality consists of dispensing with all absolute principles and standards—that there is no such thing as objective reality or permanent truth—that *truth is that which works*, and its validity can be judged only by its consequences—that no facts can be known with certainty in advance, and anything may be tried by rule-of-thumb—that reality is not firm, but fluid and "indeterminate," that there is no such thing as a distinction between an external world and a consciousness (between the perceived and the perceiver), there is only an undifferentiated package-deal labeled "experience," and whatever one wishes to be true, *is* true, whatever one wishes to exist, *does* exist, provided it works or makes one feel better.

A later school of more Kantian Pragmatists amended this philosophy as follows. If there is no such thing as an objective reality, men's metaphysical choice is whether the selfish, dictatorial whims of an individual or the democratic whims of a collective are to shape that plastic goo which the ignorant call "reality," therefore this school decided that *objectivity consists of collective subjectivism*—that knowledge is to be gained by means of public polls among special elites of "competent investigators" who can "predict and control" reality—that whatever people wish to be true, *is* true, whatever people wish to exist, *does* exist, and anyone who holds any firm convictions of his own is an arbitrary, mystic dogmatist, since reality is indeterminate and people determine its actual nature.

["For the New Intellectual," *FNI*, 35; pb 34.]

In the whirling Heraclitean flux which is the pragmatist's universe, there are no absolutes. There are no facts, no fixed laws of logic, no certainty, no objectivity.

There are no facts, only provisional "hypotheses" which for the moment facilitate human action. There are no fixed laws of logic, only mutable "conventions," without any basis in reality. (Aristotle's logic, Dewey remarks, worked so well for earlier cultures that it is now overdue for a replacement.) There is no certainty—the very quest for it, says Dewey, is a fundamental aberration, a "perversion." There is no objectivity—the object is created by the thought and action of the subject.

[Leonard Peikoff, *OP*, 130; pb 126.]

Epistemologically, their dogmatic agnosticism holds, as an absolute, that *a principle is false because it is a principle*—that conceptual integration (i.e., thinking) is impractical or "simplistic"—that an idea which is clear and simple is necessarily "extreme and unworkable." Along with Kant, their philosophic forefather, the pragmatists claim, in effect: "If you perceive it, it cannot be real," and: "If you conceive of it, it cannot be true."

What, then, is left to man? The sensation, the wish, the whim, the range and the concrete of the moment. Since no solution to any problem is possible, anyone's suggestion, guess or edict is as valid as anyone else's —provided it is narrow enough.

To give you an example: if a building were threatened with collapse and you declared that the crumbling foundation has to be rebuilt, a pragmatist would answer that your solution is too abstract, extreme, unprovable, and that immediate priority must be given to the need of putting ornaments on the balcony railings, because it would make the tenants feel better.

There was a time when a man would not utter arguments of this sort, for fear of being rightly considered a fool. Today, Pragmatism has not merely given him permission to do it and liberated him from the necessity of thought, but has elevated his mental default into an intellectual virtue, has given him the right to dismiss thinkers (or construction engineers) as naive, and has endowed him with that typically modern quality: the arrogance of the concrete-bound, who takes pride in not seeing the forest fire, or the forest, or the trees, while he is studying one inch of bark on a rotted tree stump.

["How to Read (and Not to Write)," *ARL*, I, 26, 5.]

The two points central to the pragmatist ethics are: a formal rejection of all fixed standards—and an unquestioning absorption of the prevailing standards. The same two points constitute the pragmatist approach to politics, which, developed most influentially by Dewey, became the philosophy of the Progressive movement in this country (and of most of its liberal descendants down to the present day).

[Leonard Peikoff, "Pragmatism Versus America," *ARL*, III, 17, 1.]

By itself, as a distinctive theory, the pragmatist ethics is contentless. It urges men to pursue "practicality," but refrains from specifying any "rigid" set of values that could serve to define the concept. As a result, pragmatists—despite their repudiation of all systems of morality—are compelled, if they are to implement their ethical approach at all, to rely on value codes formulated by other, non-pragmatist moralists. As a rule the pragmatist appropriates these codes without acknowledging them; he accepts them by a process of osmosis, eclectically absorbing the cultural deposits left by the moral theories of his predecessors—and protesting all the while the futility of these theories.

The dominant, virtually the only, moral code advocated by modern intellectuals in Europe and in America is some variant of *altruism*. This, accordingly, is what most American pragmatists routinely preach. . . .

In politics, also, pragmatism presents itself as opposed to "rigidity," to "dogma," to "extremes" of any kind (whether capitalist or socialist); it avows that it is relativist, "moderate," "experimental." As in ethics, however, so here: the pragmatist is compelled to employ some kind of standard to evaluate the results of his social experiments, a standard which, given his own self-imposed default, he necessarily absorbs from other, non-pragmatist trend-setters. . . . When Dewey wrote, the political principle imported from Germany and proliferating in all directions, was *collectivism*.

[Leonard Peikoff, *OP*, 131; pb 128.]

Pragmatism is the only twentieth-century philosophy to gain broad, national acceptance in the United States.

[Ibid., 138; pb 134.]

The American people were led to embrace the pragmatist philosophy not because of its actual, theoretical content (of which they were and remain largely ignorant), but because of the method by which that content was presented to them. *In its terminology and promises,* pragmatism is a philosophy calculated to appeal specifically to an American audience. . . .

The pragmatists present themselves as the exponents of a distinctively "American" approach, which consists in enshrining the basic premises of [German philosophy] while rejecting every fundamental idea, from metaphysics to politics, on which this country was founded. Most important of all, the Americans wanted ideas to be good for something on earth, to have tangible, practical significance; and, insistently, the pragmatists stress "practicality," which, according to their teachings, consists in action divorced from thought and reality.

The pragmatists stress the "cash value" of ideas. But the Americans did not know the "cash value" of the pragmatist ideas they were buying. They did not know that pragmatism could not deliver on its promise of this-worldly success because, at root, it is a philosophy which does not believe in this, or any, world.

When the Americans flocked to pragmatism, they believed that they were joining a battle to advance *their* essential view of reality and of life. They did not know that they were being marched in the opposite direction, that the battle had been calculated for a diametrically opposite purpose, or that the enemy they were being pushed to destroy was: themselves.

[Ibid., 136; pb 132.]

See also ABSOLUTES; ALTRUISM; AMERICA; ANTI-CONCEPTUAL
MENTALITY; CERTAINTY; COMPROMISE; EDUCATION; KANT, IM-
MANUEL; MORAL-PRACTICAL DICHOTOMY; MORALITY; OBJEC-
TIVITY; PRIMACY of EXISTENCE vs. PRIMACY of CONSCIOUSNESS;
PRINCIPLES; THEORY-PRACTICE DICHOTOMY; TRUTH; WHIMS/
WHIM-WORSHIP.

Prestige. The desire for the unearned has two aspects: the unearned in matter and the unearned in spirit. (By "spirit" I mean: man's
consciousness.) These two aspects are necessarily interrelated, but a
man's desire may be focused predominantly on one or the other. The
desire for the unearned in spirit is the more destructive of the two and
the more corrupt. It is a desire for *unearned greatness;* it is expressed (but
not defined) by the foggy murk of the term *"prestige."* . . .

Unearned greatness is so unreal, so neurotic a concept that the wretch
who seeks it cannot identify it even to himself: to identify it, is to make
it impossible. He needs the irrational, undefinable slogans of altruism
and collectivism to give a semiplausible form to his nameless urge and
anchor it to reality—to support his own self-deception more than to
deceive his victims.

["The Monument Builders," *VOS*, 115; pb 88.]

See also ALTRUISM; COLLECTIVISM; SECOND-HANDERS.

Pride. Pride is the recognition of the fact that you are your own
highest value and, like all of man's values, it has to be earned—that of
any achievements open to you, the one that makes all others possible is
the creation of your own character—that your character, your actions,
your desires, your emotions are the products of the premises held by
your mind—that as man must produce the physical values he needs to
sustain his life, so he must acquire the values of character that make his
life worth sustaining—that as man is a being of self-made wealth, so he
is a being of self-made soul—that to live requires a sense of self-value,
but man, who has no automatic values, has no automatic sense of self-
esteem and must earn it by shaping his soul in the image of his moral
ideal, in the image of Man, the rational being he is born able to create,
but must create by choice—that the first precondition of self-esteem is
that radiant selfishness of soul which desires the best in all things, in
values of matter and spirit, a soul that seeks above all else to achieve its
own moral perfection, valuing nothing higher than itself—and that the
proof of an achieved self-esteem is your soul's shudder of contempt and
rebellion against the role of a sacrificial animal, against the vile imper-
tinence of any creed that proposes to immolate the irreplaceable value

which is your consciousness and the incomparable glory which is your existence to the blind evasions and the stagnant decay of others.

[GS, *FNI*, 160; pb 130.]

The virtue of Pride can best be described by the term: "moral ambitiousness." It means that one must earn the right to hold oneself as one's own highest value by achieving one's own moral perfection—which one achieves by never accepting any code of irrational virtues impossible to practice and by never failing to practice the virtues one knows to be rational—by never accepting an unearned guilt and never earning any, or, if one *has* earned it, never leaving it uncorrected—by never resigning oneself passively to any flaws in one's character—by never placing any concern, wish, fear or mood of the moment above the reality of one's own self-esteem. And, above all, it means one's rejection of the role of a sacrificial animal, the rejection of any doctrine that preaches self-immolation as a moral virtue or duty.

["The Objectivist Ethics," *VOS*, 22; pb 27.]

See also AMBITION; ARISTOTLE; CHARACTER; EMOTIONS; FREE WILL; HONOR; RATIONALITY; SACRIFICE; SELF-ESTEEM; SELFISHNESS; VIRTUE.

Primacy of Existence vs. Primacy of Consciousness.

The basic metaphysical issue that lies at the root of any system of philosophy [is] *the primacy of existence* or *the primacy of consciousness*.

The primacy of existence (of reality) is the axiom that existence exists, i.e., that the universe exists independent of consciousness (of *any* consciousness), that things are what they are, that they possess a specific nature, an *identity*. The epistemological corollary is the axiom that consciousness is the faculty of perceiving that which exists—and that man gains knowledge of reality by looking outward. The rejection of these axioms represents a reversal: the primacy of consciousness—the notion that the universe has no independent existence, that it is the product of a consciousness (either human or divine or both). The epistemological corollary is the notion that man gains knowledge of reality by looking inward (either at his own consciousness or at the revelations it receives from another, superior consciousness).

The source of this reversal is the inability or unwillingness fully to grasp the difference between one's inner state and the outer world, i.e., between the perceiver and the perceived (thus blending consciousness and existence into one indeterminate package-deal). This crucial distinction is not given to man automatically; it has to be learned. It is implicit in any awareness, but it has to be grasped conceptually and held as an absolute.

["The Metaphysical Versus the Man-Made," *PWNI*, 29; pb 24.]

Observe that the philosophical system based on the axiom of the primacy of existence (i.e., on recognizing the absolutism of reality) led to the recognition of man's identity and *rights*. But the philosophical systems based on the primacy of consciousness (i.e., on the seemingly megalomaniacal notion that nature is whatever man wants it to be) lead to the view that man possesses no identity, that he is infinitely flexible, malleable, usable and disposable. Ask yourself why.

[Ibid., 34; pb 28.]

They want to cheat the axiom of existence and consciousness, they want their consciousness to be an instrument not of *perceiving* but of *creating* existence, and existence to be not the *object* but the *subject* of their consciousness—they want to be that God they created in their image and likeness, who creates a universe out of a void by means of an arbitrary whim. But reality is not to be cheated. What they achieve is the opposite of their desire. They want an omnipotent power over existence; instead, they lose the power of their consciousness. By refusing to know, they condemn themselves to the horror of a perpetual unknown.

[GS, *FNI*, 187; pb 151.]

It is important to observe the interrelation of these three axioms [existence, consciousness, and identity]. Existence is the first axiom. *The universe exists independent of consciousness.* Man is able to adapt his background to his own requirements, but "Nature, to be commanded, must be obeyed" (Francis Bacon). There is no mental process that can change the laws of nature or erase facts. The function of consciousness is not to create reality, but to apprehend it. "Existence is Identity, Consciousness is Identification."

The philosophic source of this viewpoint and its major advocate in the history of philosophy is Aristotle. Its opponents are all the other major traditions, including Platonism, Christianity, and German idealism. Directly or indirectly, these traditions uphold the notion that consciousness is the creator of reality. The essence of this notion is the denial of the axiom that existence exists.

[Leonard Peikoff, *OP*, 329; pb 303.]

See also ABSOLUTES; AXIOMATIC CONCEPTS; AXIOMS; CONSCIOUSNESS; CREATION; EVASION; EXISTENCE; GOD; IDENTITY;

IMAGINATION; KANT, IMMANUEL; METAPHYSICS; MYSTICISM; NATURE; OBJECTIVITY; PHILOSOPHY; PLATONIC REALISM; PRAGMATISM; PRIOR CERTAINTY of CONSCIOUSNESS; SUBJECTIVISM; UNIVERSE.

Principles. A principle is "a fundamental, primary, or general truth, on which other truths depend." Thus a principle is an abstraction which subsumes a great number of concretes. It is only by means of principles that one can set one's long-range goals and evaluate the concrete alternatives of any given moment. It is only principles that enable a man to plan his future and to achieve it.

The present state of our culture may be gauged by the extent to which principles have vanished from public discussion, reducing our cultural atmosphere to the sordid, petty senselessness of a bickering family that haggles over trivial concretes, while betraying all its major values, selling out its future for some spurious advantage of the moment.

To make it more grotesque, that haggling is accompanied by an aura of hysterical self-righteousness, in the form of belligerent assertions that one must compromise with anybody on anything (except on the tenet that one must compromise) and by panicky appeals to "practicality."

But there is nothing as impractical as a so-called "practical" man. His view of practicality can best be illustrated as follows: if you want to drive from New York to Los Angeles, it is "impractical" and "idealistic" to consult a map and to select the best way to get there; you will get there much faster if you just start out driving at random, turning (or cutting) any corner, taking any road in any direction, following nothing but the mood and the weather of the moment.

The fact is, of course, that by this method you will never get there at all. But while most people do recognize this fact in regard to the course of a journey, they are not so perceptive in regard to the course of their life and of their country.

["The Anatomy of Compromise," *CUI*, 144.]

Concrete problems cannot even be grasped, let alone judged or solved, without reference to abstract principles.

["Credibility and Polarization," *ARL*, I, 1, 3.]

You have no choice about the necessity to integrate your observations, your experiences, your knowledge into abstract ideas, i.e., into principles. Your only choice is whether these principles are true or false, whether they represent your conscious, rational convictions—or a grab-bag of notions snatched at random, whose sources, validity, context and consequences you do not know, notions which, more often than not, you would drop like a hot potato if you knew. . . .

You might say, as many people do, that it is not easy always to act on abstract principles. No, it is not easy. But how much harder is it, to have to act on them without knowing what they are?

["Philosophy: Who Needs It," *PWNI*, 6; pb 5.]

Consider a few rules about the working of principles in practice and about the relationship of principles to goals. . . .

1. In any *conflict* between two men (or two groups) who hold the *same* basic principles, it is the more consistent one who wins.

2. In any *collaboration* between two men (or two groups) who hold *different* basic principles, it is the more evil or irrational one who wins.

3. When opposite basic principles are clearly and openly defined, it works to the advantage of the rational side; when they are *not* clearly defined, but are hidden or evaded, it works to the advantage of the irrational side.

["The Anatomy of Compromise," *CUI*, 145.]

When men abandon principles (i.e., their conceptual faculty), two of the major results are: individually, the inability to project the future; socially, the impossibility of communication.

["Credibility and Polarization," *ARL*, I, 1, 3.]

Only fundamental principles, rationally validated, clearly understood and voluntarily accepted, can create a desirable kind of unity among men.

[Ibid., 4.]

See also ANTI-CONCEPTUAL MENTALITY; COMPROMISE; CON-CEPTS; INTEGRATION (MENTAL); PHILOSOPHY; PRAGMATISM; REASON; TRUTH.

Prior Certainty of Consciousness. Descartes began with the basic epistemological premise of every Witch Doctor (a premise he shared explicitly with Augustine): "the prior certainty of consciousness," the belief that the *existence* of an external world is not self-evident, but must be proved by deduction from the contents of one's consciousness —which means: the concept of consciousness as some faculty other than the faculty of perception—which means: the indiscriminate contents of one's consciousness as the irreducible primary and absolute, to which reality *has* to conform. What followed was the grotesquely tragic spectacle of philosophers struggling to *prove* the existence of an external world by staring, with the Witch Doctor's blind, inward stare, at the random twists of their conceptions—then of perceptions—then of sensations.

When the medieval Witch Doctor had merely ordered men to doubt the validity of their mind, the philosophers' rebellion against him consisted of proclaiming that they doubted whether man was conscious at all and whether anything existed for him to be conscious of.

["For the New Intellectual," *FNI*, 28; pb 28.]

See also AXIOMS; CONSCIOUSNESS; EXISTENCE; IRREDUCIBLE PRIMARIES; PRIMACY of EXISTENCE vs. PRIMACY of CONSCIOUSNESS; SENSATIONS.

Production. Production is the application of reason to the problem of survival.

["What Is Capitalism?" *CUI*, 17.]

Have you ever looked for the root of production? Take a look at an electric generator and dare tell yourself that it was created by the muscular effort of unthinking brutes. Try to grow a seed of wheat without the knowledge left to you by men who had to discover it for the first time. Try to obtain your food by means of nothing but physical motions —and you'll learn that man's mind is the root of all the goods produced and of all the wealth that has ever existed on earth.

But you say that money is made by the strong at the expense of the weak? What strength do you mean? It is not the strength of guns or muscles. Wealth is the product of man's capacity to think. Then is money made by the man who invents a motor at the expense of those who did not invent it? Is money made by the intelligent at the expense of the fools? By the able at the expense of the incompetent? By the ambitious at the expense of the lazy? Money is *made*—before it can be looted or mooched—made by the effort of every honest man, each to the extent of his ability. An honest man is one who knows that he can't consume more than he has produced.

["The Meaning of Money," *FNI*, 105; pb 89.]

Whether it's a symphony or a coal mine, all work is an act of creating and comes from the same source: from an inviolate capacity to see through one's own eyes—which means: the capacity to perform a rational identification—which means: the capacity to see, to connect and to make what had not been seen, connected and made before.

["The Nature of an Artist," *FNI*, 140; pb 115.]

Every type of productive work involves a combination of mental and physical effort: of thought and of physical action to translate that thought into a material form. The proportion of these two elements varies in different types of work. At the lowest end of the scale, the mental effort required to perform unskilled manual labor is minimal. At the other end, what the patent and copyright laws acknowledge is the paramount role of mental effort in the production of material values.

["Patents and Copyrights," *CUI*, 130.]

The root of production is man's mind; the mind is an attribute of the individual and it does not work under orders, controls and compulsion, as centuries of stagnation have demonstrated. Progress cannot be planned by government, and it cannot be restricted or retarded; it can only be stopped, as every statist government has demonstrated.

["The Anti-Industrial Revolution," *NL*, 140.]

See also CONSUMPTION; CREATION; CREATORS; ECONOMIC GOOD; ECONOMIC GROWTH; MONEY; PHYSICAL FORCE; PRO-DUCTIVENESS; PYRAMID OF ABILITY; REASON; STATISM.

Productiveness. The virtue of *Productiveness* is the recognition of the fact that productive work is the process by which man's mind sustains his life, the process that sets man free of the necessity to adjust himself to his background, as all animals do, and gives him the power to adjust his background to himself. Productive work is the road of man's unlimited achievement and calls upon the highest attributes of his character: his creative ability, his ambitiousness, his self-assertiveness, his refusal to bear uncontested disasters, his dedication to the goal of reshaping the earth in the image of his values. "Productive work" does not mean the unfocused performance of the motions of some job. It means the consciously chosen pursuit of a productive career, in any line of rational endeavor, great or modest, on any level of ability. It is not the degree of a man's ability nor the scale of his work that is ethically relevant here, but the fullest and most purposeful use of his mind.

["The Objectivist Ethics," *VOS*, 21; pb 26.]

Productiveness is your acceptance of morality, your recognition of the fact that you choose to live—that productive work is the process by which man's consciousness controls his existence, a constant process of acquiring knowledge and shaping matter to fit one's purpose, of translating an idea into physical form, of remaking the earth in the image of one's values—that *all* work is creative work if done by a thinking mind, and no work is creative if done by a blank who repeats in uncritical stupor a routine he has learned from others—that your work is yours to choose, and the choice is as wide as your mind, that nothing more is possible to you and nothing less is human—that to cheat your way into a job bigger than your mind can handle is to become a fear-corroded ape on borrowed motions and borrowed time, and to settle down into a job that requires less than your mind's full capacity is to cut your motor and sentence yourself to another kind of motion: decay—that your work is the process of achieving your values, and to lose your ambition for values is to lose your ambition to live—that your body is a machine, but your mind is its driver, and you must drive as far as your mind will take you, with achievement as the goal of your road—that the man who has no purpose is a machine that coasts downhill at the mercy of any boulder to crash in the first chance ditch, that the man who stifles his mind is a stalled machine slowly going to rust, that the man who lets a leader prescribe his course is a wreck being towed to the scrap heap, and the man who makes another man his goal is a hitchhiker no driver should ever pick up—that your work is the purpose of your life, and you must speed past any killer who assumes the right to stop you, that any value you might find outside your work, any other loyalty or love, can be only travelers you choose to share your journey and must be travelers going on their own power in the same direction.

[GS, *FNI*, 159; pb 130.]

Productive work is the central *purpose* of a rational man's life, the central value that integrates and determines the hierarchy of all his other values. Reason is the source, the precondition of his productive work—pride is the result.

["The Objectivist Ethics," *VOS*, 20; pb 25.]

See also AMBITION; CAREER; COMPETITION; CREATORS; LIFE; MORALITY; PRODUCTION; PURPOSE; PRIDE; RATIONALITY; REASON; VIRTUE.

Proof. "Proof," in the full sense, is the process of deriving a conclusion step by step from the evidence of the senses, each step being taken in accordance with the laws of logic.

[Leonard Peikoff, "Introduction to Logic"
lecture series (1974), Lecture 1.]

"You cannot *prove* that you exist or that you're conscious," they chatter, blanking out the fact that *proof* presupposes existence, consciousness and a complex chain of knowledge: the existence of something to know, of a consciousness able to know it, and of a knowledge that has learned to distinguish between such concepts as the proved and the unproved.

When a savage who has not learned to speak declares that existence must be proved, he is asking you to prove it by means of non-existence —when he declares that your consciousness must be proved, he is asking you to prove it by means of unconsciousness—he is asking you to step into a void outside of existence and consciousness to give him proof of both—he is asking you to become a zero gaining knowledge about a zero.

[GS, *FNI*, 192; pb 154.]

An axiomatic concept is the identification of a primary fact of reality, which cannot be analyzed, i.e., reduced to other facts or broken into component parts. It is implicit in all facts and in all knowledge. It is the fundamentally given and directly perceived or experienced, which requires no proof or explanation, but on which all proofs and explanations rest.

The first and primary axiomatic concepts are "existence," "identity" (which is a corollary of "existence") and "consciousness." One can study what exists and how consciousness functions; but one cannot analyze (or "prove") existence as such, or consciousness as such. These are irreducible primaries. (An attempt to "prove" them is self-contradictory: it is an attempt to "prove" existence by means of non-existence, and consciousness by means of unconsciousness.)

[*ITOE*, 73.]

See also AXIOMATIC CONCEPTS; AXIOMS; COROLLARIES; IRREDUCIBLE PRIMARIES; LOGIC; OBJECTIVITY; PERCEPTION; REASON; SELF-EVIDENT; VALIDATION.

Property Rights.

The right to life is the source of all rights—and the right to property is their only implementation. Without property rights, no other rights are possible. Since man has to sustain his life by his own effort, the man who has no right to the product of his effort has no means to sustain his life. The man who produces while others dispose of his product, is a slave.

Bear in mind that the right to property is a right to action, like all the others: it is not the right *to an object*, but to the action and the consequences of producing or earning that object. It is not a guarantee that a man *will* earn any property, but only a guarantee that he will own it if he earns it. It is the right to gain, to keep, to use and to dispose of material values.

["Man's Rights," *VOS*, 125; pb 94.]

Any material element or resource which, in order to become of use or value to men, requires the application of human knowledge and effort, should be private property—by the right of those who apply the knowledge and effort.

["The Property Status of Airwaves," *CUI*, 122.]

Just as man can't exist without his body, so no rights can exist without the right to translate one's rights into reality—to think, to work and to keep the results—which means: the right of property. The modern mystics of muscle who offer you the fraudulent alternative of "human rights" versus "property rights," as if one could exist without the other, are making a last, grotesque attempt to revive the doctrine of soul versus body. Only a ghost can exist without material property; only a slave can work with no right to the product of his effort. The doctrine that "human rights" are superior to "property rights" simply means that some human beings have the right to make property out of others; since the competent have nothing to gain from the incompetent, it means the right of the incompetent to own their betters and to use them as productive cattle. Whoever regards this as human and right, has no right to the title of "human."

The source of property rights is the law of causality. All property and all forms of wealth are produced by man's mind and labor. As you cannot have effects without causes, so you cannot have wealth without its source: without intelligence. You cannot force intelligence to work: those who're able to think, will not work under compulsion; those who will, won't produce much more than the price of the whip needed to keep them enslaved. You cannot obtain the products of a mind except on the owner's terms, by trade and by volitional consent. Any other policy of men toward man's property is the policy of criminals, no matter what their numbers. Criminals are savages who play it short-range and starve when their prey runs out—just as you're starving today, you who believed that crime could be "practical" if your government decreed that robbery was legal and resistance to robbery illegal.

[GS, *FNI*, 230; pb 182.]

Man has to work and produce in order to support his life. He has to support his life by his own effort and by the guidance of his own mind. If he cannot dispose of the product of his effort, he cannot dispose of his effort; if he cannot dispose of his effort, he cannot dispose of his life. Without property rights, no other rights can be practiced.

["What Is Capitalism?" *CUI*, 18.]

If some men are entitled *by right* to the products of the work of others, it means that those others are deprived of rights and condemned to slave labor.

Any alleged "right" of one man, which necessitates the violation of the rights of another, is not and cannot be a right.

No man can have a right to impose an unchosen obligation, an unrewarded duty or an involuntary servitude on another man. There can be no such thing as *"the right to enslave."*

A right does not include the material implementation of that right by other men; it includes only the freedom to earn that implementation by one's own effort. . . .

The right to property means that a man has the right to take the economic actions necessary to earn property, to use it and to dispose of it; it does *not* mean that others must provide him with property.

The right of free speech means that a man has the right to express his ideas without danger of suppression, interference or punitive action by the government. It does *not* mean that others must provide him with a lecture hall, a radio station or a printing press through which to express his ideas.

Any undertaking that involves more than one man, requires the *voluntary* consent of every participant. Every one of them has the *right* to make his own decision, but none has the right to force his decision on the others.

There is no such thing as "a right to a job"—there is only the right of free trade, that is: a man's right to take a job if another man chooses to hire him. There is no "right to a home," only the right of free trade: the right to build a home or to buy it. There are no "rights to a 'fair' wage or a 'fair' price" if no one chooses to pay it, to hire a man or to buy his product. There are no "rights of consumers" to milk, shoes, movies or champagne if no producers choose to manufacture such items (there is only the right to manufacture them oneself). There are no "rights" of special groups, there are no "rights of farmers, of workers, of business-men, of employees, of employers, of the old, of the young, of the un-born." There are only *the Rights of Man*—rights possessed by every individual man and by *all* men as individuals.

Property rights and the right of free trade are man's only "economic rights" (they are, in fact, *political* rights)—and there can be no such thing as "an *economic* bill of rights." But observe that the advocates of the latter have all but destroyed the former.

["Man's Rights," *VOS*, 129; pb 96.]

It is only on the basis of property rights that the sphere and application of individual rights can be defined in any given social situation.

Without property rights, there is no way to solve or to avoid a hopeless chaos of clashing views, interests, demands, desires, and whims.

["The Cashing-in: The Student 'Rebellion,' " *CUI*, 259.]

The right to agree with others is not a problem in any society; it is *the right to disagree* that is crucial. It is the institution of private property that protects and implements the right to disagree—and thus keeps the road open to man's most valuable attribute (valuable personally, socially, and *objectively*): the creative mind.

["What Is Capitalism?" *CUI*, 19.]

The institution of private property, in the full, legal meaning of the term, was brought into existence only by capitalism. In the pre-capitalist eras, private property existed *de facto*, but not *de jure*, i.e., by custom and sufferance, not by right or by law. In law and in principle, all property belonged to the head of the tribe, the king, and was held only by his permission, which could be revoked at any time, at his pleasure. (The king could and did expropriate the estates of recalcitrant noblemen throughout the course of Europe's history.)

[Ibid., 13.]

See also CAPITALISM; CAUSALITY; COMMUNISM; CONTRACTS; FASCISM/NAZISM; FREE SPEECH; FREEDOM; HUMAN RIGHTS and PROPERTY RIGHTS; INDIVIDUAL RIGHTS; PATENTS and COPY- RIGHTS; PRODUCTION; SOCIALISM; STATISM.

Propositions.   Since concepts, in the field of cognition, perform a function similar to that of numbers in the field of mathematics, the function of a proposition is similar to that of an equation: it applies conceptual abstractions to a specific problem.

A proposition, however, can perform this function only if the concepts of which it is composed have precisely defined meanings. If, in the field of mathematics, numbers had no fixed, firm values, if they were mere approximations determined by the mood of their users—so that "5," for instance, could mean five in some calculations, but six-and-a-half or four-and-three-quarters in others, according to the users' "convenience"—there would be no such thing as the science of mathematics.

[*ITOE*, 100.]

See also CONCEPTS; DEFINITIONS; GRAMMAR; INDUCTION and DE- DUCTION; LANGUAGE; MEANING (of CONCEPTS); NUMBERS; THOUGHT/THINKING.

Psycho-Epistemology.   Psycho-epistemology is the study of man's cognitive processes from the aspect of the interaction between the conscious mind and the automatic functions of the subconscious.

["The Psycho-Epistemology of Art," *RM*, 20; pb 18.]

"Psycho-epistemology," a term coined by Ayn Rand, pertains not to the content of a man's ideas, but to his method of awareness, i.e., the method by which his mind habitually deals with its content."

[Leonard Peikoff, editor's footnote to Ayn Rand's "The Missing Link," *PWNI*, 47; pb 39.]

The subconscious is an integrating mechanism. Man's conscious mind observes and establishes connections among his experiences; the subconscious integrates the connections and makes them become automatic. For example, the skill of walking is acquired, after many faltering attempts, by the automatization of countless connections controlling muscular movements; once he learns to walk, a child needs no conscious awareness of such problems as posture, balance, length of step, etc.—the mere decision to walk brings the integrated total into his control.

A mind's cognitive development involves a continual process of automatization. For example, you cannot perceive a table as an infant perceives it—as a mysterious object with four legs. You perceive it as a table, i.e., a man-made piece of furniture, serving a certain purpose belonging to a human habitation, etc.; you cannot separate these attributes from your sight of the table, you experience it as a single, indivisible percept—yet all you see is a four-legged object; the rest is an automatized integration of a vast amount of conceptual knowledge which, at one time, you had to learn bit by bit. The same is true of everything you perceive or experience; as an adult, you cannot perceive or experience in a vacuum, you do it in a certain automatized *context*—and the efficiency of your mental operations depends on the kind of context your subconscious has automatized.

"Learning to speak is a process of automatizing the use (i.e., the meaning and the application) of concepts. And more: all learning involves a process of automatizing, i.e., of first acquiring knowledge by fully conscious, focused attention and observation, then of establishing mental connections which make that knowledge automatic (instantly available as a context), thus freeing man's mind to pursue further, more complex knowledge." *(Introduction to Objectivist Epistemology.)*

The process of forming, integrating and using concepts is not an automatic, but a volitional process—i.e., a process which uses both new and automatized material, but which is directed volitionally. It is not an innate, but an acquired skill; it has to be *learned*—it is the most crucially important part of learning—and all of man's other capacities depend on how well or how badly he learns it.

This skill does not pertain to the particular *content* of a man's knowledge at any given age, but to the *method* by which he acquires and organizes knowledge—the method by which his mind deals with its content. The method *programs* his subconscious computer, determining how efficiently, lamely or disastrously his cognitive processes will function. The programming of a man's subconscious consists of the kind of cognitive habits he acquires; these habits constitute his psycho-epistemology.

It is a child's early experiences, observations and subverbal conclusions that determine this programming. Thereafter, the interaction of content and method establishes a certain reciprocity: the method of acquiring knowledge affects its content, which affects the further development of the method, and so on.

["The Comprachicos," *NL*, 192.]

Most people know nothing about psycho-epistemology. They take their habitual method of thought for granted, leaving it unidentified and unquestioned. Yet this kind of ignorance can be disastrous. . . . Men can automatize wrong methods of thought without even knowing it. In order to achieve intellectual control, therefore, in order to enjoy the full power over your mind that volition makes possible, you must identify your psycho-epistemological methods, and correct those, if any, which are not consonant with your adult knowledge.

This is a crucial discovery of Miss Rand's—the discovery of psycho-epistemology, and of its roots, forms, and errors. Without such knowledge, men would be left at the mercy of unidentified mental habits that they hardly even suspected—habits that perhaps derived unknowingly from childhood errors that they long since had consciously renounced. Psycho-epistemology represents a whole science, a new branch of psychology.

[Leonard Peikoff, "The Philosophy of Objectivism"
lecture series (1976), Lecture 6.]

Men's epistemology—or, more precisely, their *psycho-epistemology*, their method of awareness—is the most fundamental standard by which they can be classified. Few men are consistent in that respect; most men keep switching from one level of awareness to another, according to the circumstances or the issues involved, ranging from moments of full rationality to an almost somnambulistic stupor. But the battle of human history is fought and determined by those who are predominantly consistent, those who, for good or evil, are committed to and motivated by their chosen psycho-epistemology and its corollary view of existence.

["For the New Intellectual," *FNI*, 18; pb 21.]

While the alleged advocates of reason oppose "system-building" and haggle apologetically over concrete-bound words or mystically floating abstractions, its enemies seem to know that *integration* is the psycho-epistemological key to reason, that art is man's psycho-epistemological conditioner, and that if reason is to be destroyed, it is man's integrating capacity that has to be destroyed.

["Art and Cognition," *RM*, pb 77.]

See also ANTI-CONCEPTUAL MENTALITY; AUTOMATIZATION; CONSCIOUSNESS; EPISTEMOLOGY; FREE WILL; INTEGRATION (MENTAL); LEARNING; PSYCHOLOGY; RATIONALITY; STYLE; SUB-CONSCIOUS.

"Psychologizing."

Just as reasoning, to an irrational person, becomes rationalizing, and moral judgment becomes moralizing, so psychological theories become *psychologizing*. The common denominator is the corruption of a cognitive process to serve an ulterior motive.

Psychologizing consists in condemning or excusing specific individuals on the grounds of their psychological problems, real or invented, in the absence of or contrary to factual evidence.

["The Psychology of 'Psychologizing,' " *TO*, March 1971, 2.]

While the racket of the philosophizing mystics rested on the claim that man is unable to know the external world, the racket of the psychologizing mystics rests on the claim that man is unable to know his own motivation.

[Ibid., 4.]

Armed with a smattering, not of knowledge, but of undigested slogans, they rush, unsolicited, to diagnose the problems of their friends and acquaintances. Pretentiousness and presumptuousness are the psychologizer's invariable characteristics: he not merely invades the privacy of his victims' minds, he claims to understand their minds better than they do, to know more than they do about their own motives. With reckless irresponsibility, which an old-fashioned mystic oracle would hesitate to match, he ascribes to his victims any motivation that suits his purpose, ignoring their denials. Since he is dealing with the great "unknowable"—which used to be life after death or extrasensory perception, but is now man's subconscious—all rules of evidence, logic and proof are suspended, and anything goes (which is what attracts him to his racket).

[Ibid., 2.]

A man's moral character must be judged on the basis of his actions, his statements and his conscious convictions—not on the basis of inferences (usually, spurious) about his subconscious.

A man is not to be condemned or excused on the grounds of the state of his subconscious.

[Ibid., 5.]

See also ARGUMENT from INTIMIDATION; CHARACTER; MORAL JUDGMENT; MYSTICISM; PSYCHOLOGY; RATIONALIZATION; SUBCONSCIOUS.

Psychology.   The task of evaluating the processes of man's subconscious is the province of psychology. Psychology does not regard its subject morally, but medically—i.e., from the aspect of health or malfunction (with cognitive competence as the proper standard of health).

["The Psychology of 'Psychologizing,' " TO, March 1971, 5.]

As a science, psychology is barely making its first steps. It is still in the anteroom of science, in the stage of observing and gathering material from which a future science will come. This stage may be compared to the pre-Socratic period in philosophy; psychology has not yet found a Plato, let alone an Aristotle, to organize its material, systematize its problems and define its fundamental principles.

[Ibid., 2.]

In psychology, one school holds that man, by nature, is a helpless, guilt-ridden, instinct-driven automaton—while another school objects that this is not true, because there is no scientific evidence to prove that man is conscious.

["Faith and Force: The Destroyers of the
Modern World," PWNI, 86; pb 71.]

Psychology departments have a sprinkling of Freudians, but are dominated by Behaviorism, whose leader is B. F. Skinner. (Here the controversy is between the claim that man is moved by innate ideas, and the claim that he has no ideas at all.)

["Fairness Doctrine for Education," PWNI, 235; pb 192.]

See Conceptual Index: Psychology.

"Public Interest," the.   Since there is no such entity as "the public," since the public is merely a number of individuals, any claimed or
implied conflict of "the public interest" with private interests means that
the interests of some men are to be sacrificed to the interests and wishes
of others. Since the concept is so conveniently undefinable, its use rests
only on any given gang's ability to proclaim that "The public, *c'est moi*"
—and to maintain the claim at the point of a gun.

["The Monument Builders," *VOS,* 116; pb 88.]

So long as a concept such as "the public interest" (or the "social" or
"national" or "international" interest) is regarded as a valid principle to
guide legislation—lobbies and pressure groups will necessarily continue
to exist. Since there is no such entity as *"the public,"* since the public is
merely a number of individuals, the idea that "the public interest"
supersedes private interests and rights, can have but one meaning: that
the interests and rights of some individuals take precedence over the
interests and rights of others.

If so, then all men and all private groups have to fight to the death
for the privilege of being regarded as "the public." The government's
policy has to swing like an erratic pendulum from group to group,
hitting some and favoring others, at the whim of any given moment—
and so grotesque a profession as lobbying (selling "influence") becomes
a full-time job. If parasitism, favoritism, corruption, and greed for the
unearned did not exist, a mixed economy would bring them into existence.

Since there is no rational justification for the sacrifice of some men to
others, there is no objective criterion by which such a sacrifice can be
guided in practice. All "public interest" legislation (and any distribution
of money taken by force from some men for the unearned benefit of
others) comes down ultimately to the grant of an undefined, undefinable, non-objective, arbitrary power to some government officials.

The worst aspect of it is not that such a power can be used dishonestly,
but that *it cannot be used honestly.* The wisest man in the world, with the
purest integrity, cannot find a criterion for the just, equitable, rational
application of an unjust, inequitable, irrational principle.

["The Pull Peddlers," *CUI,* 170.]

There is no such thing as "the public interest" except as the sum of
the interests of individual men. And the basic, common interest of all
men—all *rational* men—is freedom. *Freedom* is the first requirement of
"the public interest"—not *what* men do when they are free, but *that* they
are free. All their achievements rest on that foundation—and cannot
exist without it.

The principles of a free, non-coercive social system are the only form of "the public interest."

["The Fascist New Frontier," pamphlet, 13.]

I could say to you that you do not serve the public good—that nobody's good can be achieved at the price of human sacrifices—that when you violate the rights of one man, you have violated the rights of all, and a public of rightless creatures is doomed to destruction. I could say to you that you will and can achieve nothing but universal devastation —as any looter must, when he runs out of victims. I could say it, but I won't. It is not your particular policy that I challenge, but your moral premise. If it were true that men·could achieve their good by means of turning some men into sacrificial animals, and I were asked to immolate myself for the sake of creatures who wanted to survive at the price of my blood, if I were asked to serve the interests of society apart from, above and against my own—I would refuse, I would reject it as the most contemptible evil, I would fight it with every power I possess, I would fight the whole of mankind, if one minute were all I could last before I were murdered, I would fight in the full confidence of the justice of my battle and of a living being's right to exist. Let there be no misunderstanding about me. If it is now the belief of my fellow men, who call themselves the public, that their good requires victims, then I say: The public good be damned, I will have no part of it!

["The Moral Meaning of Capitalism," *FNI*, 116; pb 98.]

See also CAPITALISM; COLLECTIVISM; "COMMON GOOD"; FREEDOM; INDIVIDUAL RIGHTS; LOBBYING; MIXED ECONOMY; SACRIFICE; SOCIETY; WELFARE STATE.

Public Property. When you clamor for public ownership of the means of production, you are clamoring for public ownership of the mind.

[GS, *FNI*, 208; pb 166.]

Since "public property" is a collectivist fiction, since the public as a whole can neither use nor dispose of its "property," that "property" will always be taken over by some political "elite," by a small clique which will then rule the public—a public of literal, dispossessed proletarians.

["The Property Status of Airwaves," *CUI*, 128.]

See also COLLECTIVISM; GOVERNMENT; PROPERTY RIGHTS.

Purchasing Power. Purchasing power is an attribute of producers, not of consumers. Purchasing power is a consequence of production: it is the power of possessing goods which one can trade for other goods. A *"purchase"* is an exchange of goods (or services) for goods (or services). Any other form of transferring goods from one person to another may belong to many different categories of transactions, but it is *not a purchase*. It may be a gift, a loan, an inheritance, a handout, a fraud, a theft, a robbery, a burglary, an expropriation. In regard to services, however (omitting temporary or occasional acts of friendship, in which the payment is the friend's value), there is only one alternative to trading: unpaid services, i.e., slavery.

["Hunger and Freedom," *ARL*, III, 22, 3.]

See also CAPITALISM; CONSUMPTION; CREDIT; ECONOMIC POWER *vs.* POLITICAL POWER; FREE MARKET; INFLATION; MONEY; PRODUCTION; TRADER PRINCIPLE.

Purpose. The three cardinal values of the Objectivist ethics—the three values which, together, are the means to and the realization of one's ultimate value, one's own life—are: Reason, Purpose, Self-Esteem, with their three corresponding virtues: Rationality, Productiveness, Pride.

Productive work is the central *purpose* of a rational man's life, the central value that integrates and determines the hierarchy of all his other values. Reason is the source, the precondition of his productive work—pride is the result.

["The Objectivist Ethics," *VOS*, 19; pb 25.]

A central purpose serves to integrate all the other concerns of a man's life. It establishes the hierarchy, the relative importance, of his values, it saves him from pointless inner conflicts, it permits him to enjoy life on a wide scale and to carry that enjoyment into any area open to his mind; whereas a man without a purpose is lost in chaos. He does not know what his values are. He does not know how to judge. He cannot tell what is or is not important to him, and, therefore, he drifts helplessly at the mercy of any chance stimulus or any whim of the moment. He can enjoy nothing. He spends his life searching for some value which he will never find. . . .

The man without a purpose is a man who drifts at the mercy of random feelings or unidentified urges and is capable of any evil, because he is totally out of control of his own life. In order to be in control of your life, you have to have a purpose—a productive purpose. . . .

The man who has no purpose, but has to act, acts to destroy others. That is not the same thing as a productive or creative purpose.

["*Playboy's* Interview with Ayn Rand," pamphlet, 6.]

See also CAREER; PRIDE; PRODUCTIVENESS; RATIONALITY; REA-
SON; STANDARD of VALUE; ULTIMATE VALUE; VALUES.

Pursuit of Happiness, Right to.   The Right to the Pursuit of
Happiness means man's right to live for himself, to choose what constitutes his own private, personal, individual happiness and to work for its
achievement, so long as he respects the same right in others. It means
that man cannot be forced to devote his life to the happiness of another
man nor of any number of other men. It means that the collective
cannot decide what is to be the purpose of a man's existence nor prescribe his choice of happiness.

["Textbook of Americanism," pamphlet, 5.]

Observe, in this context, the intellectual precision of the Founding
Fathers: they spoke of the right to *the pursuit* of happiness—*not* of the
right to happiness. It means that a man has the right to take the actions
he deems necessary to achieve his happiness; it does *not* mean that
others must make him happy.

["Man's Rights," *VOS*, 129; pb 97.]

See also FOUNDING FATHERS; HAPPINESS; INDIVIDUAL RIGHTS;
SELFISHNESS.

Pyramid of Ability.   When you live in a rational society, where
men are free to trade, you receive an incalculable bonus: the material
value of your work is determined not only by your effort, but by the
effort of the best productive minds who exist in the world around you.

When you work in a modern factory, you are paid, not only for your
labor, but for all the productive genius which has made that factory
possible: for the work of the industrialist who built it, for the work of
the investor who saved the money to risk on the untried and the new,
for the work of the engineer who designed the machines of which you
are pushing the levers, for the work of the inventor who created the
product which you spend your time on making, for the work of the
scientist who discovered the laws that went into the making of that
product, for the work of the philosopher who taught men how to think
and whom you spend your time denouncing.

The machine, the frozen form of a living intelligence, is the power
that expands the potential of your life by raising the productivity of
your time. If you worked as a blacksmith in the mystics' Middle Ages,
the whole of your earning capacity would consist of an iron bar produced by your hands in days and days of effort. How many tons of rail
do you produce per day if you work for Hank Rearden? Would you

dare to claim that the size of your pay check was created solely by your physical labor and that those rails were the product of your muscles? The standard of living of that blacksmith is all that your muscles are worth; the rest is a gift from Hank Rearden.

[GS, *FNI*, 233; pb 185.]

In proportion to the mental energy he spent, the man who creates a new invention receives but a small percentage of his value in terms of material payment, no matter what fortune he makes, no matter what millions he earns. But the man who works as a janitor in the factory producing that invention, receives an enormous payment in proportion to the mental effort that his job requires of *him*. And the same is true of all men between, on all levels of ambition and ability. The man at the top of the intellectual pyramid contributes the most to all those below him, but gets nothing except his material payment, receiving no intellectual bonus from others to add to the value of his time. The man at the bottom who, left to himself, would starve in his hopeless ineptitude, contributes nothing to those above him, but receives the bonus of all of their brains. Such is the nature of the "competition" between the strong and the weak of the intellect. Such is the pattern of "exploitation" for which you have damned the strong.

[Ibid., 234; pb 186.]

See also CAPITALISM; COMPETITION; CREATORS; FREE MARKET; INVESTMENT; MEDIOCRITY; PRODUCTION; PRODUCTIVENESS; TECHNOLOGY.

Q

Quotas. The notion of racial quotas is so obviously an expression of racism that no lengthy discussion is necessary. If a young man is barred from a school or a job because the quota for his particular race has been filled, he is barred by reason of his race. Telling him that those admitted are his "representatives," is adding insult to injury. To demand such quotas in the name of fighting racial discrimination, is an obscene mockery.

["Representation Without Authorization," *ARL*, I, 21, 2.]

The quota doctrine assumes that all members of a given physiological group are identical and interchangeable—not merely in the eyes of other people, but in their own eyes and minds. Assuming a total merging of the self with the group, the doctrine holds that it makes no difference to a man whether *he* or his "representative" is admitted to a school, gets a job, or makes a decision.

[Ibid., 3.]

The inversion of all standards—the propagation of racism as anti-racist, of injustice as just, of immorality as moral, and the reasoning behind it, which is worse than the offenses—is flagrantly evident in the policy of preferential treatment for minorities (i.e., racial quotas) in employment and education.

["Moral Inflation," *ARL*, III, 14, 1.]

No man, neither Negro nor white, has any claim to the property of another man. A man's rights are not violated by a private individual's refusal to deal with him. Racism is an evil, irrational and morally contemptible doctrine—but doctrines cannot be forbidden or prescribed by law. Just as we have to protect a communist's freedom of speech, even though his doctrines are evil, so we have to protect a racist's right to the use and disposal of his own property. Private racism is not a legal, but a moral issue—and can be fought only by private means, such as economic boycott or social ostracism.

["Racism," *VOS*, 184; pb 134.]

See also "ETHNICITY"; PROPERTY RIGHTS; RACISM; TRIBALISM.

R

Racism. Racism is the lowest, most crudely primitive form of collectivism. It is the notion of ascribing moral, social or political significance to a man's genetic lineage—the notion that a man's intellectual and characterological traits are produced and transmitted by his internal body chemistry. Which means, in practice, that a man is to be judged, not by his own character and actions, but by the characters and actions of a collective of ancestors.

Racism claims that the content of a man's mind (not his cognitive apparatus, but its *content*) is inherited; that a man's convictions, values and character are determined before he is born, by physical factors beyond his control. This is the caveman's version of the doctrine of innate ideas—or of inherited knowledge—which has been thoroughly refuted by philosophy and science. Racism is a doctrine of, by and for brutes. It is a barnyard or stock-farm version of collectivism, appropriate to a mentality that differentiates between various breeds of animals, but not between animals and men.

Like every form of determinism, racism invalidates the specific attribute which distinguishes man from all other living species: his rational faculty. Racism negates two aspects of man's life: reason and choice, or mind and morality, replacing them with chemical predestination.

["Racism," *VOS*, 172; pb 126.]

A genius is a genius, regardless of the number of morons who belong to the same race—and a moron is a moron, regardless of the number of geniuses who share his racial origin.

[Ibid., 174; pb 127.]

Like every other form of collectivism, racism is a quest for the unearned. It is a quest for automatic knowledge—for an automatic evaluation of men's characters that bypasses the responsibility of exercising rational or moral judgment—and, above all, a quest for *an automatic self-esteem* (or pseudo-self-esteem).

[Ibid.]

Today, racism is regarded as a crime if practiced by a majority—but as an inalienable right if practiced by a minority. The notion that one's culture is superior to all others solely because it represents the traditions of one's ancestors, is regarded as chauvinism if claimed by a majority—

but as "ethnic" pride if claimed by a minority. Resistance to change and progress is regarded as reactionary if demonstrated by a majority—but retrogression to a Balkan village, to an Indian tepee or to the jungle is hailed if demonstrated by a minority.

["The Age of Envy," *NL*, 167.]

See also ANTI-CONCEPTUAL MENTALITY; COLLECTIVISM; DETER-MINISM; "ETHNICITY"; FASCISM/NAZISM; FREE WILL; INDIVID-UALISM; POLYLOGISM; REASON; SELF-ESTEEM; SOVIET RUSSIA; TRIBALISM.

"Rand's Razor." The requirements of cognition determine the *objective* criteria of conceptualization. They can be summed up best in the form of an epistemological "razor": *concepts are not to be multiplied beyond necessity*—the corollary of which is: *nor are they to be integrated in disregard of necessity*.

[*ITOE*, 96.]

The requirements of cognition forbid the arbitrary grouping of existents, both in regard to isolation and to integration. They forbid the random coining of special concepts to designate any and every group of existents with any possible combination of characteristics. For example, there is no concept to designate "Beautiful blondes with blue eyes, 5'5" tall and 24 years old." Such entities or groupings are identified *descriptively*. If such a special concept existed, it would lead to senseless duplication of cognitive effort (and to conceptual chaos): everything of significance discovered about that group would apply to all other young women as well. There would be no cognitive justification for such a concept—unless some *essential* characteristic were discovered, distinguishing such blondes from all other women and requiring special study, in which case a special concept would become necessary. . . .

In the process of determining conceptual classification, neither the essential similarities nor the essential differences among existents may be ignored, evaded or omitted once they have been observed. Just as the requirements of cognition forbid the arbitrary subdivision of concepts, so they forbid the arbitrary integration of concepts into a wider concept by means of obliterating their *essential* differences—which is an error (or falsification) proceeding from definitions by non-essentials. (This is the method involved in the obliteration of valid concepts by means of "anti-concepts.")

[*ITOE*, 94.]

See also "ANTI-CONCEPTS"; CONCEPT-FORMATION; CONCEPTS; DEFINITIONS; INTEGRATION (MENTAL); INVALID CONCEPTS; OB-JECTIVITY; "PACKAGE-DEALING," FALLACY of; UNIT-ECONOMY.

Rationality. Rationality is man's basic virtue, the source of all his other virtues. Man's basic vice, the source of all his evils, is the act of unfocusing his mind, the suspension of his consciousness, which is not blindness, but the refusal to see, not ignorance, but the refusal to know. Irrationality is the rejection of man's means of survival and, therefore, a commitment to a course of blind destruction; that which is anti-mind, is anti-life.

The virtue of *Rationality* means the recognition and acceptance of reason as one's only source of knowledge, one's only judge of values and one's only guide to action. It means one's total commitment to a state of full, conscious awareness, to the maintenance of a full mental focus in all issues, in all choices, in all of one's waking hours. It means a commitment to the fullest perception of reality within one's power and to the constant, active expansion of one's perception, i.e., of one's knowledge. It means a commitment to the reality of one's own existence, i.e., to the principle that all of one's goals, values and actions take place in reality and, therefore, that one must never place any value or consideration whatsoever above one's perception of reality. It means a commitment to the principle that all of one's convictions, values, goals, desires and actions must be based on, derived from, chosen and validated by a process of thought—as precise and scrupulous a process of thought, directed by as ruthlessly strict an application of logic, as one's fullest capacity permits. It means one's acceptance of the responsibility of forming one's own judgments and of living by the work of one's own mind (which is the virtue of Independence). It means that one must never sacrifice one's convictions to the opinions or wishes of others (which is the virtue of Integrity)—that one must never attempt to fake reality in any manner (which is the virtue of Honesty)—that one must never seek or grant the unearned and undeserved, neither in matter nor in spirit (which is the virtue of Justice). It means that one must never desire effects without causes, and that one must never enact a cause without assuming full responsibility for its effects—that one must never act like a zombie, i.e., without knowing one's own purposes and motives—that one must never make any decisions, form any convictions or seek any values out of context, i.e., apart from or against the total, integrated sum of one's knowledge—and, above all, that one must never seek to get away with contradictions. It means the rejection of any form of *mysticism*, i.e., any claim to some nonsensory, nonrational, nondefinable, supernatural source of knowledge. It means a commitment to reason, not in sporadic fits or on selected issues or in special emergencies, but as a permanent way of life.

["The Objectivist Ethics," *VOS*, 20; pb 25.]

Rationality is the recognition of the fact that existence exists, that nothing can alter the truth and nothing can take precedence over that act of perceiving it, which is thinking—that the mind is one's only judge of values and one's only guide of action—that reason is an absolute that permits no compromise—that a concession to the irrational invalidates one's consciousness and turns it from the task of perceiving to the task of faking reality—that the alleged short-cut to knowledge, which is faith, is only a short-circuit destroying the mind—that the acceptance of a mystical invention is a wish for the annihilation of existence and, properly, annihilates one's consciousness.

[GS, *FNI*, 157; pb 128.]

To the extent to which a man is rational, life is the premise directing his actions. To the extent to which he is irrational, the premise directing his actions is death.

[Ibid., 156; pb 127.]

A rational process is a *moral* process. You may make an error at any step of it, with nothing to protect you but your own severity, or you may try to cheat, to fake the evidence and evade the effort of the quest—but if devotion to truth is the hallmark of morality, then there is no greater, nobler, more heroic form of devotion than the act of a man who assumes the responsibility of thinking.

[Ibid., 155; pb 126.]

See also ABSOLUTES; EXISTENCE; EVASION; EVIL; FOCUS; HONESTY; INDEPENDENCE; INTEGRITY; JUSTICE; LOGIC; MORALITY; MYSTICISM; PRIDE; PRIMACY of EXISTENCE vs. PRIMACY of CONSCIOUSNESS; PRODUCTIVENESS; REASON; THOUGHT/THINKING; VIRTUE.

Rationalism vs. Empiricism.   [Philosophers came to be divided] into two camps: those who claimed that man obtains his knowledge of the world by deducing it exclusively from concepts, which come from inside his head and are not derived from the perception of physical facts (the Rationalists)—and those who claimed that man obtains his knowledge from experience, which was held to mean: by direct perception of immediate facts, with no recourse to concepts (the Empiricists). To put it more simply: those who joined the [mystics] by abandoning reality—and those who clung to reality, by abandoning their mind.

["For the New Intellectual," *FNI*, 31; pb 30.]

See also CONCEPTS; EPISTEMOLOGY; INDUCTION and DEDUCTION; KANT, IMMANUEL; KNOWLEDGE; LOGIC; PERCEPTION; PHILOSOPHY; REASON.

Rationalization.   Since an emotion is experienced as an immediate primary, but is, in fact, a complex, derivative sum, it permits men to practice one of the ugliest of psychological phenomena: *rationalization.* Rationalization is a cover-up, a process of providing one's emotions with a false identity, of giving them spurious explanations and justifications —in order to hide one's motives, not just from others, but primarily from oneself. The price of rationalizing is the hampering, the distortion and, ultimately, the destruction of one's cognitive faculty. Rationalization is a process not of perceiving reality, but of attempting to make reality fit one's emotions.

Philosophical catch phrases are handy means of rationalization. They are quoted, repeated and perpetuated in order to justify feelings which men are unwilling to admit.

"Nobody can be certain of anything" is a rationalization for a feeling of envy and hatred toward those who *are* certain. "It may be true for you, but it's not true for me" is a rationalization for one's inability and unwillingness to prove the validity of one's contentions. "Nobody is perfect in this world" is a rationalization for the desire to continue indulging in one's imperfections, i.e., the desire to escape morality. "Nobody can help anything he does" is a rationalization for the escape from moral responsibility. "It may have been true yesterday, but it's not true today" is a rationalization for the desire to get away with contradictions. "Logic has nothing to do with reality" is a crude rationalization for a desire to subordinate reality to one's whims.

"I can't prove it, but I *feel* that it's true" is more than a rationalization: it is a description of the process of rationalizing. Men do not accept a catch phrase by a process of thought, they seize upon a catch phrase— *any* catch phrase—because it fits their emotions. Such men do not judge the truth of a statement by its correspondence to reality—they judge reality by its correspondence to their feelings.

If, in the course of philosophical detection, you find yourself, at times, stopped by the indignantly bewildered question: "How could anyone arrive at such nonsense?"—you will begin to understand it when you discover that *evil philosophies are systems of rationalization.*

["Philosophical Detection," *PWNI,* 21; pb 18.]

When a theory achieves nothing but the opposite of its alleged goals, yet its advocates remain undeterred, you may be certain that it is not a conviction or an "ideal," but a rationalization.

[Ibid., 24; pb 20.]

See also EMOTIONS; LOGIC; MORAL JUDGMENT; MORALITY; OB-
JECTIVITY; PHILOSOPHY; PROOF; RATIONALITY; SUBCONSCIOUS.

Reality.   *See Existence.*

Reason.   Reason is the faculty that identifies and integrates the material provided by man's senses.

["The Objectivist Ethics," *VOS*, 13; pb 20.]

Reason integrates man's perceptions by means of forming abstractions or conceptions, thus raising man's knowledge from the *perceptual*
level, which he shares with animals, to the *conceptual* level, which he
alone can reach. The *method* which reason employs in this process is *logic*
—and logic is the art of *non-contradictory identification.*

["Faith and Force: The Destroyers of the
Modern World," *PWNI*, 75; pb 62.]

Reason is man's only means of grasping reality and of acquiring
knowledge—and, therefore, the rejection of reason means that men
should act regardless of and/or in contradiction to the facts of reality.

["The Left: Old and New," *NL*, 84.]

The senses, concepts, logic: these are the elements of man's rational
faculty—its start, its form, its method. In essence, "follow reason"
means: base knowledge on observation; form concepts according to the
actual (measurable) relationships among concretes; use concepts according to the rules of logic (ultimately, the Law of Identity). Since each of
these elements is based on the facts of reality, the conclusions reached
by a process of reason are *objective.*
The alternative to reason is some form of mysticism or skepticism.

[Leonard Peikoff, *OP*, 332; pb 305.]

[Reason] is a faculty that man has to exercise *by choice.* Thinking is not
an automatic function. In any hour and issue of his life, man is free to
think or to evade that effort.

["The Objectivist Ethics," *VOS*, 13; pb 20.]

Man's essential characteristic is his rational faculty. Man's mind is his
basic means of survival—his only means of gaining knowledge. . . .
In order to sustain its life, every living species has to follow a certain
course of action required by its nature. The action required to sustain
human life is primarily intellectual: everything man needs has to be

discovered by his mind and produced by his effort. Production is the application of reason to the problem of survival.

["What Is Capitalism?" *CUI*, 16.]

To live, man must hold three things as the supreme and ruling values of his life: Reason—Purpose—Self-esteem. Reason, as his only tool of knowledge—Purpose, as his choice of the happiness which that tool must proceed to achieve—Self-esteem, as his inviolate certainty that his mind is competent to think and his person is worthy of happiness, which means: is worthy of living.

[GS, *FNI*, 156; pb 128.]

Reason is man's tool of knowledge, the faculty that enables him to perceive the facts of reality. To act rationally means to act in accordance with the facts of reality. Emotions are not tools of cognition. What you feel tells you nothing about the facts; it merely tells you something about your estimate of the facts. Emotions are the result of your value judgments; they are caused by your basic premises, which you may hold consciously or subconsciously, which may be right or wrong.

["*Playboy*'s Interview with Ayn Rand," pamphlet, 6.]

There is no necessary clash, no dichotomy between man's reason and his emotions—provided he observes their proper relationship. A rational man knows—or makes it a point to discover—the source of his emotions, the basic premises from which they come; if his premises are wrong, he corrects them. He never acts on emotions for which he cannot account, the meaning of which he does not understand. In appraising a situation, he knows why he reacts as he does and whether he is right. He has no inner conflicts, his mind and his emotions are integrated, his consciousness is in perfect harmony. His emotions are not his enemies, they are his means of enjoying life. But they are not his guide; the guide is his mind. This relationship cannot be reversed, however. If a man takes his emotions as the cause and his mind as their passive effect, if he is guided by his emotions and uses his mind only to rationalize or justify them somehow—*then* he is acting immorally, he is condemning himself to misery, failure, defeat, and he will achieve nothing but destruction—his own and that of others.

[Ibid.]

I have said that faith and force are corollaries, and that mysticism will always lead to the rule of brutality. The cause of it is contained in the very nature of mysticism. *Reason* is the only *objective* means of communication and of understanding among men; when men deal with one another by means of reason, reality is their *objective* standard and frame of reference. But when men claim to possess supernatural means of knowledge, no persuasion, communication or understanding are possible. Why do we kill wild animals in the jungle? Because no other way of dealing with them is open to us. And *that* is the state to which mysticism reduces mankind—a state where, in case of disagreement, men have no recourse except to physical violence.

> ["Faith and Force: The Destroyers of the
> Modern World," *PWNI*, 85; pb 70.]

Man's mind is his basic means of survival—and of self-protection. Reason is the most *selfish* human faculty: it has to be used in and by a man's own mind, and its product—truth—makes him inflexible, intransigent, impervious to the power of any pack or any ruler. Deprived of the ability to reason, man becomes a docile, pliant, impotent chunk of clay, to be shaped into any subhuman form and used for any purpose by anyone who wants to bother.

There has never been a philosophy, a theory or a doctrine that attacked (or "limited") reason, which did not also preach submission to the power of some authority. Philosophically, most men do not understand the issue to this day; but psycho-epistemologically, they have sensed it since prehistoric times. Observe the nature of mankind's earliest legends—such as the fall of Lucifer, "the light-bearer," for the sin of defying authority; or the story of Prometheus, who taught men the practical arts of survival. Power-seekers have always known that if men are to be made submissive, the obstacle is not their feelings, their wishes or their "instincts," but their minds; if men are to be ruled, then the enemy is reason.

> ["The Comprachicos," *NL*, 227.]

Only three brief periods of history were culturally dominated by a philosophy of reason: ancient Greece, the Renaissance, the nineteenth century. These three periods were the source of mankind's greatest progress in all fields of intellectual achievement—and the eras of greatest political freedom.

> ["The Intellectual Bankruptcy of Our Age," pamphlet, 5.]

Western civilization was the child and product of reason—via ancient Greece. In all other civilizations, reason has always been the menial servant—the handmaiden—of mysticism. You may observe the results. It is only Western culture that has ever been dominated—imperfectly, incompletely, precariously and at rare intervals—but still, dominated by reason. You may observe the results of that.

The conflict of reason versus mysticism is the issue of life or death—of freedom or slavery—of progress or stagnant brutality. Or, to put it another way, it is the conflict of consciousness versus unconsciousness.

["Faith and Force: The Destroyers of the Modern World," *PWNI*, 75; pb 62.]

If you rebel against reason, if you succumb to the old bromides of the Witch Doctors, such as: "Reason is the enemy of the artist" or "The cold hand of reason dissects and destroys the joyous spontaneity of man's creative imagination"—I suggest that you take note of the following fact: by rejecting reason and surrendering to the unhampered sway of their unleashed emotions (and whims), the apostles of irrationality, the existentialists, the Zen Buddhists, the non-objective artists, have not achieved a free, joyous, triumphant sense of life, but a sense of doom, nausea and screaming, cosmic terror. Then read the stories of O. Henry or listen to the music of Viennese operettas and remember that these were the products of the spirit of the nineteenth century—a century ruled by the "cold, dissecting" hand of reason. And then ask yourself: which psycho-epistemology is appropriate to man, which is consonant with the facts of reality and with man's nature?

["The Esthetic Vacuum of Our Age," *RM*, 119; pb 128.]

I am not *primarily* an advocate of capitalism, but of egoism; and I am not *primarily* an advocate of egoism, but of reason. If one recognizes the supremacy of reason and applies it consistently, all the rest follows.

This—the supremacy of reason—was, is and will be the primary concern of my work, and the essence of Objectivism. (For a definition of reason, see *Introduction to Objectivist Epistemology*.) Reason in epistemology leads to egoism in ethics, which leads to capitalism in politics.

["Brief Summary," *TO*, Sept. 1971, 1.]

See also ART; AXIOMS; CAPITALISM; CONCEPTS; EMOTIONS; EPISTEMOLOGY; FREE WILL; HISTORY; INDIVIDUAL RIGHTS; KANT, IMMANUEL; KNOWLEDGE; LOGIC; MAN; MORALITY; OBJECTIVISM; OBJECTIVITY; PERCEPTION; PHYSICAL FORCE; PRODUCTION; RATIONALISM vs. EMPIRICISM; SELF-ESTEEM; SELFISHNESS; THOUGHT/THINKING.

"Redistribution" of Wealth. If a man proposes to redistribute wealth, he means explicitly and necessarily that the wealth is his to distribute. If he proposes it in the name of the government, then the wealth belongs to the government; if in the name of society, then it belongs to society. No one, to my knowledge, did or could define a difference between that proposal and the basic principle of communism.

["The Dead End," *ARL*, I, 20, 2.]

Observe that any social movement which begins by "redistributing" income, ends up by distributing sacrifices.

["The Fascist New Frontier," pamphlet, 5.]

Whoever claims the "right" to "redistribute" the wealth produced by others is claiming the "right" to treat human beings as chattel.

["The Monument Builders," *VOS*, 120; pb 91.]

See also COLLECTIVISM; COMMUNISM; MONEY; PROPERTY RIGHTS; SACRIFICE.

Reification of the Zero *See Zero, Reification of.*

Religion. PLAYBOY: Has no religion, in your estimation, ever offered anything of constructive value to human life?
RAND: Qua religion, no—in the sense of blind belief, belief unsupported by, or contrary to, the facts of reality and the conclusions of reason. Faith, as such, is extremely detrimental to human life: it is the negation of reason. But you must remember that religion is an early form of philosophy, that the first attempts to explain the universe, to give a coherent frame of reference to man's life and a code of moral values, were made by religion, before men graduated or developed enough to have philosophy. And, as philosophies, some religions have very valuable moral points. They may have a good influence or proper principles to inculcate, but in a very contradictory context and, on a very—how should I say it?—dangerous or malevolent base: on the ground of faith.

["*Playboy*'s Interview with Ayn Rand," pamphlet, 10.]

Christ, in terms of the Christian philosophy, is the human ideal. He personifies that which men should strive to emulate. Yet, according to the Christian mythology, he died on the cross not for his own sins but for the sins of the nonideal people. In other words, a man of perfect virtue was sacrificed for men who are vicious and who are expected or supposed to accept that sacrifice. If I were a Christian, nothing could make me more indignant than that: the notion of sacrificing the ideal to the nonideal, or virtue to vice. And it is in the name of that symbol that men are asked to sacrifice themselves for their inferiors. That is precisely how the symbolism is used.

[Ibid.]

What is the nature of the guilt that your teachers call [man's] Original Sin? What are the evils man acquired when he fell from a state they consider perfection? Their myth declares that he ate the fruit of the tree of knowledge—he acquired a mind and became a rational being. It was the knowledge of good and evil—he became a moral being. He was sentenced to earn his bread by his labor—he became a productive being. He was sentenced to experience desire—he acquired the capacity of sexual enjoyment. The evils for which they damn him are reason, morality, creativeness, joy—all the cardinal values of his existence. It is not his vices that their myth of man's fall is designed to explain and condemn, it is not his errors that they hold as his guilt, but the essence of his nature as man. Whatever he was—that robot in the Garden of Eden, who existed without mind, without values, without labor, without love —he was not man.

Man's fall, according to your teachers, was that he gained the virtues required to live. These virtues, by their standard, are his Sin. His evil, they charge, is that he's man. His guilt, they charge, is that he lives.

They call it a morality of mercy and a doctrine of love for man.

No, they say, they do not preach that man is evil, the evil is only that alien object: his body. No, they say, they do not wish to kill him, they only wish to make him lose his body. They seek to help him, they say, against his pain—and they point at the torture rack to which they've tied him, the rack with two wheels that pull him in opposite directions, the rack of the doctrine that splits his soul and body.

[*GS, FNI*, 169; pb 137.]

The good, say the mystics of spirit, is God, a being whose only definition is that he is beyond man's power to conceive—a definition that invalidates man's consciousness and nullifies his concepts of existence. . . . Man's mind, say the mystics of spirit, must be subordinated to the will of God. . . . Man's standard of value, say the mystics of spirit, is the pleasure of God, whose standards are beyond man's power of comprehension and must be accepted on faith. . . . The purpose of man's life . . . is to become an abject zombie who serves a purpose he does not know, for reasons he is not to question.

[*Ibid.*, 171; pb 139.]

The kind of sense of life that produced the [papal] encyclical *"Populorum Progressio"* . . . was not produced by the sense of life of any one person, but by the sense of life of an institution.

The dominant chord of the encyclical's sense of life is hatred for man's *mind*—hence hatred for man—hence hatred for life and for this earth—hence hatred for man's enjoyment of his life on earth—and hence, as a last and least consequence, hatred for the only social system that makes all these values possible in practice: capitalism.

["Requiem for Man," *CUI*, 304.]

The encyclical is the voice of the Dark Ages, rising again in today's intellectual vacuum, like a cold wind whistling through the empty streets of an abandoned civilization.

Unable to resolve a lethal contradiction, the conflict between individualism and altruism, the West is giving up. When men give up reason and freedom, the vacuum is filled by faith and force.

No social system can stand for long without a moral base. Project a magnificent skyscraper being built on quicksands: while men are struggling upward to add the hundredth and two-hundredth stories, the tenth and twentieth are vanishing, sucked under by the muck. That is the history of capitalism, of its swaying, tottering attempt to stand erect on the foundation of the altruist morality.

It's either-or. If capitalism's befuddled, guilt-ridden apologists do not know it, two fully consistent representatives of altruism do know it: Catholicism and communism.

Their rapprochement, therefore, is not astonishing. Their differences pertain only to the supernatural, but here, in reality, on earth, they have three cardinal elements in common: the same morality, altruism—the same goal, global rule by force—the same enemy, man's mind.

There is a precedent for their strategy. In the German election of 1933, the communists supported the Nazis, on the premise that they could fight each other for power later, but must first destroy their common enemy, capitalism. Today, Catholicism and communism may well cooperate, on the premise that they will fight each other for power later, but must first destroy their common enemy, the individual, by forcing mankind to unite to form one neck ready for one leash.

[Ibid., 316.]

Is there any difference between the encyclical's philosophy and communism? I am perfectly willing, on this matter, to take the word of an eminent Catholic authority. Under the headline: "Encyclical Termed Rebuff to Marxism," *The New York Times* of March 31, 1967, reports: "The Rev. John Courtney Murray, the prominent Jesuit theologian, described Pope Paul's newest encyclical yesterday as 'the church's definitive answer to Marxism.' . . . 'The Marxists have proposed one way, and in pursuing their program they rely on man alone,' Father Murray said. 'Now Pope Paul VI has issued a detailed plan to accomplish the same goal on the basis of true humanism—humanism that recognizes man's religious nature.' "

Amen.

So much for those American "conservatives" who claim that religion is the base of capitalism—and who believe that they can have capitalism and eat it, too, as the moral cannibalism of the altruist ethics demands.

And so much for those modern "liberals" who pride themselves on being the champions of reason, science, and progress—and who smear the advocates of capitalism as superstitious, reactionary representatives of a dark past. Move over, comrades, and make room for your latest fellow-travelers, who had always belonged on *your* side—then take a look, if you dare, at the kind of past *they* represent.

[Ibid., 314.]

[There is one] possibly misleading sentence . . . in Roark's speech: "From this simplest necessity to the highest religious abstraction, from the wheel to the skyscraper, everything we are and everything we have comes from a single attribute of man—the function of his reasoning mind."

This could be misinterpreted to mean an endorsement of religion or religious ideas. I remember hesitating over that sentence, when I wrote it, and deciding that Roark's and my atheism, as well as the overall spirit of the book, were so clearly established that no one would misunderstand it, particularly since I said that religious abstractions are the product of man's mind, not of supernatural revelation.

But an issue of this sort should not be left to implications. What I was referring to was not religion as such, but a special category of abstractions, the most exalted one, which, for centuries, had been the near-monopoly of religion: *ethics*—not the particular content of religious ethics, but the abstraction "ethics," the realm of values, man's code of good and evil, with the emotional connotations of height, uplift, nobility, reverence, grandeur, which pertain to the realm of man's values, but which religion has arrogated to itself. . . .

Religion's monopoly in the field of ethics has made it extremely difficult to communicate the emotional meaning and connotations of a rational view of life. Just as religion has pre-empted the field of ethics, turning morality *against* man, so it has usurped the highest moral concepts of our language, placing them outside this earth and beyond man's reach. "Exaltation" is usually taken to mean an emotional state evoked by contemplating the supernatural. "Worship" means the emotional experience of loyalty and dedication to something higher than man. "Reverence" means the emotion of a sacred respect, to be experienced on one's knees. "Sacred" means superior to and not-to-be-touched-by any concerns of man or of this earth. Etc.

But such concepts do name actual emotions, even though no supernatural dimension exists; and these emotions are experienced as uplifting or ennobling, without the self-abasement required by religious definitions. What, then, is their source or referent in reality? It is the entire emotional realm of man's dedication to a moral ideal. Yet apart from the man-degrading aspects introduced by religion, that emotional realm is left unidentified, without concepts, words or recognition.

It is this highest level of man's emotions that has to be redeemed from the murk of mysticism and redirected at its proper object: man.

["Introduction to *The Fountainhead*," *TO*, March 1968, 4.]

Philosophy is the goal toward which religion was only a helplessly blind groping. The grandeur, the reverence, the exalted purity, the austere dedication to the pursuit of truth, which are commonly associated with religion, should properly belong to the field of philosophy.

["The Chickens' Homecoming," *NL*, 108.]

The ideology that opposes man's enjoyment of his life on earth and holds sex as such to be evil—the same ideology that is the source and cause of anti-obscenity censorship [is]: religion.

For a discussion of the profound, metaphysical reasons of religion's antagonism to sex, I refer you to my article "Of Living Death" (*The Objectivist*, September–November 1968), which deals with the papal encyclical on contraception, "Of Human Life." Today, most people who profess to be religious, particularly in this country, do not share that condemnation of sex—but it is an ancient tradition which survives, consciously or subconsciously, even in the minds of many irreligious persons, because it is a logical consequence implicit in the basic causes and motives of any form of mysticism.

["Thought Control," *ARL*, III, 1, 3.]

Since religion is a primitive form of philosophy—an attempt to offer a comprehensive view of reality—many of its myths are distorted, dramatized allegories based on some element of truth, some actual, if profoundly elusive, aspect of man's existence.

["Philosophy and Sense of Life," *RM*, 31; pb 25.]

In mankind's history, art began as an adjunct (and, often, a monopoly) of religion. Religion was the primitive form of philosophy: it provided man with a comprehensive view of existence. Observe that the art of those primitive cultures was a concretization of their religion's metaphysical and ethical abstractions.

["The Psycho-Epistemology of Art," *RM*, 23; pb 20.]

It has often been noted that a proof of God would be fatal to religion: a God susceptible of proof would have to be finite and limited; He would be one entity among others within the universe, not a mystic omnipotence transcending science and reality. What nourishes the spirit of religion is not proof, but faith, i.e., the undercutting of man's mind.

[Leonard Peikoff, " 'Maybe You're Wrong,' " *TOF*, April 1981, 12.]

See also ABORTION; AGNOSTICISM; ALTRUISM; ART; ATHEISM; BIRTH CONTROL; COMMUNISM; "CONSERVATIVES"; DARK AGES; FAITH; GOD; MAN; MAN-WORSHIP; MORALITY; MYSTICISM; ORIGINAL SIN; PHILOSOPHY; PRIMACY of EXISTENCE vs. PRIMACY of CONSCIOUSNESS; REASON; SACRED; SACRIFICE; SEX; SOUL-BODY DICHOTOMY; SUPERNATURALISM.

Renaissance. The Renaissance was specifically the *rebirth of reason*, the liberation of man's mind, the triumph of *rationality* over mysticism —a faltering, incomplete, but impassioned triumph that led to the birth of science, of individualism, of freedom.

["The Left: Old and New," *NL*, 83.]

The Renaissance—the rebirth of man's mind—blasted the rule of the [mystics] sky-high, setting the *earth* free of [their] power. The liberation was not total, nor was it immediate: the convulsions lasted for centuries, but the *cultural* influence of mysticism—of avowed mysticism—was broken. Men could no longer be told to reject their mind as an impotent tool, when the proof of its potency was so magnificently evident that the lowest perceptual-level mentality was not able fully to evade it: men were seeing the achievements of *science*.

["For the New Intellectual," *FNI*, 21; pb 24.]

The Renaissance represented a rebirth of the Aristotelian spirit. The results of that spirit are written across the next two centuries, which men describe, properly, as the Age of Reason and the Age of Enlightenment. The results include the rise of modern science; the rise of an individualist political philosophy (the work of John Locke and others); the consequent spread of freedom across the civilized world; and the birth of the freest country in history, the United States of America. The great corollary of these results, the product of men who were armed with the knowledge of the scientists and who were free at last to act, was the Industrial Revolution, which turned poverty into abundance and transformed the face of the West. The Aristotelianism released by Aquinas and the Renaissance was sweeping away the dogmas and the shackles of the past. Reason, freedom, and production were replacing faith, force, and poverty. The age-old foundations of statism were being challenged and undercut.

[Leonard Peikoff, *OP*, 22; pb 31.]

The Renaissance was the great rebirth intellectually, but not politically. Still seeking order and unity, men attempted to solve the problem of feudal tyranny by replacing many small tyrants with a single big one. This was the birth of modern absolute monarchies.

["A Nation's Unity," *ARL*, II, 2, 2.]

The Renaissance of the fifteenth and sixteenth centuries was a conscious rebellion against the anti-human, otherworldly values of medieval Christendom. In its metaphysics and epistemology, the Renaissance was essentially Aristotelian. Every aspect of the period, from science to literature to art, reflected the Aristotelian view that man is a worthy being, capable of understanding the universe, and that the universe is worthy of man's interest and study. Mysticism, which had saturated every aspect of medieval life and culture, lost its stranglehold on man's mind. A rebirth of reason and of concern with this earth, was the base of all the achievements of the Renaissance.

In terms of its morality, the Renaissance was split in two: it was part-Aristotelian, part-Christian. As Aristotelians, the men of the Renaissance displayed the virtues of intelligence and pride, and pursued the value of happiness on earth. As Christians, they upheld the virtues of humility, renunciation and self-sacrifice, and the value of rewards in Heaven. Thus the existentially brilliant era of the Renaissance was marred, spiritually, by a profound moral conflict.

That conflict appeared, in different degrees, in virtually all of the Renaissance art. For the most part, sculpture did reflect an affirmative view of man. Although the subject matter was largely Christian, sculptors abandoned the stylistic features of medieval art. They restored weight, three-dimensionality and natural proportions to the human body. They reintroduced free-standing figures. They were keenly aware of human anatomy, and created images of potentially active bodies, or of bodies engaged in energetic movement. And, equally significant, the naked body was featured in the representation of both Christian and pagan subjects.

The statues present men who have intelligence, courage, determination and strength of character; but they do not convey a sense of happiness. The moral conflict tinged the Renaissance view of life, and in the faces of the statues there is a touch of sadness or uncertainty or tragedy, an expression of longing for an ideal never fully reached.

[Mary Ann Sures, "Metaphysics in Marble," *TO*, March 1969, 11.]

See also ARISTOTLE; ART; DARK AGES; ENLIGHTENMENT, AGE of; FREEDOM; HISTORY; HUMILITY; MIDDLE AGES; MYSTICISM; REASON; RELIGION; TYRANNY.

Representative Government.   The theory of representative government rests on the principle that man is a rational being, i.e., that he is able to perceive the facts of reality, to evaluate them, to form rational judgments, to make his own choices, and to bear responsibility for the course of his life.

Politically, this principle is implemented by a man's right to choose his own agents, i.e., those whom he authorizes to represent him in the government of his country. To represent him, in this context, means to represent his views in terms of political principles. Thus the government of a free country derives its "just powers from the consent of the governed." (For the basis of this discussion, see "Man's Rights" and "The Nature of Government" in *Capitalism: The Unknown Ideal*.)

As a corroboration of the link between man's rational faculty and a representative form of government, observe that those who are demonstrably (or physiologically) incapable of rational judgment cannot exercise the right to vote. (Voting is a derivative, not a fundamental, right; it is derived from the right to life, as a political implementation of the requirements of a rational being's survival.) Children do not vote, because they have not acquired the knowledge necessary to form a rational judgment on political issues; neither do the feeble-minded or the insane, who have lost or never developed their rational faculty. (The possession of a rational faculty does not guarantee that a man will use it, only that he is *able* to use it and is, therefore, responsible for his actions.)

["Representation Without Authorization," *ARL*, I, 21, 1.]

See also CONSTITUTION; DEMOCRACY; GOVERNMENT; INDIVIDUAL RIGHTS; POLITICS; REPUBLIC; VOTING.

Republic.   The American system is *not* a democracy. It is a constitutional republic. A democracy, if you attach meaning to terms, is a system of unlimited majority rule . . . a form of collectivism, which denies individual rights. . . . The American system is a constitutionally limited republic, restricted to the protection of individual rights. In such a system, majority rule is applicable only to lesser details, such as the selection of certain personnel. But the majority has no say over the *basic* principles governing the government. It has no power to ask for or gain the infringement of individual rights.

[Leonard Peikoff, "The Philosophy of Objectivism"
lecture series (1976), Lecture 9.]

See also AMERICA; COLLECTIVISM; CONSTITUTION; DEMOCRACY; INDIVIDUAL RIGHTS; POLITICS; REPRESENTATIVE GOVERNMENT; VOTING.

Responsibility/Obligation.

In reality and in the Objectivist ethics, there is no such thing as "duty." There is only choice and the full, clear recognition of a principle obscured by the notion of "duty": *the Law of Causality.*

The proper approach to ethics, the start from a metaphysically clean slate, untainted by any touch of Kantianism, can best be illustrated by the following story. In answer to a man who was telling her that she's *got to* do something or other, a wise old Negro woman said: "Mister, there's nothing I've *got to* do except die."

Life or death is man's only fundamental alternative. To live is his basic act of choice. If he chooses to live, a rational ethics will tell him what principles of action are required to implement his choice. If he does not choose to live, nature will take its course.

Reality confronts man with a great many "musts," but all of them are conditional; the formula of realistic necessity is: "You must, if—" and the "if" stands for man's choice: "—if you want to achieve a certain goal." You must eat, if you want to survive. You must work, if you want to eat. You must think, if you want to work. You must look at reality, if you want to think—if you want to know what to do—if you want to know what goals to choose—if you want to know how to achieve them.

In order to make the choices required to achieve his goals, a man needs the constant, automatized awareness of the principle which the anti-concept "duty" has all but obliterated in his mind: the principle of causality—specifically, of Aristotelian *final causation* (which, in fact, applies only to a conscious being), i.e., the process by which an end determines the means, i.e., the process of choosing a goal and taking the actions necessary to achieve it.

In a rational ethics, it is causality—not "duty"—that serves as the guiding principle in considering, evaluating and choosing one's actions, particularly those necessary to achieve a long-range goal. Following this principle, a man does not act without knowing the purpose of his action. In choosing a goal, he considers the means required to achieve it, he weighs the value of the goal against the difficulties of the means and against the full, hierarchical context of all his other values and goals. He does not demand the impossible of himself, and he does not decide too easily which things are impossible. He never drops the context of the knowledge available to him, and never evades reality, realizing fully that his goal will not be granted to him by any power other than his own action, and, should he evade, it is not some Kantian authority that he would be cheating, but himself. . . .

A disciple of causation is profoundly dedicated to his values, knowing that he is able to achieve them. He is incapable of desiring contradictions, of relying on a "somehow," of rebelling against reality. He knows that in all such cases, it is not some Kantian authority that he would be defying and injuring, but himself—and that the penalty would be not some mystic brand of "immorality," but the frustration of his own desires and the destruction of his values. . . .

Accepting no mystic "duties" or unchosen obligations, he is the man who honors scrupulously the obligations which *he* chooses. The obligation to keep one's promises is one of the most important elements in proper human relationships, the element that leads to mutual confidence and makes cooperation possible among men. . . .

The acceptance of full responsibility for one's own choices and actions (and their consequences) is such a demanding moral discipline that many men seek to escape it by surrendering to what they believe is the easy, automatic, unthinking safety of a morality of "duty." They learn better, often when it is too late.

The disciple of causation faces life without inexplicable chains, unchosen burdens, impossible demands or supernatural threats. His metaphysical attitude and guiding moral principle can best be summed up by an old Spanish proverb: "God said: 'Take what you want and pay for it.' " But to know one's own desires, their meaning and their costs requires the highest human virtue: rationality.

["Causality Versus Duty," *PWNI*, 118; pb 98.]

See also CONTRACTS; "DUTY"; FREE WILL; KANT, IMMANUEL; LIFE; MORALITY; RATIONALITY; SELFISHNESS; VALUES.

Retaliatory Force. The basic political principle of the Objectivist ethics is: no man may *initiate* the use of physical force against others. No man—or group or society or government—has the right to assume the role of a criminal and initiate the use of physical compulsion against any man. Men have the right to use physical force *only* in retaliation and *only* against those who initiate its use. The ethical principle involved is simple and clear-cut: it is the difference between murder and self-defense. A holdup man seeks to gain a value, wealth, by killing his victim; the victim does not grow richer by killing a holdup man. The principle is: no man may obtain any values from others by resorting to physical force.

["The Objectivist Ethics," *VOS*, 31; pb 32.]

It is only as retaliation that force may be used and only against the man who starts its use. No, I do not share his evil or sink to his concept of morality: I merely grant him his choice, destruction, the only destruction he had the right to choose: his own. He uses force to seize a value; I use it only to destroy destruction.

[GS, *FNI*, 166; pb 135.]

The principle of using force only in retaliation against those who initiate its use, is the principle of subordinating might to right.

["Philosophy: Who Needs It," *PWNI*, 13; pb 10.]

See also ANARCHISM; CIVIL DISOBEDIENCE; GOVERNMENT; INDI-VIDUAL RIGHTS; JUSTICE; PACIFISM; PEACE MOVEMENTS; PHYS-ICAL FORCE; SELF-DEFENSE; WAR.

Retroactive Law. Retroactive (or *ex post facto*) law—*i.e.*, a law that punishes a man for an action which was not legally defined as a crime at the time he committed it—is rejected by and contrary to the entire tradition of Anglo-Saxon jurisprudence. It is a form of persecution practiced only in dictatorships and forbidden by every civilized code of law. It is specifically forbidden by the United States Constitution. It is not supposed to exist in the United States and it is not applied to anyone —except to businessmen. A case in which a man cannot know until he is convicted whether the action he took in the past was legal or illegal, is certainly a case of retroactive law.

["America's Persecuted Minority: Big Business," *CUI*, 50.]

See also ANTITRUST LAWS; BUSINESSMEN; CONSTITUTION; GOV-ERNMENT; LAW, OBJECTIVE AND NON-OBJECTIVE.

Revolution vs. Putsch. The New Left does not portend a revo-lution, as its press agents claim, but a *Putsch*. A revolution is the climax of a long philosophical development and expresses a nation's profound discontent; a *Putsch* is a minority's seizure of power. The goal of a revolution is to overthrow tyranny; the goal of a *Putsch* is to establish it.

Tyranny is any political system (whether absolute monarchy or fas-cism or communism) that does not recognize individual rights (which necessarily include property rights). The overthrow of a political system by force is justified only when it is directed against tyranny: it is an act of self-defense against those who rule by force. For example, the Amer-ican Revolution. The resort to force, not in defense, but in violation, of individual rights, can have no moral justification; it is not a revolution, but gang warfare.

["From a Symposium," *NL*, 96.]

See also AMERICA; DICTATORSHIP; INDIVIDUAL RIGHTS; NEW LEFT; PHYSICAL FORCE; STATISM.

"Rewriting Reality."   Unable to determine what they can or cannot change, some men attempt to "rewrite reality," i.e., to alter the nature of the metaphysically given. Some dream of a universe in which man experiences nothing but happiness—no pain, no frustration, no illness—and wonder why they lose the desire to improve their life on earth. Some feel that they would be brave, honest, ambitious in a world where everyone automatically shared these virtues—but not in the world as it is. Some dread the thought of eventual death—and never undertake the task of living.

[*"The Metaphysical Versus the Man-Made," PWNI*, 36; pb 30.]

By the "metaphysically given," we mean any fact inherent in reality as such, apart from human action (whether mental or physical)—as against "man-made facts," i.e., objects, institutions, practices, or rules of conduct that are of human origin. . . .

As soon as you say about a metaphysically given fact: *"it is"*—just that much—the whole Objectivist metaphysics is implicit. If the fact is, it is what it is (the law of identity); it is what it is independent of consciousness, of anyone's or everyone's desires, hopes, fears (the primacy of existence); and it is lawful, inherent in the identities of the relevant entities (the law of causality). Given the circumstances involved, such a fact is *necessary;* it *had to* be; any alternative would have entailed a contradiction. In short, once you say about a metaphysical fact: "it is," that means that, within the relevant circumstances, it is immutable, inexorable, inescapable, *absolute.* "Absolute" in this context means necessitated by the nature of existence and, therefore, unchangeable by human (or any other) agency. . . .

The attempt to alter the nature of the metaphysically given is described by Ayn Rand as the fallacy of "rewriting reality." Those who commit it regard metaphysical facts as non-absolute and, therefore, feel free to imagine an alternative to them. In effect, they regard the universe as though it were merely a first draft of reality, which anyone may decide at will to rewrite.

A common example is provided by those who condemn life on earth because man is capable of failure, frustration, pain, and who yearn instead for a world in which man knows nothing but happiness. But if the possibility of failure exists, it *necessarily* exists (it is inherent in the fact that achieving a value depends on a specific course of action, and that man is neither omniscient nor omnipotent in regard to such action). Anyone who holds the full context—who keeps in mind the *identity* of all the relevant entities—would be unable even to imagine an alternative to the facts as they are; the contradictions involved in such a projection would obliterate it. The rewriters, however, do not keep identity in mind; they specialize in out-of-context pining for a "heaven" that is the antonym of the metaphysically given.

> [Leonard Peikoff, "The Philosophy of Objectivism"
> lecture series (1976), Lecture 6.]

See also ABSOLUTES; AXIOMS; CAUSALITY; EXISTENCE; IDENTITY; METAPHYSICAL vs. MAN-MADE.

Right to Life. *See Life, Right to.*

Rightists vs. Leftists.
Since, today, there are no clear definitions of political terms, I use the word "rightist" to denote the views of those who are predominantly in favor of individual freedom and capitalism —and the word "leftist" to denote the views of those who are predominantly in favor of government controls and socialism. As to the middle or "center," I take it to mean "zero," i.e., no dominant position, i.e., a pendulum swinging from side to side, moment by moment.

> ["The Disfranchisement of the Right," *ARL*, I, 6, 1.]

See also CAPITALISM; COLLECTIVISM; "CONSERVATIVES" vs. "LIBERALS"; INDIVIDUAL RIGHTS; INDIVIDUALISM; POLITICS; SOCIALISM; STATISM.

Rights. *See Individual Rights.*

Rights of the Accused.
The rights of the accused are not a primary—they are a consequence derived from a man's inalienable, individual rights. A consequence cannot survive the destruction of its cause. What good will it do you to be protected in the rare emergency of a false arrest, if you are treated as the rightless subject of an unlimited government in your daily life?

> ["Moral Inflation," *ARL*, III, 13, 4.]

See also CRIME; INDIVIDUAL RIGHTS; STATISM.

Romanticism.
Romanticism is a category of art based on the recognition of the principle that man possesses the faculty of volition.

> ["What Is Romanticism?" *RM*, 81; pb 99.]

Romanticism is the *conceptual* school of art. It deals, not with the random trivia of the day, but with the timeless, fundamental, universal problems and *values* of human existence. It does not record or photograph; it creates and projects. It is concerned—in the words of Aristotle

—not with things as they are, but with things as they might be and ought to be.

["Introduction to *The Fountainhead*," *TO*, March 1968, 1.]

What the Romanticists brought to art was *the primacy of values*, an element that had been missing in the stale, arid, third- and fourth-hand (and rate) repetitions of the Classicists' formula-copying. Values (and value-judgments) are the source of emotions; a great deal of emotional intensity was projected in the work of the Romanticists and in the reactions of their audiences, as well as a great deal of color, imagination, originality, excitement and all the other consequences of a value-oriented view of life. This emotional element was the most easily perceivable characteristic of the new movement and it was taken as its defining characteristic, without deeper inquiry.

Such issues as the fact that the primacy of values in human life is not an irreducible primary, that it rests on man's faculty of volition, and, therefore, that the Romanticists, philosophically, were the champions of volition (which is the root of values) and not of emotions (which are merely the consequences)—were issues to be defined by philosophers, who defaulted in regard to esthetics as they did in regard to every other crucial aspect of the nineteenth century.

The still deeper issue, the fact that the faculty of *reason* is the faculty of volition, was not known at the time, and the various theories of free will were for the most part of an anti-rational character, thus reinforcing the association of volition with mysticism.

["What Is Romanticism?" *RM*, 88; pb 104.]

In recent times, some literary historians have discarded, as inadequate, the definition of Romanticism as an emotion-oriented school and have attempted to redefine it, but without success. Following the rule of fundamentality, it is as a *volition*-oriented school that Romanticism must be defined—and it is in terms of this essential characteristic that the nature and history of Romantic literature can be traced and understood.

[Ibid., 90; pb 106.]

If man possesses volition, then the crucial aspect of his life is his choice of values—if he chooses values, then he must act to gain and/or keep them—if so, then he must set his goals and engage in purposeful action to achieve them. The literary form expressing the essence of such action is the *plot*. (A plot is a purposeful progression of logically connected events leading to the resolution of a climax.)

The faculty of volition operates in regard to the two fundamental aspects of man's life: consciousness and existence, i.e., his psychological action and his existential action, i.e., the formation of his own character and the course of action he pursues in the physical world. Therefore, in a literary work, both the characterizations and the events are to be created by the author, according to his view of the role of values in human psychology and existence (and according to the code of values he holds to be right). His characters are abstract projections, not reproductions of concretes; they are invented conceptually, not copied reportorially from the particular individuals he might have observed. The specific characters of particular individuals are merely the evidence of their particular value-choices and have no wider metaphysical significance (except as material for the study of the general principles of human psychology); they do not exhaust man's characterological potential.

[Ibid., 82; pb 100.]

The Romanticists did not present a hero as a statistical average, but as an abstraction of man's best and highest potentiality, applicable to and achievable by all men, in various degrees, according to their individual choices.

["The Esthetic Vacuum of Our Age," *RM*, 117; pb 126.]

Philosophically, Romanticism is a crusade to glorify man's existence; psychologically, it is experienced simply as the desire to make life interesting.

["What Is Romanticism?" *RM*, 95; pb 109.]

Romanticism demands mastery of the primary element of fiction: the art of storytelling—which requires three cardinal qualities: ingenuity, imagination, a sense of drama. All this (and more) goes into the construction of an original plot integrated to theme and characterization. Naturalism discards these elements and demands nothing but characterization, in as shapeless a narrative, as "uncontrived" (i.e., purposeless) a progression of events (if any) as a given author pleases.

The value of a Romanticist's work has to be created by its author; he owes no allegiance to men (only to man), only to the metaphysical nature of reality and to his own values. The value of a Naturalist's work depends on the specific characters, choices and actions of the men he reproduces—and he is judged by the fidelity with which he reproduces them.

The value of a Romanticist's story lies in *what* might happen; the value of a Naturalist's story lies in *that* it did happen.

[Ibid., 105; pb 117.]

The major source and demonstration of moral values available to a child is Romantic art (particularly Romantic literature). What Romantic art offers him is *not* moral rules, not an explicit didactic message, but the image of a moral *person*—i.e., the *concretized abstraction* of a moral ideal. It offers a concrete, directly perceivable answer to the very abstract question which a child senses, but cannot yet conceptualize: What kind of person is moral and what kind of life does he lead?

It is not abstract principles that a child learns from Romantic art, but the precondition and the incentive for the later understanding of such principles: the emotional experience of admiration for man's highest potential, the experience of *looking up* to a hero—a view of life motivated and dominated by values, a life in which man's choices are practicable, effective and crucially important—that is, a *moral* sense of life.

["Art and Moral Treason," *RM*, 142; pb 146.]

Romantic art is the fuel and the spark plug of a man's soul; its task is to set a soul on fire and never let it go out.

[Ibid., 150; pb 152.]

It is only the superficiality of the Naturalists that classifies Romanticism as "an escape"; this is true only in the very superficial sense of contemplating a glamorous vision as a relief from the gray burden of "real-life" problems. But in the deeper, metaphysical-moral-psychological sense, it is *Naturalism* that represents an escape—an escape from choice, from values, from moral responsibility—and it is *Romanticism* that trains and equips man for the battles he has to face in reality.

["Bootleg Romanticism," *RM*, 134; pb 139.]

The (implicit) standards of Romanticism are so demanding that in spite of the abundance of Romantic writers at the time of its dominance, this school has produced very few pure, consistent Romanticists of the top rank. Among novelists, the greatest are Victor Hugo and Dostoevsky, and, as single novels (whose authors were not always consistent in the rest of their works), I would name Henryk Sienkiewicz's *Quo Vadis* and Nathaniel Hawthorne's *The Scarlet Letter*. Among playwrights, the greatest are Friedrich Schiller and Edmond Rostand.

The distinguishing characteristic of this top rank (apart from their purely literary genius) is their full commitment to the premise of volition in *both of its fundamental areas:* in regard to consciousness and to existence, in regard to man's character and to his actions in the physical world. Maintaining a perfect integration of these two aspects, unmatched in the brilliant ingenuity of their plot structures, these writers are enormously concerned with man's soul (i.e., his consciousness). They are *moralists* in the most profound sense of the word; their concern is not merely with values, but specifically with *moral* values and with the power of moral values in shaping human character. Their characters are "larger than life," i.e., they are abstract projections in terms of essentials (not always successful projections, as we shall discuss later). In their stories, one will never find action for action's sake, unrelated to moral values. The events of their plots are shaped, determined and motivated by the characters' values (or treason to values), by their struggle in pursuit of spiritual goals and by profound value-conflicts. Their themes are fundamental, universal, timeless issues of man's existence— and they are the only consistent creators of the rarest attribute of literature: the perfect integration of theme and plot, which they achieve with superlative virtuosity.

If philosophical significance is the criterion of what is to be taken seriously, then these are the most serious writers in world literature.

["What Is Romanticism?" *RM*, 91; pb 107.]

It must be noted that philosophers contributed to the confusion surrounding the term "Romanticism." They attached the name "Romantic" to certain philosophers (such as Schelling and Schopenhauer) who were avowed mystics advocating the supremacy of emotions, instincts or *will* over reason. This movement in philosophy had no significant relation to Romanticism in esthetics, and the two movements must not be confused.

["What Is Romanticism?" *RM*, 90; pb 106.]

The archenemy and destroyer of Romanticism was the altruist morality.

Since Romanticism's essential characteristic is the projection of values, particularly *moral* values, altruism introduced an insolvable conflict into Romantic literature from the start. The altruist morality cannot be practiced (except in the form of self-destruction) and, therefore, cannot be projected or dramatized convincingly in terms of man's life on earth (particularly in the realm of psychological motivation). With altruism as the criterion of value and virtue, it is impossible to create an image of man at his best—"as he might be and ought to be." The major flaw that runs through the history of Romantic literature is the failure to present a convincing hero, i.e., a convincing image of a virtuous man.

[Ibid., 100; pb 113.]

With the resurgence of mysticism and collectivism, in the later part of the nineteenth century, the Romantic novel and the Romantic movement vanished gradually from the cultural scene.

["The Esthetic Vacuum of Our Age," *RM*, 114; pb 124.]

See also ALTRUISM; ARISTOTLE; ART; CLASSICISM; EMOTIONS; FREE WILL; FUNDAMENTALITY, RULE of; LITERATURE; META- PHYSICAL VALUE-JUDGMENTS; MORALITY; NATURALISM; PLOT; POPULAR LITERATURE; REASON; THRILLERS; VALUES.

S

Sacred. I will ask you to project the look on a child's face when he grasps the answer to some problem he has been striving to understand. It is a radiant look of joy, of liberation, almost of triumph, which is unself-conscious, yet self-assertive, and its radiance seems to spread in two directions: outward, as an illumination of the world—inward, as the first spark of what is to become the fire of an earned pride. If you have seen this look, or experienced it, you know that if there is such a concept as "sacred"—meaning: the best, the highest possible to man— this look is the sacred, the not-to-be-betrayed, the not-to-be-sacrificed for anything or anyone.

["Requiem for Man," *CUI*, 303.]

[I use] the word "sanctity" not in a mystical sense, but in the sense of "supreme value."

[*WTL*, "Foreword," v.]

See also MYSTICISM; PRIDE; RELIGION; UNDERSTANDING; VALUES.

Sacrifice. "Sacrifice" is the surrender of a greater value for the sake of a lesser one or of a nonvalue. Thus, altruism gauges a man's virtue by the degree to which he surrenders, renounces or betrays his values (since help to a stranger or an enemy is regarded as more virtuous, less "selfish," than help to those one loves). The rational principle of conduct is the exact opposite: always act in accordance with the hierarchy of your values, and never sacrifice a greater value to a lesser one.

This applies to all choices, including one's actions toward other men. It requires that one possess a defined hierarchy of *rational* values (values chosen and validated by a rational standard). Without such a hierarchy, neither rational conduct nor considered value judgments nor moral choices are possible.

["The Ethics of Emergencies," *VOS*, 48; pb 44.]

"Sacrifice" does not mean the rejection of the worthless, but of the precious. "Sacrifice" does not mean the rejection of the evil for the sake of the good, but of the good for the sake of the evil. "Sacrifice" is the surrender of that which you value in favor of that which you don't.

429

If you exchange a penny for a dollar, it is *not* a sacrifice; if you exchange a dollar for a penny, it *is*. If you achieve the career you wanted, after years of struggle, it is *not* a sacrifice; if you then renounce it for the sake of a rival, it *is*. If you own a bottle of milk and give it to your starving child, it is *not* a sacrifice; if you give it to your neighbor's child and let your own die, it *is*.

If you give money to help a friend, it is *not* a sacrifice; if you give it to a worthless stranger, it *is*. If you give your friend a sum you can afford, it is *not* a sacrifice; if you give him money at the cost of your own discomfort, it is only a partial virtue, according to this sort of moral standard; if you give him money at the cost of disaster to yourself—*that* is the virtue of sacrifice in full.

If you renounce all personal desires and dedicate your life to those you love, you do not achieve full virtue: you still retain a value of your own, which is your love. If you devote your life to random strangers, it is an act of greater virtue. If you devote your life to serving men you hate—*that* is the greatest of the virtues you can practice.

A sacrifice is the surrender of a value. Full sacrifice is full surrender of all values. If you wish to achieve full virtue, you must seek no gratitude in return for your sacrifice, no praise, no love, no admiration, no self-esteem, not even the pride of being virtuous; the faintest trace of any gain dilutes your virtue. If you pursue a course of action that does not taint your life by any joy, that brings you no value in matter, no value in spirit, no gain, no profit, no reward—if you achieve this state of total zero, you have achieved the ideal of moral perfection.

You are told that moral perfection is impossible to man—and, by this standard, it is. You cannot achieve it so long as you live, but the value of your life and of your person is gauged by how closely you succeed in approaching that ideal zero which is *death*.

If you start, however, as a passionless blank, as a vegetable seeking to be eaten, with no values to reject and no wishes to renounce, you will not win the crown of sacrifice. It is not a sacrifice to renounce the unwanted. It is not a sacrifice to give your life for others, if death is your personal desire. To achieve the virtue of sacrifice, you must want to live, you must love it, you must burn with passion for this earth and for all the splendor it can give you—you must feel the twist of every knife as it slashes your desires away from your reach and drains your love out of your body. It is not mere death that the morality of sacrifice holds out to you as an ideal, but death by slow torture.

Do not remind me that it pertains only to this life on earth. I am concerned with no other. Neither are you.

If you wish to save the last of your dignity, do not call your best actions a "sacrifice": that term brands you as immoral. If a mother buys food for her hungry child rather than a hat for herself, it is *not* a sacrifice: she values the child higher than the hat; but it is a sacrifice to the kind of mother whose higher value is the hat, who would prefer her child to starve and feeds him only from a sense of duty. If a man dies fighting for his own freedom, it is *not* a sacrifice: he is not willing to live as a slave; but it *is* a sacrifice to the kind of man who's willing. If a man refuses to sell his convictions, it is *not* a sacrifice, unless he is the sort of man who has no convictions.

Sacrifice could be proper only for those who have nothing to sacrifice —no values, no standards, no judgment—those whose desires are irrational whims, blindly conceived and lightly surrendered. For a man of moral stature, whose desires are born of rational values, sacrifice is the surrender of the right to the wrong, of the good to the evil.

The creed of sacrifice is a morality for the immoral—a morality that declares its own bankruptcy by confessing that it can't impart to men any personal stake in virtues or values, and that their souls are sewers of depravity, which they must be taught to sacrifice. By its own confession, it is impotent to teach men to be good and can only subject them to constant punishment.

[GS, *FNI*, 172; pb 139.]

Concern for the welfare of those one loves is a rational part of one's selfish interests. If a man who is passionately in love with his wife spends a fortune to cure her of a dangerous illness, it would be absurd to claim that he does it as a "sacrifice" for *her* sake, not his own, and that it makes no difference to *him*, personally and selfishly, whether she lives or dies.

Any action that a man undertakes for the benefit of those he loves is *not a sacrifice* if, in the hierarchy of his values, in the total context of the choices open to him, it achieves that which is of greatest *personal* (and rational) importance to *him*. In the above example, his wife's survival is of greater value to the husband than anything else that his money could buy, it is of greatest importance to his own happiness and, therefore, his action is *not* a sacrifice.

But suppose he let her die in order to spend his money on saving the lives of ten other women, none of whom meant anything to him—as the ethics of altruism would require. *That* would be a sacrifice. Here the difference between Objectivism and altruism can be seen most clearly: if sacrifice is the moral principle of action, then that husband *should* sacrifice his wife for the sake of ten other women. What distinguishes the wife from the ten others? Nothing but her value to the husband who has to make the choice—nothing but the fact that *his* happiness requires her survival.

The Objectivist ethics would tell him: your highest moral purpose is the achievement of your own happiness, your money is yours, use it to save your wife, *that* is your moral right and your rational, moral choice.

["The Ethics of Emergencies," *VOS*, 49; pb 45.]

If the frustration of *any* desire constitutes a *sacrifice*, then a man who owns an automobile and is robbed of it, *is* being sacrificed, but so is the man who wants or "aspires to" an automobile which the owner refuses to give him—and these two "sacrifices" have equal ethical status. If so, then man's only choice is to rob or be robbed, to destroy or be destroyed, to sacrifice others to any desire of his own or to sacrifice himself to any desire of others; then man's only ethical alternative is to be a sadist or a masochist.

["The Objectivist Ethics," *VOS*, 27; pb 30.]

The failure to give to a man what had never belonged to him can hardly be described as "sacrificing his interests."

["The 'Conflicts' of Men's Interests," *VOS*, 67; pb 56.]

It stands to reason that where there's sacrifice, there's someone collecting sacrificial offerings. Where there's service, there's someone being served. The man who speaks to you of sacrifice, speaks of slaves and masters. And intends to be the master.

["The Soul of a Collectivist," *FNI*, 84; pb 73.]

See also ALTRUISM; "DUTY"; INTEGRITY; KANT, IMMANUEL; MORALITY; MYSTICISM; PRIDE; SELFISHNESS; SELFLESSNESS; STANDARD of VALUE; STATISM; ULTIMATE VALUE; VALUES.

Sanction.   To discuss evil in a manner implying neutrality, is to sanction it.

["The Argument from Intimidation," *VOS*, 198; pb 143.]

One *must* speak up in situations where silence can objectively be taken to mean agreement with or sanction of evil. When one deals with irrational persons, where argument is futile, a mere "I don't agree with you" is sufficient to negate any implication of moral sanction. When one deals with better people, a full statement of one's views may be morally required. But in no case and in no situation may one permit one's own values to be attacked or denounced, and keep silent.

["How Does One Lead a Rational Life
in an Irrational Society?" *VOS*, 92; pb 73.]

To combat petty larceny as a crucial danger, at a time when murder is being committed, is to sanction the murder.

["Antitrust: The Rule of Unreason," *TON*, Feb. 1962, 8.]

To abstain from condemning a torturer, is to become an accessory to the torture and murder of his victims.

The moral principle to adopt in this issue, is: *"Judge, and be prepared to be judged."*

["How Does One Lead a Rational Life in an Irrational Society?" *VOS*, 91; pb 72.]

A forced compliance is not a sanction. All of us are forced to comply with many laws that violate our rights, but so long as we advocate the repeal of such laws, our compliance does not constitute a sanction. Unjust laws have to be fought ideologically; they cannot be fought or corrected by means of mere disobedience and futile martyrdom.

"The Wreckage of the Consensus," *CUI*, 235.]

See also APPEASEMENT; EVIL; MORAL COWARDICE; MORAL JUDG-MENT; MORALITY; PHYSICAL FORCE; SANCTION of the VICTIM; SOVIET RUSSIA.

Sanction of the Victim.
The "sanction of the victim" is the willingness of the good to suffer at the hands of the evil, to accept the role of sacrificial victim for the "sin" of creating values.

[Leonard Peikoff, "The Philosophy of Objectivism" lecture series (1976), Lecture 8.]

Then I saw what was wrong with the world, I saw what destroyed men and nations, and where the battle for life had to be fought. I saw that the enemy was an inverted morality—and that my sanction was its only power. I saw that evil was impotent—that evil was the irrational, the blind, the anti-real—and that the only weapon of its triumph was the willingness of the good to serve it. Just as the parasites around me were proclaiming their helpless dependence on my mind and were expecting me voluntarily to accept a slavery they had no power to enforce, just as they were counting on my self-immolation to provide them with the means of their plan—so throughout the world and throughout men's history, in every version and form, from the extortions of loafing relatives to the atrocities of collectivized countries, it is the good, the able, the men of reason, who act as their own destroyers, who transfuse to evil the blood of their virtue and let evil transmit to them the poison of destruction, thus gaining for evil the power of survival, and for their own values—the impotence of death. I saw that there comes a point, in the defeat of any man of virtue, when his own consent is needed for evil to win—and that no manner of injury done to him by others can succeed if he chooses to withhold his consent. I saw that I could put an end to your outrages by pronouncing a single word in my mind. I pronounced it. The word was "No."

[GS, *FNI*, 206; pb 165.]

Every kind of ethnic group is enormously sensitive to any slight. If one made a derogatory remark about the Kurds of Iran, dozens of voices would leap to their defense. But no one speaks out for business-men, when they are attacked and insulted by everyone as a matter of routine. What causes this overwhelming injustice? The businessmen's own policies: their betrayal of their own values, their appeasement of enemies, their compromises—all of which add up to an air of moral cowardice. Add to it the fact that businessmen are creating and sup-porting their own destroyers.

The sources and centers of today's philosophical corruption are the universities. . . . It is the businessmen's money that supports American universities—not merely in the form of taxes and government hand-outs, but much worse: in the form of voluntary, private contributions, donations, endowments, etc. In preparation for this lecture, I tried to do some research on the nature and amounts of such contributions. I had to give it up: it is too complex and *too vast* a field for the efforts of one person. To untangle it now would require a major research proj-ect and, probably, years of work. All I can say is only that millions and millions and millions of dollars are being donated to universities by big business enterprises every year, and that the donors have no idea of what their money is being spent on or whom it is supporting. What is cer-tain is only the fact that some of the worst anti-business, anti-capitalism propaganda has been financed by businessmen in such projects.

Money is a great power—because, in a free or even a semi-free soci-ety, it is a frozen form of productive energy. And, therefore, the spend-ing of money is a grave responsibility. Contrary to the altruists and the advocates of the so-called "academic freedom," it is a moral crime to give money to support ideas with which you disagree; it means: ideas which you consider wrong, false, evil. It is a moral crime to give money to support your own destroyers. Yet that is what businessmen are doing with such reckless irresponsibility.

["The Sanction of the Victims," *TOF*, April 1982, 6.]

See also APPEASEMENT; BUSINESSMEN; COLLECTIVISM; COMPRO-MISE; EVIL; GOOD, the; MONEY; MORAL COWARDICE; MORALITY; SANCTION; SOVIET RUSSIA.

Savings.   Agriculture is the first step toward civilization, because it requires a significant advance in men's conceptual development: it requires that they grasp two cardinal concepts which the perceptual, concrete-bound mentality of the hunters could not grasp fully: *time* and *savings.* Once you grasp these, you have grasped the three essentials of human survival: time-savings-production. You have grasped the fact that production is not a matter confined to the immediate moment, but a continuous process, and that production is fueled by previous production. The concept of "stock seed" unites the three essentials and applies not merely to agriculture, but much, much more widely: to *all* forms of productive work. Anything above the level of a savage's precarious, hand-to-mouth existence requires *savings.* Savings buy *time.*

["Egalitarianism and Inflation," *PWNI,* 153; pb 126.]

Deferred consumption (i.e., *savings*) on a gigantic scale is required to keep industrial production going. Savings pay for machines which enable men to produce in a day an amount of goods they would not be able to produce by hand in a year (if at all). This enables the workers in turn to defer consumption and to save some of their income for their future needs or goals. The hallmark of an industrial society is its members' distance from a hand-to-mouth mode of living; the greater this distance, the greater men's progress.

The major part of this country's stock seed is not the fortunes of the rich (who are a small minority), but the savings of the middle class— i.e., of responsible men who have the ability to grasp the concept "future" and to deposit one dollar (or more) into a bank account. A man of this type saves money for his own future, but the bank invests his money in productive enterprises; thus, the goods he did not consume today, are available to him when he needs them tomorrow—and, in the meantime, these goods serve as fuel for the country's productive process.

["The Inverted Moral Priorities," *ARL,* III, 21, 1.]

Consumption is the *final,* not the *efficient,* cause of production. The efficient cause is savings, which can be said to represent the opposite of consumption: they represent *unconsumed* goods. Consumption is the end of production, and a *dead end,* as far as the productive process is concerned. The worker who produces so little that he consumes everything he earns, carries his own weight economically, but contributes nothing to future production. The worker who has a modest savings account, and the millionaire who invests a fortune (and all the men in between), are those who finance the future.

["Egalitarianism and Inflation," *PWNI,* 160; pb 132.]

See also CONSUMPTION; CREDIT; FINAL CAUSATION; GOLD STAN-
DARD; INFLATION; INTEREST (on LOANS); INVESTMENT; MIDDLE
CLASS; MONEY; PRODUCTION.

Science.   Science was born as a result and consequence of philosophy; it cannot survive without a philosophical (particularly epistemological) base. If philosophy perishes, science will be next to go.

["For the New Intellectual," *FNI*, 50; pb 44.]

It is not the special sciences that teach man to think; it is philosophy
that lays down the epistemological criteria of all special sciences.

[*ITOE*, 104.]

The disintegration of philosophy in the nineteenth century and its
collapse in the twentieth have led to a similar, though much slower and
less obvious, process in the course of modern science.

Today's frantic development in the field of technology has a quality
reminiscent of the days preceding the economic crash of 1929: riding
on the momentum of the past, on the unacknowledged remnants of an
Aristotelian epistemology, it is a hectic, feverish expansion, heedless of
the fact that its theoretical account is long since overdrawn—that in the
field of scientific theory, unable to integrate or interpret their own data,
scientists are abetting the resurgence of a primitive mysticism. In the
humanities, however, the crash is past, the depression has set in, and
the collapse of science is all but complete.

The clearest evidence of it may be seen in such comparatively young
sciences as psychology and political economy. In psychology, one may
observe the attempt to study human behavior without reference to the
fact that man is conscious. In political economy, one may observe
the attempt to study and to devise social systems without reference to
man.

It is philosophy that defines and establishes the epistemological criteria to guide human knowledge in general and specific sciences in particular.

["What Is Capitalism?" *CUI*, 11.]

See also ARISTOTLE; BEHAVIORISM; EPISTEMOLOGY; LOGIC; MYS-
TICISM; PHILOSOPHY; REASON; TECHNOLOGY; TRIBAL PREMISE
(in ECONOMICS).

Sculpture.   *Sculpture* [re-creates reality] by means of a three-dimensional form made of a solid material. . . . Sculpture [deals] with the combined fields of *sight* and *touch.* . . .

The so-called visual arts (painting, sculpture, architecture) produce concrete, perceptually available entities and make them convey an abstract, conceptual meaning.

["Art and Cognition," *RM*, pb 46.]

Compared to painting, sculpture is more limited a form of art. It expresses an artist's view of existence through his treatment of the human figure, but it is confined to the human figure. (For a discussion of sculpture's means, I will refer you to "Metaphysics in Marble" by Mary Ann Sures, *The Objectivist*, February–March 1969.)

Dealing with two senses, sight and touch, sculpture is restricted by the necessity to present a three-dimensional shape as man does *not* perceive it: without color. Visually, sculpture offers shape as an abstraction; but touch is a somewhat concrete-bound sense and confines sculpture to concrete entities. Of these, only the figure of man can project a metaphysical meaning. There is little that one can express in the statue of an animal or of an inanimate object.

Psycho-epistemologically, it is the requirements of the sense of touch that make the *texture* of a human body a crucial element in sculpture, and virtually a hallmark of great sculptors. Observe the manner in which the softness, the smoothness, the pliant resiliency of the skin is conveyed by rigid marble in such statues as the Venus de Milo or Michelangelo's Pietà.

It is worth noting that sculpture is almost a dead art. Its great day was in ancient Greece which, philosophically, was a man-centered civilization. A Renaissance is always possible, but the future of sculpture depends to a large extent on the future of architecture. The two arts are closely allied; one of the problems of sculpture lies in the fact that one of its most effective functions is to serve as architectural ornament.

[Ibid., 49.]

The history of sculpture is a history of man's view of man—of his body and spirit, i.e., of his *metaphysical* nature. Every culture, from the most primitive to the most civilized, has held an estimate of man and has wanted to see the objectified reality of that estimate. Man has been the predominant subject of sculpture, whether he was judged to be an object of pride or of shame, a hero or a sinner.

A metaphysical view of man is projected by the manner in which the sculptor presents the human figure. In the process of shaping clay or wood or stone into the form of a body, the sculptor reveals his answer to three questions: Is man a being of free will or is he a helpless puppet of fate?—Is he good or evil?—Can he achieve happiness or is he doomed to misery?—and then mounts his answer on a pedestal and puts it in a tomb or in a temple or over the portal of a church or in a living room in New York City.

[Mary Ann Sures, "Metaphysics in Marble," *TO*, Feb. 1969, 10.]

Philosophy is the sculptor of man's soul. And sculpture is philosophy in stone.

[Ibid., March 1969, 16.]

See also ANCIENT GREECE; ART; DETERMINISM; ESTHETICS; FREE WILL; MAN; METAPHYSICS; PAINTING; PHILOSOPHY; PSYCHO-EPISTEMOLOGY; VISUAL ARTS.

Secession. Some people ask whether local groups or provinces have the right to secede from the country of which they are a part. The answer is: on ethnic grounds, no. Ethnicity is not a valid consideration, morally or politically, and does not endow anyone with any special rights. As to other than ethnic grounds, remember that rights belong only to individuals and that there is no such thing as "group rights." If a province wants to secede from a dictatorship, or even from a mixed economy, in order to establish a free country—it has the right to do so. But if a local gang, ethnic or otherwise, wants to secede in order to establish its own government controls, it does not have that right. No group has the right to violate the rights of the individuals who happen to live in the same locality. A wish—individual or collective—is not a right.

["Global Balkanization," pamphlet, 14.]

See also DICTATORSHIP; "ETHNICITY"; FREEDOM; INDIVIDUAL RIGHTS; NATIONAL RIGHTS; SELF-DETERMINATION of NATIONS.

Second-Handers. Isn't that the root of every despicable action? Not selfishness, but precisely the absence of a self. Look at them. The man who cheats and lies, but preserves a respectable front. He knows himself to be dishonest, but others think he's honest and he derives his self-respect from that, second-hand. The man who takes credit for an achievement which is not his own. He knows himself to be mediocre, but he's great in the eyes of others. The frustrated wretch who professes love for the inferior and clings to those less endowed, in order to establish his own superiority by comparison. . . . They're second-handers. . . .

They have no concern for facts, ideas, work. They're concerned only with people. They don't ask: "Is this true?" They ask: "Is this what others think is true?" Not to judge, but to repeat. Not to do, but to give the impression of doing. Not creation, but show. Not ability, but friendship. Not merit, but pull. What would happen to the world without those who do, think, work, produce? Those are the egoists. You don't think through another's brain and you don't work through another's hands. When you suspend your faculty of independent judgment, you suspend consciousness. To stop consciousness is to stop life. Second-handers have no sense of reality. Their reality is not within them, but somewhere in that space which divides one human body from another. Not an entity, but a relation—anchored to nothing. That's the emptiness I couldn't understand in people. That's what stopped me whenever I faced a committee. Men without an ego. Opinion without a rational process. Motion without brakes or motor. Power without responsibility. The second-hander acts, but the source of his actions is scattered in every other living person. It's everywhere and nowhere and you can't reason with him. He's not open to reason.

["The Nature of the Second-Hander," *FNI,* 78; pb 69.]

After centuries of being pounded with the doctrine that altruism is the ultimate ideal, men have accepted it in the only way it could be accepted. By seeking self-esteem through others. By living second-hand. And it has opened the way for every kind of horror. It has become the dreadful form of selfishness which a truly selfish man couldn't have conceived. And now, to cure a world perishing from selflessness, we're asked to destroy the self. Listen to what is being preached today. Look at everyone around us. You've wondered why they suffer, why they seek happiness and never find it. If any man stopped and asked himself whether he's ever held a truly personal desire, he'd find the answer. He'd see that all his wishes, his efforts, his dreams, his ambitions are motivated by other men. He's not really struggling even for material wealth, but for the second-hander's delusion—prestige. A stamp of approval, not his own. He can find no joy in the struggle and no joy when he has succeeded. He can't say about a single thing: "This is what I wanted because *I* wanted it, not because it made my neighbors gape at me."

[Ibid., 79; pb 70.]

[In Galt's speech, below, Miss Rand discusses the second-hand nature of the psychology of mystics.]

A mystic is a man who surrendered his mind at its first encounter with the minds of others. Somewhere in the distant reaches of his childhood, when his own understanding of reality clashed with the assertions of others, with their arbitrary orders and contradictory demands, he gave in to so craven a fear of independence that he renounced his rational faculty. At the crossroads of the choice between "I know" and "They say," he chose the authority of others, he chose to submit rather than to understand, to *believe* rather than to think. Faith in the super-natural begins as faith in the superiority of others. His surrender took the form of the feeling that he must hide his lack of understanding, that others possess some mysterious knowledge of which he alone is de-prived, that reality is whatever they want it to be, through some means forever denied to him.

From then on, afraid to think, he is left at the mercy of unidentified feelings. His feelings become his only guide, his only remnant of per-sonal identity, he clings to them with ferocious possessiveness—and whatever thinking he does is devoted to the struggle of hiding from himself that the nature of his feelings is terror.

When a mystic declares that he *feels* the existence of a power superior to reason, he feels it all right, but that power is not an omniscient super-spirit of the universe, it is the consciousness of any passer-by to whom he has surrendered his own. A mystic is driven by the urge to impress, to cheat, to flatter, to deceive, *to force* that omnipotent consciousness of others. *"They"* are his only key to reality, he feels that he cannot exist save by harnessing their mysterious power and extorting their unac-countable consent. *"They"* are his only means of perception and, like a blind man who depends on the sight of a dog, he feels he must leash them in order to live. To control the consciousness of others becomes his only passion; power-lust is a weed that grows only in the vacant lots of an abandoned mind.

[GS, *FNI*, 200; pb 160.]

A [second-hander] is one who regards the consciousness of other men as superior to his own and to the facts of reality. It is to a [second-hander] that the moral appraisal of himself by others is a primary con-cern which supersedes truth, facts, reason, logic. The disapproval of others is so shatteringly terrifying to him that nothing can withstand its impact within his consciousness; thus he would deny the evidence of his own eyes and invalidate his own consciousness for the sake of any stray charlatan's moral sanction. It is only a [second-hander] who could con-ceive of such absurdity as hoping to win an intellectual argument by hinting: "But people won't *like* you!"

["The Argument from Intimidation," *VOS*, 195; pb 141.]

Notice how they'll accept anything except a man who stands alone. They recognize him at once. . . . There's a special, insidious kind of hatred for him. They forgive criminals. They admire dictators. Crime and violence are a tie. A form of mutual dependence. They need ties. They've got to force their miserable little personalities on every single person they meet. The independent man kills them—because they don't exist within him and that's the only form of existence they know. Notice the malignant kind of resentment against any idea that propounds independence. Notice the malice toward an independent man.

["The Nature of the Second-Hander," *FNI*, 79; pb 69.]

It is fear that drives them to seek the warmth, the protection, the "safety" of a herd. When they speak of merging their selves into a "greater whole," it is their fear that they hope to drown in the undemanding waves of unfastidious human bodies. And what they hope to fish out of that pool is the momentary illusion of an unearned personal significance.

["Apollo and Dionysus," *NL*, 80.]

Men were taught to regard second-handers—tyrants, emperors, dictators—as exponents of egoism. By this fraud they were made to destroy the ego, themselves and others. The purpose of the fraud was to destroy the creators. Or to harness them. Which is a synonym.

From the beginning of history, the two antagonists have stood face to face: the creator and the second-hander. When the first creator invented the wheel, the first second-hander responded. He invented altruism.

The creator—denied, opposed, persecuted, exploited—went on, moved forward and carried all humanity along on his energy. The second-hander contributed nothing to the process except the impediments. The contest has another name: the individual against the collective.

["The Soul of an Individualist," *FNI*, 97; pb 83.]

See also ALTRUISM; COLLECTIVISM; COMPETITION; CREATORS; DICTATOR; EMOTIONS; FAITH; INDEPENDENCE; INDIVIDUAL-ISM; LONELINESS; MYSTICISM; PSYCHOLOGY; REASON; SELF; SELF-ESTEEM; SELFISHNESS; SELFLESSNESS.

Self.   A man's self is his mind—the faculty that perceives reality, forms judgments, chooses values.

["Selfishness Without a Self," *PWNI*, 60; pb 50.]

The *self* you have betrayed is your mind; *self-esteem* is reliance on one's power to think. The ego you seek, that essential *"you"* which you cannot express or define, is not your emotions or inarticulate dreams, but your *intellect,* that judge of your supreme tribunal whom you've impeached in order to drift at the mercy of any stray shyster you describe as your "feeling."

[GS, *FNI*, 222; pb 177.]

Your self is your *mind;* renounce it and you become a chunk of meat ready for any cannibal to swallow.

[Ibid., 176; pb 142.]

The most *selfish* of all things is the independent mind that recognizes no authority higher than its own and no value higher than its judgment of truth.

[Ibid.]

See also REASON; SELF-ESTEEM; SELF-INTEREST; SELFISHNESS; SELFLESSNESS; THOUGHT/THINKING; VALUES.

Self-Defense. The necessary consequence of man's right to life is his right to self-defense. In a civilized society, force may be used only in retaliation and only against those who initiate its use. All the reasons which make the initiation of physical force an evil, make the retaliatory use of physical force a moral imperative.

If some "pacifist" society renounced the retaliatory use of force, it would be left helplessly at the mercy of the first thug who decided to be immoral. Such a society would achieve the opposite of its intention: instead of abolishing evil, it would encourage and reward it.

["The Nature of Government," *VOS,* 146; pb 108.]

The individual does possess the right of self-defense and *that* is the right which he delegates to the government, for the purpose of an orderly, legally defined enforcement.

["America's Persecuted Minority: Big Business," *CUI,* 46.]

A proper government is only a policeman, acting as an agent of man's self-defense, and, as such, may resort to force *only* against those who *start* the use of force.

[GS, *FNI,* 231; pb 183.]

Just as an individual has the right of self-defense, so has a free country if attacked. But this does not give its government the right to draft men into military service—which is the most blatantly statist violation of a man's right to his own life.

["The Roots of War," *CUI,* 40.]

See also DRAFT; FOREIGN POLICY; GOVERNMENT; INDIVIDUAL RIGHTS; LIFE, RIGHT to; PACIFISM; RETALIATORY FORCE; WAR.

Self-Determination of Nations. The right of "the self-determination of nations" applies only to free societies or to societies seeking to establish freedom; it does not apply to dictatorships. Just as an individual's right of free action does not include the "right" to commit crimes (that is, to violate the rights of others), so the right of a nation to determine its own form of government does not include the right to establish a slave society (that is, to legalize the enslavement of some men by others). *There is no such thing as "the right to enslave."* A nation *can* do it, just as a man *can* become a criminal—but neither can do it *by right.*

It does not matter, in this context, whether a nation was enslaved by force, like Soviet Russia, or by vote, like Nazi Germany. Individual rights are not subject to a public vote; a majority has no right to vote away the rights of a minority; the political function of rights is precisely to protect minorities from oppression by majorities (and the smallest minority on earth is the individual). Whether a slave society was conquered or *chose* to be enslaved, it can claim no national rights and no recognition of such "rights" by civilized countries—just as a mob of gangsters cannot demand a recognition of its "rights" and a legal equality with an industrial concern or a university, on the ground that the gangsters *chose* by unanimous vote to engage in that particular kind of group activity.

Dictatorship nations are outlaws. Any free nation had the *right* to invade Nazi Germany and, today, has the *right* to invade Soviet Russia, Cuba or any other slave pen. Whether a free nation chooses to do so or not is a matter of its own self-interest, *not* of respect for the non-existent "rights" of gang rulers. It is not a free nation's *duty* to liberate other nations at the price of self-sacrifice, but a free nation has the right to do it, when and if it so chooses.

[*"Collectivized 'Rights,'* " *VOS,* 139; pb 104.]

A nation that violates the rights of its own citizens cannot claim any rights whatsoever. In the issue of rights, as in all moral issues, there can be no double standard. A nation ruled by brute physical force is not a nation, but a horde—whether it is led by Attila, Genghis Khan, Hitler, Khrushchev or Castro. What rights could Attila claim and on what grounds?

[*Ibid.,* 139; pb 103.]

See also "COLLECTIVE RIGHTS"; DEMOCRACY; DICTATORSHIP; FOREIGN POLICY; FREEDOM; GOVERNMENT; INDIVIDUAL RIGHTS; NATIONAL RIGHTS; SACRIFICE; SECESSION; STATISM.

Self-Esteem.   To live, man must hold three things as the supreme and ruling values of his life: Reason—Purpose—Self-esteem. Reason, as his only tool of knowledge—Purpose, as his choice of the happiness which that tool must proceed to achieve—Self-esteem, as his inviolate certainty that his mind is competent to think and his person is worthy of happiness, which means: is worthy of living.

[GS, *FNI*, 156; pb 128.]

By a feeling he has not learned to identify, but has derived from his first awareness of existence, from his discovery that he has to make choices, man knows that his desperate need of self-esteem is a matter of life or death. As a being of volitional consciousness, he knows that he must know his own value in order to maintain his own life. He knows that he has to be *right;* to be wrong in action means danger to his life; to be wrong in person, to be *evil,* means to be unfit for existence.

Every act of man's life has to be willed; the mere act of obtaining or eating his food implies that the person he preserves is worthy of being preserved; every pleasure he seeks to enjoy implies that the person who seeks it is worthy of finding enjoyment. He has no choice about his need of self-esteem, his only choice is the standard by which to gauge it. And he makes his fatal error when he switches this gauge protecting his life into the service of his own destruction, when he chooses a standard contradicting existence and sets his self-esteem against reality.

[Ibid., 220; pb 176.]

No value is higher than self-esteem, but you've invested it in counterfeit securities—and now your morality has caught you in a trap where you are forced to protect your self-esteem by fighting for the creed of self-destruction. The grim joke is on you: that need of self-esteem, which you're unable to explain or to define, belongs to *my* morality, not yours; it's the objective token of my code, it is my proof within your own soul.

[Ibid., 220; pb 175.]

Self-esteem is reliance on one's power to think. It cannot be replaced by one's power to deceive. The self-confidence of a scientist and the self-confidence of a con man are not interchangeable states, and do not come from the same psychological universe. The success of a man who deals with reality augments his self-confidence. The success of a con man augments his panic.

["The Age of Envy," *NL*, 181.]

The man of authentic self-confidence is the man who relies on the judgment of his own mind. Such a man is not malleable; he may be mistaken, he may be fooled in a given instance, but he is *inflexible* in regard to the absolutism of reality, i.e., in seeking and demanding truth. . . .

There is only one source of authentic self-confidence: reason.

[Ibid., 182.]

The attack on "selfishness" is an attack on man's self-esteem; to surrender one, is to surrender the other.

["Introduction," *VOS*, xv; pb xi.]

Honor is self-esteem made visible in action.

["Philosophy: Who Needs It," *PWNI*, 12; pb 10.]

To love is to value. Only a rationally selfish man, a man of *self-esteem*, is capable of love—because he is the only man capable of holding firm, consistent, uncompromising, unbetrayed values. The man who does not value himself, cannot value anything or anyone.

["The Objectivist Ethics," *VOS*, 29; pb 32.]

See also ALTRUISM; FREE WILL; HUMILITY; LOVE; MENTAL HEALTH; PRIDE; PSYCHOLOGY; REASON; SACRIFICE; SELF; SELF-ISHNESS; SEX; VALUES.

Self-Evident. Nothing is self-evident except the material of sensory perception.

["Philosophical Detection," *PWNI*, 15; pb 13.]

When we speak of "direct perception" or "direct awareness," we mean the perceptual level. Percepts, not sensations, are the given, the self-evident. The knowledge of sensations as components of percepts is not direct, it is acquired by man much later: it is a scientific, *conceptual* discovery.

[*ITOE*, 5.]

See also AXIOMS; COROLLARIES; OSTENSIVE DEFINITION; PERCEPTION; PROOF; SENSATIONS; VALIDATION.

Self-Interest. Just as man cannot survive by any random means, but must discover and practice the principles which his survival requires, so man's self-interest cannot be determined by blind desires or random whims, but must be discovered and achieved by the guidance of rational principles. This is why the Objectivist ethics is a morality of *rational* self-interest—or of *rational selfishness*.

["Introduction," *VOS*, xiv; pb x.]

When one speaks of man's right to exist for his own sake, for his own rational self-interest, most people assume automatically that this means his right to sacrifice others. Such an assumption is a confession of their own belief that to injure, enslave, rob or murder others is in man's self-interest—which he must selflessly renounce. The idea that man's self-interest can be served only by a non-sacrificial relationship with others has never occurred to those humanitarian apostles of unselfishness, who proclaim their desire to achieve the brotherhood of men. And it will not occur to them, or to anyone, so long as the concept "rational" is omitted from the context of "values," "desires," "self-interest" and *ethics.*

["The Objectivist Ethics," *VOS,* 28; pb 30.]

The term "interests" is a wide abstraction that covers the entire field of ethics. It includes the issues of: man's values, his desires, his goals and their actual achievement in reality. A man's "interests" depend on the kind of goals he chooses to pursue, his choice of goals depends on his desires, his desires depend on his values—and, for a rational man, his values depend on the judgment of his mind.

Desires (or feelings or emotions or wishes or whims) are not tools of cognition; they are not a valid standard of value, nor a valid criterion of man's interests. The mere fact that a man desires something does not constitute a proof that the object of his desire is *good,* nor that its achievement is actually to his interest.

To claim that a man's interests are sacrificed whenever a desire of his is frustrated—is to hold a subjectivist view of man's values and interests. Which means: to believe that it is proper, moral and possible for man to achieve his goals, regardless of whether they contradict the facts of reality or not. Which means: to hold an irrational or mystical view of existence. Which means: to deserve no further consideration.

["The 'Conflicts' of Men's Interests," *VOS,* 57; pb 50.]

See also EMOTIONS; GOOD, the; LIFE; MORALITY; OBJECTIVISM; PRINCIPLES; RATIONALITY; SACRIFICE; SELFISHNESS; SELF-LESSNESS; VALUES.

Selfishness. The Objectivist ethics proudly advocates and upholds *rational selfishness*—which means: the values required for man's survival *qua* man—which means: the values required for *human* survival—not the values produced by the desires, the emotions, the "aspirations," the feelings, the whims or the needs of irrational brutes, who have never outgrown the primordial practice of human sacrifices, have never discovered an industrial society and can conceive of no self-interest but that of grabbing the loot of the moment.

The Objectivist ethics holds that *human* good does not require human sacrifices and cannot be achieved by the sacrifice of anyone to anyone. It holds that the *rational* interests of men do not clash—that there is no conflict of interests among men who do not desire the unearned, who do not make sacrifices nor accept them, who deal with one another as *traders*, giving value for value.

["The Objectivist Ethics," *VOS*, 28; pb 31.]

The meaning ascribed in popular usage to the word "selfishness" is not merely wrong: it represents a devastating intellectual "package-deal," which is responsible, more than any other single factor, for the arrested moral development of mankind.

In popular usage, the word "selfishness" is a synonym of evil; the image it conjures is of a murderous brute who tramples over piles of corpses to achieve his own ends, who cares for no living being and pursues nothing but the gratification of the mindless whims of any immediate moment.

Yet the exact meaning and dictionary definition of the word "selfishness" is: *concern with one's own interests.*

This concept does *not* include a moral evaluation; it does not tell us whether concern with one's own interests is good or evil; nor does it tell us what constitutes man's actual interests. It is the task of ethics to answer such questions.

["Introduction," *VOS*, ix; pb vii.]

There is a fundamental moral difference between a man who sees his self-interest in production and a man who sees it in robbery. The evil of a robber does *not* lie in the fact that he pursues his own interests, but in *what* he regards as to his own interest; *not* in the fact that he pursues his values, but in *what* he chose to value; *not* in the fact that he wants to live, but in the fact that he wants to live on a subhuman level (see "The Objectivist Ethics").

If it is true that what I mean by "selfishness" is not what is meant conventionally, then *this* is one of the worst indictments of altruism: it means that altruism *permits no concept* of a self-respecting, self-supporting man—a man who supports his life by his own effort and neither sacrifices himself nor others. It means that altruism permits no view of men except as sacrificial animals and profiteers-on-sacrifice, as victims and parasites—that it permits no concept of a benevolent co-existence among men—that it permits no concept of *justice.*

[Ibid., xii; pb ix.]

To redeem both man and morality, it is the concept of *"selfishness"* that one has to redeem.

The first step is to assert *man's right to a moral existence*—that is: to recognize his need of a moral code to guide the course and the fulfill-ment of his own life. . . .

The reasons why man needs a moral code will tell you that the pur-pose of morality is to define man's proper values and interests, that *concern with his own interests* is the essence of a moral existence, and that *man must be the beneficiary of his own moral actions.*

Since all values have to be gained and/or kept by men's actions, any breach between actor and beneficiary necessitates an injustice: the sac-rifice of some men to others, of the actors to the nonactors, of the moral to the immoral. Nothing could ever justify such a breach, and no one ever has.

The choice of the beneficiary of moral values is merely a preliminary or introductory issue in the field of morality. It is not a substitute for morality nor a criterion of moral value, as altruism has made it. Neither is it a moral *primary:* it has to be derived from and validated by the fundamental premises of a moral system.

The Objectivist ethics holds that the actor must always be the benefi-ciary of his action and that man must act for his own *rational* self-interest. But his right to do so is derived from his nature as man and from the function of moral values in human life—and, therefore, is applicable *only* in the context of a rational, objectively demonstrated and validated code of moral principles which define and determine his ac-tual self-interest. It is not a license "to do as he pleases" and it is not applicable to the altruists' image of a "selfish" brute nor to any man motivated by irrational emotions, feelings, urges, wishes or whims.

This is said as a warning against the kind of "Nietzschean egoists" who, in fact, are a product of the altruist morality and represent the other side of the altruist coin: the men who believe that any action, regardless of its nature, is good if it is intended for one's own benefit. Just as the satisfaction of the irrational desires of others is *not* a criterion of moral value, neither is the satisfaction of one's own irrational desires. Morality is not a contest of whims . . .

A similar type of error is committed by the man who declares that since man must be guided by his own independent judgment, any action he chooses to take is moral if *he* chooses it. One's own independent judgment is the *means* by which one must choose one's actions, but it is not a moral criterion nor a moral validation: only reference to a demon-strable principle can validate one's choices.

Just as man cannot survive by any random means, but must discover and practice the principles which his survival requires, so man's self-interest cannot be determined by blind desires or random whims, but must be discovered and achieved by the guidance of rational principles. This is why the Objectivist ethics is a morality of *rational* self-interest—or of *rational selfishness.*

Since selfishness is "concern with one's own interests," the Objectivist ethics uses that concept in its exact and purest sense. It is not a concept that one can surrender to man's enemies, nor to the unthinking misconceptions, distortions, prejudices and fears of the ignorant and the irrational. The attack on "selfishness" is an attack on man's self-esteem; to surrender one, is to surrender the other.

[Ibid., xiii; pb ix.]

Do you ask what moral obligation I owe to my fellow men? None—except the obligation I owe to myself, to material objects and to all of existence: rationality. I deal with men as my nature and theirs demands: by means of reason. I seek or desire nothing from them except such relations as they care to enter of their own voluntary choice. It is only with their mind that I can deal and only for my own self-interest, when they see that my interest coincides with theirs. When they don't, I enter no relationship; I let dissenters go their way and I do not swerve from mine. I win by means of nothing but logic and I surrender to nothing but logic. I do not surrender my reason or deal with men who surrender theirs.

[GS, *FNI*, 163; pb 133.]

Men have been taught that the ego is the synonym of evil, and selflessness the ideal of virtue. But the creator is the egoist in the absolute sense, and the selfless man is the one who does not think, feel, judge or act. These are functions of the self.

Here the basic reversal is most deadly. The issue has been perverted and man has been left no alternative—and no freedom. As poles of good and evil, he was offered two conceptions: egoism and altruism. Egoism was held to mean the sacrifice of others to self. Altruism—the sacrifice of self to others. This tied man irrevocably to other men and left him nothing but a choice of pain: his own pain borne for the sake of others or pain inflicted upon others for the sake of self. When it was added that man must find joy in self-immolation, the trap was closed. Man was forced to accept masochism as his ideal—under the threat that sadism was his only alternative. This was the greatest fraud ever perpetrated on mankind.

This was the device by which dependence and suffering were perpetuated as fundamentals of life.

The choice is not self-sacrifice or domination. The choice is independence or dependence. The code of the creator or the code of the second-hander. This is the basic issue. It rests upon the alternative of life or death. The code of the creator is built on the needs of the reasoning mind which allows man to survive. The code of the second-hander is built on the needs of a mind incapable of survival. All that which proceeds from man's independent ego is good. All that which proceeds from man's dependence upon men is evil.

The egoist in the absolute sense is not the man who sacrifices others. He is the man who stands above the need of using others in any manner. He does not function through them. He is not concerned with them in any primary matter. Not in his aim, not in his motive, not in his thinking, not in his desires, not in the source of his energy. He does not exist for any other man—and he asks no other man to exist for him. This is the only form of brotherhood and mutual respect possible between men.

["The Soul of an Individualist," *FNI*, 94; pb 81.]

The moral purpose of a man's life is the achievement of his own happiness. This does not mean that he is indifferent to all men, that human life is of no value to him and that he has no reason to help others in an emergency. But it *does* mean that he does not subordinate his life to the welfare of others, that he does not sacrifice himself to their needs, that the relief of their suffering is not his primary concern, that any help he gives is an *exception*, not a rule, an act of generosity, not of moral duty, that it is *marginal* and *incidental*—as disasters are marginal and incidental in the course of human existence—and that *values*, not disasters, are the goal, the first concern and the motive power of his life.

["The Ethics of Emergencies," *VOS*, 55; pb 49.]

Love, friendship, respect, admiration are the emotional response of one man to the virtues of another, the spiritual *payment* given in exchange for the personal, selfish pleasure which one man derives from the virtues of another man's character. Only a brute or an altruist would claim that the appreciation of another person's virtues is an act of selflessness, that as far as one's own selfish interest and pleasure are concerned, it makes no difference whether one deals with a genius or a fool, whether one meets a hero or a thug, whether one marries an ideal woman or a slut. In spiritual issues, a trader is a man who does not seek to be loved for his weaknesses or flaws, only for his virtues, and who does not grant his love to the weaknesses or the flaws of others, only to their virtues.

["The Objectivist Ethics," *VOS*, 29; pb 31.]

The first right on earth is the right of the ego. Man's first duty is to himself. His moral law is never to place his prime goal within the persons of others. His moral obligation is to do what he wishes, provided his wish does not depend *primarily* upon other men. This includes the whole sphere of his creative faculty, his thinking, his work. But it does not include the sphere of the gangster, the altruist and the dictator.

A man thinks and works alone. A man cannot rob, exploit or rule— alone. Robbery, exploitation and ruling presuppose victims. They imply dependence. They are the province of the second-hander.

Rulers of men are not egoists. They create nothing. They exist entirely through the persons of others. Their goal is in their subjects, in the activity of enslaving. They are as dependent as the beggar, the social worker and the bandit. The form of dependence does not matter.

["The Soul of an Individualist," *FNI*, 96; pb 82.]

See also ALTRUISM; AMORALISM; CAPITALISM; CHARITY; COLLEC- TIVISM; CREATORS; "DUTY"; EMOTIONS; GOOD, the; HAPPINESS; INDEPENDENCE; INDIVIDUALISM; LIFE; LOVE; MAN; MORALITY; NIETZSCHE, FRIEDRICH; "PACKAGE-DEALING," FALLACY of; PRIDE; PRODUCTIVENESS; RATIONALITY; REASON; RESPONSIBILITY/ OBLIGATION; SACRIFICE; SECOND-HANDERS; SELF; SELF-ESTEEM; SELF-INTEREST; SELFLESSNESS; STANDARD OF VALUE; TRADER PRINCIPLE; VALUES; VIRTUE; WHIMS/WHIM-WORSHIP.

Selflessness.   Men have been taught that the ego is the synonym of evil, and selflessness the ideal of virtue. But the creator is the egoist in the absolute sense, and the selfless man is the one who does not think, feel, judge or act. These are functions of the self.

["The Soul of an Individualist," *FNI*, 94; pb 81.]

[Peter Keating is] paying the price and wondering for what sin and telling himself that he's been too selfish. In what act or thought of his has there ever been a self? What was his aim in life? Greatness—in other people's eyes. Fame, admiration, envy—all that which comes from others. Others dictated his convictions, which he did not hold, but he was satisfied that others believed he held them. Others were his motive power and his prime concern. He didn't want to be great, but to be thought great. He didn't want to build, but to be admired as a builder. He borrowed from others in order to make an impression on others. There's your actual selflessness. It's his ego that he's betrayed and given up. But everybody calls him selfish. . . .

Isn't that the root of every despicable action? Not selfishness, but precisely the absence of a self. Look at them. The man who cheats and lies, but preserves a respectable front. He knows himself to be dishonest, but others think he's honest and he derives his self-respect from that, second-hand. The man who takes credit for an achievement which is not his own. He knows himself to be mediocre, but he's great in the eyes of others. The frustrated wretch who professes love for the inferior and clings to those less endowed, in order to establish his own superiority by comparison.

["The Nature of the Second-Hander," *FNI*, 78; pb 68.]

When you are in love, it means that the person you love is of great personal, selfish importance to you and to your life. If you were selfless, it would have to mean that you derive no personal pleasure or happiness from the company and the existence of the person you love, and that you are motivated only by self-sacrificial pity for that person's need of you. I don't have to point out to you that no one would be flattered by, nor would accept, a concept of that kind. Love is not self-sacrifice, but the most profound assertion of your own needs and values. It is for your *own* happiness that you need the person you love, and that is the greatest compliment, the greatest tribute you can pay to that person.

["*Playboy's* Interview with Ayn Rand," pamphlet, 7.]

See also ALTRUISM; LOVE; SECOND-HANDERS; SELF; SELFISH-NESS; SELF-ESTEEM.

Self-Sacrifice. *See Altruism; Sacrifice; Selflessness.*

Sensations. The lower of the conscious species possess only the faculty of *sensation*, which is sufficient to direct their actions and provide for their needs. A sensation is produced by the automatic reaction of a sense organ to a stimulus from the outside world; it lasts for the duration of the immediate moment, as long as the stimulus lasts and no longer. Sensations are an automatic response, an automatic form of knowledge, which a consciousness can neither seek nor evade. An organism that possesses only the faculty of sensation is guided by the pleasure-pain mechanism of its body. . . .

The higher organisms possess a much more potent form of consciousness: they possess the faculty of *retaining* sensations, which is the faculty of *perception*. A "perception" is a group of sensations automatically retained and integrated by the brain of a living organism, which gives it the ability to be aware, not of single stimuli, but of *entities*, of things. An animal is guided, not merely by immediate sensations, but by *percepts*. Its actions are not single, discrete responses to single, separate stimuli, but are directed by an integrated awareness of the *perceptual* reality confronting it.

["The Objectivist Ethics," *VOS*, 9; pb 18.]

Although, chronologically, man's consciousness develops in three stages: the stage of sensations, the perceptual, the conceptual—epistemologically, the base of all of man's knowledge is the *perceptual* stage.

Sensations, as such, are not retained in man's memory, nor is man able to experience a pure isolated sensation. As far as can be ascertained, an infant's sensory experience is an undifferentiated chaos. Discriminated awareness begins on the level of percepts. . . .

Percepts, not sensations, are the given, the self-evident. The knowledge of sensations as components of percepts is not direct, it is acquired by man much later: it is a scientific, *conceptual* discovery . . .

(It may be supposed that the concept "existent" is implicit even on the level of sensations—if and to the extent that a consciousness is able to discriminate on that level. A sensation is a sensation of *something*, as distinguished from the *nothing* of the preceding and succeeding moments. A sensation does not tell man *what* exists, but only *that* it exists.)

[*ITOE*, 5.]

Sensations are the primary material of consciousness and, therefore, cannot be communicated by means of the material which is derived from them. The existential causes of sensations can be described and defined in conceptual terms (e.g., the wavelengths of light and the structure of the human eye, which produce the sensations of color), but one cannot communicate what color is like, to a person who is born blind. To define the meaning of the concept "blue," for instance, one must point to some blue objects to signify, in effect: "I mean *this*." Such an identification of a concept is known as an "ostensive definition."

[Ibid., 53.]

See also CONCEPTS; ENTITY; INTEGRATION (MENTAL); OSTENSIVE DEFINITION; PERCEPTION; PLEASURE AND PAIN.

Sense of Life.   A sense of life is a pre-conceptual equivalent of metaphysics, an emotional, subconsciously integrated appraisal of man and of existence. It sets the nature of a man's emotional responses and the essence of his character.

Long before he is old enough to grasp such a concept as metaphysics, man makes choices, forms value-judgments, experiences emotions and acquires a certain *implicit* view of life. Every choice and value-judgment implies some estimate of himself and of the world around him—most particularly, of his capacity to deal with the world. He may draw conscious conclusions, which may be true or false; or he may remain mentally passive and merely react to events (i.e., merely feel). Whatever the case may be, his subconscious mechanism sums up his psychological activities, integrating his conclusions, reactions or evasions into an emotional sum that establishes a habitual pattern and becomes his automatic response to the world around him. What began as a series of single, discreet conclusions (or evasions) about his own particular problems, becomes a generalized feeling about existence, an implicit *metaphysics* with the compelling motivational power of a constant, basic emotion—an emotion which is part of all his other emotions and underlies all his experiences. *This* is a sense of life.

["Philosophy and Sense of Life," *RM*, 31; pb 25.]

If one saw, in real life, a beautiful woman wearing an exquisite evening gown, with a cold sore on her lips, the blemish would mean nothing but a minor affliction, and one would ignore it.

But a painting of such a woman would be a corrupt, obscenely vicious attack on man, on beauty, on all values—and one would experience a feeling of immense disgust and indignation at the artist. (There are also those who would feel something like approval and who would belong to the same moral category as the artist.)

The emotional response to that painting would be instantaneous, much faster than the viewer's mind could identify all the reasons involved. The psychological mechanism which produces that response (and which produced the painting) is a man's sense of life.

(A sense of life is a pre-conceptual equivalent of metaphysics, an emotional, subconsciously integrated appraisal of man and of existence.)

It is the artist's sense of life that controls and integrates his work, directing the innumerable choices he has to make, from the choice of subject to the subtlest details of style. It is the viewer's or reader's sense of life that responds to a work of art by a complex, yet automatic reaction of acceptance and approval, or rejection and condemnation.

This does not mean that a sense of life is a valid criterion of esthetic merit, either for the artist or the viewer. A sense of life is *not* infallible. But a sense of life is the source of art, the psychological mechanism which enables man to create a realm such as art.

The emotion involved in art is not an emotion in the ordinary meaning of the term. It is experienced more as a "sense" or a "feel," but it has two characteristics pertaining to emotions: it is automatically immediate and it has an intense, profoundly personal (yet undefined) value-meaning to the individual experiencing it. The value involved is life, and the words naming the emotion are: "*This* is what life means to *me*."

Regardless of the nature or content of an artist's metaphysical views, what an art work expresses, fundamentally, under all of its lesser aspects is: "*This* is life as *I* see it." The essential meaning of a viewer's or reader's response, under all of its lesser elements, is: "*This* is (or is *not*) life as I see it."

["Art and Sense of Life," *RM*, 43; pb 34.]

A sense of life is formed by a process of emotional generalization which may be described as a subconscious counterpart of a process of abstraction, since it is a method of classifying and integrating. But it is a process of *emotional* abstraction: it consists of classifying things *according to the emotions they invoke*—i.e., of tying together, by association or connotation, all those things which have the power to make an individual experience the same (or a similar) emotion. For instance: a new neighborhood, a discovery, adventure, struggle, triumph—or: the folks next door, a memorized recitation, a family picnic, a known routine, comfort. On a more adult level: a heroic man, the skyline of New York, a sunlit landscape, pure colors, ecstatic music—or: a humble man, an old village, a foggy landscape, muddy colors, folk music. . . . The subverbal, subconscious criterion of selection that forms his emotional abstractions is: "That which is important to *me*" or: "The kind of universe which is right for *me*, in which *I* would feel at home." . . .

It is only those values which he regards or grows to regard as "important," those which represent his implicit view of reality, that remain in a man's subconscious and form his sense of life.

"It is important to understand things"—"It is important to obey my parents"—"It is important to act on my own"—"It is important to please other people"—"It is important to fight for what I want"—"It is important not to make enemies"—"My life is important"—"Who am I to stick my neck out?" Man is a being of self-made soul—and it is of such conclusions that the stuff of his soul is made. (By "soul" I mean "consciousness.")

The integrated sum of a man's basic values is his sense of life.

["Philosophy and Sense of Life," *RM*, 33; pb 27.]

A given person's sense of life is hard to identify conceptually, because it is hard to isolate: it is involved in everything about that person, in his every thought, emotion, action, in his every response, in his every choice and value, in his every spontaneous gesture, in his manner of moving, talking, smiling, in the total of his personality. It is that which makes him a "personality."

Introspectively, one's own sense of life is experienced as an absolute and an irreducible primary—as that which one never questions, because *the thought of questioning it never arises*. Extrospectively, the sense of life of another person strikes one as an immediate, yet undefinable, impression—on very short acquaintance—an impression which often feels like certainty, yet is exasperatingly elusive, if one attempts to verify it.

This leads many people to regard a sense of life as the province of some sort of special intuition, as a matter perceivable only by some special, non-rational insight. The exact opposite is true: a sense of life is *not* an irreducible primary, but a very complex sum; it can be felt, but it cannot be understood, by an automatic reaction; to be understood, it has to be analyzed, identified and verified conceptually. That automatic impression—of oneself or of others—is only a lead; left untranslated, it can be a very deceptive lead. But if and when that intangible impression is supported by and unites with the conscious judgment of one's mind, the result is the most exultant form of certainty one can ever experience: it is the integration of mind and values.

There are two aspects of man's existence which are the special province and expression of his sense of life: love and art.

[Ibid., 39; pb 31.]

A culture, like an individual, has a sense of life or, rather, the equivalent of a sense of life—an emotional atmosphere created by its dominant philosophy, by its view of man and of existence. This emotional atmosphere represents a culture's dominant values and serves as the leitmotif of a given age, setting its trends and its style.

Thus Western civilization had an Age of Reason and an Age of Enlightenment. In those periods, the quest for reason and enlightenment was the dominant intellectual drive and created a corresponding emotional atmosphere that fostered these values.

Today, we live in the Age of Envy.

["The Age of Envy," *NL*, 152.]

A nation's sense of life is formed by every individual child's early impressions of the world around him: of the ideas he is taught (which he may or may not accept) and of the way of acting he observes and evaluates (which he may evaluate correctly or not). And although there are exceptions at both ends of the psychological spectrum—men whose sense of life is better (truer philosophically) or worse than that of their fellow-citizens—the majority develop the essentials of the same subconscious philosophy. This is the source of what we observe as "national characteristics." . . .

Just as an individual's sense of life can be better or worse than his conscious convictions, so can a nation's. And just as an individual who has never translated his sense of life into conscious convictions is in terrible danger—no matter how good his subconscious values—so is a nation.

This is the position of America today.

If America is to be saved from destruction—specifically, from dictatorship—she will be saved by her sense of life.

["Don't Let It Go," *PWNI*, 251; pb 206.]

A sense of life is not a substitute for explicit knowledge. Values which one cannot identify, but merely senses implicitly, are not in one's control. One cannot tell what they depend on or require, what course of action is needed to gain and/or keep them. One can lose or betray them without knowing it.

[Ibid., 256; pb 210.]

See also AMERICA; ART; ARTISTIC CREATION; BENEVOLENT UNIVERSE PREMISE; EMOTIONS; ENLIGHTENMENT, AGE OF; ENVY/ HATRED of the GOOD for BEING the GOOD; ESTHETIC ABSTRACTIONS; ESTHETIC JUDGMENT; LOVE; MALEVOLENT UNIVERSE PREMISE; METAPHYSICAL VALUE-JUDGMENTS; METAPHYSICS; PHILOSOPHY; SEX; SUBCONSCIOUS.

Service.   The concept of "service" has been turned into a collectivist "package-deal" by means of a crude equivocation and a cruder evasion. In the language of economics, the word "service" means *work* offered for trade on a free market, to be paid for by those who choose to buy it. In a free society, men deal with one another by voluntary, uncoerced exchange, by mutual consent to mutual profit, each man pursuing his own rational self-interest, none sacrificing himself or others; and all values—whether goods or services—are *traded,* not given away.

This is the opposite of what the word "service" means in the language of altruist ethics: to an altruist, "service" means unrewarded, self-sacrificial, unilateral *giving,* while receiving nothing in return. It is this sort of selfless "service" to "society" that collectivists demand of all men.

["How *Not* to Fight Against Socialized Medicine,"
TON, March 1963, 12.]

See also ALTRUISM; CAPITALISM; COLLECTIVISM; "PACKAGE-DEALING," FALLACY of; SACRIFICE; SELFISHNESS; TRADER PRINCIPLE.

Sex.   Sex is a physical capacity, but its exercise is determined by man's mind—by his choice of values, held consciously or subconsciously. To a rational man, sex is an expression of self-esteem—*a celebration of himself and of existence.* To the man who lacks self-esteem, sex is an attempt to fake it, to acquire its momentary illusion.

Romantic love, in the full sense of the term, is an emotion possible only to the man (or woman) of unbreached self-esteem: it is his response to his own highest values in the person of another—an integrated response of mind and body, of love and sexual desire. Such a man (or woman) is incapable of experiencing a sexual desire divorced from spiritual values.

["Of Living Death," *TO*, Oct. 1968, 2.]

Just as an idea unexpressed in physical action is contemptible hypocrisy, so is platonic love—and just as physical action unguided by an idea is a fool's self-fraud, so is sex when cut off from one's code of values. . . . Only the man who extols the purity of a love devoid of desire, is capable of the depravity of a desire devoid of love.

["The Meaning of Sex," *FNI*, 120; pb 100.]

The man who despises himself tries to gain self-esteem from sexual adventures—which can't be done, because sex is not the cause, but an effect and an expression of a man's sense of his own value . . .

The men who think that wealth comes from material resources and has no intellectual root or meaning, are the men who think—for the same reason—that sex is a physical capacity which functions independently of one's mind, choice or code of values. They think that your body creates a desire and makes a choice for you—just about in some such way as if iron ore transformed itself into railroad rails of its own volition. Love is blind, they say; sex is impervious to reason and mocks the power of all philosophers. But, in fact, a man's sexual choice is the result and the sum of his fundamental convictions. Tell me what a man finds sexually attractive and I will tell you his entire philosophy of life. Show me the woman he sleeps with and I will tell you his valuation of himself. No matter what corruption he's taught about the virtue of selflessness, sex is the most profoundly selfish of all acts, an act which he cannot perform for any motive but his own enjoyment—just try to think of performing it in a spirit of selfless charity!—an act which is not possible in self-abasement, only in self-exaltation, only in the confidence of being desired and being worthy of desire. It is an act that forces him to stand naked in spirit, as well as in body, and to accept his real ego as his standard of value. He will always be attracted to the woman who reflects his deepest vision of himself, the woman whose surrender permits him to experience—or to fake—a sense of self-esteem. . . . Love is our response to our highest values—and can be nothing else.

[Ibid., 118; pb 99.]

The doctrine that man's sexual capacity belongs to a lower or animal part of his nature . . . is the necessary consequence of the doctrine that man is not an integrated entity, but a being torn apart by two opposite, antagonistic, irreconcilable elements: his body, which is of this earth, and his soul, which is of another, supernatural realm. According to that doctrine, man's sexual capacity—regardless of how it is exercised or motivated, not merely its abuses, not unfastidious indulgence or promiscuity, but *the capacity as such*—is sinful or depraved.

["Of Living Death," *TO*, Sept. 1968, 1.]

Sex is one of the most important aspects of man's life and, therefore, must never be approached lightly or casually. A sexual relationship is proper only on the ground of the highest values one can find in a human being. Sex must not be anything other than a response to values. And that is why I consider promiscuity immoral. Not because sex is evil, but because sex is too good and too important. . . .

[Sex should] involve . . . a very serious relationship. Whether that relationship should or should not become a marriage is a question which depends on the circumstances and the context of the two persons' lives. I consider marriage a very important institution, but it is important *when* and *if* two people have found the person with whom they wish to spend the rest of their lives—a question of which no man or woman can be automatically certain. When one is certain that one's choice is final, then marriage is, of course, a desirable state. But this does *not* mean that any relationship based on less than total certainty is improper. I think the question of an affair or a marriage depends on the knowledge and the position of the two persons involved and should be left up to them. Either is moral, provided only that both parties take the relationship seriously and that it is based on values.

["*Playboy*'s Interview with Ayn Rand," pamphlet, 8.]

See also ABORTION; BIRTH CONTROL; EMOTIONS; FEMININITY; FREUD; LOVE; MARRIAGE; PHILOSOPHY; RELIGION; SELF-ESTEEM; SELFISHNESS; SENSE of LIFE; SOUL-BODY DICHOTOMY; VALUES.

Similarity. The element of *similarity* is crucially involved in the formation of every concept; similarity, in this context, is the relationship between two or more existents which possess the same characteristic(s), but in different measure or degree. . . .

Similarity is grasped *perceptually;* in observing it, man is not and does not have to be aware of the fact that it involves a matter of measurement. It is the task of philosophy and of science to identify that fact.

[*ITOE*, 15.]

See also CONCEPT-FORMATION; MEASUREMENT; PERCEPTION.

Singing. *See Performing Arts.*

Skepticism. "We know that we know nothing," they chatter, blanking out the fact that they are claiming knowledge—"There are no absolutes," they chatter, blanking out the fact that they are uttering an absolute—"You cannot *prove* that you exist or that you're conscious," they chatter, blanking out the fact that *proof* presupposes existence, consciousness and a complex chain of knowledge: the existence of something to know, of a consciousness able to know it, and of a knowledge that has learned to distinguish between such concepts as the proved and the unproved.

[GS, *FNI*, 192; pb 154.]

In the history of philosophy—with some very rare exceptions—epistemological theories have . . . taught either that knowledge is impossible (skepticism) or that it is available without effort (mysticism). These two positions appear to be antagonists, but are, in fact, two variants on the same theme, two sides of the same fraudulent coin: the attempt to escape the responsibility of rational cognition and the absolutism of reality—the attempt to assert the primacy of consciousness over existence. . . .

The mystic is usually an exponent of the *intrinsic* (revealed) school of epistemology; the skeptic is usually an advocate of epistemological *subjectivism.*

[*ITOE*, 105.]

The crusading skepticism of the modern era; the mounting attack on absolutes, certainty, reason itself; the insistence that firm convictions are a disease and that compromise in any dispute is men's only recourse— all this, in significant part, is an outgrowth of Descartes' basic approach to philosophy. To reclaim the self-confidence of man's mind, the first modern to refute is Kant (see *Introduction to Objectivist Epistemology*); the second is Descartes.

Observe that Descartes starts his system by using "error" and its synonyms or derivatives as "stolen concepts."

Men have been wrong, and therefore, he implies, they can never know what is right. But if they cannot, how did they ever discover that they were wrong? How can one form such concepts as "mistake" or "error" while wholly ignorant of what is correct? "Error" signifies a departure from truth; the concept of "error" logically presupposes that one has already grasped some truth. If truth were unknowable, as Descartes implies, the idea of a departure from it would be meaningless.

The same point applies to concepts denoting specific forms of error.

If we cannot ever be certain that an argument is logically valid, if validity is unknowable, then the concept of "invalid" reasoning is impossible to reach or apply. If we cannot ever know that a man is sane, then the concept of "insanity" is impossible to form or define. If we cannot recognize the state of being awake, then we cannot recognize or conceptualize a state of *not* being awake (such as dreaming). If man cannot grasp X, then "non-X" stands for nothing.

Fallibility does not make knowledge impossible. Knowledge is what makes possible the discovery of fallibility.

[Leonard Peikoff, " 'Maybe You're Wrong,' " *TOF*, April 1981, 8.]

It is possible, the skeptic argument declares, *for* man to be in error; therefore, it is possible *that* every individual is in error on every question. This argument is a non sequitur; it is an equivocation on the term "possible."

What is possible to a species under some circumstances, is not necessarily possible to every individual member of that species under every set of circumstances. Thus, it is possible for a human being to run the mile in less than four minutes; and it is possible for a human being to be pregnant. I cannot, however, go over to a crippled gentleman in his wheelchair and say: "Perhaps you'll give birth to a son next week, after you've run the mile to the hospital in 3.9 minutes—after all, you're human, and it is possible for human beings to do these things."

The same principle applies to the possibility of error—or of truth. If someone maintains that New York City is made of mushroom soup, he cannot defend his idea by saying: "It is possible for human beings to reach the truth, I am human, so maybe this is the truth." No matter what is possible under some conditions, a man cannot be "possibly" right when he is blatantly wrong. By the same token, no skeptic can declare that you are possibly wrong, when you are blatantly right. "It is possible *for man* . . ." does not justify "It is possible *that you* . . ." The latter claim depends on the individual involved, and on the conditions.

"Maybe you're wrong" is an accusation that must be supported by specific evidence. It cannot be uttered without context, grounds, or basis, i.e., arbitrarily.

[Ibid., 10.]

Doubting without a basis is the equivalent of—is indeed a form of—asserting without a basis. Both procedures, being arbitrary, are disqualified by the very nature of human cognition. In reason, certainty must precede doubt, just as a grasp of truth must precede the detection of error. To establish a claim to knowledge, what one must do is to prove an idea positively, on the basis of the full context of evidence available;

i.e., a man must prove that he *is* right. It is not incumbent on anyone—nor is it possible—to prove that he is *not* wrong, when no evidence of error has been offered.

[Ibid., 12.]

See also ABSOLUTES; AGNOSTICISM; ARBITRARY; AXIOMS; CERTAINTY; CONTEXT; EPISTEMOLOGY; FALSEHOOD; KANT, IMMANUEL; MYSTICISM; "OPEN MIND" *and* "CLOSED MIND"; PERCEPTION; POSSIBLE; PROOF; REASON; SELF-EVIDENT; "STOLEN CONCEPT," FALLACY *of;* SUBJECTIVISM; TRUTH.

Social System.

A social system is a set of moral-political-economic principles embodied in a society's laws, institutions, and government, which determine the relationships, the terms of association, among the men living in a given geographical area. It is obvious that these terms and relationships depend on an identification of man's nature, that they would be different if they pertain to a society of rational beings or to a colony of ants. It is obvious that they will be radically different if men deal with one another as free, independent individuals, on the premise that every man is an end in himself—or as members of a pack, each regarding the others as the means to *his* ends and to the ends of "the pack as a whole."

There are only two fundamental questions (or two aspects of the same question) that determine the nature of any social system: Does a social system recognize individual rights?—and: Does a social system ban physical force from human relationships? The answer to the second question is the practical implementation of the answer to the first.

["What Is Capitalism?" *CUI,* 18.]

A social system is a code of laws which men observe in order to live together. Such a code must have a basic principle, a starting point, or it cannot be devised. The starting point is the question: *Is the power of society limited or unlimited?*

Individualism answers: The power of society is limited by the inalienable, individual rights of man. Society may make only such laws as do not violate these rights.

Collectivism answers: The power of society is unlimited. Society may make any laws it wishes, and force them upon anyone in any manner it wishes.

["Textbook of Americanism," pamphlet, 3.]

See also CAPITALISM; COLLECTIVISM; GOVERNMENT; IDEOLOGY; INDIVIDUALISM; MORALITY; POLITICS; SOCIETY.

Social Theory of Ethics. The social theory of ethics substitutes "society" for God—and although it claims that its chief concern is life on earth, it is *not* the life of man, not the life of an individual, but the life of a disembodied entity, *the collective*, which, in relation to every individual, consists of everybody except himself. As far as the individual is concerned, *his* ethical duty is to be the selfless, voiceless, rightless slave of any need, claim or demand asserted by others. The motto "dog eat dog"—which is *not* applicable to capitalism nor to dogs—*is* applicable to the social theory of ethics. The existential monuments to *this* theory are Nazi Germany and Soviet Russia.

["The Objectivist Ethics," *VOS*, 33; pb 34.]

The avowed mystics held the arbitrary, unaccountable "will of God" as the standard of the good and as the validation of their ethics. The neomystics replaced it with "the good of society," thus collapsing into the circularity of a definition such as "the standard of the good is that which is good for society." This meant, in logic—and, today, in world-wide practice—that "society" stands above any principles of ethics, since *it* is the source, standard and criterion of ethics, since "the good" is whatever *it* wills, whatever *it* happens to assert as its own welfare and pleasure. This meant that "society" may do anything it pleases, since "the good" is whatever it chooses to do *because* it chooses to do it. And— since there is no such entity as "society," since society is only a number of individual men—this meant that *some* men (the majority or any gang that claims to be its spokesman) are ethically entitled to pursue any whims (or any atrocities) they desire to pursue, while *other* men are ethically obliged to spend their lives in the service of that gang's desires.

[Ibid., 3; pb 14.]

See also GOD; GOOD, the; INDIVIDUALISM; INTRINSIC THEORY of VALUES; MORALITY; MYSTICAL ETHICS; OBJECTIVE THEORY of VALUES; SOCIETY; STANDARD of VALUE; STATISM; VALUES.

Socialism. Socialism is the doctrine that man has no right to exist for his own sake, that his life and his work do not belong to *him*, but belong to society, that the only justification of his existence is his service to society, and that society may dispose of him in any way it pleases for the sake of whatever it deems to be its own tribal, collective good.

["For the New Intellectual," *FNI*, 48; pb 43.]

The essential characteristic of socialism is the denial of individual property rights; under socialism, the right to property (which is the right of use and disposal) is vested in "society as a whole," i.e., in the collective, with production and distribution controlled by the state, i.e., by the government.

Socialism may be established by force, as in the Union of Soviet Socialist Republics—or by vote, as in Nazi (National Socialist) Germany. The degree of socialization may be total, as in Russia—or partial, as in England. Theoretically, the differences are superficial; practically, they are only a matter of time. The basic principle, in all cases, is the same.

The alleged goals of socialism were: the abolition of poverty, the achievement of general prosperity, progress, peace and human brotherhood. The results have been a terrifying failure—terrifying, that is, if one's motive is men's welfare.

Instead of prosperity, socialism has brought economic paralysis and/ or collapse to every country that tried it. The degree of socialization has been the degree of disaster. The consequences have varied accordingly.

["The Monument Builders," *VOS*, 112; pb 86.]

There is no difference between the principles, policies and practical results of socialism—and those of any historical or prehistorical tyranny. Socialism is merely democratic absolute monarchy—that is, a system of absolutism without a fixed head, open to seizure of power by all comers, by any ruthless climber, opportunist, adventurer, demagogue or thug.

When you consider socialism, do not fool yourself about its nature. Remember that there is no such dichotomy as "human rights" versus "property rights." No human rights can exist without property rights. Since material goods are produced by the mind and effort of individual men, and are needed to sustain their lives, if the producer does not own the result of his effort, he does not own his life. To deny property rights means to turn men into property owned by the state. Whoever claims the "right" to "redistribute" the wealth produced by others is claiming the "right" to treat human beings as chattel.

[Ibid., 120; pb 91.]

When one observes the nightmare of the desperate efforts made by hundreds of thousands of people struggling to escape from the socialized countries of Europe, to escape over barbed-wire fences, under machine-gun fire—one can no longer believe that socialism, in any of its forms, is motivated by benevolence and by the desire to achieve men's welfare.

No man of authentic benevolence could evade or ignore so great a horror on so vast a scale.

Socialism is not a movement of the people. It is a movement of the intellectuals, originated, led and controlled by the intellectuals, carried by them out of their stuffy ivory towers into those bloody fields of practice where they unite with their allies and executors: the thugs.

[Ibid., 115; pb 87.]

The socialists had a certain kind of logic on their side: if the collective sacrifice of all to all *is* the moral ideal, then they wanted to establish this ideal in practice, here and on this earth. The arguments that socialism would not and could not work, did not stop them: neither has altruism ever worked, but this has not caused men to stop and question it. Only *reason* can ask such questions—and *reason*, they were told on all sides, has nothing to do with morality, morality lies outside the realm of reason, no *rational* morality can ever be defined.

The fallacies and contradictions in the economic theories of socialism were exposed and refuted time and time again, in the Nineteenth Century as well as today. This did not and does not stop anyone: it is not an issue of economics, but of morality. The intellectuals and the so-called idealists were determined to make socialism work. How? By that magic means of all irrationalists: *somehow.*

["Faith and Force: The Destroyers of the Modern World," *PWNI*, 82; pb 68.]

There is no difference between communism and socialism, except in the means of achieving the same ultimate end: communism proposes to enslave men by force, socialism—by vote. It is merely the difference between murder and suicide.

["Foreign Policy Drains U.S. of Main Weapon," *Los Angeles Times*, Sept. 9, 1962, G2.]

Both "socialism" and "fascism" involve the issue of property rights. The right to property is the right of use and disposal. Observe the difference in those two theories: socialism negates private property rights altogether, and advocates "the vesting of *ownership and control*" in the community as a whole, i.e., in the state; fascism leaves *ownership* in the hands of private individuals, but transfers *control* of the property to the government.

Ownership without control is a contradiction in terms: it means "property," without the right to use it or to dispose of it. It means that the citizens retain the responsibility of holding property, without any of its advantages, while the government acquires all the advantages without any of the responsibility.

In this respect, socialism is the more honest of the two theories. I say "more honest," *not* "better"—because, *in practice*, there is no difference between them: both come from the same collectivist-statist principle, both negate individual rights and subordinate the individual to the collective, both deliver the livelihood and the lives of the citizens into the power of an omnipotent government—and the differences between them are only a matter of time, degree, and superficial detail, such as the choice of slogans by which the rulers delude their enslaved subjects.

["The New Fascism: Rule by Consensus," *CUI*, 202.]

The Nazis defended their policies, and the country did not rebel; it accepted the Nazi argument. Selfish individuals may be unhappy, the Nazis said, but what we have established in Germany is the ideal system, *socialism*. In its Nazi usage this term is not restricted to a theory of economics; it is to be understood in a fundamental sense. "Socialism" for the Nazis denotes the principle of collectivism as such and its corollary, statism—in every field of human action, including but not limited to economics.

"To be a socialist," says Goebbels, "is to submit the I to the thou; socialism is sacrificing the individual to the whole."

By this definition, the Nazis practiced what they preached. They practiced it at home and then abroad. No one can claim that they did not sacrifice enough individuals.

[Leonard Peikoff, *OP*, 10; pb 19.]

See also ALTRUISM; CAPITALISM; COLLECTIVISM; DICTATORSHIP; ECONOMIC POWER *vs.* POLITICAL POWER; EGALITARIANISM; FASCISM *and* COMMUNISM/SOCIALISM; GUILD SOCIALISM; HUMAN RIGHTS *and* PROPERTY RIGHTS; INDIVIDUAL RIGHTS; "LIBERALS"; NEW LEFT; POVERTY; PROPERTY RIGHTS; "PUBLIC PROPERTY"; "REDISTRIBUTION" *of* WEALTH; SOCIETY; SOVIET RUSSIA; STATISM; TRIBALISM; TYRANNY.

Society.   Society is a large number of men who live together in the same country, and who deal with one another.

["Textbook of Americanism," pamphlet, 9.]

Modern collectivists . . . see society as a super-organism, as some supernatural entity apart from and superior to the sum of its individual members.

["Collectivized 'Rights,' " *VOS*, 138; pb 103.]

A great deal may be learned about society by studying man; but this process cannot be reversed: nothing can be learned about man by studying society—by studying the inter-relationships of entities one has never identified or defined.

["What Is Capitalism?" *CUI*, 15.]

See also COLLECTIVISM; INDIVIDUALISM.

Soul-Body Dichotomy.   They have cut man in two, setting one half against the other. They have taught him that his body and his consciousness are two enemies engaged in deadly conflict, two antagonists of opposite natures, contradictory claims, incompatible needs, that to benefit one is to injure the other, that his soul belongs to a supernatural realm, but his body is an evil prison holding it in bondage to this earth—and that the good is to defeat his body, to undermine it by years of patient struggle, digging his way to that glorious jail-break which leads into the freedom of the grave.

They have taught man that he is a hopeless misfit made of two elements, both symbols of death. A body without a soul is a corpse, a soul without a body is a ghost—yet such is their image of man's nature: the battleground of a struggle between a corpse and a ghost, a corpse endowed with some evil volition of its own and a ghost endowed with the knowledge that everything known to man is non-existent, that only the unknowable exists.

Do you observe what human faculty that doctrine was designed to ignore? It was man's mind that had to be negated in order to make him fall apart. Once he surrendered reason, he was left at the mercy of two monsters whom he could not fathom or control: of a body moved by unaccountable instincts and of a soul moved by mystic revelations—he was left as the passively ravaged victim of a battle between a robot and a dictaphone.

[GS, *FNI*, 170; pb 138.]

You are an indivisible entity of matter and consciousness. Renounce your consciousness and you become a brute. Renounce your body and you become a fake. Renounce the material world and you surrender it to evil.

[Ibid., 175; pb 142.]

As products of the split between man's soul and body, there are two kinds of teachers of the Morality of Death: the mystics of spirit and the mystics of muscle, whom you call the spiritualists and the materialists, those who believe in consciousness without existence and those who believe in existence without consciousness. Both demand the surrender of your mind, one to their revelations, the other to their reflexes. No matter how loudly they posture in the roles of irreconcilable antagonists, their moral codes are alike, and so are their aims: in matter—the enslavement of man's body, in spirit—the destruction of his mind.

[Ibid., 171; pb 138.]

The New Intellectual . . . will discard . . . the soul-body dichotomy. He will discard its irrational conflicts and contradictions, such as: mind *versus* heart, thought *versus* action, reality *versus* desire, the practical *versus* the moral. He will be an *integrated man*, that is: a thinker who is a man of action. He will know that ideas divorced from consequent action are fraudulent, and that action divorced from ideas is suicidal. He will know that the conceptual level of psycho-epistemology—the volitional level of reason and thought—is the basic necessity of man's survival and his greatest moral virtue. He will know that men need philosophy for the purpose of *living on earth*.

["For the New Intellectual," *FNI*, 59; pb 51.]

See also ANALYTIC-SYNTHETIC DICHOTOMY; CONSCIOUSNESS; EMOTIONS; EXISTENCE; HUMAN RIGHTS and PROPERTY RIGHTS; LIFE; MAN; MORAL-PRACTICAL DICHOTOMY; MYSTICS of SPIRIT and of MUSCLE; RATIONALISM vs. EMPIRICISM; RELIGION; REASON; THEORY-PRACTICE DICHOTOMY.

Soviet Russia.   The essential characteristic of socialism is the denial of individual property rights; under socialism, the right to property (which is the right of use and disposal) is vested in "society as a whole," i.e., in the collective, with production and distribution controlled by the state, i.e., by the government.

Socialism may be established by force, as in the Union of Soviet Socialist Republics—or by vote, as in Nazi (National Socialist) Germany. The degree of socialization may be total, as in Russia—or partial, as in England. Theoretically, the differences are superficial; practically, they are only a matter of time. The basic principle, in all cases, is the same.

The alleged goals of socialism were: the abolition of poverty, the achievement of general prosperity, progress, peace and human brotherhood. The results have been a terrifying failure—terrifying, that is, if one's motive is men's welfare.

Instead of prosperity, socialism has brought economic paralysis and/or collapse to every country that tried it. The degree of socialization has been the degree of disaster. The consequences have varied accordingly.

In more fully socialized countries, *famine* was the start, the insignia announcing socialist rule—as in Soviet Russia, as in Red China, as in Cuba. In those countries, socialism reduced the people to the unspeakable poverty of the pre-industrial ages, to literal starvation, and has kept them on a stagnant level of misery.

No, it is not "just temporary," as socialism's apologists have been saying—for half a century. After forty-five years of government planning, Russia is still unable to solve the problem of feeding her population.

As far as superior productivity and speed of economic progress are concerned, the question of any comparisons between capitalism and socialism has been answered once and for all—for any honest person— by the present difference between West and East Berlin.

Instead of peace, socialism has introduced a new kind of gruesome lunacy into international relations—the "cold war," which is a state of chronic war with undeclared periods of peace between wantonly sudden invasions—with Russia seizing one-third of the globe, with socialist tribes and nations at one another's throats, with socialist India invading Goa, and communist China invading socialist India.

An eloquent sign of the moral corruption of our age is the callous complacency with which most of the socialists and their sympathizers, the "liberals," regard the atrocities perpetrated in socialistic countries and accept rule by terror as a way of life—while posturing as advocates of "human brotherhood." . . .

In the name of "humanity," they condone and accept the following: the abolition of all freedom and all rights, the expropriation of all property, executions without trial, torture chambers, slave-labor camps, the mass slaughter of countless millions in Soviet Russia—and the bloody horror of East Berlin, including the bullet-riddled bodies of fleeing children.

When one observes the nightmare of the desperate efforts made by hundreds of thousands of people struggling to escape from the socialized countries of Europe, to escape over barbed-wire fences, under machine-gun fire—one can no longer believe that socialism, in any of its forms, is motivated by benevolence and by the desire to achieve men's welfare.

No man of authentic benevolence could evade or ignore so great a horror on so vast a scale.

["The Monument Builders," *VOS*, 112; pb 86.]

The collectivization of Soviet agriculture was achieved by means of a government-planned famine—planned and carried out deliberately to force peasants into collective farms; Soviet Russia's enemies claim that fifteen million peasants died in that famine; the Soviet government admits the death of seven million.

At the end of World War II, Soviet Russia's enemies claimed that thirty million people were doing forced labor in Soviet concentration camps (and were dying of planned malnutrition, human lives being cheaper than food); Soviet Russia's apologists admit to the figure of twelve million people.

["What Is Capitalism?" *CUI*, 34.]

When you hear the liberals mumble that Russia is not *really* socialistic, or that it was all Stalin's fault, or that socialism never had a *real* chance in England, or that what *they* advocate is something that's different *somehow*—you know that you are hearing the voices of men who haven't a leg to stand on, men who are reduced to some vague hope that "somehow, *my* gang would have done it better."

The secret dread of modern intellectuals, liberals and conservatives alike, the unadmitted terror at the root of their anxiety, which all of their current irrationalities are intended to stave off and to disguise, is the unstated knowledge that Soviet Russia is the full, actual, literal, consistent embodiment of the morality of altruism, that Stalin did *not* corrupt a noble ideal, that this is the only way altruism has to be or can ever be practiced. If service and self-sacrifice are a moral ideal, and if the "selfishness" of human nature prevents men from leaping into sacrificial furnaces, there is no reason—no reason that a mystic moralist could name—why a dictator should not push them in at the point of bayonets—for their own good, or the good of humanity, or the good of posterity, or the good of the latest bureaucrat's latest five-year plan. There is no reason that they can name to oppose *any* atrocity. The value of a man's life? His right to exist? His right to pursue his own happiness? These are concepts that belong to individualism and capitalism—to the antithesis of the altruist morality.

> ["Faith and Force: The Destroyers of the
> Modern World," *PWNI*, 84; pb 69.]

Half a century ago, the Soviet rulers commanded their subjects to be patient, bear privations, and make sacrifices for the sake of "industrializing" the country, promising that this was only temporary, that industrialization would bring them abundance, and Soviet progress would surpass the capitalistic West.

Today, Soviet Russia is still unable to feed her people—while the rulers scramble to copy, borrow, or steal the technological achievements of the West. Industrialization is not a static goal; it is a dynamic process with a rapid rate of obsolescence. So the wretched serfs of a planned tribal economy, who starved while waiting for electric generators and tractors, are now starving while waiting for atomic power and interplanetary travel. Thus, in a "people's state," the progress of science is a threat to the people, and every advance is taken out of the people's shrinking hides.

> ["What Is Capitalism?" *CUI*, 29.]

Under the inept government of the Czars and with the most primitive methods of agriculture, Russia was a major grain exporter. The unusually fertile soil of the Ukraine alone was (and is) capable of feeding the entire world. Whatever natural conditions are required for growing wheat, Russia had (and has) them in overabundance. That Russia should now be on a list of hungry, wheat-begging importers, is the most damning indictment of a collectivist economy that reality can offer us.

["Hunger and Freedom," *ARL,* III, 22, 4.]

Early in 1960, Anatoly Marchenko, a twenty-two-year-old laborer in the Union of Soviet Socialist Republics, happened to be present when a brawl erupted among some workers in a hostel. Every person found on the scene—innocent or guilty—was arrested and sent to a Siberian prison camp. Marchenko was one of them. He escaped from the camp and fled toward the Iranian border. Fifty yards from it, he was captured. While Western "humanitarians" were loudly applauding the "new liberalism" of the Khrushchev regime, Anatoly Marchenko was convicted of high treason and sentenced to six years in Russia's concentration camps.

My Testimony is Marchenko's report on those years. "When I was locked up in Vladimir Prison I was often seized by despair," he writes in his preface. "Hunger, illness, and above all helplessness, the sheer impossibility of struggling against evil, provoked me to the point where I was ready to hurl myself upon my jailers with the sole aim of being killed. Or to put an end to myself in some other way. Or to maim myself as I had seen others do.

"One thing alone prevented me, one thing alone gave me the strength to live through that nightmare: the hope that I would eventually come out and tell the whole world what I had seen and experienced. I promised myself that for the sake of this aim I would suffer and endure everything. And I gave my word on this to my comrades who were doomed to spend many more years behind bars and barbed wire." ...

Marchenko's account of his life in Vladimir [prison] is so horrifying that it becomes, at times, almost impossible to continue reading. Anyone who doubts the nature of the Soviet system should read every word. ...

For more than fifty years, the West's liberal intellectuals have proclaimed their love for mankind, while being bored by the rivers of blood pouring out of the Soviet Union. Professing their compassion for human suffering, they have none for the victims in Russia. Unable or unwilling to give up their faith in collectivism, they evade the existence of Soviet atrocities, of terror, secret police and concentration camps—and publish glowing tributes to Soviet technology, production and art. Posturing as humanitarians, they man the barricades to fight the "injustice," "exploitation," "repression," and "persecution" they claim to find *in America;* as to the full reality of such things in Russia, they keep silent.

If anyone has any doubts about the moral meaning of the liberals' position, let him read—and reread—every detail of Marchenko's experiences. Let him remember that these horrors are not accidental in the Soviet Union and are not a matter of a particular dictator's character. They are inherent in the system. They are the inevitable products of a fully collectivist society.

If anyone has any doubts about the evil of establishing cultural exchange programs or of building "trade-bridges" to the Soviet Union or of buying the products of slave labor, let him remember how Marchenko felt when he stood in front of a shop window in Moscow, after his release. "That television set has cost my friends our sweat, our health, roasting in the cooler and long hours during roll-call in the rain and snow. Look closely at that polished surface: can you not see reflected in it the close-shaven head, the yellow, emaciated face, and the black cotton tunic of a convict? Maybe it's a former friend of yours?"

[Susan Ludel, review of Anatoly Marchenko's
My Testimony, TO, July 1970, 10.]

I would advocate that which the Soviet Union fears above all else: economic boycott. I would advocate a blockade of Cuba and an economic boycott of Soviet Russia; and you would see both those regimes collapse without the loss of a single American life.

["*Playboy's* Interview with Ayn Rand," pamphlet, 13.]

It is immoral for the U.S. (and for all free or semi-free countries) to engage in any undertaking with Soviet Russia as a partner. It is particularly immoral if the undertaking is intellectual or cultural. Such a partnership necessarily implies and proclaims the acceptance of Soviet Russia as a peaceful, well-meaning, civilized country.

["Comments on the Moscow Olympics,"
The Intellectual Activist, Feb. 1, 1980, p. 1.]

There is only one form of protest open to the men of goodwill in the semi-free world: *do not sanction the Soviet jailers of [the dissidents]*—do not help them to pretend that they are the morally acceptable leaders of a civilized country. Do not patronize or support the evil pretense of the so-called "cultural exchanges"—any Soviet-government-sponsored scientists, professors, writers, artists, musicians, dancers (who are either vicious bootlickers or doomed, tortured victims). Do not patronize, support or deal with any Soviet supporters and apologists in this country: *they* are the guiltiest men of all.

["The 'Inexplicable Personal Alchemy,' " *NL,* 125.]

See also ALTRUISM; AMERICA; COLLECTIVISM; COMMUNISM; COMPROMISE; DICTATORSHIP; FASCISM *and* COMMUNISM/SOCIALISM; FOREIGN POLICY; INDIVIDUALISM; "LIBERALS"; PROPERTY RIGHTS; SACRIFICE; SANCTION; SOCIALISM; STATISM; TYRANNY; UNITED NATIONS.

Space. "Space," like "time," is a relational concept. It does not designate an entity, but a relationship, which exists only within the universe. The universe is not in space any more than it is in time. To be "in a position" means to have a certain relationship to the boundary of some container. E.g., you are *in* New York: there is a point of the earth's surface on which you stand—that's your spatial position: your relation to this point. All it means to say "There is space between two objects" is that they occupy different positions. In this case, you are focusing on two relationships—the relationship of one entity to its container and of another to its container—simultaneously.

The universe, therefore, cannot be *anywhere*. Can the universe be in Boston? Can it be in the Milky Way? Places are in the universe, not the other way around.

Is the universe then unlimited in size? No. Everything which exists is finite, including the universe. What then, you ask, is outside the universe, if it is finite? This question is invalid. The phrase "outside the universe" has no referent. The universe is everything. "Outside the universe" stands for "that which is where everything isn't." There is no such place. There isn't even nothing "out there"; there is no "out there."

[Leonard Peikoff, "The Philosophy of Objectivism"
lecture series (1976), Lecture 2.]

See also ENTITY; EXISTENCE; METAPHYSICS; TIME; UNIVERSE.

Standard of Measurement. *See Measurement.*

Standard of Value. The Objectivist ethics holds man's life as the *standard* of value—and *his own life* as the ethical *purpose* of every individual man.

The difference between "standard" and "purpose" in this context is as follows: a "standard" is an abstract principle that serves as a measurement or gauge to guide a man's choices in the achievement of a concrete, specific purpose. "That which is required for the survival of man *qua* man" is an abstract principle that applies to every individual man. The task of applying this principle to a concrete, specific purpose—the purpose of living a life proper to a rational being—belongs to every individual man, and the life he has to live is his own.

Man must choose his actions, values and goals by the standard of that which is proper to man—in order to achieve, maintain, fulfill and enjoy that ultimate value, that end in itself, which is his own life.

["The Objectivist Ethics," *VOS*, 19; pb 25.]

The standard of value of the Objectivist ethics—the standard by which one judges what is good or evil—is *man's life*, or: that which is required for man's survival *qua* man.

Since reason is man's basic means of survival, that which is proper to the life of a rational being is the good; that which negates, opposes or destroys it is the evil.

[Ibid., 16; pb 23.]

"Man's survival *qua* man" means the terms, methods, conditions and goals required for the survival of a rational being through the whole of his lifespan—in all those aspects of existence which are open to his choice.

[Ibid., 18; pb 24.]

See also ABSTRACTIONS *and* CONCRETES; *LIFE; MAN; MORALITY; OBJECTIVISM; RATIONALITY; REASON; TELEOLOGICAL MEASUREMENT; ULTIMATE VALUE; VALUES; VIRTUE.*

States' Rights.   The constitutional concept of "states' rights" pertains to the division of power between local and national authorities, and serves to protect the states from the Federal government; it does not grant to a state government an unlimited, arbitrary power over its citizens or the privilege of abrogating the citizens' individual rights.

["Racism," *VOS*, 180; pb 131.]

[George Wallace] is not a defender of *individual* rights, but merely of *states'* rights—which is far, far from being the same thing. When he denounces "Big Government," it is not the unlimited, arbitrary power of the state that he is denouncing, but merely its centralization—and he seeks to place the same unlimited, arbitrary power in the hands of many little governments. The break-up of a big gang into a number of warring small gangs is not a return to a constitutional system nor to individual rights nor to law and order.

["The Presidential Candidates, 1968," *TO*, June 1968, 5.]

See also "COLLECTIVE RIGHTS"; "CONSERVATIVES"; CONSTITUTION; GOVERNMENT; INDIVIDUAL RIGHTS.

Statism.   The political expression of altruism is collectivism or *statism*, which holds that man's life and work belong to the state—to society, to the group, the gang, the race, the nation—and that the state may dispose of him in any way it pleases for the sake of whatever it deems to be its own tribal, collective good.

["Introducing Objectivism," *TON,* Aug. 1962, 35.]

A statist system—whether of a communist, fascist, Nazi, socialist or "welfare" type—is based on the . . . government's unlimited power, which means: on the rule of brute force. The differences among statist systems are only a matter of time and degree; the principle is the same. Under statism, the government is not a policeman, but a legalized criminal that holds the power to use physical force in any manner and for any purpose it pleases against legally disarmed, defenseless victims.

Nothing can ever justify so monstrously evil a theory. Nothing can justify the horror, the brutality, the plunder, the destruction, the starvation, the slave-labor camps, the torture chambers, the wholesale slaughter of statist dictatorships.

["War and Peace," *TON,* Oct. 1962, 44.]

Government control of a country's economy—any kind or degree of such control, by any group, for any purpose whatsoever—rests on the basic principle of *statism*, the principle that man's life belongs to the state.

["Conservatism: An Obituary," *CUI,* 192.]

A statist is a man who believes that some men have the right to force, coerce, enslave, rob, and murder others. To be put into practice, this belief has to be implemented by the political doctrine that the government—the state—has the right to *initiate* the use of physical force against its citizens. How often force is to be used, against whom, to what extent, for what purpose and for whose benefit, are irrelevant questions. The basic principle and the ultimate results of all statist doctrines are the same: dictatorship and destruction. The rest is only a matter of time.

["America's Persecuted Minority: Big Business," *CUI,* 47.]

If the term "statism" designates concentration of power in the state at the expense of individual liberty, then Nazism in politics was a form of statism. In principle, it did not represent a new approach to government; it was a continuation of the political absolutism—the absolute monarchies, the oligarchies, the theocracies, the random tyrannies—which has characterized most of human history.

In degree, however, the total state does differ from its predecessors: it represents statism pressed to its limits, in theory and in practice, devouring the last remnants of the individual.

[Leonard Peikoff, *OP,* 6; pb 16.]

The ideological root of statism (or collectivism) is the *tribal premise* of primordial savages who, unable to conceive of individual rights, believed that the tribe is a supreme, omnipotent ruler, that it owns the lives of its members and may sacrifice them whenever it pleases to whatever it deems to be its own "good." Unable to conceive of any social principles, save the rule of brute force, they believed that the tribe's wishes are limited only by its physical power and that other tribes are its natural prey, to be conquered, looted, enslaved, or annihilated. The history of all primitive peoples is a succession of tribal wars and intertribal slaughter. That this savage ideology now rules nations armed with nuclear weapons, should give pause to anyone concerned with mankind's survival.

Statism is a system of institutionalized violence and perpetual civil war. It leaves men no choice but to fight to seize political power—to rob or be robbed, to kill or be killed. When brute force is the only criterion of social conduct, and unresisting surrender to destruction is the only alternative, even the lowest of men, even an animal—even a cornered rat—will fight. There can be no peace within an enslaved nation.

["The Roots of War," *CUI*, 36.]

The degree of statism in a country's political system, is the degree to which it breaks up the country into rival gangs and sets men against one another. When individual rights are abrogated, there is no way to determine who is entitled to what; there is no way to determine the justice of anyone's claims, desires, or interests. The criterion, therefore, reverts to the tribal concept of: one's wishes are limited only by the power of one's gang.

[Ibid.]

Statism—in fact and in principle—is nothing more than gang rule. A dictatorship is a gang devoted to looting the effort of the productive citizens of its own country. When a statist ruler exhausts his own country's economy, he attacks his neighbors. It is his only means of postponing internal collapse and prolonging his rule. A country that violates the rights of its own citizens, will not respect the rights of its neighbors. Those who do not recognize individual rights, will not recognize the rights of nations: a nation is only a number of individuals.

Statism *needs* war; a free country does not. Statism survives by looting; a free country survives by production.

Observe that the major wars of history were started by the more controlled economies of the time against the freer ones. For instance, World War I was started by monarchist Germany and Czarist Russia, who dragged in their freer allies. World War II was started by the alliance of Nazi Germany with Soviet Russia and their joint attack on Poland.

Observe that in World War II, both Germany and Russia seized and dismantled entire factories in conquered countries, to ship them home —while the freest of the mixed economies, the semi-capitalistic United States, sent billions worth of lend-lease equipment, including entire factories, to its allies.

Germany and Russia needed war; the United States did not and gained nothing. (In fact, the United States lost, economically, even though it won the war: it was left with an enormous national debt, augmented by the grotesquely futile policy of supporting former allies and enemies to this day.) Yet it is capitalism that today's peace-lovers oppose and statism that they advocate—in the name of peace.

[Ibid., 37.]

The human characteristic required by statism is *docility*, which is the product of hopelessness and intellectual stagnation. Thinking men cannot be ruled; ambitious men do not stagnate.

["Tax-Credits for Education," *ARL,* I, 12, 1.]

The first choice—and the only one that matters—is: freedom or dictatorship, *capitalism* or *statism.*

That is the choice which today's political leaders are determined to evade. The "liberals" are trying to put statism over by stealth—statism of a semi-socialist, semi-fascist kind—without letting the country realize what road they are taking to what ultimate goal. And while such a policy is reprehensible, there is something more reprehensible still: the policy of the "conservatives," who are trying to defend *freedom* by stealth.

["Conservatism: An Obituary," *CUI,* 193.]

The statists' epistemological method consists of endless debates about single, concrete, out-of-context, range-of-the-moment issues, never allowing them to be integrated into a sum, never referring to basic principles or ultimate consequences—and thus inducing a state of intellectual disintegration in their followers. The purpose of that verbal fog is to conceal the evasion of two fundamentals: (a) that production and prosperity are the product of men's intelligence, and (b) that government power is the power of coercion by physical force.

Once these two facts are acknowledged, the conclusion to be drawn is inevitable: that intelligence does not work under coercion, that man's mind will not function at the point of a gun.

["Let Us Alone!" *CUI,* 141.]

See also ALTRUISM; CAPITALISM; COLLECTIVISM; COMMUNISM; "CONSERVATIVES"; DICTATORSHIP; FASCISM/NAZISM; GOVERN- MENT; INDIVIDUAL RIGHTS; INDIVIDUALISM; INTERVENTION- ISM (ECONOMIC); "LIBERALS"; PHYSICAL FORCE; TRIBALISM; TYRANNY; WAR; WELFARE STATE.

"Stolen Concept," Fallacy of.

The "stolen concept" fallacy, first identified by Ayn Rand, is the fallacy of using a concept while denying the validity of its genetic roots, i.e., of an earlier concept(s) on which it logically depends.

[Leonard Peikoff, editor's footnote to Ayn Rand's "Philosophical Detection," *PWNI*, 26; pb 22.]

As they feed on stolen wealth in body, so they feed on stolen concepts in mind, and proclaim that honesty consists of refusing to know that one is stealing. As they use effects while denying causes, so they use our concepts while denying the roots and the existence of the concepts they are using.

[GS, *FNI*, 191; pb 154.]

When modern philosophers declare that axioms are a matter of arbi- trary choice, and proceed to choose complex, derivative concepts as the alleged axioms of their alleged reasoning, one can observe that their statements imply and depend on "existence," "consciousness," "iden- tity," which they profess to negate, but which are smuggled into their arguments in the form of unacknowledged, "stolen" concepts.

[*ITOE*, 79.]

They proclaim that there are no entities, that nothing exists but mo- tion, and blank out the fact that *motion* presupposes the thing which moves, that without the concept of entity, there can be no such concept as "motion."

. . . They proclaim that there is no law of identity, that nothing exists but change, and blank out the fact that *change* presupposes the concepts of what changes, from what and to what, that without the law of identity no such concept as "change" is possible.

. . . "You cannot *prove* that you exist or that you're conscious," they chatter, blanking out the fact that *proof* presupposes existence, con- sciousness and a complex chain of knowledge: the existence of some- thing to know, of a consciousness able to know it, and of a knowledge that has learned to distinguish between such concepts as the proved and the unproved.

[GS, *FNI*, 191; pb 154.]

The arguments of those who attack the senses are merely variants of the fallacy of the "stolen concept."

[*ITOE*, 4.]

Observe that Descartes starts his system by using "error" and its synonyms or derivatives as "stolen concepts."

Men have been wrong, and therefore, he implies, they can never know what is right. But if they cannot, how did they ever discover that they were wrong? How can one form such concepts as "mistake" or "error" while wholly ignorant of what is correct? "Error" signifies a departure from truth; the concept of "error" logically presupposes that one has already grasped some truth. If truth were unknowable, as Descartes implies, the idea of a departure from it would be meaningless.

The same point applies to concepts denoting specific forms of error. If we cannot ever be certain that an argument is logically valid, if validity is unknowable, then the concept of "invalid" reasoning is impossible to reach or apply. If we cannot ever know that a man is sane, then the concept of "insanity" is impossible to form or define. If we cannot recognize the state of being awake, then we cannot recognize or conceptualize a state of *not* being awake (such as dreaming). If man cannot grasp *X*, then "non-*X*" stands for nothing.

[Leonard Peikoff, " 'Maybe You're Wrong,' " *TOF*, April 1981, 9.]

Particularly since Kant, the philosophical technique of concept stealing, of attempting to negate reason by means of reason, has become a general bromide, a gimmick worn transparently thin.

[*ITOE*, 81.]

See also AXIOMATIC CONCEPTS; AXIOMS; CONCEPTS; HIERARCHY of KNOWLEDGE; INVALID CONCEPTS; KANT, IMMANUEL; LOGIC; PERCEPTION; TRUTH.

Style. "Style" is a particular, distinctive or characteristic mode of execution.

["Art and Sense of Life," *RM*, 51; pb 40.]

Two distinct, but interrelated, elements of a work of art are the crucial means of projecting its sense of life: the *subject* and the *style—what* an artist chooses to present and *how* he presents it.

The subject of an art work expresses a view of man's existence, while the style expresses a view of man's consciousness. The subject reveals an artist's *metaphysics*, the style reveals his *psycho-epistemology*. . . .

The theme of an art work is the link uniting its subject and its style. "Style" is a particular, distinctive or characteristic mode of execution. An artist's style is the product of his own psycho-epistemology—and, by implication, a projection of his view of man's consciousness, of its efficacy or impotence, of its proper method and level of functioning.

Predominantly (though not exclusively), a man whose normal mental state is a state of full focus, will create and respond to a style of radiant clarity and ruthless precision—a style that projects sharp outlines, cleanliness, purpose, an intransigent commitment to full awareness and clearcut identity—a level of awareness appropriate to a universe where A is A, where everything is open to man's consciousness and demands its constant functioning.

A man who is moved by the fog of his feelings and spends most of his time out of focus will create and respond to a style of blurred, "mysterious" murk, where outlines dissolve and entities flow into one another, where words connote anything and denote nothing, where colors float without objects, and objects float without weight—a level of awareness appropriate to a universe where A can be any non-A one chooses, where nothing can be known with certainty and nothing much is demanded of one's consciousness.

Style is the most complex element of art, the most revealing and, often, the most baffling psychologically. The terrible inner conflicts from which artists suffer as much as (or, perhaps, more than) other men are magnified in their work. As an example: Salvador Dali, whose style projects the luminous clarity of a rational psycho-epistemology, while most (though not all) of his subjects project an irrational and revoltingly evil metaphysics. A similar, but less offensive, conflict may be seen in the paintings of Vermeer, who combines a brilliant clarity of style with the bleak metaphysics of Naturalism. At the other extreme of the stylistic continuum, observe the deliberate blurring and visual distortions of the so-called "painterly" school, from Rembrandt on down—down to the rebellion against consciousness, expressed by a phenomenon such as Cubism which seeks specifically to disintegrate man's consciousness by painting objects as man *does not* perceive them (from several perspectives at once).

A writer's style may project a blend of reason and passionate emotion (Victor Hugo)—or a chaos of floating abstractions, of emotions cut off from reality (Thomas Wolfe)—or the dry, bare, concrete-bound, humor-tinged raucousness of an intelligent reporter (Sinclair Lewis)—or the disciplined, perceptive, lucid, yet muted understatement of a represser (John O'Hara)—or the carefully superficial, over-detailed precision of an amoralist (Flaubert)—or the mannered artificiality of a second-hander (several moderns not worthy of mention).

Style conveys what may be called a "psycho-epistemological sense of life," i.e., an expression of that level of mental functioning on which the artist feels most at home. This is the reason why style is crucially important in art—both to the artist and to the reader or viewer—and why its importance is experienced as a profoundly *personal* matter. To the artist, it is an expression, to the reader or viewer a confirmation, of his own consciousness—which means: of his efficacy—which means: of his self-esteem (or pseudo-self-esteem).

[Ibid., 50; pb 40.]

Style is not an end in itself, it is only a means to an end—the means of telling a story. The writer who develops a beautiful style, but has nothing to say, represents a kind of arrested esthetic development; he is like a pianist who acquires a brilliant technique by playing finger-exercises, but never gives a concert.

The typical literary product of such writers—and of their imitators, who possess no style—are so-called "mood-studies," popular among today's literati, which are little pieces conveying nothing but a certain mood. Such pieces are not an art-form, they are merely finger-exercises that never develop into art.

["Basic Principles of Literature," *RM*, 78; pb 96.]

See also ART; FOCUS; IDENTITY; METAPHYSICS; PSYCHO-EPISTE-MOLOGY; SENSE of LIFE; STYLIZATION; SUBJECT (in ART).

Stylization.   "Stylized" means condensed to essential characteristics, which are chosen according to an artist's view of man.

["Art and Cognition," *RM*, pb 67.]

An artist does not fake reality—he *stylizes* it. He selects those aspects of existence which he regards as metaphysically significant—and by isolating and stressing them, by omitting the insignificant and accidental, he presents *his* view of existence. His concepts are not divorced from the facts of reality—they are concepts which integrate the facts *and* his metaphysical evaluation of the facts.

["Art and Sense of Life," *RM*, 46; pb 36.]

The dance is the silent partner of music and participates in a division of labor: music presents a stylized version of man's consciousness in action—the dance presents a stylized version of man's body in action.

["Art and Cognition," *RM*, pb 66.]

See also ART; DANCE; METAPHYSICAL VALUE-JUDGMENTS; PAINT-ING; STYLE.

Subconscious.   Your subconscious is like a computer—more complex a computer than men can build—and its main function is the integration of your ideas. Who programs it? Your conscious mind. If you default, if you don't reach any firm convictions, your subconscious is programmed by chance—and you deliver yourself into the power of ideas you do not know you have accepted. But one way or the other, your computer gives you print-outs, daily and hourly, in the form of *emotions*—which are lightning-like estimates of the things around you, calculated according to your values. If you programmed your computer by conscious thinking, you know the nature of your values and emotions. If you didn't, you don't.

Many people, particularly today, claim that man cannot live by logic alone, that there's the emotional element of his nature to consider, and that they rely on the guidance of their emotions. Well, . . . the joke is on . . . them: man's values and emotions are determined by his fundamental view of life. The ultimate programmer of his subconscious is *philosophy*—the science which, according to the emotionalists, is impotent to affect or penetrate the murky mysteries of their feelings.

The quality of a computer's output is determined by the quality of its input. If your subconscious is programmed by chance, its output will have a corresponding character. You have probably heard the computer operators' eloquent term "gigo"—which means: "Garbage in, garbage out." The same formula applies to the relationship between a man's thinking and his emotions.

A man who is run by emotions is like a man who is run by a computer whose print-outs he cannot read. He does not know whether its programming is true or false, right or wrong, whether it's set to lead him to success or destruction, whether it serves his goals or those of some evil, unknowable power. He is blind on two fronts: blind to the world around him and to his own inner world, unable to grasp reality or his own motives, and he is in chronic terror of both. Emotions are not tools of cognition. The men who are not interested in philosophy need it most urgently: they are most helplessly in its power.

["Philosophy: Who Needs It," *PWNI*, 7; pb 5.]

The subconscious is an integrating mechanism. Man's conscious mind observes and establishes connections among his experiences; the subconscious integrates the connections and makes them become automatic. For example, the skill of walking is acquired, after many faltering attempts, by the automatization of countless connections controlling muscular movements; once he learns to walk, a child needs no conscious awareness of such problems as posture, balance, length of step, etc.— the mere decision to walk brings the integrated total into his control.

A mind's cognitive development involves a continual process of automatization. For example, you cannot perceive a table as an infant perceives it—as a mysterious object with four legs. You perceive it as a table, i.e., a man-made piece of furniture, serving a certain purpose belonging to a human habitation, etc.; you cannot separate these attributes from your sight of the table, you experience it as a single, indivisible percept—yet all you see is a four-legged object; the rest is an automatized integration of a vast amount of conceptual knowledge which, at one time, you had to learn bit by bit. The same is true of everything you perceive or experience; as an adult, you cannot perceive or experience in a vacuum, you do it in a certain automatized *context*—and the efficiency of your mental operations depends on the kind of context your subconscious has automatized.

"Learning to speak is a process of automatizing the use (i.e., the meaning and the application) of concepts. And more: all learning involves a process of automatizing, i.e., of first acquiring knowledge by fully conscious, focused attention and observation, then of establishing mental connections which make that knowledge automatic (instantly available as a context), thus freeing man's mind to pursue further, more complex knowledge." *(Introduction to Objectivist Epistemology.)*

The process of forming, integrating and using concepts is not an automatic, but a volitional process—i.e., a process which uses both new and automatized material, but which is directed volitionally. It is not an innate, but an acquired skill; it has to be *learned*—it is the most crucially important part of learning—and all of man's other capacities depend on how well or how badly he learns it.

This skill does not pertain to the particular *content* of a man's knowledge at any given age, but to the *method* by which he acquires and organizes knowledge—the method by which his mind deals with its content. The method *programs* his subconscious computer, determining how efficiently, lamely or disastrously his cognitive processes will function. The programming of a man's subconscious consists of the kind of cognitive habits he acquires; these habits constitute his psycho-epistemology.

It is a child's early experiences, observations and subverbal conclusions that determine this programming. Thereafter, the interaction of content and method establishes a certain reciprocity: the method of acquiring knowledge affects its content, which affects the further development of the method, and so on.

["The Comprachicos," *NL*, 192.]

Man's values control his subconscious emotional mechanism that functions like a computer adding up his desires, his experiences, his fulfillments and frustrations—like a sensitive guardian watching and constantly assessing his relationship to reality. The key question which this computer is programmed to answer, is: What is *possible* to me? . . .

Man's emotional mechanism works as the barometer of the efficacy or impotence of his actions.

["Our Cultural Value-Deprivation," *TO*, April 1966, 3.]

[Objectivism rejects the Freudian] theory of a dynamic unconscious— i.e., the unconscious as a mystic entity, with a will and purpose of its own unknown to the conscious mind, like an inborn demon that continually raises Hell. Strictly speaking, Objectivism does not subscribe to the idea of an *un*conscious at all. We use the term "subconscious" instead— and that is simply a name for the content of your mind that you are not focused on at any given moment. It is simply a repository for past information or conclusions that you were once conscious of in some form, but that are now stored beneath the threshold of consciousness. There is nothing in the subconscious besides what you acquired by conscious means. The subconscious does perform automatically certain important integrations (sometimes these are correct, sometimes not), but the conscious mind is always able to know what these are (and to correct them, if necessary). The subconscious has no purposes or values of its own, and it does not engage in diabolical manipulations behind the scenes. In that sense, it is certainly not "dynamic."

[Leonard Peikoff, "The Philosophy of Objectivism" lecture series (1976), question period, Lecture 12.]

See also AUTOMATIZATION; CONSCIOUSNESS; CONTEXT; EMOTIONS; FREE WILL; FREUD; INTEGRATION (MENTAL); INTROSPECTION; LOGIC; PHILOSOPHY; PSYCHO-EPISTEMOLOGY; "PSYCHOLOGIZING"; PSYCHOLOGY; SENSE of LIFE; VALUES.

Subject (in Art).   Two distinct, but interrelated, elements of a work of art are the crucial means of projecting its sense of life: the *subject* and the *style*—*what* an artist chooses to present and *how* he presents it.

The subject of an art work expresses a view of man's existence, while the style expresses a view of man's consciousness. The subject reveals an artist's *metaphysics*, the style reveals his *psycho-epistemology*.

The choice of subject declares what aspects of existence the artist regards as important—as worthy of being re-created and contemplated. He may choose to present heroic figures, as exponents of man's nature —or he may choose statistical composites of the average, the undistinguished, the mediocre—or he may choose crawling specimens of depravity. He may present the triumph of heroes, in fact or in spirit (Victor Hugo), or their struggle (Michelangelo), or their defeat (Shakespeare). He may present the folks next door: next door to palaces (Tolstoy), or to drugstores (Sinclair Lewis), or to kitchens (Vermeer), or to sewers (Zola). He may present monsters as objects of moral denunciation (Dostoevsky), or as objects of terror (Goya)—or he may demand sympathy for his monsters, and thus crawl outside the limits of the realm of values, including esthetic ones.

Whatever the case may be, it is the subject (qualified by the theme) that projects an art work's view of man's place in the universe.

["Art and Sense of Life," *RM*, 50; pb 40.]

The subject is not the only attribute of art, but it is the fundamental one, it is the end to which all the others are the means. In most esthetic theories, however, the end—the subject—is omitted from consideration, and only the means are regarded as esthetically relevant. Such theories set up a false dichotomy and claim that a slob portrayed by the technical means of a genius is preferable to a goddess portrayed by the technique of an amateur. I hold that *both* are esthetically offensive; but while the second is merely esthetic incompetence, the first is an esthetic crime.

There is no dichotomy, no necessary conflict between ends and means. The end does *not* justify the means—neither in ethics nor in esthetics. And neither do the means justify the end: there is no esthetic justification for the spectacle of Rembrandt's great artistic skill employed to portray a side of beef.

That particular painting may be taken as a symbol of everything I am opposed to in art and in literature. At the age of seven, I could not understand why anyone would wish to paint or to admire pictures of dead fish, garbage cans or fat peasant women with triple chins. Today, I understand the psychological causes of such esthetic phenomena—and the more I understand, the more I oppose them.

In art, and in literature, the end and the means, or the subject and the style, must be worthy of each other.

That which is not worth contemplating in life, is not worth re-creating in art.

Misery, disease, disaster, evil, all the negatives of human existence, are proper subjects of *study* in life, for the purpose of understanding and correcting them—but are not proper subjects of *contemplation* for contemplation's sake. In art, and in literature, these negatives are worth re-creating only in relation to some positive, as a foil, as a contrast, as a means of stressing the positive—but *not* as an end in themselves.

["The Goal of My Writing," *RM*, 166; pb 166.]

See also *ART; LITERATURE; METAPHYSICS; PAINTING; PSYCHO-EPISTEMOLOGY; SCULPTURE; SENSE OF LIFE; STYLE.*

Subjectivism.

In Metaphysics and Epistemology

Subjectivism is the belief that reality is not a firm absolute, but a fluid, plastic, indeterminate realm which can be altered, in whole or in part, by the consciousness of the perceiver—i.e., by his feelings, wishes or whims. It is the doctrine which holds that man—an entity of a specific nature, dealing with a universe of a specific nature—can, somehow, live, act and achieve his goals apart from and/or in contradiction to the facts of reality, i.e., apart from and/or in contradiction to his own nature and the nature of the universe. (This is the "mixed," moderate or middle-of-the-road version of subjectivism. Pure or "extreme" subjectivism does not recognize the concept of identity, i.e., the fact that man or the universe or anything possesses a specific nature.)

· ["Who Is the Final Authority in Ethics?" *TON*, Feb. 1965, 7.]

The *subjective* means the arbitrary, the irrational, the blindly emotional.

["Art and Moral Treason," *RM*, 148; pb 150.]

In metaphysics, "subjectivism" is the view that reality (the "object") is dependent on human consciousness (the "subject"). In epistemology, as a result, subjectivists hold that a man need not concern himself with the facts of reality; instead, to arrive at knowledge or truth, he need merely turn his attention inward, consulting the appropriate contents of consciousness, the ones with the power to make reality conform to their dictates. According to the most widespread form of subjectivism, the elements which possess this power are *feelings*.

In essence, subjectivism is the doctrine that feelings are the creator of facts, and therefore men's primary tool of cognition. If men feel it, declares the subjectivist, that makes it so.

The alternative to subjectivism is the advocacy of objectivity—an attitude which rests on the view that reality exists independent of human consciousness; that the role of the subject is not to create the object, but to perceive it; and that knowledge of reality can be acquired only by directing one's attention outward to the facts.

[Leonard Peikoff, *OP*, 58; pb 62.]

The subjectivist denies that there is any such thing as "*the* truth" on a given question, the truth which corresponds to the facts. On his view, truth varies from consciousness to consciousness as the processes or contents of consciousness vary; the same statement may be true for one consciousness (or one type of consciousness) and false for another. The virtually infallible sign of the subjectivist is his refusal to say, of a statement he accepts: "It is true"; instead, he says: "It is true—*for* me (or *for* us)." There is no truth, only truth relative to an individual or a group —truth for me, for you, for him, for her, for us, for them.

[Leonard Peikoff, "Nazism and Subjectivism," *TO*, Jan. 1971, 9.]

Your teachers, the mystics of both schools, have reversed causality in their consciousness, then strive to reverse it in existence. They take their emotions as a cause, and their mind as a passive effect. They make their emotions their tool for perceiving reality. They hold their desires as an irreducible primary, as a fact superseding all facts. An honest man does not desire until he has identified the object of his desire. He says: "It is, therefore I want it." They say: "I want it, therefore it is."

They want to cheat the axiom of existence and consciousness, they want their consciousness to be an instrument not of *perceiving* but of *creating* existence, and existence to be not the *object* but the *subject* of their consciousness—they want to be that God they created in their image and likeness, who creates a universe out of a void by means of an arbitrary whim. But reality is not to be cheated. What they achieve is the opposite of their desire. They want an omnipotent power over existence; instead, they lose the power of their consciousness. By refusing to know, they condemn themselves to the horror of a perpetual unknown.

[GS, *FNI*, 187; pb 150.]

There are two different kinds of subjectivism, distinguished by their answers to the question: *whose* consciousness creates reality? Kant rejected the older of these two, which was the view that each man's feelings create a private universe for him. Instead, Kant ushered in the era of *social* subjectivism—the view that it is not the consciousness of individuals, but of *groups,* that creates reality. In Kant's system, mankind as a whole is the decisive group; what creates the phenomenal world is not the idiosyncrasies of particular individuals, but the mental structure common to all men.

Later philosophers accepted Kant's fundamental approach, but carried it a step further. If, many claimed, the mind's structure is a brute given, which cannot be explained—as Kant had said—then there is no reason why all men should have the same mental structure. There is no reason why mankind should not be splintered into *competing* groups, each defined by its own distinctive type of consciousness, each vying with the others to capture and control reality.

The first world movement thus to pluralize the Kantian position was Marxism, which propounded a social subjectivism in terms of competing economic classes. On this issue, as on many others, the Nazis follow the Marxists, but substitute race for class.

[Leonard Peikoff, *OP*, 59; pb 63.]

In Ethics

Today, as in the past, most philosophers agree that the ultimate standard of ethics is *whim* (they call it "arbitrary postulate" or "subjective choice" or "emotional commitment")—and the battle is only over the question of *whose* whim: one's own or society's or the dictator's or God's. Whatever else they may disagree about, today's moralists agree that ethics is a *subjective* issue and that the three things barred from its field are: reason—mind—reality.

If you wonder why the world is now collapsing to a lower and ever lower rung of hell, *this* is the reason.

If you want to save civilization, it is *this* premise of modern ethics— and of all ethical history—that you must challenge.

["The Objectivist Ethics," *VOS*, 4; pb 15.]

There are, in essence, three schools of thought on the nature of the good: the intrinsic, the subjective, and the objective.

["What Is Capitalism?" *CUI*, 21.]

The *subjectivist* theory holds that the good bears no relation to the facts of reality, that it is the product of a man's consciousness, created by his feelings, desires, "intuitions," or whims, and that it is merely an "arbitrary postulate" or an "emotional commitment."

The intrinsic theory holds that the good resides in some sort of reality, independent of man's consciousness; the subjectivist theory holds that the good resides in man's consciousness, independent of reality.

[Ibid.]

Ethical subjectivism, which holds that a *desire* or a *whim* is an irreducible moral primary, that every man is entitled to any desire he might feel like asserting, that all desires have equal moral validity, and that the only way men can get along together is by giving in to anything and "compromising" with anyone. It is not hard to see who would profit and who would lose by such a doctrine.

["Doesn't Life Require Compromise?" *VOS*, 86; pb 69.]

The subjectivist theory of ethics is, strictly speaking, not a theory, but a negation of ethics. And more: it is a negation of reality, a negation not merely of man's existence, but of *all* existence. Only the concept of a fluid, plastic, indeterminate, Heraclitean universe could permit anyone to think or to preach that man needs no *objective* principles of action—that reality gives him a blank check on values—that anything he cares to pick as the good or the evil, will do—that a man's whim is a valid moral standard, and that the only question is how to get away with it. The existential monument to *this* theory is the present state of our culture.

["The Objectivist Ethics," *VOS*, 34; pb 34.]

In Esthetics

A work of art is a specific entity which possesses a specific nature. If it does not, it is not a work of art. If it is merely a material object, it belongs to some category of material objects—and if it does not belong to any particular category, it belongs to the one reserved for such phenomena: junk.

"Something made by an artist" is *not* a definition of art. A beard and a vacant stare are *not* the defining characteristics of an artist.

"Something in a frame hung on a wall" is *not* a definition of painting.

"Something with a number of pages in a binding" is *not* a definition of literature.

"Something piled together" is *not* a definition of sculpture.

"Something made of sounds produced by anything" is *not* a definition of music.

"Something glued on a flat surface" is *not* a definition of any art. There is no art that uses glue as a medium. Blades of grass glued on a sheet of paper to represent grass might be good occupational therapy for retarded children—though I doubt it—but it is *not* art.

"Because I felt like it" is *not* a definition or validation of anything.

There is no place for *whim* in any human activity—if it is to be regarded as human. There is no place for the unknowable, the unintelligible, the undefinable, the non-objective in any human product.

["Art and Cognition," *RM*, pb 78.]

See also AMORALISM; ANARCHISM; ARBITRARY; ART; AXIOMS; CAUSALITY; CONSCIOUSNESS; EXISTENCE; GOD; IDENTITY; EMOTIONS; INTRINSIC THEORY of VALUES; KANT, IMMANUEL; "LIBERTARIANS"; MODERN ART; MORALITY; OBJECTIVE THEORY of VALUES; OBJECTIVISM; OBJECTIVITY; PRAGMATISM; PRIMACY of EXISTENCE vs. PRIMACY of CONSCIOUSNESS; PRIOR CERTAINTY of CONSCIOUSNESS; REASON; SKEPTICISM; WHIMS/WHIM-WORSHIP.

Subjectivism (Psychological).

Do not confuse [amoralism] with psychological subjectivism. A psychological subjectivist is unable fully to identify his values or to prove their objective validity, but he may be profoundly consistent and loyal to them in practice (though with terrible psycho-epistemological difficulty). The amoralist does not hold subjective values; he does not hold *any* values.

["Selfishness Without a Self," *PWNI*, 57; pb 47.]

See also AMORALISM; PSYCHO-EPISTEMOLOGY; PSYCHOLOGY.

Suffering.

Suffering as such is not a value; only man's fight against suffering, is. If you choose to help a man who suffers, do it only on the ground of his virtues, of his fight to recover, of his rational record, or of the fact that he suffers unjustly; then your action is still a trade, and his virtue is the payment for your help. But to help a man who has no virtues, to help him on the ground of his suffering as such, to accept his faults, his *need*, as a claim—is to accept the mortgage of a zero on your values.

[GS, *FNI*, 226; pb 180.]

See also ALTRUISM; BENEVOLENT UNIVERSE PREMISE; COMPAS-SION; EMOTIONS; HAPPINESS; MALEVOLENT UNIVERSE PREM-ISE; MERCY; PLEASURE and PAIN; VIRTUE.

Supernaturalism.

What is meant by "the supernatural"? Suppos-edly, a realm that transcends nature. What is nature? Nature is existence —the sum of that which is. It is usually called "nature" when we think of it as a system of interconnected, interacting entities governed by law. So "nature" really means the universe of entities acting and interacting in accordance with their identities. What, then, is "super-nature"? Some-thing beyond the universe, beyond entities, beyond identity. It would have to be: a form of existence beyond existence—a kind of entity beyond anything man knows about entities—a something which contra-dicts everything man knows about the identity of that which is. In short, a contradiction of every metaphysical essential.

[Leonard Peikoff, "The Philosophy of Objectivism"
lecture series (1976), Lecture 2.]

They claim that they perceive a mode of being superior to your exis-tence on this earth. The mystics of spirit call it "another dimension," which consists of denying dimensions. The mystics of muscle call it "the future," which consists of denying the present. To exist is to possess identity. What identity are they able to give to their superior realm? They keep telling you what it is *not*, but never tell you what it *is*. All their identifications consist of negating: God is that which no human mind can know, they say—and proceed to demand that you consider it knowledge—God is non-man, heaven is non-earth, soul is non-body, virtue is non-profit, A is non-A, perception is non-sensory, knowledge is non-reason. Their definitions are not acts of defining, but of wiping out.

[GS, *FNI*, 184; pb 148.]

There is no way to prove a "super-existence" by inference from existence; supernaturalism can be accepted only on faith.

[Leonard Peikoff, "The Philosophy of Objectivism" lecture series (1976), Lecture 2.]

See also ATHEISM; CAUSALITY; DEFINITIONS; EXISTENCE; FAITH; GOD; IDENTITY; METAPHYSICS; MIRACLES; MYSTICISM; NATURE; REASON.

T

Tabula Rasa. Since man has no automatic knowledge, he can have no automatic values; since he has no innate ideas, he can have no innate value judgments.

Man is born with an emotional mechanism, just as he is born with a cognitive mechanism; but, at birth, *both* are "tabula rasa." It is man's cognitive faculty, his mind, that determines the *content* of both.

["The Objectivist Ethics," *VOS*, 23; pb 28.]

At birth, a child's mind is tabula rasa; he has the potential of awareness—the mechanism of a human consciousness—but no content. Speaking metaphorically, he has a camera with an extremely sensitive, unexposed film (his conscious mind), and an extremely complex computer waiting to be programmed (his subconscious). Both are blank. He knows nothing of the external world. He faces an immense chaos which he must learn to perceive by means of the complex mechanism which he must learn to operate.

If, in any two years of adult life, men could learn as much as an infant learns in his first two years, they would have the capacity of genius. To focus his eyes (which is not an innate, but an acquired skill), to perceive the things around him by integrating his sensations into percepts (which is not an innate, but an acquired skill), to coordinate his muscles for the task of crawling, then standing upright, then walking—and, ultimately, to grasp the process of concept-formation and learn to speak—these are some of an infant's tasks and achievements whose magnitude is not equaled by most men in the rest of their lives.

["The Comprachicos," *NL*, 190.]

No one is born with any kind of "talent" and, therefore, every skill has to be acquired. Writers are *made*, not born. To be exact, writers are self-made.

["Foreword," *WTL*, v.]

See also ARISTOTLE; CONSCIOUSNESS; HIERARCHY of KNOWLEDGE; "INSTINCT"; PERCEPTION; RATIONALISM vs. EMPIRICISM; VALUES.

Tactfulness. Do not confuse appeasement with tactfulness or generosity. Appeasement is not consideration for the feelings of others, it is *consideration for and compliance with the unjust, irrational and evil feelings of others.* It is a policy of exempting the emotions of others from moral judgment, and of willingness to sacrifice innocent, virtuous victims to the evil malice of such emotions.

Tactfulness is consideration extended only to rational feelings. A tactful man does not stress his success or happiness in the presence of those who have suffered failure, loss or unhappiness; not because he suspects them of envy, but because he realizes that the contrast can revive and sharpen their pain. He does not stress his virtues in anyone's presence: he takes for granted that they are recognized.

["The Age of Envy," *NL*, 160.]

See also APPEASEMENT; COMPROMISE; JUSTICE.

Taxation.   In a fully free society, taxation—or, to be exact, payment for governmental services—would be *voluntary.* Since the proper services of a government—the police, the armed forces, the law courts—are demonstrably needed by individual citizens and affect their interests directly, the citizens would (and should) be willing to pay for such services, as they pay for insurance.

The question of how to implement the principle of voluntary government financing—how to determine the best means of applying it in practice—is a very complex one and belongs to the field of the philosophy of law. The task of political philosophy is only to establish the nature of the principle and to demonstrate that it is practicable. The choice of a specific method of implementation is more than premature today—since the principle will be practicable only in a *fully* free society, a society whose government has been constitutionally reduced to its proper, basic functions.

["Government Financing in a Free Society," *VOS*, 157; pb 116.]

Any program of voluntary government financing has to be regarded as a goal for a distant future.

What the advocates of a fully free society have to know, at present, is only the principle by which that goal can be achieved.

The principle of voluntary government financing rests on the following premises: that the government is *not* the owner of the citizens' income and, therefore, cannot hold a blank check on that income—that the nature of the proper governmental services must be constitutionally defined and delimited, leaving the government no power to enlarge the scope of its services at its own arbitrary discretion. Consequently, the principle of voluntary government financing regards the government as the servant, not the ruler, of the citizens—as an *agent* who must be paid for his services, not as a benefactor whose services are gratuitous, who dispenses something for nothing.

[Ibid., 160; pb 118.]

In view of what they hear from the experts, the people cannot be blamed for their ignorance and their helpless confusion. If an average housewife struggles with her incomprehensibly shrinking budget and sees a tycoon in a resplendent limousine, she might well think that just one of his diamond cuff links would solve all her problems. She has no way of knowing that if all the personal luxuries of all the tycoons were expropriated, it would not feed her family—and millions of other, similar families—for one week; and that the entire country would starve on the first morning of the week to follow. . . . How would she know it, if all the voices she hears are telling her that we must soak the rich?

No one tells her that higher taxes imposed on the rich (and the semi-rich) will not come out of their consumption expenditures, but out of their investment capital (i.e., their savings); that such taxes will mean less investment, i.e., less production, fewer jobs, higher prices for scarcer goods; and that by the time the rich have to lower their standard of living, hers will be gone, along with *her* savings and her husband's job—and no power in the world (no *economic* power) will be able to revive the dead industries (there will be no such power left).

["The Inverted Moral Priorities," *ARL*, III, 21, 3.]

See also CAPITALISM; DEFICIT FINANCING; FREEDOM; GOVERN-MENT; INDIVIDUAL RIGHTS; INFLATION; INVESTMENT; PHYSI-CAL FORCE; PROPERTY RIGHTS; "REDISTRIBUTION" of WEALTH; SAVINGS.

Technology.   Technology is an applied science, i.e., it translates the discoveries of theoretical science into practical application to man's life. As such, technology is not the first step in the development of a given body of knowledge, but the last; it is not the most difficult step, but it is the ultimate step, the implicit purpose, of man's quest for knowledge.

["Apollo 11," *TO*, Sept. 1969, 9.]

Nothing can raise a country's productivity except technology, and technology is the final product of a complex of sciences (including philosophy), each of them kept alive and moving by the achievements of a few independent minds.

["The Moratorium on Brains," *ARL*, I, 3, 5.]

The enemies of the Industrial Revolution—its displaced persons—were of the kind that had fought human progress for centuries, by every means available. In the Middle Ages, their weapon was the fear of God. In the nineteenth century, they still invoked the fear of God—for instance, they opposed the use of anesthesia on the grounds that it defies God's will, since God intended men to suffer. When this weapon wore out, they invoked the will of the collective, the group, the tribe. But since this weapon has collapsed in their hands, they are now reduced, like cornered animals, to baring their teeth and their souls, and to proclaiming that man has no right to exist—by the divine will of inanimate matter.

The demand to "restrict" technology is the demand to *restrict* man's mind. It is nature—i.e., reality—that makes both these goals impossible to achieve. Technology can be destroyed, and the mind can be paralyzed, but neither can be restricted. Whenever and wherever such restrictions are attempted, it is the mind—not the state—that withers away.

[*"The Anti-Industrial Revolution," NL*, 145.]

If you consider, not merely the length, but the kind of life men have to lead in the undeveloped parts of the world—"the *quality* of life," to borrow, with full meaning, the ecologists' meaningless catch phrase—if you consider the squalor, the misery, the helplessness, the fear, the unspeakably hard labor, the festering diseases, the plagues, the starvation, you will begin to appreciate the role of technology in man's existence.

Make no mistake about it: it is *technology* and *progress* that the nature-lovers are out to destroy. To quote again from the *Newsweek* survey: "What worries ecologists is that people now upset about the environment may ultimately look to technology to solve everything . . ." This is repeated over and over again; technological solutions, they claim, will merely create new problems.

[*Ibid.*, 138.]

Whom and what are [the ecological crusaders] attacking? It is not the luxuries of the "idle rich," but the availability of "luxuries" to the broad masses of people. They are denouncing the fact that automobiles, air conditioners and television sets are no longer toys of the rich, but are within the means of an average American worker—a beneficence that does not exist and is not fully believed anywhere else on earth.

What do they regard as the proper life for working people? A life of unrelieved drudgery, of endless, gray toil, with no rest, no travel, no pleasure—above all, no pleasure. Those drugged, fornicating hedonists do not know that man cannot live by toil alone, that pleasure is a necessity, and that television has brought more enjoyment into more lives than all the public parks and settlement houses combined.

What do they regard as luxury? Anything above the "bare necessities" of physical survival—with the explanation that men would not have to labor so hard if it were not for the "artificial needs" created by "commercialism" and "materialism." In reality, the opposite is true: the less the return on your labor, the harder the labor. It is much easier to acquire an automobile in New York City than a meal in the jungle. Without machines and technology, the task of mere survival is a terrible, mind-and-body-wrecking ordeal. In "nature," the struggle for food, clothing and shelter consumes all of a man's energy and spirit; it is a losing struggle—the winner is any flood, earthquake or swarm of locusts. (Consider the 500,000 bodies left in the wake of a single flood in Pakistan; they had been men who lived without technology.) To work only for bare necessities is a *luxury* that mankind cannot afford.

[Ibid., 148.]

See also ECOLOGY/ENVIRONMENTAL MOVEMENT; ECONOMIC GROWTH; NEW LEFT; POLLUTION; SCIENCE; SOUL-BODY DICHOTOMY.

Teleological Measurement. In regard to the concepts pertaining to evaluation ("value," "emotion," "feeling," "desire," etc.), the hierarchy involved is of a different kind and requires an entirely different type of measurement. It is a type applicable only to the psychological process of evaluation, and may be designated as *"teleological measurement."*

Measurement is the identification of a relationship—a quantitative relationship established by means of a standard that serves as a unit. Teleological measurement deals, not with cardinal, but with *ordinal* numbers—and the standard serves to establish a graded relationship of means to end.

For instance, a moral code is a system of teleological measurement which grades the choices and actions open to man, according to the degree to which they achieve or frustrate the code's standard of value. The standard is the end, to which man's actions are the means.

A moral code is a set of abstract principles; to practice it, an individual must translate it into the appropriate concretes—he must choose the particular goals and values which he is to pursue. This requires that he define his particular hierarchy of values, in the order of their importance, and that he act accordingly. Thus all his actions have to be guided by a process of teleological measurement. (The degree of uncertainty and contradictions in a man's hierarchy of values is the degree to which he will be unable to perform such measurements and will fail in his attempts at value calculations or at purposeful action.)

Teleological measurement has to be performed in and against an enormous context: it consists of establishing the relationship of a given choice to all the other possible choices and to one's hierarchy of values.

The simplest example of this process, which all men practice (with various degrees of precision and success), may be seen in the realm of material values—in the (implicit) principles that guide a man's spending of money. On any level of income, a man's money is a limited quantity; in spending it, he weighs the value of his purchase against the value of every other purchase open to him for the same amount of money, he weighs it against the hierarchy of all his other goals, desires and needs, then makes the purchase or not accordingly.

The same kind of measurement guides man's actions in the wider realm of moral or spiritual values. (By "spiritual" I mean "pertaining to consciousness." I say "wider" because it is man's hierarchy of values in this realm that determines his hierarchy of values in the material or economic realm.) But the currency or medium of exchange is different. In the spiritual realm, the currency—which exists in limited quantity and must be teleologically measured in the pursuit of any value—is *time*, i.e., *one's life*.

[*ITOE*, 42.]

See also CONSCIOUSNESS; LIFE; MEASUREMENT; MONEY; MORAL-ITY; PRINCIPLES; STANDARD of VALUE; ULTIMATE VALUE; VALUES.

Teleology. *See Goal-Directed Action.*

Thanksgiving. Thanksgiving is a typically *American* holiday. In spite of its religious form (giving thanks to God for a good harvest), its essential, secular meaning is *a celebration of successful production*. It is a producers' holiday. The lavish meal is a symbol of the fact that abundant consumption is the result and reward of production. Abundance is (or was and ought to be) America's pride—just as it is the pride of American parents that their children need never know starvation.

["Cashing in on Hunger," *ARL*, III, 23, 1.]

See also AMERICA; CHRISTMAS; PRODUCTION; RELIGION.

Theme (Literary). The four essential attributes of a novel are: Theme—Plot—Characterization—Style.

These are *attributes*, not separable parts. They can be isolated conceptually for purposes of study, but one must always remember that they are interrelated and that a novel is their sum. (If it is a good novel, it is an indivisible sum.)

[*"Basic Principles of Literature," RM,* 57; pb 80.]

A theme is the summation of a novel's abstract meaning. For instance, the theme of *Atlas Shrugged* is: "The role of the mind in man's existence." The theme of Victor Hugo's *Les Misérables* is: "The injustice of society toward its lower classes." The theme of *Gone With the Wind* is: "The impact of the Civil War on Southern society."

A theme may be specifically philosophical or it may be a narrower generalization. It may present a certain moral-philosophical position or a purely historical view, such as the portrayal of a certain society in a certain era. There are no rules or restrictions on the choice of a theme, provided it is communicable in the form of a novel. But if a novel has no discernible theme—if its events add up to nothing—it is a bad novel; its flaw is lack of integration.

Louis H. Sullivan's famous principle of architecture, "Form follows function," can be translated into: "Form follows purpose." The theme of a novel defines its purpose. The theme sets the writer's standard of selection, directing the innumerable choices he has to make and serving as the integrator of the novel.

Since a novel is a re-creation of reality, its theme has to be dramatized, i.e., presented in terms of action. Life is a process of action. The entire content of man's consciousness—thought, knowledge, ideas, values—has only one ultimate form of expression: in his actions; and only one ultimate purpose: to guide his actions. Since the theme of a novel is an idea about or pertaining to human existence, it is in terms of its effects on or expression in human actions that that idea has to be presented.

[*Ibid.,* 58; pb 81.]

A cardinal principle of good fiction [is]: *the theme and the plot of a novel must be integrated*—as thoroughly integrated as mind and body or thought and action in a rational view of man.

The link between the theme and the events of a novel is an element which I call the *plot-theme.* It is the first step of the translation of an abstract theme into a story, without which the construction of a plot would be impossible. A "plot-theme" is the central conflict or "situation" of a story—a conflict in terms of action, corresponding to the theme and complex enough to create a purposeful progression of events.

The *theme* of a novel is the core of its abstract meaning—the *plot-theme* is the core of its events.

[*Ibid.,* 63; pb 85.]

The theme of a novel can be conveyed only through the events of the plot, the events of the plot depend on the characterization of the men who enact them—and the characterization cannot be achieved except through the events of the plot, and the plot cannot be constructed without a theme.

This is the kind of integration required by the nature of a novel. And this is why a good novel is an indivisible sum: every scene, sequence and passage of a good novel has to involve, contribute to and advance all three of its major attributes: theme, plot, characterization.

[Ibid., 74; pb 93.]

Those who may be interested in the chronological development of my thinking . . . may observe the progression from a political theme in *We the Living* to a metaphysical theme in *Atlas Shrugged.*

["Preface," *FNI*, ii; pb viii.]

[*We the Living*] was published in 1936 and reissued in 1959. Its theme is: the individual against the state; the supreme value of a human life and the evil of the totalitarian state that claims the right to sacrifice it.

[*FNI*, 69; pb 60.]

[*Anthem*] was first published in England in 1938. Its theme is: the meaning of man's ego.

[Ibid., 73; pb 64.]

[*The Fountainhead*] was published in 1943. Its theme is: individualism versus collectivism, not in politics, but in man's soul; the psychological motivations and the basic premises that produce the character of an individualist or a collectivist.

[Ibid., 77; pb 68.]

[*Atlas Shrugged*] was published in 1957. Its theme is: the role of the mind in man's existence—and, as corollary, the demonstration of a new moral philosophy: the morality of rational self-interest.

[Ibid., 103; pb 88.]

See also ART; CHARACTERIZATION; INTEGRATION (MENTAL); LIT-ERATURE; PLOT; PLOT-THEME; SOUL-BODY DICHOTOMY; STYLE; SUBJECT (IN ART).

Theory-Practice Dichotomy.   [Consider the catch phrase:] "This may be good in theory, but it doesn't work in practice." What is a theory? It is a set of abstract principles purporting to be either a correct description of reality or a set of guidelines for man's actions. Correspondence to reality is the standard of value by which one estimates a theory. If a theory is inapplicable to reality, by what standard can it be estimated as "good"? If one were to accept that notion, it would mean: a. that the activity of man's mind is unrelated to reality; b. that the purpose of thinking is neither to acquire knowledge nor to guide man's actions. (The purpose of that catch phrase is to invalidate man's conceptual faculty.)

["Philosophical Detection," *PWNI*, 17; pb 14.]

*See also PLATONIC REALISM; PRAGMATISM; PRINCIPLES; RATION-
ALISM vs. EMPIRICISM; SOUL-BODY DICHOTOMY.*

Thought/Thinking. The process of *thinking* . . . is the process of defining *identity* and discovering *causal connections*.

[GS, *FNI*, 189; pb 152.]

The faculty that works by means of concepts, is: *reason*. The process is *thinking*.

["The Objectivist Ethics," *VOS*, 12; pb 20.]

All thinking is a process of identification and integration. Man perceives a blob of color; by integrating the evidence of his sight and his touch, he learns to identify it as a solid object; he learns to identify the object as a table; he learns that the table is made of wood; he learns that the wood consists of cells, that the cells consist of molecules, that the molecules consist of atoms. All through this process, the work of his mind consists of answers to a single question: *What* is it? His means to establish the truth of his answers is logic, and logic rests on the axiom that existence exists. Logic is the art of *non-contradictory identification*. A contradiction cannot exist. An atom is itself, and so is the universe; neither can contradict its own identity; nor can a part contradict the whole. No concept man forms is valid unless he integrates it without contradiction into the total sum of his knowledge. To arrive at a contradiction is to confess an error in one's thinking; to maintain a contradiction is to abdicate one's mind and to evict oneself from the realm of reality.

[GS, *FNI*, 153; pb 125.]

That which you call your soul or spirit is your consciousness, and that which you call "free will" is your mind's freedom to think or not, the only will you have, your only freedom, the choice that controls all the choices you make and determines your life and your character.

[Ibid., 155; pb 127.]

Thinking is not an automatic function. In any hour and issue of his life, man is free to think or to evade that effort. Thinking requires a state of full, focused awareness. The act of focusing one's consciousness is volitional.

["The Objectivist Ethics," *VOS*, 13; pb 20.]

Psychologically, the choice "to think or not" is the choice "to focus or not." Existentially, the choice "to focus or not" is the choice "to be conscious or not." Metaphysically, the choice "to be conscious or not" is the choice of life or death.

[Ibid., 13; pb 21.]

Thinking is man's only basic virtue, from which all the others proceed. And his basic vice, the source of all his evils, is that nameless act which all of you practice, but struggle never to admit: the act of blanking out, the willful suspension of one's consciousness, the refusal to think—not blindness, but the refusal to see; not ignorance, but the refusal to know. It is the act of unfocusing your mind and inducing an inner fog to escape the responsibility of judgment—on the unstated premise that a thing will not exist if only you refuse to identify it, that A will not be A so long as you do not pronounce the verdict "It *is*." Non-thinking is an act of annihilation, a wish to negate existence, an attempt to wipe out reality. But existence exists; reality is not to be wiped out, it will merely wipe out the wiper. By refusing to say "It is," you are refusing to say "I am." By suspending your judgment, you are negating your person. When a man declares: 'Who am I to know?'—he is declaring: "Who am I to live?"

This, in every hour and every issue, is your basic moral choice: thinking or non-thinking, existence or non-existence, A or non-A, entity or zero.

[GS, *FNI*, 155; pb 127.]

If devotion to truth is the hallmark of morality, then there is no greater, nobler, more heroic form of devotion than the act of a man who assumes the responsibility of thinking.

[Ibid.]

Thinking is a delicate, difficult process, which man cannot perform unless knowledge is his goal, logic is his method, and the judgment of *his* mind is his guiding absolute. Thought requires *selfishness*, the fundamental selfishness of a rational faculty that places nothing above the integrity of its own function.

A man cannot think if he places something—anything—above his perception of reality. He cannot follow the evidence unswervingly or uphold his conclusions intransigently, while regarding compliance with other men as his moral imperative, self-abasement as his highest virtue, and sacrifice as his primary duty. He cannot use his brain while surrendering his sovereignty over it, i.e., while accepting his neighbors as its owner and term-setter.

[Leonard Peikoff, *OP*, 334; pb 308.]

The concept "thought" is formed by retaining the distinguishing characteristics of the psychological action (a purposefully directed process of cognition) and by omitting the particular contents as well as the degree of the intellectual effort's intensity.

[*ITOE*, 41.]

The intensity of a process of thought and of the intellectual effort required varies according to the *scope* of its content; it varies when one grasps the concept "table" or the concept "justice," when one grasps that $2 + 2 = 4$ or that $e = mc^2$.

[Ibid., 40.]

See also CAUSALITY; CONCEPT-FORMATION; CONCEPTS; CREATION; EVASION; FOCUS; FREE WILL; IDENTITY; IMAGINATION; INTEGRATION (MENTAL); IRRATIONALITY; LOGIC; RATIONALITY; REASON; SELFISHNESS; UNDERSTANDING; VIRTUE.

Thrillers.   "Thrillers" are detective, spy or adventure stories. Their basic characteristic is *conflict,* which means: a clash of goals, which means: purposeful action in pursuit of *values.* Thrillers are the product, the popular offshoot, of the *Romantic* school of art that sees man, not as a helpless pawn of fate, but as a being who possesses volition, whose life is directed by his own value-choices. Romanticism is a value-oriented, morality-centered movement: its material is not journalistic minutiae, but the abstract, the essential, the universal principles of man's nature —and its basic literary commandment is to portray man "as he might be and ought to be."

Thrillers are a simplified, elementary version of Romantic literature. They are not concerned with a delineation of values, but, taking certain fundamental values for granted, they are concerned with only one aspect of a moral being's existence: the battle of good against evil in terms of purposeful action—a dramatized abstraction of the basic pattern of: choice, goal, conflict, danger, struggle, victory.

Thrillers are the kindergarten arithmetic, of which the higher mathematics is the greatest novels of world literature. Thrillers deal only with the skeleton—the plot structure—to which serious Romantic literature adds the flesh, the blood, the mind. The plots in the novels of Victor Hugo or Dostoevsky are pure thriller-plots, unequaled and unsurpassed by the writers of thrillers. . . .

Thrillers are the last refuge of the qualities that have vanished from modern literature: life, color, imagination; they are like a mirror still holding a distant reflection of man.

["Bootleg Romanticism," *RM*, 124; pb 132.]

Nobody takes thrillers literally, nor cares about their specific events, nor harbors any frustrated desire to become a secret agent or a private eye. Thrillers are taken symbolically; they dramatize one of man's widest and most crucial abstractions: the abstraction of *moral conflict*.

What people seek in thrillers is the spectacle of *man's efficacy:* of his ability to fight for his values and to achieve them. What they see is a condensed, simplified pattern, reduced to its essentials: a man fighting for a vital goal—overcoming one obstacle after another—facing terrible dangers and risks—persisting through an excruciating struggle—and winning.

[Ibid., 133; pb 138.]

What men find in the spectacle of the ultimate triumph of the good is the inspiration to fight for one's own values in the moral conflicts of one's own life.

[Ibid., 134; pb 139.]

See also LITERATURE; POPULAR LITERATURE; ROMANTICISM; VALUES.

Time.   Time is a measurement of motion; as such, it is a type of relationship. Time applies only within the universe, when you define a standard—such as the motion of the earth around the sun. If you take that as a unit, you can say: "This person has a certain relationship to that motion; he has existed for three revolutions; he is three years old." But when you get to the universe as a whole, obviously no standard is applicable. You cannot get outside the universe. The universe is eternal in the literal sense: non-temporal, out of time.

[Leonard Peikoff, "The Philosophy of Objectivism"
lecture series (1976), question period, Lecture 2.]

See also EXISTENCE; MEASUREMENT; MOTION; SPACE; UNIVERSE.

Trader Principle.   The symbol of all relationships among [rational] men, the moral symbol of respect for human beings, is *the trader*. We, who live by values, not by loot, are traders, both in matter and in spirit. A trader is a man who earns what he gets and does not give or take the undeserved. A trader does not ask to be paid for his failures, nor does he ask to be loved for his flaws. A trader does not squander his body as fodder or his soul as alms. Just as he does not give his work except in trade for material values, so he does not give the values of his spirit—his love, his friendship, his esteem—except in payment and in trade for human virtues, in payment for his own selfish pleasure, which he receives from men he can respect. The mystic parasites who have, throughout the ages, reviled the traders and held them in contempt, while honoring the beggars and the looters, have known the secret motive of their sneers: a trader is the entity they dread—a man of justice.

[GS, *FNI*, 163; pb 133.]

There is no conflict of interests among men who do not desire the unearned, who do not make sacrifices nor accept them, who deal with one another as *traders*, giving value for value.

The principle of *trade* is the only rational ethical principle for all human relationships, personal and social, private and public, spiritual and material. It is the principle of *justice*.

A trader is a man who earns what he gets and does not give or take the undeserved. He does not treat men as masters or slaves, but as independent equals. He deals with men by means of a free, voluntary, unforced, uncoerced exchange—an exchange which benefits both parties by their own independent judgment. A trader does not expect to be paid for his defaults, only for his achievements. He does not switch to others the burden of his failures, and he does not mortgage his life into bondage to the failures of others.

In spiritual issues—(by "spiritual" I mean: "pertaining to man's consciousness")—the currency or medium of exchange is different, but the principle is the same. Love, friendship, respect, admiration are the emotional response of one man to the virtues of another, the spiritual *payment* given in exchange for the personal, selfish pleasure which one man derives from the virtues of another man's character. Only a brute or an altruist would claim that the appreciation of another person's virtues is an act of selflessness, that as far as one's own selfish interest and pleasure are concerned, it makes no difference whether one deals with a genius or a fool, whether one meets a hero or a thug, whether one marries an ideal woman or a slut. In spiritual issues, a trader is a man who does not seek to be loved for his weaknesses or flaws, only for his virtues, and who does not grant his love to the weaknesses or the flaws of others, only to their virtues.

["The Objectivist Ethics," *VOS*, 28; pb 31.]

The trader and the warrior have been fundamental antagonists throughout history. Trade does not flourish on battlefields, factories do not produce under bombardments, profits do not grow on rubble. Capitalism is a society of *traders*—for which it has been denounced by every would-be gunman who regards trade as "selfish" and conquest as "noble."

[*"The Roots of War," CUI, 38.*]

See also ALTRUISM; CAPITALISM; ECONOMIC POWER vs. POLITICAL POWER; FREE MARKET; FREEDOM; JUSTICE; LOVE; MARKET VALUE; PHYSICAL FORCE; PURCHASING POWER; SELFISHNESS; SERVICE; SOUL-BODY DICHOTOMY; VALUES; WAR.

Tradition. The "neo-conservatives" are now trying to tell us that America was the product of "faith in revealed truths" and of uncritical respect for the traditions of the past (!).

It is certainly irrational to use the *"new"* as a standard of value, to believe that an idea or a policy is good merely because it is new. But it is much more preposterously irrational to use the *"old"* as a standard of value, to claim that an idea or a policy is good merely because it is ancient. The "liberals" are constantly asserting that they represent the future, that they are "new," "progressive," "forward-looking," etc.—and they denounce the "conservatives" as old-fashioned representatives of a dead past. The "conservatives" concede it, and thus help the "liberals" to propagate one of today's most grotesque inversions: collectivism, the ancient, frozen, status society, is offered to us in the name of *progress*— while capitalism, the only free, dynamic, creative society ever devised, is defended in the name of *stagnation.*

The plea to preserve *"tradition"* as such, can appeal only to those who have given up or to those who never intended to achieve anything in life. It is a plea that appeals to the worst elements in men and rejects the best: it appeals to fear, sloth, cowardice, conformity, self-doubt— and rejects creativeness, originality, courage, independence, self-reliance. It is an outrageous plea to address to human beings anywhere, but particularly outrageous here, in America, the country based on the principle that man must stand on his own feet, live by his own judgment, and move constantly forward as a productive, creative innovator.

The argument that we must respect "tradition" as such, respect it *merely* because it is a "tradition," means that we must accept the values other men have chosen, *merely* because other men have chosen them— with the necessary implication of: who are *we* to change them? The affront to a man's self-esteem, in such an argument, and the profound contempt for man's nature are obvious.

[*"Conservatism: An Obituary," CUI, 198.*]

America was created by men who broke with all political traditions and who originated a system unprecedented in history, relying on nothing but the "unaided" power of their own intellect.

[Ibid.]

See also AMERICA; ANTI-CONCEPTUAL MENTALITY; "CONSERVA-TIVES"; CULTURE; "ETHNICITY"; FAITH; HISTORY; INDIVIDUAL-ISM; TRIBALISM.

Tribal Premise (in Economics).

The basic premise of crude, primitive *tribal collectivism* [is] the notion that wealth belongs to the tribe or to society as a whole, and that every individual has the "right" to "participate" in it.

[Review of Shirley Scheibla's *Poverty Is Where the Money Is, TO,* Aug. 1969, 11.]

The tribal premise underlies today's political economy. That premise is shared by the enemies and the champions of capitalism alike; it provides the former with a certain inner consistency, and disarms the latter by a subtle, yet devastating aura of moral hypocrisy—as witness, their attempts to justify capitalism on the ground of "the common good" or "service to the consumer" or "the best allocation of resources." (*Whose* resources?)

If capitalism is to be understood, it is this *tribal premise* that has to be checked—and challenged.

Mankind is not an entity, an organism, or a coral bush. The entity involved in production and trade is *man*. It is with the study of man—not of the loose aggregate known as a "community"—that any science of the humanities has to begin.

["What Is Capitalism?" *CUI,* 14.]

Political economists—including the advocates of capitalism—defined their science as the study of the management or direction or organization or manipulation of a "community's" or a nation's "resources." The nature of these "resources" was not defined; their communal ownership was taken for granted—and the goal of political economy was assumed to be the study of how to utilize these "resources" for "the common good."

The fact that the principal "resource" involved was man himself, that he was an entity of a specific nature with specific capacities and requirements, was given the most superficial attention, if any. Man was regarded simply as one of the factors of production, along with land, forests, or mines—as one of the less significant factors, since more study was devoted to the influence and quality of these others than to *his* role or quality.

Political economy was, in effect, a science starting in midstream: it observed that men were producing and trading, it took for granted that they had always done so and always would—it accepted this fact as the given, requiring no further consideration—and it addressed itself to the problem of how to devise the best way for the "community" to dispose of human effort.

[Ibid., 12.]

A great deal may be learned about society by studying man; but this process cannot be reversed: nothing can be learned about man by studying society—by studying the inter-relationships of entities one has never identified or defined. Yet that is the methodology adopted by most political economists. Their attitude, in effect, amounts to the unstated, implicit postulate: "Man is that which fits economic equations." Since he obviously does not, this leads to the curious fact that in spite of the practical nature of their science, political economists are oddly unable to relate their abstractions to the concretes of actual existence.

[Ibid., 15.]

See also CAPITALISM; COLLECTIVISM; "COMMON GOOD"; INDIVID-UALISM; MAN; PRODUCTION; "REDISTRIBUTION" of WEALTH; SERVICE; TRIBALISM.

Tribalism. Tribalism (which is the best name to give to all the group manifestations of the anti-conceptual mentality) is a dominant element in Europe, as a reciprocally reinforcing cause and result of Europe's long history of caste systems, of national and local (provincial) chauvinism, of rule by brute force and endless, bloody wars. As an example, observe the Balkan nations, which are perennially bent upon exterminating one another over minuscule differences of tradition or language. Tribalism had no place in the United States—until recent decades. It could not take root here, its imported seedlings were withering away and turning to slag in the melting pot whose fire was fed by two inexhaustible sources of energy: individual rights and objective law; these two were the only protection man needed.

["The Missing Link," *PWNI*, 51; pb 42.]

What are the nature and the causes of modern tribalism? Philosophically, tribalism is the product of irrationalism and collectivism. It is a logical consequence of modern philosophy. If men accept the notion that reason is not valid, what is to guide them and how are they to live?

Obviously, they will seek to join some group—any group—which claims the ability to lead them and to provide some sort of knowledge acquired by some sort of unspecified means. If men accept the notion that the individual is helpless, intellectually and morally, that he has no mind and no rights, that he is nothing, but the group is all, and his only moral significance lies in selfless service to the group—they will be pulled obediently to join a group. But which group? Well, if you believe that you have no mind and no moral value, you cannot have the confidence to make choices—so the only thing for you to do is to join an *unchosen* group, the group into which you were born, the group to which you were predestined to belong by the sovereign, omnipotent, omniscient power of your body chemistry.

This, of course, is racism. But if your group is small enough, it will not be called "racism": it will be called "*ethnicity*."

["Global Balkanization," pamphlet, 5.]

A symptom of the tribal mentality's self-arrested, perceptual level of development may be observed in the tribalists' position on *language*.

Language is a conceptual tool—a code of visual-auditory symbols that denote concepts. To a person who understands the function of language, it makes no difference what sounds are chosen to name things, provided these sounds refer to clearly defined aspects of reality. But to a tribalist, language is a mystic heritage, a string of sounds handed down from his ancestors and memorized, not understood. To him, the importance lies in the perceptual concrete, the *sound* of a word, not its meaning. He would kill and die for the privilege of printing on every postage stamp the word "postage" for the English-speaking and the word "postes" for the French-speaking citizens of his bilingual Canada. Since most of the ethnic languages are not full languages, but merely dialects or local corruptions of a country's language, the distinctions which the tribalists fight for are not even as big as that.

But, of course, it is not for their language that the tribalists are fighting: they are fighting to protect their level of awareness, their mental passivity, their obedience to the tribe, and their desire to ignore the existence of outsiders.

[Ibid., 8.]

It is obvious why the morality of *altruism* is a tribal phenomenon. Prehistorical men were physically unable to survive without clinging to a tribe for leadership and protection against other tribes. The cause of altruism's perpetuation into civilized eras is not physical, but psycho-epistemological: the men of self-arrested, perceptual mentality are unable to survive without tribal leadership and "protection" against reality.

The doctrine of self-sacrifice does not offend them: they have no sense of self or of personal value—they do not know what it is that they are asked to sacrifice—they have no firsthand inkling of such things as intellectual integrity, love of truth, personally chosen values, or a passionate dedication to an idea. When they hear injunctions against "selfishness," they believe that what they must renounce is the brute, mindless whim-worship of a tribal lone wolf. But their leaders—the theoreticians of altruism—know better. Immanuel Kant knew it; John Dewey knew it; B. F. Skinner knows it; John Rawls knows it. Observe that it is not the mindless brute, but reason, intelligence, ability, merit, self-confidence, self-esteem that they are out to destroy.

Today, we are seeing a ghastly spectacle: a magnificent scientific civilization dominated by the morality of prehistorical savagery.

["Selfishness Without a Self," *PWNI*, 61; pb 50.]

See also ALTRUISM; AMERICA; AMORALISM; ANTI-CONCEPTUAL MENTALITY; COLLECTIVISM; "ETHNICITY"; INDIVIDUALISM; IRRATIONALISM; KANT, IMMANUEL; LANGUAGE; PSYCHO-EPISTEMOLOGY; RACISM; REASON; SELF; SELF-ESTEEM; SELFISHNESS; STATISM.

Truth.　Truth is the recognition of reality; reason, man's only means of knowledge, is his only standard of truth.

[GS, *FNI*, 154; pb 126.]

Truth is the product of the recognition (i.e., identification) of the facts of reality. Man identifies and integrates the facts of reality by means of concepts. He retains concepts in his mind by means of definitions. He organizes concepts into propositions—and the truth or falsehood of his propositions rests, not only on their relation to the facts he asserts, but also on the truth or falsehood of the definitions of the concepts he uses to assert them, which rests on the truth or falsehood of his designations of *essential* characteristics.

[*ITOE*, 63.]

The truth or falsehood of all of man's conclusions, inferences, thought and knowledge rests on the truth or falsehood of his definitions.

[Ibid., 65.]

Every truth about a given existent(s) reduces, in basic pattern, to: "X is: one or more of the things which it is." The predicate in such a case states some characteristic(s) of the subject; but since it *is* a characteristic of the subject, the *concept(s)* designating the subject in fact includes the predicate from the outset. If one wishes to use the term "tautology" in this context, then *all* truths are "tautological." (And, by the same reasoning, all falsehoods are self-contradictions.)

When making a statement about an existent, one has, ultimately, only two alternatives: "X (which means X, the existent, including all its characteristics) *is* what it is"—or: "X *is not* what it is." The choice between truth and falsehood is the choice between "tautology" (in the sense explained) and self-contradiction.

In the realm of propositions, there is only one basic epistemological distinction: *truth vs. falsehood,* and only one fundamental issue: By what method is truth discovered and validated? To plant a dichotomy at the base of human knowledge—to claim that there are opposite *methods* of validation and opposite *types* of truth [as do the advocates of the "analytic-synthetic" dichotomy] is a procedure without grounds or justification.

[Leonard Peikoff, "The Analytic-Synthetic Dichotomy," *ITOE*, 136.]

The existence of human volition cannot be used to justify the theory that there is a dichotomy of *propositions* or of *truths*. Propositions about metaphysical facts, and propositions about man-made facts, do not have different characteristics *qua propositions*. They differ merely in their subject matter, but then so do the propositions of astronomy and of immunology. Truths about metaphysical and about man-made facts are learned and validated by the same process: by observation; and, *qua truths*, both are equally necessary. Some *facts* are not necessary, but all *truths* are.

Truth is the identification of a fact of reality. Whether the fact in question is metaphysical or man-made, the fact determines the truth: if the fact exists, there is no alternative in regard to what is true. For instance, the fact that the U.S. has 50 states was not metaphysically necessary—but as long as this is men's choice, the proposition that "The U.S. has 50 states" is necessarily *true*. A true proposition *must* describe the facts as they are. In this sense, a "necessary truth" is a redundancy, and a "contingent truth" a self-contradiction.

[Ibid., 150.]

[Consider the catch phrase:] "It may be true for you, but it's not true for me." What is the meaning of the concept "truth"? Truth is the recognition of reality. (This is known as the correspondence theory of truth.) The same thing cannot be true and untrue at the same time and in the same respect. That catch phrase, therefore, means: a. that the Law of Identity is invalid; b. that there is no objectively perceivable reality, only some indeterminate flux which is nothing in particular, i.e., that there is no reality (in which case, there can be no such thing as truth); or c. that the two debaters perceive two different universes (in which case, no debate is possible). (The purpose of the catch phrase is the destruction of objectivity.)

["Philosophical Detection," *PWNI*, 16; pb 14.]

See also ANALYTIC-SYNTHETIC DICHOTOMY; CONCEPTS; CONTRA-DICTIONS; DEFINITIONS; EXISTENCE; FALSEHOOD; HONESTY; IDENTITY; LOGIC; METAPHYSICAL vs. MAN-MADE; NECESSITY; OBJECTIVITY; PRIMACY of EXISTENCE vs. PRIMACY of CON-SCIOUSNESS; PROPOSITIONS; REASON.

Tyranny. Tyranny is any political system (whether absolute monarchy or fascism or communism) that does not recognize individual rights (which necessarily include property rights). The overthrow of a political system by force is justified only when it is directed against tyranny: it is an act of self-defense against those who rule by force. For example, the American Revolution.

["From a Symposium," *NL*, 96.]

See also DICTATORSHIP; GOVERNMENT; INDIVIDUAL RIGHTS; PHYSICAL FORCE; POLITICS; PROPERTY RIGHTS; STATISM.

U

Ultimate Value. An *ultimate* value is that final goal or end to which all lesser goals are the means—and it sets the standard by which all lesser goals are *evaluated*. An organism's life is its *standard of value:* that which furthers its life is the *good,* that which threatens it is the *evil.*

Without an ultimate goal or end, there can be no lesser goals or means: a series of means going off into an infinite progression toward a nonexistent end is a metaphysical and epistemological impossibility. It is only an ultimate goal, an *end in itself,* that makes the existence of values possible. Metaphysically, *life* is the only phenomenon that is an end in itself: a value gained and kept by a constant process of action. Epistemologically, the concept of "value" is genetically dependent upon and derived from the antecedent concept of "life." To speak of "value" as apart from "life" is worse than a contradiction in terms. "It is only the concept of 'Life' that makes the concept of 'Value' possible."

["The Objectivist Ethics," *VOS*, 7; pb 17.]

The maintenance of life and the pursuit of happiness are not two separate issues. To hold one's own life as one's ultimate value, and one's own happiness as one's highest purpose are two aspects of the same achievement. Existentially, the activity of pursuing rational goals is the activity of maintaining one's life; psychologically, its result, reward and concomitant is an emotional state of happiness. It is by experiencing happiness that one lives one's life, in any hour, year or the whole of it. And when one experiences the kind of pure happiness that is an end in itself—the kind that makes one think: "*This* is worth living for"—what one is greeting and affirming in emotional terms is the metaphysical fact that *life* is an end in itself.

[Ibid., 25; pb 29.]

See also EMOTIONS; GOAL-DIRECTED ACTION; HAPPINESS; HIER-ARCHY of KNOWLEDGE; LIFE; METAPHYSICAL; STANDARD of VALUE; "STOLEN CONCEPT," FALLACY of; VALUES.

Understanding. To understand means to focus on the content of a given subject (as against the sensory—visual or auditory—form in which it is communicated), to isolate its essentials, to establish its relationship to the previously known, and to integrate it with the appropriate categories of other subjects. Integration is the essential part of understanding.

The predominance of memorizing is proper only in the first few years of a child's education, while he is observing and gathering perceptual material. From the time he reaches the conceptual level (i.e., from the time he learns to speak), his education requires a progressively larger scale of understanding and progressively smaller amounts of memorizing.

["The Comprachicos," *NL*, 208.]

See also CONCEPTS; EDUCATION; INTEGRATION (MENTAL); KNOWLEDGE; LEARNING; PERCEPTION; REASON.

Unemployment. *See Unions.*

Unions. The artificially high wages forced on the economy by compulsory unionism imposed economic hardships on other groups—particularly on non-union workers and on unskilled labor, which was being squeezed gradually out of the market. Today's widespread unemployment is the result of organized labor's privileges and of allied measures, such as minimum wage laws. For years, the unions supported these measures and sundry welfare legislation, apparently in the belief that the costs would be paid by taxes imposed on the rich. The growth of inflation has shown that the major victim of government spending and of taxation is the middle class. Organized labor is part of the middle class—and the actual value of labor's forced "social gains" is now being wiped out.

["A Preview," *ARL*, I, 23, 2.]

Organized labor has been much more sensitive to the danger of government power and much more aware of ideological issues. Its spokesmen have fought the government in proper, morally confident terms whenever they saw a threat to their rights. (To name a few examples of such occasions: the attempt at labor conscription in World War II, the issue of U.S. contributions to the Soviet-dominated International Labor Organization, President Kennedy's attempt to impose guidelines in the steel crisis of 1962.) Labor's concern was aroused only in defense of *its* rights; still, whoever defends his own rights defends the rights of all. But labor was pursuing a contradictory policy, which could not be maintained for long. In many issues—notably in its support of welfare-state legislation—labor violated the rights of others and fertilized the growth of the government's power. And, today, labor is in line to become the next major victim of advancing statism.

It was business, not labor, that initiated the policy of government intervention in the economy (as long ago as the nineteenth century)—

and business was the first victim. Labor adopted the same policy and will meet the same fate. He who lives by a legalized sword, will perish by a legalized sword.

["The Moratorium on Brains," *ARL*, I, 3, 2.]

See also CAPITALISM; FREE MARKET; INFLATION; MIDDLE CLASS; MONEY; POVERTY.

Unit. *The ability to regard entities as units is man's distinctive method of cognition,* which other living species are unable to follow.

A unit is an existent regarded as a separate member of a group of two or more similar members. (Two stones are two units; so are two square feet of ground, if regarded as distinct parts of a continuous stretch of ground.) Note that the concept "unit" involves an act of consciousness (a selective focus, a certain way of regarding things), but that it is *not* an arbitrary creation of consciousness: it is a method of identification or classification according to the attributes which a consciousness observes in reality. This method permits any number of classifications and cross-classifications: one may classify things according to their shape or color or weight or size or atomic structure; but the criterion of classification is not invented, it is perceived in reality. Thus the concept "unit" is a bridge between metaphysics and epistemology: units do not exist *qua* units, what exists are things, but *units are things viewed by a consciousness in certain existing relationships.*

[*ITOE*, 7.]

With the grasp of the (implicit) concept "unit," man reaches the conceptual level of cognition which consists of two interrelated fields: the *conceptual* and the *mathematical.* The process of concept-formation is, in large part, a mathematical process.

[Ibid., 8.]

A "number" is a mental symbol that integrates units into a single larger unit (or subdivides a unit into fractions) with reference to the basic number of "one," which is the basic mental symbol of "unit." Thus "5" stands for | | | | |. (Metaphysically, the referents of "5" are any five existents of a specified kind; epistemologically, they are represented by a single symbol.)

[Ibid., 84.]

See also CONCEPT-FORMATION; CONCEPTS; EPISTEMOLOGY; IM-PLICIT KNOWLEDGE; INTEGRATION (MENTAL); MEASUREMENT; METAPHYSICS; NUMBER; UNIT-ECONOMY; WORDS.

Unit-Economy. Since consciousness is a specific faculty, it has a specific nature or identity and, therefore, its range is limited: it cannot perceive everything at once; since awareness, on all its levels, requires an active process, it cannot do everything at once. Whether the units with which one deals are percepts or concepts, the range of what man can hold in the focus of his conscious awareness at any given moment, is limited. The essence, therefore, of man's incomparable cognitive power is the ability to reduce a vast amount of information to a minimal number of units—which is the task performed by his conceptual faculty. And the principle of *unit-economy* is one of that faculty's essential guiding principles.

[*ITOE*, 83.]

In any given moment, concepts enable man to hold in the focus of his conscious awareness much more than his purely perceptual capacity would permit. The range of man's perceptual awareness—the number of percepts he can deal with at any one time—is limited. He may be able to visualize four or five units—as, for instance, five trees. He cannot visualize a hundred trees or a distance of ten light-years. It is only his conceptual faculty that makes it possible for him to deal with knowledge of that kind.

["The Psycho-Epistemology of Art," *RM*, 19; pb 17.]

Conceptualization is a method of expanding man's consciousness by reducing the number of its content's units—a systematic means to an unlimited integration of cognitive data.

A concept substitutes one symbol (one word) for the enormity of the perceptual aggregate of the concretes it subsumes. In order to perform its unit-reducing function, the symbol has to become automatized in a man's consciousness, i.e., the enormous sum of its referents must be instantly (implicitly) available to his conscious mind whenever he uses that concept, without the need of perceptual visualization or mental summarizing—in the same manner as the concept "5" does not require that he visualize five sticks every time he uses it.

For example, if a man has fully grasped the concept "justice," he does not need to recite to himself a long treatise on its meaning, while he listens to the evidence in a court case. The mere sentence "I must be just" holds that meaning in his mind automatically, and leaves his conscious attention free to grasp the evidence and to evaluate it according to a complex set of principles. (And, in case of doubt, the conscious recall of the precise meaning of "justice" provides him with the guidelines he needs.)

It is the principle of unit-economy that necessitates the definition of concepts in terms of *essential* characteristics. If, when in doubt, a man recalls a concept's definition, the essential characteristic(s) will give him an instantaneous grasp of the concept's meaning, i.e., of the nature of its referents.

[*ITOE.*, 85.]

See also AUTOMATIZATION; CONSCIOUSNESS; DEFINITIONS; IDENTITY; MEANING (*of CONCEPTS*); PSYCHO-EPISTEMOLOGY; "RAND'S RAZOR"; WORDS.

United Nations. Psychologically, the U.N. has contributed a great deal to the gray swamp of demoralization—of cynicism, bitterness, hopelessness, fear and nameless guilt—which is swallowing the Western world. But the communist world has gained a moral sanction, a stamp of civilized respectability from the Western world—it has gained the West's assistance in deceiving its victims—it has gained the status and prestige of an equal partner, thus establishing the notion that the difference between human rights and mass slaughter is merely a difference of political opinion.

The declared goal of the communist countries is the conquest of the world. What they stand to gain from a collaboration with the (relatively) free countries is the latter's material, financial, scientific, and intellectual resources; the free countries have nothing to gain from the communist countries. Therefore, the only form of common policy or compromise possible between two such parties is the policy of property owners who make piecemeal concessions to an armed thug in exchange for his promise not to rob them.

The U.N. has delivered a larger part of the globe's surface and population into the power of Soviet Russia than Russia could ever hope to conquer by armed force. The treatment accorded to Katanga versus the treatment accorded to Hungary, is a sufficient example of U.N. policies. An institution allegedly formed for the purpose of using the united might of the world to stop an aggressor, has become means of using the united might of the world to force the surrender of one helpless country after another into the aggressor's power.

Who, but a concrete-bound epistemological savage, could have expected any other results from such an "experiment in collaboration"? What would you expect from a crime-fighting committee whose board of directors included the leading gangsters of the community?

["The Anatomy of Compromise," *CUI*, 148.]

When an institution reaches the degree of corruption, brazen cynicism and dishonor demonstrated by the U.N. in its shameful history, to discuss it at length is to imply that its members and supporters may possibly be making an innocent error about its nature—which is no longer possible. There is no margin for error about a monstrosity that was created for the alleged purpose of preventing wars by uniting the world against any aggressor, but proceeded to unite it against any victim of aggression. The expulsion of a *charter member*, the Republic of China —an action forbidden by the U.N.'s own Charter—was a "moment of truth," a naked display of the United Nations' soul.

What was Red China's qualification for membership in the U.N.? The fact that her government seized power by force, and has maintained it for twenty-two years by terror. What disqualified Nationalist China? The fact that she was a friend of the United States.

[*"The Shanghai Gesture," ARL*, I, 14, 1.]

See also COMMUNISM; COMPROMISE; FOREIGN POLICY; SANCTION; SOVIET RUSSIA; WAR.

Universe. The universe is the total of that which exists—not merely the earth or the stars or the galaxies, but everything. Obviously then there can be no such thing as the "cause" of the universe. . . .

Is the universe then unlimited in size? No. Everything which exists is finite, including the universe. What then, you ask, is outside the universe, if it is finite? This question is invalid. The phrase "outside the universe" has no referent. The universe is everything. "Outside the universe" stands for "that which is where everything isn't." There is no such place. There isn't even nothing "out there": there is no "out there."

[Leonard Peikoff, "The Philosophy of Objectivism" lecture series (1976), Lecture 2.]

To grasp the axiom that existence exists, means to grasp the fact that nature, i.e., the universe as a whole, cannot be created or annihilated, that it cannot come into or go out of existence. Whether its basic constituent elements are atoms, or subatomic particles, or some yet undiscovered forms of energy, it is not ruled by a consciousness or by will or by chance, but by the Law of Identity. All the countless forms, motions, combinations and dissolutions of elements within the universe—from a floating speck of dust to the formation of a galaxy to the emergence of life—are caused and determined by the identities of the elements involved. Nature is the *metaphysically given*—i.e., the nature of nature is outside the power of any volition.

[*"The Metaphysical Versus the Man-Made," PWNI*, 30; pb 25.]

See also CAUSALITY; EXISTENCE; IDENTITY; INFINITY; METAPHYSICAL vs. MAN-MADE; METAPHYSICS; NATURE; SPACE; TIME.

U.S.S.R.   *See Soviet Russia.*

Utilitarianism.   Utilitarianism is a union of hedonism and Christianity. The first teaches man to love pleasure; the second, to love his neighbor. The union consists in teaching man to love his neighbor's pleasure. To be exact, the Utilitarians teach that an action is moral if its result is to maximize pleasure among men in general. This theory holds that man's duty is to serve—according to a purely quantitative standard of value. He is to serve not the well-being of the nation or of the economic class, but "the greatest happiness of the greatest number," regardless of who comprise it in any given issue. As to one's *own* happiness, says [John Stuart] Mill, the individual must be "disinterested" and "strictly impartial"; he must remember that he is only one unit out of the dozens, or millions, of men affected by his actions. "All honor to those who can abnegate for themselves the personal enjoyment of life," says Mill, "when by such renunciation they contribute worthily to increase the amount of happiness in the world."

[Leonard Peikoff, *OP*, 122; pb 119.]

"The greatest good for the greatest number" is one of the most vicious slogans ever foisted on humanity.

This slogan has no concrete, specific meaning. There is no way to interpret it benevolently, but a great many ways in which it can be used to justify the most vicious actions.

What is the definition of "the good" in this slogan? None, except: whatever is good for the greatest number. Who, in any particular issue, decides what is good for the greatest number? Why, the greatest number.

If you consider this moral, you would have to approve of the following examples, which are exact applications of this slogan in practice: fifty-one percent of humanity enslaving the other forty-nine; nine hungry cannibals eating the tenth one; a lynching mob murdering a man whom they consider dangerous to the community.

There were seventy million Germans in Germany and six hundred thousand Jews. The greatest number (the Germans) supported the Nazi government which told them that their greatest good would be served by exterminating the smaller number (the Jews) and grabbing their property. This was the horror achieved in practice by a vicious slogan accepted in theory.

But, you might say, the majority in all these examples did not achieve any real good for itself either? No. It didn't. Because "the good" is not determined by counting numbers and is not achieved by the sacrifice of anyone to anyone.

["Textbook of Americanism," pamphlet, 10.]

See also ALTRUISM; COLLECTIVISM; GOOD, the; HAPPINESS; HEDONISM; INDIVIDUAL RIGHTS; MILL, JOHN STUART; MORALITY; PLEASURE and PAIN; SACRIFICE; SELFISHNESS.

V

Validation. "Validation" in the broad sense includes any process of relating mental contents to the facts of reality. Direct perception, the method of validating axioms, is one such process. "Proof" designates another type of validation. Proof is the process of deriving a conclusion logically from antecedent knowledge.

[Leonard Peikoff, "The Philosophy of Objectivism" lecture series (1976), question period, Lecture 3.]

See also AXIOMS; COROLLARIES; EPISTEMOLOGY; INDUCTION *and* DEDUCTION; LOGIC; OBJECTIVITY; PROOF; SELF-EVIDENT.

Values. To challenge the basic premise of any discipline, one must begin at the beginning. In ethics, one must begin by asking: What are *values?* Why does man need them?

"Value" is that which one acts to gain and/or keep. The concept "value" is not a primary; it presupposes an answer to the question: of value to *whom* and for *what?* It presupposes an entity capable of acting to achieve a goal in the face of an alternative. Where no alternative exists, no goals and no values are possible.

I quote from Galt's speech: "There is only one fundamental alternative in the universe: existence or nonexistence—and it pertains to a single class of entities: to living organisms. The existence of inanimate matter is unconditional, the existence of life is not: it depends on a specific course of action. Matter is indestructible, it changes its forms, but it cannot cease to exist. It is only a living organism that faces a constant alternative: the issue of life or death. Life is a process of self-sustaining and self-generated action. If an organism fails in that action, it dies; its chemical elements remain, but its life goes out of existence. It is only the concept of 'Life' that makes the concept of 'Value' possible. It is only to a living entity that things can be good or evil."

To make this point fully clear, try to imagine an immortal, indestructible robot, an entity which moves and acts, but which cannot be affected by anything, which cannot be changed in any respect, which cannot be damaged, injured or destroyed. Such an entity would not be able to have any values; it would have nothing to gain or to lose; it could not regard anything as *for* or *against* it, as serving or threatening its welfare, as fulfilling or frustrating its interests. It could have no interests and no goals.

["The Objectivist Ethics," *VOS*, 5; pb 15.]

"Value" is that which one acts to gain and keep, "virtue" is the action by which one gains and keeps it. "Value" presupposes an answer to the question: of value to whom and for what? "Value" presupposes a standard, a purpose and the necessity of action in the face of an alternative. Where there are no alternatives, no values are possible.

[GS, *FNI*, 147; pb 121.]

It is only an ultimate goal, an *end in itself*, that makes the existence of values possible. Metaphysically, *life* is the only phenomenon that is an end in itself: a value gained and kept by a constant process of action. Epistemologically, the concept of "value" is genetically dependent upon and derived from the antecedent concept of "life." To speak of "value" as apart from "life" is worse than a contradiction in terms. "It is only the concept of 'Life' that makes the concept of 'Value' possible."

In answer to those philosophers who claim that no relation can be established between ultimate ends or values and the facts of reality, let me stress that the fact that living entities exist and function necessitates the existence of values and of an ultimate value which for any given living entity is its own life. Thus the validation of value judgments is to be achieved by reference to the facts of reality. The fact that a living entity *is*, determines what it *ought* to do. So much for the issue of the relation between "*is*" and "*ought*."

Now in what manner does a human being discover the concept of "*value*"? By what means does he first become aware of the issue of "*good or evil*" in its simplest form? By means of the physical sensations of *pleasure* or *pain*. Just as sensations are the first step of the development of a human consciousness in the realm of *cognition*, so they are its first step in the realm of *evaluation*.

The capacity to experience pleasure or pain is innate in a man's body; it is part of his *nature*, part of the kind of entity he *is*. He has no choice about it, and he has no choice about the standard that determines what will make him experience the physical sensation of pleasure or of pain. What is that standard? *His life.*

["The Objectivist Ethics," *VOS*, 7; pb 17.]

Since a value is that which one acts to gain and/or keep, and the amount of possible action is limited by the duration of one's lifespan, it is a part of one's life that one invests in everything one values. The years, months, days or hours of thought, of interest, of action devoted to a value are the currency with which one pays for the enjoyment one receives from it.

[*ITOE*, 44.]

Material objects as such have neither value nor disvalue; they acquire value-significance only in regard to a living being—particularly, in regard to serving or hindering man's goals.

["From the Horse's Mouth," *PWNI*, 96; pb 79.]

Values are the motivating power of man's actions and a *necessity* of his survival, psychologically as well as physically.

Man's values control his subconscious emotional mechanism that functions like a computer adding up his desires, his experiences, his fulfillments and frustrations—like a sensitive guardian watching and constantly assessing his relationship to reality. The key question which this computer is programmed to answer, is: What is *possible* to me?

There is a certain similarity between the issue of sensory perception and the issue of values. . . .

If severe and prolonged enough, the absence of a normal, active flow of sensory stimuli may disintegrate the complex organization and the interdependent functions of man's consciousness.

Man's emotional mechanism works as the barometer of the efficacy or impotence of his actions. If severe and prolonged enough, the absence of a normal, active flow of *value-experiences* may disintegrate and paralyze man's consciousness—by telling him that no action is possible.

The form in which man experiences the reality of his values is *pleasure*.

["Our Cultural Value-Deprivation," *TO*, April 1966, 3.]

The objective theory of values is the only moral theory incompatible with rule by force. Capitalism is the only system based implicitly on an objective theory of values—and the historic tragedy is that this has never been made explicit.

If one knows that the good is *objective*—i.e., determined by the nature of reality, but to be discovered by man's mind—one knows that an attempt to achieve the good by physical force is a monstrous contradiction which negates morality at its root by destroying man's capacity to recognize the good, i.e., his capacity to value. Force invalidates and paralyzes a man's judgment, demanding that he act against it, thus rendering him morally impotent. A value which one is forced to accept at the price of surrendering one's mind, is not a value to anyone; the forcibly mindless can neither judge nor choose nor value. An attempt to achieve the good by force is like an attempt to provide a man with a picture gallery at the price of cutting out his eyes. Values cannot exist (cannot be valued) outside the full context of a man's life, needs, goals, and *knowledge*.

["What Is Capitalism?" *CUI*, 23.]

Virtue. "Value" is that which one acts to gain and keep, "virtue" is the action by which one gains and keeps it.

[GS, *FNI*, 147; pb 121.]

Man has a single basic choice: to think or not, and *that* is the gauge of his virtue. Moral perfection is an *unbreached rationality*—not the degree of your intelligence, but the full and relentless use of your mind, not the extent of your knowledge, but the acceptance of reason as an absolute.

[Ibid., 224; pb 178.]

My morality, the morality of reason, is contained in a single axiom: existence exists—and in a single choice: to live. The rest proceeds from these. To live, man must hold three things as the supreme and ruling values of his life: Reason—Purpose—Self-esteem. Reason, as his only tool of knowledge—Purpose, as his choice of the happiness which that tool must proceed to achieve—Self-esteem, as his inviolate certainty that his mind is competent to think and his person is worthy of happiness, which means: is worthy of living. These three values imply and require all of man's virtues, and all his virtues pertain to the relation of existence and consciousness: rationality, independence, integrity, honesty, justice, productiveness, pride.

[Ibid., 156; pb 128.]

Virtue is not an end in itself. Virtue is not its own reward or sacrificial fodder for the reward of evil. *Life* is the reward of virtue—and happi-ness is the goal and the reward of life.

[Ibid., 161; pb 131.]

TICE; MORALITY; PRIDE; PRODUCTIVENESS; RATIONALITY; VALUES.

Visual Arts.   The so-called visual arts (painting, sculpture, architecture) produce concrete, perceptually available entities and make them convey an abstract, conceptual meaning. . . .

The visual arts do not deal with the sensory field of awareness as such, but with *the sensory field as perceived by a conceptual consciousness.*

The sensory-perceptual awareness of an adult does not consist of mere sense data (as it did in his infancy), but of automatized integrations that combine sense data with a vast context of conceptual knowledge. The visual arts refine and direct the sensory elements of these integrations. By means of selectivity, of emphasis and omission, these arts lead man's sight to the conceptual context intended by the artist. They teach man to see more precisely and to find deeper meaning in the field of his vision.

It is a common experience to observe that a particular painting—for example, a still life of apples—makes its subject "more real than it is in reality." The apples seem brighter and firmer, they seem to possess an almost self-assertive character, a kind of heightened reality which neither their real-life models nor any color photograph can match. Yet if one examines them closely, one sees that no real-life apple ever looked like that. What is it, then, that the artist has done? He has created a *visual abstraction.*

He has performed the process of concept-formation—of isolating and integrating—but in exclusively visual terms. He has isolated the *essential,* distinguishing characteristics of apples, and integrated them into a single visual unit. He has brought the conceptual method of functioning to the operations of a single sense organ, the organ of sight.

["Art and Cognition," *RM,* pb 47.]

See also ABSTRACTION (PROCESS of); ART; ARTISTIC CREATION; CONCEPTS; DECORATIVE ARTS; INTEGRATION (MENTAL); PAINTING; PERCEPTION; PHOTOGRAPHY; SCULPTURE; STYLIZATION.

Volition.   *See Free Will.*

Volitional.   "Volitional" means selected from two or more alternatives that were possible under the circumstances, the difference being made by the individual's decision, which could have been otherwise.

[Leonard Peikoff, "The Philosophy of Objectivism" lecture series (1976), Lecture 3.]

See also FREE WILL.

Voting. The right to vote is a *consequence*, not a primary cause, of a free social system—and its value depends on the constitutional structure implementing and strictly delimiting the voters' power; unlimited majority rule is an instance of the principle of tyranny.

["The Lessons of Vietnam," *ARL*, III, 24, 3.]

A majority vote is not an epistemological validation of an idea. Voting is merely a proper political device—within a strictly, constitutionally delimited sphere of action—for choosing the practical *means* of implementing a society's basic principles. But those principles are not determined by vote.

["Who Is the Final Authority in Ethics?" *TON*, Feb. 1965, 8.]

Individual rights are not subject to a public vote; a majority has no right to vote away the rights of a minority.

["Collectivized 'Rights,' " *VOS*, 140; pb 104.]

The citizens of a free nation may disagree about the specific legal procedures or *methods* of implementing their rights (which is a complex problem, the province of political science and of the philosophy of law), but they agree on the basic principle to be implemented: the principle of individual rights. When a country's constitution places individual rights outside the reach of public authorities, the sphere of political power is severely delimited—and thus the citizens may, safely and properly, agree to abide by the decisions of a majority vote in this delimited sphere. The lives and property of minorities or dissenters are not at stake, are not subject to vote and are not endangered by any majority decision; no man or group holds a blank check on power over others.

[Ibid., 138; pb 103.]

See also CONSTITUTION; DEMOCRACY; ECONOMIC POWER vs. PO-LITICAL POWER; GOVERNMENT; INDIVIDUAL RIGHTS; REPRE-SENTATIVE GOVERNMENT; REPUBLIC; STATISM; TYRANNY.

W

War. Wars are the second greatest evil that human societies can perpetrate. (The first is dictatorship, the enslavement of their own citizens, which is the cause of wars.)

["The Wreckage of the Consensus," *CUI*, 224.]

Laissez-faire capitalism is the only social system based on the recognition of individual rights and, therefore, the only system that bans force from social relationships. By the nature of its basic principles and interests, it is the only system fundamentally opposed to war.

Men who are free to produce, have no incentive to loot; they have nothing to gain from war and a great deal to lose. Ideologically, the principle of individual rights does not permit a man to seek his own livelihood at the point of a gun, inside or outside his country. Economically, wars cost money; in a free economy, where wealth is privately owned, the costs of war come out of the income of private citizens—there is no overblown public treasury to hide that fact—and a citizen cannot hope to recoup his own financial losses (such as taxes or business dislocations or property destruction) by winning the war. Thus his own economic interests are on the side of peace.

In a statist economy, where wealth is "publicly owned," a citizen has no economic interests to protect by preserving peace—he is only a drop in the common bucket—while war gives him the (fallacious) hope of larger handouts from his master. Ideologically, he is trained to regard men as sacrificial animals; he is one himself; he can have no concept of why foreigners should not be sacrificed on the same public altar for the benefit of the same state.

The trader and the warrior have been fundamental antagonists throughout history. Trade does not flourish on battlefields, factories do not produce under bombardments, profits do not grow on rubble. Capitalism is a society of *traders*—for which it has been denounced by every would-be gunman who regards trade as "selfish" and conquest as "noble."

Let those who are actually concerned with peace observe that *capitalism gave mankind the longest period of peace in history*—a period during which there were no wars involving the entire civilized world—from the end of the Napoleonic wars in 1815 to the outbreak of World War I in 1914.

["The Roots of War," *CUI*, 38.]

Statism—in fact and in principle—is nothing more than gang rule. A dictatorship is a gang devoted to looting the effort of the productive citizens of its own country. When a statist ruler exhausts his own country's economy, he attacks his neighbors. It is his only means of postponing internal collapse and prolonging his rule. A country that violates the rights of its own citizens, will not respect the rights of its neighbors. Those who do not recognize individual rights, will not recognize the rights of nations: a nation is only a number of individuals.

Statism *needs* war; a free country does not. Statism survives by looting; a free country survives by production.

Observe that the major wars of history were started by the more controlled economies of the time against the freer ones. For instance, World War I was started by monarchist Germany and Czarist Russia, who dragged in their freer allies. World War II was started by the alliance of Nazi Germany with Soviet Russia and their joint attack on Poland.

Observe that in World War II, both Germany and Russia seized and dismantled entire factories in conquered countries, to ship them home —while the freest of the mixed economies, the semi-capitalistic United States, sent billions worth of lend-lease equipment, including entire factories, to its allies.

Germany and Russia needed war; the United States did not and gained nothing. (In fact, the United States lost, economically, even though it won the war: it was left with an enormous national debt, augmented by the grotesquely futile policy of supporting former allies and enemies to this day.) Yet it is capitalism that today's peace-lovers oppose and statism that they advocate—in the name of peace.

[Ibid., 37.]

If men want to oppose war, it is *statism* that they must oppose. So long as they hold the tribal notion that the individual is sacrificial fodder for the collective, that some men have the right to rule others by force, and that some (any) alleged "good" can justify it—there can be no peace *within* a nation and no peace among nations.

[Ibid., 42.]

Just as, in domestic affairs, all the evils caused by statism and government controls were blamed on capitalism and the free market—so, in foreign affairs, all the evils of statist policies were blamed on and ascribed to capitalism. Such myths as "capitalistic imperialism," "war-profiteering," or the notion that capitalism has to win "markets" by military conquest are examples of the superficiality or the unscrupulousness of statist commentators and historians.

The essence of capitalism's foreign policy is *free trade*—i.e., the abolition of trade barriers, of protective tariffs, of special privileges—the opening of the world's trade routes to free international exchange and competition among the private citizens of all countries dealing directly with one another. During the nineteenth century, it was free trade that liberated the world, undercutting and wrecking the remnants of feudalism and the statist tyranny of absolute monarchies.

[Ibid., 38.]

Capitalism wins and holds its markets by free competition, at home and abroad. A market conquered by war can be of value (temporarily) only to those advocates of a mixed economy who seek to close it to international competition, impose restrictive regulations, and thus acquire special privileges by force.

[Ibid., 39.]

Remember that private citizens—whether rich or poor, whether businessmen or workers—have no power to start a war. That power is the exclusive prerogative of a government. Which type of government is more likely to plunge a country into war: a government of limited powers, bound by constitutional restrictions—or an unlimited government, open to the pressure of any group with warlike interests or ideologies, a government able to command armies to march at the whim of a single chief executive?

[Ibid., 40.]

It is true that nuclear weapons have made wars too horrible to contemplate. But it makes no difference to a man whether he is killed by a nuclear bomb or a dynamite bomb or an old-fashioned club. Nor does the number of other victims or the scale of the destruction make any difference to him.

[Ibid., 42.]

If nuclear weapons are a dreadful threat and mankind cannot afford war any longer, then *mankind cannot afford statism any longer*. Let no man of good will take it upon his conscience to advocate the rule of force—outside or *inside* his own country. Let all those who are actually concerned with peace—those who do love *man* and do care about his survival—realize that if war is ever to be outlawed, it is *the use of force* that has to be outlawed.

[Ibid., 43.]

See also CAPITALISM; DICTATORSHIP; DRAFT; FOREIGN POLICY; FREEDOM; GENOCIDE; NINETEENTH CENTURY; PEACE

MOVEMENTS; PHYSICAL FORCE; SOVIET RUSSIA; STATISM; TRADER PRINCIPLE; TRIBALISM; UNITED NATIONS.

Welfare State.   Since the things man needs for survival have to be produced, and nature does not guarantee the success of any human endeavor, there is not and cannot be any such thing as a *guaranteed economic security*. The employer who gives you a job, has no guarantee that his business will remain in existence, that his customers will continue to buy his products or services. The customers have no guarantee that they will always be able and willing to trade with him, no guarantee of what their needs, choices and incomes will be in the future. If you retire to a self-sustaining farm, you have no guarantee to protect you from what a flood or a hurricane might do to your land and your crops. If you surrender everything to the government and give it total power to plan the whole economy, this will not guarantee your economic security, but it *will* guarantee the descent of the entire nation to a level of miserable poverty—as the practical results of every totalitarian economy, communist or fascist, have demonstrated.

Morally, the promise of an impossible "right" to economic security is an infamous attempt to abrogate the concept of rights. It can and does mean only one thing: a promise to enslave the men who produce, for the benefit of those who don't. "If some men are entitled *by right* to the products of the work of others, it means that those others are deprived of rights and condemned to slave labor." ("Man's Rights" in *Capitalism: The Unknown Ideal.*) There can be no such thing as the right to enslave, i.e., the right to destroy rights.

["A Preview," *ARL,* I, 22, 2.]

It is true that the welfare-statists are not socialists, that they never advocated or intended the socialization of private property, that they want to "preserve" private property—with government control of its use and disposal. But *that* is the fundamental characteristic of fascism.

["The New Fascism: Rule by Consensus," *CUI,* 211.]

The gold standard is incompatible with chronic deficit spending (the hallmark of the welfare state). Stripped of its academic jargon, the welfare state is nothing more than a mechanism by which governments confiscate the wealth of the productive members of a society to support a wide variety of welfare schemes. . . .

The financial policy of the welfare state requires that there be no way for the owners of wealth to protect themselves.

This is the shabby secret of the welfare statists' tirades against gold.

Deficit spending is simply a scheme for the "hidden" confiscation of wealth. Gold stands in the way of this insidious process. It stands as a protector of property rights. If one grasps this, one has no difficulty in understanding the statists' antagonism toward the gold standard.

[Alan Greenspan, "Gold and Economic Freedom," *CUI*, 100.]

Morally and economically, the welfare state creates an ever accelerating downward pull. Morally, the chance to satisfy demands by force spreads the demands wider and wider, with less and less pretense at justification. Economically, the forced demands of one group create hardships for all others, thus producing an inextricable mixture of actual victims and plain parasites. Since need, not achievement, is held as the criterion of rewards, the government necessarily keeps sacrificing the more productive groups to the less productive, gradually chaining the top level of the economy, then the next level, then the next. (How else are unachieved rewards to be provided?)

There are two kinds of *need* involved in this process: the need of the group making demands, which is openly proclaimed and serves as cover for another need, which is never mentioned—the need of the power-seekers, who require a group of dependent favor-recipients in order to rise to power. Altruism feeds the first need, statism feeds the second, Pragmatism blinds everyone—including victims and profiteers—not merely to the deadly nature of the process, but even to the fact that a process is going on.

["A Preview," *ARL*, I, 23, 1.]

[A] real turning point came when the welfare statists switched from economics to physiology: they began to seek a new power base in deliberately fostered racism, the racism of minority groups, then in the hatreds and inferiority complexes of women, of "the young," etc. The significant aspect of this switch was *the severing of economic rewards from productive work.* Physiology replaced the conditions of employment as the basis of social claims. The demands were no longer for "just compensation," but just for compensation, with no work required.

So long as the power-seekers clung to the basic premises of the welfare state, holding need as the criterion of rewards, logic forced them, step by step, to champion the interests of the less and less productive groups, until they reached the ultimate dead end of turning from the role of champions of "honest toil" to the role of champions of open parasitism, parasitism on principle, parasitism as a "right" (with their famous slogan turning into: "Who does not toil, shall eat those who do").

[Ibid., 2.]

In business, the rise of the welfare state froze the status quo, perpetuating the power of the big corporations of the pre-income-tax era, placing them beyond the competition of the tax-strangled newcomers. A similar process took place in the welfare state of the intellect. The results, in both fields, are the same.

["The Establishing of an Establishment," *PWNI*, 207; pb 170.]

See also ALTRUISM; CHARITY; COMPASSION; FASCISM and COMMUNISM/SOCIALISM; GOLD STANDARD; INDIVIDUAL RIGHTS; INFLATION; INTERVENTIONISM (ECONOMIC); LOBBYING; MINORITY RIGHTS; PITY; POVERTY; PRAGMATISM; PRINCIPLES; PROPERTY RIGHTS; RACISM; "REDISTRIBUTION" of WEALTH; SACRIFICE; SELFISHNESS; STATISM; TAXATION.

Whims/Whim-Worship.
A "whim" is a desire experienced by a person who does not know and does not care to discover its cause.

["The Objectivist Ethics," *VOS*, 3; pb 14.]

Automatic omniscience [is what] a whim-worshiper ascribes to his emotions.

["Philosophical Detection," *PWNI*, 23; pb 19.]

What does it mean, to act on whim? It means that a man acts like a zombie, without any knowledge of what he deals with, what he wants to accomplish, or what motivates him. It means that a man acts in a state of temporary insanity. Is this what you call juicy or colorful? I think the only juice that can come out of such a situation is blood. To act against the facts of reality can result only in destruction.

["*Playboy's* Interview with Ayn Rand," pamphlet, 6.]

What is the nature of that superior world to which they sacrifice the world that exists? The mystics of spirit curse matter, the mystics of muscle curse profit. The first wish men to profit by renouncing the earth, the second wish men to inherit the earth by renouncing all profit. Their non-material, non-profit worlds are realms where rivers run with milk and coffee, where wine spurts from rocks at their command, where pastry drops on them from clouds at the price of opening their mouth. On this material, profit-chasing earth, an enormous investment of virtue —of intelligence, integrity, energy, skill—is required to construct a railroad to carry them the distance of one mile; in their non-material, non-profit world, they travel from planet to planet at the cost of a wish. If an honest person asks them: "How?"—they answer with righteous scorn that a "how" is the concept of vulgar realists; the concept of superior spirits is "Somehow." On this earth restricted by matter and profit, rewards are achieved by thought; in a world set free of such restrictions, rewards are achieved by wishing.

And *that* is the whole of their shabby secret. The secret of all their esoteric philosophies, of all their dialectics and super-senses, of their evasive eyes and snarling words, the secret for which they destroy civilization, language, industries and lives, the secret for which they pierce their own eyes and eardrums, grind out their senses, blank out their minds, the purpose for which they dissolve the absolutes of reason, logic, matter, existence, reality—is to erect upon that plastic fog a single holy absolute: their *Wish*.

[GS, *FNI*, 185; pb 149.]

See also AMORALISM; EMOTIONS; FINAL CAUSATION; HEDONISM; IRRATIONALITY; MYSTICISM; RATIONALITY; SUBJECTIVISM.

"Window Dressing." The non-philosophical attitude of most rightists, who surrendered the intellect to the leftists . . . permitted the intellectuals to play the game of "window dressing," i.e., to preach political tolerance or impartiality and to practice it, on suitable occasions, by featuring the weakest, most befuddled champion of capitalism as a representative of the right. (Which led people to the conclusion: "If *this* is the best that can be said for the right, then the leftist position must be true.")

["The Disfranchisement of the Right," *ARL*, I, 6, 1.]

See also CAPITALISM; "CONSERVATIVES"; "CONSERVATIVES" vs. "LIBERALS"; RIGHTISTS vs. LEFTISTS.

Words. In order to be used as a single unit, the enormous sum integrated by a concept has to be given the form of a single, specific, *perceptual* concrete, which will differentiate it from all other concretes and from all other concepts. This is the function performed by language. Language is a code of visual-auditory symbols that serves the psycho-epistemological function of converting concepts into the mental equivalent of concretes. Language is the exclusive domain and tool of concepts. Every word we use (with the exception of proper names) is a symbol that denotes a concept, i.e., that stands for an unlimited number of concretes of a certain kind.

[*ITOE*, 11.]

The first words a child learns are words denoting visual objects, and he retains his first concepts *visually*. Observe that the visual form he gives them is reduced to those *essentials* which distinguish the particular kind of entities from all others—for instance, the universal type of a child's drawing of man in the form of an oval for the torso, a circle for the head, four sticks for extremities, etc. Such drawings are a visual record of the process of abstraction and concept-formation in a mind's transition from the perceptual level to the full vocabulary of the conceptual level.

There is evidence to suppose that written language originated in the form of drawings—as the pictographic writing of the Oriental peoples seems to indicate. With the growth of man's knowledge and of his power of abstraction, a pictorial representation of concepts could no longer be adequate to his conceptual range, and was replaced by a fully symbolic code.

[Ibid., 15.]

The process of forming a concept is not complete until its constituent units have been integrated into a single mental unit by means of a specific word. The first concepts a child forms are concepts of perceptual entities; the first words he learns are words designating them. Even though a child does not have to perform the feat of genius performed by some mind or minds in the prehistorical infancy of the human race: the invention of language—every child has to perform independently the feat of grasping the nature of language, the process of symbolizing concepts by means of words.

Even though a child does not (and need not) originate and form every concept on his own, by observing every aspect of reality confronting him, he has to perform the process of differentiating and integrating perceptual concretes, in order to grasp the meaning of words. If a child's brain is physically damaged and unable to perform that process, he does not learn to speak.

Learning to speak does not consist of memorizing sounds—*that* is the process by which a parrot learns to "speak." Learning consists of grasping meanings, i.e., of grasping the *referents* of words, the kinds of existents that words denote in reality. In this respect, the learning of words is an invaluable accelerator of a child's cognitive development, but it is not a substitute for the process of concept-formation; nothing is.

[Ibid., 24.]

Words transform concepts into (mental) entities; *definitions* provide them with *identity*. (Words without definitions are not language but inarticulate sounds.)

[Ibid., 12.]

It is often said that definitions state the meaning of words. This is true, but it is not exact. A word is merely a visual-auditory symbol used to represent a concept; a word has no meaning other than that of the concept it symbolizes, and the meaning of a concept consists of its units. It is not words, but concepts that man defines—by specifying their referents.

[*Ibid.*, 52.]

See also COMMUNICATION; CONCEPT-FORMATION; CONCEPTS; DEFINITIONS; GRAMMAR; LANGUAGE; LINGUISTIC ANALYSIS; MEANING (*of* CONCEPTS); NOMINALISM; PERCEPTION; PSYCHO-EPISTEMOLOGY; UNIT; UNIT-ECONOMY.

X

Xenophobia. *See Anti-Conceptual Mentality.*

Z

Zero, Reification of. A vulgar variant of concept stealing, prevalent among avowed mystics and irrationalists, is a fallacy I call the *Reification of the Zero.* It consists of regarding "nothing" as a *thing,* as a special, different kind of *existent.* (For example, see Existentialism.) This fallacy breeds such symptoms as the notion that presence and absence, or being and non-being, are metaphysical forces of equal power, and that being is the absence of non-being. E.g., "Nothingness is prior to being." (Sartre)—"Human finitude is the presence of the *not* in the being of man." (William Barrett)—"Nothing is more real than nothing." (Samuel Beckett)—*"Das Nichts nichtet"* or "Nothing noughts." (Heidegger). "Consciousness, then, is not a stuff, but a *negation.* The subject is not a thing, but a *non-*thing. The subject carves its own world out of Being by means of negative determinations. Sartre describes consciousness as a 'noughting nought' (*néant néantisant*). It is a form of being other than its own: a mode 'which has yet to be what it is, that is to say, which is what it is, that is to say, which is what it is not and which is not what it is.' " (Hector Hawton, *The Feast of Unreason,* London: Watts & Co., 1952, p. 162.)

(The motive? "Genuine utterances about the nothing must always remain unusual. It cannot be made common. It dissolves when it is placed in the cheap acid of mere logical acumen." Heidegger.)

[*ITOE*, 80.]

See also AXIOMATIC CONCEPTS; AXIOMS; EXISTENCE; IDENTITY; NON-EXISTENCE; "STOLEN CONCEPT," FALLACY of.